CLASSICS

OF

INTERNATIONAL

RELATIONS

CLASSICS
OF
INTERNATIONAL
RELATIONS

Edited by

JOHN A. VASQUEZ

Rutgers University

Prentice-Hall, Inc., Englewood Cliffs, New Jersey 07632

Library of Congress Cataloging in Publication Data
Main entry under title:

Classics of international relations.

Includes bibliographies and index.
1. International relations—Addresses, essays, lectures.   I. Vasquez, John A. (date)
JX1308.C63   1986   327   85-6285
ISBN 0-13-135336-5

Editorial/production supervision and
    interior design: Mark Stevens
Cover design: Wanda Lubelska
Manufacturing buyer: Barbara Kelly Kittle

Printed in the Unted States of America

10   9   8   7   6   5   4

ISBN   0-13-135336-5   01

Prentice-Hall International (UK) Limited, *London*
Prentice-Hall of Australia Pty. Limited, *Sydney*
Editora Prentice-Hall do Brasil, Ltda., *Rio de Janeiro*
Prentice-Hall Canada Inc., *Toronto*
Prentice-Hall Hispanoamericana, S.A., *Mexico*
Prentice-Hall of India Private Limited, *New Delhi*
Prentice-Hall of Japan, Inc., *Tokyo*
Prentice-Hall of Southeast Asia Pte. Ltd., *Singapore*
Whitehall Books Limited, *Wellington, New Zealand*

In memory of

Sean Henehan Vasquez

d.
b. October 12, 1982

CONTENTS (Topical)

Chapter Six: Crisis

Chapter Seven: War

Chapter Eight: Imperialism

IV.   THE SEARCH FOR PEACE

Chapter Nine: The Balance of Power

CONTENTS (Chronological)

REACTIONS TO WORLD WAR, 1914–1948

THE 1950s

THE 1960s

THE 1970s

PREFACE

My purpose in editing this book has been to present some of the best analyses of the most enduring questions of international relations. In doing so, I hope to capture the essence of what the field has to say to humankind. I have chosen to do this by bringing together the reflections of the great thinkers and the analyses of twentieth-century scholars on a common set of problems. In selecting the works of the great thinkers, I have tried to select those works that are regarded as classics of Western civilization and essential to a liberal education. In selecting more recent works, I have tried to select classics of the discipline—representatives of the most influential work published on international relations in each of the last four decades. The resulting volume, I believe, constitutes one of the most efficient and comprehensive sources through which the student or general reader can gain an overview of international relations inquiry. Hence, the volume is meant to stand by itself and does not need a supplemental textbook. For readers or instructors who nevertheless feel the need for further treatment of the subject, collateral reading is suggested for each section at the end of the volume.

The book is divided into four parts, each of which is devoted to a central issue. Part I focuses on the perennial question of whether morality should or can govern political behavior. Chapters on how the just-war, idealist, realist, and radical traditions have addressed this question in different historical contexts are included. Part II treats the questions of how international relations should be studied, whether knowledge about the subject can be acquired, and whether a science of international relations is possible; the debate among idealists, traditionalists, and behavioralists is presented. Part III is devoted to the primary empirical concerns of the field—the conduct of foreign policy and its relationship to global conflict. The chapters on the making of foreign policy, crisis, war, and imperialism provide a distillation of the most important theories and research on each of these questions. Part IV reflects the main concern of the field—how peace can be achieved and maintained. Chapters on the balance of power, nuclear deterrence, international law and world government, and world community present and evaluate the major proposals for the mitigation or elimination of war.

Although this book is lengthy, there were still many important pieces that could not be included because of space limitation. Among the works of the great thinkers, only classics from the Western tradition have been included; a separate volume would be needed to do justice to the rich tradition of non-Western thought. The only exception has been the inclusion of Gandhi, whose ideas have had a tremendous impact in the West, particularly upon peace movements. As for more recent scholarship, the emphasis has been placed on the Anglo-American tradition, or on works that have directly affected that tradition. But even after applying these rather restrictive selection criteria, many significant thinkers who met them could not be included; their works have been recommended for further reading in the introduction to each section.

My greatest debt in preparing this volume is to my former students in my introductory course on Global Peace and War and in my graduate core course on Theories of International Relations. Both of these courses have challenged me to present, at different levels, the most important work in the field within the constraint of a single semester. My students' reactions to my various efforts have had a major impact on the content of this volume. As has become increasingly common in my work, my colleague and partner Marie T. Henehan has shared in both the burden and the pleasure of preparing this book. Her advice, encouragement, patience, and criticism have had a major impact on my selection and my commentary. My thanks also to Roy Licklider and to Carl Larsen, each of whom read the introductory material and provided valuable suggestions, and to Van Coufoudakis, Frank C. Darling, and Waltraud Queiser Morales, the reviewers for Prentice-Hall. Jay Shafritz's *Classics of Public Administration* provided the inspiration for this work, and his advice was valuable in my own effort to collect classics in a single volume. Stan Wakefield and the editorial staff at Prentice-Hall have provided encouragement and have handled the manuscript so smoothly and professionally that it made publishing with them truly a pleasure. The Block Island Writers' Workshop provided a sounding board for some of the introductory material during the all-too-short winter of 1983–84. Diane Swartz, my efficient typist, proved once again that a good typist can not only reduce the frustrations of preparing a manuscript for publication but also give it the joy it naturally deserves. Of course, despite the aid of all these people, I accept the final responsibility for the volume.

Lastly, this book is dedicated to our stillborn son. In a world in which millions can lie only a few minutes away from annihilation, his death has reminded us of the fragility and miracle of human life.

JOHN A. VASQUEZ

I

Morality and Politics

The most persistent philosophical question that has plagued those who have thought about international relations has been whether the foreign policy of a state ought to be based on the norms and principles of moral conduct. While there are few who would say that the individual should not be bound by moral rules in his or her everyday life, or even that the government should not follow basic standards of decency in the way it treats its citizens, many would say that in questions of international affairs, the state should do whatever is in its interest without the hindrance of ethical strictures. This position is often referred to as *raison d'état* or "reason of state." Whether reason of state should take precedence over moral rules has been an issue from the time of ancient Greece to our own day.

A closely related issue is the question of whether it is possible for a state to follow moral rules in its global conduct. What would a moral foreign policy look like, and would it work? Historically, there have been two approaches toward developing a guideline for a moral foreign policy. The first argues that a foreign policy is moral so long as no immoral acts are committed. Elements of this approach can be found in the just war tradition, which is based on a Judeo-Christian ethic and is illustrated in the selection by Saint Thomas Aquinas. The second approach goes a step further, maintaining that the goal of foreign policy should be to promote the Good. This is the approach of idealism and is illustrated in the selection by Woodrow Wilson.

In the West, the just war tradition has been primarily a religious one. Faced with the ethical requirements outlined both in the Old and in the New Testaments and the political demands first of pagan Rome and then of Christian Rome and Medieval Europe, Christian theologians attempted to develop a set of rules for determining when, if ever, killing for political purposes could be justified. The work of Thomas Aquinas (ca. 1225–1274) was pivotal in this process, because he systematized previous thought on the question and laid the foundation for all subsequent doctrine on just war within the Roman Catholic Church. He addressed the question from the perspective of how Christians should behave on earth in order to insure eternal salvation. Protestant positions have been more varied, ranging from absolute pacifism to acquiescence and obedience to state demands.

Toward the end of World War I, Woodrow Wilson developed a different approach, one that placed the blame for war on power politics, the machinations of secret diplomacy, and the sinister interests of undemocratic leaders. If these things could be changed, war could be ended, because war was fundamentally irrational; that is, war was not in the interests of most people, and most conflicts were resolvable through the use of reason. Wilson believed that, by spreading democracy (through the creation of the Weimar Republic in Germany and of new states in Eastern Europe) and creating a League of Nations to inhibit aggression and peacefully resolve disputes, a revolution in the conduct of world politics would be brought about. It was in this context that the academic discipline of international relations was born, breaking away from diplomatic history, theology, and philosophy, upon which it had previously been based. These scholars, who were later labeled idealists and utopians by the realists, pursued and advanced many of the ideas initially suggested by Wilson.

The critics of these two moral approaches have taken a reason-of-state position, which maintains not only that the state is exempt from morality, but also that if the state does rely on morality, morality will fail to protect it. Some critics have even gone on to argue that attempts to promote the Good actually create more suffering in the world than there would be if everyone simply followed their selfish interests. The selection by Thucydides (ca. 460–ca. 400 B.C.) illustrates the position that morality in and of itself is not sufficient against power; the selection can also be interpreted as making a similar point against reason in the face of action. The selection by Machiavelli (1513) makes the case that self-interest should be the prince's main goal, and that nothing, particularly morality, should stand in its way.

The notions that power and action are the key to international politics and that morality and reason can be utopian and impotent are the hallmarks of the approach to international relations known as *realism* or *realpolitik*. In the twentieth century, realism has been a direct reaction to the failure of Wilson and other idealists to prevent World War II. Their use of reason was seen as utopian because they underestimated the role of power in enforcing a new order and preventing war. In addition, idealists were perceived as exaggerating the influence of reason by assuming a fundamental harmony of interests, when in fact, according to the realists, there are often profound conflicts of interest that can only be resolved by a struggle for power. The ways in which these insights percolated through the inter-war generation that had to deal with Hitler are demonstrated in the selection by Reinhold Niebuhr (1940), who makes the case for Christian realism against those within the Church taking a more pacifistic and/or isolationist position. Niebuhr's work in the United States and E.H. Carr's work in Britain the year before (see selection 12) were critical in setting the stage for the idealist-realist debate of the 1940s, which resulted in the ascendancy of realism.

The definitive contemporary statement on realism, and the work that is usually credited with converting the field from idealist advocacy to realist analysis, is Hans Morgenthau's (1948) *Politics Among Nations*. In the selection reprinted here, Morgenthau defines international politics in terms of power, makes the case against idealism, and argues for the primacy of realpolitik over morality in affairs of the state.

George Kennan (1951) takes up many of the insights of Morgenthau and the other realists to analyze the failure of an American diplomacy based on the legalistic-moralistic approach. He points out that the emphasis on moral rather than self-interest goals makes foreign policy more dangerous and more prone to wars that seek total victory. In a more theoretical vein, Morgenthau (1952; see selection 16) makes the case for basing foreign policy solely on national interest. In the same year, Arnold Wolfers (1952; see selection 17) in a prescient essay, points out the dangers inherent in this concept.

The realists were very successful in dominating both the academic discipline and policy-making circles in the United States and Great Britain in the fifties and sixties. This domination was due in part to the fact that realism was a natural ideology for an ascending status-quo power like the United States. With the onset of the Vietnam War, however, it became increasingly clear to Americans outside the intellectual and policy-making establishment that the realist argument—that morality has no place in international politics, and that power and interest are all that are important—was too facile and convenient. Instead of looking back to Thucydides and Machiavelli, these scholars reexamined the just war tradition, and looked at a radical tradition that emphasized the interests of the common person rather than the interests of the prince or decision-making elite.

It is the strong tendency of analysts and students of international relations to do as Machiavelli did—to pretend that we are princes or decision makers, define problems through those eyes, and then recommend accordingly. Most of us are not decision makers, however, and it is not very clear that their interests are ours, or that the way they define the world should be the way we define it; this is one of the starting points of the radical critique of realism. This critique then goes on to insist that moral rules serve the interests of common people, particularly on the question of war, and that intellectuals, instead of helping people to see this truth, help the elite to deceive people into becoming cannon fodder.

The selections from the essays of Leo Tolstoy make these points strikingly and are steeped in the tradition of Christian pacifism and political anarchism. His message to citizens and common soldiers everywhere is: It is not only wrong to kill, but there is also no need to kill, because wars serve only the interests of the state, and not the people. Their emphasis on this message is one of the reasons Tolstoy, like other antiwar thinkers such as Thoreau and Mark Twain, was read widely in the United States in the late 1960s.

Even more influential has been the work of Gandhi. Gandhi insisted, particularly through his example, that the means by which a goal is sought has an effect on what is obtained. Political means, especially violent ones, produce a number of consequences, only one of which is attainment of a goal. The other consequences may undermine, or even destroy, the value of the original goal. From this perspective, violence is not simply a means; it is evil. To engage in violence, no matter what the reason, is to lose the battle, to become corrupted, to become part of the problem. To believe that the end can justify the means is to become deluded into thinking that the immediate goal is more important than the ultimate goal, the Good. Our actions as we attempt to attain a goal determine what we attain, because our behavior in political action shapes who we are (that is, our moral character). For Gandhi, a true revolution must not only result in political independence but also free people from the evils of violence and hatred. For many Americans involved in the civil rights and antiwar movements of the 1960s, nonviolence was not only a technique but also a strategy designed to change the spirit that had given rise to oppression of American blacks at home and support of counterrevolutionary dictatorships abroad. Gandhi's prophecy looms as a final warning in the nuclear age, as billions are spent in the United States and in the Soviet Union on the weapons of complete destruction, and as more and more nations seek nuclear capability.

The essays by Howard Zinn (1966) and Noam Chomsky (1966) are attempts to apply the insights of the radical tradition to an ongoing Vietnam War. Both were highly influential at the time, and the essays continue to be important statements about the role of morality in guiding both foreign policy and intellectual inquiry about international politics. Together the essays demonstrate the limits of realism for an important segment of a new generation of Americans.

Underlying many of the arguments in this section is the question of the relationship between the individual and the state. Must the state serve the interests of the individual? Must it serve the interests of all or just some? Is an individual obliged to meet the demands of the state or the larger community? Can the state morally require individuals or certain groups to risk their lives in a war? For Aquinas and for many others within the just war tradition, obligation to the moral principles of God and the Church clearly takes precedence over the demands of the state or the individual, both of which had little status within medieval Christendom. For liberal idealists like Wilson, the individual has an obligation not only to defend the community but also to fight for the Good. For realists, individuals are often seen as resources for the state, much like coal and steel. The feelings of individuals are handled more from the perspective of morale rather than morality. For some radicals, particularly those who are anarchists rather than collectivists, individuals not only have no obligations to the state, but also must come to realize that the state is an enemy of the individual.

The selections in Part I demonstrate that there is no simple answer to the question of the role of morality in politics. The selections do, however, offer some important lessons for consideration. First, there appear to be no a priori grounds for choosing realism over an approach that imparts a greater role to morality. Realism is no less value-laden than moral approaches are. Both offer prescriptions as to what *should* be done and what is the best foreign policy. It is more accurate to describe realism as a counterethic than as a set of solely factual statements and explanations, as is sometimes implied.

How does one choose one ethic over another? There are two ways of trying to answer this question. One way is to ask, What is, intrinsically, the best way to live? One then does what is right. The other way is to ask, What are the consequences of a particular action? One then takes the action that produces the most good. It is possible to assess different ethical systems, including the just war tradition, idealism, realism, and the radical critique, by examining, in terms of these two questions, the global quality of life to which they give rise. Is the global quality of life that is established by following these prescriptions intrinsically the best way to live, or at least a good way to live, given historical possibilities? Are the consequences of following the prescriptions beneficial, or disastrous?

As the selections are examined in light of these questions, the lessons the writer is trying to derive become clearer. To the realists, it is evident that history has shown that following the dictates of reason or morality is not beneficial because, all too frequently, there are powerful states who will not obey these dictates and will simply take what they want through force of arms. In this situation, which according to the realists is typical in international politics, only power can ensure survival. To be without power is to court disaster, as the Melians did in the Peloponnesian War.

While it is difficult to argue, except on religious grounds, in favor of following a morality that no one obeys, it is equally true that realism tends to reduce the number of individuals and groups who will be restrained by moral considerations. It does this by increasing the number of individuals who have no motivation to obey moral rules, and by making it difficult for individuals who want to follow the rules to do so. Today, for example, we all accept the rule that in the classroom, intellectual disagreements should not be settled by dueling. If a group of students began to bring pistols to class and challenged and killed students with whom they disagreed, and, for some hypothetical reason, law enforcement agencies did nothing about it, then it would be difficult for the rest of us to refrain from bringing pistols to class, even if we accepted the general rule against dueling. Once the ideology of dueling has been accepted, it is hard to resist the practice of dueling; in the absence of the practice of dueling, however, the ideology makes little sense.

In this manner, realism acts, in part, as a self-fulfilling prophecy, by helping to bring about the very world it deplores but accepts out of necessity. While it may be true that the worlds of the Peloponnesian War, Renaissance Italy, and World War II were realpolitik worlds, things do not always have to be that way, nor have they always been that way—that is the basic insight of the idealists. There are some ways of acting at the global level that establish a higher quality of life than other ways of acting. To the extent that these more beneficial actions can be institutionalized into a set of rules, realpolitik worlds can be superseded. This is precisely what the just war tradition has attempted to do, and was successful in doing for much of the medieval period.

It should be clear that, to the extent that it provides insights to the naive, realism will have beneficial consequences in that it will alert the naive to danger. To the extent that realism provides a rationalization for the strong, it will be pernicious. One of the points made by American radicals during the Vietnam War was that American interests in Vietnam were not morally acceptable, and to respond, as realists do, that morality has no place in international politics was simply self-serving. Both radicals and those who take a just war approach place the burden of proof on those who wish to use the common people to fight wars, making them establish their case upon something other than the interests of the decision maker. Since decision makers are often advised to lie and to deceive, it behooves the rest of us to have some sort of independent basis for assessing their actions. The just war tradition and the radical critique provide such a basis.

Finally, the realists appear to be correct in arguing that idealist foreign policies that promulgate moral, religious, or ideological goals are more apt to produce total wars than are policies based only on protecting the territorial integrity and political independence of the state. Contemporary realists like Niebuhr, Morgenthau, and Kennan prescribe avoidance of messianic missions and limiting international politics to issues of survival. The problem, of course, is that most decision makers are not willing to restrict their policies in this manner. The idea that tolerance is better than fighting is, nevertheless, a particularly important lesson to remember in the nuclear age.

It must be kept in mind that the four approaches discussed in this section—just war, idealism, realism, and the radical critique—are intellectual positions that are only occasionally applied in a consistent fashion by political leaders. In recent times, just war and radical approaches have been influential primarily with religious institutions and mass movements, respectively, and not with the leaders of the most powerful states. Leaders of these states have been torn between the contradictory tendencies of idealism and realism in trying to spread their own ideologies and yet needing to confront the realities of world politics. In the United States, for example, the attempts to make the world safe for democracy, to protect small states from aggression, to aid economic development, and to promote human rights all reflect idealist goals in foreign policy that go beyond the narrow interests of territorial integrity and political independence. At the same time, there has been a recognition that moralistic condemnations, like the nonrecognition of the People's Republic of China, can be impotent, and that more messianic crusades, like Dulles's desire to "roll back the iron curtain," can be dangerous. There has been a constant tension in American foreign policy between idealism and realism, with presidents using idealism to justify their actions and realism to calculate their interests. On the whole, realism has held the upper hand when the United States has taken action against strong states, like the Soviet Union. At other times, the ideology of anticommunism has been so pervasive that it has led to involvements, as in Vietnam, where, from the realist perspective, there was no clear threat.

Similarly, there has been a tension in the Soviet Union between the spreading of communism and the supporting of revolution and, on the other hand, protecting the Russian state. At the end of World War II, Stalin's policy in Eastern Europe seemed to be aimed at creating a Russian sphere of influence to protect it from a rebuilt Germany, rather than an attempt to conquer the world. Likewise, Stalin was more than ready before 1949 to sacrifice Mao's revolution in China in order to gain advantages with the West. On the other hand, the Soviet Union has found itself supporting revolutionary regimes that have hurt its overall strategic position, as in the case of its support of the current regime in Ethiopia at the cost of losing its base in Somalia.

These examples serve to emphasize the point that the realm of practice rarely has the clarity, consistency, or purpose that is present in the realm of ideas. This is partly because governments are eclectic in the ideas they employ; more importantly, though, it is because putting ideas into practice is very difficult, given domestic and global constraints.

FOR FURTHER READING

Just War: 1. AUGUSTINE, AURELIUS, BISHOP OF HIPPO. *De Libero Arbitrio* (Freedom of the Will) 1.5 (A.D. 395), Letter to Publicola (No. 47) (A.D. 398), Letter to Boniface (No. 189) (A.D. 418).

2. *Corpus Juris Canonici*, Pars Prior, *Decretum Magistri Gratiani* (Code of Canon Law, Decretals of Gratian) (ca. 1140).

3. FRANCISCUS DE VITORIA (ca. 1487–1546). *De Indis; De Jure Belli Relectiones*. Reprinted in *Classics of International Law*, edited by Ernest Nys. Washington, D.C.: The Carnegie Institution, 1917.

4. *The Challenge of Peace: God's Promise and Our Response.* (Pastoral letter on nuclear war by the U.S. Catholic bishops.) Washington, D.C.: U.S. Catholic Conference, 1983.

5. MICHAEL WALZER. *Just and Unjust Wars: A Moral Argument with Historical Illustrations.* New York: Basic Books, 1977.

Idealism: 6. NORMAN ANGELL. *The Great Illusion.* New York: G.P. Putnam's Sons, 1911.

7. M. MOOS AND T. I. COOK. *Power Through Purpose: The Realism of Idealism as a Basis for Foreign Policy.* Baltimore: Johns Hopkins University Press, 1954.

8. RICHARD A. FALK. *A Study of Future Worlds.* New York: The Free Press, 1975.

Realism:

9. GEORG SCHWARZENBERGER. *Power Politics*. London: Jonathan Cape, Ltd., 1941.

10. NICHOLAS SPYKMAN. *America's Strategy in World Politics*. New York: Harcourt, Brace & World, 1942.

11. MARTIN WIGHT. *Power Politics*. London: Royal Institute of International Affairs, 1946.

12. JOHN HERZ. *Political Realism and Political Idealism*. Chicago: University of Chicago Press, 1951.

13. HERBERT BUTTERFIELD. *Christianity, Diplomacy and War*. London: Epworth Press, 1953.

14. FRIEDRICH MEINECHE. *Machiavellianism: The Doctrine of Raison d'Etat and Its Place in Modern History*. New Haven: Yale University Press, 1957.

15. ARNOLD WOLFERS. *Discord and Collaboration*. Baltimore: Johns Hopkins University Press, 1962.

Radical Critique:

16. HENRY DAVID THOREAU. Civil Disobedience (1849). In *Walden and Civil Disobedience*. New York: Signet, 1960.

17. M. K. GANDHI . (1869–1948). *Non-violent Resistance (Satyagraha)*. New York: Schocken Books, 1961.

18. ALBERT CAMUS. Neither Victims Nor Executioners. *Combat* (the daily newspaper of the French Resistance), 1946. Translated in *Politics* (July–August 1947); *Liberation* (February 1960).

19. C. WRIGHT MILLS. *The Power Elite*. New York: Oxford University Press, 1956.

20. WILLIAM A. WILLIAMS. *The Tragedy of American Diplomacy*. New York: Delta Books, 1959.

21. GENE SHARP. The Political Equivalent of War: Civilian Defense. *International Conciliation* (November 1965).

22. GABRIEL KOLKO. *The Roots of American Foreign Policy*. New York: Delta Books, 1959.

23. HOWARD ZINN. *The Politics of History*. Boston: Beacon Press, 1971.

1
JUST WAR AND IDEALISM

1. Of War

THOMAS AQUINAS

QUESTION XL

ARTICLE I. Whether It is Always Sinful To Wage War?

We proceed thus to the First Article: It seems that it is always sinful to wage war.

Objection 1. Because punishment is not inflicted except for sin. Now those who wage war are threatened by Our Lord with punishment, according to Matt. 26. 52: *All that take the sword shall perish with the sword.* Therefore all wars are unlawful.

Obj. 2. Further, Whatever is contrary to a Divine precept is a sin. But war is contrary to a Divine precept, for it is written (Matt. 5. 39): *But I say to you not to resist evil;* and (Rom. 12.19): *Not revenging yourselves, my dearly beloved, but give place unto wrath.* Therefore war is always sinful.

From *Summa Theologica*, Part II of Second Part. Translated by the Fathers of the English Dominican Province. First published in the U.S. in 1917 by Benziger Brothers. Footnotes deleted.

Obj. 3. Further, Nothing, except sin, is contrary to an act of virtue. But war is contrary to peace. Therefore war is always a sin.

Obj. 4. Further, The exercise of a lawful thing is itself lawful, as is evident in exercises of the sciences. But warlike exercises which take place in tournaments are forbidden by the Church, since those who are slain in these trials are deprived of ecclesiastical burial. Therefore it seems that war is a sin absolutely.

On the contrary, Augustine says in a sermon on the son of the centurion: "If the Christian Religion forbade war altogether, those who sought salutary advice in the Gospel would rather have been counselled to cast aside their arms, and to give up soldiering altogether. On the contrary, they were told: 'Do violence to no man; . . . and be content with your pay' (Luke 3. 14). If he commanded them to be content with their pay, he did not forbid soldiering."

I answer that, In order for a war to be just, three things are necessary. First, the authority of the sovereign by whose command the war is to be waged. For it is not the business of a private person to declare war, because he can seek for redress of his rights from the tribunal of his superior. Moreover it is not the business of a private person to summon together the people, which has to be done in wartime. And as the care of the common weal is committed to those who are in authority, it is their business to watch over the common weal of the city, kingdom or province subject to them. And just as it is lawful for them to have recourse to the material sword in defending that common weal against internal disturbances, when they punish evil-doers, according to the words of the Apostle (Rom. 13.4): *He beareth not the sword in vain: for he is God's minister, an avenger to execute wrath upon him that doth evil;* so too, it is their business to have recourse to the sword of war in defending the common weal against external enemies. Hence it is said to those who are in authority (Ps. 81. 4): *Rescue the poor: and deliver the needy out of the hand of the sinner;* and for this reason Augustine says (*Contra Faust.* xxii, 75): "The natural order conducive to peace among mortals demands that the power to declare and counsel war should be in the hands of those who hold the supreme authority."

Secondly, a just cause is required, namely that those who are attacked should be attacked because they deserve it on account of some fault. Therefore Augustine says (Q. X, *super Jos.*): "A just war is usually described as one that avenges wrongs, when a nation or state has to be punished, for refusing to make amends for the wrongs inflicted by its subjects, or to restore what it has seized unjustly."

Thirdly, it is necessary that the belligerents should have a right intention, so that they intend the advancement of good, or the avoidance of evil. Hence Augustine says (*De Verb. Dom.*): "True religion does not look upon as sinful those wars that are waged not for motives of aggrandisement, or cruelty, but with the object of securing peace, of punishing evildoers, and of uplifting the good." For it may happen that the war is declared by the legitimate authority, and for a just cause, and yet be rendered unlawful through a wicked intention. Hence Augustine says (*Contra Faust.* xxii). "The passion for inflicting harm, the cruel thirst for vengeance, an unpacific and relentless spirit, the fever of revolt, the lust of

power, and such things, all these are rightly condemned in war."

Reply Obj. 1. As Augustine says (*Contra Faust.* xxii). "To take the sword is to arm oneself in order to take the life of anyone, without the command or permission of superior or lawful authority." On the other hand, to have recourse to the sword (as a private person) by the authority of the sovereign or judge, or (as a public person) through zeal for justice, and by the authority, so to speak, of God, is not to *take the sword*, but to use it as commissioned by another, and so it does not deserve punishment. And yet even those who make sinful use of the sword are not always slain with the sword, but they always perish with their own sword, because, unless they repent, they are punished eternally for their sinful use of the sword.

Reply Obj. 2. Precepts of this kind, as Augustine observes (*De Serm. Dom. in Monte,* i), should always be borne in readiness of mind, so that we be ready to obey them, and, if necessary, to refrain from resistance or self-defence. Nevertheless it is necessary sometimes for a man to act otherwise for the common good, or for the good of those with whom he is fighting. Hence Augustine says (*Ep. ad Marcellin.*): "Those whom we have to punish with a kindly severity, it is necessary to handle in many ways against their will. For when we are stripping a man of the lawlessness of sin, it is good for him to be vanquished, since nothing is more hopeless than the happiness of sinners, whence arises a guilty impunity, and an evil will, like an internal enemy."

Reply Obj. 3. Those who wage war justly aim at peace, and so they are not opposed to peace, except to the evil peace, which Our Lord *came not to send upon earth* (Matt. 10. 34). Hence Augustine says (*Ep. ad Bonif.* clxxxix): "We do not seek peace in order to be at war, but we go to war that we may have peace. Be peaceful, therefore, in warring, so that you may vanquish those whom you war against, and bring them to the prosperity of peace."

Reply Obj. 4. Manly exercises in warlike feats of arms are not all forbidden, but those which are inordinate and perilous, and end in slaying or plundering. In olden times warlike exercises presented no such danger, and hence they were called exercises of arms or bloodless wars, as Jerome states in an epistle (cf. Veget.,—*De Re Milit.* i).

ARTICLE 2. Whether It Is Lawful for Clerics and Bishops To Fight?

We proceed thus to the Second Article: It seems lawful for clerics and bishops to fight.

Objection 1. For, as stated above (A. I), wars are lawful and just in so far as they protect the poor and the entire common weal from suffering at the hands of the foe. Now this seems to be above all the duty of prelates, for Gregory says (*Hom. in Ev.* xiv). "The wolf comes upon the sheep, when any unjust and rapacious man oppresses those who are faithful and humble. But he who was thought to be the shepherd, and was not, leaveth the sheep, and flieth, for he fears lest the wolf hurt him, and dares not stand up against his injustice." Therefore it is lawful for prelates and clerics to fight.

Obj. 2. Further, Pope Leo IV writes (xxiii, qu. 8, can. *Igitur*): "As adverse tidings had frequently come from the Saracen side, some said that the Saracens would come to the port of Rome secretly and covertly; for which reason we commanded our people to gather together, and ordered them to go down to the sea-shore." Therefore it is lawful for bishops to fight.

Obj. 3. Further, It seems to be the same whether a man does a thing himself, or consents to its being done by another, according to Rom. I. 32: *They who do such things, are worthy of death, and not only they that do them, but they also that consent to them that do them.* Now those, above all, seem to consent to a thing, who induce others to do it. But it is lawful for bishops and clerics to induce others to fight, for it is written (xxiii, qu. 8, can. *Hortatu*) that "Charles went to war with the Lombards at the instance and entreaty of Adrian, bishop of Rome." Therefore they also are allowed to fight.

Obj. 4. Further, Whatever is right and meritorious in itself is lawful for prelates and clerics. Now it is sometimes right and meritorious to make war, for it is written (xxiii, qu. 8, can. *Omni timore*) that "if a man die for the true faith, or to save his country, or in defence of Christians, God will give him a heavenly reward." Therefore it is lawful for bishops and clerics to fight.

On the contrary, It was said to Peter as representing bishops and clerics (Matt. 26. 52): *Put up again thy sword into the scabbard* (Vulg.,—*its place*). Therefore it is not lawful for them to fight.

I answer that, Several things are requisite for the good of a human society, and a number of things are done better and quicker by a number of persons than by one, as the Philosopher observes, while certain occupations are so inconsistent with one another, that they cannot be fittingly exercised at the same time; hence those who are assigned to important duties are forbidden to occupy themselves with things of small importance. Thus according to human laws, soldiers who are assigned to warlike pursuits are forbidden to engage in commerce.

Now warlike pursuits are altogether incompatible with the duties of a bishop and a cleric for two reasons. The first reason is a general one, because, namely, warlike pursuits are full of unrest, so that they hinder the mind very much from the contemplation of Divine things, the praise of God, and prayers for the people, which belong to the duties of a cleric. Therefore just as commercial enterprises are forbidden to clerics, because they entangle the mind too much, so too are warlike pursuits, according to II Tim. 2. 4: *No man being a soldier to God, entangleth himself with secular business.* The second reason is a special one, because, namely, all the clerical Orders are directed to the ministry of the altar, on which the Passion of Christ is represented sacramentally, according to I Cor. 11. 26: *As often as you shall eat this bread, and drink the chalice, you shall show the death of the Lord, until He come.* Therefore it is unbecoming for them to slay or shed blood, and it is more fitting that they should be ready to shed their own blood for Christ, so as to imitate in deed what they portray in their ministry. For this reason it has been decreed that those who shed blood, even without sin, become irregular. Now no man who has a certain duty to perform can lawfully do that which renders him unfit for that duty. Therefore it is altogether unlawful for clerics to fight, because war is directed to the shedding of blood.

Reply Obj. 1. Prelates ought to withstand not only the wolf who brings spiritual death upon the flock, but also the pillager and the oppressor who work bodily harm; not, however, by having recourse themselves to material arms, but by means of spiritual weapons, according to the saying of the Apostle (II Cor. 10. 4): *The weapons of our warfare are not carnal, but mighty through God.* Such are salutary warnings, devout prayers, and, for those who are obstinate, the sentence of excommunication.

Reply Obj. 2. Prelates and clerics may, by the authority of their superiors, take part in wars, not indeed by taking up arms themselves, but by affording spiritual help to those who fight justly, by exhorting and absolving them, and by other like spiritual helps. Thus in the Old Testament (Jos. 6. 4) the priests were commanded to sound the sacred trumpets in the battle. It was for this purpose that bishops or clerics were first allowed to go to war; and it is an abuse of this permission, if any of them take up arms themselves.

Reply Obj. 3. As stated above (Q. XXIII, A. 4, Reply 2) every power, art or virtue that pertains to the end, has to dispose that which is directed to the end. Now, among the faithful, carnal wars should be considered as having for their end the Divine spiritual good to which clerics are deputed. Therefore it is the duty of clerics to dispose and counsel other men to engage in just wars. For they are forbidden to take up arms, not as though it were a sin, but because such an occupation is unbecoming their persons.

Reply Obj. 4. Although it is meritorious to wage a just war, nevertheless it is rendered unlawful for clerics, by reason of their being assigned to works more meritorious still. Thus the marriage act may be meritorious; and yet it becomes reprehensible in those who have vowed virginity, because they are bound to a yet greater good.

ARTICLE 3. Whether It Is Lawful To Lay Ambushes in War?

We proceed thus to the Third Article: It seems that it is unlawful to lay ambushes in war.

Objection 1. For it is written (Deut. 16. 20): *Thou shalt follow justly after that which is just.* But ambushes, since they are a kind of deception, seem to pertain to injustice. Therefore it is unlawful to lay ambushes even in a just war.

Obj. 2. Further, Ambushes and deception seem to be opposed to faithfulness even as lies are. But since we are bound to keep faith with all men, it is wrong to lie to anyone, as Augustine states (*Contra Mend.* xv). Therefore, as "one is bound to keep faith with one's enemy," as Augustine states (*Ep. ad Bonifac.* clxxxix) it seems that it is unlawful to lay ambushes for one's enemies.

Obj. 3. Further, It is written (Matt. 7. 12): *Whatsoever you would that men should do to you, do you also to them,* and we ought to observe this in all our dealings with our neighbour. Now our enemy is our neighbour. Therefore, since no man wishes ambushes or deceptions to be prepared for himself, it seems that no one ought to carry on war by laying ambushes.

On the contrary, Augustine says (*QQ. in Heptateuch., qu.* x, *super Jos.*): "Provided the war be just, it is no concern of justice whether it be carried on openly or by ambushes," and he proves this by the authority of the Lord, Who commanded Joshua to lay ambushes for the city of Hai (Jos. 8. 2).

I answer that, The object of laying ambushes is in order to deceive the enemy. Now a man may be deceived by another's word or deed in two ways. First, through being told something false, or through the breaking of a promise, and this is always unlawful. No one ought to deceive the enemy in this way, for there are certain rights of war and covenants, which ought to be observed even among enemies, as Ambrose states (*De Offic.* i, 29).

Secondly, a man may be deceived by what we say or do, because we do not declare our purpose or meaning to him. Now we are not always bound to do this, since even in the Sacred Doctrine many things have to be concealed, especially from unbelievers, lest they deride it, according to Matt. 7. 6: *Give not that which is holy, to dogs.* Therefore much more ought the plan of campaign to be hidden from the enemy. For this reason among other things that a soldier has to learn is the art of concealing his purpose lest it come to the enemy's knowledge, as stated in the Book on *Strategy* by Frontinus. Concealment of this kind is what is meant by an ambush which may be lawfully employed in a just war. Nor can these ambushes be properly called deceptions, nor are they contrary to justice or to a well-ordered will. For a man would have an inordinate will if he were unwilling that others should hide from him.

This suffices for the *Replies to the Objections*.

ARTICLE 4. Whether It Is Lawful To Fight on Holy Days?

We proceed thus to the Fourth Article: It seems unlawful to fight on holy days.

Objection 1. For holy days are instituted that we may give our time to the things of God. Hence they are included in the keeping of the Sabbath prescribed (Exod. 20. 8), for Sabbath is interpreted rest. But wars are full of unrest. Therefore by no means is it lawful to fight on holy days.

Obj. 2. Further, Certain persons are reproached (Isa. 58. 3) because on fast-days they exacted what was owing to them, were guilty of strife, and of striking with their fists. Much more, therefore, is it unlawful to fight on holy days.

Obj. 3. Further, No inordinate deed should be done to avoid temporal harm. But fighting on a holy day seems in itself to be an inordinate deed. Therefore no one should fight on a holy day even through the need of avoiding temporal harm.

On the contrary, It is written (I Machab. 2. 41): *The Jews rightly determined . . . saying: Whosoever shall come up against us to fight on the Sabbath-day, we will fight against him.*

I answer that, The observance of holy days is no hindrance to those things which are ordered to man's safety, even that of his body. Hence Our Lord argued with the Jews, saying (John 7. 23): *Are you angry at Me because I have healed the whole man on the Sabbath-day?* Hence physicians may lawfully attend to their patients on holy days. Yet much more reason is there for safeguarding the common weal (by which many are saved from being slain, and innumerable evils both temporal and spiritual prevented), than the bodily safety of an individual. Therefore, for the purpose of safeguarding the common weal of the faithful, it is lawful to carry on a war on holy days, provided there be need for doing so; because it would be to tempt God, if notwithstanding such a need, one were to choose to refrain from fighting. However, as soon as the need ceases, it is no longer lawful to fight on a holy day, for the reasons given. And this suffices for the *Replies to the Objections*.

2. The World Must be Made Safe for Democracy
The Fourteen Points
The Final Triumph

WOODROW WILSON

THE WORLD MUST BE MADE SAFE FOR DEMOCRACY

I have called the Congress into extraordinary session because there are serious, very serious, choices of policy to be made, and made immediately, which it was neither right nor constitutionally permissible that I should assume the responsibility of making.

On the third of February last I officially laid before you the extraordinary announcement of the Imperial German Government that on and after the first day of February it was its purpose to put aside all restraints of law or of humanity and use its submarines to sink every vessel that sought to approach either the ports of Great Britain and Ireland or the western coasts of Europe or any of the ports controlled by the enemies of Germany within the Mediterranean. That had seemed to be the object of the German submarine warfare earlier in the war, but since April of last year the Imperial Government had somewhat restrained the commanders of its undersea craft in conformity with its promise then given to us that passenger boats should not be sunk and that due warning would be given to all other vessels which

its submarines might seek to destroy, when no resistance was offered or escape attempted, and care taken that their crews were given at least a fair chance to save their lives in their open boats. The precautions taken were meager and haphazard enough, as was proved in distressing instance after instance in the progress of the cruel and unmanly business, but a certain degree of restraint was observed. The new policy has swept every restriction aside. Vessels of every kind, whatever their flag, their character, their cargo, their destination, their errand, have been ruthlessly sent to the bottom without warning and without thought of help or mercy for those on board, the vessels of friendly neutrals along with those of belligerents. Even hospital ships and ships carrying relief to the sorely bereaved and stricken people of Belgium, though the latter were provided with safe conduct through the proscribed areas by the German Government itself and were distinguished by unmistakable marks of identity, have been sunk with the same reckless lack of compassion or of principle.

I was for a little while unable to believe that such things would in fact be done by any government that had hitherto subscribed to the humane practices of civilized nations. International law

From, respectively, Address to Congress Asking for Declaration of War, April 2, 1917; Address to Congress, January 8, 1918; Address at the Metropolitan Opera House in New York City, September 27, 1918.

had its origin in the attempt to set up some law which would be respected and observed upon the seas, where no nation had right of dominion and where lay the free highways of the world. By painful stage after stage has that law been built up, with meager enough results, indeed, after all was accomplished that could be accomplished, but always with a clear view, at least, of what the heart and conscience of mankind demanded. This minimum of right the German Government has swept aside under the plea of retaliation and necessity and because it had no weapons which it could use at sea except these which it is impossible to employ as it is employing them without throwing to the winds all scruples of humanity or of respect for the understandings that were supposed to underlie the intercourse of the world. I am not now thinking of the loss of property involved, immense and serious as that is, but only of the wanton and wholesale destruction of the lives of noncombatants, men, women, and children, engaged in pursuits which have always, even in the darkest periods of modern history, been deemed innocent and legitimate. Property can be paid for; the lives of peaceful and innocent people cannot be. The present German submarine warfare against commerce is a warfare against mankind.

It is a war against all nations. American ships have been sunk, American lives taken, in ways which it has stirred us very deeply to learn of, but the ships and people of other neutral and friendly nations have been sunk and overwhelmed in the waters in the same way. There has been no discrimination. The challenge is to all mankind. Each nation must decide for itself how it will meet it. The choice we make for ourselves must be made with a moderation of counsel and a temperateness of judgment befitting our character and our motives as a nation. We must put excited feeling away. Our motive will not be revenge or the victorious assertion of the physical might of the nation, but only the vindication of right, of human right, of which we are only a single champion.

When I addressed the Congress on the twenty-sixth of February last I thought that it would suffice to assert our neutral rights with arms, our right to use the seas against unlawful interference,

our right to keep our people safe against unlawful violence. But armed neutrality, it now appears, is impracticable. . . . There is one choice we cannot make, we are incapable of making: we will not choose the path of submission and suffer the most sacred rights of our Nation and our people to be ignored or violated. The wrongs against which we now array ourselves are no common wrongs; they cut to the very roots of human life.

With a profound sense of the solemn and even tragical character of the step I am taking and of the grave responsibilities which it involves, but in unhesitating obedience to what I deem my constitutional duty, I advise that the Congress declare the recent course of the Imperial German Government to be in fact nothing less than war against the Government and people of the United States; that it formally accept the status of belligerent which has thus been thrust upon it; and that it take immediate steps not only to put the country in a more thorough state of defense but also to exert all its power and employ all its resources to bring the Government of the German Empire to terms and end the war. . . .

While we do these things, these deeply momentous things, let us be very clear, and make very clear to all the world what our motives and our objects are. My own thought has not been driven from its habitual and normal course by the unhappy events of the last two months, and I do not believe that the thought of the Nation has been altered or clouded by them. I have exactly the same things in mind now that I had in mind when I addressed the Senate on the twenty-second of January last; the same that I had in mind when I addressed the Congress on the third of February and on the twenty-sixth of February. Our object now, as then, is to vindicate the principles of peace and justice in the life of the world as against selfish and autocratic power and to set up amongst the really free and self-governed peoples of the world such a concert of purpose and of action as will henceforth insure the observance of those principles. Neutrality is no longer feasible or desirable where the peace of the world is involved and the freedom of its peoples, and the menace to that peace and freedom lies in the existence of autocratic governments backed by organized force which is controlled wholly by their will, not by the will of their people. We have seen the last of neutrality in such circumstances. We are at the beginning of an age in which it will be insisted that the same standards of conduct and of responsibility for wrong done shall be observed among nations and their governments that are observed among the individual citizens of civilized states.

We have no quarrel with the German people. We have no feeling towards them but one of sympathy and friendship. It was not upon their impulse that their government acted in entering the war. It was not with their previous knowledge or approval. It was a war determined upon as wars used to be determined upon in the old, unhappy days when people were nowhere consulted by their rulers and wars were provoked and waged in the interest of dynasties or of little groups of ambitious men who were accustomed to use their fellow men as pawns and tools. Self-governed nations do not fill their neighbor states with spies or set the course of intrigue to bring about some critical posture of affairs which will give them an opportunity to strike and make conquest. Such designs can be successfully worked out only under cover and where no one has the right to ask questions. Cunningly contrived plans of deception or aggression, carried, it may be, from generation to generation, can be worked out and kept from the light only within the privacy of courts or behind the carefully guarded confidences of a narrow and privileged class. They are happily impossible where public opinion commands and insists upon full information concerning all the nation's affairs.

A steadfast concert for peace can never be maintained except by a partnership of democratic nations. No autocratic government could be trusted to keep faith within it or observe its covenants. It must be a league of honor, a partnership of opinion. Intrigue would eat its vitals away; the plottings of inner circles who could plan what they would and render account to no one would be a corruption seated at its very heart. Only free peoples can hold their purpose and their honor steady to a common end and prefer the interests of mankind to any narrow interest of their own.

Does not every American feel that assurance has been added to our hope for the future peace

of the world by the wonderful and heartening things that have been happening within the last few weeks in Russia? Russia was known by those who knew it best to have been always in fact democratic at heart, in all the vital habits of her thought, in all the intimate relationships of her people that spoke their natural instinct, their habitual attitude towards life. The autocracy that crowned the summit of her political structure, long as it had stood and terrible as was the reality of its power, was not in fact Russian in origin, character, or purpose; and now it has been shaken off and the great, generous Russian people have been added in all their naïve majesty and might to the forces that are fighting for freedom in the world, for justice, and for peace. Here is a fit partner for a League of Honor.

One of the things that has served to convince us that the Prussian autocracy was not and could never be our friend is that from the very outset of the present war it has filled our unsuspecting communities and even our offices of government with spies and set criminal intrigues everywhere afoot against our national unity of counsel, our peace within and without, our industries and our commerce. Indeed, it is now evident that its spies were here even before the war began; and it is unhappily not a matter of conjecture but a fact proved in our courts of justice that the intrigues which have more than once come perilously near to disturbing the peace and dislocating the industries of the country have been carried on at the instigation, with the support, and even under the personal direction of official agents of the Imperial Government accredited to the Government of the United States. Even in checking these things and trying to extirpate them we have sought to put the most generous interpretation possible upon them because we knew that their source lay not in any hostile feeling or purpose of the German people towards us (who were no doubt as ignorant of them as we ourselves were), but only in the selfish designs of a Government that did what it pleased and told its people nothing. But they have played their part in serving to convince us at last that that Government entertains no real friendship for us and means to act against our peace and security at its convenience. That it means to stir up enemies against us at our very doors the intercepted note to the German Minister at Mexico City is eloquent evidence.

We are accepting this challenge of hostile purpose because we know that in such a Government, following such methods, we can never have a friend; and that in the presence of its organized power, always lying in wait to accomplish we know not what purpose, there can be no assured security for the democratic Governments of the world. We are now about to accept gage of battle with this natural foe to liberty and shall, if necessary, spend the whole force of the Nation to check and nullify its pretensions and its power. We are glad now that we see the facts with no veil of false pretense about them, to fight thus for the ultimate peace of the world and for the liberation of its peoples, the German peoples included: for the rights of nations great and small and the privilege of men everywhere to choose their way of life and of obedience. The world must be made safe for democracy. Its peace must be planted upon the tested foundations of political liberty. We have no selfish ends to serve. We desire no conquest, no dominion. We seek no indemnities for ourselves, no material compensation for the sacrifices we shall freely make. We are but one of the champions of the right of mankind. We shall be satisfied when those rights have been made as secure as the faith and the freedom of nations can make them.

Just because we fight without rancor and without selfish object, seeking nothing for ourselves but what we shall wish to share with all free people, we shall, I feel confident, conduct our operations as belligerents without passion and ourselves observe with proud punctilio the principles of right and of fair play we profess to be fighting for. . . .

It is a distressing and oppressive duty, Gentlemen of the Congress, which I have performed in thus addressing you. There are, it may be, many months of fiery trial and sacrifice ahead of us. It is a fearful thing to lead this great peaceful people into war, into the most terrible and disastrous of all wars, civilization itself seeming to be in the balance. But the right is more precious than peace, and we shall fight for the things which we have always carried nearest our hearts—for democracy, for the right of those who submit to authority to have a voice in their own Governments, for the rights and liberties of small nations, for a universal dominion of right by such a concert of free peoples as shall bring peace and safety to all nations and make the world itself at last free. To such a task we can dedicate our lives and our fortunes, everything that we are and everything that we have, with the pride of those who know that the day has come when America is privileged to spend her blood and her might for the principles that gave her birth and happiness and the peace which she has treasured. God helping her, she can do no other.

THE FOURTEEN POINTS

. . . It will be our wish and purpose that the processes of peace, when they are begun, shall be absolutely open and that they shall involve and permit henceforth no secret understandings of any kind. The day of conquest and aggrandizement is gone by; so is also the day of secret covenants

entered into in the interest of particular governments and likely at some unlooked-for moment to upset the peace of the world. It is this happy fact, now clear to the view of every public man whose thoughts do not still linger in an age that is dead and gone, which makes it possible for every nation whose purposes are consistent with justice and the peace of the world to avow now or at any other time the objects it has in view.

We entered this war because violations of right had occurred which touched us to the quick and made the life of our own people impossible unless they were corrected and the world secured once for all against their recurrence. What we demand in this war, therefore, is nothing peculiar to ourselves. It is that the world be made fit and safe to live in; and particularly that it be made safe for every peace-loving nation which, like our own, wishes to live its own life, determine its own institutions, be assured of justice and fair dealing by the other people of the world as against force and selfish aggression. All the peoples of the world are in effect partners in this interest, and for our own part we see very clearly that unless justice be done to others it will not be done to us. The program of the world's peace, therefore, is our program; and that program, the only possible program, as we see it, is this:

I. Open covenants of peace, openly arrived at, after which there shall be no private international understandings of any kind but diplomacy shall proceed always frankly and in the public view.

II. Absolute freedom of navigation upon the seas, outside territorial waters, alike in peace and in war, except as the seas may be closed in whole or in part by international action for the enforcement of international covenants.

III. The removal, so far as possible, of all economic barriers and the establishment of an equality of trade conditions among all the nations consenting to the peace and associating themselves for its maintenance.

IV. Adequate guarantees given and taken that national armaments will be reduced to the lowest point consistent with domestic safety.

V. A free, open-minded, and absolutely impartial adjustment of all colonial claims, based upon a strict observance of the principle that in determining all such questions of sovereignty the interests of the populations concerned must have equal weight with the equitable claims of the government whose title is to be determined.

VI. The evacuation of all Russian territory and such a settlement of all questions affecting Russia as will secure the best and freest cooperation of the other nations of the world in obtaining for her an unhampered and unembarrassed opportunity for the independent determination of her own political development and national policy and assure her of a sincere welcome into the society of free nations under institutions of her own choosing; and, more than a welcome, assistance also of every kind that she may need and may herself desire. The treatment accorded Russia by her sister nations in the months to come will be the acid test of their good will, of their comprehension of her needs as distinguished from their own interests, and of their intelligent and unselfish sympathy.

VII. Belgium, the whole world will agree, must be evacuated and restored, without any attempt to limit the sovereignty which she enjoys in common with all other free nations. No other single act will serve as this will serve to restore confidence among the nations in the laws which they have themselves set and determined for the government of their relations with one another. Without this healing act the whole structure and validity of international law is forever impaired.

VIII. All French territory should be freed and the invaded portions restored, and the wrong done to France by Prussia in 1871 in the matter of Alsace-Lorraine, which has unsettled the peace of the world for nearly fifty years, should be righted, in order that peace may once more be made secure in the interest of all.

IX. A readjustment of the frontiers of Italy should be effected along clearly recognizable lines of nationality.

X. The peoples of Austria-Hungary, whose place among the nations we wish to see safeguarded and assured, should be accorded the freest opportunity of autonomous development.

XI. Rumania, Serbia, and Montenegro should be evacuated; occupied territories restored; Serbia accorded free and secure access to the sea; and the relations of the several Balkan states to one another determined by friendly counsel along historically established lines of allegiance and nationality; and international guarantees of the political and economic independence and territorial integrity of the several Balkan states should be entered into.

XII. The Turkish portions of the present Ottoman Empire should be assured a secure sovereignty, but the other nationalities which are now under Turkish rule should be assured an undoubted security of life and an absolutely unmolested opportunity of autonomous development, and the Dardanelles should be permanently opened as a free passage to the ships and commerce of all nations under international guarantees.

XIII. An independent Polish state should be erected which should include the territories inhabited by indisputably Polish populations, which should be assured a free and secure access to the sea, and whose political and economic independence and territorial integrity should be guaranteed by international covenant.

XIV. A general association of nations must be formed under specific covenants for the purpose of affording mutual guarantees of political independence and territorial integrity to great and small states alike.

In regard to these essential rectifications of wrong and assertions of right we feel ourselves to be intimate partners of all the governments and peoples associated together against the imperialists. We cannot be separated in interest or divided in purpose. We stand together until the end.

For such arrangements and covenants we are willing to fight and to continue to fight until they are achieved; but only because we wish the right to prevail and desire a just and stable peace such as can be secured only by removing the chief provocations to war, which this program does remove. We have no jealousy of German greatness, and there is nothing in this program that impairs it. We grudge her no achievement or distinction of learning or of pacific enterprise such as have made her record very bright and very enviable. We do not wish to injure her or to block in any way her legitimate influence or power. We do not wish to fight her either with arms or with hostile arrangements of trade if she is willing to associate herself with us and the other peace-loving nations of the world in covenants of justice and law and fair dealing. We wish her only to accept a place of equality among the peoples of the world—the new world in which we now live—instead of a place of mastery.

Neither do we presume to suggest to her any alteration or modification of her institutions. But it is necessary, we must frankly say, and necessary as a preliminary to any intelligent dealings with her on our part, that we should know whom her spokesmen speak for when they speak to us, whether for the Reichstag majority or for the military party and the men whose creed is imperial domination.

We have spoken now, surely, in terms too concrete to admit of any further doubt or question. An evident principle runs through the whole program I have outlined. It is the principle of justice to all peoples and nationalities, and their right to live on equal terms of liberty and safety with one another, whether they be strong or weak. Unless this principle be made its foundation no part of the structure of international justice can stand. The people of the United States could act upon no other principle; and to the vindication of this principle they are ready to devote their lives, their honor, and everything that they possess. The moral climax of this the culminating and final war for human liberty has come, and they are ready to put their own strength, their own highest purpose, their own integrity and devotion to the test.

THE FINAL TRIUMPH

. . . At every turn of the war we gain a fresh consciousness of what we mean to accomplish by it. When our hope and expectation are most excited we think more definitely than before of the issues that hang upon it and of the purposes which must be realized by means of it. For it has positive and well-defined purposes which we did not determine and which we cannot alter. No statesman or assembly created them; no statesman or assembly can alter them. They have arisen out of the very nature and circumstances of the war. The most that statesmen or assemblies can do is to carry them out or be false to them. They were perhaps not clear at the outset; but they are clear now. The war has lasted more than four years and the whole world has been drawn into it. The common will of mankind has been substituted for the particular purposes of individual states. Individual statesmen may have started the conflict, but neither they nor their opponents can stop it as they please. It has become a peoples' war, and peoples of all sorts and races, of every degree of power and variety of fortune, are involved in its sweeping processes of change and settlement. We came into it when its character had become fully defined and it was plain that no nation could stand apart or be indifferent to its outcome. Its challenge drove to the heart of everything we cared for and lived for. The voice of the war had become clear and gripped our hearts. Our brothers from many lands, as well as our own murdered dead under the sea, were calling to us, and we responded, fiercely and of course.

The air was clear about us. We saw things in their full, convincing proportions as they were; and we have seen them with steady eyes and unchanging comprehension ever since. We accepted the issues of the war as facts, not as any group of men either here or elsewhere had defined them, and we can accept no outcome which does not squarely meet and settle them. Those issues are these:

Shall the military power of any nation or group of nations be suffered to determine the fortunes of peoples over whom they have no right to rule except the right of force?

Shall strong nations be free to wrong weak nations and make them subject to their purpose and interest?

Shall peoples be ruled and dominated, even in their own internal affairs, by arbitrary and irresponsible force or by their own will and choice?

Shall there be a common standard of right and privilege for all peoples and nations or shall the strong do as they will and the weak suffer without redress?

Shall the assertion of right be haphazard and by casual alliance or shall there be a common concert to oblige the observance of common rights?

No man, no group of men, chose these to be the issues of the struggle. They *are* the issues of it; and they must be settled—by no arrangement or compromise or adjustment of interests, but definitely and once for all and with a full and unequivocal acceptance of the principle that the interest of the weakest is as sacred as the interest of the strongest.

This is what we mean when we speak of a permanent peace, if we speak sincerely, intelligently, and with a real knowledge and comprehension of the matter we deal with.

We are all agreed that there can be no peace obtained by any kind of bargain or compromise with the governments of the Central Empires, because we have dealt with them already and have seen them deal with other governments that were parties to this struggle, at Brest-Litovsk and Bucharest. They have convinced us that they are without honor and do not intend justice. They observe no covenants, accept no principle but force and their own interest. We cannot "come to terms" with them. They have made it impossible. The German people must by this time be fully aware that we cannot accept the word of those who forced this war upon us. We do not think the same thoughts or speak the same language of agreement.

It is of capital importance that we should also be explicitly agreed that no peace shall be obtained by any kind of compromise or abatement of the principles we have avowed as the principles for which we are fighting. There should exist no doubt about that. I am, therefore, going to take the liberty of speaking with the utmost frankness about the practical implications that are involved in it. . . .

It is the peculiarity of this great war that while statesmen have seemed to cast about for definitions of their purpose and have sometimes seemed to shift their ground and their point of view, the thought of the mass of men, whom statesmen are supposed to instruct and lead, has grown more and more unclouded; more and more certain of what it is that they are fighting for. National purposes have fallen more and more into the background and the common purpose of enlightened mankind has taken their place. The counsels of plain men have become on all hands more simple and straightforward and more unified than the counsels of sophisticated men of affairs, who still retain the impression that they are playing a game of power and playing for high stakes. That is why I have said that this is a peoples' war, not a statesmen's. Statesmen must follow the clarified common thought or be broken.

I take that to be the significance of the fact that assemblies and associations of many kinds made up of plain workaday people have demanded, almost every time they came together, and are still demanding, that the leaders of their Governments declare to them plainly what it is, exactly what it is, that they were seeking in this war, and what they think the items of the final settlement should be. They are not yet satisfied with what they have been told. They still seem to fear that they are getting what they ask for only in statesmen's terms—only in the terms of territorial arrangements and divisions of power, and not in terms of broad-visioned justice and mercy and peace and the satisfaction of those deep-seated longings of oppressed and distracted men and women and enslaved peoples that seem to them the only things worth fighting a war for that engulfs the world. Perhaps statesmen have not always recognized this changed aspect of the whole world of policy and action. Perhaps they have not always spoken in direct reply to the questions asked because they did not know how searching those questions were and what sort of answers they demanded. . . .

. . . "Peace drives" can be effectively neutralized and silenced only by showing that every victory of the nations associated against Germany brings the nations nearer the sort of peace which will bring security and reassurance to all peoples and make the recurrence of another such struggle of pitiless force and bloodshed forever impossible, and that nothing else can. Germany is constantly intimating the "terms" she will accept; and always finds that the world does not want terms. It wishes the final triumph of justice and fair dealing.

2
REALISM

3.   The Melian Debate

THUCYDIDES

[416 B.C.] **84.** The next summer went Alcibiades to Argos with twenty galleys and took thence the suspected Argives and such as seemed to savour of the Lacedaemonian faction, to the number of three hundred, and put them into the nearest of the islands subject to the Athenian state.

The Athenians made war also against the isle of Melos, with thirty galleys of their own, six of Chios, and two of Lesbos. Wherein were of their own twelve hundred men of arms, three hundred archers, and twenty archers on horseback; and of their confederates and islanders, about fifteen hundred men of arms. The Melians are a colony of the Lacedaemonians, and therefore refused to be subject, as the rest of the islands were, unto the Athenians, but rested at the first neutral; and afterwards, when the Athenians put them to it by wasting of their land, they entered into open war.

Now the Athenian commanders, Cleomedes, the son of Lycomedes, and Tisias, the son of Tisimachus, being encamped upon their land with

these forces, before they would hurt the same sent ambassadors to deal with them first by way of conference. These ambassadors the Melians refused to bring before the multitude, but commanded them to deliver their message before the magistrates and the few; and they accordingly said as followeth:

85. *Athenians*. "Since we may not speak to the multitude, for fear lest when they hear our persuasive and unanswerable arguments all at once in a continued oration, they should chance to be seduced (for we know that this is the scope of your bringing us to audience before the few), make surer yet that point, you that sit here; answer you also to every particular, not in a set speech, but presently interrupting us whensoever anything shall be said by us which shall seem unto you to be otherwise. And first answer us whether you like this motion or not?"

86. Whereunto the council of the Melians answered: "The equity of a leisurely debate is not to be found fault withal; but this preparation of war, not future but already here present, seemeth not to agree with the same. For we see

---

From *The Peloponnesian War*, fifth book, the Thomas Hobbes translation.

that you are come to be judges of the conference, and that the issue of it, if we be superior in argument and therefore yield not, is likely to bring us war, and if we yield, servitude.''

87. *Ath.* ''Nay, if you be come together to reckon up suspicions of what may be, or to any other purpose than to take advice upon what is present and before your eyes, how to save your city from destruction, let us give over. But if this be the point, let us speak to it.''

88. *Melians.* ''It is reason, and pardonable for men in our cases, to turn both their words and thoughts upon divers things. Howsoever, this consultation being held only upon the point of our safety, we are content, if you think good, to go on with the course you have propounded.''

89. *Ath.* ''As we therefore will not, for our parts, with fair pretences, as, that having defeated the Medes, our reign is therefore lawful, or that we come against you for injury done, make a long discourse without being believed; so would we have you also not expect to prevail by saying either that you therefore took not our parts because you were a colony of the Lacedaemonians or that you have done us no injury. But out of those things which we both of us do really think, let us go through with that which is feasible, both you and we knowing that in human disputation justice is then only agreed on when the necessity is equal; whereas they that have odds of power exact as much as they can, and the weak yield to such conditions as they can get.''

90. *Mel.* ''Well then (seeing you put the point of profit in the place of justice), we hold it profitable for ourselves not to overthrow a general profit to all men, which is this: that men in danger, if they plead reason and equity, nay, though somewhat without the strict compass of justice, yet it ought ever to do them good. And the same most of all concerneth you, forasmuch as you shall else give an example unto others of the greatest revenge that can be taken if you chance to miscarry.''

91. *Ath.* ''As for us, though our dominion should cease, yet we fear not the sequel. For not they that command, as do the Lacedaemonians, are cruel to those that are vanquished by them (yet we have nothing to do now with the Lacedaemonians), but such as having been in sub-

jection have assaulted those that commanded them and gotten the victory. But let the danger of that be to ourselves. In the meantime we tell you this: that we are here now both to enlarge our own dominion and also to confer about the saving of your city. For we would have dominion over you without oppressing you, and preserve you to the profit of us both.''

92. *Mel.* ''But how can it be profitable for us to serve, though it be so for you to command?''

93. *Ath.* ''Because you, by obeying, shall save yourselves from extremity; and we, not destroying you, shall reap profit by you.''

94. *Mel.* ''But will you not accept that we remain quiet and be your friends (whereas before we were your enemies), and take part with neither?''

95. *Ath.* ''No. For your enmity doth not so much hurt us as your friendship will be an argument of our weakness and your hatred of our power amongst those we have rule over.''

96. *Mel.* ''Why? Do your subjects measure equity so, as to put those that never had to do with you, and themselves, who for the most part have been your own colonies, and some of them after revolt conquered, into one and the same consideration?''

97. *Ath.* ''Why not? For they think they have reason on their side, both the one sort and the other, and that such as are subdued are subdued by force, and such as are forborne are so through our fear. So that by subduing you, besides the extending of our dominion over so many more subjects, we shall assure it the more over those we had before, especially being masters of the sea, and you islanders, and weaker (except you can get the victory) than others whom we have subdued already.''

98. *Mel.* ''Do you think then, that there is no assurance in that which we propounded? For here again (since driving us from the plea of equity you persuade us to submit to your profit), when we have shewed you what is good for us, we must endeavour to draw you to the same, as far forth as it shall be good for you also. As many therefore as now are neutral, what do you but make them your enemies, when, beholding these your proceedings, they look that hereafter you will also turn your arms upon them? And what is this, but to make greater the enemies you have already, and to make others your enemies, each against their wills, that would not else have been so?''

99. *Ath.* ''We do not think that they shall be ever the more our enemies, who inhabiting anywhere in the continent, will be long ere they so much as keep guard upon their liberty against us. But islanders unsubdued, as you be, or islanders offended with the necessity of subjection which they are already in, these may indeed, by unadvised courses, put both themselves and us into apparent danger.''

100. *Mel.* ''If you then to retain your command, and your vassals to get loose from you, will undergo the utmost of danger, would it not in us, that be already free, be great baseness and cowardice if we should not encounter anything whatsoever rather than suffer ourselves to be brought into bondage?''

101. *Ath.* ''No, if you advise rightly. For you have not in hand a match of valour upon equal terms, wherein to forfeit your honour, but rather a consultation upon your safety that you resist not such as be so far your overmatches.''

102. *Mel.* ''But we know that, in matter of war, the event is sometimes otherwise than according to the difference of number in sides; and that if we yield presently, all our hope is lost; whereas if we hold out, we have yet a hope to keep ourselves up.''

103. *Ath.* ''Hope, the comfort of danger, when such use it as have to spare, though it hurt them, yet it destroys them not. But to such as set their rest upon it (for it is a thing by nature prodigal), it at once by failing maketh itself known; and known, leaveth no place for future caution. Which let not be your own case, you that are but weak and have no more but this one stake. Nor be you like unto many men, who, though they may presently save themselves by human means, will yet, when upon pressure of the enemy their most apparent hopes fail them, betake themselves to blind ones, as divination, oracles, and other such things which with hopes destroy men.''

104. *Mel.* ''We think it, you well know, a hard matter for us to combat your power and fortune, unless we might do it on equal terms. Nevertheless we believe that, for fortune, we shall be nothing inferior, as having the gods on our side, because we stand innocent against men unjust; and for power, what is wanting in us will be supplied by our league with the Lacedaemonians, who are of necessity obliged, if for no other cause, yet for consanguinity's sake and for their own honour, to defend us. So that we are confident, not altogether so much without reason as you think.''

105. *Ath.* ''As for the favour of the gods, we expect to have it as well as you; for we neither do nor require anything contrary to what mankind hath decreed, either concerning the worship of the gods or concerning themselves. For of the gods we think according to the common opinion; and of men, that for certain by necessity of nature they will everywhere reign over such as they be too strong for. Neither did we make this law nor are we the first that use it made; but as we found it, and shall leave it to posterity for ever, so also we use it, knowing that you likewise, and others that should have the same power which we have, would do the same. So that forasmuch as toucheth the favour of the gods, we have in reason no fear of being inferior. And as for the opinion you have of the Lacedaemonians, in that you believe they will help you for their own honour, we bless your innocent minds, but affect not your folly. For the Lacedaemonians, though in respect of themselves and the constitutions of their own country they are wont for the most part to be generous; yet in respect of others, though much might be alleged, yet the shortest way one might say it all thus: that most apparently of all men, they hold for honourable that which pleaseth, and for just that which profiteth. And such an opinion maketh nothing for your now absurd means of safety.''

106. *Mel.* ''Nay, for this same opinion of theirs, we now the rather believe that they will not betray their own colony, the Melians, and thereby become perfidious to such of the Grecians as be their friends and beneficial to such as be their enemies.''

107. *Ath.* ''You think not, then, that what is profitable must be also safe, and that which is just and honourable must be performed with danger, which commonly the Lacedaemonians are least willing of all men to undergo [for others].''

108. *Mel.* ''But we suppose that they will

undertake danger for us rather than for any other; and that they think that we will be more assured unto them than unto any other, because for action, we lie near to Peloponnesus, and for affection, are more faithful than others for our nearness of kin."

109. *Ath.* "The security of such as are at wars consisteth not in the good will of those that are called to their aid, but in the power of those means they excel in. And this the Lacedaemonians themselves use to consider more than any; and therefore, out of diffidence in their own forces, they take many of their confederates with them, though to an expedition but against their neighbours. Wherefore it is not likely, we being masters of the sea, that they will ever pass over into an island."

110. *Mel.* "Yea, but they may have others to send; and the Cretic sea is wide, wherein to take another is harder for him that is master of it than it is for him that will steal by to save himself. And if this course fail, they may turn their arms against your own territory or those of your confederates not invaded by Brasidas. And then you shall have to trouble yourselves no more about a territory that you have nothing to do withal, but about your own and your confederates."

111. *Ath.* "Let them take which course of these they will that you also may find by experience and not be ignorant that the Athenians never yet gave over siege for fear of any diversion upon others. But we observe that, whereas you said you would consult of your safety, you have not yet in all this discourse said anything which a man relying on could hope to be preserved by; the strongest arguments you use are but future hopes; and your present power is too short to defend you against the forces already arranged against you. You shall therefore take very absurd counsel, unless, excluding us, you make amongst yourselves some more discreet conclusion; for [when you are by yourselves], you will no more set your thoughts upon shame, which, when dishonour and danger stand before men's eyes, for the most part undoeth them. For many, when they have foreseen into what dangers they were entering, have nevertheless been so overcome by that forcible word dishonour that that which is but called dishonour hath caused them to fall willingly

into immedicable calamities, and so to draw upon themselves really, by their own madness, a greater dishonour than could have befallen them by fortune. Which you, if you deliberate wisely, will take heed of, and not think shame to submit to a most potent city, and that upon so reasonable conditions as of league and of enjoying your own under tribute; and seeing choice is given you of war or safety, do not out of peevishness take the worse. For such do take the best course who, though they give no way to their equals, yet do fairly accommodate to their superiors, and towards their inferiors use moderation. Consider of it, therefore, whilst we stand off; and have often in your mind that you deliberate of your country, which is to be happy or miserable in and by this one consultation."

112. So the Athenians went aside from the conference; and the Melians, after they had decreed the very same things which before they had spoken, made answer unto them in this manner: "Men of Athens, our resolution is no other than what you have heard before; nor will we, in a small portion of time, overthrow that liberty in which our city hath remained for the space of seven hundred years since it was first founded. But trusting to the fortune by which the gods have preserved it hitherto and unto the help of men, that is, of the Lacedaemonians, we will do our best to maintain the same. But this we offer: to be your friends, enemies to neither side, and you to depart out of our land, after agreement such as we shall both think fit."

113. Thus the Melians answered. To which the Athenians, the conference being already broken off, replied thus: "You are the only men, as it seemeth to us, by this consultation, that think future things more certain than things seen, and behold things doubtful, through desire to have them true, as if they were already come to pass. As you attribute and trust the most unto the Lacedaemonians, and to fortune and hopes, so will you be the most deceived."

114. This said, the Athenian ambassadors departed to their camp. And the commanders, seeing that the Melians stood out, fell presently to the war, and dividing the work among the several cities, encompassed the city of the Melians with a wall. The Athenians afterwards left some forces of their own and of their confederates for a guard both by sea and land, and with the greatest part of their army went home. The rest that were left besieged the place.

115. About the same time the Argives, making a road into Phliasia, lost about eighty of their men by ambush laid for them by the men of Phlius and the outlaws of their own city. And the Athenians that lay in Pylus fetched in thither a great booty from the Lacedaemonians. Notwithstanding which, the Lacedaemonians did not war upon them [as] renouncing the peace, but gave leave by edict only to any of their people that would to take booties reciprocally in the territory of the Athenians. The Corinthians also made war upon the Athenians; but it was for certain controversies of their own, and the rest of Peloponnesus stirred not.

The Melians also took that part of the wall of the Athenians, by an assault in the night, which looked towards the market place, and having slain the men that guarded it, brought into the town both corn and other provision, whatsoever they could buy for money, and so returned and lay still. And the Athenians from thenceforth kept a better watch. And so this summer ended.

116. The winter following, the Lacedaemonians being about to enter with their army into the territory of the Argives, when they perceived that the sacrifices which they made on the border for their passage were not acceptable, returned. And the Argives, having some of their own city in suspicion in regard of this design of the Lacedaemonians, apprehended some of them, and some escaped.

About the same time the Melians took another part of the wall of the Athenians, they that kept the siege being then not many. But this done, there came afterwards some fresh forces from Athens, under the conduct of Philocrates, the son of Demeas. And the town being now strongly besieged, there being also within some that practised to have it given up, they yielded themselves to the discretion of the Athenians, who slew all the men of military age, made slaves of the women and children, and inhabited the place with a colony sent thither afterwards of five hundred men of their own.

4.   From *The Prince*

Niccolò Machiavelli

CHAPTER 5: HOW CITIES OR PRINCIPALITIES ARE TO BE GOVERNED THAT PREVIOUS TO BEING CONQUERED HAD LIVED UNDER THEIR OWN LAWS.

Conquered states that have been accustomed to liberty and the government of their own laws can be held by the conqueror in three different ways. The first is to ruin them; the second, for the conqueror to go and reside there in person; and the third is to allow them to continue to live under their own laws, subject to a regular tribute, and to create in them a government of a few, who will keep the country friendly to the conqueror. Such a government, having been established by the new prince, knows that it cannot maintain itself without the support of his power and friendship, and it becomes its interest therefore to sustain him. A city that has been accustomed to free institutions is much easier held by its own citizens than in any other way, if the conqueror desires to preserve it. The Spartans and the Romans will serve as examples of these different

Translated by Christian E. Detmold; first published in the United States in 1882.

ways of holding a conquered state.

The Spartans held Athens and Thebes, creating there a government of a few; and yet they lost both these states again. The Romans, for the purpose of retaining Capua, Carthage, and Numantia, destroyed them, but did not lose them. They wished to preserve Greece in somewhat the same way that the Spartans had held it, by making her free and leaving her in the enjoyment of her own laws, but did not succeed; so that they were obliged to destroy many cities in that country for the purpose of holding it. In truth there was no other safe way of keeping possession of that country but to ruin it. And whoever becomes master of a city that has been accustomed to liberty, and does not destroy it, must himself expect to be ruined by it. For they will always resort to rebellion in the name of liberty and their ancient institutions, which will never be effaced from their memory, either by the lapse of time, or by benefits bestowed by the new master. No matter what he may do, or what precautions he may take, if he does not separate and disperse the inhabitants, they will on the first occasion invoke the name of liberty and the memory of their ancient institutions, as was done by Pisa after having been held over a hundred years in subjection by the Florentines.

But it is very different with states that have been accustomed to live under a prince. When the line of the prince is once extinguished, the inhabitants, being on the one hand accustomed to obey, and on the other having lost their ancient sovereign, can neither agree to create a new one from amongst themselves, nor do they know how to live in liberty; and thus they will be less prompt to take up arms, and the new prince will readily be able to gain their good will and to assure himself of them. But republics have more vitality, a greater spirit of resentment and desire of revenge, for the memory of their ancient liberty neither can nor will permit them to remain quiet, and therefore the surest way of holding them is either to destroy them, or for the conqueror to go and live there. . . .

CHAPTER 15: OF THE MEANS BY WHICH MEN, AND ESPECIALLY PRINCES, WIN APPLAUSE, OR INCUR CENSURE.

It remains now to be seen in what manner a prince should conduct himself towards his subjects and his allies; and knowing that this matter has already been treated by many others, I apprehend that my writing upon it also may be deemed presumptuous, especially as in the discussion of the same I shall differ from the rules laid down by others. But as my aim is to write something that may be useful to him for whom it is intended, it seems to me proper to pursue the real truth of the matter, rather than to indulge in mere speculation on the same; for many have imagined republics and principalities such as have never been known to exist in reality. For the manner in which men live is so different from the way in which they ought to live, that he who leaves the common course for that which he ought to follow will find that it leads him to ruin rather than to safety. For a man who, in all respects, will carry out only his professions of good, will be apt to be ruined amongst so many who are evil. A prince therefore who desires to maintain himself must learn to be not always good, but to be so or not as necessity may

require. Leaving aside then the imaginary things concerning princes, and confining ourselves only to the realities, I say that all men when they are spoken of, and more especially princes, from being in a more conspicuous position, are noted for some quality that brings them either praise or censure. Thus one is deemed liberal, another miserly (*misero*) to use a Tuscan expression (for avaricious is he who by rapine desires to gain, and miserly we call him who abstains too much from the enjoyment of his own). One man is esteemed generous, another rapacious; one cruel, another merciful; one faithless, and another faithful; one effeminate and pusillanimous, another ferocious and brave; one affable, another haughty; one lascivious, another chaste; one sincere, the other cunning; one facile, another inflexible; one grave, another frivolous; one religious, another sceptical; and so on.

I am well aware that it would be most praiseworthy for a prince to possess all of the above-named qualities that are esteemed good; but as he cannot have them all, nor entirely observe them, because of his human nature which does not permit it, he should at least be prudent enough to know how to avoid the infamy of those vices that would rob him of his state; and if possible also to guard against such as are likely to endanger it. But if that be not possible, then he may with less hesitation follow his natural inclinations. Nor need he care about incurring censure for such vices, without which the preservation of his state may be difficult. For, all things considered, it will be found that some things that seem like virtue will lead you to ruin if you follow them; whilst others, that apparently are vices, will, if followed, result in your safety and well-being. . . .

CHAPTER 17: OF CRUELTY AND CLEMENCY, AND WHETHER IT IS BETTER TO BE LOVED THAN FEARED.

Coming down now to the other aforementioned qualities, I say that every prince ought to desire the reputation of being merciful, and not cruel; at the same time, he should be careful not to misuse that mercy. Cesar Borgia was reputed cruel, yet by his cruelty he reunited the Romagna to his states, and restored that province to order, peace, and loyalty; and if we carefully examine his course, we shall find it to have been really much more merciful than the course of the people of Florence, who to escape the reputation of cruelty, allowed Pistoja to be destroyed. A prince, therefore, should not mind the ill repute of cruelty, when he can thereby keep his subjects united and loyal; for a few displays of severity will really be more merciful than to allow, by an excess of clemency, disorders to occur, which are apt to result in rapine and murder; for these injure a whole community, whilst the executions ordered by the prince fall only upon a few individuals. And, above all others, the new prince will find it almost impossible to avoid the reputation of cruelty, because new states are generally exposed to many dangers . . . .

A prince, however, should be slow to believe and to act; nor should he be too easily alarmed by his own fears, and should proceed moderately and with prudence and humanity, so that an excess of confidence may not make him incautious, nor too much mistrust make him intolerant. This, then, gives rise to the question "whether it be better to be beloved than feared, or "to be feared than beloved." It will naturally be answered that it would be desirable to be both the one and the other; but as it is difficult to be both at the same time, it is much more safe to be feared than to be loved, when you have to choose between the two. For it may be said of men in general that they are ungrateful and fickle, dissemblers, avoiders of danger, and greedy of gain. So long as you shower benefits upon them, they are all yours; they offer you their blood, their substance, their lives, and their children, provided the necessity for it is far off; but when it is near at hand, then they revolt. And the prince who relies upon their words, without having otherwise provided for his security, is ruined; for friendships that are won by rewards, and not by greatness and nobility of soul, although deserved, yet are not real, and cannot be depended upon in time of adversity.

Besides, men have less hesitation in offending one who makes himself beloved than one who makes himself feared; for love holds by a bond of obligation which, as mankind is bad, is broken on every occasion whenever it is for the interest of the obliged party to break it. But fear holds by the apprehension of punishment, which never leaves men. A prince, however, should make himself feared in such a manner that, if he has not won the affections of his people, he shall at least not incur their hatred; for the being feared, and not hated, can go very well together, if the prince abstains from taking the substance of his subjects, and leaves them their women. And if you should be obliged to inflict capital punishment upon any one, then be sure to do so ony when there is manifest cause and proper justification for it; and, above all things, abstain from taking people's property, for men will sooner forget the death of their fathers than the loss of their patrimony. Besides, there will never be any lack of reasons for taking people's property; and a prince who once begins to live by rapine will ever find excuses for seizing other people's property. On the other hand, reasons for taking life are not so easily found, and are more readily exhausted. But when a prince is at the head of his army, with a multitude of soldiers under his command, then it is above all things necessary for him to disregard the reputation of cruelty; for without such severity an army cannot be kept together, nor disposed for any successful feat of arms. . . .

To come back now to the question whether it be better to be beloved than feared, I conclude that, as men love of their own free will, but are inspired with fear by the will of the prince, a wise prince should always rely upon himself, and not upon the will of others; but, above all, should he always strive to avoid being hated, as I have already said above.

CHAPTER 18: IN WHAT MANNER PRINCES SHOULD KEEP THEIR FAITH.

It must be evident to every one that it is more praiseworthy for a prince always to maintain good faith, and practise integrity rather than craft and deceit. And yet the experience of our own times has shown that those princes have achieved great things who made small account of good faith, and who understood by cunning to circumvent the intelligence of others; and that in the end they got the better of those whose actions were dictated by loyalty and good faith. . . .

A sagacious prince then cannot and should not fulfil his pledges when their observance is contrary to his interest, and when the causes that induced him to pledge his faith no longer exist. If men were all good, then indeed this precept would be bad; but as men are naturally bad, and will not observe their faith towards you, you must, in the same way, not observe yours to them; and no prince ever yet lacked legitimate reasons with which to color his want of good faith. Innumerable modern examples could be given of this; and it could easily be shown how many treaties of peace, and how many engagements, have been made null and void by the faithlessness of princes; and he who has best known how to play the fox has ever been the most successful.

But it is necessary that the prince should know how to color this nature well, and how to be a great hypocrite and dissembler. For men are so simple, and yield so much to immediate necessity, that the deceiver will never lack dupes. . . .

It is not necessary, however, for a prince to possess all the above-mentioned qualities; but it is essential that he should at least seem to have them. I will even venture to say, that to have and to practise them constantly is pernicious, but to seem to have them is useful. For instance, a prince should seem to be merciful, faithful, humane, religious, and upright, and should even be so in reality; but he should have his mind so trained that, when occasion requires it, he may know how to change to the opposite. And it must be understood that a prince, and especially one who has but recently acquired his state, cannot perform all those things which cause men to be esteemed as good; he being often obliged, for the sake of maintaining his state, to act contrary to humanity, charity, and religion. And therefore is it necessary that he should have a versatile mind, capable of changing readily, according as the winds and changes of fortune bid him; and, as has been said above, not to swerve from the good if possible, but to know how to resort to evil if necessity demands it.

A prince then should be very careful never to allow anything to escape his lips that does not abound in the above-named five qualities, so that

to see and to hear him he may seem all charity, integrity, and humanity, all uprightness, and all piety. And more than all else it is necessary for a prince to seem to possess the last quality; for mankind in general judge more by what they see and hear than by what they feel, every one being capable of the former, and but few of the latter. Everybody sees what you seem to be, but few really feel what you are; and these few dare not oppose the opinion of the many, who are protected by the majesty of the state; for the actions of all men, and especially those of princes, are judged by the result, where there is no other judge to whom to appeal.

A prince then should look mainly to the successful maintenance of his state. The means which he employs for this will always be accounted honorable, and will be praised by everybody; for the common people are always taken by appearances and by results, and it is the vulgar mass that constitutes the world. But a very few have rank and station, whilst the many have nothing to sustain them. A certain prince of our time, whom it is well not to name, never preached anything but peace and good faith; but if he had always observed either the one or the other, it would in most instances have cost him his reputation or his state. . . .

CHAPTER 21: HOW PRINCES SHOULD CONDUCT THEMSELVES TO ACQUIRE A REPUTATION.

. . . It is also important for a prince to give striking examples of his interior administration, (similar to those that are related of Messer Bernabo di Milano,) when an occasion presents itself to reward or punish any one who has in civil affairs either rendered great service to the state, or committed some crime, so that it may be much talked about. But, above all, a prince should endeavor to invest all his actions with a character of grandeur and excellence. A prince, furthermore, becomes esteemed when he shows himself either a true friend or a real enemy; that is, when, regardless of consequences, he declares himself openly for or against another, which will always be more creditable to him than to remain neutral. For if two of your neighboring potentates should come to war amongst themselves, they are either of such character that, when either of them has been defeated, you will have cause to fear the conqueror, or not. In either case, it will always be better for you to declare yourself openly and make fair war; for if you fail to do so, you will be very apt to fall a prey to the victor, to the delight and satisfaction of the defeated party, and you will have no claim for protection or assistance from either the one or the other. For the conqueror will want no doubtful friends, who did not stand by him in time of trial; and the defeated party will not forgive you for having refused, with arms in hand, to take the chance of his fortunes.

When Antiochus came into Greece, having been sent by the Ætolians to drive out the Romans, he sent ambassadors to the Achaians, who were friends of the Romans, to induce them to remain neutral; whilst the Romans, on the other hand, urged them to take up arms in their behalf. When the matter came up for deliberation in the council of the Achaians, and the ambassadors of Antiochus endeavored to persuade them to remain neutral, the Roman legate replied: "As to the course which is said to be the best and most advantageous for your state, not to intervene in our war, I can assure you that the very reverse will be the case; for by not intervening you will, without thanks and without credit, remain a prize to the victor."

And it will always be the case that he who is not your friend will claim neutrality at your hands, whilst your friend will ask your armed intervention in his favor. Irresolute princes, for the sake of avoiding immediate danger, adopt most frequently the course of neutrality, and are generally ruined in consequence. But when a prince declares himself boldly in favor of one party, and that party proves victorious, even though the victor be powerful, and you are at his discretion, yet is he bound to you in love and obligation; and men are never so base as to repay these by such flagrant ingratitude as the oppressing you under these circumstances would be.

Moreover, victories are never so complete as to dispense the victor from all regard for justice. But when the party whom you have supported loses, then he will ever after receive you as a friend, and, when able, will assist you in turn; and thus you will have become the sharer of a fortune which in time may be retrieved.

In the second case, when the contending parties are such that you need not fear the victor, then it is the more prudent to give him your support; for you thereby aid one to ruin the other, whom he should save if he were wise; for although he has defeated his adversary, yet he remains at your discretion, inasmuch as without your assistance victory would have been impossible for him. And here it should be noted, that a prince ought carefully to avoid making common cause with any one more powerful than himself, for the purpose of attacking another power, unless he should be compelled to do so by necessity. For if the former is victorious, then you are at his mercy; and princes should, if possible, avoid placing themselves in such a position.

The Venetians allied themselves with France against the Duke of Milan, an alliance which they could easily have avoided, and which proved their ruin. But when it is unavoidable, as was the case with the Florentines when Spain and the Pope united their forces to attack Lombardy, then a prince ought to join the stronger party, for the reasons above given. Nor is it to be supposed that a state can ever adopt a course that is entirely safe; on the contrary, a prince must make up his mind to take the chance of all the doubts and uncertainties; for such is the order of things that one inconvenience cannot be avoided except at the risk of being exposed to another. And it is the province of prudence to discriminate amongst these inconveniences, and to accept the least evil for good.

A prince should also show himself a lover of virtue, and should honor all who excel in any one of the arts, and should encourage his citizens quietly to pursue their vocations, whether of commerce, agriculture, or any other human industry; so that the one may not abstain from embellishing his possessions for fear of their being taken from him, nor the other from opening new sources of commerce for fear of taxes. But the prince should provide rewards for those who are willing to do these things, and for all who strive to enlarge his city or state. And besides this, he should at suitable periods amuse his people with festivities and

5. The War and American Churches

REINHOLD NIEBUHR

The Christian Church of America has never been upon a lower level of spiritual insight and moral sensitivity than in this tragic age of world conflict. Living in a suffering world, with its ears assailed by the cries of the miserable victims of tyranny and conflict, it has chosen to identify the slogan "Keep America out of the War" with the Christian gospel. . . .

. . . It is important of course that religion should not involve itself again in a holy war. It is important that Christianity should recognize that all historic struggles are struggles between sinful men and not between the righteous and the sinners; but it is just as important to save what relative decency and justice the western world still has, against the most demonic tyranny of history. Obviously the Nazis could never have gained a position in Europe from which they can place the whole of a continent under their ban if western society were really healthy. Obviously there is decay in the democratic world and there

is no certainty that the capitalistic democracies will be able to rescue what is decent and just in their societies, either from internal corruption or external peril. History, however, does not present us with ideals and clear-cut choices.

There was a time when the socialists of Austria rightly declared that the difference between Hitler's and Schuschnigg's fascism was not very great. But when actually confronted with the peril of having Hitler's worse tyranny fastened upon Austria they wisely (though too tardily) decided that the difference might be all-important in that particular moment of history. That situation was symbolic of all historic decisions. The idea that it is possible to find a vantage point of guiltlessness from which to operate against the world is not a Christian idea but a modern rationalistic one. Ever since the eighteenth century modern secularists have been trying to find the specific causes of social sin and to eliminate them. Injustice was supposed to be caused solely by unjust governments or by faulty economic organization of society, or by human ignorance. Democracy was supposed to be the force of righteousness against monarchy. Socialism was assumed to be

Excerpted from *Christianity and Power Politics* by Reinhold Niebuhr (New York: Charles Scribner's Sons, 1940), pp. 33,35–38,39,40–41,42–47. Reprinted by permission of the author's estate.

free of all imperialistic passions while capitalism was supposed to be the sole source of the imperial will.

"If we can't find the real cause of social injustice," said a typical modern recently, "we would be forced to go back to the absurd doctrine of original sin." That remark is a revelation of the scientific "objectivity" of modernity. The Christian idea of original sin is ruled out *a priori*. This is understandable enough in a non-Christian world. What is absurd is that modern Christianity should have accepted this modern rejection of the doctrine of original sin with such pathetic eagerness and should have spent so much energy in seeking to prove that a Christian can be just as respectable and modern as a secularist. Does he not hold to the same absurd dogma of the goodness of human nature and does he not have the same pathetic hope that if only this or that fault in the educational, social, political or economic system is corrected man will cease to be a peril to himself and to his fellowmen?

The difficulty with such optimism in regard to human nature is that it confuses every political issue in the modern world. Modern Christianity, far from offering corrective insights to this optimism, makes confusion worse confounded by exaggerating it. The secularist believes in the gradual emergence of a universal mind. The Christian believes that every man is potentially a Christ. He has forgotten that in the profoundest versions of Christianity, every man sees in Christ not only what he is and ought to be but also the true reality to which his own life stands in contradiction. Christianity does not believe, as the pessimists do, that men are by nature egotists. Nor does it hold with the optimists that egotism can be easily transcended. It believes rather that men are egotists in contradiction to their essential nature. That is the doctrine of original sin, stripped of literalistic illusions. . . .

International peace, political and economic justice and every form of social achievement represent precarious constructs in which the egoism of man is checked and yet taken for granted; and in which human sympathy and love must be exploited to the full and yet discounted. Universal peace can wait upon neither universal culture nor universal love. There can be in fact no such thing

as universal peace, if we mean by it a frictionless harmony between nations and a perfect justice between men. It ought to be possible for western society to achieve a higher degree of social and political cohesion and to avoid complete anarchy. But such a possibility depends upon a degree of political realism which is lacking today in both our religious and our secular culture. It depends upon a realism which understands how tenuous and tentative every form of social peace and justice is. . . .

In one sense the logic of this isolationism is of course perfectly correct. It is not possible to make discriminate choices in politics without running the risk of ultimate involvement in conflict, because all social tensions may result in overt conflict and all forms supporting one side or the other may have the consequence of requiring a more direct support. The logic of isolationism is plausible enough but the moral implications are intolerable. If it were followed through consistently in the whole of social life each family would seek to build itself a haven of isolation lest it become involved in the horrid realities of political struggle, which are a part of every national existence. American peace as a symbol of the goodness of man can be maintained only at the price of accentuating every vice in American character, particularly the vices of Pharisaism and self-righteousness which have developed in a nation saved by two oceans from a too obvious involvement in international strife and saved by its wealth from a too obvious display of an internal social struggle. . . .

The moral and political confusion, created by religious and secular perfectionists who do not understand the involvement of all mankind in the sinful realities of history, is aggravated by perfectionists' illusions about peace. It has become almost a universal dogma of American Christianity that any kind of peace is better than war. This always means in the end that tyranny is preferred to war; for submission to the foe is the only certain alternative to resistance against the foe.

That the dogmatic assumption that nothing can be worse than war leads inevitably to an implied or explicit acceptance of tyranny is revealed by many current pronouncements in the religious world. A study conference of the Churches on the international situation held under the auspices of the Federal Council of Churches at the beginning of 1940 declared: "We are convinced that there is ground for hope that a just peace is now possible by negotiation. It is important for the welfare of mankind that the conflict end, not in a dictated but in a negotiated peace based upon the interests of all the people concerned."

This statement, which was commended by the leading Christian journal in America as containing the very essence of Christian counsel in the war situation was completely divorced from all political realities. The fact is that Hitler wanted a negotiated peace from the time he invaded Poland to the time the great offensive began. Being in possession of the continent, with the exception of France, it was obvious that a negotiated peace would have been possible only upon the basis of leaving him in possession of all the loot he had taken. If such a peace had been made the smaller nations, not yet under the Nazi heel, would have been gradually conquered by economic and political pressure. They would have had no power to resist and no incentive to resist, since they could not have looked forward to any aid in stemming the tide of Nazism. A negotiated peace, when the Churches desired it, would have been merely an easy Nazi victory.

The alternative effort to dislodge the Nazis may wreck Europe even if it succeeds, and it may fail and thus come to the same result as premature capitulation through a negotiated peace. This fact is supposed to justify the hysterical demand for peace on any terms. But our American moralists fail to understand that peoples and nations which face an imminent threat of enslavement do not make nice calculations of alternative consequences. There are critical moments in history when such calculations become irrelevant. Every instinct of survival and every decent impulse of humanity becomes engaged and prompts resistance, no matter what the consequences. The result may be tragic; but only a very vapid moralism fails to appreciate the beauty and nobility in such tragedy and continues to speculate on how much better it would have been to accept slavery without resistance than to accept it after resistance.

Just as the dogmatic insistence that nothing can possibly be worse than war leads to the explicit or implicit acceptance of tyranny, so the uncritical identification of neutrality with the Christian ethic leads to a perverse obfuscation of important moral distinctions between contending forces. *The Christian Century* has consistently criticized President Roosevelt for not being absolutely neutral. It seems not to realize that this means to condone a tyranny which has destroyed freedom, is seeking to extinguish the Christian religion, debases its subjects to robots who have no opinion and judgment of their own, threatens the Jews of Europe with complete annihilation and all the nations of Europe with subordination under the imperial dominion of a "master race."

The Christian Century answers the arguments of those who believe that civilization is imperilled by the victory of Germany with the simple assertion that this cannot be true since it is war which imperils civilization. Recognizing a certain uneasiness of conscience among Americans it counsels them to hold firm to their resolution not to have anything to do with the conflict and seeks to ease their conscience by advising them that the "Protestant conscience" of Holland and Switzerland arrived at the same conclusions. Most of the neutrals of Europe to whose conscience *The Christian Century* pointed were destroyed while it was holding them up as glorious examples.

In its simple moralism *The Christian Century* had failed to illumine the basic problem of international relations. This problem is the necessity of an obvious coincidence between national and ideal interests before nations embark upon the hazards of war. There was no question in the minds of any of the small neutral nations about the decisive character of the present conflict. Most of them hoped that Europe would be saved without their aid. Their vital interests were in every case involved ultimately but not immediately. When they became involved immediately, namely by invasion of the foe, it was too late to serve either national interest or the values of civilization which transcend national interest.

The fact that there must be some coincidence between national and ideal interests to prompt national action in a crisis is an inevitable political fact, but it is morally dubious and politically ambiguous in its import. It is morally dubious because it leaves other nations to carry the brunt of defending a civilization which transcends the mere existence of those nations. Politically it is ambiguous because the vital interests of a nation may be ultimately imperilled without being immediately imperilled. To wait until ultimate perils become immediate means to wait too long.

The Scandinavian nations would have been well advised to offer united resistance to aggression rather than wait for the extinction of the liberties of each. Holland and Belgium sought to ward off disaster by constructing a neutrality program which pretended to find equal peril in the designs of contending imperial powers. The peril was not equal. There was in fact no peril from the one side at all. The consequence of a policy which obscured the real facts was the invasion of these nations and the break-through of the German army into France. America is of course in the same position. It pretended that its vital interests would be no more endangered by a German victory than by an Allied one. The real situation is that both the ultimate cause of civilization and our own vital interests are much more seriously imperilled by Germany than the Allies. Since the victory of the German armies in Holland, Belgium and France we have gradually awakened to this fact, but probably too late.

In other words the neutrality policy which *The Christian Century* and its kind have praised as representing some kind of Christian ultimate is not only bad morals but bad politics. It represents the cardinal weakness of democracy in facing the perils of tyranny. Democracy, which must take account of the fears and apprehensions of the common people as dictatorships need not, cannot act in time. It can act in time only if it has leaders who are willing and able to anticipate perils which the common man cannot see. By the time the man in the street sees how great the peril is, the danger is so imminent as to make adequate defense preparations impossible.

This natural weakness of democracy as a form of government when dealing with foreign policy is aggravated by liberalism as the culture which has informed the life of the democratic nations. In this liberalism there is little understanding of the depth to which human malevolence may sink and the heights to which malignant power may rise. Some easy and vapid escape is sought from the terrors and woes of a tragic era.

The fact is that moralistic illusions of our liberal culture have been so great and its will-to-live has been so seriously enervated by a confused pacifism, in which Christian perfectionism and bourgeois love of ease have been curiously compounded, that our democratic world does not really deserve to survive. It may not survive. If it does it will be only because it came to its senses in the final hour and because the weaknesses of tyranny may finally outweigh its momentary advantages.

6. Political Power

A Realist Theory
of International Politics

HANS J. MORGENTHAU

POLITICAL POWER

WHAT IS POLITICAL POWER?

Its Relation to the Nation as a Whole

International politics, like all politics, is a struggle for power. Whatever the ultimate aims of international politics, power is always the immediate aim. Statesmen and peoples may ultimately seek freedom, security, prosperity, or power itself. They may define their goals in terms of a religious, philosophic, economic, or social ideal. They may hope that this ideal will materialize through its own inner force, through divine intervention, or through the natural development of human affairs. They may also try to further its realization through nonpolitical means, such as technical co-operation with other nations or international organizations. But

Excerpted from *Politics Among Nations: The Struggle for Power and Peace*, Third Edition, by Hans J. Morgenthau (New York: Knopf, 1960), pp. 27–29,31–35,3–4,10–12,14. Copyright 1948,1954, © 1960 by Alfred A. Knopf, Inc. Reprinted by permission of the publisher. Footnotes deleted.

whenever they strive to realize their goal by means of international politics, they do so by striving for power. The Crusaders wanted to free the holy places from domination by the Infidels; Woodrow Wilson wanted to make the world safe for democracy; the Nazis wanted to open Eastern Europe to German colonization, to dominate Europe, and to conquer the world. Since they all chose power to achieve these ends, they were actors on the scene of international politics.

Two conclusions follow from this concept of international politics. First, not every action that a nation performs with respect to another nation is of a political nature. . . .

Second, not all nations are at all times to the same extent involved in international politics. . . .

Its Nature

. . . When we speak of power, we mean man's control over the minds and actions of other men.

By political power we refer to the mutual relations of control among the holders of public authority and between the latter and the people at large. . . .

Political power is a psychological relation between those who exercise it and those over whom it is exercised. It gives the former control over certain actions of the latter through the influence which the former exert over the latter's minds. That influence derives from three sources: the expectation of benefits, the fear of disadvantages, the respect or love for men or institutions. It may be exerted through orders, threats, persuasion, the authority or charisma of a man or of an office, or a combination of any of these.

While it is generally recognized that the interplay of these factors, in ever changing combinations, forms the basis of all domestic politics, the importance of these factors for international politics is less obvious, but no less real. . . .

THE DEPRECIATION OF POLITICAL POWER

The aspiration for power being the distinguishing element of international politics, as of all politics, international politics is of necessity power politics. While this fact is generally recognized in the practice of international affairs, it is frequently denied in the pronouncements of scholars, publicists, and even statesmen. . . .

In recent times, the conviction that the struggle for power can be eliminated from the international scene has been connected with the great attempts at organizing the world, such as the League of Nations and the United Nations. . . .

. . . It is sufficient to state that the struggle for power is universal in time and space and is an undeniable fact of experience. It cannot be denied that throughout historic time, regardless of social, economic, and political conditions, states have met each other in contests for power. Even though anthropologists have shown that certain primitive peoples seem to be free from the desire for power, nobody has yet shown how their state of mind and the conditions under which they live can be recreated on a worldwide scale so as to eliminate the struggle for power from the international scene. It would be useless and even self-destructive to free one or the other of the peoples of the earth from the desire for power while leaving it extant in others. If the desire for power cannot be abolished everywhere in the world, those who might be cured would simply fall victims to the power of others. . . .

Regardless of particular social conditions, the decisive argument against the opinion that the struggle for power on the international scene is a mere historic accident must be derived from the nature of domestic politics. The essence of international politics is identical with its domestic counterpart. Both domestic and international politics are a struggle for power, modified only by the different conditions under which this struggle takes place in the domestic and in the international spheres.

The tendency to dominate, in particular, is an element of all human associations, from the family through fraternal and professional associations and local political organizations, to the state. On the family level, the typical conflict between the mother-in-law and her child's spouse is in its essence a struggle for power, the defense of an established power position against the attempt to establish a new one. As such it foreshadows the conflict on the international scene between the policies of the status quo and the policies of imperialism. . . .

In view of this ubiquity of the struggle for power in all social relations and on all levels of social organization, is it surprising that international politics is of necessity power politics? And would it not be rather surprising if the struggle for power were but an accidental and ephemeral attribute of international politics when it is a permanent and necessary element of all branches of domestic politics?

A REALIST THEORY OF INTERNATIONAL POLITICS

This book purports to present a theory of international politics. The test by which such a theory must be judged is not *a priori* and abstract but empirical and pragmatic. The theory, in other words, must be judged not by some preconceived abstract principle or concept unrelated to reality, but by its purpose: to bring order and meaning to a mass of phenomena which without it would remain disconnected and unintelligible. It must meet a dual test, an empirical and a logical one: Do the facts as they actually are lend themselves to the interpretation the theory has put upon them, and do the conclusions at which the theory arrives follow with logical necessity from its premises? In short, is the theory consistent with the facts and within itself?

The issue this theory raises concerns the nature of all politics. The history of modern political thought is the story of a contest between two schools that differ fundamentally in their conceptions of the nature of man, society, and politics. One believes that a rational and moral political order, derived from universally valid abstract principles, can be achieved here and now. It assumes the essential goodness and infinite malleability of human nature, and blames the failure of the social order to measure up to the rational standards on lack of knowledge and understanding, obsolescent social institutions, or the depravity of certain isolated individuals or groups. It trusts in education, reform, and the sporadic use of force to remedy these defects.

The other school believes that the world, imperfect as it is from the rational point of view, is the result of forces inherent in human nature. To improve the world one must work with those forces, not against them. This being inherently a world of opposing interests and of conflict among them, moral principles can never be fully realized, but must at best be approximated through the ever temporary balancing of interests and the ever precarious settlement of conflicts. This school, then, sees in a system of checks and balances a universal principle for all pluralist societies. It appeals to historic precedent rather than to abstract principles, and aims at the realization of the lesser evil rather than of the absolute good. . . .

Political realism believes that politics, like society in general, is governed by objective laws that have their roots in human nature. In order to improve society it is first necessary to understand the laws by which society lives. The operation of these laws being impervious to our preferences, men will challenge them only at the risk of failure.

Realism, believing as it does in the objectivity of the laws of politics, must also believe in the possibility of developing a rational theory that reflects, however imperfectly and one-sidedly, these objective laws. It believes also, then, in the possibility of distinguishing in politics between truth and opinion—between what is true objectively and rationally, supported by evidence and illuminated by reason, and what is only a subjective judgment, divorced from the facts as they are and informed by prejudice and wishful thinking. . . .

Political realism is aware of the moral significance of political action. It is also aware of the ineluctable tension between the moral command and the requirements of successful political action. And it is unwilling to gloss over and obliterate that tension and thus to obfuscate both the moral and the political issue by making it appear as though the stark facts of politics were morally more satisfying than they actually are, and the moral law less exacting than it actually is.

Realism maintains that universal moral principles cannot be applied to the actions of states in their abstract universal formulation, but that they must be filtered through the concrete circumstances of time and place. The individual may say for himself: "*Fiat justitia, pereat mundus* (Let justice be done, even if the world perish)," but the state has no right to say so in the name of those who are in its care. Both individual and state must judge political action by universal moral principles, such as that of liberty. Yet while the individual has a moral right to sacrifice himself in defense of such a moral principle, the state has no right to let its moral disapprobation of the infringement of liberty get in the way of successful political action, itself inspired by the moral principle of national survival. There can be no political morality without prudence; that is, without consideration of the political consequences of seemingly moral action. Realism, then, considers prudence—the weighing of the consequences of alternative political actions—to be the supreme virtue in politics. Ethics in the abstract judges action by its conformity with the moral law; political ethics judges action by its political consequences. . . .

Political realism refuses to identify the moral aspirations of a particular nation with the moral laws that govern the universe. As it distinguishes between truth and opinion, so it distinguishes between truth and idolatry. All nations are tempted—and few have been able to resist the temptation for long—to clothe their own particular aspirations and actions in the moral purposes of the universe. To know that nations are subject to the moral law is one thing, while to pretend to know with certainty what is good and evil in the relations among nations is quite another. There is a world of difference between the belief that all nations stand under the judgment of God, inscrutable to the human mind, and the blasphemous conviction that God is always on one's side and that what one wills oneself cannot fail to be willed by God also.

The lighthearted equation between a particular nationalism and the counsels of Providence is morally indefensible, for it is that very sin of pride against which the Greek tragedians and the Biblical prophets have warned rulers and ruled. That equation is also politically pernicious, for it is liable to engender the distortion in judgment which, in the blindness of crusading frenzy, destroys nations and civilizations—in the name of moral principle, ideal, or God himself.

On the other hand, it is exactly the concept of interest defined in terms of power that saves us from both that moral excess and that political folly. For if we look at all nations, our own included, as political entities pursuing their respective interests defined in terms of power, we are able to do justice to all of them. And we are able to do justice to all of them in a dual sense: We are able to judge other nations as we judge our own and, having judged them in this fashion, we are then capable of pursuing policies that respect the interests of other nations, while protecting and promoting those of our own. Moderation in

policy cannot fail to reflect the moderation of moral judgment.

The difference, then, between political realism and other schools of thought is real and it is profound. However much the theory of political realism may have been misunderstood and misinterpreted, there is no gainsaying its distinctive intellectual and moral attitude to matters political.

Intellectually, the political realist maintains the autonomy of the political sphere, as the economist, the lawyer, the moralist maintain theirs. . . .

The political realist is not unaware of the existence and relevance of standards of thought other than political ones. As political realist, he cannot but subordinate these other standards to those of politics. And he parts company with other schools when they impose standards of thought appropriate to other spheres upon the political sphere. It is here that political realism takes issue with the "legalistic-moralistic approach" to international politics. That this issue is not, as has been contended, a mere figment of the imagination, but goes to the very core of the controversy, can be shown from many historical examples. . . .

This realist defense of the autonomy of the political sphere against its subversion by other modes of thought does not imply disregard for the existence and importance of these other modes of thought. It rather implies that each should be assigned its proper sphere and function. Political realism is based upon a pluralistic conception of human nature. Real man is a composite of "economic man," "political man," "moral man," "religious man," etc. A man who was nothing but "political man" would be a beast, for he would be completely lacking in moral restraints. A man who was nothing but "moral man" would be a fool, for he would be completely lacking in prudence. A man who was nothing but "religious man" would be a saint, for he would be completely lacking in worldly desires.

Recognizing that these different facets of human nature exist, political realism also recognizes that in order to understand one of them one has to deal with it on its own terms. That is to say, if I want to understand "religious man," I must for the time being abstract from the other aspects of human nature and deal with its religious aspect as if it were the only one. Furthermore, I must apply to the religious sphere the standards of thought appropriate to it, always remaining aware of the existence of other standards and their actual influence upon the religious qualities of man. What is true of this facet of human nature is true of all the others. No modern economist, for instance, would conceive of his science and its relations to other sciences of man in any other way. It is exactly through such a process of emancipation from other standards of thought, and the development of one appropriate to its subject matter, that economics has developed as an autonomous theory of the economic activities of man. To contribute to a similar development in the field of politics is indeed the purpose of political realism. . . .

7. Diplomacy in the Modern World

George F. Kennan

. . . As you have no doubt surmised, I see the most serious fault of our past policy formulation to lie in something that I might call the legalistic-moralistic approach to international problems. This approach runs like a red skein through our foreign policy of the last fifty years. It has in it something of the old emphasis on arbitration treaties, something of the Hague Conferences and schemes for universal disarmament, something of the more ambitious American concepts of the role of international law, something of the League of Nations and the United Nations, something of the Kellogg Pact, something of the idea of a universal "Article 51" pact, something of the belief in World Law and World Government. But it is none of these, entirely. Let me try to describe it.

It is the belief that it should be possible to suppress the chaotic and dangerous aspirations of governments in the international field by the ac-

ceptance of some system of legal rules and restraints. This belief undoubtedly represents in part an attempt to transpose the Anglo-Saxon concept of individual law into the international field and to make it applicable to governments as it is applicable here at home to individuals. It must also stem in part from the memory of the origin of our own political system—from the recollection that we were able, through acceptance of a common institutional and juridical framework, to reduce to harmless dimensions the conflicts of interest and aspiration among the original thirteen colonies and to bring them all into an ordered and peaceful relationship with one another. Remembering this, people are unable to understand that what might have been possible for the thirteen colonies in a given set of circumstances might not be possible in the wider international field.

It is the essence of this belief that, instead of taking the awkward conflicts of national interest and dealing with them on their merits with a view to finding the solutions least unsettling to the stability of international life, it would be better to find some formal criteria of a juridical nature by

Reprinted from *American Diplomacy, 1900–1950* by George F. Kennan (Chicago: University of Chicago Press, 1951), pp. 95–103, by permission of The University of Chicago Press. Copyright © 1951 The University of Chicago Press.

which the permissible behavior of states could be defined. There would then be judicial entities competent to measure the actions of governments against these criteria and to decide when their behavior was acceptable and when unacceptable. Behind all this, of course, lies the American assumption that the things for which other peoples in this world are apt to contend are for the most part neither creditable nor important and might justly be expected to take second place behind the desirability of an orderly world, untroubled by international violence. To the American mind, it is implausible that people should have positive aspirations, and ones that they regard as legitimate, more important to them than the peacefulness and orderliness of international life. From this standpoint, it is not apparent why other peoples should not join us in accepting the rules of the game in international politics, just as we accept such rules in the competition of sport in order that the game may not become too cruel and too destructive and may not assume an importance we did not mean it to have.

If they were to do this, the reasoning runs, then the troublesome and chaotic manifestations of the national ego could be contained and rendered either unsubstantial or subject to easy disposal by some method familiar and comprehensible to our American usage. Departing from this background, the mind of American statesmanship, stemming as it does in so large a part from the legal profession in our country, gropes with unfailing persistence for some institutional framework which would be capable of fulfilling this function.

I cannot undertake in this short lecture to deal exhaustively with this thesis or to point out all the elements of unsoundness which I feel it contains. But some of its more outstanding weaknesses are worthy of mention.

In the first place, the idea of the subordination of a large number of states to an international juridical regime, limiting their possibilities for aggression and injury to other states, implies that these are all states like our own, reasonably content with their international borders and status, at least to the extent that they would be willing to refrain from pressing for change without international agreement. Actually, this has generally been true only of a portion of international society. We tend to underestimate the violence of national maladjustments and discontents elsewhere in the world if we think that they would always appear to other people as less important than the preservation of the juridical tidiness of international life.

Second, while this concept is often associated with a revolt against nationalism, it is a curious thing that it actually tends to confer upon the concept of nationality and national sovereignty an absolute value it did not have before. The very principle of "one government, one vote," regardless of physical or political differences between states, glorifies the concept of national sovereignty and makes it the exclusive form of participation in international life. It envisages a world composed exclusively of sovereign national states with a full equality of status. In doing this, it ignores the tremendous variations in the firmness and soundness of national divisions: the fact that the origins of state borders and national personalities were in many instances fortuitous or at least poorly related to realities. It also ignores the law of change. The national state pattern is not, should not be, and cannot be a fixed and static thing. By nature, it is an unstable phenomenon in a constant state of change and flux. History has shown that the will and the capacity of individual peoples to contribute to their world environment is constantly changing. It is only logical that the organizational forms (and what else are such things as borders and governments?) should change with them. The function of a system of international relationships is not to inhibit this process of change by imposing a legal strait jacket upon it but rather to facilitate it: to ease its transitions, to temper the asperities to which it often leads, to isolate and moderate the conflicts to which it gives rise, and to see that these conflicts do not assume forms too unsettling for international life in general. But this is a task for diplomacy, in the most old-fashioned sense of the term. For this, law is too abstract, too inflexible, too hard to adjust to the demands of the unpredictable and the unexpected.

By the same token, the American concept of world law ignores those means of international offense—those means of the projection of power and coercion over other peoples—which by-pass institutional forms entirely or even exploit them against themselves: such things as ideological attack, intimidation, penetration, and disguised seizure of the institutional paraphernalia of national sovereignty. It ignores, in other words, the device of the puppet state and the set of techniques by which states can be converted into puppets with no formal violation of, or challenge to, the outward attributes of their sovereignty and their independence.

This is one of the things that have caused the peoples of the satellite countries of eastern Europe to look with a certain tinge of bitterness on the United Nations. The organization failed so completely to save them from domination by a great neighboring country, a domination no less invidious by virtue of the fact that it came into being by processes we could not call "aggression." And there is indeed some justification for their feeling, because the legalistic approach to international affairs ignores in general the international significance of political problems and the deeper sources of international instability. It assumes that civil wars will remain civil and not grow into international wars. It assumes the ability of each people to solve its own internal political problems in a manner not provocative of its international environment. It assumes that each nation will always be able to construct a government qualified to speak for it and cast its vote in the international arena and that this government will be acceptable to the rest of the international community in this capacity. It assumes, in other words, that domestic issues will not become international issues and that the world community will not be put in the position of having to make choices between rival claimants for power within the confines of the individual state.

Finally, this legalistic approach to international relations is faulty in its assumptions concerning the possibility of sanctions against offenses and violations. In general, it looks to collective action to provide such sanction against the bad behavior of states. In doing so, it forgets the limitations on the effectiveness of military coalition. It forgets that, as a circle of military associates widens in any conceivable political-military venture, the theoretical total of available military strength may increase, but only at the cost of compactness and ease of control. And the wider a coalition becomes, the more difficult it becomes to retain political unity and general agreement on the purposes and effects of what is being done. As we are seeing in the case of Korea, joint military operations against an aggressor have a different meaning for each participant and raise specific political issues for each one which are extraneous to the action in question and affect many other facets of international life. The wider the circle of military associates, the more cumbersome the problem of political control over their actions, and the more circumscribed the least common denominator of agreement. This law of diminishing returns lies so heavily on the possibilities for multilateral military action that it makes it doubtful whether the participation of smaller states can really add very much to the ability of the great powers to assure stability of international life. And this is tremendously important, for it brings us back to the realization that even under a system of world law the sanction against destructive international behavior might continue to rest basically, as it has in the past, on the alliances and relationships among the great powers themselves. There might be a state, or perhaps more than one state, which all the rest of the world community together could not successfully coerce into following a line of action to which it was violently averse. And if this is true, where are we? It seems to me that we are right back in the realm of the forgotten art of diplomacy from which we have spent fifty years trying to escape.

These, then, are some of the theoretical deficiencies that appear to me to be inherent in the legalistic approach to international affairs. But there is a greater deficiency still that I should like to mention before I close. That is the inevitable association of legalistic ideas with moralistic ones: the carrying-over into the affairs of states of the concepts of right and wrong, the assumption that state behavior is a fit subject for moral judgment. Whoever says there is a law must of course be indignant against the lawbreaker and feel a moral superiority to him. And when such indignation spills over into military contest, it knows no bounds short of the reduction of the lawbreaker to the point of complete submissiveness— namely, unconditional surrender. It is a curious thing, but it is true, that the legalistic approach to world affairs, rooted as it unquestionably is in a desire to do away with war and violence, makes violence more enduring, more terrible, and more destructive to political stability than did the older motives of national interest. A war fought in the name of high moral principle finds no early end short of some form of total domination.

In this way, we see that the legalistic approach to international problems is closely identified with the concept of total war and total victory, and the manifestations of the one spill over only too easily into the manifestations of the other. And the concept of total war is something we would all do well to think about a little in these troubled times. This is a relatively new concept, in Western civilization at any rate. It did not really appear on the scene until World War I. It characterized both of these great world wars, and both of them—as I have pointed out—were followed by great instability and disillusionment. But it is not only a question now of the desirability of this concept; it is a question of its feasibility. Actually, I wonder whether even in the past total victory was not really an illusion from the standpoint of the victors. In a sense, there is not total victory short of genocide, unless it be a victory over the minds of men. But the total military victories are rarely victories over the minds of men. And we now face the fact that it is very questionable whether in a new global conflict there could ever be any such thing as total *military* victory. I personally do not believe that there could. There might be a great weakening of the armed forces of one side or another, but I think it out of the question that there should be such a thing as a general and formal submission of the national will on either side. The attempt to achieve this unattainable goal, however, could wreak upon civilization another set of injuries fully as serious as those caused by World War I or World War II, and I

leave it to you to answer the question as to how civilization could survive them.

It was asserted not long ago by a prominent American that "war's very object is victory" and that "in war there can be no substitute for victory." Perhaps the confusion here lies in what is meant by the term "victory." Perhaps the term is actually misplaced. Perhaps there can be such a thing as "victory" in a battle, whereas in war there can be only the achievement or nonachievement of your objectives. In the old days, wartime objectives were generally limited and practical ones, and it was common to measure the success of your military operations by the extent to which they brought you closer to your objectives. But where your objectives are moral and ideological ones and run to changing the attitudes and traditions of an entire people or the personality of a regime, then victory is probably something not to be achieved entirely by military means or indeed in any short space of time at all; and perhaps that is the source of our confusion.

In any case, I am frank to say that I think there is no more dangerous delusion, none that has done us a greater disservice in the past or that threatens to do us a greater disservice in the future, than the concept of total victory. And I fear that it springs in large measure from the basic faults in the approach to international affairs which I have been discussing here. If we are to get away from it, this will not mean that we shall have to abandon our respect for international law, or our hopes for its future usefulness as the gentle civilizer of events which I mentioned in one of the earlier lectures. Nor will it mean that we have to go in for anything that can properly be termed "appeasement"—if one may use a word so cheapened and deflated by the abuse to which it has been recently subjected. But it will mean the emergence of a new attitude among us toward many things outside our borders that are irritating and unpleasant today—an attitude more like that of the doctor toward those physical phenomena in the human body that are neither pleasing nor fortunate—an attitude of detachment and soberness and readiness to reserve judgment. It will mean that we will have the modesty to admit that our own na-

CHAPTER

3

THE RADICAL CRITIQUE

8. Address to the Swedish Peace Congress in 1909

Patriotism and Government

Patriotism and Christianity

LEO TOLSTOY

ADDRESS TO THE SWEDISH PEACE CONGRESS IN 1909

Dear Brothers:

We have met here to fight against war. War, the thing for the sake of which all the nations of the earth—millions and millions of people—place at the uncontrolled disposal of a few men or sometimes only one man, not merely milliards of rubles, talers, francs, or yen (representing a very large share of their labour), but also their very lives. And now we, a score of private people gathered from the various ends of the earth, possessed of no special privileges and above all having no power over anyone, intend to fight—and as we wish to fight we wish also to conquer—this immense power not of one government but of all the governments, which have at their disposal these milliards of money and millions of soldiers and who are well aware that the exceptional position of those who form the governments rests on

These essays are translated respectively by Aylmer Maude, Leo Wiener (1905), and Aylmer Maude et al. (1899 version).

the army alone: the army which has a meaning and purpose only if there is a war, the very war against which we wish to fight and which we wish to abolish.

For us to struggle, the forces being so unequal, must appear insane. But if we consider our opponents' means of strife and our own, it is not our intention to fight that will seem absurd but that the thing we mean to fight against can still exist. They have millions of money and millions of obedient soldiers; we have only one thing, but that is the most powerful thing in the world—Truth.

Therefore, insignificant as our forces may appear in comparison with those of our opponents, our victory is as sure as the victory of the light of the rising sun over the darkness of night.

Our victory is certain, but on one condition only—that when uttering the truth we utter it all, without compromise, concession, or modification. The truth is so simple, so clear, so evident, and so incumbent not only on Christians but on all reasonable men, that it is only necessary to speak it out completely in its full significance for it to be irresistible.

The truth in its full meaning lies in what was said thousands of years ago (in the law accepted among us as the Law of God) in four words: *Thou Shalt Not Kill.* The truth is that man may not and should not in any circumstances or under any pretext kill his fellow man.

That truth is so evident, so binding, and so generally acknowledged, that it is only necessary to put it clearly before men for the evil called war to become quite impossible.

And so I think that if we who are assembled here at this Peace Congress should, instead of clearly and definitely voicing this truth, address ourselves to the governments with various proposals for lessening the evils of war or gradually diminishing its frequency, we should be like men who having in their hand the key to a door, should try to break through walls they know to be too strong for them. Before us are millions of armed men, ever more and more efficiently armed and trained for more and more rapid slaughter. We know that these millions of people have no wish to kill their fellows and for the most part do not even know why they are forced to do that repulsive work, and that they are weary of their position of subjection and compulsion; we know that the murders committed from time to time by these men are committed by order of the governments; and we know that the existence of the governments depends on the armies. Can we, then, who desire the abolition of war, find nothing more conducive to our aim than to propose to the governments which exist only by the aid of armies and consequently by war—measures which would destroy war? Are we to propose to the governments that they should destroy themselves?

The governments will listen willingly to any speeches of that kind, knowing that such discussions will neither destroy war nor undermine their own power, but will only conceal yet more effectually what must be concealed if wars and armies and themselves in control of armies are to continue to exist.

"But," I shall be told, "this is anarchism; people never have lived without governments and States, and therefore governments and States and military forces defending them are necessary for the existence of the nations.''

But leaving aside the question of whether the life of Christian and other nations is possible without armies and wars to defend their governments and States, or even supposing it to be necessary for their welfare that they should slavishly submit to institutions called governments (consisting of people they do not personally know), and publish an appeal to all men, and especially to the Christian nations, in which we clearly and definitely express what everybody knows but hardly anyone says: namely that war is not—as most people now assume—a good and laudable affair, but that like all murder, it is a vile and criminal business not only for those who voluntarily choose a military career but for those who submit to it from avarice or fear of punishment.

With regard to those who voluntarily choose a military career, I would propose to state clearly and definitely in that appeal that notwithstanding all the pomp, glitter, and general approval with which it is surrounded, it is a criminal and shameful activity; and that the higher the position a man holds in the military profession the more criminal and shameful is his occupation. In the same way with regard to men of the people who are drawn into military service by bribes or by threats of punishments, I propose to speak clearly and definitely of the gross mistake they make—contrary to their faith, morality, and common sense—when they consent to enter the army; contrary to their faith, because by entering the ranks of murderers they infringe the Law of God which they acknowledge; contrary to morality, because for pay or from fear of punishment they agree to do what in their souls they know to be wrong; and contrary to common sense, because if they enter the army and war breaks out they risk having to suffer consequences as bad or worse than those they are threatened with if they refuse. Above all they act contrary to common sense in that they join that caste of people which deprives them of freedom and compels them to become soldiers.

With reference to both classes I propose in this appeal to express clearly the thought that for men of true enlightenment, who are therefore free from the superstition of military glory (and their number is growing every day) the military profession and calling, notwithstanding all the efforts to hide its real meaning, is as shameful a business as an executioner's and even more so. For the executioner only holds himself in readiness to kill those who have been adjudged harmful and criminal, while a soldier promises to kill all whom he is told to kill, even though they be those dearest to him or the best of men.

Humanity in general, and our Christian humanity in particular, has reached a stage of such acute contradiction between its moral demands and the existing social order, that a change has become inevitable, and a change not in society's moral demands which are immutable, but in the social order which can be altered. The demand for a different social order, evoked by that inner contradiction which is so clearly illustrated by our preparations for murder, becomes more and more insistent every year and every day. The tension which demands that alteration has reached such a degree that, just as sometimes only a slight shock is required to change a liquid into a solid body, so perhaps only a slight effort or even a single word may be needed to change the cruel and irrational life of our time—with its divisions, armaments, and armies—into a reasonable life in keeping with the consciousness of contemporary humanity. Every such effort, every such word, may be the shock which will instantly solidify the supercooled liquid. Why should not our gathering be that shock? In Andersen's fairy tale, when the King went in triumphal procession through the streets of the town and all the people were delighted with his beautiful new clothes, a word from a child who said what everybody knew but had not said, changed everything. He said: "He has nothing on!" and the spell was broken and the King became ashamed and all those who had been assuring themselves that they saw him wearing beautiful new clothes perceived that he

was naked! We must say the same. We must say what everybody knows but does not venture to say. We must say that by whatever name men may call murder—murder always remains murder and a criminal and shameful thing. And it is only necessary to say that clearly, definitely, and loudly, as we can say it here, and men will cease to see what they thought they saw and will see what is really before their eyes. They will cease to see the service of their country, the heroism of war, military glory, and patriotism, and will see what exists: the naked, criminal business of murder! And if people see that, the same thing will happen as in the fairy tale: those who do the criminal thing will feel ashamed, and those who assure themselves that they do not see the criminality of murder will perceive it and cease to be murderers.

But how will nations defend themselves against their enemies, how will they maintain internal order, and how can nations live without an army?

What form the life of men will take if they repudiate murder, we do not and cannot know; but one thing is certain: that it is more natural for men to be guided by the reason and conscience with which they are endowed, than to submit slavishly to people who arrange wholesale murders; and that therefore the form of social order assumed by the lives of those who are guided in their actions not by violence based on threats of murder but by reason and conscience, will in any case be no worse than that under which they now live.

That is all I want to say. I shall be very sorry if it offends or grieves anyone or evokes any ill feeling. But for me, a man eighty years old, expecting to die at any moment, it would be shameful and criminal not to speak out the whole truth as I understand it—the truth which, as I firmly believe, is alone capable of relieving mankind from the incalculable ills produced by war.

PATRIOTISM AND GOVERNMENT (1900)

1

I have several times had occasion to express the idea that patriotism is in our time an unnatural, irrational, harmful sentiment, which causes the greater part of those calamities from which humanity suffers, and that, therefore, this sentiment ought not to be cultivated, as it now is, but, on the contrary, ought to be repressed and destroyed with all means that sensible people can command. But, strange to say, in spite of the evident and incontestable relation of the universal armaments and destructive wars, which ruin the nations, to this exclusive sentiment, all my arguments as to the obsoleteness, untimeliness, and harm of patriotism have been met either with silence or with intentional misunderstanding, or, again, with the same strange retort: "What is said is that there is harm in the bad patriotism, jingoism, chauvinism, but the real, good patriotism is a very elevated, moral sentiment, which it is not only senseless, but even criminal to condemn." But as to what this real, good patriotism consists in, . . . nothing is said. . . .

The army, the money, the school, the religion, the press, is in the hands of the ruling classes. In the schools they fan patriotism in the children by means of history, by describing their nation as the best of all the nations and always in the right; in the adults the same sentiment is roused by means of spectacles, celebrations, monuments, and a patriotic, lying press; but patriotism is chiefly roused in them by this, that, committing all kinds of unjust acts and cruelties against other nations, they provoke in these nations a hatred for their own nation, and then use this hatred for provoking such a hatred in their own nation.

The fanning of this terrible sentiment of patriotism has proceeded in the European nations in a rapidly increasing progression, and in our time has reached a stage beyond which it cannot go.

4

Within the memory of all, not merely old men of our time, there took place an event which in the most obvious manner showed the striking stupefaction to which the men of the Christian world were brought by means of patriotism.

The German ruling classes fanned the patriotism of their popular masses to such an extent that in the second half of the century a law was proposed to the people, according to which all men without exception were to become soldiers; all sons, husbands, fathers, were to study murder and to become submissive slaves of the first highest rank, and to be prepared for the murder of those whom they would be ordered to kill,—the men of the oppressed nationalities and their own labourers who should defend their rights,—their fathers and brothers, as the most impudent of all rulers, William II., publicly announced.

This terrible measure, which in the rudest way offends all the best sentiments of men, has, under the influence of patriotism, been accepted without a murmur by the nation of Germany.

The consequence of this was the victory over the French. This victory still more fanned the patriotism of Germany, and later of France, Russia, and other powers, and all the people of the Continental powers without a murmur submitted to the introduction of a universal military service, that is, to slavery, which for the degree of degradation and loss of will cannot be compared with any of the ancient conditions of slavery. . . .

But more than that. Every increase of the army of one state (and every state, being on account of patriotism in danger, wishes to increase it) compels the neighbouring state to increase its army also for the sake of patriotism, which again calls forth a new increase of the first. . . .

7

To free people from those terrible calamities of armaments and wars, which they suffer now, and which keep growing greater and greater, we do not need congresses, nor conferences, nor treaties and tribunals, but the abolition of that implement of violence which is called the governments, and from which originate all the greatest calamities of men.

To abolish the governments[1] only one thing is needed: it is necessary that men should understand that the sentiment of patriotism, which alone maintains this implement of violence, is a coarse, harmful, disgraceful, and bad, and above all, immoral sentiment. It is coarse, because it is characteristic of only such men as stand on the lowest stage of morality and who expect from other nations the same acts of violence that they want to practise themselves; it is harmful, because it violates the advantageous and joyous peaceful relations with other nations, and, above all, produces that organization of the governments, in which the worst man can acquire and always acquires the power; it is disgraceful, because it transforms the man not only into a slave, but also into a fighting cock, bull, gladiator, who ruins his forces and his life, not for his own purposes, but for those of his government; it is immoral, because, instead of recognizing himself as the son of God, as Christianity teaches us, or at least as a free man, who is guided by his reason,—every man, under the influence of patriotism, recognizes himself as the son of his country, the slave of his government, and commits acts which are contrary to his reason and to his conscience. . . .

9

. . . Whoever you may be,—a Frenchman, Russian, Pole, Englishman, Irishman, German, Bohemian,—you must understand that all our real human interests, whatever they be,—agricultural, industrial, commercial, artistic, or scientific,—all these interests, like all the pleasures and joys, in no way oppose the interests of the other nations and states, and that you are, by means of a mutual interaction, exchange of services, the joy of a broad brotherly communion, of an exchange not only of wares, but also of sentiments, united with the men of the other nations.

You must understand that the questions as to who succeeds in seizing Wei-hai-wei, Port Arthur, or Cuba—whether it is your government or another—are by no means a matter of indifference to you, but that every seizure made by your government is detrimental to you, because it inevitably brings with it all kinds of influences, which your government will exert against you, in order to compel you to take part in robberies and acts of violence, which are necessary for the seizures and for the retention of what has been seized. You must understand that your life can in no way be improved by this, that Alsace will be German or French, and that Ireland and Poland are free or enslaved: no matter whose they may be, you can live wherever you please; even if you were an Alsatian, an Irishman, or a Pole,—you must understand that every fanning of patriotism will only make your position worse, because the enslavement of your nation has resulted only from the struggle of patriotisms, and that every manifestation of patriotism in one nation increases the reaction against it in another. You must understand that you can save yourselves from all your calamities only when you free yourselves from the obsolete idea of patriotism and from the obedience to the governments which is based upon it, and when you shall boldly enter into the sphere of that higher idea of the brotherly union of the nations, which has long ago entered into life and is calling you to itself from all sides.

Let men understand that they are not the sons of any countries or governments, but the sons of God, and that, therefore, they cannot be slaves, nor enemies of other men, and all those senseless, now quite useless, pernicious institutions, bequeathed by antiquity, which are called governments, and all those sufferings, acts of violence, degradations, crimes, which they bring with them, will disappear of their own accord.

---

[1]Should read ''To abolish the governments' violence''—ED.

PATRIOTISM AND CHRISTIANITY (1899)

15

It would seem that, owing to the spread of education, of speedier locomotion, of greater intercourse between different nations, to the widening of literature, and chiefly to the decrease of danger from other nations, the fraud of patriotism ought daily to become more difficult and at length impossible to practise.

But the truth is that these very means of general external education, facilitated locomotion and intercourse, and especially the spread of literature, being captured and constantly more and more controlled by government, confer on the latter such possibilities of exciting a feeling of mutual animosity between nations, that in degree as the uselessness and harmfulness of patriotism have become manifest, so also has increased the power of the government and ruling class to excite patriotism among the people. . . .

And so, thanks to the development of literature, reading, and the facilities of travel, governments which have their agents everywhere, by means of statutes, sermons, schools, and the press, inculcate everywhere upon the people the most barbarous and erroneous ideas as to their advantages, the relationship of nations, their qualities and intentions; and the people, so crushed by labor that they have neither the time nor the power to understand the significance or test the truth of the ideas which are forced upon them or of the demands made upon them in the name of their welfare, put themselves unmurmuringly under the yoke.

Whereas working-men who have freed themselves from unremitting labor and become educated, and who have, therefore, it might be supposed, the power of seeing through the fraud which is practised upon them, are subjected to such a coercion of threats, bribes, and all the hypnotic influence of governments, that, almost without exception, they desert to the side of the government, and by entering some well-paid and profitable employment, as priest, schoolmaster, officer, or functionary, become participators in spreading the deceit which is destroying their comrades.

It is as if the nets were laid at the entrances to education, in which those who by some means or other escape from the masses bowed down by labor, are inevitably caught.

At first, when one understands the cruelty of all this deceit, one feels indignant in spite of oneself against those who from personal ambition or greedy advantage propagate this cruel fraud which destroys the souls as well as the bodies of men, and one feels inclined to accuse them of a sly craftiness; but the fact is that they are deceitful with no wish to deceive, but because they cannot be otherwise. And they deceive, not like Machiavellians, but with no consciousness of their deceit, and usually with the naïve assurance that they are doing something excellent and elevated, a view in which they are persistently encouraged by the sympathy and approval of all who surround them.

It is true that, being dimly aware that on this fraud is founded their power and advantageous position, they are unconsciously drawn toward it; but their action is not based on any desire to delude the people, but because they believe it to be of service to the people.

Thus emperors, kings, and their ministers, with all their coronations, manœuvers, reviews, visiting one another, dressing up in various uniforms, going from place to place, and delibrating with serious faces as to how they may keep peace between nations supposed to be inimical to each other,—nations who would never dream of quarreling,—feel quite sure that what they are doing is very reasonable and useful.

In the same way the various ministers, diplomatists, and functionaries—dressed up inn uniforms, with all sorts of ribbons and crosses, writing and docketing with great care, upon the best paper, their hazy, involved, altogether needless communications, advices, projects—are quite assured that, without their activity, the entire existence of nations would halt or become deranged.

In the same manner military men, got up in ridiculous costumes, arguing seriously with what rifle or cannon men can be most expeditiously destroyed, are quite certain that their field-days and reviews are most important and essential to the people.

So likewise the priests, journalists, writers of patriotic songs and class-books, who preach patriotism and receive liberal remuneration, are equally satisfied.

And no doubt the organizers of festivities—like the Franco-Russian fêtes—are sincerely affected while pronouncing their patriotic speeches and toasts.

All these people do what they are doing unconsciously, because they must, all their life being founded upon deceit, and because they know not how to do anything else. . . .

. . . Not long ago, Wilhelm II. ordered a new throne for himself, with some special kind of ornamentation, and having dressed up in a white uniform, with a cuirass, tight breeches, and a helmet with a bird on the top, and enveloped himself in a red mantle, came out to his subjects, and sat down on this new throne, perfectly assured that his act was most necessary and important; and his subjects not only saw nothing ridiculous in it, but thought the sight most imposing.

16

For some time the power of the government over the people has not been maintained by force, as was the case when one nation conquered another and ruled it by force of arms, or when the rulers of an unarmed people had separate legions of janizaries or guards.

The power of the government has for some time been maintained by what is termed public opinion.

A public opinion exists that patriotism is a fine moral sentiment, and that it is right and our duty to regard one's own nation, one's own state, as the best in the world; and flowing naturally from this public opinion is another, namely, that it is right and our duty to acquiesce in the control of a government over ourselves, to subordinate ourselves to it, to serve in the army and submit ourselves to discipline, to give our earnings to the government in the form of taxes, to submit to the decisions of the law-courts, and to consider the edicts of the government as divinely right. And when such public opinion exists, a strong governmental power is formed possessing milliards of money, an organized mechanism of administration, the postal service, telegraphs, telphones, disciplined armies, law-courts, police, submissive, clergy, schools, even the press; and this power maintains in the people the public opinion which it finds necessary. . . .

And indeed, one has only to remember what we profess, both as Christians and merely as men of our day, those fundamental moralities by which we are directed in our social, family, and personal existence, and the position in which we place ourselves in the name of patriotism, in order to see what a degree of contradiction we have placed between our conscience and what, thanks to an energetic government influence in this direction, we regard as our public opinion.

One has only thoughtfully to examine the most ordinary demands of patriotism, which are expected of us as the most simple and natural affair, in order to understand to what extent these requirements are at variance with that real public opinion which we already share. We all regard ourselves as free, educated, humane men, or even as Christians, and yet we are all in such a position that were Wilhelm to-morrow to take offense against Alexander, or Mr. N. to write a lively article on the Eastern Question, or Prince So-and-so to plunder some Bulgarians or Servians, or some queen or empress to be put out by something or other, all we educated humane Christians must go and kill people of whom we have no knowledge, and toward whom we are as amicably disposed as to the rest of the world. . . .

17

No feats of heroism are needed to achieve the greatest and most important changes in the existence of humanity; neither the armament of millions of soldiers, nor the construction of new roads and machines, nor the arrangement of exhibitions, nor the organization of workmen's unions, nor revolutions, nor barricades, nor explosions, nor the perfection of aërial navigation; but a change in public opinion.

And to accomplish this change no exertions of the mind are needed, nor the refutation of anything in existence, nor the invention of any extraordinary novelty; it is only needful that we should not succumb to the erroneous, already defunct, public opinion of the past, which governments have induced artificially; it is only needful that each individual should say what he really feels or thinks, or at least that he should not say what he does not think.

And if only a small body of the people were to do so at once, of their own accord, outworn public opinion would fall off us of itself, and a new, living, real opinion would assert itself. And when public opinion should thus have changed without the slightest effort, the internal condition of men's lives which so torments them would change likewise of its own accord.

One is ashamed to say how little is needed for all men to be delivered from those calamities which now oppress them; it is only needful not to lie.

Let people only be superior to the falsehood which is instilled into them, let them decline to say what they neither feel nor think, and at once such a revolution of all the organization of our life will take place as could not be attained by all the efforts of revolutionists during centuries, even were complete power within their hands.

If people would only believe that strength is not in force but in truth, would only not shrink from it either in word or deed, not say what they do not think, not do what they regard as foolish and as wrong! . . .

The governments know this, and tremble before this force, and strive in every way they can to counteract or become possessed of it.

They know that strength is not in force, but in thought and in clear expression of it, and, therefore, they are more afraid of the expression of independent thought than of armies; hence they institute censorships, bribe the press, and monopolize the control of religion and of the schools. . . .

We all complain of the senseless order of life, which is at variance with our being, and yet we refuse to use the unique and powerful weapon within our hands—the consciousness of truth and its expression; but on the contrary, under the pretext of struggling with evil, we destroy the weapon, and sacrifice it to the exigencies of an imaginary conflict.

One man does not assert the truth which he knows, because he feels himself bound to the people with whom he is engaged; another, because the truth might deprive him of the profitable position by which he maintains his family; a third, because he desires to attain reputation and authority, and then use them in the service of mankind; a fourth, because he does not wish to destroy old sacred traditions; a fifth, because he has no desire to offend people; a sixth, because the expression of the truth would arouse persecution, and disturb the excellent social activity to which he has devoted himself.

One serves as emperor, king, minister, government functionary, or soldier, and assures himself and others that the deviation from truth indispensable to his condition is redeemed by the good he does. Another, who fulfils the duties of a spiritual pastor, does not in the depths of his soul believe all he teaches, but permits the deviation from truth in view of the good he does. A third instructs men by means of literature, and notwithstanding the silence he must observe with regard to the whole truth, in order not to stir up the government and society against himself, has no doubt as to the good he does. A fourth struggles resolutely with the existing order as revolutionist or anarchist, and is quite assured that the aims he pursues are so beneficial that the neglect of the truth, or even of the falsehood, by silence, indispensable to the success of his activity, does not destroy the utility of his work. . . .

If only men were boldly and clearly to express the truth already manifest to them of the brotherhood of all nations, and the crime of exclusive devotion to one's own people, that defunct, false public opinion would slough off of itself like a dried skin,—and upon it depends the power of governments, and all the evil produced by them; and the new public opinion would stand forth, which is even now but awaiting that dropping off of the old to put forth manifestly and powerfully its demand, and establish new forms of existence in conformity with the consciousness of mankind. . . .

9.   Means and Ends
Passive Resistance
The Atom Bomb, America and Japan

MOHANDAS K. GANDHI

MEANS AND ENDS

Reader: Why should we not obtain our goal, which is good, by any means whatsoever, even by using violence? Shall I think of the means when I have to deal with a thief in the house? My duty is to drive him out anyhow. You seem to admit that we have received nothing, and that we shall receive nothing by petitioning. Why, then, may we not do so by using brute force? And, to retain what we may receive we shall keep up the fear by using the same force to the extent that it may be necessary. You will not find fault with a continuance of force to prevent a child from thrusting its foot into fire? Somehow or other we have to gain our end.

Editor: Your reasoning is plausible. It has deluded many. I have used similar arguments before now. But I think I know better now, and I shall

The first two selections are from *Hind Swaraj or Indian Home Rule* (1909), Chapters 16 and 17. The third is from *Harijan* (July 7, 1946). All are reprinted by permission of the Navajivan Trust (Ahmedabad, India).

endeavour to undeceive you. Let us first take the argument that we are justified in gaining our end by using brute force because the English gained theirs by using similar means. It is perfectly true that they used brute force and that it is possible for us to do likewise, but by using similar means we can get only the same thing that they got. You will admit that we do not want that. Your belief that there is no connection between the means and the end is a great mistake. Through that mistake even men who have been considered religious have committed grievous crimes. Your reasoning is the same as saying that we can get a rose through planting a noxious weed. If I want to cross the ocean, I can do so only by means of a vessel; if I were to use a cart for that purpose, both the cart and I would soon find the bottom. "As is the God, so is the votary", is a maxim worth considering. Its meaning has been distorted and men have gone astray. The means may be likened to a seed, the end to a tree; and there is just the same inviolable connection between the means and the end as there is between the seed and the tree. I am not likely to obtain the result flowing from the worship of God by laying myself prostrate before Satan. If, therefore, any one were to say: "I want to worship God; it does not matter that I do so by means of Satan," it would be set down as ignorant folly. We reap exactly as we sow. The English in 1833 obtained greater voting power by violence. Did they by using brute force better appreciate their duty? They wanted the right of voting, which they obtained by using physical force. But real rights are a result of performance of duty; these rights they have not obtained. We, therefore, have before us in England the force of everybody wanting and insisting on his rights, nobody thinking of his duty. And, where everybody wants rights, who shall give them to whom? I do not wish to imply that they do no duties. They don't perform the duties corresponding to those rights; and as they do not perform that particular duty, namely, acquire fitness, their rights have proved a burden to them. In other words, what they have obtained is an exact result of the means they adopted. They used the means corresponding to the end. If I want to deprive you of your watch, I shall certainly have to fight for it; if I want to buy your watch, I shall have to pay for it; and if I want a gift, I shall have to plead for it; and, according to the means I employ, the watch is stolen property, my own property, or a donation. Thus we see three different results from three different means. Will you still say that means do not matter?

Now we shall take the example given by you of the thief to be driven out. I do not agree with you that the thief may be driven out by any means. If it is my father who has come to steal I shall use one kind of means. If it is an acquaintance I shall use another; and in the case of a perfect stranger I shall use a third. If it is a white man, you will perhaps say you will use means different from those you will adopt with an Indian thief. If it is a weakling, the means will be different from those to be adopted for dealing with an equal in physical strength; and if the thief is armed from top to toe, I shall simply remain quiet. Thus we have a variety of means between the father and the armed man. Again, I fancy that I should pre-

tend to be sleeping whether the thief was my father or that strong armed man. The reason for this is that my father would also be armed and I should succumb to the strength possessed by either and allow my things to be stolen. The strength of my father would make me weep with pity; the strength of the armed man would rouse in me anger and we should become enemies. Such is the curious situation. From these examples we may not be able to agree as to the means to be adopted in each case. I myself seem clearly to see what should be done in all these cases, but the remedy may frighten you. I therefore hesitate to place it before you. For the time being I will leave you to guess it, and if you cannot, it is clear you will have to adopt different means in each case. You will also have seen that any means will not avail to drive away the thief. You will have to adopt means to fit each case. Hence it follows that your duty is not to drive away the thief by any means you like.

Let us proceed a little further. That well-armed man has stolen your property; you have harboured the thought of his act; you are filled with anger; you argue that you want to punish that rogue, not for your own sake, but for the good of your neighbours; you have collected a number of armed men, you want to take his house by assault; he is duly informed of it, he runs away; he too is incensed. He collects his brother robbers, and sends you a defiant message that he will commit robbery in broad daylight. You are strong, you do not fear him, you are prepared to receive him. Meanwhile, the robber pesters your neighbours. They complain before you. You reply that you are doing all for their sake, you do not mind that your own goods have been stolen. Your neighbours reply that the robber never pestered them before, and that he commenced his depredations only after you declared hostilities against him. You are between Scylla and Charybdis. You are full of pity for the poor men. What they say is true. What are you to do? You will be disgraced if you now leave the robber alone. You, therefore, tell the poor men: "Never mind. Come, my wealth is yours, I will give you arms, I will teach you how to use them; you should belabour the rogue; don't you leave him alone." And so the battle grows; the robbers increase in numbers;

your neighbours have deliberately put themselves to inconvenience. Thus the result of wanting to take revenge upon the robber is that you have disturbed your own peace; you are in perpetual fear of being robbed and assaulted; your courage has given place to cowardice. If you will patiently examine the argument, you will see that I have not overdrawn the picture. This is one of the means. Now let us examine the other. You set this armed robber down as an ignorant brother; you intend to reason with him at a suitable opportunity; you argue that he is, after all, a fellow man; you do not know what prompted him to steal. You, therefore, decide that, when you can, you will destroy the man's motive for stealing. Whilst you are thus reasoning with yourself, the man comes again to steal. Instead of being angry with him you take pity on him. You think that this stealing habit must be a disease with him. Henceforth, you, therefore, keep your doors and windows open, you change your sleeping-place, and you keep your things in a manner most accessible to him. The robber comes again and is confused as all this is new to him; nevertheless, he takes away your things. But his mind is agitated. He inquires about you in the village, he comes to learn about you broad and loving heart, he repents, he begs your pardon, returns you your things, and leaves off the stealing habit. He becomes your servant, and you will find for him honourable employment. This is the second method. Thus, you see, different means have brought about totally different results. I do not wish to deduce from this that robbers will act in the above manner or that all will have the same pity and love like you, but I only wish to show that fair means alone can produce fair results, and that, at least in the majority of cases, if not indeed in all, the force of love and pity is infinitely greater than the force of arms. There is harm in the exercise of brute force, never in that of pity.

Now we will take the question of petitioning. It is a fact beyond dispute that a petition, without the backing of force, is useless. However, the late Justice Ranade used to say that petitions served a useful purpose because they were a means of educating people. They give the latter an idea of their condition and warn the rulers. From this point of view, they are not altogether useless. A petition of an equal is a sign of courtesy; a petition from a slave is a symbol of his slavery. A petition backed by force is a petition from an equal and, when he transmits his demand in the form of a petition, it testifies to his nobility. Two kinds of force can back petitions. "We shall hurt you if you do not give this," is one kind of force; it is the force of arms, whose evil results we have already examined. The second kind of force can thus be stated: "If you do not concede our demand, we shall be no longer your petitioners. You can govern us only so long as we remain the governed; we shall no longer have any dealings with you." The force implied in this may be described as love-force, soul-force, or, more popularly but less accurately, passive resistance.[1] This force is indestructible. He who uses it perfectly understands his position. We have an ancient proverb which literally means: "One negative cures thirty-six diseases." The force of arms is powerless when matched against the force of love or the soul.

Now we shall take your last illustration, that of the child thrusting its foot into fire. It will not avail you. What do you really do to the child? Supposing that it can exert so much physical force that it renders you powerless and rushes into fire, then you cannot prevent it. There are only two remedies open to you—either you must kill it in order to prevent it from perishing in the flames, or you must give your own life because you do not wish to see it perish before your very eyes. You will not kill it. If your heart is not quite full of pity, it is possible that you will not surrender yourself by preceding the child and going into the fire yourself. You, therefore, helplessly allow it to go to the flames. Thus, at any rate, you are not using physical force. I hope you will not consider that it is still physical force, though of a low order, when you would forcibly prevent the child from rushing towards the fire if you could. That force is of a different order and we have to understand what it is.

Remember that, in thus preventing the child, you are minding entirely its own interest, you are

---

[1]*Satyagraha*, what Gandhi in later years preferred to label "nonviolent resistance," to emphasize that it was an activist and not a passive strategy—ED.

exercising authority for its sole benefit. Your example does not apply to the English. In using brute force against the English you consult entirely your own, that is the national, interest. There is no question here either of pity or of love. If you say that the actions of the English, being evil, represent fire, and that they proceed to their actions through ignorance, and that therefore they

occupy the position of a child and that you want to protect such a child, then you will have to overtake every evil action of that kind by whomsoever committed and, as in the case of the evil child, you will have to sacrifice yourself. If you are capable of such immeasurable pity, I wish you well in its exercise.

PASSIVE RESISTANCE

Reader: Is there any historical evidence as to the success of what you have called soul-force or truth-force? No instance seems to have happened of any nation having risen through soul-force. I still think that the evil-doers will not cease doing evil without physical punishment.

Editor: The poet Tulsidas has said: "Of religion, pity, or love, is the root, as egotism of the body. Therefore, we should not abandon pity so long as we are alive." This appears to me to be a scientific truth. I believe in it as much as I believe in two and two being four. The force of love is the same as the force of the soul or truth. We have evidence of its working at every step. The universe would disappear without the existence of that force. But you ask for historical evidence. It is, therefore, necessary to know what history means. The Gujarati equivalent means: "It so happened." If that is the meaning of history, it is possible to give copious evidence. But, if it means the doings of kings and emperors, there can be no evidence of soul-force or passive resistance in such history. You cannot expect silver ore in a tin mine. History, as we know it, is a record of the wars of the world, and so there is a proverb among Englishmen that a nation which has no history, that is, no wars, is a happy nation. How kings played, how they became enemies of one another, how they murdered one

another, is found accurately recorded in history, and if this were all that had happened in the world, it would have been ended long ago. If the story of the universe had commenced with wars, not a man would have been found alive today. Those people who have been warred against have disappeared as, for instance, the natives of Australia of whom hardly a man was left alive by the intruders. Mark, please, that these natives did not use soul-force in self-defence, and it does not require much foresight to know that the Australians will share the same fate as their victims. "Those that take the sword shall perish by the Sword." With us the proverb is that professional swimmers will find a watery grave.

The fact that there are so many men still alive in the world shows that it is based not on the force of arms but on the force of truth or love. Therefore, the greatest and most unimpeachable evidence of the success of this force is to be found in the fact that, in spite of the wars of the world, it still lives on.

Thousands, indeed tens of thousands, depend for their existence on a very active working of this force. Little quarrels of millions of families in their daily lives disappear before the exercise of this force. Hundreds of nations live in peace. History does not and cannot take note of this fact. History is really a record of every interruption of the even working of the force of love or of the soul. Two brothers quarrel; one of them repents and re-awakens the love that was lying dormant in him; the two again begin to live in peace; nobody takes note of this. But if the two brothers, through the intervention of solicitors or some other reason, take up arms or go to law—which is another form of the exhibition of brute force—their doing would be immediately noticed in the press, they would be the talk of their neighbours and would probably go down to history. And what is true of families and communities is true of nations. There is no reason to believe that there is one law for families and another for nations. History, then, is a record of an interruption of the course of nature. Soul-force, being natural, is not noted in history. . . .

THE ATOM BOMB, AMERICA AND JAPAN

It has been suggested by American friends that the atom bomb will bring in Ahimsa (non-violence) as nothing else can. It will, if it is meant that its destructive power will so disgust the world that it will turn it away from violence for the time being. This is very like a man glutting himself with dainties to the point of nausea and turning away from them only to return with redoubled zeal after the effect of nausea is well over. Precisely in the same manner will the world return to violence with renewed zeal after the effect of disgust is worn out.

So far as I can see, the atomic bomb has deadened the finest feeling that has sustained mankind for ages. There used to be the so-called laws of war which made it tolerable. Now we know the naked truth. War knows no law except that of might. The atom bomb brought an empty victory to the allied arms but it resulted for the time being in destroying the soul of Japan. What has happened to the soul of the destroying nation is yet too early to see. Forces of nature act in a mysterious manner. We can but solve the mystery by deducing the unknown result from the known results of similar events. A slaveholder cannot hold a slave without putting himself or his deputy in the cage holding the slave. Let no one run away with the idea that I wish to put in a defense of Japanese misdeeds in pursuance of Japan's unworthy ambition. The difference was only one of degree. I assume that Japan's greed was more unworthy. But the greater unworthiness conferred no right on the less unworthy of destroying without mercy men, women and children of Japan in a particular area.

The moral to be legitimately drawn from the supreme tragedy of the bomb is that it will not be destroyed by counter-bombs even as violence cannot be by counter-violence. Mankind has to get out of violence only through non-violence. Hatred can be overcome only by love. Counter-hatred only increases the surface as well as the depth of hatred. I am aware that I am repeating what I have many times stated before and practiced to the best of my ability and capacity. What I first stated was itself nothing new. It was as old as the hills. Only I recited no copy-book maxim but definitely announced what I believed in every fibre of my being. Sixty years of practice in various walks of life has only enriched the belief which experience of friends has fortified. It is however the central truth by which one can stand alone without flinching. I believe in what Max Müller said years ago, namely that truth needed to be repeated as long as there were men who disbelieved it.

10.   Vietnam: Setting the Moral Equation

Howard Zinn

. . . I would start such a discussion from the supposition that it is logically indefensible to hold to an absolutely nonviolent position, because it is at least theoretically conceivable that a small violence might be required to prevent a larger one. Those who are immediately offended by this statement should consider: World War II; the assassination attempt on Hitler; the American, French, Russian, Chinese, Cuban revolutions; possible armed revolt in South Africa; the case of Rhodesia; the Deacons in Louisiana. Keep in mind that many who support the war in Vietnam may do so on grounds which they believe similar to those used in the above cases.

The terrible thing is that once you stray from absolute nonviolence you open the door for the most shocking abuses. It is like distributing scalpels to an eager group, half of whom are surgeons and half butchers. But that is man's constant problem—how to release the truth without being devoured by it.

How can we tell butchers from surgeons, distinguish between a healing and a destructive act of violence? The first requirement is that our starting point must always be nonviolence, and that the burden of proof, therefore, is on the advocate of violence to show, with a high degree of prob-

ability, that he is justified. In modern American civilization, we demand unanimity among twelve citizens before we will condemn a single person to death, but we will destroy thousands of people on the most flimsy of political assumptions (like the domino theory of revolutionary contagion).

What proof should be required? I suggest four tests:

1. Self-defense, against outside attackers or a counterrevolutionary force within, using no more violence than is needed to repel the attack, is justified. This covers that Negro housewife who several years ago in a little Georgia town, at home alone with her children, fired through the door at a gang of white men carrying guns and chains, killing one, after which the rest fled. It would sacrifice the Rhineland to Hitler in 1936, and even Austria (for the Austrians apparently preferred not to fight), but demands supporting the Loyalist government in Spain, and defending Czechoslovakia in 1938. And it applies to Vietnamese fighting against American attackers who hold the strings of a puppet government.

2. Revolution is justified, for the purpose of overthrowing a deeply entrenched oppressive regime, unshakable by other means. Outside aid is permissible (because rebels, as in the American Revolution, are almost always at a disadvantage against the holders of power), but with the requirement that the manpower for the revolution be indigenous, for this in itself is a test of how popu-

Excerpted from "Vietnam: Setting the Moral Equation," by Howard Zinn, in *The Nation* (January 17, 1966), pp. 64–69. Copyright 1966 *The Nation* magazine, The Nation Associates, Inc. Reprinted with the permission of the publisher and author.

lar the revolution is. This could cover the French, American, Mexican, Russian, Chinese, Cuban, Algerian cases. It would also cover the Vietcong rebellion. And a South African revolt, should it break out.

3. Even if one of the above conditions is met, there is no moral justification for visiting violence on the innocent. Therefore, violence in self-defense or in revolution must be focused on the evildoers, and limited to that required to achieve the goal, resisting all arguments that extra violence might speed victory. This rules out the strategic bombing of German cities in World War II, the atom bombing of Hiroshima and Nagasaki; it rules out terrorism against civilians even in a just revolution. Violence even against the guilty, when undertaken for sheer revenge, is unwarranted which rules out capital punishment for any crime. The requirement of focused violence makes nonsensical the equating of the killing of village chiefs in South Vietnam by the Vietcong and the bombing of hospitals by American fliers; yet the former is also unjustifed if it is merely an act of terror or revenge and not specifically required for a change in the social conditions of the village.

4. There is an additional factor which the conditions of modern warfare make urgent. Even if all three of the foregoing principles are met, there is a fourth which must be considered if violence is to be undertaken: the costs of self-defense or social change must not be so high, because of the intensity or the prolongation of violence, or because of the risk of proliferation, that the victory is not worth the cost. For the Soviets to defend Cuba from attack—though self-defense was called for—would not have been worth a general war; for the United States to defend Hungary from attack—though self-defense was called for—would not have been worth a general war. For China or Soviet Russia to aid the Vietcong with troops though the Vietcong cause is just, would be wrong if it seriously risked a general war. Under certain conditions, nations should be captive rather than be destroyed, or revolutionaries should bide their time. Indeed, because of the omnipresence of the great military powers—the United States and the USSR

(perhaps this is not so true for the countries battling England, France, Holland, Belgium, Portugal)—revolutionary movements may have to devise tactics short of armed revolt to overturn an oppressive regime.

The basic principle I want to get close to is that violence is most clearly justified when those whose own lives are at stake make the decision on whether the prize is worth dying for. Self-defense and guerrilla warfare, by their nature, embody this decision. Conscript armies and unfocused warfare violate it. And no one has a right to decide that someone else is better off dead than Red, or that someone else should die to defend his way of life, or that an individual (like Norman Morrison) should choose to live rather than die.

It would be foolish to pretend that this summary can be either precise or complete. Those involved in self-defense or in a revolution need no intellectual justification; their emotions reflect some inner rationality. It is those outside the direct struggle, deciding whether to support one side or stay out, who need to think clearly about principles. Americans, therefore, possessing the greatest power and being furthest removed from the problems of self-defense or revolution, need thoughtful deliberation most. All we can do in social analysis is to offer rough guides to replace nonthinking, to give the beginnings of some kind of moral calculus.

However, it takes no close measurement to conclude that the American bombings in Vietnam, directed as they are to farming areas, villages, hamlets, fit none of the criteria listed, and so are deeply immoral, whatever else is true about the situation in Southeast Asia or the world. The silence of the government's supporters on this—from Hubert Humphrey to the academic signers of advertisements—is particularly shameful, because it requires no surrender of their other arguments to concede that this is unnecessary bestiality.

Bombings aside, none of the American military activity against the Vietcong could be justified unless it were helping a determined people to defend itself against an outside attacker. That is why the Administration, hoping to confirm by verbal repetition what cannot be verified in fact, continually uses the term "aggression" to describe the Vietnamese guerrilla activities. The expert evidence, however, is overwhelming on this question:

1. Philippe Devillers, the French historian, says "the insurrection existed before the Communists decided to take part. . . . And even among the Communists, the initiative did not originate in Hanoi, but from the grass roots, where the people were literally driven by Diem to take up arms in self-defense."

2. Bernard Fall says "anti-Diem guerrillas were active long before infiltrated North Vietnamese elements joined the fray."

3. The correspondent for *Le Monde*, Jean Lacouture (in *Le Viet Nam entre deux paix*) confirms that local pressure, local conditions led to guerrilla activity.

4. Donald S. Zagoria, a specialist on Asian communism at Columbia University, wrote recently that "it is reasonably clear that we are dealing with an indigenous insurrection in the South, and that this, not Northern assistance; is the main trouble."

One test of "defense against aggression" is the behavior of the official South Vietnamese army—the "defenders" themselves. We find: a high rate of desertions; a need to herd villagers into concentration-camp "strategic hamlets" in order to control them; the use of torture to get information from other South Vietnamese, whom you might expect to be enthusiastic about "defending" their country; and all of this forcing the United States to take over virtually the entire military operation in Vietnam.

The ordinary people of Vietnam show none of the signs of a nation defending itself against "aggression," except in their noncooperation with the government and the Americans. A hundred thousand Vietnamese farmers were conducting a rebellion with mostly captured weapons (both David Halberstam and Hanson Baldwin affirmed this in *The New York Times*, contradicting quietly what I. F. Stone demolished statistically—the State Department's White Paper on "infiltration"). Then they matched the intrusion of 150,000 American troops with 7,500 North Vietnamese soldiers (in November, 1965, American military officials estimated that five regiments of North Vietnamese, with 1,500 in each regiment, were in South Vietnam). Weapons were acquired from Communist countries, but not a single plane to match the horde of American bombers filling the skies over Vietnam. This adds up not to North Vietnamese aggression (if indeed North Vietnamese can be considered outsiders at all) but to American aggression, with a puppet government fronting for American power.

Thus, there is no valid principle on which the United States can defend either its bombing, or its military presence, in Vietnam. It is the factual emptiness of its moral claim which then leads it to seek a one-piece substitute, that comes prefabricated with its own rationale, surrounded by an emotional aura sufficient to ward off inspectors. This transplanted fossil is the Munich analogy, which, speaking with all the passion of Churchill in the Battle of Britain, declares: to surrender in Vietnam is to do what Chamberlain did at Munich; that is why the villagers must die.

The great value of the Munich analogy to the Strangeloves is that it captures so many American liberals, among many others. It backs the Vietnamese expedition with a coalition broad enough to include Barry Goldwater, Lyndon Johnson, George Meany and John Roche (thus reversing World War II's coalition, which excluded the far Right and included the radical Left). This bloc justifies the carnage in Vietnam with a huge image of invading armies, making only one small change in the subtitle: replacing the word "Fascist" with the word "Communist." Then, the whole savage arsenal of World War II—the means both justified and unjustifiable—supported by that great fund of indignation built against the Nazis, can be turned to the uses of the American Century.

To leave the Munich analogy intact, to fail to discuss communism and fascism, is to leave untouched the major premise which supports the present policy of near genocide in Vietnam. I propose here at least to initiate such a discussion.

Let's refresh our memories on what happened at Munich. Chamberlain of England and Daladier of France met Hitler and Mussolini (this was September 30, 1938) and agreed to surrender the Sudeten part of Czechoslovakia, inhabited by German-speaking people, hoping thus to prevent a general war in Europe. Chamberlain returned to England, claiming he had brought "peace in our time." Six months later, Hitler had gobbled up the rest of Czechoslovakia; then he began presenting ultimatums to Poland, and by September 3, 1939, general war had broken out in Europe.

There is strong evidence that if the Sudetenland had not been surrendered at Munich—with it went Czechoslovakia's powerful fortifications, seventy percent of its iron, steel and electric power, eighty-six percent of its chemicals, sixty-six percent of its coal—and had Hitler then gone to war, he would have been defeated quickly, with the aid of Czechoslovakia's thirty-five well-trained divisions. And if he chose, at the sign of resistance, not to go to war, then at least he would have been stopped in his expansion.

And so, the analogy continues, to let the Communist-dominated National Liberation Front win in South Vietnam (for the real obstacle in the sparring over negotiations is the role of the NLF in a new government) is to encourage more Communist expansion in Southeast Asia and beyond, and perhaps lead to a war more disastrous than the present one; to stop communism in South Vietnam is to discourage its expansion elsewhere.

We should note, first, some of the important differences between the Munich situation in 1938 and Vietnam today:

1. In 1938, the main force operating against the Czech *status quo* was an outside force, Hitler's Germany: the supporting force was the Sudeten group inside led by Konrad Henlein. Since 1958 (and traceable back to 1942), the major force operating against the *status quo* in South Vietnam has been an inside force, formed in 1960 into the NLF: the chief supporter is not an outside nation but another part of the same nation, North Vietnam. The largest outside force in Vietnam consists of the American troops (who, interestingly, are referred to in West Germany as *Bandenkampfverbande*, Bandit Fighting Units, the name used in World War II by the Waffen-S.S. units to designate the guerrillas whom they specialized in killing). To put it another way, in 1938, the Germans were trying to take over part of another country. Today, the Vietcong are trying to take over part of their own country. In 1938, the outsider was Germany. Today it is the United States.

2. The Czech government, whose interests the West surrendered to Hitler in 1938, was a strong, effective, prosperous, democratic government—the government of Benes and Masaryk. The South Vietnamese government which we support is a hollow shell of a government, unstable, unpopular, corrupt, a dictatorship of bullies and torturers, disdainful of free elections and representative government (recently they opposed establishing a National Assembly on the ground that it might lead to communism), headed by a long line of tyrants from Bao Dai to Diem to Ky, who no more deserve to be ranked with Benes and Masaryk than Governor Wallace of Alabama deserves to be compared with Robert E. Lee. It is a government whose perpetuation is not worth the loss of a single human life.

3. Standing firm in 1938 meant engaging, in order to defeat once and for all, the central threat of that time, Hitler's Germany. Fighting in Vietnam today, even if it brings total victory, does not at all engage what the United States considers the central foes—the Soviet Union and Communist China. Even if international communism *were* a single organism, to annihilate the Vietcong would be merely to remove a toenail from an elephant. To engage what we think is the source of our difficulties (Red China one day, Soviet Russia the next) would require nuclear war, and even Robert Strange McNamara doesn't seem up to that.

4. There is an important difference between the historical context of Munich, 1938, and that of Vietnam, 1966. Munich was the culmination of a long line of surrenders and refusals to act: when Japan invaded China in 1931, when Mussolini invaded Ethiopia in 1935, when Hitler remilitarized the Rhineland in 1936, when Hitler and Mussolini supported the Franco attack on Republican Spain 1936–39, when Japan attacked China in 1937, when Hitler took Austria in the spring of 1938. The Vietnam crisis, on the other hand, is the culmination of a long series of events in which the West has on occasion held back (as in Czechoslovakia in 1948, or Hungary in 1956), but more often taken firm action, from the Truman Doctrine to the Berlin blockade, to the Korean conflict, to the Cuban blockade of 1962. So, withdrawing from Vietnam would not reinforce a pattern in the way that the Munich pact did. It would be another kind of line in that jagged graph which represents recent foreign policy.

5. We have twenty years of cold-war history to test the proposition derived from the Munich analogy—that a firm stand in Vietnam is worth the huge loss of life, because it will persuade the Communists there must be no more uprisings elsewhere. But what effect did our refusal to allow the defeat of South Korea (1950–53), or our aid in suppressing the Huk rebellion in the Philippines (1947–55), or the suppression of guerrillas in Malaya (1948–60), have on the guerrilla warfare in South Vietnam which started around 1958 and became consolidated under the National Liberation Front in 1960? If our use of subversion and arms to overthrow Guatemala in 1954 showed the Communists in Latin America that we meant business, then how did it happen that Castro rebelled and won in 1959? Did our invasion of Cuba in 1961, our blockade in 1962, show other revolutionaries in Latin America that they must desist? Then how explain the Dominican uprising in 1965? And did our dispatch of Marines to Santo Domingo end the fighting of guerrillas in the mountains of Peru?

One touches the Munich analogy and it falls apart. This suggests something more fundamental: that American policy makers and their supporters simply do not understand either the nature of communism or the nature of the various uprisings that have taken place in the postwar world. They are not able to believe that hunger, homelessness, oppression are sufficient spurs to revolution, without outside instigation, just as Dixie governors could not believe that Negroes marching in the streets were not led by outside agitators.

So, communism and revolution require discussion. They are sensitive questions, which some in the protest movement hesitate to broach for fear of alienating allies. But they are basic to that inversion of morality which enables the United States to surround the dirty war in Vietnam with the righteous glow of the war against Hitler.

A key assumption in this inversion is that communism and Nazism are sufficiently identical to be treated alike. However, communism as a set of ideals has attracted good people—not racists

or bullies or militarists—all over the world. One may argue that in Communist countries citizens had better affirm their allegiance to it, but that doesn't account for the fact that millions in France, Italy and Indonesia are Communist party members, that countless others all over the world have been inspired by Marxian ideals. And why should they not? These ideals include peace, brotherhood, racial equality, the classless society, the withering away of the state.

If Communists behave much better out of power than in it, that is a commentary not on their ideals but on weaknesses which they share with non-Communist wielders of power. If, presumably in pursuit of their ideals, they have resorted to brutal tactics, maintained suffocating bureaucracies and rigid dogmas, that makes them about as reprehensible as other nations, other social systems which, while boasting of the Judeo-Christian heritage, have fostered war, exploitation, colonialism and race hatred. We judge ourselves by our ideals; others by their actions. It is a great convenience.

The ultimate values of the Nazis, let us recall, included racism, elitism, militarism and war as ends in themselves. Unlike either the Communist nations or the capitalist democracies, there is here no ground for appeal to higher purposes. The ideological basis for coexistence between Communist and capitalist nations is the rough consensus of ultimate goals which they share. While war is held off, the citizens on both sides—it is to be hoped and indeed it is beginning to occur—will increasingly insist that their leaders live up to these values.

One of these professed values—which the United States is trying with difficulty to conceal by fragile arguments and feeble analogies—is the self-determination of peoples. Self-determination justifies the overthrow of entrenched oligarchies—whether foreign or domestic—in ways that will not lead to general war. China, Egypt, Indonesia, Algeria and Cuba are examples. Such revolutions tend to set up dictatorships, but they do so in the name of values which can be used to erode that same dictatorship. They therefore deserve as much general support and specific criticism as did the American revolutionaries, who set up a slave-holding government, but with a commitment to freedom which later led it, *against its wishes*, to abolitionism.

The easy use of the term "totalitarian" to cover both Nazis and Communists, or to equate the South Vietnamese regime with that of Ho Chi Minh, fails to make important distinctions, just as dogmatists of the Left sometimes fail to distinguish between Fascist states and capitalist democracies.

This view is ahistorical on two counts. First, it ignores the fact that, for the swift economic progress needed by new nations today, a Communist-led regime does an effective job (though it is not the only type of new government that can). In doing so, it raises educational and living standards and thus paves the way (as the USSR and Eastern Europe already show) for attacks from within on its own thought-control system. Second, this view forgets that the United States and Western Europe, now haughty in prosperity, with a fair degree of free expression, built their present status on the backs of either slaves or colonial people, and subjected their own laboring populations to several generations of misery before beginning to look like welfare states.

The perspective of history suggests that a united Vietnam under Ho Chi Minh is preferable to the elitist dictatorship of the South, just as Maoist China with all its faults is preferable to the rule of Chiang, and Castro's Cuba to Batista's. We do not have pure choices in the present, although we should never surrender those values which can shape the future. Right now, for Vietnam, a Communist government is probably the best avenue to that whole packet of human values which make up the common morality of mankind today: the preservation of human life, self-determination, economic security, the end of race and class oppression, that freedom of speech which an educated population begins to demand.

This is a conclusion which critics of government policy have hesitated to make. With some, it is because they simply don't believe it, but with others, it is because they don't want to rock the boat of "coalition." Yet the main obstacle to United States withdrawal is a fear that is real—that South Vietnam will then go Communist. If we

fail to discuss this honestly, we leave untouched a major plank in the structure that supports U.S. action.

When the jump is made from real fears to false ones, we get something approaching lunacy in American international behavior. Richard Hofstadter, in *The Paranoid Style in American Politics*, writes of "the central preconception of the paranoid style—the existence of a vast, insidious, preternaturally effective international conspiratorial network designed to perpetrate acts of the most fiendish character."

Once, the center of the conspiracy was Russia. A political scientist doing strategic research for the government told me recently with complete calm that his institute decided not too long ago that they had been completely wrong about the premise which underlay much of American policy in the postwar period—the premise that Russia hoped to take over Western Europe by force. Yet now, with not a tremor of doubt, the whole kit and caboodle of the invading-hordes theory is transferred to China.

Paranoia starts from a base of facts, but then leaps wildly to an absurd conclusion. It is a fact that China is totalitarian in its limitation of free expression, is fierce in its expressions of hatred for the United States, that it crushed opposition in Tibet, and fought for a strip of territory on the Indian border. But let's consider India briefly: it crushed an uprising in Hyderabad, took over the state of Kerala, initiated attacks on the China border, took Goa by force, and is fierce in its insistence on Kashmir. Yet we do not accuse it of wanting to take over the world.

Of course, there is a difference. China is emotionally tied to and sometimes aids obstreperous rebellions all over the world. However, China is not the source of these rebellions. The problem is not that China wants to take over the world, but that various peoples want to take over their parts of the world, and without the courtesies that attend normal business transactions. What if the Negroes in Watts really rose up and tried to take over Los Angeles? Would we blame that on Castro?

Not only does paranoia lead the United States to see international conspiracy where there is a diversity of Communist nations based on indigenous Communist movements. It also confuses communism with a much broader movement of this century—the rising of hungry and harassed people in Asia, Africa, Latin America (and the American South). Hence we try to crush radicalism in one place (Greece, Iran, Guatemala, the Philippines, etc.) and apparently succeed, only to find a revolution—whether Communist or Socialist or nationalist or of indescribable character—springing up somewhere else. We surround the world with our navy, cover the sky with our planes, fling our money to the winds, and then a revolution takes place in Cuba, 90 miles from home. We see every rebellion everywhere as the result of some devilish plot concocted in Moscow or Peking, when what is really happening is that people everywhere want to eat and to be free, and will use desperate means and any one of a number of social systems to achieve their ends.

The other side makes the same mistake. The Russians face a revolt in Hungary or Poznan, and attribute it to bourgeois influence, or to American scheming. Stalin's paranoia led him to send scores of old Bolsheviks before the firing squad. The Chinese seem to be developing obsessions about the United States; but in their case we are doing our best to match their wildest accusations with reality. It would be paranoid for Peking to claim that the United States is surrounding China with military bases, occupying countries on its border, keeping hundreds of thousands of troops within striking distance, contemplating the bombing of its population—if it were not largely true.

A world-wide revolution is taking place, aiming to achieve the very values that all major countries, East and West, claim to uphold: self-determination, economic security, racial equality, freedom. It takes many forms—Castro's, Mao's, Nasser's, Sukarno's, Senghor's, Kenyatta's. That it does not realize all its aims from the start makes it hardly more imperfect than we were in 1776. The road to freedom is stony, but people are going to march along it. What we need to do is improve the road, not blow it up.

The United States Government has tried hard to cover its moral nakedness in Vietnam. But the signs of its failure grow by the day. Facts have a way of coming to light. Also, we have recently had certain experiences which make us less naive about governments while we become more hopeful about people: the civil rights movement, the student revolt, the rise of dissent inside the Communist countries, the emergence of fresh, brave spirits in Africa, Asia, Latin America, and in our own country.

It is not our job, as citizens, to point out the difficulties of our military position (this, when true, is quite evident), or to work out clever bases for negotiating (the negotiators, when they *must*, will find a way), or to dissemble what we know is true in order to build a coalition (coalitions grow naturally from what is common to a heterogeneous group, and require each element to represent its colors as honestly as possible to make the mosaic accurate and strong). As a sign of the strange "progress" the world has made, from now on all moral transgressions take the form of irony, because they are committed against officially proclaimed values. The job of citizens, in any society, any time, is simply to point this out.

11. The Responsibility of Intellectuals

Noam Chomsky

About twenty years ago, Dwight MacDonald published a series of articles in *Politics* on the responsibility of peoples and, specifically, the responsibility of intellectuals. I read them as an undergraduate, in the immediate post-war years, and had occasion to reread them a few months ago in connection with a course I was teaching. They seem to me to have lost none of their power or persuasiveness. MacDonald is concerned with the question of war guilt. He asks the question: to what extent were the German or Japanese people responsible for the atrocities committed by their governments? And, quite properly, he turns the question back to home: to what extent are the British or American people responsible for the vicious terror bombings of civilians, perfected as a technique of warfare by the Western democracies and reaching their culmination in Hiroshima and Nagasaki, surely among the most unspeakable crimes in history. For an undergraduate in 1945–46—for anyone whose political and moral consciousness had been formed by the

horrors of the 1930's, by the war in Ethiopia, the Russian purge, the "China Incident," the Spanish Civil War, the Nazi atrocities, the Western reaction to these events and, in part, complicity in them—these questions had particular significance and poignancy.

With respect to the responsibility of intellectuals, there are still other, equally disturbing questions. Intellectuals are in a position to expose the lies of governments, to analyze actions in terms of their causes and motives and often hidden intentions. In the Western world, at least, they have the power that comes from political liberty, from access to information and freedom of expression. For a privileged minority, Western democracy provides the leisure, the facilities, and the training to seek the truth that lies hidden behind the veil of distortion and misrepresentation, ideology and class interest through which the events of current history are presented to us. The responsibilities of intellectuals, then, are much deeper than what MacDonald calls the "responsibility of peoples," given the unique privileges that they enjoy.

The issues that MacDonald raises are as pertinent today as they were twenty years ago. We can hardly avoid asking ourselves to what extent the American people bear responsibility for the savage American assault on a largely helpless rural population in Vietnam, still another atrocity of what Asians see as the "Vasco da Gama era" of world history. As for those of us who stood by in silence and apathy as this catastrophe slowly

This is the text of a talk given at the Harvard Hillel Foundation in March, 1966 as published in *Mosaic* 7/1 (Spring 1966) and later reprinted by the Students for a Democratic Society. The talk was the basis of an expanded and fully documented essay of about twice the length, which can be found in Noam Chomsky, *American Power and the New Mandarins* (New York: Pantheon, 1969), pp. 323–366. Copyright © 1967 by Noam Chomsky. Reprinted by permission of the author and by Pantheon Books, a Division of Random House, Inc.

took shape over the past dozen years, on what page of history do we find our proper place? Only the most insensible can escape these questions. I want to return to them, later on, after a few scattered remarks about the role and responsibility of intellectuals.

It is the responsibility of intellectuals to speak the truth and to expose lies. This, at least, may seem enough of a truism to pass without comment. Not so, however. For the modern intellectual, it is not at all obvious. Thus we have a Martin Heidegger writing, in a pro-Hitler declaration of 1933, that "truth is the revelation of that which makes a people certain, clear, and strong in its action and knowledge;" it is only this kind of "truth" that one has a responsibility to speak. Americans tend to be more forthright. Thus when Arthur Schlesinger was asked by the *New York Times*, last Thanksgiving, to explain the fact that his published account of the Bay of Pigs incident contradicted the story he had given the press at the time of the attack, he simply remarked that he had lied; and a few days later, he went on to compliment the *Times* for also having suppressed information on the planned invasion, in "the national interest," as this was defined by the group of arrogant and foolish men of whom Schlesinger gives such a flattering portrait in his recent book. It is of no particular interest that one man is quite happy to lie in behalf of a cause which—by his own account—he knows to be unjust; but it is significant that such events occasion so little response in the intellectual community, no feeling, for example, that there is something strange in the offer of a major chair in humanities to a historian who feels it to be his duty to persuade the world that an American sponsored invasion of a nearby country is nothing of the sort. And what of the incredible sequence of lies on the part of our government and its spokesmen concerning such matters as negotiations in Vietnam? The facts are known to all who care to know. The press, foreign and domestic, has presented documentation to refute each falsehood as it appears. But the power of the government propaganda apparatus is such that the citizen who does not undertake a research project of the subject can hardly hope to confront government pronouncements with fact. One might expect that this situation

would cause some concern in such an organization as, for example, the Congress for Cultural Freedom, which was brought together by "two things: a love of liberty and a respect for that part of human endeavour that goes by the name of culture." One would hope for this in vain, however.

Alongside of this growing lack of concern for truth, we find, in recent statements, a degree of naïveté with regard to American actions that is shocking beyond description. For example, Arthur Schlesinger, according to the *Times*, February 6, characterized our Vietnamese policies of 1954 "as part of our general program of international good will." Unless intended as rather bitter irony, this remark shows either a colossal cynicism, or an inability, on a scale that defies comment, to comprehend elementary phenomena of contemporary history. Similarly, what is one to make of the testimony of Thomas Schelling before the House Foreign Affairs Committee, January 27, 1966, where he discusses the two great dangers if all Asia "goes Communist?" First, this would exclude "the United States and what we call Western civilization from a large part of the world that is poor and colored and potentially hostile." Second, "a country like the United States probably cannot maintain self-confidence if just about the greatest thing it ever attempted, namely to create the basis for decency and prosperity and democratic government in the underdeveloped world, had to be acknowledged as a failure or as an attempt that we wouldn't try again." It surpasses belief that a person with even a minimal acquaintance with the record of American imperialism, political or economic, could produce such statements. It surpasses belief, that is, unless we look at the matter from a more historical point of view, and place such statements in the context of the hypocritical moralism of the past; for example, of Woodrow Wilson, who was going to teach the Latin Americans the art of good government and who wrote (1902) that it is "our peculiar duty" to teach colonial peoples "order and self-control . . . [and] . . . the drill and habit of law and obedience . . . ;" or of the missionaries of the 1840's who described the hideous and degrading opium wars "as the result of a great design of Providence to make the wickedness of men subserve his purposes of mercy towards China, in breaking through her wall of exclusion, and bringing the empire into more immediate contact with western and Christian nations.'' As a final example of this failure of skepticism, to use the most polite term that I can call to mind, consider the remarks of Henry Kissinger in concluding his presentation in a recent Harvard-Oxford television debate on American Vietnam policies. He observed, rather sadly, that what disturbs him most is that others question not our judgment, but our motives—a most remarkable comment on the part of one whose professional concern is political analysis, analysis of the actions of governments in terms of motives that are, obviously, unexpressed in official propaganda and may even be only dimly perceived by those who act from these motives. No one would be disturbed by an analysis of the political behavior of Russians, French, or Tanzanians, which questioned their motives and sought to interpret actions in terms of long-range interests, perhaps well-concealed behind official rhetoric. But it is an article of faith that American motives are pure and not subject to analysis. Although it is nothing new in American intellectual history—or, for that matter, in the general history of imperialist apologia—this touching innocence becomes increasingly disgusting as the power it serves grows more dominant in world affairs, and more capable, therefore, of unconstrained viciousness of the sort that we read about, every day, on the front pages. We are hardly the first power in history to combine material interests, massive technological capacity, and an utter disregard for the suffering and misery of the lower orders. The long tradition of naïveté and self-righteousness that disfigures our intellectual history, however, must serve as a warning to the third world, if such a warning is needed, as to how our protestations of sincerity and benign intention are to be interpreted.

A striking feature of the recent debate on Southeast Asian policy has been the distinction that is commonly drawn between ''responsible criticism,'' on the one hand, and ''sentimental,'' or ''emotional,'' or ''hysterical'' criticism, on the other. There is much to be learned from a careful study of the terms in which this distinction is drawn. The ''hysterical critics'' are to be identified, apparently, by their irrational refusal to accept one fundamental political axiom, namely, that the United States has the right to extend its power and control without limit, insofar as is feasible—from the purest of motives, of course. Responsible criticism does not challenge this assumption, but argues, rather, that we probably can't ''get away with it'' at this particular time and place.

A distinction of this sort seems to be what Irving Kristol has in mind, for example, in his analysis of the protest over Vietnam policy, in *Encounter*, August, 1965. He contrasts the responsible critics, such as Walter Lippmann, the *Times*, and Senator Fulbright, with the ''teach-in movement.'' ''Unlike the university protestors,'' he points out, ''Mr. Lippmann engages in no presumptuous suppositions as to 'what the Vietnamese people really want'—he obviously doesn't much care—or in legalistic exegesis as to whether, or to what extent, there is 'aggression' or 'revolution' in South Vietnam. His is a *realpolitik* point of view; and he will apparently even contemplate the possibility of a *nuclear* war against China in extreme circumstances.'' This is commendable, and contrasts favorably, for Kristol, with the talk of the ''unreasonable, ideological types'' in the teach-in movement, who often seem to be motivated by such absurdities as ''simple, virtuous 'anti-imperialism,' '' who deliver ''harangues on 'the power structure,' '' and who even sometimes stoop so low as to read ''articles and reports from the foreign press on the American presence in Vietnam.'' Furthermore, these nasty types are often ''mathematicians, chemists, or philosophers'' (just as, incidentally, those most vocal in protest in the Soviet Union are generally physicists, literary intellectuals, etc.), rather than people with Washington contacts, who, of course, realize that ''had they a new, good idea about Vietnam, they would get a prompt and respectful hearing'' in Washington.

I am not interested here in whether Kristol's description of the protest movement (or of international affairs) is accurate, but rather in the assumptions that it expresses with respect to such questions as these: is the purity of American motives a matter that is beyond discussion, or that is irrelevant to discussion? Should decisions be left to ''experts'' with Washington contacts—that is, assuming that they command the necessary knowledge and principles to make the "best" decision, will they invariably do so? And, a logically prior question, is expertise applicable; specifically, is there a body of theory and of relevant information, not in the public domain, that can be applied to the determination of foreign policy (or that demonstrates the correctness of present actions) in some way that the mathematicians, chemists, and philosophers are incapable of comprehending? Although Kristol does not examine these questions directly, his attitudes presuppose answers, answers which are wrong in all cases. American aggressiveness, however it may be masked in pious rhetoric, is a dominant force in world affairs and must be analyzed in terms of its causes and motives; there is no body of theory or significant body of relevant information, beyond the comprehension or awareness of the layman, which makes policy immune from criticism; to the extent that expert knowledge is applied to world affairs, it is surely appropriate—for a person of any integrity, quite necessary—to question its quality and the goals that it serves. These facts seem too obvious to require extended discussion.

Having settled the issue of the political irrelevance of the protest movement, Kristol turns to the question of what motivates it—more generally, the question of what has made students and junior faculty "go left," as he sees it, amidst general prosperity and under liberal, welfare state administrations. This, he notes, "is a riddle to which no sociologist has as yet come up with an answer." Since these young people are well-off, have good futures, etc., their protest must be irrational, in his view. It must be the result of boredom, of too much security, or something of this sort.

Other possibilities come to mind. It might be, for example, that as honest men the students and junior faculty are attempting to find out the truth for themselves rather than ceding the responsibility to "experts" or to government; and it might be that they react with indignation to what they discover. These possibilities Kristol does not reject. They are simply unthinkable, unworthy of consideration. More accurately, these possibilities are inexpressible; the categories in which they are formulated (honesty, indignation) simply

do not exist for the tough-minded social scientist. One is reminded of a favorite quotation of Daniel Bell's, namely, Max Scheler's "generalization" that moral indignation is a disguised form of repressed envy. Although quite ridiculous, this "generalization," to which Bell ascribes "much truth" (elsewhere, only "some truth") has the merit of eliminating this irritating phenomenon from serious attention.

In this implicit disparagement of traditional intellectual values, Kristol reflects attitudes that are fairly widespread in academic circles. I do not doubt that in part these attitudes are a result of the desperate, often ludicrous attempt of the social and behavioral sciences—my own field among them—to imitate the surface features of the sciences that really have significant intellectual content. In part, they have other sources. Anyone can be a moral individual, concerned with human rights and problems; but only a college professor, a trained expert, can solve technical problems by "sophisticated" methods. Ergo, it is only problems of the latter sort that are important or real. Responsible, non-ideological experts will give advice on tactical questions; irresponsible, "ideological types" will "harangue" about principle and trouble themselves over moral issues and human rights, or over the traditional problems of man and society concerning which social and behavioral science have nothing to offer beyond trivialities. Obviously, these emotional, ideological types are irrational, since, being well-off and having power in their grasp, they shouldn't worry about such matters.

It is a curious and depressing fact that the "anti-war movement" all too often falls prey to a similar trust and faith in technical expertise. Last fall, for example, there was an International Conference on Alternative Perspectives on Vietnam, which circulated a pamphlet to potential participants stating its assumptions. The plan was to set up study groups in which three "types of intellectual tradition" will be represented: (1) area specialists; (2) "social theory, with special emphasis on theories of the international system, of social change and development, of conflict and conflict resolution, or of revolution;" (3) "the analysis of public policy in terms of basic human values, rooted in various theological, philosophical and humanist traditions." The second intellectual tradition will provide "general propositions, derived from social theory and tested against historical, comparative, or experimental data;" the third "will provide the framework out of which fundamental value questions can be raised and in terms of which the moral implications of societal actions can be analyzed." The hope was that "by approaching the questions [of Vietnam policy] from the moral perspectives of all great religions and philosophical systems, we may find solutions that are more consistent with fundamental human values than current American policy in Vietnam has turned out to be." In short, the experts on values (i.e., spokesmen for the great religions and philosophical systems) will provide fundamental insights on moral perspectives, and the experts on social theory will provide general empirical well-validated propositions and "general models of conflict." From this interplay, new policies will emerge, presumably from application of the canons of scientific method. The only debatable issue, it seems to me, is whether it is more ridiculous to turn to experts in social theory for general well-confirmed propositions, or to specialists in the great religions and philosophical systems for insights into fundamental human values.

There is much more that can be said about this topic, but, without continuing, I would simply like to emphasize that, as is no doubt fairly obvious, the cult of the expert is both self-serving, for those who propound it, and quite fraudulent. Obviously, one must learn from social and behavioral science whatever one can; obviously, these fields should be pursued in as serious a way as is possible. But it will be quite unfortunate, and highly dangerous, if they are not accepted and judged on their merits and in terms of their actual, not pretended accomplishments. In particular, if there is a body of theory, well-tested and verified, that applies to the conduct of foreign affairs or the resolution of domestic or international conflict, its existence has been kept a well-guarded secret. In the case of Vietnam, if those who feel themselves to be experts have access to principles or information that would justify what the American government is doing in that unfortunate country, they have been singularly ineffective in making this fact known. To anyone who has any familiarity with the social and behavioral

sciences (or the "policy sciences") the claim that there are certain considerations and principles too deep for the outsider to comprehend is simply an absurdity, unworthy of comment.

When we consider the responsibility of intellectuals, our basic concern must be their role in the creation and unmasking of ideology. And, in fact, Kristol's contrast between the unreasonable ideological types and the responsible experts is formulated in terms that immediately bring to mind Daniel Bell's interesting and influential essay "The End of Ideology," an essay which is as important for what it leaves unsaid as for its actual content. Bell presents and discusses the Marxist analysis of ideology as a mask for class interest, in particular, quoting Marx's well-known conclusion that the petty-bourgeoisie believes "that the *special* conditions of its emancipation are the *general* conditions through which alone modern society can be saved and the class struggle avoided." He then argues that the age of ideology is at an end, supplanted, at least in the West, by a general agreement that each issue must be settled in its own individual terms, within the framework of a Welfare State in which, presumably, experts in the conduct of public affairs will have a prominent role. Bell is quite careful, however, in characterizing the precise sense of "ideology" in which "ideologies are exhausted." He is referring only to ideology as "the conversion of ideas into social levers," to ideology as "a set of beliefs, infused with passion, . . . [which] . . . seeks to transform the whole of a way of life." The crucial words are "transform" and "convert into social levers." Intellectuals in the West, he argues, have lost interest in converting ideas into social levers for the radical transformation of society, and they are justified in having given up this interest. Now that we have achieved the pluralistic society of the Welfare State, there is no longer any need for a radical transformation of society; we may tinker with our way of life here and there, but it would be wrong to try to modify it in any significant way. With this consensus of intellectuals, ideology is dead.

There are several striking facts about Bell's essay. First, he does not point out that the consensus of the intellectuals to which he alludes is entirely self-serving. He does not relate his claim that intellectuals have given up all thought of transforming society to the fact that they play an increasingly prominent role in running the Welfare State—he does not, for example, relate the general acceptance of the Welfare State to his observation, elsewhere, that "America has become an affluent society, offering place . . . and prestige . . . to the onetime radicals" (to an extent which he much underestimates, I believe, in what I have seen of his work). This is a curious omission in an essay that opens with a discussion of ideology as a mask for class interest. Secondly, he offers no argument whatsoever to show that intellectuals are somehow "right" or "objectively justified," in terms of anything but self-interest, in reaching the consensus to which he alludes, with its rejection of the notion that society should be transformed. In fact, although Bell is fairly sharp about the empty rhetoric of the "new left," he seems to have a rather touching, in fact, quite utopian faith that technical experts will be able to come to grips with the few minor problems which, he feels, still remain; for example, the fact that labor is treated as a commodity, and the problems of "alienation" (see his "Work and its Discontents"—he apparently does not discuss the problem of poverty in the midst of plenty, another major concern of those who initiated the "age of ideology").

In fact, it seems fairly obvious that the classical problems are very much with us; one might plausibly argue that they have even been enhanced in severity and scale. For example, the classical paradox of poverty in the midst of plenty is now an ever-increasing problem on an international scale. Whereas one might conceive, at least in principle, of a solution within national boundaries, a sensible idea as to how to transform international society in such a way as to cope with the vast and apparently increasing human misery is hardly likely to develop within the framework of the intellectual consensus that Bell describes.

Thus it would seem accurate to describe the consensus of Bell's intellectuals in somewhat different terms than his. Using the terminology of the first part of his essay, we may say that the Welfare State technician finds justification for his special and prominent social status in his "science," specifically, in the claim that social science can support a technology of social tinkering

on a domestic or international scale. He then takes a further step, proceeding, in the familiar way, to claim universal validity for what is in fact a class interest, to argue that the special conditions on which his claim to power and authority are based are, in fact, the general conditions through which alone modern society can be saved. He argues that tinkering within a Welfare State framework must replace the commitment to the ideologies of the past, ideologies which were concerned with a transformation of society. Having found his position of power, having achieved security and affluence, he has no further need for ideologies that look to change. The scholar-expert replaces the "free-floating intellectual" who "felt that the wrong values were being honored, and rejected the society," and who has now lost his political role (now, that is, that the right values are being honored).

Conceivably, it is correct that the technical experts will be able to come to grips with the classical problems without a radical transformation of society. Just so, it is conceivably true that the petty-bourgeoisie was right in regarding the special conditions of its emancipation as the general conditions through which alone modern society would be saved. But Bell presents not the slightest argument for this conclusion, and does not point out that the conclusion is entirely self-serving, a mask for special interest.

Within the same framework of general utopianism, Bell goes on to pose the issue between the progressive, Western, Welfare State scholar-experts and the benighted, third world ideologists, in a rather curious way. He points out, quite correctly, that there is no issue of Communism, the content of that doctrine having been "long forgotten by friends and foes alike." Rather, he says, "the question is an older one: whether new societies can grow by building democratic institutions and allowing people to make choices—and sacrifices—voluntarily, or whether the new elites, heady with power, will impose totalitarian means to transform their societies." The question is an interesting one; it is odd, however, to see it referred to as "an older one," the implication being, apparently, that the West chose the democratic way—as, for example, in the England of the industrial revolution, when farmers voluntarily made the choice of leaving the land, giving up cottage industry, becoming an industrial proletariat, and voluntarily decided, within the framework of the existing democratic institutions, to make the sacrifices that are graphically described in the classic literature on nineteenth century industrial society. One may debate the question whether authoritarian control is necessary to permit capital accumulation in the underdeveloped world; it is sheer hypocrisy, in more than one respect, to propose, with pride, the Western model for development.

The point of view that Bell describes, and lauds, is not an ideology in his sense—it is not a system of ideas that can be used, or that is intended to be used as a "social lever" for the transformation of society. Rather, a good case can be made for the conclusion that his consensus is that of the intellectuals who have already achieved power and affluence, or who sense that they can achieve them by "accepting society" as it is and promoting the values that are "being honored" in this society. If so, then this consensus is the domestic analogue to that proposed, in the international arena, by a significant segment of the intellectual community, for example, those who justify expansion of American power in Asia, whatever the human cost, on the grounds that it is necessary to contain the "expansion of China" (an "expansion" which is, to be sure, totally hypothetical for the time being)—to translate from State Department Newspeak, on the grounds that it is essential to reverse the Asian nationalist revolutions, or at least, to prevent them from spreading. The analogy becomes clear when we look carefully at the rhetoric in which this proposal is phrased. With his usual lucidity, Churchill outlined the general position in a remark to his colleague of the moment, Joseph Stalin, at Teheran in 1943: "The government of the world must be entrusted to satisfied nations, who wished nothing more for themselves than what they had. If the world-government were in the hands of hungry nations there would always be danger. But none of us had any reason to seek for anything more. . . . Our power placed us above the rest. We were like the rich men dwelling at peace within their habitations." For a translation of Churchill's biblical rhetoric into the social science

jargon of the Rand Corporation, I refer you to the testimony of Charles Wold, Senior Economist of the Rand Corporation, at the Congressional Committee Hearings cited earlier: "I am dubious that China's fears of encirclement are going to be abated, eased, relaxed in the long-term future. But I would hope that what we do in Southeast Asia would help to develop within the Chinese body politic more of a realism and willingness to live with this fear than to indulge it by support for liberation movements, which admittedly depend on a great deal more than external support . . . the operational question for American foreign policy is not whether that fear can be eliminated or substantially alleviated, but whether China can be faced with a structure of incentives, of penalties and rewards, of inducements that will make it willing to live with this fear." The point is further clarified by Thomas Schelling: "There is growing experience, which the Chinese can profit from, that although the United States may be interested in encircling them, may be interested in defending nearby areas from them, it is, nevertheless, prepared to behave peaceably if they are."

In short, we are prepared to live peaceably in our—to be sure, rather extensive—habitations. And if, let us say, a peasant-based revolutionary movement tries to achieve independence from foreign domination or to overthrow the semi-feudal structures supported by foreign powers, or if the Chinese irrationally refuse to respond properly to the schedule of reinforcement that we have prepared for them, if they object to being encircled by the benign and peace-loving "rich men" who control the territories on their borders as a natural right, then, evidently, we must respond to this belligerence with appropriate force.

If it is the responsibility of the intellectual to insist upon the truth, it is also his duty to see events in their historical perspective. Thus one must applaud the insistence of the Secretary of State on the importance of historical analogies, the Munich analogy, for example. As Munich showed, a powerful and aggressive nation with a fanatic belief in its manifest destiny will regard each victory, each extension of its power and authority, as a prelude to the next step. The matter was very well put by Adlai Stevenson, when he spoke of "the old, old route whereby expansive powers push at more and more doors, believing they will open until, at the ultimate door, resistance is unavoidable and major war breaks out." Here lies the danger of appeasement, as the Chinese tirelessly point out to the Soviet Union, which, they claim, is playing Chamberlain to our Hitler in Vietnam. Of course, the aggressiveness of liberal imperialism is not that of Nazi Germany, though the distinction may seem rather academic to a Vietnamese peasant who is being gassed or incinerated. We do not want to occupy Asia; we merely wish, to return to Mr. Wolf, "to help the Asian countries progress toward economic modernization, as relatively 'open' and stable societies, to which our access, as a country and as individual citizens, is free and comfortable" (it need not be emphasized that when he speaks of "access," he is not referring to tourism). The formulation is appropriate. Recent history shows that we care little what form of government a country has so long as it remains an "open society," in our peculiar sense of this term—a society, that is, that remains open to American economic penetration and political control. If it is necessary to approach genocide in Vietnam to achieve this objective, then this is the price we must pay in defense of freedom and the rights of man.

In pursuing these aims, we are breaking no new ground. Few imperialist countries have had explicit territorial ambitions. Thus in 1784, the British Parliament announced that: "To pursue schemes on conquest and extension of dominion in India are measures repugnant to the wish, honor, and policy of this nation." Shortly after, the conquest of India was in full swing. A century later, Britain announced its intentions in Egypt under the slogan "intervention, reform, withdrawal." It is unnecessary to comment on which parts of this promise were fulfilled, within the next half-century. In 1936, on the eve of hostilities in North China, the Japanese stated their Basic Principles of National Policy. These included the use of moderate and peaceful means to extend her strength, to promote social and economic development, to eradicate the menace of Communism, to correct the aggressive policies of the great powers, and to secure her position as the stabilizing power in East Asia. Of course, even

in 1937, the Japanese government had "no territorial designs upon China." In short, we follow a well-trodden path.

It is useful to remember, incidentally, that the U.S. was apparently quite willing, as late as 1939, to negotiate a commercial treaty with Japan and arrive at a *modus vivendi* if Japan would "change her attitude and practice towards our rights and interests in China," as Secretary Hull put it. The bombing of Chunking and the rape of Nanking were rather unpleasant, to be sure, but our rights and interests in China are what is really important, as the responsible, unhysterical men of the day saw quite clearly. It was the closing of the open door by Japan that let directly to the Pacific war, just as it is the closing of the open door by "Communist" China itself that may very well lead to the next, and no doubt last, Pacific war.

But let me return to MacDonald and the responsibility of intellectuals. MacDonald quotes an interview with a death-camp paymaster who bursts into tears when told that the Russians will hang him, asking "Why should they? What have I done?" And MacDonald concludes: "Only those who are willing to resist authority themselves when it conflicts too intolerably with their personal moral code, only they have the right to condemn the death-camp paymaster." The question "What have I done?" is one that we may well ask ourselves, as we read, each day, of fresh atrocities in Vietnam—as we create, or mouth, or tolerate, whether with amusement or contempt, the deceptions that will be used to justify the next defense of freedom.

Quite often, the statements of sincere and devoted technical experts give surprising insight into the intellectual attitudes that lie in the background of the latest savagery. Consider, for example, the following comment by economist Richard Lindholm, in 1959, expressing his frustration over the failure of economic development in "free Vietnam": ". . . the use of American aid is determined by how the Vietnamese use their incomes and their savings. The fact that a large portion of the Vietnamese imports financed with American aid are either consumer goods or raw materials used rather directly to meet consumer demands is an indication that the Vietnamese people desire these goods, for they have shown their desire by their willingness to use their piasters to purchase them.''

In short, the Vietnamese *people* desire Buicks and air-conditioners, rather than sugar refining equipment or road-building machinery, as they have shown by their behavior in a free market. And much as we may deplore their free choice, we must allow the people to have their way. Of course, there are also those two-legged beasts of burden that one stumbles on in the countryside; but as any graduate student of political science can explain to you, they are not part of a responsible modernizing elite, and therefore have only a superficial biological resemblance to the human race.

In no small measure, it is attitudes like this that lie behind the butchery in Vietnam, and we had better face up to them with candor, or we will find our government leading us towards a ''final solution'' in Vietnam, and in the many Vietnams that inevitably lie ahead.

II

The Science
of International
Relations

Perhaps because international relations as a field of inquiry dates back to the times of Thucydides, it has, in the twentieth century, been very conscious of the lack of progress that has been made in producing cumulative knowledge. Thus, along with discussions on policy, theory, and research, the following epistemological and methodological questions have periodically been debated: How do we know that we know? What constitutes knowledge? How do we study international relations in order to gain knowledge? Since most of the debating parties have, at one time or another, claimed the label *science*, the debate can be interpreted as a controversy over the extent to which international politics can be studied scientifically.

In the twentieth century, the realists were the first to insist that the lack of progress in the field was due to the failure to study world politics in a sufficiently scientific manner. In *The Twenty Years' Crisis*, E.H. Carr attacked utopianism for confusing aspiration with reality, and maintained that a true science must first endeavor to understand how things actually are. Carr's work helped to make international relations primarily empirical instead of merely normative. Later realists, like Morgenthau, went on to insist that a science of international politics must be general and theoretical, and not narrowly historical; they contended, in other words, that it must delineate the fundamental laws that govern human behavior (see selection 6).

While the realists were responsible for the adoption of the general goals of science, they were more resistant to the scientific method itself. Harold Guetzkow's

(1950) essay became an early rallying point for an emerging group of behavioralists who wanted to follow a systematic scientific strategy for acquiring cumulative knowledge about world politics. By the early 1960s, the behavioralists were having a major impact, and the field divided, sometimes bitterly, on the question of quantitative methods. The essay by Hedley Bull (1966) crystallizes most of the concerns of traditional scholars in the field. The defense of quantitative analysis by J. David Singer (1969) centers on the notion that, regardless of how elegant, insightful, or apparently relevant traditional work might be, it cannot be accepted as knowledge unless it is true, and it cannot be accepted as true unless there is systematic evidence to support it. For Singer, quantitative analysis involves following scientific rules to test hypotheses so that evidence can be used to assess the truth-claims of scholars.

The debate over scientific principles raises fundamental questions concerning intellectual inquiry, and some important lessons have been derived as a result. Realism produced two lasting results on the way in which inquiry has been conducted in the field. First, it rejected the very descriptive and narrowly factual analysis of diplomatic history and current events; in its place, it established a mode of inquiry that attempts to delineate general patterns—or what some realists called laws—from history. Thereafter, inquiry focused on explaining *why* events happened, rather than on describing *how* they occurred. Second, realism pushed normative and legalistic analysis to the periphery of the field. Realists like E.H. Carr argued that the field had to first understand and explain the fundamental laws of international politics before policy recommendations could usefully be made. Unfortunately, this advice was followed neither by the realists themselves nor by others. Consequently, the field has been plagued by attempts to apply untested theories or preliminary research findings to policy questions. Sometimes these suggestions have even been adopted by governments, as they were in the development of Western nuclear strategy (see Chapter 10).

Here the behavioralists' insistence that scholars explain how they know that they know becomes critical. Unless explanations can be formulated so that they can be tested and researched systematically, rather than illustrated with a few anecdotes, the so-called knowledge of the field remains little more than informed and well-argued opinion. Indeed, some traditionalists, like Hedley Bull, came close to asserting that, for very important questions, informed opinion is all that is possible. The behavioralists felt that studying international relations scientifically would produce the kind of systematic body of knowledge that exists in the physical sciences. This is ultimately an empirical question, and we will just have to wait to see if behavioralists will produce the kind of knowledge that will enable us to manipulate global politics as physical scientists are able to manipulate nature. It has been, after all, only a few centuries since some of the wisest philosophers argued that a science of nature was impossible!

For the present, however, scientific testing does serve some critical functions: Unless we at least attempt to collect and assess evidence in a nonbiased fashion, we are in danger of engaging in mythmaking. In social inquiry, there is often the risk that statements will assume the aura of truth because of the way in which they are phrased, because they are widely repeated, or because they serve the interests of certain groups. When this happens, social inquiry can easily become the captive of prevailing dogma or ideology. The scientific method is one of the few means by which humankind can protect itself from these kinds of self-delusion.

A problem with the behavioralist movement that has served to alienate traditionalists is that some scholars have defined science too narrowly, confining it to quantitative analysis. Science consists not so much of using numbers as it does of formulating testable claims, following procedures that are open and replicable, collecting evidence in a systematic and unbiased fashion, and making valid inferences. There is no a priori reason why nonquantitative comparative historical case studies cannot fall under this rubric (see selection 43). The main point of scientific inquiry is not quantitative analysis, but to reject unsupported speculation in favor of a method that produces systematic and replicable findings.

FOR FURTHER READING

1.   ANATOL   RAPAPORT. Various Meanings of 'Theory.' *American Political Science Review*, 52 (1958):972–988.

2.   STANLEY HOFFMANN. International Relations: The Long Road to Theory. *World Politics* 11 (1959):346–377.

3.   MORTON   KAPLAN.   The   New   Great   Debate: Traditionalism vs. Science in International Relations. *World Politics* 19 (1966):1–20.

4.   KLAUS KNORR AND JAMES N. ROSENAU, EDS. *Contending Approaches to International Politics*. Princeton: Princeton University Press, 1969.

5.   ORAN YOUNG. Professor Russett: Industrious Tailor to a Naked Emperor. *World Politics* 21 (1969):486–511.

6.   BRUCE RUSSETT. The Young Science of International Politics. *World Politics* 22 (1969):87–94.

7.   DINA A. ZINNES. *Contemporary Research in International Relations: A Perspective and a Critical Appraisal*. New York: The Free Press, 1976.

8.   KENNETH WALTZ. *Theory of International Politics*. Reading, Mass: Addison-Wesley, 1979.

CHAPTER

4
THE DEBATE OVER SCIENCE

12.   The Beginnings of a Science

E. H. CARR

The science of international politics is in its infancy. Down to 1914, the conduct of international relations was the concern of persons professionally engaged in it. In democratic countries, foreign policy was traditionally regarded as outside the scope of party politics; and the representative organs did not feel themselves competent to exercise any close control over the mysterious operations of foreign offices. In Great Britain, public opinion was readily aroused if war occurred in any region traditionally regarded as a sphere of British interest, or if the British navy momentarily ceased to possess that margin of superiority over potential rivals which was then deemed essential. In continental Europe, conscription and the chronic fear of foreign invasion had created a more general and continuous popular awareness of international problems. But this awareness found expression mainly in the labour movement,

which from time to time passed somewhat academic resolutions against war. The constitution of the United States of America contained the unique provision that treaties were concluded by the President "by and with the advice and consent of the Senate". But the foreign relations of the United States seemed too parochial to lend any wider significance to this exception. The more picturesque aspects of diplomacy had a certain news value. But nowhere, whether in universities or in wider intellectual circles, was there organised study of current international affairs. War was still regarded mainly as the business of soldiers; and the corollary of this was that international politics were the business of diplomats. There was no general desire to take the conduct of international affairs out of the hands of the professionals or even to pay serious and systematic attention to what they were doing.

The war of 1914–18 made an end of the view that war is a matter which affects only professional soldiers and, in so doing, dissipated the corresponding impression that international politics could safely be left in the hands of professional diplomats. The campaign for the popularisation

Reprinted from *The Twenty Years' Crisis* by E.H. Carr (London: Macmillan, 1939), pp. 1–2,8–10, by permission of Macmillan, London and Basingstoke and by permission of St. Martin's Press, Inc., New York. Copyright © 1939 Macmillan. Footnotes deleted.

of international politics began in the English-speaking countries in the form of an agitation against secret treaties, which were attacked, on insufficient evidence, as one of the causes of the war. The blame for the secret treaties should have been imputed, not to the wickedness of the governments, but to the indifference of the peoples. Everybody knew that such treaties were concluded. But before the war of 1914 few people felt any curiosity about them or thought them objectionable. The agitation against them was, however, a fact of immense importance. It was the first symptom of the demand for the popularisation of international politics and heralded the birth of a new science. . . .

THE IMPACT OF REALISM

No science deserves the name until it has acquired sufficient humility not to consider itself omnipotent, and to distinguish the analysis of what is from aspiration about what should be. Because in the political sciences this distinction can never be absolute, some people prefer to withhold from them the right to the title of science. In both physical and political sciences, the point is soon reached where the initial stage of wishing must be succeeded by a stage of hard and ruthless analysis. The difference is that political sciences can never wholly emancipate themselves from utopianism, and that the political scientist is apt to linger for a longer initial period than the physical scientist in the utopian stage of development. This is perfectly natural. For while the transmutation of lead into gold would be no nearer if everyone in the world passionately desired it, it is undeniable that if everyone really desired a "world-state" or "collective security" (and meant the same thing by those terms), it would be easily attained; and the student of international politics may be forgiven if he begins by supposing that his task is to make everyone desire it. It takes him some time to understand that no progress is likely to be made along this path, and that no political utopia will achieve even the most limited

success unless it grows out of political reality. Having made the discovery, he will embark on that hard ruthless analysis of reality which is the hallmark of science; and one of the facts whose causes he will have to analyse is the fact that few people do desire a "world-state" or "collective security", and that those who think they desire it mean different and incompatible things by it. He will have reached a stage when purpose by itself is seen to be barren, and when analysis of reality has forced itself upon him as an essential ingredient of his study.

The impact of thinking upon wishing which, in the development of a science, follows the breakdown of its first visionary projects, and marks the end of its specifically utopian period, is commonly called realism. Representing a reaction against the wish-dreams of the initial stage, realism is liable to assume a critical and somewhat cynical aspect. In the field of thought, it places its emphasis on the acceptance of facts and on the analysis of their causes and consequences. It tends to depreciate the role of purpose and to maintain, explicitly or implicitly, that the function of thinking is to study a sequence of events which it is powerless to influence or to alter. In the field of action, realism tends to emphasise the irresistible strength of existing forces and the inevitable character of existing tendencies, and to insist that the highest wisdom lies in accepting, and adapting oneself to, these forces and these tendencies. Such an attitude, though advocated in the name of "objective" thought, may no doubt be carried to a point where it results in the sterilisation of thought and the negation of action. But there is a stage where realism is the necessary corrective to the exuberance of utopianism, just as in other periods utopianism must be invoked to counteract the barrenness of realism. Immature thought is predominantly purposive and utopian. Thought which rejects purpose altogether is the thought of old age. Mature thought combines purpose with observation and analysis. Utopia and reality are thus the two facets of political science. Sound political thought and sound political life will be found only where both have their place.

13. Long Range Research in International Relations

Harold Guetzkow

This article has no practical suggestions for the conduct of either the cold or hot war with Russia. Instead it asserts that man's search for relief from wars needs to be directed by an adequate, basic theory of international relations. In lieu of offering as theory only another opinion the writer will attempt to outline some of the characteristics which an adequate theory may have eventually.

Top foreign policy makers probably feel they live in too urgent a world to concern themselves with the theories of modern social science. They devote little, if any, of their organizations' resources to theoretical studies which have no immediate bearing on day-to-day decisions. Yet, in making decisions, statesmen use assumptions about social behavior which they learned early in life and which may be valid only with reference to one ethnic group or not at all. As a result, their actions and policies are often self-defeating and their solutions to problems are severely circumscribed. In most cases the policy-maker is no

doubt unaware of his assumptions about group behavior. It may be this unawareness which makes him content with inadequate and unworkable theories of international relations.

This article contends that the surest and quickest way to world peace is an indirect one—the patient construction over the years of a basic theory of international relations. From this theory may come new and unthought-of solutions to end wars and to guide international relations on a peaceful course.

The value of the scientific approach was emphatically underlined in World War II. The superiority of the United States' operations stemmed in large measure from successful exploitation of the world's scientific resources as they existed in 1940. Many authorities were impressed with the way in which basic natural science theory made military developments possible. Unfortunately, the reservoir of social theory is small and poor in quality, and little effort is being made to build it into a scientific resource.

This article will first consider areas in which the methodological tools used by the present-day worker in international relations must be

Reprinted from *The American Perspective* 4 (Fall 1950), pp. 421–440, by permission of the author.

broadened and sharpened. Then, it will suggest a few ingredients of a basic theory in international relations.

1. CONSIDERATIONS ON METHODS

Political scientists, in whose domain research on international relations has been concentrated, are in a ferment over methods. This was vividly demonstrated in the 1948 panel reports on research of the American Political Science Association. More recently the International Relations Committee of the Social Science Research Council has reviewed the impact of this development on contemporary international relations research. The following remarks come in part from these sources and in part from personal convictions regarding the direction of social science research. It is the author's belief that the following changes in our methodologies are necessary to the sound construction of basic theories in international relations.

A. The present-day trend toward analytic rather than descriptive theories of international relations needs to be reinforced.

B. The move toward theories that synthesize many causes should be emphasized.

C. Dynamic mechanisms which are assumed to explain international behavior need to be made concrete and free from vague generalities.

D. States should no longer be personified as though they behaved like individual human beings.

E. Gradually the exclusive devotion to *post-facto* explanations must give way to posing theoretical propositions which may be used for prediction and then subjected to the test of experience.

A. In the early phases of the development of a science, there must be systematic classification and description of phenomena. At first this description tends to be verbal, and only gradually do the characteristics become measurable in dimensions which are distinct from each other. In international relations, current theory tends to be descriptive. Most contemporary works are anchored to particulars—for instance, chapters on the international relations of specific states. This approach permits detailed narration with much attention to the substance of foreign relations; but it then is very difficult to construct propositions useful in analyzing more than the single concrete situation under discussion.

The latter phases of the development of a science are marked by the construction of analytic theories. The science is no longer content with descriptive generalizations but attempts to analyze relations and to develop general dynamic theories of how underlying forces bring about the phenomena observed in the earlier phases of the science. In international relations there are few signs today of such analytic theory developments. Even the more advanced power theories, which analyze international relations as the influence of one nation upon another because of the operation of national power (resources, population, and technology), are usually offered by political scientists as descriptive accounts, not as dynamic analyses. Moreover, the most advanced exponent of power theory today limits his concepts to the Western European countries.

The development of an analytical theory gives the scientist a powerful tool for discovering the mainsprings of action within a system of international relations. For instance, understanding is needed of the way in which communication, cultural uniformity, and social solidarity interact and affect the relations between nations. An analytic theory including such factors would be a valuable addition to a more fully formulated power theory. Such theory often provides unexpected derivations and quite new approaches to international affairs. One modern theorist has constructed a mathematical model of relations between states from which he deduces that military preparedness *decreases* security within the inter-nation system—a quite unconventional conclusion! His theoretical constructions also indicate the way in which an armaments race might be slackened.

B. Many of the older theories of international relations are unrealistic because they consider only one or a few causes. The century old balance-of-power theories, involving such concepts as "sphere of influence" and "land-vs.-sea power," tend toward one-cause explanations. Within recent years, however, there has been much progress in broadening the number of variables and the types of forces which are included in international relations theory.

The impetus for this broadening seems to have stemmed from two sources: the eminently successful German geopoliticians, and the recent rapid advances of the social sciences in the United States. When the German Academy established and the Nazis bounteously subsidized a *Laboratorium für Weltpolitik*, Haushofer and Ranse gradually incorporated the findings of more and more academic disciplines into their imperialistic geo-strategies. American social scientists are now demonstrating the fruitfulness of that "cluster of closely related disciplines called social psychology—cultural analysis—sociology." It becomes clearer that such disciplines will need to be used in the construction of basic theories of international relations.

The problems of working with a theory become more difficult as it expands to include more variables. Because "other things are not equal," it is difficult to evaluate the relative importance of one variable as contrasted with another. However, in economics, where this state of affairs grows increasingly acute, the recent methodological inventions of the Cowles Commission make it possible to handle theoretical systems involving many variables which act simultaneously. One economist has recently constructed a model of some 31 variables all included in a system of 16 simultaneous equations. He then proceeded to solve the system and to check the adequacy of his postulates against existing data. Other social sciences, on a more modest scale, are making rapid strides in handling problems which twenty years ago were thought to be impossibly complex. It will be feasible to adapt these techniques to problems in international relations.

C.   Explanations in theories of international relations are often vague. But recently there has been a tendency toward closer observation of political processes. For instance, detailed analysis of the "psychological potential" from which U.S. foreign policy springs has been made on the basis of attitude and public opinion surveys. Another development in some detail is the "self-fulfilling prophecy." The expectations (which may often

be inaccurate) about the behavior of another nation are seen inducing this nation to fulfill these expectations because of acts which such a prediction leads the predictor-nation to perform. One political scientist has explored the operation of this mechanism in detail, applying the analysis to U.S. relations with Russia. His documentation suggests that the avoidance of reactions to particular expectations may eliminate self-fulfillment of the prophecy.

Such miniature systems, of course, do not cope directly with such monumental tasks as the construction of a basic theory of international relations. But the most useful theories will have to be, at first, small conceptual systems dealing with a restricted range of phenomena.

D.   The social scientist often treats the nation as though it were an individual in theorizing about international relations. This tendency has roots in the period when the acts of monarchs were identical with the acts of nations, and no distinction was necessary. Later, during neo-Darwinian times, the concept of the state as an organism became common. The lack of knowledge of the fundamental characteristics of functioning organizations allows our thinking about nations as nations to be loose and unstructured—and this vacuum in our knowledge forces us to use only those concepts available within common-sense culture.

Psychiatrists and psychologists whose work is gradually becoming valuable to the political scientists, readily treat the nation in this personalist way. The social scientist must be alert to this bias. Despite the incautious generalizations and free extrapolations of many persuasive writers, there is not sufficient evidence to warrant such a statement as "Thus we know that the 'personality' of a nation is largely determined by the fact that parents regularly channel the behavior of their children toward the local culture patterns." By treating organizations as though they were persons, we unconsciously attribute characteristics to organizations which may be quite contrary to fact. Perhaps the results of such confusion between personality and nation have been most ridiculously demonstrated in the recent treatment of the German nation as paranoid.

E. Few theorists venture to make predictions about future international events. Instead, they prudently limit themselves to *post facto* explanations of events. This is a realistic recognition of the limitations of our present state of social science. Lack of prediction, however, makes it difficult to test the validity of theories. In the long run, the usefuness of a theory depends upon its reliability in prediction.

Lack of interest in prediction partially stems from the background and training of students of international relations in the fields of philosophy, history and law. Distaste of predictions undoubtedly also comes from the bitter, unsuccessful attempts which lie scattered alongside the development of international relations theory. Because of the urgent demand for practical application, interest and effort have been centered on predictions of the grand strategies—just as now attention of the social scientist is focused on the American-Russian struggle.

It would be fruitful to limit at first the predictions to minor international occurrences, rather than risking an attempt to forecast important global events. Confirmation and denials of parts of theories might gradually lead to a more firmly bulwarked system, eventually enabling the social scientist to predict more and more imposing events in international relations. An aide to the policy-maker, the worker in international relations must make predictions. Yet he has never consolidated his propositions into a predictive system, so that he might test the validity of his theorizing. Until this is done, how can substantial progress be made in the construction of a testable theory of international relations?

In conclusion, what is advocated is a more thorough application of scientific methods to research in international relations. Emphasis should be given to the construction of analytic theories which specify concretely the dynamic mechanisms underlying various types of international relations. The mere building of analogies as exemplified in the personification of nations should be avoided. New theories should be capable of yielding predictions so that their validity may eventually be tested.

2. ELEMENTS NEEDED FOR THEORY CONSTRUCTION

But is it possible to construct a theory of international relations with the extension of methods proposed? What form would such theorizing take? How would it be possible to construct small islands of theory, which eventually might be tied together into a more definitive theory-system? This article can not answer these questions but presents only some explorations.

The process of theory construction requires three stages. First, using the nation as the primary unit, propositions would be developed to explain how national behaviors in the international scene originate within the state. Then, a general theory of the relations between any two states might be erected. Later, as one becomes more sure of his footing, this artificially restricted, binary theory might be elaborated into a multi-nation theory. This latter development would undoubtedly be accompanied by research on the functioning of international agencies as dynamic, supra-nation organizations.

Even the simplest theory will probably need to include propositions about four types of factors which operate to determine the foreign policy and behavior of a state:

(1) Domestic forces which are the wellspring of the state's inter-nation behaviors.
(2) The nature of the nation's decision-apparatus which translate the basic forces into foreign policies.
(3) The personal dynamics of the nation's leaders which mold the operation of the decision-making apparatus.
(4) The state of the nation's technology.

Of course, these groupings overlap. And undoubtedly much predictive potential of a theory constructed with them will come eventually from the interrelations which exist among variables.

Domestic forces. The distinction between "domestic" and "international" affairs, sharply drawn in the 18th and 19th century, is being gradually replaced by more realistic approaches.

There are many domestic forces which pressure a nation's foreign policies into particular channels . . .

National Decision-Apparatus. How are these domestic factors, which constitute the mainspring of the nation's foreign relations, translated into national behaviors? In large measure, these forces affect foreign policies and behaviors through the decision-making and decision-executing apparatuses within the state. Hence, a basic theory of international relations needs to conceptualize these processes. . . .

Leadership Dynamics. The "great man" theory of history has long emphasized that international relations would have been quite different had different actors played the lead parts. Contemporary social scientists adopt a more moderate viewpoint. They recognize that the personal characteristics of the leader interact with social events to produce history. It will be valuable to develop a theory on how the manner in which the leader plays his role modifies the functioning of the decision-apparatus. In nations with highly centralized, monolithic administrative structures, empirical tests of this type of theory will be difficult but possible. In democratic-type organizations with multiple leadership, would it ever be possible to trace through the permutating interactions which must occur when a major foreign policy decision is reached and executed? . . .

Technology. Because the social scientist—especially the social theorist—is seldom an engineer or anthropologist, it is easy for him to forget the powerful impact the technological achievements of a nation have upon its human and social behavior systems. Although we are all impressed with the importance of atomic energy, no definitive report has yet been prepared by the social scientists on the implications of this technological advance. . . .

This outline indicates the types of forces which determine the foreign behaviors of a nation. Implicit in this formulation, of course, is the fact that the behaviors of other nations are received and interpreted through the same mechanisms.

The leader characteristics, the decision-apparatus, the technological state, and the underlying needs and desires of the people all function to determine how the foreign behaviors of other nations inpinge upon the state. The processes involved in interpreting the behavior of other nations are not simple. Perhaps many of the same forces which initiate foreign behaviors will also determine the way in which the foreign behaviors of other states are received. However, these forces do not operate in completely identical ways in the two situations.

After theories of the factors influencing foreign behaviors have been elaborated within particular areas, it may be found that the effects of "interaction" are important. An example is found in demographic theories of "felt" population pressure where "absolute" population pressure becomes a factor influencing foreign behavior only under certain social and economic conditions. It is the interaction of the absolute pressure and the economic conditions which makes the population pressure "felt." The enumeration of the four areas above implies a set of interrelationships among them: within a given technology the domestic forces initiate foreign behaviors through the national decision-apparatuses, all molded by the personal characteristics of the nation's leadership.

3. COMPONENTS OF AN INTER-NATION THEORY

In theorizing about the intra-nation formulation of foreign policy, one necessarily illuminates certain aspects of an inter-nation theory. At the least it seems necessary to differentiate two types of inter-nation behaviors: the more formal behavior of the state's decision-apparatus, and the informal relationships which exist between peoples of different nationalities.

Some of the same factors involved in an intra-nation theory will also determine inter-nation relations. For instance, interpersonal relations (as determined by the personality characteristics of the statesmen) will influence the outcome of international conferences. The state of technology will make changes in the traditional methods of handling inter-national relations, as exemplified by the transformation of the ambassador from plenipotentiary to mouthpiece as a result of rapid communication between home government and delegates abroad. Finally, economic factors are known to determine power interrelations among nations, as has been so dramatically illustrated in the operation of the Marshall plan.

While these parallelisms can be extended, it is more helpful to turn now to the new types of problems which arise in considering inter-nation theory. Our intention is to indicate the applicability of social science research techniques even to these difficult problems.

Binary Theories of Inter-Nation Relations.
In order to simplify the theory construction in its early phases, miniature systems might be established using pairs of nations, which would make it easier to form a concept of the problems. The pairs might be selected in such a way that empirical checks of the theory could be made with minimum cost and maximum information. As a series of binary systems were developed, the bridge to simple three-nation constructions might be made. The multi-nation theory would be very difficult to construct, but after the development of binary theories, a means would eventually suggest itself. . . .

International Organization Processes. As international contacts multiply, relationships tend to be institutionalized. Exchange of notes gradually gives way to international conferences, and conferences often acquire permanent character through the adoption of standing committees. Finally, unifying organizations arise, such as the International Labor Organization, the World Health Organization, the League of Nations or the United Nations.

It is very likely that the theory of international organization will borrow heavily from the theory of public administration. However, a separate theory will be required because of such special factors in international organization as sovereignty. Nor is there any question that these international processes are suitable for theoretical and empirical research. . . .

Problems of International Cohesion. The necessity of examining the informal relations between the populations of different states has already been noted. Public opinion not only affects the foreign policy of one state but sometimes also operates across national boundaries. A case in point is the 1948 Italian elections, which were unquestionably influenced by American public opinion as expressed in a vigorous letter-writing campaign.

These informal relations or interactions are especially relevant to the problem of developing solidarity and cohesion among nations. Although nationalist loyalty has been studied intensively, little serious work has been done on the problem of creating wider loyalties. Current work by social psychologists on the processes by which people maintain membership in multiple groups may prove to be applicable to problems of the compatibility or incompatibility of national and international loyalties.

Both the loyalty and public opinion factors indicate the way in which the direct relationship of the individual to other nations or international organizations need be considered in constructing a theory of international relations. Both would be factors in making predictions of the extent to which there is international solidarity, but it would also be necessary to give weight to the many nonpersonal forces that produce varying degrees of international cohesion. As nations become more interdependent and their international institutions develop effectiveness, another important theoretical problem emerges. To what extent does the interdependence create solidarity? Sociologists long have been concerned with this problem among groups within a nation and have come to regard interdependence as one of the main sources of group consolidation. The international version of the problem awaits sociological appraisal.

4. THE ORGANIZATION OF RESEARCH ACTIVITIES TO CONSTRUCT BASIC THEORIES OF INTERNATIONAL RELATIONS

It has been contended that with an extended methodology, it should be quite possible to construct an integrated set of theories about international relations. The formulation and testing of such theories would not, however, be easy. The sponsors of the research would need the patience of a Job and the determination of a Horatio Alger. The basic considerations implicit in the first two sections of this article would determine some characteristics of the organization which would carry out the proposed research. What follows is an attempt to focus these implications and to indicate in a tentative way how actual research might be organized.

Integrative Nature of Research Activity. The first two sections of this article stress how dependent the development of basic theories of international relations is upon the state of theoretical work on human and social behavior. The research activity will consequently need to be broad and eclectic in its orientation.

It will avoid recruiting the scientist who feels his own substantive viewpoint is a panacea. Because of difficulties always experienced in doing team research between disciplines, it may be well to devote some years to the training of mature scholars in one or two areas besides their own, so that aspects of the cross-discipline endeavour can be integrated within a single person. This may relieve some of the strains usually arising within inter-disciplinary research units.

Because of the size of the task, safeguards must be taken to avoid the growth of a research organization so large and difficult to co-ordinate that its right hand doesn't know what its left hand is doing. Full advantage should be taken of the islandic features pointed out in the second section. For instance, each time the central, integrating team of researchers uncovers a theoretical pocket, this project might be isolated for a time and become administratively divorced from the central program. The integrating team would have its hands full bringing together the developed islands of theory.

There already exist important centers devoted to fundamental research related to international relations. An example is found in the Hoover Institute and Library research on the mechanism of revolution, an essential ingredient of both the intra-national and inter-national formulations suggested in the second section. By building careful liaison relationships, the results of such specialized centers could be profitably incorporated into the integrating team's formulations. As the central team made progress on its own, certain ramifications might appear which could be discussed with the more specialized centers. At times, these independent units might make changes in their own programs, so that their results would more readily fit into the developing global theory.

Reality-Orientation of the Research Endeavour. The mere spinning of theoretical webs is a fascinating occupation. Hence, precaution must be taken to check the extent to which the concepts conform to reality. As pointed out in section 1, the scientific method is the vehicle *par excellence* for the accomplishment of this purpose. It will be necessary to maintain a close relationship between the theoretical work and the empirical, hypothesis-checking endeavours of the research program. Only in this way can the erroneous theories be corrected, and the compounding of mistaken ideas prevented. . . .

Skeptics often claim that the social sciences will never make fundamental tests of their hypotheses because they can not experiment. Undoubtedly such limitations will make it difficult to test theories of international relations—but not impossible. Although the social scientist cannot conduct experiments at the time and place he desires them and with all scientific controls, often the events of the world can yield tests of his theories. For instance, would it not have been possible to test the validity of theoretical work on the interplay of economic and power factors in international relations at the 1950 trade agreements meetings? One might make preliminary, orientational checks of his theory on the results of the Annecy trade conferences in 1948. Then, with a revised theory, the scientist might make predictions of the outcomes of the 1950 meetings. The adequacy of one's theories would be "experimentally" checked by the deviation of the predictions from the actual outcomes. . . .

Influence of the Sponsors on the Research Work. In the end the keeper of the purse plays the tune. It is vital to the well-being of basic research in international relations that the sponsor of the activity be relatively free of biasing pressures. These pressures will probably be of two kinds: pressures to be practical and to be nationalistic. There will be forces constantly seducing the research endeavour into more practical, policy-oriented direction. Because this area is of such vital concern to governments and citizens, there will be incessant demands for devotion of the program's resources to premature application of its findings. The history of the social sciences is replete with submissions to such pressure. Yet, the basic reason we have made little world progress toward peace is that we never allow our social scientists to work with sufficient energy on the basic theoretical problems.

There will be constant pressure toward disturbance of the basic theories with nationalistic bias. The internal struggles in UNESCO arising from this source—and Russia does not even belong to UNESCO—has dissipated much of the energies of that organization. Hence, it would seem advisable to establish the research organization on a private basis, staffed with men from a number of nations whose objectivity as scientists might help them override their national biases.

Undoubtedly the German Academy's theoretical efforts in geopolitics were never allowed to reach their full potential because of the fearful operation of these two types of pressures. Yet despite these forces, in 1941 Haushofer was bold enough to stand by his quasi-scientific prediction of Nazi disaster should a Russian campaign be undertaken, even though he lost his sponsorship in so doing.

I am as fearful as my readers of the utilization of the results of basic research in international relations for immoral purposes. Derivations from the basic postulates might give rise to astoundingly successful psychological warfare programs. Perhaps some safeguard will be obtained, if the results are available simultaneously to all nations and all peoples. But even such openness in the scientist's proceedings will hardly guarantee the prevention of Machiavellian acts. The basic assumptions and many of the derivations of Nazi policy were forthrightly explained to the world in *Mein Kampf*, and particular campaigns were spelled out in some detail in books published some

ten years before the operations were undertaken. Yet, statesmen remained blind and persisted in their stereotyped thinking about inter-nation relations until World War II was upon them.

The Organization Outlined. The Research Organization might consist of an inter-disciplinary Executive Integrating Team, headed by the Organization's Director, whose main task would be construction of an over-all, integrated basic theory of international relations. One member of the Executive Team would be Director of the Theory-Islands Division. Another member would be Director of an Empirical-Tests Division. The Executive Team would be assisted by an internal secretariat, which would aid the team in keeping itself appraised of both division's work. It would be helped in its liaison work by consultation conferences of outside experts organized for particular purposes, as well as a Liaison Staff, who would constantly search throughout the world for new theoretic and empirical developments made by other investigators, both private and in government. So that the Executive Team could devote its full energies to the creative task of constructing an integrated basic theory, the administrative functions of the Research Organization would be in the hands of an Administrative Officer and staff. In one sense, the Executive Team would be somewhat analogous to the Atomic Warfare Exploration Staff which Eisenhower set up to consider the implications of atomic weapons for military operations, without prejudice from old-line preconceptions. However, the international relations team would be much more theoretic in its interests.

In order to keep the size of the Research Organization manageable, it would be wise to allow both divisions to contract work with independent research units. By judicious selection of projects, over-lapping in research could be held to a minimum, and work stimulated in areas in which results most desperately are needed. The present operations of the Office of Naval Research might be profitably studied to gain insights on how this type of contract-stimulation of basic research could be carried out.

Although both divisions of the Research Organization would eventually function simultaneously, at first there would be emphasis upon the Theory-Islands work. Then as theories were made ready for testing by the Executive Team, the Empirical-Tests Division would undertake their validation. This Division's results would be fed back to the Executive Integrating Team to guide theory revision. Often unexpected leads obtained by the Empirical-Tests Division would need to be assigned to the Theory-Island Division for development.

Techniques for Increasing Applicability of Research Findings. After five to seven years of operation the Executive Team may decide it is time to establish a third division—the Engineering and Invention Division. It would put the basic theoretical formulations into practical applications which would aid the nations in developing better relations.

The Engineering committee within this Division would serve as consultants, perhaps on a fee basis, to governments, international organizations, and private agencies. It would help them utilize the results of the research in handling their day-to-day international relations problems. It would help such local units establish their own research operations to aid in applying the general theory to their own special needs.

Most solid scientific theories prove fruitful in providing ideas which probably would never have been conceived had there been no special frame-of-reference provided by the theory. The Invention committee would have few definite responsibilities except to exploit creatively the basic theory. Their task would be to invent new devices and techniques for the conduct of international relations in ways that would eliminate the need for violent, world-devastating operations as instruments of foreign policy. Although the Executive Team will on occasion produce ideas allowing entirely new approaches to certain problems in international relations, the Invention group would be charged with the responsibility not only of developing the ideas proposed by the Executive Team but of suggesting original notions on their own.

5. CONCLUSION

In summary, a basic theory of international relations will need to be supplemented with a theory on the operation of international organizations. Because international relations are not confined to relations among nations, the final formulations will include the operation of forces deriving directly from individuals as persons. It will even be necessary to construct propositions about the effects of the operations of private economic and educational agencies on the international scene.

Out of the process of developing, integrating, and testing these bodies of theory, it is to be expected that ideas will spring which probably would never be conceived without the frame of reference provided by the theory. These ideas may concern practical applications of the theory which will aid nations in the day-to-day handling of international problems; or they may lead to new devices and techniques for the conduct of international relations. There appears to be no other approach which holds any promise of enabling men of good will to understand and control the present system of international relations, whose breakdown now threatens the world with utter devastation.

14.   International Theory:
The Case for a Classical Approach

HEDLEY BULL

1

Two approaches to the theory of international relations at present compete for our attention. The first of these I shall call the classical approach. By this I do not mean the study and criticism of the "classics" of international relations, the writings of Hobbes, Grotius, Kant, and other great thinkers of the past who have turned their attention to international affairs. Such study does indeed exemplify the classical approach, and it provides a method that is particularly fruitful and important. What I have in mind, however, is something much wider than this: the approach to theorizing that derives from philosophy, history, and law, and that is characterized above all by explicit reliance upon the exercise of judgment and by the assumptions that if we confine ourselves to strict standards of verification and proof there is very little of significance that can be said about international relations, that general propositions about this subject must therefore derive from a scientifically imperfect process of perception or intuition, and that these general propositions cannot be accorded anything more than the tentative

Excerpted from "International Theory: The Case for a Classical Approach," in *World Politics* 18/3 (April 1966), pp. 361–377. Copyright © 1966 by Princeton University Press. Excerpts reprinted by permission of Princeton University Press. Footnotes deleted.

and inconclusive status appropriate to their doubtful origin.

Until very recently virtually all attempts at theorizing about international relations have been founded upon the approach I have just described. We can certainly recognize it in the various twentieth-century systematizations of international theory—in works like those of Alfred Zimmern, E. H. Carr, Hans Morgenthau, Georg Schwarzenberger, Raymond Aron, and Martin Wight. And it is clearly also the method of their various precursors, whose scattered thoughts and partial treatments they have sought to draw together: political philosophers like Machiavelli and Burke, international lawyers like Vattel and Oppenheim, pamphleteers like Gentz and Cobden, historians like Heeren and Ranke. It is because this approach has so long been the standard one that we may call it classical.

The second approach I shall call the scientific one. I have chosen to call it scientific rather than scientistic so as not to prejudge the issue I wish to discuss by resort to a term of opprobrium. In using this name for the second approach, however, it is the aspirations of those who adopt it that I have in mind rather than their performance. They aspire to a theory of international relations whose propositions are based either upon logical or mathematical proof, or upon strict, empirical procedures of verification. Some of them dismiss the classical theories of international relations as worthless, and clearly conceive themselves to be the founders of a wholly new science. Others concede that the products of the classical approach were better than nothing, and perhaps even regard them with a certain affection, as the owner of a 1965 model might look at a vintage motor car. But in either case they hope and believe that their own sort of theory will come wholly to supersede the older type; like the logical positivists when they sought to appropriate English philosophy in the 1930's, or like Mr. McNamara's Whiz Kids when they moved into the Pentagon, they see themselves as tough-minded and expert new men, taking over an effete and woolly discipline, or pseudo-discipline, which has so far managed by some strange quirk to evade the scientific method but has always been bound to succumb to it in the end. . . .

2

. . . the scientific approach has contributed and is likely to contribute very little to the theory of international relations, and in so far as it is intended to encroach upon and ultimately displace the classical approach, it is positively harmful. In support of this conclusion I wish to put forward seven propositions.

The first proposition is that by confining themselves to what can be logically or mathematically proved or verified according to strict procedures, the practitioners of the scientific approach are denying themselves the only instruments that are at present available for coming to grips with the substance of the subject. In abstaining from what Morton Kaplan calls "intuitive guesses" or what William Riker calls "wisdom literature" they are committing themselves to a course of intellectual puritanism that keeps them (or would keep them if they really adhered to it) as remote from the substance of international politics as the inmates of a Victorian nunnery were from the study of sex.

To appreciate our reliance upon the capacity for judgment in the theory of international relations we have only to rehearse some of the central questions to which that theory is addressed. Some of these are at least in part moral questions, which

cannot by their very nature be given any sort of objective answer, and which can only be probed, clarified, reformulated, and tentatively answered from some arbitrary standpoint, according to the method of philosophy. Others of them are empirical questions, but of so elusive a nature that any answer we provide to them will leave some things unsaid, will be no more than an item in a conversation that has yet to be concluded. It is not merely that in *framing* hypotheses in answer to these empirical questions we are dependent upon intuition or judgment (as has often been pointed out, this is as true in the natural as in the social sciences); it is that in the *testing* of them we are utterly dependent upon judgment also, upon a rough and ready observation, of a sort for which there is no room in logic or strict science, that things are this way and not that.

For example, does the collectivity of sovereign states constitute a political society or system, or does it not? If we can speak of a society of sovereign states, does it presuppose a common culture or civilization? And if it does, does such a common culture underlie the worldwide diplomatic framework in which we are attempting to operate now? What is the place of war in international society? Is all private use of force anathema to society's working, or are there just wars which it may tolerate and even require? Does a member state of international society enjoy a right of intervention in the internal affairs of another, and if so in what circumstances? Are sovereign states the sole members of international society, or does it ultimately consist of individual human beings, whose rights and duties override those of the entities who act in their name? To what extent is the course of diplomatic events at any one time determined or circumscribed by the general shape or structure of the international system; by the number, relative weight, and conservative or radical disposition of its constituent states, and by the instruments for getting their way that military technology or the distribution of wealth has put into their hands; by the particular set of rules of the game underlying diplomatic practice at that time? And so on.

These are typical of the questions of which the theory of international relations essentially consists. But the scientific theorists have forsworn the means of coming directly to grips with them. When confronted with them they do one of two things. Either they shy away and devote themselves to peripheral subjects—methodologies for dealing with the subject, logical extrapolations of conceptual frameworks for thinking about it, marginalia of the subject that are susceptible of measurement or direct observation—or they break free of their own code and resort suddenly and without acknowledging that this is what they are doing to the methods of the classical approach—methods that in some cases they employ very badly, their preoccupations and training having left them still strangers to the substance of the subject.

This congenital inability of the scientific approach to deal with the crux of the subject while yet remaining true to its own terms leads me to an observation about the teaching of the subject in universities. Whatever virtues one might discern in the scientific approach, it is a wholly retrograde development that it should now form the basis of undergraduate courses of instruction in international politics, as in some universities in the United States it now does. The student whose study of international politics consists solely of an introduction to the techniques of systems theory, game theory, simulation, or content analysis is simply shut off from contact with the subject, and is unable to develop any feeling either for the play of international politics or for the moral dilemmas to which it gives rise.

The second proposition I wish to put forward arises out of the first: It is that where practitioners of the scientific approach have succeeded in casting light upon the substance of the subject it has been by stepping beyond the bounds of that approach and employing the classical method. What there is of value in their work consists essentially of judgments that are not established by the mathematical or scientific methods they employ, and which may be arrived at quite independently of them. . . .

My third proposition is that the practitioners of the scientific approach are unlikely to make progress of the sort to which they aspire. Some of the writers I have been discussing would be ready enough to admit that so far only peripheral topics have been dealt with in a rigidly scientific way. But their claim would be that it is not by

its performance so far that their approach should be judged, but by the promise it contains of ultimate advance. They may even say that the modesty of their beginnings shows how faithful they are to the example of natural science: Modern physics too, Morton Kaplan tells us, "has reared its present lofty edifice by setting itself problems that it has the tools or techniques to solve."

The hope is essentially that our knowledge of international relations will reach the point at which it becomes genuinely cumulative: that from the present welter of competing terminologies and conceptual frameworks there will eventually emerge a common language, that the various insignificant subjects that have now been scientifically charted will eventually join together and become significant, and that there will then exist a foundation of firm theory on which newcomers to the enterprise will build.

No one can say with certainty that this will not happen, but the prospects are very bleak indeed. The difficulties that the scientific theory has encountered do not appear to arise from the quality that international relations is supposed to have of a "backward" or neglected science, but from characteristics inherent in the subject matter which have been catalogued often enough: the unmanageable number of variables of which any generalization about state behavior must take account; the resistance of the material to controlled experiment; the quality it has of changing before our eyes and slipping between our fingers even as we try to categorize it; the fact that the theories we produce and the affairs that are theorized about are related not only as subject and object but also as cause and effect, thus ensuring that even our most innocent ideas contribute to their own verification or falsification.

A more likely future for the theory of international politics is that it will remain indefinitely in the philosophical stage of constant debate about fundamentals; that the works of the new scientific theorists will not prove to be solid substructure on which the next generation will build, but rather that those of them that survive at all will take their place alongside earlier works as partial and uncertain guides to an essentially intractable subject; and that successive thinkers, while learning what they can from what has gone before, will continue to feel impelled to build their own houses of theory from the foundations up.

A fourth proposition that may be advanced against many who belong to the scientific school is that they have done a great disservice to theory in this field by conceiving of it as the construction and manipulation of so-called "models." Theoretical inquiry into an empirical subject normally proceeds by way of the assertion of general connections and distinctions between events in the real world. But it is the practice of many of these writers to cast their theories in the form of a deliberately simplified abstraction from reality, which they then turn over and examine this way and that before considering what modifications must be effected if it is to be applied to the real world. A model in the strict sense is a deductive system of axioms and theorems; so fashionable has the term become, however, that it is commonly used also to refer to what is simply a metaphor or an analogy. It is only the technique of constructing models in the strict sense that is at issue here. However valuable this technique may have proved in economics and other subjects, its use in international politics is to be deplored.

The virtue that is supposed to lie in models is that by liberating us from the restraint of constant reference to reality, they leave us free to set up simple axioms based on a few variables and thenceforward to confine ourselves to rigorous deductive logic, thereby generating wide theoretical insights that will provide broad signposts to guide us in the real world even if they do not fill in the details.

I know of no model that has assisted our understanding of international relations that could not just as well have been expressed as an empirical generalization. This, however, is not the reason why we should abstain from them. The freedom of the model-builder from the discipline of looking at the world is what makes him dangerous; he slips easily into a dogmatism that empirical generalization does not allow, attributing to the model a connection with reality it does not have, and as often as not distorting the model itself by importing additional assumptions about the world in the guise of logical axioms. The very intellectual completeness and logical tidiness of the model-building operation lends it an air of author-

ity which is often quite misleading as to its standing as a statement about the real world. . . .

The fashion for constructing models exemplifies a much wider and more long-standing trend in the study of social affairs: the substitution of methodological tools and the question "Are they useful or not?" for the assertion of propositions about the world and the question "Are they true or not?" Endemic though it has become in recent thinking, I believe this change to have been for the worse. The "usefulness" of a tool has in the end to be translated as the truth of a proposition, or a series of propositions, advanced about the world, and the effect of the substitution is simply to obscure the issue of an empirical test and to pave the way for shoddy thinking and the subordination of inquiry to practical utility. However, this is a theme that requires more amplification than it can be given here, and in introducing it I am perhaps taking on more antagonists than I need do for my present purpose.

A fifth proposition is that the work of the scientific school is in some cases distorted and impoverished by a fetish for measurement. For anyone dedicated to scientific precision, quantification of the subject must appear as the supreme ideal, whether it takes the form of the expression of theories themselves in the form of mathematical equations or simply that of the presentation of evidence amassed in quantitative form. Like the Anglican bishop a year or so ago who began his sermon on morals by saying that he did not think all sexual intercourse is necessarily wrong, I wish to take a liberal view of this matter. There is nothing inherently objectionable, just as there is nothing logically peculiar, in a theoretical statement about international politics cast in mathematical form. Nor is there any objection to the counting of phenomena that do not differ from one another in any relevant respect, and presenting this as evidence in support of a theory. The difficulty arises where the pursuit of the measurable leads us to ignore relevant differences between the phenomena that are being counted, to impute to what has been counted a significance it does not have, or to be so distracted by the possibilities that do abound in our subject for counting as to be diverted from the qualitative inquiries that are in most cases more fruitful. . . .

My sixth proposition is that there is a need for rigor and precision in the theory of international politics, but that the sort of rigor and precision of which the subject admits can be accommodated readily enough within the classical approach. Some of the targets at which the scientific theorists aim their barbs are quite legitimate ones. The classical theory of international relations has often been marked by failure to define terms, to observe logical canons of procedure, or to make assumptions explicit. It has sometimes also, especially when associated with the philosophy of history, sought to pursue into international politics implications of a fundamentally unscientific view of the world. The theory of international relations should undoubtedly attempt to be scientific in the sense of being a coherent, precise, and orderly body of knowledge, and in the sense of being consistent with the philosophical foundations of modern science. Insofar as the scientific approach is a protest against slipshod thinking and dogmatism, or against a residual providentialism, there is everything to be said for it. But much theorizing in the classical mold is not open to this sort of objection. The writings of the great international lawyers from Vitoria to Oppenheim (which, it may be argued, form the basis of the traditional literature of the subject) are rigorous and critical. There are plenty of contemporary writers who are logical and rigorous in their approach and yet do not belong to the school I have called the scientific one: Raymond Aron, Stanley Hoffmann, and Kenneth Waltz are examples. Moreover, it is not difficult to find cases where writers in the scientific vein have failed to be rigorous and critical in this sense.

My seventh and final proposition is that the practitioners of the scientific approach, by cutting themselves off from history and philosophy, have deprived themselves of the means of self-criticism, and in consequence have a view of their subject and its possibilities that is callow and brash. I hasten to add that this is not true, or not equally true, of them all. But their thinking is certainly characterized by a lack of any sense of inquiry into international politics as a continuing tradition to which they are the latest recruits; by an insensitivity to the conditions of recent history that have produced them, provided them with the preoccupations and perspectives they have, and colored these in ways of which they might not be aware; by an absence of any disposition to wonder why, if the fruits their researches promise are so great and the prospects of translating them into action so favorable, this has not been accomplished by anyone before; by an uncritical attitude toward their own assumptions, and especially toward the moral and political attitudes that have a central but unacknowledged position in much of what they say.

The scientific approach to international relations would provide a very suitable subject for the sort of criticism that Bernard Crick has applied to a wider target in his admirable book *The American Science of Politics*—criticism that would, by describing its history and social conditions, isolate the slender and parochial substructure of moral and political assumption that underlies the enterprise. There is little doubt that the conception of a science of international politics, like that of a science of politics generally, has taken root and flourished in the United States because of attitudes towards the practice of international affairs that are especially American—assumptions, in particular about the moral simplicity of problems of foreign policy, the existence of "solutions" to these problems, the receptivity of policy-makers to the fruits of research, and the degree of control and manipulation that can be exerted over the whole diplomatic field by any one country. . . .

3

Having stated the case against the scientific approach I must return to the qualifications I introduced at the outset. I am conscious of having made a shotgun attack upon a whole flock of assorted approaches, where single rifle shots might have brought down the main targets more efficiently and at the same time spared others that may have been damaged unnecessarily. Certainly, there are many more approaches to the theory of international relations than two, and the dichotomy that has served my present purpose obscures many other distinctions that it is important to bear in mind.

Students of international relations are divided

by what are in some cases simply barriers of mis-understanding or academic prejudice that cut across the whole field of social studies at the present time. No doubt it is desirable that such barriers be lowered. But in the present controversy, eclecticism, masquerading as tolerance, is the greatest danger of all; if we are to be hospitable to every approach (because "something may come of it some day") and extend equal rights to every cliché (because "there is, after all, a grain of truth in what he says"), there will be no end to the absurdities thrust upon us. There are grains of truth to be had from a speaker at Hyde Park Corner or a man on a Clapham omnibus, but the question is "What place do they have in the hierarchy of academic priorities?"

I hope I have made it clear that I see a good deal of merit in a number of the contributions that have been made by theorists who adopt a scientific approach. The argument is not that these contributions are worthless, but that what is of value in them can be accommodated readily enough within the classical approach. Moreover, the distinctive methods and aspirations these theorists have brought to the subject are leading them down a false path, and to all appeals to follow them down it we should remain resolutely deaf.

15. The Incompleat Theorist: Insight Without Evidence

J. David Singer

1. SOME DELICATE DECISIONS

. . . In Professor Bull's inventory of the scientific school's deadly sins, seven allegedly discrete propositions emerge, but despite claims to rigor and precision we quickly discover that at least one traditionalist is quite indifferent to the requirement that categories be conceptually comparable, logically exhaustive, and mutually exclusive. Rather than try to impose a degree of order on the scattershot arraignment, let me show how uncompulsive we behavioral science types can be, and skip about just as casually as the most discursive intuitionist.

After responding to these arguments with epistemological counterarguments and some anecdotal illustrations, I will try to formulate a position

Excerpted from "The Incompleat Theorist: Insight Without Evidence" by J. David Singer, in James N. Rosenau and Klaus Knorr, eds., *Contending Approaches to International Politics* (Princeton: Princeton University Press, 1969), pp. 63–86. Copyright © 1969 by Princeton University Press. Excerpts reprinted by permission of Princeton University Press and the author. Footnotes deleted.

which may hopefully command not only the assent of the reader but of the prosecutor himself. In the process, I hope to demonstrate that the war between rigor and imagination in international politics is not only over, but that it was to some extent a "phony war" all along—a war which, despite its similarity to that which most other disciplines have been through, need not have been fought but for the recalcitrance of some and the exuberance of others.

2. ALLEGATIONS AND REJOINDERS

....

The Puritan Intellect

The first fantasy one encounters in this morose recitation is the assertion that the scientific approach is so intellectually puritanical that it eschews the use of wisdom, insight, intuition, and judgment. Nonsense! If this were true, we would not only never write a word, but we would never address a class, consult for a government agency, cast a ballot, or even get up in the morning. The scientific view is that, while we can never be satisfied until the proposition in doubt (for example) has indeed been verified, we need hardly decline into cerebral immobility while waiting for the final word. The important difference is that the prescientific chap equates "Eureka!" with divine revelation, while the more rigorous type permits himself that moment of pleasure for basking in the warmth of private discovery, and then gets on with the job of publicly visible, explicit, reproducible authentication.

Our classicist also urges that most of the important moral, as well as theoretical, questions "cannot by their very nature be given any sort of objective answer". While I concur with his aside that the conversations of science and of ethics are always inconclusive (a somewhat milder charge), that is no reason to stop where we are, barely beyond the edge of superstition. On matters moral, scholar and layman alike have been emasculated by the folklore which sees the world of values and the world of facts as deeply and forever separate and distinct. At a certain level of generality, almost all men can find ethical consensus, but as we move toward the specific, we inevitably begin to part company. However, much of the division turns out to be not so much a matter of preference as it is one of prediction.

Very few western diplomats in 1939, for instance, *preferred* Nazi expansion in Central Europe, but most of them *predicted* that the Munich agreement would avoid it. And while few American leaders *preferred* a continuation of the war in Vietnam, many *predicted* in 1965 that rapid military escalation would terminate it. These were errors in prediction—which a more solid research base might have helped us avoid—more than disagreements over ends. To be more general, very few of those court astrologers who have urged the doctrine of "*Si vis pacem, para bellum*" on their leaders have actually preferred war; they merely predicted poorly in almost every case. In other words, even though there will inevitably be differences among men as to their preferred ultimate outcomes, or ends, the bulk of our disagreements turn on the different consequences which we expect (or predict) from the means we advo-

cate and select. My view here is that, as our knowledge base expands and is increasingly integrated in the theoretical sense, the better our predictions will be, and therefore, the fewer policy disagreements we will have. That is, more and more value conflicts will be translatable into the more tractable form of predictive conflicts, thus bridging the gap between fact and value, and liberating our predictions from our preferences.

I certainly do not mean to argue that whenever men, individually or collectively, find themselves pursuing incompatible ends, it is always due to a failure in their knowledge. All too often we do actually want the same object (one type of scarcity) or a different set of environmental conditions (another type of scarcity). But even in those cases, greater knowledge might lead to the calculation that compromise in the short run is less costly than victory in the middle or long run. And in situations which do not now permit the translation of conflicts into predictions, and hence into compromise and cooperation, greater knowledge would help us to so modify the structure and culture of diplomacy that the payoff matrix would indeed be more conducive to mutually advantageous resolution of international conflict. If nations behave as they do largely because it's a dog-eat-dog Hobbesian environment, why not investigate those system changes which might make it a safer one for vigorous—but informed—pursuit of the national interests? Even the highway safety people are beginning to understand that the structure (roads, exits, and embankments) and culture (norms and expectations) may have as much to do with vehicle fatalities as the skill or aggressiveness of individual drivers.

To sum up this first point, then, I defer to no one in my condemnation of a curriculum which embraces "systems theory, game theory, simulation, or content analysis" at the expense of any "contact with the subject" or "any feeling either for the play of international politics or for the moral dilemmas to which it gives rise," but utterly reject the notion that a scientific approach requires us to choose between the two. Our mission in both teaching and research is nothing more than an effective amalgamation of insight with evidence, and of substance with technique. When one of the most eminent of our traditionalists describes his method as the art of "mustering all the evidence that history, personal experience, introspection, common sense and . . . logical reasoning" make available, it is difficult to quarrel. But, it must be added that history, experience, introspection, common sense, and logic do not in themselves generate *evidence*, but ideas which must then be examined in the light of evidence.

If This Be Plagiarism

The second and closely related allegation is that the scientific approach only succeeds in casting any light upon substantive matters when it steps "beyond the bounds of that approach" and employs the classical method. As suggested above, classical concepts and historical insights are very much *within* (and not beyond) the bounds of the scientific spirit. We cannot confirm or disconfirm a proposition until it has been formulated, and the first draft of any such formulation almost invariably finds its expression in the classical mode. A great deal of careful empiricism, and a considerable amount of conceptual integration of such facts have been done by observant, experienced, sophisticated scholars from Thucydides through Carr, Wolfers, Claude, and Morgenthau. While these scholars have actually "pinned down" very little in the way of verified generalizations, they have brought shreds of partial evidence together, have developed conceptual schemes of some elegance and clarity, and have raised an impressive array of important questions. No responsible scientist would throw away that fund of wisdom and insist on beginning all over again, *tabula rasa*.

Let me try to illustrate the continuity of the prescientific and the scientific approaches by brief reference to a study of my own. In close collaboration with a diplomatic historian, I have begun a systematic inquiry into those events and conditions which most frequently coincided with the outbreak of interstate war during the period 1815–1945. Beginning with a survey of the traditional literature, we gradually assembled a number of propositions which seem to be: (a) widely accepted by historians and political scientists; (b) quite plausible on their face; and (c) generally borne out by the illustrations which their propo-

nents have selected. By converting the traditional insights into operational language and gathering data on all relevant cases, we have already begun to find evidence which supports certain propositions, casts serious doubt on others, and leads to the revision of still others. . . .[Here Singer discusses findings from the Correlates of War project. See selection 31.]

I think that even this small sample of only one project's results should suffice for the nonce to illustrate the value of combining the traditional and the scientific approaches. There are, of course, a few people who will look at the results of this and similar research and tell us that they "knew it all along." My retort is of two kinds. First, and rhetorically, if the traditionalists knew this, that, or the other thing all along, how come so many of them "knew" exactly the opposite at the same time? More seriously, such a response to data-based findings reveals an alarming insensitivity to the crucial distinction between subjective belief and verifiable knowledge. Again, we are not likely to do much interesting research unless we have, and act upon, our hunches and insights, but we will never build much of a theory, no matter how high and wide we stack our *beliefs*. Conversely, a few strategically selected empirical studies can produce the evidence necessary to complete an existing theoretical edifice. It is also essential to remember that we made as many important discoveries by the incremental accumulation of modest, limited studies, many of which may seen trivial by themselves, as we do by attacking the big questions directly and all at once. Unfortunately, very few scholars make even a single great discovery in their lifetimes, regardless of discipline, but all competent resarch *contributes*, directly or indirectly, to those great discoveries.

The Triumph of Trivia

The third deadly sin is that our work has been, and will continue to be, restricted to peripheral and to insignificant subjects. This weakness is due, we are given to understand, not to the traditional neglect of scientific method, but to the "characteristics inherent in the subject matter." Among those factors which make our prospects "very bleak indeed" are: the unmanageable number of variables of which any generalization must take account; the difficulty of controlled experiment; the transitory and elusive nature of our material; and the extent to which our research affects the empirical world, such that "even our most innocent ideas contribute to their own verification and falsification."

As to the large number of variables, three points are worth noting. First, modern analytical tools permit us to work with as many independent and intervening variables as we care to when seeking to account for the frequency of any particular type of outcome. Second, we can always reduce this number by combining those variables which *seem* to be conceptually similar, and more to the point, we can then ascertain—via such techniques as factor analysis—the extent to which they actually are highly similar; if a dozen variables all show an extremely high covariation, we can either drop eleven of them for the moment or use them all to create a single combined variable. Third, and most important, we often start out with a large number of variables because our theory is relatively weak, but once the data are in on a sufficiently large number of cases, we can proceed to analyze them in a search for correlational patterns or causal linkages. Beginning with fairly standard bivariate techniques, we can ascertain: whether there is any statistical relationship between the observed outcome and each alleged predictor, such that it could not have occurred by sheer chance; whether that relationship is linear or more complicated; and most important, which predictor (independent variable) accounts for most of the variance, and is therefore most potent in influencing the observed result. Somewhat more complex are those techniques which permit us to combine a number of independent and intervening variables in a wide variety of ways in order to determine which ones in which pattern or sequence covary most strongly with the observed outcome, and therefore constitute the most powerful determinants. . . .

Regarding the difficulty of catching and categorizing our material, the evidence is beginning to mount that it may not be all that elusive. Many of us in comparative, as well as international, politics have begun to enjoy some fair success in observing, measuring, and recording much of the phenomena which, according to the traditionalists, would always be beyond the scientific reach, available only to the practised eye and sophisticated antennae of scholarly wisdom. If they could stop persuading themselves how "impossible" certain things are and how "intangible" the important variables are, and merely look at the literature, they would discover that the pessimism was probably unwarranted; of course, it is one thing to think that one has developed a measure of certain national or global attributes, or relationships, or behavioral events, but quite another to demonstrate that the measure is not only reliable, but valid. A measure is described as *reliable* if it is used by different observers at the same time, or the same observer at different times, and it always produces essentially the same score when applied to the same state of affairs; among familiar measures whose reliability is well demonstrated are the Dow-Jones stock market index, the United States Department of Commerce cost-of-living index, the gross national product of many industrial societies, and the periodic Gallup survey on how well the United States' President is "doing his job." To achieve that sort of acceptance and the opportunity to demonstrate its continuing reliability, a measure must embody a theoretical concept which seems important and do it in a fashion which is not only operational but persuasive. In the next several years, we may well find a few measures around which such a consensus has developed.

But reliability is far and away the simpler of the two demands one must make of a quantitative index; more difficult to satisfy and to evaluate is the demand of validity. An indicator is *valid* to the extent that it actually does measure the phenomena it is alleged to measure. There is, for example, the recent controversy over whether certain "intelligence tests" used in the United States really measure intelligence as it is generally defined and conceptualized in psychology or whether it measures achievement, or social class, or parent's educational level. The same challenges can be addressed to Galtung's measure of social position, Hart's measure of technological advancement, the Rummel and Tanter measures of foreign conflict, or the Singer and Small measures of lateral mobility, alliance aggregation, bipolarity, diplomatic status, or magnitude of war. The trouble with validity is that we never really pin it down in any final fashion. A measure may seem intuitively reasonable (and we therefore say it has "face validity"), or it may predict consistently to another variable in accord with our theory, or it may covary consistently with an "independent" measure of the same concept. None of these is really conclusive evidence of a measure's validity, but all help to make it a useful and widely accepted indicator; whereas reliability is strictly a methodological attribute, validity falls precisely at the juncture of theory and method.

The Model Is Not for Marrying

Turning to the fourth of our intellectual vices, I find some possible grounds for convergence, as well as collision, with our critic. Here we are reminded of all the things that can be—and in our field, often are—wrong with models. On the convergence side, let me readily admit that many of those we find are indeed lacking in internal rigor and consistency, often constitute little more than an intellectual exercise, and do occasionally bootleg some invisible assumptions. But lots of people do lots of things badly, especially when they are just learning, but many do these same things well; should historians be forbidden to think and should lawyers be forbidden to write merely because some performances are on the inadequate side? Granting the flaws which are all too often present, would he have us believe that knowledge comes to those who insist on gazing only at the "real" world through the conventional and culture-bound lenses passed on to us by either the ancients or by the practitioners of the moment? Did the early disciples have the clearest picture of Christianity? Does the boy with his finger in the dike best comprehend hydraulics?

Models, paradigms, and conceptual schemes are merely intellectual tools by which we order and codify that which would otherwise remain a buzzing welter. Some bring us clarity and others only add to our confusion, but no matter what we call them, each of us uses abstractions to give meaning—or the illusion of meaning—to that which our senses detect. Furthermore, as generations of philosophers (East and West) have reminded us, we can never describe the "real" world; all we can do is record and exchange symbolic representations of it. Those symbols may be verbal, numerical, pictorial, and even photographic, but they remain only *representations* of reality. Even though we must (and do) strive for the truest representation, we can never be certain that we have found it. Thus, it is as legitimate to ask whether our models are useful as it is to ask if they are true; the physical and biological sciences, for example, advanced rather nicely with tentative models that were more useful than true. In sum, I concur that our models leave much to be desired, and that they would probably be more useful were they designed to be more representational, but insist that the promising path here is to build them around concepts that are more operational, rather than more familiar, and to discard them when more accurate or more useful ones come along.

By Gauge or by Guess

Our fifth alleged flaw is the "fetish for measurement". . . . We are arraigned here on three subsidiary counts. First, we tend to "ignore relevant differences between the phenomena that are being counted." This is partly an empirical question and partly an epistemological one; in due course the various measurement efforts will show us where we have erred in lumping the unlumpable. But it seems to me that this undue preoccupation, yea obsession, with the unique, the discrete, the non-comparable, is what has largely kept history from developing into a cumulative discipline, and has led to so much frivolous debate between the quantifiers and the antiquantifiers in sociology, psychology, economics, and political science. The fact is that no two events, conditions, or relationships are ever exactly alike; they must always differ in *some* regard, even if it is only in time-space location. The question is whether they are sufficiently similar to permit comparison and combination for the theoretical purposes at hand. To borrow a metaphor of which the antiquantifiers are quite fond, there is absolutely nothing wrong with adding apples and oranges if fruit is the subject at hand! And if we want to generalize at a more restricted level, we had better distinguish not only between apples and oranges, but between McIntosh and Golden Delicious as well. If we cannot combine and aggregate, with due attention to the matter of relevant differences, we cannot make empirical generalizations; and in the absence of such generalizations, we may generate a great deal of speculation, but blessed little theory.

The second allegation here is that we attach more significance to a quantitative indicator or a statistical regularity than it deserves. This, too, is primarily an empirical question, and if we can discover that a common enemy unifies a nation only under certain limited conditions, that the percentage of national product going to foreign trade decreases rather than increases as productivity rises, that domestic conditions correlate with a nation's foreign policy only under special conditions, that estimates of relative military power become distorted as diplomatic tension rises, or that nations are more war-prone when their status is falling rather than rising, we must conclude that the quantifying exercises were useful. Once more, there is something to the charge, and, as suggested above, we must be careful not to equate reliability and plausibility with validity in our measures. Likewise, because we can engage in a wider variety of statistical analyses with interval scales than with ordinal ones, which give nothing more than a rank ordering, there is some temptation to develop such measures even when the situation does not justify the degree of precision implied in an interval scale.

A final point here is Bull's willingness to take seriously only those quantitative results which "confirm some intuitive impression." Here again is the old faith in the folklore and conventional wisdom of a particular time and place. When rigorous methods produce results which are intuitively reasonable, we should not only find this reassuring, but should be careful to avoid pointing out that we "knew it all along." As I suggested above, it would be most instructive to go through our scholarly literature and see how often we have known one thing all along in one section or chapter and something quite different in the following section or chapter. The fact is, we seldom even know what we know, because our assertions are usually made in regard to a small and highly selective sample of cases and in an extremely limited context.

No Monopoly on Precision

The sixth item in Bull's "propositional inventory" is his allegation that the practitioners of the classical approach are as likely to be precise, coherent, and orderly as are members of the scientific school. He reminds us that in the past many classicists (especially the international lawyers) have indeed shown real conceptual rigor, and that the self-styled scientists have often failed in this regard. The claim is all too true, but beside the point. First, the ratio of high-to-low verbal and conceptual precision in the literature of the two schools would certainly not be flattering to those on the classicist side. When social scientists do historical work, we set up our coding rules and then examine *all* the cases which qualify; there is much less of a tendency to ransack history in search of those isolated cases which satisfy one's theoretical or rhetorical requirements of the moment. We need only glance through both sets of literature for tentative but striking evidence of this difference. Closely related, and perhaps an inevitable corollary of this difference, is the fact that when most traditionalists do a serious historical analysis, it takes the form of a case study, whereas the scientist knows that: (a) one can never describe all the variables relevant to a given case, and (b) that what happened only once before is not much of a guide to what will happen in the future. Thus, we tend to select a *few* variables on (please note) intuitive grounds or on the basis of prior research findings, and then examine their interrelationship over *many* historical cases.

Second, and in addition to specific procedures, the scientific researcher usually has an intellectual style that substantially increases the probability of better performance in this regard. Even when we deal with a variable that need not be operationalized in the study at hand, we tend to ask how it *could* be so refined and clarified. Once in the habit of thinking operationally, it is difficult to settle for constructs and propositions that are not—or could not be translated into—"machine readable" form. As the traditionally trained scholar moves further in this direction, and looks at propositions as interesting problems to be investigated or hypotheses to be tested—rather than as the revealed truth—the gap will begin to close. But vague and fuzzy notions cannot be put to the test, and whatever respect for precision there is in the classical tradition will have to be resurrected and mobilized.

The Rootless Wanderers

Our seventh deadly sin is that we have often cut ourselves off from history and philosophy, with certain dire consequences, among which is the loss of some basis for stringent self-criticism. I take the charge to mean that it is from those two intellectual *disciplines*—rather than the phenomena they study—that the severance has occurred. I would hope so on two grounds. First, if we in the scientific school *have* neglected the political and diplomatic past, or such philosophical concerns as ethics, the "big picture," and the long view, then we are indeed in trouble. The fact is, unhappily, that the charge of our being ahistorical is far from unfounded, and an appreciable fraction of the modernists do indeed restrict themselves to the study of only the most recent past or the more trivial problems, and largely for the reason implied in Bull's earlier point: because the data are more available or the cases are more amenable to our methods. But this criticism applies equally to the more traditional scholars. For reasons too complex to explore here, almost all training in political science (with perhaps the exception of political philosophy) is weak in historical depth and extremely restricted in its time frame, particularly in England and America.

As to our philosophical rootlessness, the picture seems to be more mixed, with the modernists quite alert to the epistemological concerns of philosophy but often indifferent to its normative concerns. For example, the traditionalists seem much more willing than the modernists to speak out on matters of public policy, with the latter often hiding behind the argument that our knowledge is still much to inadequate, or that we should not use our status as "experts" to exercise more political influence than other citizens. These

counsels of perfection and of misguided egalitarianism are, to me at least, a source of embarrassment if not dismay. Of course, American political science (as a professional discipline) has been "hung up" on these issues for many decades. My generation, for example, was largely taught that political commitment implied emotional involvement, and that such involvement destroyed scholarly objectivity. The argument only holds water if there are no mechanisms for avoiding the pitfalls of political involvement, and if our field remains one in which most issues of importance *are* merely matters of opinion and belief. The whole point of scientific method is to permit us to investigate whatever problems interest and excite us, while largely eliminating the possibility that we will come out where we *want* to come out.

The more ethical position, it seems to me, is to recognize that individual responsibility cannot be put on the shelf until we are absolutely certain of our political perceptions and predictions. First, most social events will always retain an element of the probabilistic, and since we are—as citizens or consultants—usually called on for judgments about a single case, rather than the large number of cases around which science is built, certainty is something we will rarely experience. In the meantime, of course, the thing to do is advance our data and theory base so that we *can* be more knowledgeable on matters of public policy. Second, if we withhold expression of our judgments until our science is more fully developed, we run a fairly high risk that so many errors in judgment will have been made that the situations we face then will be even less tractable than those of the present, or—and it is not impossible—we will already have stumbled into Armageddon.

As to the modernist's concern that we might "exploit" our status and prestige (itself a dubious quality) by speaking out publicly and identifiably, and therefore put the layman at a disadvantage in influencing the policy process, the anxiety is neither logical nor historically justified. On matters of bridge design, the hazards of smoking, auto safety, construction of the SST, or real estate zoning, the specialist in international politics is no more powerful than most of his fellow citizens, with decisions inevitably made on the basis of some mix of political pressure and expertise. As retarded as our discipline may be, we have as great a right and responsibility to take public stands in our area of special competence as the engineer, medical researcher, lobbyist, sales manager, planner, or land speculator have in theirs. In my view, knowledge is meant to energize, not paralyze.

Thus, I would part company with Professor Bull when he suggests earlier in his paper that most moral questions are "by their very nature" not open to any objective answer, but wholeheartedly concur with his warning on the dangers of remaining "as remote from the substance of international politics as the inmates of a Victorian nunnery were from the study of sex."

Returning to the original charge, my other reason for hoping that he refers not to the substance, but the style, of history and philosophy is that we probably have little more to learn from them in terms of method or concept. At the risk of alienating some of my favorite colleagues, I would say that these disciplines have gone almost as far as they can go in adding to social science knowledge in any appreciable way. True, the historian can continue to pile up facts and do his case studies, but only as he borrows from the social sciences can he produce hard evidence or compelling interpretations of the past; one reason that we must heed Bull's implied advice and move into historical research is that otherwise our understanding of the past will remain in the hands of the literati, responding to one revisionist or counter-revisionist interpretation after another, as the consensus ebbs and flows. Of course, some historians are beginning to shift to the scientific mode now, but while encouraging that trend, it is up to the social scientists to meet them half-way, chronologically as well as methodologically. As to the philosophers, their discipline is too broad and diverse to permit any sweeping statements, ranging as it does from theology to philosophy of science, but logic, deduction, speculation and introspection can only carry us so far. Thus, while new formulations in philosophy (and mathematics) can be expected, the odds are that the scientist himself will continue to be his own best

philosopher and theorist, as long as he looks up from his data matrix and statistical significance tables periodically, and asks "what does it all mean?"

So much for Professor Bull's critique for the moment; while his attack, as he courageously admits, was more shotgun than rifle, he did bring down some worthy targets, and if a few already dead horses are somewhat more riddled than before, the ammunition was certainly expended with style and flair. Let me try now to summarize my position on the general issues, adding the hope that this volume may represent the last round in what has been considerably less than a "great debate."

3. CONCLUSION

My thesis should now be quite clear, but in the unlikely event that my touch has been too light or my rhetoric too subtle, let me reiterate it here in the baldest terms. All kinds of men contemplate and think about all kinds of problems. Some are intrigued with physical problems, ranging from biology to celestial mechanics; some are more preoccupied with social phenomena, from child development to world politics; and some are intrigued with that elusive interface at which the physical and the social domains appear to meet, whether in psychophysiology or human ecology. When men first began to think about any of these problems, they had little to go on. There was not much in the way of recorded experiences, philosophical schemes, tools of observation, or techniques of measurement. Over the centuries, however, some knowledge began to accumulate; witch doctors, court astrologers, and theologians all contributed—even in their errors—to the growth in understanding of the world around us. Philosophical schemes and cosmologies, inclined planes and brass instruments, psychoanalysis and mathematical statistics all tended to further the increase in knowledge. In some fields of inquiry, progress was quite rapid. In others, due to social taboos as well as the inherent complexity of the phenomena, things did not move quite as well. Thus, long after Lavoisier had demonstrated the fallaciousness of the phlogiston theory, and the systematic observations of Galileo and Brahe had discredited the Ptolemaic conception of astronomy, students of social phenomena—relying on authority rather than evidence—continued to accept notions that were equally inaccurate.

Where do we stand now? In some of the social sciences, progress has been steady and impressive; in others, it has been more halting. It would seem that those disciplines which are most advanced are precisely those in which imagination and insight have been combined with—not divorced from—rigor and precision. In each of these, one finds that the early work, no matter how creative, remained largely speculative, with several theoretical schemes—often equally plausible—contending for position. Until systematic observation, operationally derived evidence, and replicable analytical procedures were introduced, skillful rhetoric and academic gamesmanship often carried the day. Thus, in sociology, Comte and Spencer played a key role in the transition from speculation to measurement; Hume and Smith come to mind as those who represent the convergence of theoretical insight and systematic quantification in economics; and in psychology, one might select Wundt and Titchener as the scholars who bridged the gap between the preoperational and the operational. At the other pole, such social science disciplines as anthropology and psychiatry remain largely impressionistic—but far from nonempirical—in their evidence, and thus unimpressive in their theory.

We in political science stand very much at the threshold. In certain subfields, operational measurement and the quantitative evidence which result are more or less taken for granted now; opinion surveys, voting studies, and roll-call analyses are, except in the intellectual backwaters, seen as necessary—but not sufficient—ingredients in the growth of political theory. But in international politics, there are still those few who raise the same old spectres, rattle the same old skeletons, and flog the same old horses. They sometimes tell us that Thucydides or Machiavelli or Mahan knew all there was to know and at other times they tell us that the subject matter is intrinsically unknowable. Perhaps the best answer to both assertions is to "look at the record"; a decade ago there was little published scientific research beyond the pioneering work of Quincy Wright's *Study of War* and Lewis Richardson's scattered articles. Five years ago, a handful of us were getting underway and perhaps a dozen or so data-based papers had appeared. In mid-1967, I find . . . in the English language journals almost 100 articles that bring hard evidence to bear on theoretically significant questions, and more than a dozen books. Whether the traditionalists will find these persuasive—or as Bull recognizes, whether they will even read them—is uncertain. The quality if clearly uneven, the theoretical relevance is mixed, the methodological sophistication ranges from naïve to fantastic, the policy payoffs seem to differ enormously, and the craftsmanship runs from slovenly to compulsive, but the work is already beginning to add up. . . .

My point, then, is that there is no longer much doubt that we can make the study of international politics (or better still, world politics) into a scientific discipline worthy of the name. But it requires the devotees of both warring camps to come together in collaboration if not in sublime unity. We on the scientific side have little ground for exultation. Whatever progress we have already made is due in large measure to the wisdom, insight, and creativity of those from whom we have learned. What is more, the war would not be over if the traditionalists had waited for us to meet them half way. It is a tribute to the classical tradition, in which many of us were of course reared, that its heritage is rich and strong enough to permit the sort of growth and development which now is well along. All that remains is for those in the scientific camp to shift from the digital to the analog computer and recognize that every serious scholar's work is on the same continuum. If we modernists can master the substantive, normative, and judgmental end of it as well as the traditionalists are mastering the concepts and methods at our end, convergence will be complete, and the "war" will not have been in vain.

III

Foreign Policy
and Global Conflict

Understanding foreign policy and explaining global conflict have been the two main empirical endeavors of the field of international relations. As the following selections elucidate, these are interrelated questions. Chapter 5 begins with general explanations of foreign policy. Some of the path-breaking work that has been done on the subject of crisis is presented in Chapter 6. Chapter 7 presents selections from a variety of disciplines and historical periods to address the field's central problem: the causes of war. Chapter 8 covers the subject of imperialism. While other empirical research has been conducted, these areas embody the best and most influential work.

The selections in Chapter 5 can be grouped into three categories. Morgenthau (1952) and Wolfers (1952) deal with the concept of national interest both as an explanation of foreign policy and as a basis for conducting foreign affairs. Snyder et al. (1954), Guetzkow and Valadez (1968, 1981), and Allison and Halperin (1972) analyze the process by which foreign policy decisions are made. Finally, Rosenau (1966) and Rummel (1977) present general explanations of foreign policy behavior.

The end of World War II, the creation of the United Nations, the emergence of the Cold War, and the onset of the Korean War provided severe tests for the application of idealist and realist ideas about foreign policy. The shattered hopes for a postwar era of peace, and the circumlocution that the Korean War was a police action did much to insure the intellectual triumph of realism. Both Morgenthau's (1952) essay and his book *In Defense of the National Interest* cogently present the case for basing foreign policy on the national interest, although, with his typical acumen, he recognizes the potential problems posed by the ambiguity of the concept. In a series of articles later collected in *Discord and Collaboration* (1962), Arnold Wolfers elucidates and often reformulates some of the fundamental assumptions and concepts of realism. In the selection reprinted here, he details the empirical obfuscations and policy risks inherent in the concept of national interest. Many of the problems he outlines were to later materialize during the Vietnam and Watergate era to haunt the American polity. Ironically, Wolfers's analysis eventually led most political scientists to abandon the concept just at the time when Morgenthau's analysis provided the intellectual rationale for policymakers to embrace it. While scholars have developed other concepts to explain foreign policy, no other concept that can be used to make and evaluate foreign policy has gained wide acceptance. The most closely related concept has been that of class interest, which shares many of the same conceptual problems. Clearly, the need for new concepts to evaluate policy stands as one of the major challenges to the field.

During the fifties and sixties, the behavioralists focused attention on empirical questions rather than on questions related purely to policy. The work of Snyder, Bruck, and Sapin introduced the decision-making approach to the field in 1954. Instead of attempting to deduce a country's foreign policy on the basis of its national interest, Snyder et al. try to explain foreign policy by examining the factors that influence officials to make a particular decision. This emphasis on official decision makers reduces the anthropomorphic tendency to consider a nation as a single entity rather than as a collection of leaders, elites, and publics. Finally, the Snyder selection reflects an attempt to move away from explaining the foreign policy of one state (American foreign policy, for example), and to develop a framework within which the foreign policy of any state could be analyzed.

Studying foreign policy decision making is difficult, however, because the process is usually inaccessible to scholarly observation, and often secret. One of the more innovative attempts to resolve this problem was through the use of simulation. This technique was introduced into the field in the late fifties by Harold Guetzkow, who, with others, developed the Inter-Nation Simulation as a way of producing theory and research. In the selection presented here, Guetzkow and Valadez review some of the findings on the factors that may influence individuals and groups in making foreign policy decisions. While the selection deals with only one aspect of the research, the reader can nevertheless gain a sense of the scope and rigor of one of the major projects in the field.

The work on bureaucratic politics also deals with foreign policy decision making, but from a different perspective and without employing the scientific method. In their important essay, Allison and Halperin (1972) attack the realist idea that the nation is a unitary rational actor that produces foreign policy in the national interest. Instead, they see foreign policy as a product of the pulling and hauling of bureaucratic actors, each with its own organizational interests. Because this indicates that foreign policy is often formulated primarily for domestic or organizational reasons, the assumption that foreign policy is basically a set of rational communications and interactions between two states is erroneous. While the insight associated with this approach has not given rise to a general explanation of foreign policy, it has undercut confidence in deductive attempts to explain decisions on the basis of national interest.

As the focus on decision making evolved from the fifties through the seventies, others attempted to develop a general explanation of foreign policy. The most influential of these attempts was Rosenau's "pre-theory." His work makes two essential advances over that of Snyder et al. First, he reduces the long checklist of factors to five variable clusters; second, he rank-orders the potency of these factors on the basis of the nation's attributes and the issue under contention. Rosenau's contribution is particularly important because it moved the field toward the creation of testable hypotheses that could explain the behavior of states. In doing so, Rosenau gave rise to a school of comparative foreign policy that has researched and reformulated many of his propositions.

The other major attempt to explain foreign policy behavior came out of Rummel's Dimensionality of Nations (DON) project, the major project in the field devoted to analyzing foreign conflict. Unlike Rosenau's work, Rummel's began with data collection and quantitative analysis and then moved toward theory construction. Rummel looked first at the effects of one national attribute—internal conflict—on foreign conflict behavior, then at a variety of national attributes, and finally, at attribute distances and the role of status. As part of this process, Rummel made an important contribution by introducing data analysis techniques, particularly factor analysis, to the field. The selection reprinted here is the theoretical introduction to one of the most successful quantitative analyses published in the field. In it, Rummel is able to account for a considerable amount of the variation in United States foreign policy behavior.

Because the United States was involved in a number of dramatic crises during the Cold War, and because many wars are preceded by crises, it is not an accident that crisis research became a focus of the behavioralists. Chapter 6 includes three representative selections from some of the best work on this topic. The article by Charles Hermann has continued to receive wide attention; in it, he defines *crisis* as a situation that, as a decision maker perceives it, involves a high threat to the state, a short time in which to decide, and the element of surprise. Using these three dimensions, he develops a typology of situations that a decision maker could face, and then offers propositions to explain and predict how these situations would affect foreign policy decision making. In his other work, Hermann used the Inter-Nation Simulation to test his propositions; later in the seventies, he was instrumental in collecting event data (quantitative analysis of news reports) in the CREON project, which linked his focus on decision making with Rosenau's pre-theory of foreign policy behavior.

The selection by Holsti, North, and Brody attempts to delineate the role of perception in the escalation of crisis to war. This selection was one of the most important articles to come out of the Stanford Studies on Conflict and Integration, directed by Robert North. The project was significant because it was the first to use the technique of content analysis to gather data from previously secret government documents. It not only serves as an exemplar of scientific research, but also elucidates the dynamics of hostile spirals that lead to war. Later, Robert North and Nazli Choucri (see selection 34), supplemented this research with an investigation of the long-term factors that, from 1870 to 1914, led to World War I.

In contrast to the previous two writers, Charles McClelland did not take a decision maker's perspective in studying crises, but instead developed a systems approach. In the selection reprinted here, he provides a definition of crisis and a method for detecting crises based on the increase and changed nature of communication patterns. He then uses these data to describe how crises in Berlin and the Formosa Strait abated so that war was avoided. Clearly, this work complements the study on the 1914 crisis. McClelland's work was also significant for its methodological contribution. Trained as a diplomatic historian, McClelland felt the need for the creation of data to test many of the theoretical statements made in the fifties. His solution was to create "event data" through a content analysis, first of the *New York Times Index* and then of the *Times* itself. Known as WEIS (World Event Interaction Survey), the work set the pattern for an event-data movement within the discipline in the early 1970s.

The three articles in this chapter demonstrate that important pieces of knowledge can be created by the application of scientific and statistical techniques. Although much remains to be accomplished, these efforts represented a significant early step.

The work on war has been of concern for a longer period of time; the attention it has received from a number of disciplines has had an impact within the field. The works in Chapter 7 were selected to reflect this richness: their authors are practitioners of political philosophy, psychology, anthropology, physics, and political science.

The selection by Hobbes (1651) provides an insight that has been central in analyses of world politics; namely, that in a state of anarchy, war is constant and insecurity is prevalent. Although Hobbes was reacting to the English Civil War, his notion that the state of nature is anarchic, and that without government there is nothing to prevent war, has long been seen by many as an accurate image of the international system. For Hobbes, war is a natural condition, given human nature, which he sees as "a perpetuall and restlesse desire of Power after power, that ceaseth onely in Death."[1] The solution to war is for all individuals to disarm and to give complete obedience to an all-powerful sovereign. At the global level, this solution would entail a world government. Hobbes's contribution is that he not only provided the basis for much of the work on global anarchy, but also developed one of the main explanations of the need for government.

Freud also asserts that the causes of war are within human nature, but his explanation is more precise. Reacting to the conflagration of World War I and later to the rise of Hitler, Freud sees war not only as inevitable, but also as becoming more severe. Freud believes that the intensity of war is a function of the intensity of repression within civilization. As civilization becomes more complex, more repression of basic drives would be required. War, for Freud, is an explosive release of those drives; the greater the previous repression, the greater the explosive release.

---

[1] Thomas Hobbes, *Leviathan*, Part I, Chapter 11, second paragraph.

In part, Freud also views war as a reflection of a death instinct by which humans attempt to escape the burdens of life. Freud wonders whether war is a way for the human species periodically to kill its members because of the increasing burdens of civilization. While his thoughts on these questions are highly speculative, his thinking is particularly relevant and ominous in the nuclear age.[2]

Unlike Freud and Hobbes, Margaret Mead does not believe that war is inherent in human nature. If this were the case, she cogently points out in her essay, then it should be found in all societies; but it is not. She and other anthropologists have located peaceful societies. To Mead, war is a learned custom that does not have a biological basis. Her focus on peaceful societies is representative of an area of inquiry in the field that explains war by looking at what has enabled peaceful societies to avoid it.

The work of Lewis Fry Richardson was the first major attempt to investigate war through the application of the scientific method and statistical procedures. As with many others whose work is included in this volume, Richardson reacted to World War I with horror and resolved to find the causes of war. A Quaker, he retired from a very successful career in physics and meteorology to investigate the subject of war. His two major works, *Statistics of Deadly Quarrels* and *Arms and Insecurity*, were published posthumously in 1960. In the former, he collected data on deadly quarrels and then examined their common attributes. His analysis was particularly important for the *way* in which he studied war and for his use of statistical models and reasoning. In *Arms and Insecurity*, a portion of which is reprinted here, he attempts to use mathematics to explain arms races as an action-reaction process that often results in war. His specific model as well as his use of mathematical deduction provided the foundation for much of the work on arms races.

The work on war that received the most attention in the field of political science during the forties, fifties, and sixties was Quincy Wright's monumental tome, *A Study of War*. Begun in 1926 at the University of Chicago in response to World War I, and completed in 1942 with institutional assistance and recognition, it remained until the late 1970s the most systematic and comprehensive social science study of war. It drew from a variety of disciplines, including animal behavior, for its insights. Its significance lies in its search for the general causes and consequences of war as a phenomenon, and in collecting data on war that dates back to the fifteenth century. The selection reprinted here from the abridged edition summarizes what Wright believed were the major causes of war.

In the middle 1960s, J. David Singer initiated the Correlates of War project, which involved several scholars and a host of graduate students. This project has been the main source of scientific data on the frequency, magnitude, and severity of war, including civil war, since 1815. It has also been the main source of data on alliances, arms races, national capability, and serious disputes. While the collection of highly reliable and valid data would be, in itself, a significant contribution, this project, unlike many other data-collection efforts, has made an even more significant contribution to hypothesis testing and the accumulation of scientific

---

[2]Freud's views on war varied from optimism to pessimism. The latter attitude seems to predominate and is particularly evident in *Civilization and Its Discontents*. For a much more optimistic view, see his letter to Einstein, "Why War?"

findings. In the reprinted article, Singer summarizes the findings that had been produced by 1980. Although still active and ongoing, the Correlates of War is already the most significant and successful project not only within international relations, but in all of political science.

Closely related to the study of war has been the analysis of imperialism, the subject of Chapter 8. Imperialism, which has been perceived as a cause of war, is also a subject of inquiry in its own right. Although imperialism was a concern in ancient times, the seminal modern study is that of Hobson. His work greatly influenced Lenin, who made it the basis of his own analysis, *Imperialism: The Highest Stage of Capitalism*, which remains the best-known work on the subject and the starting point for most leftist analyses of imperialism.

Primarily because of the political climate within the United States and because of the influence of the Cold War, most studies on imperialism were not conducted by international-relations scholars. Johan Galtung's *A Structural Theory of Imperialism*, published in 1971, renewed interest in the study of the subject. In it he employs sociological concepts to analyze the imperialistic relationship between the center and the periphery in today's world. In so doing, he shows that the ending of colonialism has not ended imperialism, which has continued in more subtle ways.

In the mid-1970s, behavioralists within the United States became more interested in testing and reformulating propositions on imperialism. One of the most significant efforts was that of Choucri and North, who examined the relationship among domestic factors, expansion, imperial rivalries, and the onset of World War I. Their work is particularly important in linking the earlier work on the 1914 crisis with the more structural approach of contemporary Marxists.

Meanwhile, the relationship between center and periphery continued as a focus of inquiry. Latin American researchers, including André Gunder Frank and Cardoso and Faletto, saw this relationship as one of dependency, and used it to explain why Third World countries are not industrializing more rapidly. A more global and historical explanation is provided by Immanuel Wallerstein, who argues that the economy of one nation can only be understood in terms of the dominant global political economy, which has been controlled by Western capitalist nations since the sixteenth century. Like many classics in this area, Wallerstein's work comes from outside the field of international relations. With the decline of American economic hegemony, as indicated by the abandonment of the gold standard and then by the Arab oil embargo, his work received wide attention and helped to promote a new emphasis on political economy within the field. The selection reprinted here is the concluding chapter of *The Modern World System*.

FOR FURTHER READING

Foreign Policy:

1. CHARLES A. BEARD. *The Idea of the National Interest.* New York: Macmillan, 1934.

2. HAROLD NICOLSON. *Diplomacy*. London: T. Butterworth, 1939.

3.   ROBERT E. OSGOOD. *Ideals and Self-Interest in America's Foreign Relations*. Chicago: University of Chicago Press, 1953.

4.   HAROLD GUETZKOW, AND OTHERS. *Simulation in International Relations*. Englewood Cliffs, N.J.: Prentice-Hall, Inc., 1963.

5.   HERBERT C. KELMAN, ED. *International Behavior: A Social Psychological Analysis*. New York: Holt, Rinehart & Winston, 1965.

6.   JAMES N. ROSENAU. *The Scientific Study of Foreign Policy*. New York: The Free Press, 1968.

7.   GLENN PAIGE. *The Korean Decision: June 24–30, 1950*. New York: The Free Press, 1968.

8.   JONATHAN WILKENFELD. Domestic and Foreign Conflict Behavior of Nations. *Journal of Peace Research* 1 (1968): 56–69.

9.   JOHN D. STEINBRUNER. *The Cybernetic Theory of Decision*. Princeton: Princeton University Press, 1974.

10.   ROBERT JERVIS. *Perception and Misperception in International Relations*. Princeton: Princeton University Press, 1976.

11.   R. J. RUMMEL. *Field Theory Evolving*. Beverly Hills, Calif.: Sage Publications, 1977.

Crisis: 12.   CHARLES F. HERMANN, ED. *International Crises: Insights from Behavioral Research*. New York: The Free Press, 1972.

13.   EDWARD AZAR. Conflict Escalation and Conflict Reduction in an International Crisis: Suez, 1956. *Journal of Conflict Resolution* 16 (1972): 183–201.

14.   RAYMOND TANTER. *Modelling and Managing International Conflicts*. Beverly Hills, Calif.: Sage Publications, 1974.

15.   GLENN SNYDER AND PAUL DIESING. *Conflict Among Nations: Bargaining, Decision Making, and System Structure*. Princeton: Princeton University Press, 1977.

War: 16.   SIGMUND FREUD. *Civilization and Its Discontents*. London: Hogarth Press, 1930.

17.   PITIRIM A. SOROKIN. *Social and Cultural Dynamics*, Vol. 3. New York: American Book, 1937.

18.   KENNETH N. WALTZ. *Man, the State, and War*. New York: Columbia University Press, 1959.

19.   RAYMOND ARON. *Peace and War*. New York: Doubleday, 1966.

20.   J. DAVID SINGER, ED. *The Correlates of War*, Vols. 1 & 2. New York: The Free Press, 1979, 1980.

21.   R.J. RUMMEL. *War, Power, Peace*, Vol. 4: *Understanding Conflict and War*. Beverly Hills, Calif.: Sage Publications, 1979.

22.   MICHAEL D. WALLACE. Armaments and Escalation: Two Conflicting Hypotheses. *International Studies Quarterly* 26 (1982):37–56.

Imperialism:

23.   J.A. HOBSON. *Imperialism: A Study* (1902). London: George Allen and Unwin, 1938.

24.   JOSEPH SCHUMPETER. ''The Sociology of Imperialism,'' in *Imperialism and Social Classes*. New York: Meridian Books, 1958 (essay originally published in 1919).

25.   RONALD ROBINSON AND JOHN GALLAGHER. *Africa and the Victorians*. London: Macmillan, 1961.

26.   LIN PIAO. Long Live the Victory of People's War! *The Peking Review*. September 3, 1965.

27.   HARRY MAGDOFF. *The Age of Imperialism*. New York: Monthly Review Press, 1969.

28.   ANDRÉ GUNDER FRANK. *Capitalism and Underdevelopment in Latin America*. New York: Monthly Review Press, 1969.

29.   FERNANDO HENRIQUE CARDOSO AND ENZO FALETTO. *Dependency and Development in Latin America*. Berkeley: University of California Press, 1979.

5

THEORIES OF FOREIGN POLICY

16. Another "Great Debate": The National Interest of the United States

HANS J. MORGENTHAU

1

. . . The issue which the present debate raises concerns the nature of all politics and, more particularly, of the American tradition in foreign policy. The history of modern political thought is the story of a contest between two schools which differ fundamentally in their conception of the nature of man, society, and politics. One believes that a rational and moral political order, derived from universally valid abstract principles, can be achieved here and now. It assumes the essential goodness and infinite malleability of human nature and attributes the failure of the social order to measure up to the rational standards to lack of knowledge and understanding, obsolescent social institutions, or the depravity of certain isolated individuals or groups. It trusts in education, reform, and the sporadic use of force to remedy these deficiencies.

The other school believes that the world, imperfect as it is from the rational point of view, is

Excerpted from "Another 'Great Debate': The National Interest of the United States," by Hans J. Morgenthau, *American Political Science Review*, 46 (1952), pp. 961–978. Reprinted by permission of the publisher. Footnotes deleted.

the result of forces which are inherent in human nature. To improve the world one must work with those forces, not against them. This being inherently a world of opposing interests and of conflict among them, moral principles can never be fully realized, but at best approximated through the ever temporary balancing of interests and the ever precarious settlement of conflicts. This school, then, sees in a system of checks and balances a universal principle for all pluralist societies. It appeals to historic precedent rather than to abstract principles, and aims at achievement of the lesser evil rather than of the absolute good. . . .

2

Yet what is the national interest? How can we define it and give it the content which will make it a guide for action? This is one of the relevant questions to which the current debate has given rise.

It has been frequently argued against the realist conception of foreign policy that its key concept, the national interest, does not provide an acceptable standard for political action. This argument is in the main based upon two grounds: the elusiveness of the concept and its susceptibility to interpretations, such as limitless imperialism and narrow nationalism, which are not in keeping with the American tradition in foreign policy. The argument has substance as far as it goes, but it does not invalidate the usefulness of the concept.

The concept of the national interest is similar in two respects to the "great generalities" of the Constitution, such as the general welfare and due process. It contains a residual meaning which is inherent in the concept itself, but beyond these minimum requirements its content can run the whole gamut of meanings which are logically compatible with it. That content is determined by the political traditions and the total cultural context within which a nation formulates its foreign policy. The concept of the national interest, then, contains two elements, one that is logically required and in that sense necessary, and one that is variable and determined by circumstances.

Any foreign policy which operates under the standard of the national interest must obviously have some reference to the physical, political, and cultural entity which we call a nation. In a world where a number of sovereign nations compete with and oppose each other for power, the foreign policies of all nations must necessarily refer to their survival as their minimum requirements. Thus all nations do what they cannot help but do: protect their physical, political, and cultural identity against encroachments by other nations. . . .

The survival of a political unit, such as a nation, in its identity is the irreducible minimum, the necessary element of its interests vis-à-vis other units. Taken in isolation, the determination of its content in a concrete situation is relatively simple; for it encompasses the integrity of the nation's territory, of its political institutions, and of its culture. Thus bipartisanship in foreign policy, especially in times of war, has been most easily achieved in the promotion of these minimum requirements of the national interest. The situation is different with respect to the variable elements of the national interests. All the cross currents of personalities, public opinion, sectional interests, partisan politics, and political and moral folkways are brought to bear upon their

determination. In consequence, the contribution which science can make to this field, as to all fields of policy formation, is limited. It can identify the different agencies of the government which contribute to the determination of the variable elements of the national interest and assess their relative weight. It can separate the long-range objectives of foreign policy from the short-term ones which are the means for the achievement of the former and can tentatively establish their rational relations. Finally, it can analyze the variable elements of the national interest in terms of their legitimacy and their compatibility with other national values and with the national interest of other nations. We shall address ourselves briefly to the typical problems with which this analysis must deal.

The legitimacy of the national interest must be determined in the face of possible usurpation by subnational, other-national, and supranational interests. On the subnational level we find group interests, represented particularly by ethnic and economic groups, who tend to identify themselves with the national interest. Charles A. Beard has emphasized, however one-sidedly, the extent to which the economic interests of certain groups have been presented as those of the United States. Group interests exert, of course, constant pressure upon the conduct of our foreign policy, claiming their identity with the national interest. It is, however, doubtful that, with the exception of a few spectacular cases, they have been successful in determining the course of American foreign policy. It is much more likely, given the nature of American domestic politics, that American foreign policy, insofar as it is the object of pressures by sectional interests, will normally be a compromise between divergent sectional interests. The concept of the national interest, as it emerges from this contest as the actual guide for foreign policy, may well fall short of what would be rationally required by the overall interests of the United States. Yet the concept of the national interest which emerges from this contest of conflicting sectional interests is also more than any particular sectional interest or their sum total. It is, as it were, the lowest common denominator where sectional interests and the national interest meet in an uneasy compromise which may leave much to be desired in view of all the interests concerned. . . .

The more acute problem arises at the present time from the importance which the public and government officials, at least in their public utterances, attribute to the values represented and the policies pursued by international organizations either as alternatives or supplements to the values and policies for which the national government stands. It is frequently asserted that the foreign policy of the United States pursues no objectives apart from those of the United Nations, that, in other words, the foreign policy of the United States is actually identical with the policy of the United Nations. This assertion cannot refer to anything real in actual politics to support it. For the constitutional structure of international organizations, such as the United Nations, and their procedural practices make it impossible for them to pursue interests apart from those of the member-states which dominate their policy-forming bodies. . . .

The real issue in view of the problem that concerns us here is not whether the so-called interests of the United Nations, which do not exist apart from the interests of its most influential members, have superseded the national interests of the United States, but for what kind of interests the United States has secured United Nations support. While these interests cannot be United Nations interests, they do not need to be national interests either. Here we are in the presence of that modern phenomenon which has been variously described as "utopianism," "sentimentalism," "moralism," the "legalistic-moralistic approach." The common denominator of all these tendencies in modern political thought is the substitution for the national interest of a supranational standard of action which is generally identified with an international organization, such as the United Nations. The national interest is here not being usurped by sub- or supranational interests which, however inferior in worth to the national interest, are nevertheless real and worthy of consideration within their proper sphere. What challenges the national interest here is a mere figment of the imagination, a product of wishful thinking,

which is postulated as a valid norm for international conduct, without being valid either there or anywhere else. At this point we touch the core of the present controversy between utopianism and realism in international affairs; we shall return to it later in this paper.

The national interest as such must be defended against usurpation by non-national interests. Yet once that task is accomplished, a rational order must be established among the values which make up the national interest and among the resources to be committed to them. While the interests which a nation may pursue in its relation with other nations are of infinite variety and magnitude, the resources which are available for the pursuit of such interests are necessarily limited in quantity and kind. No nation has the resources to promote all desirable objectives with equal vigor; all nations must therefore allocate their scarce resources as rationally as possible. The indispensable precondition of such rational allocation is a clear understanding of the distinction between the necessary and variable elements of the national interest. Given the contentious manner in which in democracies the variable elements of the national interest are generally determined, the advocates of an extensive conception of the national interest will inevitably present certain variable elements of the national interest as though their attainment were necessary for the nation's survival. In other words, the necessary elements of the national interest have a tendency to swallow up the variable elements so that in the end all kinds of objectives, actual or potential, are justified in terms of national survival. . . .

The concept of the national interest presupposes neither a naturally harmonious, peaceful world nor the inevitability of war as a consequence of the pursuit by all nations of their national interest. Quite to the contrary, it assumes continuous conflict and threat of war, to be minimized through the continuous adjustment of conflicting interests by diplomatic action. No such assumption would be warranted if all nations at all times conceived of their national interest only in terms of their survival and, in turn, defined their interest in survival in restrictive and rational terms. As it is, their conception of the national interest is subject to all the hazards of misinterpretation, usurpation, and misjudgment to which reference has been made above. To minimize these hazards is the first task of a foreign policy which seeks the defense of the national interest by peaceful means. Its second task is the defense of the national interest, restrictively and rationally defined, against the national interests of other nations which may or may not be thus defined. If they are not, it becomes the task of armed diplomacy to convince the nations concerned that their legitimate interests have nothing to fear from a restrictive and rational foreign policy and that their illegitimate interests have nothing to gain in the face of armed might rationally employed. . . .

17. "National Security" as an Ambiguous Symbol

ARNOLD WOLFERS

Statesmen, publicists and scholars who wish to be considered realists, as many do today, are inclined to insist that the foreign policy they advocate is dictated by the national interest, more specifically by the national security interest. It is not surprising that this should be so. Today any reference to the pursuit of security is likely to ring a sympathetic chord.

However, when political formulas such as "national interest" or "national security" gain popularity they need to be scrutinized with particular care. They may not mean the same thing to different people. They may not have any precise meaning at all. Thus, while appearing to offer guidance and a basis for broad consensus they may be permitting everyone to label whatever policy he favors with an attractive and possibly deceptive name.

In a very vague and general way "national interest" does suggest a direction of policy which can be distinguished from several others which may present themselves as alternatives. It indicates that the policy is designed to promote demands which are ascribed to the nation rather than to individuals, sub-national groups or mankind as a whole. In emphasizes that the policy subordinates other interests to those of the nation. But beyond this, it has very little meaning. . . .

. . . The question is raised, therefore, whether this seemingly more precise formula of national security offers statesmen a meaningful guide for action. Can they be expected to know what it means? Can policies be distinguished and judged on the ground that they do or do not serve this interest?

The term national security, like national interest, is well enough established in the political discourse of international relations to designate an objective of policy distinguishable from others. We know roughly what people have in mind if they complain that their government is neglecting national security or demanding excessive sacrifices for the sake of enhancing it. Usually those who raise the cry for a policy oriented exclusively toward this interest are afraid their country underestimates the external dangers facing it or is being

Reprinted from *Political Science Quarterly* 67 (December 1952), pp. 481–502, by permission of the publisher. Footnotes deleted.

diverted into idealistic channels unmindful of these dangers. Moreover, the symbol suggests protection through power and therefore figures more frequently in the speech of those who believe in reliance on national power than of those who place their confidence in model behavior, international cooperation, or the United Nations to carry their country safely through the tempests of international conflict. For these reasons it would be an exaggeration to claim that the symbol of national security is nothing but a stimulus to semantic confusion, though closer analysis will show that if used without specifications it leaves room for more confusion than sound political counsel or scientific usage can afford.

The demand for a policy of national security is primarily normative in character. It is supposed to indicate what the policy of a nation should be in order to be either expedient—a rational means toward an accepted end—or moral, the best or least evil course of action. The value judgments implicit in these normative exhortations will be discussed.

Before doing so, attention should be drawn to an assertion of fact which is implicit if not explicit in most appeals for a policy guided by national security. Such appeals usually assume that nations in fact have made security their goal except when idealism or utopianism of their leaders has led them to stray from the traditional path. If such conformity of behavior actually existed, it would be proper to infer that a country deviating from the established pattern of conduct would risk being penalized. This would greatly strengthen the normative arguments. The trouble with the contention of fact, however, is that the term ''security'' covers a range of goals so wide that highly divergent policies can be interpreted as policies of security.

Security points to some degree of protection of values previously acquired. In Walter Lippmann's words, a nation is secure to the extent to which it is not in danger of having to sacrifice core values, if it wishes to avoid war, and is able, if challenged, to maintain them by victory in such a war. What this definition implies is that security rises and falls with the ability of a nation to deter an attack, or to defeat it. This is in accord with common usage of the term.

Security is a value, then, of which a nation can have more or less and which it can aspire to have in greater or lesser measure. It has much in common, in this respect, with power or wealth, two other values of great importance in international affairs. But while wealth measures the amount of a nation's material possessions, and power its ability to control the actions of others, security, in an objective sense, measures the absence of threats to acquired values, in a subjective sense, the absence of fear that such values will be attacked. In both respects a nation's security can run a wide gamut from almost complete insecurity or sense of insecurity at one pole, to almost complete security or absence of fear at the other. . . .

This point, however, should not be overstressed. There can be no quarrel with the generalization that most nations, most of the time—the great Powers particularly—have shown, and had reason to show, an active concern about some lack of security and have been prepared to make sacrifices for its enhancement. Danger and the awareness of it have been, and continue to be, sufficiently widespread to guarantee some uniformity in this respect. But a generalization which leaves room both for the frantic kind of struggle for more security which characterized French policy at times and for the neglect of security apparent in American foreign policy after the close of both World Wars throws little light on the behavior of nations. The demand for conformity would have meaning only if it could be said—as it could under the conditions postulated in the working hypothesis of pure power politics—that nations normally subordinate all other values to the maximization of their security, which, however, is obviously not the case.

There have been many instances of struggles for more security taking the form of an unrestrained race for armaments, alliances, strategic boundaries and the like; but one need only recall the many heated parliamentary debates on arms appropriations to realize how uncertain has been the extent to which people will consent to sacrifice for additonal increments of security. Even when there has been no question that armaments would mean more security, the cost in taxes, the reduction in social benefits or the sheer discomfort involved has militated effectively against further effort. . . .

It might be objected that in the long run nations are not so free to choose the amount of effort they will put into security. Are they not under a kind of compulsion to spare no effort provided they wish to survive? This objection again would make sense only if the hypothesis of pure power politics were a realistic image of actual world affairs. In fact, however, a glance at history will suffice to show that survival has only exceptionally been at stake, particularly for the major Powers. If nations were not concerned with the protection of values other than their survival as independent states, most of them, most of the time, would not have had to be seriously worried about their security, despite what manipulators of public opinion engaged in mustering greater security efforts may have said to the contrary. What "compulsion" there is, then, is a function not merely of the will of others, real or imagined, to destroy the nation's independence but of national desires and ambitions to retain a wealth of other values such as rank, respect, material possessions and special privileges. It would seem to be a fair guess that the efforts for security by a particular nation will tend to vary, other things being equal, with the range of values for which protection is being sought.

In respect to this range there may seem to exist a considerable degree of uniformity. All over the world today peoples are making sacrifices to protect and preserve what to them appear as the minimum national core values, national independence and territorial integrity. But there is deviation in two directions. Some nations seek protection for more marginal values as well. There was a time when United States policy could afford to be concerned mainly with the protection of the foreign investments or markets of its nationals, its "core values" being out of danger, or when Britain was extending its national self to include large and only vaguely circumscribed "regions of special interest." It is a well-known and portentous phenomenon that bases, security zones and the like may be demanded and acquired for the purpose of protecting values acquired earlier; and they then become new national values requiring protection themselves. Pushed to its logical

conclusion, such spatial extension of the range of values does not stop short of world domination. . . .

The lack of uniformity does not end here. A policy is not characterized by its goal, in this case security, alone. In order to become imitable, the means by which the goal is pursued must be taken into account as well. Thus, if two nations were both endeavoring to maximize their security but one were placing all its reliance on armaments and alliances, the other on meticulous neutrality, a policy maker seeking to emulate their behavior would be at a loss where to turn. Those who call for a policy guided by national security are not likely to be unaware of this fact, but they take for granted that they will be understood to mean a security policy based on power, and on military power at that. Were it not so, they would be hard put to prove that their government was not already doing its best for security, though it was seeking to enhance it by such means as international coöperation or by the negotiation of compromise agreements—means which in one instance may be totally ineffective or utopian but which in others may have considerable protective value. . . .

After all that has been said little is left of the sweeping generalization that in actual practice nations, guided by their national security interest, tend to pursue a uniform and therefore imitable policy of security. . . .

The actual behavior of nations, past and present, does not affect the normative proposition, to which we shall now turn our attention. According to this proposition nations are called upon to give priority to national security and thus to consent to any sacrifice of value which will provide an additional increment of security. It may be expedient, moral or both for nations to do so even if they should have failed to heed such advice in the past and for the most part are not living up to it today.

The first question, then, is whether some definable security policy can be said to be generally expedient. Because the choice of goals is not a matter of expediency, it would seem to make no sense to ask whether it is expedient for nations to be concerned with the goal of security itself; only the means used to this end, so it would seem, can be judged as to their fitness—their instrumental rationality—to promote security. Yet, this is not so. Security, like other aims, may be an intermediate rather than an ultimate goal, in which case it can be judged as a means to these more ultimate ends.

Traditionally, the protection and preservation of national core values have been considered ends in themselves, at least by those who followed in the footsteps of Machiavelli or, for other reasons of political philosophy, placed the prince, state or nation at the pinnacle of their hierarchy of values. Those who do so today will be shocked at the mere suggestion that national security should have to be justified in terms of higher values which it is expected to serve. But there is a large and perhaps growing current of opinion—as a matter of fact influential in this country for a long time—which adheres to this idea. We condemn Nazis and Communists for defending their own totalitarian countries instead of helping to free their people from tyranny; we enlist support for armaments, here and in Allied countries, not so much on the grounds that they will protect national security but that by enhancing such security they will serve to protect ultimate human values like individual liberty. Again, opposition in Europe and Asia to military security measures is based in part on the contention that it would help little to make national core values secure, if in the process the liberties and the social welfare of the people had to be sacrificed; the prevention of Russian conquest, some insist, is useless, if in the course of a war of defense a large part of the people were to be exterminated and most cities destroyed. . . .

When one sets out to define in terms of expediency the level of security to which a nation should aspire, one might be tempted to assume that the sky is the limit. Is not insecurity of any kind an evil from which any rational policy maker would want to rescue his country? Yet, there are obvious reasons why this is not so.

In the first place, every increment of security must be paid by additional sacrifices of other values usually of a kind more exacting than the mere expenditure of precious time on the part of policy makers. At a certain point, then, by something like the economic law of diminishing returns, the gain in security no longer compensates for the added costs of attaining it. As in the case of economic value comparisons and preferences, there is frequently disagreement among different layers of policy makers as to where the line should be drawn. This is true particularly because absolute security is out of the question unless a country is capable of world domination, in which case, however, the insecurities and fears would be "internalized" and probably magnified. Because nations must "live dangerously," then, to some extent, whatever they consent to do about it, a modicum of additional but only relative security may easily become unattractive to those who have to bear the chief burden. Nothing renders the task of statesmen in a democracy more difficult than the reluctance of the people to follow them very far along the road to high and costly security levels.

In the second place, national security policies when based on the accumulation of power have a way of defeating themselves if the target level is set too high. This is due to the fact that "power of resistance" cannot be unmistakably distinguished from "power of aggression." What a country does to bolster its own security through power can be interpreted by others, therefore, as a threat to their security. If this occurs, the vicious circle of what John Herz has described as the "security dilemma" sets in: the efforts of one side provoke countermeasures by the other which in turn tend to wipe out the gains of the first. Theoretically there seems to be no escape from this frustrating consequence; in practice, however, there are ways to convince those who might feel threatened that the accumulation of power is not intended and will never be used for attack. The chief way is that of keeping the target level within moderate bounds and of avoiding placing oneself in a position where it has to be raised suddenly and drastically. The desire to escape from this vicious circle presupposes a security policy of much self-restraint and moderation, especially in the choice of the target level. It can never be expedient to pursue a security policy which by the fact of provocation or incentive to others fails to increase the nation's relative power position and capability of resistance. . . .

The reason why "power of resistance" is not the general panacea which some believe it to be lies in the nature of security itself. If security, in the objective sense of the term at least, rises and falls with the presence or absence of aggressive intentions on the part of others, the attitude and behavior of those from whom the threat emanates are of prime importance. Such attitude and behavior need not be beyond the realm of influence by the country seeking to bolster its security. Whenever they do not lie beyond this realm the most effective and least costly security policy consists in inducing the opponent to give up his aggressive intentions.

While there is no easy way to determine when means can and should be used which are directed not at resistance but at the prevention of the desire of others to attack, it will clarify the issue to sketch the type of hypotheses which would link specific security policies, as expedient, to some of the most typical political constellations.

One can think of nations lined up between the two poles of maximum and minimum "attack propensity," with those unalterably committed to attack, provided it promises success, at one pole and those whom no amount of opportunity for successful attack could induce to undertake it at the other. While security in respect to the first group can come exclusively as a result of "positions of strength" sufficient to deter or defeat attack, nothing could do more to undermine security in respect to the second group than to start accumulating power of a kind which would provoke fear and countermoves.

Unfortunately it can never be known with certainty, in practice, what position within the continuum one's opponent actually occupies. Statesmen cannot be blamed, moreover, if caution and suspicion lead them to assume a closer proximity to the first pole than hindsight proves to have been justified. We believe we have ample proof that the Soviet Union today is at or very close to the first pole, while Canadian policy makers probably place the United States in its intentions toward Canada at the second pole.

It is fair to assume that, wherever the issue of security becomes a matter of serious concern, statesmen will usually be dealing with potential opponents who occupy a position somewhere between but much closer to the first of the two poles. This means, then, that an attack must be feared as a possibility, even though the intention to launch it cannot be considered to have crystallized to the point where nothing could change it. If this be true, a security policy in order to be expedient cannot avoid accumulating power of resistance and yet cannot let it go at that. Efforts have to be made simultaneously toward the goal of removing the incentives to attack. This is only another way of saying that security policy must seek to bring opponents to occupy a position as close to the second pole as conditions and capabilities permit.

Such a twofold policy presents the greatest dilemmas because efforts to change the intentions of an opponent may run counter to the efforts to build up strength against him. The dangers of any policy of concessions, symbolized by "Munich," cannot be underestimated. The paradox of this situation must be faced, however, if security policy is to be expedient. It implies that national security policy, except when directed against a country unalterably committed to attack, is the more rational the more it succeeds in taking the interests, including the security interests, of the other side into consideration. Only in doing so can it hope to minimize the willingness of the other to resort to violence. Rather than to insist, then, that under all conditions security be sought by reliance on nothing but defensive power and be pushed in a spirit of national selfishness toward the highest targets, it should be stressed that in most instances efforts to satisfy legitimate demands of others are likely to promise better results in terms of security. . . .

We can now focus our attention on the moral issue, if such there be. Those who advocate a policy devoted to national security are not always aware of the fact—if they do not explicitly deny it—that they are passing moral judgment when they advise a nation to pursue the goal of national security or when they insist that such means as the accumulation of coercive power—or its use—should be employed for this purpose.

Nations like individuals or other groups may value things not because they consider them good or less evil than their alternative; they may value them because they satisfy their pride, heighten their sense of self-esteem or reduce their fears. However, no policy, or human act in general, can escape becoming a subject for moral judgment—whether by the conscience of the actor himself or by others—which calls for the sacrifice of other values, as any security policy is bound to do. Here is becomes a matter of comparing and weighing values in order to decide which of them are deemed sufficiently good to justify the evil of sacrificing others. If someone insists that his country should do more to build up its strength, he is implying, knowingly or not, that more security is sufficiently desirable to warrant such evils as the cut in much-needed social welfare benefits or as the extension of the period of military service. . . .

The moral issue will be resolved in one of several ways depending on the ethical code upon which the decision is based. From one extreme point of view it is argued that every sacrifice, especially if imposed on other nations, is justified provided it contributes in any way to national security. Clearly this implies a position that places national security at the apex of the value pyramid and assumes it to constitute an absolute good to which all other values must be subordinated. Few will be found to take this position because if they subscribed to a nationalistic ethics of this extreme type they would probably go beyond security—the mere preservation of values—and insist that the nation is justified in conquering whatever it can use as *Lebensraum* or otherwise. At the opposite extreme are the absolute pacifists who consider the use of coercive power an absolute evil and condemn any security policy, therefore, which places reliance on such power.

For anyone who does not share these extreme views the moral issue raised by the quest for national security is anything but clear-cut and simple. He should have no doubts about the right of a nation to protect and preserve values to which it has a legitimate title or even about its moral duty to pursue a policy meant to serve such preservation. But he cannot consider security the supreme law as Machiavelli would have the statesmen regard the *ragione di stato*. Somewhere a line is drawn, which in every instance he must seek to discover, that divides the realm of neglect, the "too-little," from the realm of excess, the "too-much." Even Hans Morgenthau who extols the moral duty of self-preservation seems to take

it for granted that naked force shall be used for security in reaction only to violent attack, not for preventive war.

Decision makers are faced with the moral problem, then, of choosing first the values which deserve protection, with national independence ranking high not merely for its own sake but for the guarantee it may offer to values like liberty, justice and peace. He must further decide which level of security to make his target. This will frequently be his most difficult moral task though terms such as adequacy or fair share indicate the kind of standards that may guide him. Finally, he must choose the means and thus by scrupulous computation of values compare the sacrifices, which his choice of means implies, with the security they promise to provide.

It follows that policies of national security, far from being all good or all evil, may be morally praiseworthy or condemnable depending on their specific character and the particular circumstances of the case. They may be praised for their self-restraint and the consideration which this implies for values other than security; they may instead be condemned for being inadequate to protect national values. Again, they may be praised in one instance for the consideration given to the interests of others, particularly of weaker nations, or condemned in another because of the recklessness with which national values are risked on the altar of some chimera. The target level falls under moral judgment for being too ambitious, egotistical and provocative or for being inadequate; the means employed for being unnecessarily costly in other values or for being ineffective. This wide range of variety which arises out of the multitude of variables affecting the value computation would make it impossible, and in fact meaningless, to pass moral judgment, positive or negative, on "national security policy in general."

It is this lack of moral homogeneity which in matters of security policy justifies attacks on so-called moralism, though not on moral evaluation. The "moralistic approach" is taken to mean a wholesale condemnation either of any concern with national security—as being an expression of national egotism—or of a security policy relying on coercive and therefore evil power. The exponent of such "moralism" is assumed to believe that security for all peoples can be had today by the exclusive use of such "good" and altruistic means as model behavior and persuasion, a spirit of conciliation, international organization or world government. If there are any utopians who cling to this notion, and have influence on policy, it makes sense to continue to disabuse them of what can surely be proved to be dangerous illusions.

It is worth emphasizing, however, that the opposite line of argument, which without regard for the special circumstances would praise everything done for national security or more particularly everything done for the enhancement of national power of resistance, is no less guilty of applying simple and abstract moral principles and of failing to judge each case realistically on its merits.

In conclusion, it can be said, then, that normative admonitions to conduct a foreign policy guided by the national security interest are no less ambiguous and misleading than the statement of fact concerning past behavior which was discussed earlier. In order to be meaningful such admonitions would have to specify the degree of security which a nation shall aspire to attain and the means by which it is to be attained in a given situation. It may be good advice in one instance to appeal for greater effort and more armaments; it may be no less expedient and morally advisable in another instance to call for moderation and for greater reliance on means other than coercive power. Because the pendulum of public opinion swings so easily from extreme complacency to extreme apprehension, from utopian reliance on "good will" to disillusioned faith in naked force only, it is particularly important to be wary of any simple panacea, even of one that parades in the realist garb of a policy guided solely by the national security interest.

18. Decision-Making as an Approach to the Study of International Politics

Richard C. Snyder, H.W. Bruck, and Burton Sapin

"THE STATE AS ACTOR IN A SITUATION"
This diagram will serve as a partial indication of
the fundamental approach adopted in this essay.
A complete analysis of the diagram and its major
implications must be reserved for the longer
monograph.

Commentary

1. The first aspect of this diagrammatic
presentation of an analytical scheme is the *assumption* that the most effective way to gain perspective on international politics and to find ways
of grasping the complex determinants of state behavior is to pitch the analysis on the level of *any
state*. An understanding of *all* states is to be
founded on an understanding of *any one* state
through the use of a scheme which will permit

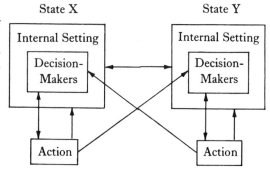

FIGURE 5.1

the analytical construction of properties of action
which will be shared in common by all specific
states. That is, the model is a fictional state whose
characteristics are such as to enable us to say
certain things about all real states regardless of
how different they may appear to be in some
ways. Therefore, if the scheme is moderately successful, we should be able to lay the foundation
for analyzing the impact of cultural values on
British foreign policy and on Soviet foreign policy

even though the values are different in each case and produce quite different consequences. "State X," then, stands for all states or for any one state. We have rejected the assumption that two different analytical schemes are required simply because two states behave differently.

It should be added immediately that theoretical progress in the study of international politics will require eventually a *typology* of states based on basic political organization, range of decision-making systems, strengths and weaknesses of decision-making systems, and types of foreign policy strategies employed. This will facilitate comparison, of course, but it will also make it possible to take into account certain significant differences among states while at the same time analyzing the behavior of all states in essentially the same way.

2.   We are also assuming that the nation-state is going to be the significant unit of political action for many years to come. Strategies of action and commitment of resources will continue to be decided at the national level. This assumption is made on grounds of analytical convenience and is not an expression of preference by the authors. Nor does it blind us to the development or existence of supranational forces and organizations. The basic question is solely how the latter are to be treated. We prefer to view the United Nations as a special mode of interaction in which the identity and policy-making capacity of individual national states are preserved but subject to different conditioning factors. The collective action of the United Nations can hardly be explained without reference to actions in various capitals.

3.   The phrase "state as actor in a situation" is designed primarily as a shorthand device to alert us to certain perspectives while still adhering to the notion of the state as a collectivity. Explicit mention must be made of our employment of action analysis and (both here and in the detailed treatment of decision-making) *of some of the vocabulary* of the now well-known Parsons-Shils scheme. We emphasize vocabulary for two reasons. First, as new schemes of social analysis are developed (mostly outside of political science), there is a great temptation to apply such schemes quickly, one result being the use of new words without comprehension of the theoretical

system of which they are a part. Second, we have rejected a general application of the Parsons-Shils approach as an organizing concept—for reasons which will emerge later. At this point we may simply note that our intellectual borrowings regarding fundamental questions of method owe much more to the works of Alfred Schuetz.

Basically, action exists (analytically) when the following components can be ascertained: actor (or actors), goals, means, and situation. The situation is defined by the actor (or actors) in terms of the way the actor (or actors) relates himself to other actors, to possible goals, and to possible means, and in terms of the way means and ends are formed into strategies of action subject to relevant factors in the situation. These ways of relating himself to the situation (and thus of defining it) will depend on the nature of the actor—or his orientations. Thus, "state X" mentioned above may be regarded as a participant in an action system comprising other actors; state X is the focus of the observer's attention. State X orients to action according to the manner in which the particular situation is viewed by certain officials and according to what they want. The actions of other actors, the actor's goals and means, and the other components of the situation are related meaningfully by the actor. His action flows from his definition of the situation.

4.   We need to carry the actor-situation scheme one step further in an effort to rid ourselves of the troublesome abstraction "state." It is one of our basic methodological choices to define the state as its official decision-makers—those whose authoritative acts are, to all intents and purposes, the acts of the state. *State action is the action taken by those acting in the name of the state.* Hence, the state is its decision-makers. State X as *actor* is translated into its decision-makers as actors. It is also one of our basic choices to take as our prime analytical objective the re-creation of the "world" of the decision-makers as *they* view it. The manner in which *they* define situations becomes another way of saying how the state is oriented to action and why. This is a quite different approach from trying to recreate the situation and interpretation of it *objectively*, that is, by the observer's judgment rather than that of the actors themselves.

To focus on the individual actors who are the state's decision-makers and to reconstruct the situation as defined by the decision-makers requires, of course, that a central place be given to the analysis of the behavior of these officials. One major significance of the diagram is that it calls attention to the sources of state action and to the essentially subjective (that is, from the standpoint of the decision-makers) nature of our perspective.

5.   Now let us try to clarify a little further. We have said that the key to the explanation of why the state behaves the way it does lies in the way its decision-makers as actors define their situation. *The definition of the situation* is built around the projected action as well as the reasons for the action. Therefore, it is necessary to analyze the actors (the official decision-makers) in the following terms: (a) their *discrimination* and *relating* of objects, conditions, and other actors—various things are perceived or expected in a relational context; (b) the existence, establishment, or definition of *goals*—various things are wanted from the situation; (c) attachment of *significance* to various courses of action suggested by the situation according to some criteria of estimation; and (d) application of *"standards of acceptability"* which (1) narrow the range of perceptions, (2) narrow the range of objects wanted, and (3) narrow the number of alternatives.

Three features of all orientations emerge: *perception, choice,* and *expectation.*

Perhaps a translation of the vocabulary of action theory will be useful. We are saying that the actors' orientations to action are reconstructed when the following kinds of questions are answered: what did the decision-makers think was relevant in a particular situation? how did they determine this? how were the relevant factors related to each other—what connections did the decision-makers see between diverse elements in the situation? how did they establish the connections? what wants and needs were deemed involved in or affected by the situation? what were the sources of these wants and needs? how were they related to the situation? what specific or general goals were considered and selected? what courses of action were deemed fitting and effective? how were fitness and effectiveness decided?

6.   We have defined international politics as processes of state interaction at the governmental level. However, there are nongovernmental factors and relationships which must be taken into account by any system of analysis, and there are obviously nongovernmental effects of state action. Domestic politics, the nonhuman environment, cross-cultural and social relationships are important in this connection. We have chosen to group such factors under the concept of *setting.* This is an analytic term which reminds us that the decision-makers act upon and respond to conditions and factors which exist outside themselves and the governmental organization of which they are a part. Setting has two aspects: *external* and *internal.* We have deliberately chosen setting instead of environment because the latter term is either too inclusive or has a technical meaning in other sciences. Setting is really a set of categories of *potentially relevant factors and conditions* which may affect the action of any state.

External setting refers, in general, to such factors and conditions beyond the territorial boundaries of the state—the actions and reactions of other states (their decision-makers), the societies for which they act, and the physical world. Relevance of particular factors and conditions *in general* and *in particular situations* will depend on the attitudes, perceptions, judgments, and purposes of state X's decision-makers, that is, on how they react to various stimuli. It should be noted that our conception of setting does *not* exclude certain so-called environmental limitations such as the state of technology, morbidity ratio, and so on, which *may* limit the achievement of objectives or which *may* otherwise become part of the conditions of action *irrespective* of *whether* and *how* the decision-makers perceive them. However—and this is important—this does not in our scheme imply the substitution of an omniscient observer's judgment for that of the decision-maker. Setting is an analytical device to suggest certain enduring kinds of relevances and to limit the number of nongovernmental factors with which the student of international politics must be concerned. The external setting is constantly changing and will be composed of *what the decision-makers decide is important.* This "deciding'' can mean simply that certain lacks—such as minerals or guns—not imposed on them, that is, must be *accepted*. A serious native revolt in South Africa in 1900 was not a feature of the external setting of United States decision-makers; it would be in 1963. Compare, too, the relatively minor impact of Soviet foreign activities on the United States decision-makers in the period of 1927 to 1933 with the present impact.

Usually the factors and conditions referred to by the term *internal setting* are loosely labeled ''domestic politics,'' ''public opinion,'' or ''geographical position.'' A somewhat more adequate formulation might be: some clues to the way any state behaves toward the world must be sought in the way its society is organized and functions, in the character and behavior of its people, and in its physical habitat. The list of categories under B [see figure 5.2] may be somewhat unfamiliar. There are two reasons for insisting that the analysis of the society for which state X acts be pushed to this fundamental level. First, the list invites attention to a much wider range of potentially relevant factors than the more familiar terms like morale, attitudes, national power, party politics, and so on. For example, the problem of vulnerability to subversive attack is rarely discussed by political scientists in terms of the basic social structure of a particular nation, that is, in terms of B3. Nor is the recruitment of manpower often connected with the way the roles of the sexes are differentiated in a society. Second, if one is interested in the fundamental ''why'' of state behavior, the search for reliable answers must go beyond the *derived* conditions and factors (morale, pressure groups, production, attitudes, and so on) which are normally the focus of attention.

7.   The diagram suggests another important point. Line BC is a two-way arrow connoting rightly an interaction between social organization and behavior on the one hand and decision-making on the other. Among other things this arrow represents the impact of domestic social forces on the formulation and execution of foreign policy. BC implies that the influence of conditions and factors in the society is felt through the decision-making process. But line DB is also impor-

tant because it indicates that a nation experiences its own external actions. State action is designed primarily to alter factors and behavior or to otherwise affect conditions in the external setting, yet it may have equally serious consequences for the society itself. We need only suggest the range of possibilities here. Extensive foreign relations may enhance the power of the central government relative to other regulatory institutions. Particular programs may contribute to the redistribution of resources, income, and social power. For example, the outpouring of billions in foreign aid by the United States since 1945 has contributed to the increased power and influence of scientists, military leaders, engineers, and the managerial group. The people of a state experience foreign policy in other ways—they may feel satisfaction, alarm, guilt, exhilaration, or doubt about it. There will be nongovernmental *interpretations*— perhaps several major ones—shared by various members or groups of the society. Such interpretations may or may not be identical with the prevailing official interpretation. There will also be nongovernmental expectations concerning state action which, again, may or may not correspond to official expectations. Discrepancies between nongovernmental and governmental interpretations and expectations may have important ramifications. For one thing, public support and confidence may be undermined if state action produces consequences which fundamentally violate public expectations.

The point to be made here is that the diagrammatic expression of our scheme shows that the impact of domestic social factors (line BCD) must be viewed also as a part of a larger feedback process as indicated by line BCDBC.

8.   Another significant set of relationships emerges from the diagram in line ABE. The external and internal settings are related to each other. Among others, two implications may be stressed here. First, because we have defined international politics as interaction process at the governmental level, it may appear that we are making the focus unduly narrow, thus ignoring a whole host of private, nongovernmental interactions. Nothing could be further from the truth. Societies interact with each other in a wide range

of ways through an intricate network of communications—trade, family ties, professional associations, shared values, cultural exchanges, travel, mass media, and migration. While all of these patterns may be subject to governmental regulation (in some form), they *may* have very little to do with the origins and forms of state action. At any rate, the question of the political significance of intersocietal, intercultural, nongovernmental interactions requires an analytical scheme which will make possible some understanding of how such interactions condition official action. This in turn requires a much more systematic description of interactions than we now have, plus a way of accounting for their connection with state action.

One can, however, study the interactions connoted by line ABE for their own sake with only a slight interest in their political aspects. In this case, it seems proper to say that the focus is international relations rather than international politics.

Nongovernmental international relations do not enter the analysis of state behavior *unless* it can be shown that the behavior of the decision-makers is in some manner determined by or directed toward such relations. For example, assume a bitter, hostile campaign against a foreign government by powerful United States newspapers and assume the campaign is well publicized in the other nation. By itself this would constitute an asymmetrical interaction between two societies. It would not become a matter of state interaction unless or until the following happened: (a) an official protest to the U.S. State Department by the foreign government; (b) retaliation against United States citizens in the foreign country; (c) disturbance of negotiations between the two governments on quite another issue; (d) arousal of public opinion in the foreign country to the point where the effectiveness of United States policies toward that country was seriously affected; (e) the pressure generated by the campaign in the United States caused the decision-makers to modify their actions and reactions vis-à-vis the other state; (f) the United States government officially repudiated the criticism and apologized to the

other government. This same *kind* of argument would hold for all types of nongovernmental relations except that there would be varying degrees of directness (that is, change in intersocietal relations $\rightarrow$ change in state action) and indirectness (that is, change in intersocietal relations $\rightarrow$ change in social organization and behavior $\rightarrow$ derived condition or factor $\rightarrow$ change in state action) and therefore different time-sequences.

Second, while the most obvious consequences of state action are to be looked for in the reactions of other states along the lines CDE4C in the diagram, changes in the external setting can influence state action along the lines CDE3A3BC, that is, indirectly through changes in nongovernmental relations which ultimately are recognized and taken into account by the decision-makers.

9.   To get back to the center of the diagram, it should be noted that CD is a two-way arrow. The rest of this essay is concerned with the nature of decision-making, but it can be said here that in addition to the feedback relationships CDBC and CDE3A3, DC connotes a direct feedback from an awareness by the decision-makers of their own action and from assessments of the progress of action. This is to say that state action has an impact on decision-making apart from subsequent reactions of other states and apart from effects mediated through the state's social organization and behavior.

10.   So far as this diagram is concerned, most attention in the field of international politics is paid to interactions CDE4CD. CD represents action(s); DE (particularly DE4) represents consequences for, or impact upon, the external setting; EC represents new conditions or stimuli—reactions or new actions (E4C). Therefore, CDECD represents the action-reaction-interaction sequence.

Obviously these lines stand for a wide range of relationships and kinds of action. What should be emphasized here is that interactions can be really understood fully only in terms of the decision-making responses of states to situations, problems, and the actions of other states. The combination of interaction and decision-making can be diagrammed as:

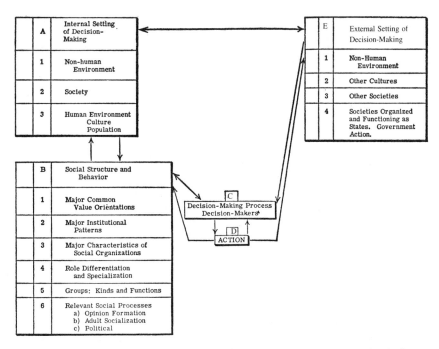

FIGURE 5.2 State "X" as Actor in a Situation (Situation is comprised of a combination of selectively relevant factors in the external and internal setting as interpreted by the decision-makers.)

Naturally if one thinks of all the separate actions and reactions, and all the combinations involved in the governmental relationships between one state and all others, it seems unrealistic and somewhat absurd to let a few lines on a diagram represent so much. Indeed, all would be lost unless one could speak of *patterns* and *systems*. Patterns refer to *uniformities* and *persistence* of actions and sets of relationships. "Nationalism," "imperialism," "internationalism," "aggression," "isolationism," "peace," "war," "conflict," and "cooperation" are familiar ways of characterizing kinds of actions and reactions as well as patterned relationships among states. These terms are, of course, both descriptive and judgmental—they are shorthand expressions covering complicated phenomena and also may imply approval or disapproval, goodness or badness.

System in this context refers to the modes, rules, and nature of reciprocal influence which structure the interaction between states. Five kinds of system—there are others—may be mentioned: *coalitions* (temporary and permanent); *supranational organization; bilateral; multilateral* (unorganized); and *ordination-subordination* (imperial relationships and satellites). Once again, the way these interactions and relationships arise and the particular form or substance they take would seem to be explainable in terms of the way the decision-makers in the participating political organisms "define their situation." As we have said elsewhere there seem to be only two ways of scientifically studying international politics: (1) the description and measurement of interaction; and (2) decision-making—the formulation and execution of policy. Interaction patterns can be studied by themselves without reference to decision-making except that the "why" of the patterns cannot be answered.

Summary

To conclude this brief commentary, it may be said that the diagram . . . is designed in the first instance to portray graphically the basic perspectives of our frame of reference: *any* state as a way of saying something about *all* states; the central position of the decision-making focus; and the integration of a wide range of factors which may explain state action, reaction, and interaction.

The lines of the diagram carry *two* suggestive functions. First, they alert the observer to possible (known and hypothetical) relationships among empirical factors. Thus, the diagram simultaneously invites attention to three interrelated, intersecting empirical processes—state interaction (CDEC) at the governmental level, intersocietal interaction (ABE) at the nongovernmental level, and intrasocietal interaction (BCDB) at both the governmental and nongovernmental level. These processes arise, to put the matter another way, from decision-makers interacting with factors which constitute the dual setting, from state interaction as normally conceived, and from the factors which constitute internal and external settings acting upon each other.

Second, the diagram is intended to suggest possible analytic and theoretical relationships as well. The boxes indicate ways of specifying the relevant factors in state behavior through the employment of certain concepts—decision-making, action, setting, situation, society, culture, and so on—which provide, if they are successfully developed, criteria of relevance and ways of handling the empirical phenomena and their interrelationships. There are in existence a large number of tested and untested hypotheses, general and "middle range" theories, applicable within each of the categories comprising the diagram. The central concept of decision-making may provide a basis for linking a group of theories which hitherto have been applicable only to a segment of international politics or have not been susceptible of application at all. We may cite two examples. The concept of culture is clearly suggested by A2, B2, and E2 which specify empirical phenomena branded analytically as cultural in the technical sense. Based on this important social science concept is the derived concept of National Character—typical behavior patterns uniquely (or allegedly so) characteristic of one nation. Suggestive as national character analysis has been, it has been thus far impossible to bridge the analytic gap between behavior patterns at the cultural level and state action on the governmental level. Communication theory (really a cluster of related theories) has been applied almost exclusively to mass media (B6) and to techniques of state action (D). Only recently has an attempt been made to apply recent developments in communication theory to intersocietal interaction and to decision-making. . . .

RECAPITULATION

We began the brief exposition of our frame of reference by stating our conviction that the analysis of international politics should be centered, in part, on the behavior of those whose action is the action of the state, namely, the decision-makers. We insisted, further, that state action grew out of and was embodied in the "definition of the situation" by the decision-makers. Finally, we have attempted to demonstrate that the definition of the situation resulted from a decision-making process which took place within a decisional unit. In our scheme, decision-making is accounted for in terms of the activities and relationships of the members of the unit. The unit is viewed as functioning in an internal and external setting. . . .

19. Simulation and "Reality": Validity Research

HAROLD GUETZKOW AND JOSEPH J. VALADEZ

. . . A simulated construction is but theory. It provides no shortcut or magical route to the "proof" of the validity of the verbal and mathematical components it contains. Thus, there is a need for a systematic examination of the extent of the congruences between empirical analyses of world processes and simulations of international relations. This essay attempts such an examination.

It is still convenient to employ the definition of simulation of behavioral processes written some years ago: "an operating representation, in reduced and/or simplified form, of relations among social units (or entities) by means of symbolic and/or replicate component parts" (Guetzkow, 1959: 184).

Within the perspective that simulation is operating theory, let us proceed with our central task: To what extent are simulations of international processes being verified? . . .

INTER-NATION SIMULATION

"Decision-Makers and Their Nations"

In considering "Decision-Makers and Their Nations," it is convenient first to discuss individuals serving in the INS as surrogates for the decision-makers of the world. Attention will be given next to these humans assembled in groups, along with the political, economic, and military programs which function together as representations of the nation-state.

Humans as Surrogates. Because of the difficulties involved in programming the decision-making within a nation, given the present de-

Excerpted from Harold Guetzkow and Joseph J. Valadez, eds. *Simulated International Processes: Theories and Research in Global Modeling* (Beverly Hills, Calif.: Sage Publications, 1981), pp. 253–327. Copyright © 1981 Sage Publications, Inc. Reprinted by permission of the publisher and the authors. This essay is an updated and revised version of Harold Guetzkow's "Some Correspondences between Simulations and 'Realities' in International Relations," in Morton A. Kaplan, ed., *New Approaches in International Relations* (New York: St. Martin's Press, 1968), pp. 202–269. This excerpt contains only some of the findings from INS and none of the more recent findings reported from IPS and SIPER. Footnotes deleted.

velopment of work in "artificial intelligence" (Feigenbaum and Feldman, 1963; Schank and Colby, 1973), humans are used in the Inter-Nation Simulation to handle these activities. . . .

PERSONAL CHARACTERISTICS. Perhaps the most focused evidence available on the impact of personal style on outputs from the humans who constitute the decision-making units within the Inter-Nation Simulation is presented by Michael J. Driver (1965, 1977) in his essays, "A Structure Analysis of Aggression, Stress, and Personality in an Inter-Nation Simulation" and "Individual Differences as Determinants of Aggression in the Inter-Nation Simulation." Richard A. Brody (1963) and Driver selected 336 participants for their sixteen runs of the simulation on the basis of each individual's cognitive simplicity/complexity. Driver found that outputs of the high school seniors and graduates who served as his decision-makers conformed to the findings obtained in many other situations (Harvey et al., 1961; Schroder et al., 1967). Driver (1977: Table 13.1; 342) noted how those surrogates with simpler conceptual structures, as determined on a pretest, tended to involve their nations in more aggressive behavior than did those with more complex, abstract conceptual structures ($\chi^2 = 7.1**^3$ ρ <.005; correspondence rating: much).

This same characteristic was investigated by Hermann et al. (1974) in a study of decision-making in response to an unidentified attack. The simulators hypothesized that cognitive complexity of the participating 325 U.S. Naval petty officers would be inversely related to the decision to counterattack a suspected foe. This prediction was found to be consistent with Driver's conclusion that individuals with less complex cognitive structures tend to exhibit more aggressive behavior than the more complex thinkers. The correlation, though in the predicted direction ($\beta = -.13$, $b = -.12$, $s = .15$, $t = .84$, df = 11/27) was weak (correspondence rating: little).

The success of Suedfeld and his associates in adapting the complexity concepts and techniques to historical, archival materials (Suedfeld and Tetlock, 1977; Suedfeld and

Rank, 1976) gives one further confidence in the homomorphy of the simulation and the reference materials offered by Driver and the Hermanns. "Complexity of the messages produced by governmental leaders was significantly lower in crises that ended in war" (Suedfeld and Tetlock, 1977: 169).

The operation of personal characteristics of surrogates within simulations may be pinpointed, too, both in terms of a particular set of personality traits, namely "self-esteem" and "defensiveness," and in terms of a particular situation, namely "crisis." Personal characteristics are related intimately to the way in which individuals handle crises (Basowitz et al., 1955; Funkenstein et al., 1957; Janis, 1958; Lazarus, 1964; and Selye, 1956). Margaret G. Hermann (1965) has replicated aspects of these phenomena (Lazarus and Baker, 1956) concerned with self-esteem and defensiveness in her observations of 163 U.S. Naval petty officers (average age, 32.5 years) who conducted decision-making in eleven replications of a crisis-permeated simulation of policy-making (C. F. Hermann, 1969: Ch. 3). Along with many other outcomes she found that as the simulated crisis produced more negative affect, the decision-makers high in self-esteem and high in defensiveness ("avoiders") decreased their attempts to seek aid from other nations and they decreased their search for information about the threat. Conversely, those low in self-esteem but high in defensiveness ("affiliators") increased their attempts to affiliate and increased their search for information (M. G. Hermann, 1965: 73). . . . The results are statistically significant ($F = 4.37**$; correspondence rating: much).

Self-esteem, independent of defensiveness, has been found to be associated with avoidance behavior (Hermann and Hermann, 1967; Block and Thomas, 1955; Cohen, 1959; Leventhal and Perloe, 1962; Silverman, 1964). Hermann et al. (1974) examined this personality characterisitic in U.S. Naval petty officers as it related to the decision to launch nuclear weapons in response to a simulated unidentified attack. Predicting self-esteem to be inversely related to this decision, the simulators monitored some ten INS runs conducted at the Great Lakes Naval Training Center. Statistical results strongly supported this hypothesis ($\beta = -.35$, b $= -.33$, s $= .13$, t $= 2.56$, df $= 6/32$, p $< .05$; correspondence rating: much; Hermann et al., 1974: 88).

Hermann-like findings corresponding to field and laboratory work reported by Harold M. Schroder et al. (1967) have been obtained in a "tactical game situation" less rich than the Inter-Nation Simulation, in which crisis was created by increasing information loads. Using three measures of information-handling (delegated information searches; self-initiated information searches . . . and integrated utilization of sought-for information in subsequent decision-making), Streufert et al. (1965) obtained statistically significant impact of levels of information load upon information-handling by 185 college students, assembled into fourteen teams serving as decision-makers. And using the same personality measures employed by Driver in his operation with Brody of the Inter-Nation Simulation, the researchers obtained dramatic as well as statistically significant differences in the effects of crisis upon information-handling for those surrogates with structurally complex styles, as contrasted with those with structurally simple styles (. . . correspondence rating: much).

Thus, both in ordinary and in crisis situations within two simulations, the surrogate decision-makers behaved in ways similar to ways other individuals act in field and laboratory studies. In the end, however, it may be expeditious to use surrogates who match particular international actors for work within the Inter-Nation Simulation. An attempt to encompass the entire personality of the participants was made by M. G. Hermann (Hermann and Hermann, 1967) in her use of a semantic differential instrument and the California Psychological Inventory (CPI), which yielded a profile of some thirteen traits in a disguised simulation of the activities within and among the countries that became involved in World War I during the summer of 1914. Working as a clinical psychologist, Hermann prepared personality profiles for each of ten actors who played significant roles in the 1914 crisis, on the basis of personal letters, autobiographical materials, and biographies. Then she matched these profiles to those of potential par-

ticipants, choosing ten from an available population of 101 high school graduates for use as surrogates. The findings from this pilot study are suggestive: One realization with matched participants (M-Run) came closer to producing an output similar to the unfolding of historical events, as they are described by the historian Luigi Albertini (1953), than did a second realization (A-Run), in which another ten surrogates were less well matched than in the M-Run (correspondence rating: some). More definitive validation study covering key personal characteristics of relevance to policy-makers acting in the international scene awaits the production of comparable research in reference materials. . . .

To this point our review of the operation of personal characteristics in the Inter-Nation Simulation has focused on their impact upon the outputs of the surrogates. It is also of interest to know to what extent the very processes producing the consequences are themselves homomorphic to those which create outcomes in the reference system. Are the "right" outputs being produced for the "wrong" reasons? There are three researches of relevance which examine how processes of perception mediate the impact of personal characteristics upon outcomes in the simulation.

1. Studies of President Woodrow Wilson and Secretary of State John Foster Dulles made by other researchers suggested to Michael J. Shapiro that their personal styles exemplified the frequently verified relations between cognitive rigidity and a tendency to perceive conflicts in moral rather than instrumental terms, and also to be relatively unreceptive to change. Using Driver's measures of cognitive style, as derived from the Adorno/California F-Scale and the Schroder/Streufert Situational Interpretation Test (SIT), 1966: Table 1; 10). Shapiro checked whether the same processes held within these Brody-Driver simulations. He found that cognitive rigidity correlated significantly (r $=$ .51** for the F-Scale; r $= .69**$ for SIT) with the extent to which 336 high school students, serving as participants, evaluated environmental stimuli in moral categories, as revealed in coding the messages generated in the course of

the simulation. But he found that neither rigidity measure was correlated with fixity of beliefs and attitudes about decision-makers in other nations (the r's being −.01 and .12, respectively; correspondence rating: some, 1966: Table 2; 12).

2.   Using a model developed by Ledyard Tucker and Samuel L. Messick (1963), Driver (1977) was able to measure changes in the dimensionality of the perceptions of the nations' decision-makers as they moved from ordinary to tense to dangerous situations within the 112 simulated nations in his research with Brody (1963). Corresponding to the findings in laboratory and field situations, including those analyzed in studies of natural disasters (such as panics during fires and floods), Driver noted that the dimensionality of the perceptions of the 336 high school students used as surrogates changed curvilinearly, from simple to more complex to less complex, as the inter-nation situation moved from run-of-the-day interaction through conflict and into war (Schroder et al., 1967: 66–81; Driver, 1977: 353). Driver found that even the content of the framework, in terms of which of the other nations were perceived as similar or different from one another, varied as the distinctions among the nations were made in terms of two to three, and then three to five, and then reduced to two or three dimensions again. For example, Driver (1962: 243) noted that "economic power dimensions are first transformed into military power and finally replaced altogether by alliance concerns as the clouds of war gather" (correspondence rating: much).

3.   In quite a different way, C. F. Hermann obtained findings which converge with those of Driver, and noted that in crisis as compared with noncrisis there was a tendency— slight, but statistically significant—for his petty officers to perceive "events as involving a number of different alternatives or only one or two alternatives" . . . even though content coding revealed no such differences in frequency in alternatives found in messages and conference statements exchanged in the course of the simulation (Hermann, 1969: 171). In his

illustrations from the literature on international crisis behavior of political decision-makers, Hermann listed observations (1969: 161–165) that also are congruent with Driver's findings (correspondence rating: some).

In all three of these sets of findings there is somewhat convergent evidence as to how processes of perception operate within the surrogate decision-makers in realizations of the Inter-Nation Simulation. Two processes are displayed: the correlation of cognitive rigidity with the extent to which participants evaluate environmental stimuli in moral categories, and the tendency toward reduction in the perceived richness of the situation in crisis. The reference data used in making the comparisons with the simulations consisted of case materials, along with anecdotal observations. The evidence samples but limited aspects of perceptual phenomena, even though both ordinary and political decision-makers were compared with the surrogates. A codification of perceptions and misperceptions in international politics was completed by Jervis (1976) after the studies reviewed immediately above were undertaken. Its use of both laboratory experiments and international cases summarizes rich evidence of the common ways in which the "processes of perception" operate in the human, whether the individual is in the (simulation) laboratory or the foreign office. Within these confines, it seems the outputs deriving from the personal charateristics are being produced for at least some of the "right" reasons. . . .

Surrogate Groups and Programs as "Nations." In making an assessment of "decision-makers and their nations," it is useful not only to consider the decision-makers per se, but also to explore how the surrogates function when assembled as decision-making groups, as well as how the consequences of their decisions are programmed as the outputs of their nations. "Individual and group components of the Inter-Nation Simulation are meshed into an operating model through both structured and free, self-developing interactive processes. In general, programmed assumptions are used for setting the foundations of the simulation, serving to provide operating rules for the decision-makers whereby they may handle the political, economic, and military aspects of their nations" (Guetzkow, 1981b: 64). Let us now examine aspects of the validity of the processes within these "nations" in the simulation. In addition to giving attention to the extent of the congruences occurring between simulations and "realities" with respect to the roles, group structures, and internal communication patterns within the decision-making organization involved, we will give an evaluation of the national programs.

ORGANIZATIONAL CHARACTERISTICS: DECISION-MAKING GROUPS AND ROLES THEREIN. In their East Algonian Exercise, Crow and Noel (1977: 400–401) demonstrated the effects of an organizational context upon their decision-makers, at least in one experiment with respect to one output—the level of military response used to control a simulated military insurrection. Those with high-risk preferences tended to respond throughout at a higher level than those with low-risk preferences ($F = 9.27**$, $df = 1/24$). But in both instances, as the individual moved from private decision-making to a situation in which there was a high probability of winning the war and in which he needed to come to consensus with three other "top-level leaders of Algo, all equal in authority and responsibility" (1977: 387), there was a reduction in the level of response ($F = 4.29*$, $df = 1/24$). Some writers about politics (e.g., Acheson, 1960; Neustadt, 1960) believe that a committee system tends "to inhibit innovation, boldness, and creativity with the result that any decision is a consensus or compromise based on the lowest common denominator of agreement" (Crow and Noel, 1977: 396). As Henry Kissinger (1962: 356) speculates, "the system stresses avoidance of risk rather than boldness of conception."

In two of Crow and Noel's other experiments in the East Algonian Exercise, in which military response levels made in the course of rendering individual "pregroup" judgments were compared with the outcomes of group consensus, there were no clear effects of organizational context shown, despite the similarity of these experiments to the one mentioned earlier. In one, there was an interaction effect between the simulated situation and the organizational context, but in a contrary direction. When the opponent was presented as highly aggressive the decision-makers shifted to a significantly ($F = 11.1*$, $df = 1/20$) higher level of military response as a result of group decision—in this experiment, from a level of 7.4 to 9.2 (1977: Table 15.4; 401)—a result contrary to current verbal speculation among students of politics. Yet, such findings are in keeping with results from social psychological experiments by M. A. Wallach and N. Kogan (1965), in which group discussions permit shifts to accept greater risks because "each individual can feel less than proportionally to blame for the possible failure of a risky decision" (Crow and Noel, 1977: 396; correspondence rating: incongruent). Both results may be valued, although there is dissatisfaction with the limitations of both criteria: the unsystematic nature of field observation and the lack of "richness" of the laboratory.

More in line with the results from these social psychological experiments were simulation outputs reported by Hermann et al. (1974: 89). In accordance with Kogan and Wallach's (1967) findings, the simulators expected that group decision-makers were less likely to respond aggressively to an unidentified attack and accept the risk of delay. Statistical analysis of simulation outputs did not contradict this hypothesis that groups mitigate aggressive decision-making ($\beta = -.32$, $b = -.31$, $s = .12$, $t = 2.61$, $p < .05$; correspondence rating: much . . .).

In his simulation study of crises in foreign policy-making, C. F. Hermann (1969) probed the development of consensus within sixty-six decision-making groups comprising eleven runs of an Inter-Nation Simulation with U.S. Naval petty officers as participants (see pp. 261–266). In an "event and decision form," Hermann (1969: 206–207) queried his participants a number of times as to whether a crisis they "recently or are now experiencing" had made the nation's goals "easier/harder to attain," covering such goals as "office-holding," "alliance development," and an ability to "preserve nation as separate unit." Although this experimenter demanded no actual group decision after focused discussion on the matter, as was the case in the East Algonian Exercise conducted by Crow and Noel (1977), crisis induced considerably more consensus, as measured by the agreement among three or four office-holders within each nation that "one or more goals had been made more difficult to attain" (1969: 159). In a set of forty-eight paired samples of crisis versus noncrisis events, consensus existed for two-thirds of the noncrisis situations; the consensus increased significantly ($\chi^2 = 7.2$, p. $= .004$) to 100 percent in the crisis situations (1969: Table 18; 159). In discussing his hypothesis that "In crisis as compared to non-crisis, the frequency of consensus among decision-makers as to the national goals affected by the situation is increased," Hermann (1969: 155–157) indicated that such a tendency toward increased consensus is documented by the general literature on conflict (Mack and Snyder, 1957: 234) and on disaster (Thompson and Hawkes, 1962: 278), and by the specific case studies of U.S. decision-making within the Korean (Snyder and Paige, 1958: 375) and the Cuban (Larson, 1963: 225) crises (correspondence rating: some).

This relationship between crisis conditions and intra-group communication processes was further investigated in the Robinson et al. (1969) study of intervening variables influencing group consensus in two sets of INS simulations—at the Great Lakes Naval Training Station and the Western Behavioral Sciences Institute—and the all-person MIT political game. The acts of searching for information and alternatives are typically characteristic of decision-making (Lasswell, 1956); the simulators expected that the time pressures of crisis situations may inhibit these, thus accelerating group decision. It was suggested that this decision-making may thus be based on a deficient intelligence system. Previous research has reported that one reason the search for alternative courses of action becomes limited in crisis is that decision-makers tend to

be satisfied earlier than during times of stability (Simon, 1957; March, 1962). Though the MIT game produced nonsignificant results ($\chi^2 = .10$, n.s.), both INS studies produced findings corresponding to empirical research suggesting that there is less search for alternative courses of action in crisis (Great Lakes: $\chi^2 = 4.22$, p. $< .05$; WBSI: $\chi^2 = 13.60$, p $< .01$; correspondence rating: much). The number of alternatives open to national leaders is perceived by them to be significantly less in crisis (Snyder and Paige, 1958; Holsti, 1965). This same reduction occurred in the simulation studies (Great Lakes: $\chi^2 = 5.62$, p $< .01$; WBSI: $\chi^2 = 9.77$, p $< .01$). As before, the MIT game exhibited nonsignificant findings ($\chi^2 = .10$, n.s.; correspondence rating: much).

As part of the starting conditions within the Inter-Nation Simulation, roles are designated within each group responsible for the nation's decision-making—a procedure which contrasts with the usual RAND/MIT practice of having each "team" work without assigned activities for any participant in their political-military exercises. In this way, an attempt is made within INS to induce a "division of labor" among the participants so that each position gains its perspective, as commonly occurs in roles found in bureaucracies (Katz and Kahn, 1966: Ch. 7, 171–198). Thus, the group as a surrogate tends to function less as a small, "face-to-face" group, instead taking on some characteristics of an organization (Guetzkow and Bowes, 1957).

Druckman's (1965, 1968) study of ethnocentrism indicated that tendencies toward "bias" as found in laboratory and field studies (Rosenblatt, 1964) occur among the roles within the simulation. For example, those in low status roles within the simulated executive decision-making groups in WINSAFE II (Raser and Crow, 1964), especially the marginal decision-maker who was aspiring to office, were found to be "most favorably disposed toward the in-group and least favorably disposed toward all out-groups, allies and enemies" (Druckman, 1968: 62). Likewise, following observations made by Gordon Allport, Leonard Berkowitz, Robert

Hamblin, and George Homans, Druckman (1968: 61) theorized that "the role with the most international contacts with opposite members of equal status . . . should be least ethnocentric." Druckman found that "the foreign minister or external decision-maker was the least ethnocentric role" (1965: 124–125; cf. Druckman, 1968: 62). The external decision-maker rated his own group least favorably and the out-group's allies and enemies most favorably (correspondence rating: much). Thus, role differentiations in the Inter-Nation Simulation may be homomorphic to those which occur in government offices handling decision-making for countries within the international system, although there is no direct evidence on this matter from a study (Argyris, 1967) made within the U.S. Department of State. . . .

EPILOG

Given the barefoot quality of our assessments of correspondences between outcomes of the simulations and the reference materials, it is easy to realize that our listing of congruences is but a first step in the task of making adequate estimates of the validities involved. In the perspective of a sophisticated philosophical analysis, "the confirmation of scientific hypotheses" by one of Reichenbach's students, in which both Popper and Hanson's seemingly contradictory stances are reconciled within a Bayesian framework, it is reassuring to note that "logically prior to the use of Bayes's theorem some generalizations must have been established through induction and enumeration. These are hypotheses based upon crude inductive generalization, but they constitute the logical starting point. Each of them is rather shaky, owing to the childish quality of the induction by enumeration which supports it, but the more sophisticated inferences that follow can be well founded. As evidence accumulates and further inductions are made, the results become more and more securely established" (Salmon, 1967: 131–132). It is to be hoped that others will join in meeting the exciting challenges posed by our

validity problems, moving beyond mere enumeration.

Now that we have apparently entered an era in which the construction and application of simulations is blooming, might this not also be the time to refine methods with which our as yet coarse models might increase in validity? Following completion of the project on Simulated International Processes (see Guetzkow, 1981a), a second project, Computer Simulations for Decision-Making in International Affairs (CSDMIA), commenced at Northwestern University to move in this direction. Through construction of modular simulations, various components of international relations processes can be individually formulated and refined. "Once analyzed, these 'mini-modules' are specified as computer simulation modules operable both independently and within the context of a more comprehensive simulation framework, i.e., Bremer's SIPER" (Guetzkow et al., 1977: 6). Each mini-simulation constitutes a mini-theory; through experimentation each may be individually refined. Will such an effort increase the overall validity of the entire simulation, despite Bremer's difficulty in his utilization of a somewhat comparable strategy in the economic realm of SIPER?

Improvements and extensions of extant simulations, however, depend upon how well our colleagues assume the burdens of validating their work. To date, emphasis among simulation builders has been more upon the venture of model construction, with the scholar working as an artist, rather than upon involvement in checking correspondences between the simulations and their respective reference systems, as is incumbent upon the scholar who works as a social scientist or policy-influencer. This obligation, however, does not belong solely to the simulator. As Morton Gorden (1967) pointed out, the verbal theorist shares in the same obligations. When simulator and verbal theorist ground their work in empirical materials, then they may fruitfully join hands with mathematical and simulation theorists in constructing homomorphic models of the international system which will have fidelity. Then their constructions will represent the world more adequately, as it is now and as it may evolve with simulated alternative futures, unfolding the "realities" of the decades ahead.

REFERENCES

ACHESON, D. G. 1960. The President and the Secretary of State. In D. K. Price, ed., *The Secretary of State*. Englewood Cliffs, N.J.: Prentice-Hall, Inc.

ALBERTINI, L. 1953. *The Origins of the War of 1914*. Ed. and trans. by I. M. Massy. London: Oxford University Press.

ARGYRIS, C. 1967. *Some Causes of Organizational Ineffectiveness Within the Department of State*. Washington, D.C.: Government Printing Office (for the Center for International Systems Research; DS Publication 8180).

BASOWITZ, H., H. PERSKY, S. KORCHIN, and R. GRINKER. 1955. *Anxiety and Stress*. New York: McGraw-Hill.

BLOCK, J., AND H. THOMAS. 1955. Is satisfaction with self a measure of adjustment? *Journal of Abnormal and Social Psychology* 51: 254–259.

*BRODY, R. A. 1963. Some systemic effects of the spread of nuclear-weapons technology: A study through simulation of a multinuclear future. *Journal of Conflict Resolution* 7(4): 663–753.

COHEN, A. R. 1959. Situation structure, self-esteem, and threat-oriented reactions to power. In D. Cartwright, ed. *Studies in Social Power*. Ann Arbor: University of Michigan Press.

CROW, W. J., AND R. NOEL. 1977. An experiment in simulated historical decision-making. In M. G. Hermann with T. Milburn, eds., *A Psychological Examination of Political Leaders*, pp. 385–405. New York: Macmillan.

*DRIVER, M. J. 1962. Conceptual structure and group processes in an Inter-Nation Simulation, Part 1: 'The perception of simulated nations: A multidimensional analysis of social perceptions as affected by situational stress and characteristic levels of complexity in perceivers,' Ph.D. dissertation, Princeton University.

*——— . 1965. A structure analysis of aggression, stress, and personality in an Inter-Nation Simulation. Paper 97, Institute for Research in the Behavioral, Economic, and Management Sciences, Herman C. Krannert Graduate School of Industrial Administration, Purdue University.

*——— . 1977. Individual differences as determinants of aggression in the Inter-Nation Simulation. In M. G. Hermann with T. Milburn, eds., *A Psychological Examination of Political Leaders*, pp. 337–353. New York: Macmillan.

*DRUCKMAN, D. 1965. Ethnocentric bias in the Inter-Nation Simulation. M.A thesis, Northwestern University.

*——— . 1968. Ethnocentrism in the Inter-Nation Simulation. *Journal of Conflict Resolution* 12 (March): 45–68.

FEIGENBAUM, E. A. AND J. FELDMAN, eds. 1963. *Computers and Thought*. New York: McGraw-Hill.

FUNKENSTEIN, D. H., S. H. KING, AND M. E. DROLETTE. 1957. *Mastery of Stress*. Cambridge, Mass.: Harvard University Press.

*GORDEN, M. 1967. International relations theory in the TEMPER simulation. Evanston, Ill.: Simulated International Processes project, Northwestern University.

*GUETZKOW, H. 1959. A use of simulation in the study of inter-nation relations. *Behavioral Science* 4(3): 183–191.

——— . 1981a. Simulated International Processes: An incomplete history, pp. 13–21 in H. Guetzkow and J. J. Valadez, eds., *Simulated International Processes: Theories and Research in Global Modeling*. Beverly Hills, Calif: Sage.

——— . 1981b. The Inter-Nation Simulation, pp. 23–64 in H. Guetzkow and J. J. Valadez (eds.) *Simulated International Processes: Theories and Research in Global Modeling*. Beverly Hills, Calif.: Sage.

——— AND A. E. BOWES. 1957. The development of organizations in a laboratory. *Management Science* 3: 380–402.

——— , W. L. HOLLIST, AND M. D. WARD. 1977. Computer simulations for decision-making in international affairs: Moving toward consolidation of research in international relations through empirical analysis and computer simulation. *International Peace Research Newsletter* 25/3: 5–13.

HARVEY, O. J., D. E. HUNT, AND H. M. SCHRODER. 1961. *Conceptual Systems and Personality Organization*. New York: John Wiley.

*HERMANN, C. F. 1969. *Crises in Foreign Policy: An Analysis*. Indianapolis: Bobbs-Merrill.

_____, AND M. G. HERMANN. 1967. An attempt to simulate the outbreak of World War I. *American Political Science Review* 61/2: 400–416.

_____, _____, AND R. CANTOR. 1974. Counterattack or delay: Characteristics influencing decision-makers' responses to the simulation of an unidentified attack. *Journal of Conflict Resolution* 18: 75–106.

*HERMANN, M. G. 1965. Stress, self-esteem and defensiveness in an Inter-Nation Simulation. Ph.D. dissertation, Northwestern University.

HOLSTI, O. R. 1965. The 1914 case. *American Political Science Review* 59/2: 365–378.

JANIS, I. L. 1958. *Psychological Stress*. New York: John Wiley.

JERVIS, R. 1976. *Perceptions and Misperceptions in International Politics*. Princeton, N.J.: Princeton University Press.

KATZ, D. AND R. L. KAHN. 1966. *The Social Psychology of Organizations*. New York: John Wiley.

KISSINGER, H. A. 1961. *The Necessity for Choice: Prospects of American Foreign Policy*. New York: Harper & Row.

KOGAN, N. AND M. A. WALLACH. 1967. Risk taking as a function of the situation, the person, and the group. In *New Directions in Psychology*. New York: Holt, Rinehart & Winston.

LARSON, D. L. 1963. *The "Cuban Crisis" of 1962*. Boston: Houghton Mifflin.

LASSWELL, H. D. 1956. *The Decision Process*. College Park, Md.: Bureau of Governmental Research.

LAZARUS, R. S. 1964. A laboratory approach to the dynamics of psychological stress. *American Psychologist* 19: 400–411.

_____ AND R. W. BAKER. 1956 Personality and psychological stress: A theoretical and methodological framework. *Psychology Newsletter* 8: 21–32.

LEVENTHAL, H. AND S. I. PERLOE. 1962. A relationship between self-esteem and persuasibility. *Journal of Abnormal and Social Psychology* 64: 385–388.

MACK, R. W. AND R. C. SNYDER. 1957. The analysis of social conflict: Toward an overview and synthesis. *Journal of Conflict Resolution* 1: 212–248.

MARCH, J. G. 1962. Some recent substantive and methodological developments in theory of organizational decision-making. In A. Ranney, ed., *Essays on the Behavioral Study of Politics*. Urbana: University of Illinois Press.

NEUSTADT, R. 1960. *Presidential Power*. New York: John Wiley.

*RASER, J. R. AND W. J. CROW. 1964. WINSAFE II: An Inter-Nation Simulation study of deterrence postures embodying capacity to delay response. La Jolla, Calif.: Western Behavioral Sciences Institute.

*ROBINSON, J. A., C. F. HERMANN, AND M. G. HERMANN. 1969. Search under crisis in political gaming and simulation. pp. 80–94 in D. G. Pruitt and R. C. Snyder, eds. *Theory and Research on the Causes of War*. Englewood Cliffs, N.J.: Prentice-Hall, Inc.

ROSENBLATT, P. C. 1964. Origins and effects of group ethnocentrism and nationalism. *Journal of Conflict Resolution* 8/2: 131–146.

SALMON, W. C. 1967. *The Foundations of Scientific Inference*. Pittsburgh: University of Pittsburgh Press.

SCHANK, R. C. AND K. M. COLBY, eds. 1973. *Computer Models of Thought and Language*. San Francisco: Freeman.

SCHRODER, H. M., M. J. DRIVER, AND S. STREUFERT. 1967. *Human Information Processing*. New York: Holt, Rinehart & Winston.

*SHAPIRO, M. J. 1966b. Cognitive rigidity and moral judgments in an inter-nation simulation. Evanston, Ill.: Northwestern University.

SILVERMAN, I. 1964. Differential effects of ego threat upon persuasibility for high and low self-esteem subjects. *Journal of Abnormal and Social Psychology* 69: 567–572.

SIMON, H. A. 1957. *Models of Man*. New York: John Wiley.

SNYDER, R. C. AND G. D. PAIGE. 1958. The United States decision to resist aggression in Korea: The application of an analytical scheme. *Administrative Science Quarterly* 3: 341–378.

STREUFERT, S., M. A. CLARDY, M. J. DRIVER, M. KARLINS, H. M. SCHRODER, AND P. SUEDFELD. 1965. A tactical game for the analysis of complex decision-making in individuals and groups. *Psychological Reports* 17: 723–727.

SUEDFELD, P. AND A. D. RANK. 1976. Revolutionary leaders: Long-term success as a function of changes in conceptual complexity. *Journal of Personality and Social Psychology* 34/2: 169–178.

_____, AND P. TETLOCK. 1977. Integrative complexity of communications in international crises. *Journal of Conflict Resolution* 21/1: 169–184.

THOMPSON, J. D. AND R. W. HAWKES. 1962. Disaster, community organization, and administrative process. In G. W. Baker and D. W. Chapman, eds.

Man and Society in Disaster. New York: Basic Books.

TUCKER, L. R. AND S. L. MESSICK. 1963. An individual differences model for multi-dimensional scaling. *Psychometrika* 28/4: 333–367.

WALLACH, M. A. AND N. KOGAN. 1965. The roles of information, discussion, and consensus in group risk taking. *Journal of Experimental Social Psychology* 65: 75–86.

_____

*Asterisked entries are studies involving the Northwestern project on Simulated International Processes.

20. Bureaucratic Politics: A Paradigm and Some Policy Implications

Graham T. Allison and Morton H. Halperin[1]

During the Tet holiday of 1968, North Vietnamese troops launched massive attacks on a large number of South Vietnamese cities. *Why?*

In December 1950, the Chinese Communists intervened in the Korean War. Today some Senators raise the specter of Chinese Communist intervention in the Vietnamese War. Will Communist China intervene in Vietnam? Specifically, if the U.S. were to renew the bombing of North

Excerpted from "Bureaucratic Politics: A Paradigm and Some Policy Implications," by Graham T. Allison and Morton H. Halperin, *World Politics* 24 (Spring 1972), Supplement. Excerpts reprinted by permission of Princeton University Press.

[1]This presentation of a bureaucratic politics approach to foreign policy builds upon previous works of both authors. Specifically, it takes as a point of departure Allison's "Conceptual Models and the Cuban Missile Crisis," *American Political Science Review*, LXIII (September 1970) and *Essence of Decision: Explaining the Cuban Missile Crisis* (Boston 1971); and Halperin's *Bureaucratic Politics and Foreign Policy*, forthcoming. Here we focus on the further development of "Model III," recognizing that organizations can be included as players in the game of bureaucratic politics, treating the factors emphasized by an organizational process approach as constraints, developing the notion of shared attitudes, and introducing a distinction between "decision games" and "action games."

Vietnam with a vengeance, destroying the dikes and closing Haiphong, and South Vietnamese troops were to invade North Vietnam—both unlikely contingencies—would large units of Communist Chinese troops enter the war?

In the mid-1960's, the U.S. put a lid on American strategic weapons: 1000 Minutemen, 54 Titans, and 640 Polaris, and a limited number of bombers. Administration officials announced these limits, recognizing that the Soviets would build up to a position of parity but hoping that Moscow would not go for superiority. If in the mid-1960's a Secretary of Defense had wanted to persuade the Soviet Union not to deploy an ICBM fleet that would seriously threaten U.S. forces, how might he have proceeded?

The first question asks for an explanation; the second for a prediction; the third for a plan. These are three central activities in which both analysts of international politics and makers of foreign policy engage. In response to the first question, most analysts begin by considering various objectives that the North Vietnamese might have had in mind: for example, to shock the American public and thereby affect the presidential election; to collapse the government of South Vietnam; to cause a massive uprising of military and civilians in South Vietnam, thus bringing total victory; or to take the cities and keep them. By examining the problems that Hanoi faced and the character of the action they chose, analysts eliminate some of these aims as implausible. Explanation then consists in constructing a calculation that permits us to understand why, in the particular situation, with certain objections, one would have chosen to launch the Tet offensive. In attempting to predict whether the Communist Chinese will intervene in the Vietnamese War, and if so, in what fashion, most analysts would consider (1) Chinese national security interests in Vietnam, (2) the likelihood of the collapse of the North Vietnamese in the absence of Chinese Communist intervention, (3) the contribution of Chinese Communist troops to the North Vietnamese efforts, and (4) indications of Chinese Communist intentions, for example, warnings to the U.S., pledges to the North Vietnamese, statements about Chinese interests, etc. These considerations would then be combined in some intuitive fashion to yield a prediction. In recommending U.S. actions to persuade the Soviets to stop with rough parity, and not to push for "superiority," many analysts would have focused on Soviet national security interests. They would then consider American actions that would affect those interests in such a way that deploying larger strategic forces would be counterproductive.

Characteristic of each of these three answers is a basic approach: a fundamental set of assumptions and categories for thinking about foreign affairs. This approach depends primarily on the assumption that events in international politics consist of the more or less purposive acts of unified national governments and that governmental behavior can be understood by analogy with the intelligent, coordinated acts of individual human beings. Following this approach, analysts focus on the interests and goals of a nation, the alternative courses of actions available, and the costs and benefits of each alternative. An event has been explained when the analyst has shown, for example, how the Tet offensive was a reasonable choice, given Hanoi's strategic objectives. Predictions are generated by calculating the rational thing to do in a certain situation, given specified

objectives. Recommended plans concentrate on analyzing other nations' strategic interests and ways of affecting their calculations about the consequences of actions.

Let the reader consider, for example, how he would explain the Soviet invasion of Czechoslovakia in 1968, or North Vietnamese activity in Laos and Cambodia. One typically puts himself in the place of the nation or the national government confronted with a problem of foreign affairs and tries to figure out how he might have chosen the action in question. If I had been the Soviet Union faced with the threat of Czech liberalization, or the Czech threat to the economy of the Bloc, what would I have done? Moreover, this is not simply the way we react to current events. It is the way most analysts, most of the time, structure their most careful explanations and predictions of important occurrences in foreign affairs.

Few readers will find the simple assertion of this point persuasive. Obviously there are several variants of this basic approach. Obviously the approach does not capture the entire analysis of those who employ it. Obviously not all analysts rely on this approach all of the time. But as one of us has argued at much greater length elsewhere, this framework, which has been labelled Model I, has been the dominant approach to the study of foreign policy and international politics. (Even analysts primarily concerned with discovering causal relations between variables—for example, between environmental or intra-national factors— and specific outcomes, when called upon to explain or predict, display a tendency to rely on the assumption of purposive unitary nations coping within the constraints established by these causal relations.)

This traditional approach to international politics has much to recommend it. As a "lens" it reduces the organizational and political complications of government to the simplification of a single actor. The array of details about a happening can be seen to cluster around the major features of an action. Through this lens, the confused and even contradictory factors that influence an occurrence become a single dynamic: the *choice* of the alternative that achieved a certain goal. This approach permits a quick, imaginative sorting out of the problem of explanation or prediction. It serves as a productive shorthand, requiring a minimum of information. It can yield an informative summary of tendencies, for example, by identifying the weight of strategic costs and benefits.

But this simplification—like all simplifications—obscures as well as reveals. In particular, it obscures the persistently neglected fact of bureaucracy: the "maker" of government policy is not one calculating decision-maker, but rather a conglomerate of large organizations and political actors who differ substantially about what their government should do on any particular issue and who compete in attempting to affect both governmental decisions and the actions of their government.

The purpose of this paper is to present an alternative approach that focuses on intra-national factors, in particular Bureaucratic Politics, in explaining national behavior in international relations. The argument is that these factors are very important, underemphasized in the current literature, yet critical when one is concerned with planning policy. Section 1 of this paper presents the alternative approach: a Bureaucratic Politics Model. Our hope is that the framework is sufficiently general to apply to the behavior of most modern governments in industrialized nations, though it will be obvious that our primary base is the U.S. government. Section 2 suggests how this approach can be applied to understand how one nation influences the behavior of another. Section 3 states a number of policy implications of this alternative approach.

1

A BUREAUCRATIC POLITICS MODEL

Our purpose here is to outline a rough-cut framework for focusing primarily on the individuals within a government, and the interaction among them, as determinants of the actions of a government in international politics. What a government does in any particular instance can be understood largely as a result of bargaining among players positioned hierarchically in the government. The bargaining follows regularized circuits.

Both the bargaining and the results are importantly affected by a number of constraints, in particular, organizational processes and shared values.

In contrast with Model I, this Bureaucratic Politics Model sees no unitary actor but rather many actors as players—players who focus not on a single strategic issue but on many diverse intra-national problems as well. Players choose in terms of no consistent set of strategic objectives, but rather according to various conceptions of national security, organizational, domestic, and personal interests. Players make governmental decisions not by a single rational choice, but by pulling and hauling. (This by no means implies that individual players are not acting rationally, given their interests.) . . .

Suggestive Propositions
About Decisions

1. Decisions of a government seldom reflect a single coherent, consistent set of calculations about national security interests.

2. Decisions by definition assign specific actions to specific players, but they typically leave considerable leeway both about which subordinates should be involved and what specific actions should be taken.

3. Decisions typically reflect considerable compromise. Compromise results from a need to gain adherence, a need to avoid harming strongly felt interests (including organizational interests), and the need to hedge against the dire predictions of other participants.

4. Decisions are rarely tailored to facilitate monitoring. As a result, senior players have great difficulty in checking on the faithful implementation of a decision.

5. Decisions that direct substantial changes in action typically reflect a coincidence of (a) a deadline for a President or senior players that focuses them on a problem and fuels the search for a solution and (b) the interests of junior players committed to a specific solution and in search of a problem.

About Actions

1. Presidential decisions will be faithfully implemented when: a President's involvement is unambiguous, his words are unambiguous, his order is widely publicized, the men who receive it have control of everything needed to carry it out, and those men have no apparent doubt of his authority to issue the decision.

2. Major new departures in foreign policy typically stem from some decision by central players. But the specific details of the action taken are determined in large part by standard operating procedure and programs existing in the organizations at the time.

3. Ambassadors and field commanders feel less obliged to faithfully implement decisions because they typically have not been involved in the decision game. They feel they know better what actions one should want from another government and how to get those actions.

4. The larger the number of players who can act independently on an issue, the less the government's action will reflect decisions of the government on that issue.

5. Where a decision leaves leeway for the organization that is implementing it, that organization will act so as to maximize its organizational interest within constraints. . . .

2

INTERACTION BETWEEN NATIONS

How does the behavior of one nation affect that of another?

Most analysts of international politics approach this question by applying a version of Model I to the behavior of each nation. This approach leads them to treat the interaction between nations as if it resulted from a competition between two purposive individuals. Each nation's actions are seen to be an attempt to influence the actions of the other by affecting its strategic calculus. The behavior of each nation is explained as a reaction to the behavior of the other.

Consider how analysts who take this approach explain arms races. Nation A builds military forces for the purpose of influencing nation B. If it fears that nation B is stronger and hence may be tempted to attack or to exploit its military superiority, nation A will increase the size of its own forces. Nation B, observing this buildup, and fearful of the increased strength of nation A, in turn increases its own forces.

The Bureaucratic Politics Model suggests an alternative answer to the question of how one nation's behavior affects the behavior of another. Explanation focuses primarily on processes internal to each nation. The actions of a nation result not from an agreed upon calculus of strategic interests, but rather from pulling and hauling among individuals with differing perceptions and stakes. These arise not only from differing conceptions of national security interest but also from differing domestic, organizational and personal interests. The influence of one nation's actions on another result from the actions' impact on the stands, or on the power of players in decision or action games in the other nation.

From this alternative perspective, the explanation of an "arms race" is to be found primarily within each nation—in particular in the process by which each one procures and deploys military forces. At any given time some players in nation A will take stands in favor of increasing defense expenditures and procuring particular weapons systems. The interests that lead them to these stands will be diverse. Career officers in the armed services, for example, will seek additional funds for forces controlled by their services. Other players' stands will be affected by their perceptions of how particular decisions will affect the influence of particular players. Actions by another nation will be interpreted by those seeking additional weapons to enhance their arguments and influence. These actions will affect decisions to increase defense spending if they affect senior players' perceptions of what is necessary for national security or of what is necessary to promote their other interests.

Model I analysis can be relied on to predict the fact that a large increase in nation A's defense budget will produce an increase in nation B's defense spending. But the size of that increase and, even more importantly, the specific characteristics of weapons purchased with the increase are better explained or predicted by the Bureaucratic Politics Model. In general, Model I is more useful for explaining actions where national security interests dominate, where shared values lead to a consensus on what the national security requires, and where actions flow rather directly from decisions. The bureaucratic politics model is more useful where there is data on the interests of players and the rules of the game, where organizational and domestic interests predominate, or where one wishes to treat the details of action.

The Bureaucratic Politics Model suggests a number of propositions about the way actions of one nation affect the actions of another. We shall attempt to formulate these propositions explicitly. But before presenting propositions, it should be useful to consider in a more general manner the process of national interaction as it looks through the lens of bureaucratic politics.

The Bureaucratic Politics Model's emphasis on intra-national processes stems not only from the fact that individuals within nations do the acting, but also from the observation that the satisfaction of players' interests are to be found overwhelmingly at home. Political leaders of a nation rise and fall depending on whether they satisfy domestic needs. Individuals advance in the bureaucracy when they meet the standards set by political leaders or by career ladders. Organizations prosper or decline depending on domestic support in that bureaucracy and beyond it—but within the nation. These struggles are what preoccupy players in foreign-policy bureaucracies. Threats to interests from rival organizations, or competing political groups, are far more real than threats from abroad.

This is not to say that players do not have national security interests. No leader wants to see his nation attacked, and few desire to send their soldiers off to fight in distant wars. Some leaders are committed to a conception of world order. Some players have a wide range of interests beyond the borders of the nation. Even when players are concerned about national security interests, however, they are likely to see the battles as being won or lost mainly at home. This has become a truism of the Vietnam war, but it is true for other policies as well. For President Harry S. Truman the problem of the Marshall Plan was how to get Congress to establish the program and vote the funds, not how to get European governments to take the money or use it wisely. For President Dwight D. Eisenhower the problem of arms control was how to get imaginative proposals

from his associates. For planners in the Pentagon, the drive to get the forces necessary to defend the nation is stymied, not by foreign governments, but by rival services, the Secretary of Defense, and the President.

It is not that actions of other nations do not matter, but rather they matter if and when they influence domestic struggles. A player's efforts to accomplish his objectives—whether to advance domestic political interests, organizational interests, personal interests, or national security interests—are sometimes affected by what he and other players come to believe about the actions of other nations. A German chancellor whose domestic position depends upon his reputation for being able to get what the Federal Republic needs from the United States will be concerned about American actions that lead his colleagues and opponents to conclude Washington no longer listens to him. An American Secretary of Defense or President who wishes to cut defense spending will see that his position requires Soviet actions that permit him to argue that the nation's security can be protected with reduced forces. A State Department official who believes his government's security requires European unification will fear that his efforts to get the United States to promote this cause could be undercut by Common Market trade policies, since these offer an opportunity for others to point to the adverse economic consequences of European unification. Since actions by other nations can affect the stands players take, and thereby affect decisions and actions, we must consider how actions of other nations enter into the process of decision bargaining and how they affect actions.

Many nations are doing many things at any given time. Not all of these foreign activities become relevant to decision or action games within a nation. Those that do are the actions reported by the nation's foreign office or intelligence organizations, or by senior players directly. Intelligence organizations are not perfect and neutral transmission belts. They notice what their images of the world lead them to think will be important to senior players. They report events and opinions according to established procedures and in ways designed to protect their own organizational interests. Senior players notice what may help them or their opponents and relate mainly to the former. If a new interpretation of another nation's actions comes to be accepted among senior players, some players will see new opportunities to seek decisions or actions. Others will see threats to ongoing actions or desired new ones; still others will be unconcerned.

Reports of the actions of other nations will never be more than one of many influences on decisions and actions. However, when players are evenly divided, or new action suggests to many a substantial change in anticipated future actions, these reports of another nation's actions can be decisive. The Japanese attack on Pearl Harbor, to take an extreme example, affected the perceptions of many Americans about whether the national security required American forces to engage in war against Japan. The Soviet ABM deployment may well have tipped the balance in the hard-fought American controversy over whether to deploy an ABM. President Lyndon Johnson's estimate of the effect of not deploying an American ABM system on his reelection prospects may have been substantially changed by the possibility that he could be charged with permitting an "ABM gap."

When the actions of one nation are effective in changing the behavior of a second, the new action is rarely what was intended by any player in the first nation. Changes in stands will lead to desired changes in action, which in turn will produce desired changes in the action of another nation only: when a clear signal is sent, when someone in the other nation already wants to take the desired action and the action increases that player's influence. More often, the effects are marginal or unintended.

Propositions About National Interaction

1.   The actions of nation *A* that appear to an outside observer to be designed to influence the actions of nation *B* will in fact be a combination of: (a) routine patterns of behavior; (b) man-

euvers in decision games that are incidentally visible to other nations or deliberately visible, since to be effective they must appear to be a "signal"; (c) actions by players in the absence of decisions; (d) actions following a decision game not related to influence nation *B*; as well as (e) actions following a decision game related to influencing nation *B*.

2.   Reports and interpretations of these actions provided to senior players by participants in nation *B* (in the Foreign Office and Intelligence) charged with observing, reporting, explaining and predicting actions of other nations, will be affected by (a) the perceptual tendencies of all individuals; (b) the use of Model I analysis or (c) even if not, the lack of required data and understanding; and (d) the standard operating procedures and interests of these organizations.

A.   These players share the perceptual tendencies of all individuals. This means, for example, that

(1) New information will be fitted into their existing attitudes and images:
(2) Reports that should lead to a change in plans will be distorted so as to "save their theory";
(3) Clues that signal a significant change in the probabilities of events will be lost in the surrounding noise.

Examples: Evidence of a Japanese attack on Pearl Harbor was explained away. One senior military officer urged that the United States proceed to invade Cuba even after the Soviets agreed to remove their missiles.

B.   Because these players use Model I they tend to assume that the actions were: (1) designed and executed, in effect, by a single individual; (2) designed carefully to influence their nation; (3) designed with a world view like their own; and (4) designed without regard to the domestic and bureaucratic politics of nation *A*.

Examples: Khrushchev warned Kennedy of the difficulty he had during the Cuban missile crisis of convincing his associates that an American U-2 which crossed into Soviet territory was not an indication that the United States was about to attack. The American intelligence community persists in predicting Soviet force structure on the basis of Model I analysis. . . .

6.   Changes in actions of one nation will succeed in changing the actions of a second nation in a desired direction only to the extent that (a) the actions of the first nation send a clear, consistent, simple signal and (b) some participants in the other nation want, in pursuit of their own interests, to change behavior in the desired way, and (c) this signal serves to increase the influence of these participants.

21. Pre-Theories and Theories of Foreign Policy

JAMES N. ROSENAU

. . . .

3

. . . Two basic shortcomings, one philosophical and the other conceptual, would appear to be
holding back the development of foreign policy
theory. Let us look first at the philosophical short-
coming. If theoretical development in a field is
to flourish, empirical materials which have been
similarly processed must be available. It is no
more possible to construct models of human behavior out of raw data than it is to erect a building
out of fallen trees and unbaked clay. The trees
must be sawed and the clay must be baked, and
the resulting lumber and bricks must be the same
size, shape, and color if a sturdy and coherent
building is to be erected. Note that the design and
function of the structure are not determined by
the fact that the materials comprising it have been

Excerpted from R. Barry Farrell, ed., *Approaches to Comparative and International Politics* (Evanston, Illinois: Northwestern University Press, 1966), pp. 27–93. Copyright © 1966
Northwestern University Press. Reprinted by permission of
the publisher and the author. Most footnotes deleted.

similarly processed. The same bricks and lumber
can be used to build houses or factories, large
structures or small ones, modern buildings or traditional ones. So it is with the construction and
use of social theories. There must be, as it were,
pre-theory which renders the raw materials comparable and ready for theorizing. The materials
may serve as the basis for all kinds of theories—
abstract or empirical, single- or multi-country,
pure or applied—but until they have been similarly processed, theorizing is not likely to occur,
or, if it does, the results are not likely to be very
useful.

Unlike economics, sociology, and other areas
of political science, the field of foreign policy
research has not subjected its materials to this
preliminary processing. Instead, as noted above,
each country and each international situation in
which it participates is normally treated as unique
and nonrecurrent, with the result that most available studies do not treat foreign policy phenomena
in a comparable way. Thus it is that the same
data pertaining to the external behavior of the
Soviet Union are interpreted by one observer as
illustrative of Khrushchev's flexibility, by another

as reflective of pent-up consumer demands, and by still another as indicative of the Sino-Soviet conflict. To recur to the analogy of physical materials, it is as if one person cut up the fallen trees for firewood, another used them as the subject of a painting, and still another had them sawed for use in the building of a frame house.

It must be emphasized that the preliminary processing of foreign policy materials involves considerably more than methodological tidiness. We are not referring here to techniques of gathering and handling data, albeit there is much that could be said about the need for standardization in this respect. Nor do we have in mind the desirability of orienting foreign policy research toward the use of quantified materials and operationalized concepts, albeit again good arguments could be advanced on behalf of such procedures. Rather, the preliminary processing to which foreign policy materials must be subjected is of a much more basic order. It involves the need to develop an explicit conception of where causation is located in international affairs. Should foreign policy researchers proceed on the assumption that identifiable human beings are the causative agents? Or should they treat political roles, governmental structures, societal processes, or international systems as the source of external behavior? And if they presume that causation is located in all these sources, to what extent and under what circumstances is each source more of less causal than the others? Few researchers in the field process their materials in terms of some kind of explicit answer to these questions. Most of them, in other words, are not aware of the philosophy of foreign policy analysis they employ, or, more broadly, they are unaware of their pre-theories of foreign policy.

To be sure, foreign policy researchers are not so unsophisticated as to fail to recognize that causation can be attributed to a variety of actors and entities. For years now it has been commonplace to avoid single-cause deterministic explanations and to assert the legitimacy of explaining the same event in a variety of ways. Rather than serving to discipline research, however, this greater sophistication has in some ways supplied a license for undisciplined inquiry. Now it is equally commonplace to assume that one's obligations as a researcher are discharged by articulating the premise that external behavior results from a combination of many factors, both external and internal, *without* indicating how the various factors combine under different circumstances. Having rejected single-cause explanations, in other words, most foreign policy researchers seem to feel they are therefore free *not* to be consistent in their manner of ascribing causation. Deterministic theories have philosophical roots, much foreign policy research seems to say, so that in abandoning the theories it is also necessary to give up the practice of locating one's work in a pre-theoretical context. Thus, as previously indicated, rare is the observer who is troubled by the discrepancy between his attribution of causation to De Gaulle's personal qualities and not to Khrushchev's. On the contrary, many apparently believe that such discrepancies are the mark of flexibility in research and the surest sign of having avoided deterministic modes of thought.

Nothing could be further from the truth. The development and employment of a pre-theory of foreign policy does not, as noted below, necessarily lead to determinism or even to greater rigidity. It merely provides a basis for comparison in the examination of the external behavior of various countries in various situations and, to repeat, there can be no real flourishing of theory until the materials of the field are processed—i.e., rendered comparable—through the use of pre-theories of foreign policy.

Perhaps the best way to indicate exactly what a pre-theory of foreign policy involves is by outlining the main ingredients of any pre-theory and then indicating how the author has integrated these ingredients into his own particular pre-theory. Although the statement is subject to modification and elaboration, it does not seem unreasonable to assert that all pre-theories of foreign policy are either five-dimensional or translatable into five dimensions. That is, all foreign policy analysts either explain the external behavior of societies in terms of five sets of variables, or they proceed in such a way that their explanations can be recast in terms of the five sets. Listed in order of increasing temporal and spatial distance from the external behaviors for which they serve as sources, the five sets are what we shall call the idiosyncratic, role, governmental, societal, and systemic variables.

The first set encompasses the idiosyncracies of the decision-makers who determine and implement the foreign policies of a nation. Idiosyncratic variables include all those aspects of a decision-maker—his values, talents, and prior experiences—that distinguish his foreign policy choices or behavior from those of every other decision-maker. John Foster Dulles' religious values, De Gaulle's vision of a glorious France, and Khrushchev's political skills are frequently mentioned examples of idiosyncratic variables. The second set of variables pertains to the external behavior of officials that is generated by the roles they occupy and that would be likely to occur irrespective of the idiosyncracies of the role occupants. Regardless of who he is, for example, the U.S. ambassador to the United Nations is likely to defend American and Western positions in the Security Council and General Assembly. Governmental variables refer to those aspects of a government's structure that limit or enhance the foreign policy choices made by decision-makers. The impact of executive-legislative relations on American foreign policy exemplifies the operation of governmental variables. The fourth cluster of variables consists of those nongovernmental aspects of a society which influence its external behavior. The major value orientations of a society, its degree of national unity, and the extent of its industrialization are but a few of the societal variables which can contribute to the contents of a nation's external aspirations and policies. As for systemic variables, these include any nonhuman aspects of a society's external environment or any actions occurring abroad that condition or otherwise influence the choices made by its officials. Geographical "realities" and ideological challenges from potential aggressors are obvious examples of systemic variables which can shape the decisions and actions of foreign policy officials.

But these are only the ingredients of a pre-theory of foreign policy. To formulate the pre-theory itself one has to assess their *relative potencies*. That is, one has to decide which set

of variables contributes most to external behavior, which ranks next in influence, and so on through all the sets. There is no need to specify exactly how large a slice of the pie is accounted for by each set of variables. Such precise specifications are characteristics of theories and not of the general framework within which data are organized. At this pre-theoretical level it is sufficient merely to have an idea of the relative potencies of the main sources of external behavior.

Note that constructing a pre-theory of foreign policy is not a matter of choosing to employ only one set of variables. We are not talking about levels of analysis but, in effect, about philosophies of analysis with respect to one particular level, that of national societies. We assume that at this level behavior is shaped by individual, role, government, societal, and systemic factors and that the task is thus one of choosing how to treat each set of variables relative to the others. Many choices are possible. One hundred and twenty pre-theories can be constructed out of the 120 possible ways in which the five sets of variables can be ranked. Some analysts may prefer to use one or another of the rankings to analyze the external behavior of all societies at all times. Others may work out more complex pre-theories in which various rankings are applied to different societies under different circumstances. Whatever the degree of complexity, however, the analyst employs a pre-theory of foreign policy when he attaches relative potencies to the main sources of external behavior.

Attaching causal priorities to the various sets of variables is extremely difficult. Most of us would rather treat causation as idiographic than work out a consistent pre-theory to account for the relative strength of each variable under different types of conditions. One way to overcome this tendency and compel oneself to differentiate the variables is that of engaging in the exercise of mentally manipulating the variables in actual situations. Consider, for example, the U.S.-sponsored invasion of Cuba's Bay of Pigs in April 1961. To what extent was that external behavior a function of the idiosyncratic characteristics of John F. Kennedy (to cite, for purposes of simplicity, only one of the actors who made the invasion decision)? Were his youth, his commitments to action, his affiliations with the Democratic party, his self-confidence, his close election victory—and so on through an endless list—relevant to the launching of the invasion and, if so, to what extent? Would any President have undertaken to oust the Castro regime upon assuming office in 1961? If so, how much potency should be attributed to such role-derived variables? Suppose everything else about the circumstances of April 1961 were unchanged except that Warren Harding or Richard Nixon occupied the White House; would the invasion have occurred? Or hold everything constant but the form of government. Stretch the imagination and conceive of the U.S. as having a cabinet system of government with Kennedy as prime minister; would the action toward Cuba have been any different? Did legislative pressure derived from a decentralized policy-making system generate an impulse to "do something" about Castro, and, if so, to what extent did these governmental variables contribute to the external behavior? Similarly, in order to pre-theorize about the potency of the societal variables, assume once more a presidential form of government. Place Kennedy in office a few months after a narrow election victory, and imagine the Cuban situation as arising in 1921, 1931, or 1951; would the America of the roaring twenties, the depression, or the McCarthy era have "permitted," "encouraged," or otherwise become involved in a refugee-mounted invasion? If the United States were a closed, authoritarian society rather than an open, democratic one, to what extent would the action toward Cuba have been different? Lastly, hold the idiosyncratic, role, governmental, and societal variables constant in the imagination, and posit Cuba as 9000 rather than 90 miles off the Florida coast; would the invasion have nevertheless been launched? If it is estimated that no effort would have been made to span such a distance, does this mean that systemic variables should always be treated as overriding, or is their potency diminished under certain conditions?

The formulation of a pre-theory of foreign policy can be further stimulated by expanding this mental exercise to include other countries and other situations. Instead of Kennedy, the presidency, and the U.S. of 1961 undertaking action toward Cuba, engage in a similar process of hold-

ing variables constant with respect to the actions taken by Khrushchev, the monolithic Russian decision-making structure, and the U.S.S.R. of 1956 toward the uprising in Hungary. Or apply the exercise to the actions directed at the Suez Canal by Eden, the cabinet system, and the England of 1956. Or take still another situation, that of the attack on Goa carried out by the charismatic Nehru and the modernizing India of 1961. In all four cases a more powerful nation initiated military action against a less powerful neighbor that had come to represent values antagonistic to the interests of the attacker. Are we therefore to conclude that the external behavior of the U.S., Russia, England, and India stemmed from the same combination of external and internal sources? Should the fact that the attacked society was geographically near the attacking society in all four instances be interpreted as indicating that systemic variables are always relatively more potent than any other type? Or is it reasonable to attribute greater causation to idiosyncratic factors in one instance and to societal factors in another? If so, what is the rationale for subjecting these seemingly similar situations to different kinds of analysis?

Reflection about questions similar to those raised in the two previous paragraphs has led this observer to a crude pre-theory of foreign policy in which the relative potencies of the five sets of variables are assessed in terms of distinctions between large and small countries, between developed and underdeveloped economies, and between open and closed political systems. As can be seen in Table 5.1, these three continua give rise to eight types of countries and eight different rankings of relative potency. There is no need here to elaborate at length on the reasoning underlying each ranking.[1] The point is not to demon-

---

[1] Suffice it to note that the potency of a systemic variable is considered to vary inversely with the size of a country (there being greater resources available to larger countries and thus lesser dependence on the international system than is the case with smaller countries), that the potency of an idiosyncratic factor is assumed to be greater in less developed economies (there being fewer of the restraints which bureaucracy and large-scale organization impose in more developed economies), that for the same reason a role variable is accorded greater potency in more developed economies, that a societal variable is considered to be more potent in open polities than

TABLE 5.1   An Abbreviated Presentation of the Author's Pre-Theory of Foreign Policy, in Which Five Sets of Variables Underlying the External Behavior of Societies Are Ranked According to Their Relative Potencies in Eight Types of Societies

Geography and physical resources	LARGE COUNTRY				SMALL COUNTRY			
State of the economy	Developed		Underdeveloped		Developed		Underdeveloped	
State of the polity.	Open	Closed	Open	Closed	Open	Closed	Open	Closed
Rankings of the variables	Role Societal Governmental Systemic Idiosyncratic	Role Idiosyncratic Governmental Systemic Societal	Idiosyncratic Role Societal Systemic Governmental	Idiosyncratic Role Governmental Systemic Societal	Role Systemic Societal Governmental Idiosyncratic	Role Systemic Idiosyncratic Governmental Societal	Idiosyncratic Systemic Role Societal Governmental	Idiosyncratic Systemic Role Governmental Societal
Illustrative examples	U.S	U.S.S.R.	India	Red China	Holland	Czechoslovakia	Kenya	Ghana

strate the validity of the rankings but rather to indicate what the construction of a pre-theory of foreign policy involves and why it is a necessary prerequisite to the development of theory. Indeed, given the present undeveloped state of the field, the rankings can be neither proved nor disproved. They reflect the author's way of organizing materials for close inspection and not the inspections themselves. To be theoretical in nature, the rankings would have to specify *how much* more potent each set of variables is than those below it on each scale, and the variables themselves would have to be causally linked to specific forms of external behavior.

To be sure, as in all things, it is possible to have poor and unsound pre-theories of foreign policy as well as wise and insightful ones. The author's pre-theory may well exaggerate the potency of some variables and underrate others, in which case the theories which his pre-theory generates or supports will in the long run be less productive and enlightening than those based on pre-theories which more closely approximate empirical reality. Yet, to repeat, this pre-theory is not much more than an orientation and is not at present subject to verification.

One suspects that many foreign policy analysts would reject this pre-theory, not because they conceive of different rankings or even different sets of variables but rather because the very idea of explicating a pre-theory strikes them as premature or even impossible. Those committed to the single-country, historical approach to foreign affairs would no doubt object that developing a pre-theory is a fruitless endeavor, since every situation is different from every other and no pre-theory can possibly be so coherent as to account for the infinite variation that marks international life. Other analysts, including some who are more social-scientific in their orientation, reject the possibility of pre-theorizing on the grounds that the same events can be explained in several ways and that therefore the problem of determining the relative potencies of different sets of variables can never be satisfactorily solved.

The fact is, however, that one cannot avoid having a pre-theory of foreign policy whenever one takes on the task of tracing causation. Even the most historical-minded analyst makes the initial assumption that events derive from an under-

---

in closed ones (there being a lesser need for officials in the latter to heed nongovernmental demands in the former), and that for the same reason governmental variables are more potent than societal variables in closed polities than in open ones.

lying order, that every external behavior of every society stems from some source and is therefore, at least theoretically, explicable. To assume otherwise—to view the external behaviors of societies as random and impulsive, as occurring for no reason, and as therefore unknowable—is to render analysis useless and to condemn the analyst to perpetual failure. Since we cannot avoid the presumption of an underlying order, neither can we avoid having some conception of its nature. Yet causation is not self-revealing. The underlying order does not simply manifest itself for the diligent analyst who gathers every scrap of evidence and then takes a long, hard look at what he has accumulated. Inevitably he must organize the evidence in terms of some frame of reference, crude and premature as it may seem. There may be infinite variety in international life, but analysts are not so infinitely flexible. They cannot, and they do not, ignore their prior knowledge about foreign affairs and start over, so to speak, each time they undertake to analyze an external behavior. Furthermore, even if one were to assume that each international situation is different from every other situation, it is still necessary to have some basis for recognizing and explaining the differences. Similarly, even if one assumes that the same event is subject to a variety of interpretations, depending on the perspective of the observer, it is nevertheless necessary to adopt a particular perspective if any interpretation is to be made.

While it is thus impossible to avoid possession of a pre-theory of foreign policy, it is quite easy to avoid awareness of one's pre-theory and to proceed as if one started over with each situation. Explicating one's conception of the order that underlies the external behavior of societies can be an excruciating process. As in psychoanalysis, bringing heretofore implicit and unexamined assumptions into focus may compel one to face considerations which one has long sought to ignore. Some of the assumptions may seem utterly ridiculous when exposed to explicit and careful perusal. Others may seem unworkable in the light of new knowledge. Still others may involve mutually exclusive premises, so that to recognize them would be to undermine one's previous work and to obscure one's present line of inquiry.

Nor are matters greatly simplified by emotional readiness to live with the results of explication. There still remains the intellectually taxing task of identifying the variables which one regards as major sources of external behavior and of then coming to some conclusions about their relative potencies under varying circumstances. Such a task can be very difficult indeed. Long-standing habits of thought are involved, and the analyst may have become so accustomed to them that for him the habits are part of ongoing reality and not of his way of perceiving reality. In addition, if these habits provide no experience in pre-theorizing about the processes of causation, it will not be easy to tease out variables and assess their potencies. For example, while it is relatively simple to observe that a De Gaulle is less restrained in foreign policy than a Khrushchev, many analysts—especially those who insist that every situation is unique and that therefore they do not possess a pre-theory of foreign policy—would have a hard time discerning that the observation stems from their pre-theoretical premise that idiosyncratic variables have greater potency in France than in the Soviet Union.

Great as the obstacles to explication may be, however, they are not insurmountable. Patience and continual introspection can eventually bring implicit and unexamined premises to the surface. The first efforts may result in crude formulations, but the more one explicates, the more elaborate does one's pre-theory become.

But, it may be asked, if the purpose of all this soul searching and anguish is that of facilitating the development of general theory, how will the self-conscious employment of pre-theories of foreign policy allow the field to move beyond its present position? As previously implied, the answer lies in the assumption that the widespread use of explicit pre-theories will result in the accumulation of materials that are sufficiently processed to provide a basis for comparing the external behavior of societies. If most researchers were to gather and present their data in the context of their views about the extent to which individuals, roles, governments, societies, and international systems serve as causal agents in foreign affairs, then even though these views might represent a variety of pre-theories, it should be possible to discern patterns and draw contrasts among diverse types of policies and situations. Theoretical development is not in any way dependent on the emergence of a consensus with respect to the most desirable pre-theory of foreign policy. Comparison and theorizing can ensue as long as each researcher makes clear what variables he considers central to causation and the relative potencies he ascribes to them. For even if one analyst ascribes the greatest potency to idiosyncratic variables, while another views them as having relatively little potency and still another regards them as impotent, they will have all provided data justifying their respective assumptions, and in so doing they will have given the theoretician the materials he needs to fashion if-then propositions and to move to ever higher levels of generalization.

4

But all will not be solved simply by the explication of pre-theories. This is a necessary condition of progress toward general theory, but it is not a sufficient one. Research in the foreign policy field would appear to be hindered by conceptual as well as philosophical shortcomings, and we will not be able to move forward until these more specific obstacles are also surmounted. Not only must similarly processed materials be available if general theory is to flourish, but researchers must also possess appropriate concepts for compiling them into meaningful patterns. Although rendered similar through the explication of pre-theories, the materials do not fall in place by themselves. Concepts are necessary to give them structure and thereby facilitate the formulation of if-then propositions. . . .

Two interrelated conceptual problems seem to be holding back the development of general theories of external behavior. One concerns the tendency of researchers to maintain a rigid distinction between national and international political systems in the face of mounting evidence that the distinction is breaking down. The second difficulty involves an inclination to ignore the implications of equally clear-cut indications that the functioning of political systems can vary significantly from one type of issue to another. Let us anticipate much of the ensuing discussion by noting that the interrelationship of the two problems is such that a new kind of political system, the *penetrated system*, is needed to comprehend the fusion of national and international systems in certain kinds of *issue-areas*.

Myriad are the data that could be cited to illustrate the increasing obscuration of the boundaries between national political systems and their international environments. These boundaries may consist of the activities that result in "the authoritative allocation of values for a society," or of the interacting roles that sustain a society "by means of the employment, or threat of employment, of more or less legitimate physical compulsion," or of the processes in a society that "mobilizes its resources in the interest of (positively sanctioned) goals," or "of the more inclusive structures in a society that have recognized responsibility for performing, at a minimum, the function of goal-attainment by means of legitimate decisions." But however such boundaries may be drawn, ever since World War II they have been constantly transgressed by nonsocietal actors. The manner of transgression, moreover, has been quite varied. . . .

. . . As has already been indicated, the national society is now so penetrated by the external world that it is no longer the only source of legitimacy or even of the employment of coercive techniques. The probability that most social processes will culminate at the national level has diminished, and instead the "most inclusive" structures through which groups strive to attain goals are increasingly becoming a composite of subnational, national, and supranational elements.

It must be emphasized that these changes involve considerably more than a significant increase in the influence wielded by nonmembers of national societies. We are not simply asserting the proposition that the external world impinges ever more pervasively on the life of national societies, albeit such a proposition can hardly be denied. Nor are we talking merely about the growing interdependence of national political systems. Our contention is rather that in certain respects national political systems now permeate, as well as depend on, each other and that their functioning now embraces actors who are not formally members of the system. These nonmembers not only exert influence upon national systems but actually participate in the processes through which such systems allocate values, coordinate goal-directed efforts, and legitimately employ coercion. They not only engage in bargaining with the system, but they actually bargain within the system, taking positions on behalf of one or another of its components. Most important, the participation of nonmembers of the society in value-allocative and goal-attainment processes is accepted by both its officialdom and its citizenry, so that the decisions to which nonmembers contribute are no less authoritative and legitimate than are those in which they do not participate. Such external penetration may not always be gladly accepted by the officials and citizens of a society, but what renders decisions legitimate and authoritative is that they are felt to be binding, irrespective of whether they are accepted regretfully or willingly. No doubt both the Finnish president and the people were less than delighted by the aforementioned participation of Soviet officials in their electoral processes, but the decisions that resulted from such participation do not appear to have been more widely challenged in Finland than are other decisions made exclusively by members of the society.

One could, of course, reject this line of reasoning on narrow legal grounds. From the perspective of the law, the participation of nonmembers in a society's deliberations can never be regarded as more than the exercise of external influence. Strictly speaking, Soviet officials have no "right" to participate directly in Finnish affairs. They cannot vote in Finnish elections, and they are not entitled to nominate candidates for office. They are *non*members, not members, of Finnish society, and thus their actions in Finland can never be viewed as legitimate or authoritative from a strict juridical standpoint. To repeat, however, the functioning of national political systems contrasts so sharply with this narrow legal construction that the latter is hardly adequate as a basis of political conceptualization. The boundaries of political systems are defined by activities and processes, not by legalities. Our interest is in political science and not in legal science, albeit the two

need not be as discrepant as the situations discussed here.

The foregoing considerations not only lead to the conclusion that cogent political analysis requires a readiness to treat the functioning of national systems as increasingly dependent on external events and trends, but they also suggest the need to identify a new type of political system that will account for phenomena which not even a less rigid use of the national-international distinction renders comprehensible. Such a system might be called the *penetrated political system,* and its essential characteristics might be defined in the following way: A penetrated political system is one in which *nonmembers of a national society participate directly and authoritatively, through actions taken jointly with the society's members, in either the allocation of its values or the mobilization of support on behalf of its goals.* The political processes of a penetrated system are conceived to be structurally different from both those of an international political system and those of a national political system. In the former, nonmembers indirectly and nonauthoritatively influence the allocation of a society's values and the mobilization of support for its goals through autonomous rather than through joint action. In the latter, nonmembers of a society do not direct action toward it and thus do not contribute in any way to the allocation of its values or the attainment of its goals.

Obviously operationalization of these distinctions will prove difficult. When does an interaction between two actors consist of autonomous acts, and when does it amount to joint action? When are nonmembers of a society participants in its politics, and when are they just influential nonparticipants? Furthermore, how extensive must the participation by nonmembers be in order that a penetrated political system may come into existence? . . .

. . . One final point with respect to penetrated systems needs to be made. As it stands at present, our formulation suffers from a lack of differentiation. While the analysis points to the conclusion that all national societies in the modern world are susceptible of swift transformation into penetrated systems, it treats all such systems as if they were similarly transformed and structured. Yet obviously there is a vast difference between the penetrated systems that have developed in Vietnam and the Congo and those that have evolved with respect to British or Indian defenses. In the former cases penetration is thorough-going, whereas in the latter it is limited to the allocation of a highly restricted set of values. Nonmembers may participate directly in the determination and attainment of Indian military goals, but clearly they are not a party to the processes whereby India's linguistic problems are handled. In Vietnam, on the other hand, nonmembers have been centrally involved in efforts to mobilize support for certain religious values as well as for a military campaign. Accordingly, so as to differentiate degrees of penetration as well as the structural differences to which they give rise, it seems appropriate to distinguish between multi-issue and single-issue penetrated systems, the distinction being based on whether nonmembers participate in the allocation of a variety of values or of only a selected set of values.

5

The conclusion that national societies can be organized as penetrated political systems with respect to some types of issues—or issue-areas—and as national political systems with respect to others is consistent with mounting evidence that the functioning of any type of political system can vary significantly from one issue-area to another. Data descriptive of local, party, legislative, national, and international systems are converging around the finding that different types of issue-areas elicit different sets of motives on the part of different actors in a political system, that different system members are thus activated in different issue-areas, and that the different interaction patterns which result from these variations produce different degrees of stability and coherence for each of the issue-areas in which systemic processes are operative. . . .

. . . In the foreign policy field, too, there are numerous indications that the nature of the issue constitutes a crucial variable in the processes whereby the external behavior of national societies is generated. In the United States, for example, the complex of internal influences brought to bear in the ratification of treaties would seem to be entirely different from that which underlies the allocation of economic and military assistance to other countries. One has the impression that much the same could be said about other societies that maintain foreign aid programs.

Whether they are impressionistic or systematic, in short, the data on issue-areas are too impressive to ignore. Conceptual allowance must be made for them if theorizing in the foreign policy field is to flourish. Indeed, the emergence of issue-areas is as pronounced and significant as is the breakdown of the national-international distinction. Taken together, the two trends point to the radical conclusion that the boundaries of political systems ought to be drawn vertically in terms of issue-areas as well as horizontally in terms of geographic areas. Stated in the context of the present world scene, the data compel us to cast our analyses as much in terms of, say, civil-rights political systems, economic-development political systems, and health-and-welfare political systems as we do in terms of local, national, and international systems. . . .

. . . In short, further elaboration, rather than continued neglect, of the issue-area concept would seem to be in order. None of the arguments against the construction of vertical political systems out of identifiable issue-areas fully offset the compelling evidence that horizontal systems function differently in different areas. Let us turn, therefore, to the task of specifying more precisely the nature of issue-areas and the location of vertical systems within them.

Stated formally, an issue-area is conceived to consist of *(1) a cluster of values, the allocation or potential allocation of which (2) leads the affected or potentially affected actors to differ so greatly over (a) the way in which the values should be allocated or (b) the horizontal levels at which the allocations should be authorized that (3) they engage in distinctive behavior designed to mobilize support for the attainment of their particular values.* If a cluster of values does not lead to differences among those affected by it, then the issue-area is not considered to exist for that group of actors, and their relationships with respect to the values are not considered to form a vertical system. If a cluster of values does divide the actors affected by it but if their differences are not so great as to induce support-building behavior, then the issue-area, and its vertical systems, is considered to be dormant until such time as one of the actors activates it by pressing for a reallocation of the value cluster. If a cluster of values induces support building on the part of the affected actors but if their behavior is not distinctive from that induced by another cluster of values, then the issue-area is considered to encompass both clusters, and both are also regarded as being processed by the same vertical system.

It will be noted that the boundaries of vertical systems are delineated not by the common membership of the actors who sustain them (as horizontal systems are), but rather by the distinctiveness of the values and the behavior they encompass. The actors determine the state of a vertical system—whether it is active, dormant, or nonexistent—but the boundaries of the system are independent of the identity of the actors who are active within it. In fact, the horizontal affiliations of its actors may be quite varied. Some might be members of local systems. Others might belong to national systems. Still others might be participants in penetrated or international systems. The cluster of values associated with economic development provides an example of an issue-area that encompasses actors at every horizontal level.

This is not to imply, of course, that either the actors, the values, or the behavior that form the parameters of a vertical system are simple to identify. A number of operational problems will have to be resolved before empirical research on vertical phenomena yield worthwhile results. In particular, answers to three questions must be developed: How are the values over which men differ to be clustered together into issue-areas? At what level of abstraction should they be clustered? What characteristics render the behavior evoked by one cluster of values distinctive from that stimulated by other clusters?

The general line of response to the first two questions seems reasonably clear. A typology of issue-areas ought to be something more than a mere cataloguing of the matters over which men are divided at any moment in time. For vertical systems to be of analytic utility, they must persist

beyond the life of particular actors. As has already been implied, not much would be accomplished if "issue-area" meant nothing more than the conventional usage, in which an "issue" is equated with any and every concrete historical conflict that ensues between identifiable individuals or groups. In brief, a typology of issue-areas must be cast in sufficiently abstract terms to encompass past and future clusters of values as well as present ones. Obviously, too, the level of abstraction must be high enough to allow for clusters of values that evoke behavior within all types of horizontal systems, from local communities to the global community. At the same time the typology cannot be so generalized as to erase the distinctiveness of the behavior which characterizes the vertical systems in each of its areas.

For the present, of course, any typology must be largely arbitrary. Until systematic and extensive data on the distinctive nature of certain issue-areas are accumulated, the lines dividing them cannot be drawn with much certainty. In order to suggest further dimensions of the concept, however, let us adopt a simple typology which seems to meet the above criteria. Let us conceive of all behavior designed to bring about the authoritative allocation of values as occurring in any one of four issue-areas: the *territorial, status, human resources*, and *nonhuman resources* areas, each of which encompasses the distinctive motives, actions, and interactions evoked by the clusters of values that are linked to, respectively, the allocation of territorial jurisdiction, the allocation of status within horizontal political systems or within nonpolitical systems, the development and allocation of human resources, and the development and allocation of nonhuman resources. Examples of vertical systems located in the territorial area are the persistent conflict over Berlin, the continuing Arizona-California controversy over rights to the Colorado River, and the recurring efforts to effect a merger of the Township and Borough of Princeton, New Jersey. Status-area systems are exemplified by the long-standing problem of whether Red China should be admitted to the United Nations, the unending racial conflict in South Africa, and the perennial question of higher pay for policemen faced by every American town. Enduring efforts to provide medical care for the aged, unceasing problems of population control, and periodic disputes over the training of teachers are illustrative of vertical systems that fall in the human resources area. Certain foreign aid programs, most housing and highway programs, and many agricultural policies illustrate the kinds of vertical systems that are classified in the nonhuman resources area.

In other words, each of the four issue-areas is conceived to embrace a number of vertical political systems, and the boundaries of each vertical system are in turn conceived to be determined by the scope of the interaction that occurs within it. Thus, as implied above, some vertical systems may function exclusively at local horizontal levels; others may be national in scope; still others may be confined to interaction at the international level. . . .

. . . But how, it may well be asked, does this particular typology meet the criterion that the value clusters in each area must evoke distinctive motives, actions, and interactions on the part of the affected actors? Granted that the values themselves differ, why should it be presumed that these differences are sufficient to produce differentiation in the functioning of the systems that allocate the values in each issue-area? As previously indicated, the answers to these questions must of necessity be somewhat vague. Since the issue-area concept has not been the focus of systematic inquiry, data which would allow for comparisons of the functioning of vertical systems are not available, and any typology has perforce to be constructed out of crude impressions about the reasons for the findings uncovered by Dahl and others. In the case of the foregoing typology the four issue-areas were derived from an impression that the motives, actions, and interactions of political actors are crucially related to the degree of tangibility of both the values which have to be allocated and the means which have to be employed to effect allocation. With respect to motives and actions, it was reasoned that the affected actors would be more strongly motivated and more persistently active the *greater* the tangibility of the *means* (since the rewards and costs to the actor of allocating a particular cluster of values are likely to be clearer the more easily comprehensible are the means necessary to realize the values); and that the more actors affected and active, the *lesser* the tangibility of the *ends* (since tangibility involves specificity, and thus the aspirations of a greater number of actors are likely to be encompassed by issues in which intangible goals are at stake). With respect to interaction, the presumption was made that the *greater* the tangibility of both the *ends* and *means* involved in an allocative process, the more the tendency to bargain among the affected actors would increase. In short, among the distinctive characteristics of an issue-area are the number of affected actors, the intensity of their motivations to act, the frequency with which they act, and the extent of their readiness to bargain with each other.

That four main issue-areas derive from the foregoing is readily apparent. The processes of allocating tangible values through the use of tangible means will differ significantly from those in which intangible ends and means are involved; both of these will in turn be distinguished from the processes whereby tangible values are allocated through the utilization of intangible means; and still a fourth pattern of distinctive motives, actions, and interactions will occur whenever tangible means are employed to achieve intangible ends. In short, we have fashioned a 2 x 2 matrix, each cell of which corresponds more or less closely to one of the four kinds of values that are presumed to sustain political behavior:

FIGURE 5-3

		MEANS	
		Intangible	Tangible
ENDS	Intangible	Status area	Human resources area
	Tangible	Territorial area	Nonhuman resources area

Although crude and impressionistic, this derivation of the distinctiveness of the issue-area does seem to hold up when one engages in the exercise of locating empirical findings in the matrix. Let us take Dahl's data as an example, and assume for purposes of illustration that the tangible-intangible scale of ends is operationalized in terms of whether the values involved can be photographed with a camera and that the tangibility of means is measured by the extent to which money must be expended in order to acquire the values. The values represented by education cannot be photographed, albeit money is necessary to build the schools and pay the teachers—prerequisites to the realization of educational values. Hence vertical systems designed to process educational issues fall in the human resources areas of the matrix. Similarly, nominations in New Haven are not photographable, and, unlike the building and maintenance of a school system, money is not needed to have them allocated in a desired fashion. Thus they would be classified in the status area. Likewise, urban redevelopment in New Haven—or the need for it—is readily photographable, and great quantities of money must be committed to its realization, thereby locating it in the nonhuman resources area. Since Dahl offers no data for the territorial area, let us conclude this exercise with the example of Berlin as a vertical political system. In this case recent history—especially since the erection of the wall in August 1961—testifies poignantly to the photographability of the values involved. Yet diplomatic persuasion, rather than money and the military capabilities it buys, must obviously serve as the means through which a Berlin settlement will ultimately be accomplished.

The impression that the fit between this formulation and empirical phenomena is sufficient to warrant further development of the typology is reinforced by one other consideration. The assumption that the tangibility of ends and means determines the number of affected actors and the extent of their readiness to bargain with each other permits specific conclusions about distinctive characteristics of at least two of the issue-areas. On the one hand, the status area, being composed of both intangible ends and means, is likely to evoke more uncompromising political behavior on the part of more actors than any of the other three; on the other hand, the nonhuman resources area, being composed of both tangible ends and means, is likely to evoke more bargaining on the part of fewer actors than any of the other areas. That these two conclusions correspond to the differences between concrete vertical systems in each area can be readily demonstrated. Compare, for instance, the processes whereby values pertaining to civil rights are allocated with those that mark the allocation of values in the field of transportation (e.g., the development of rivers, harbors, and roads). Clearly more persons are aroused by the former cluster than by the latter, and plainly, too, uncompromising positions are as characteristic of civil rights issues as horse-trading is of rivers and harbors allocations.

Indeed, it is noteworthy that these characteristics of the status area would seem to be so powerful as to create still another distinctive characteristic of that area: The boundaries of vertical systems in the status area would appear to be more capable of expansion than are systems in any other area. Because they arouse a greater number of actors and a more uncompromising set of orientations, status issues can quickly move upward, downward, and sideward, once they are activated. The demand for civil rights in Angola, the attempt of James Meredith to enter the University of Mississippi, and the recognition of Communist China are illustrative of the vertical dynamism of status issues. Their horizontal dynamism—their capacity for intruding upon other issue-areas—is exemplified by the current civil rights debate in the United States. It was equally apparent in November 1963, when the arrest of Professor Frederick C. Barghoorn proved to be far more unsettling to the U.S.-U.S.S.R. system (as it was then being sustained in wheat and disarmament negotiations) than a concurrent flare-up of the Berlin crisis.

6

The implications of the foregoing conceptual adjustments for the construction of foreign policy theory are clear. If the above formulation has any

validity, the external behavior of horizontal systems at the national level is likely to vary so greatly in scope, intensity, and flexibility in each of the four issue-areas that any theory of foreign policy will have to include if-then propositions which reflect these variations. Similarly theoretical account will have to be taken of the external behavior of penetrated systems. Their relations with the rest of the world will obviously be partly a function of differences in the degree and nature of the penetration they experience. Moreover, since the extent and manner of penetration are likely to vary from one issue-area to the next, any theory will have to encompass these additional differences.

Indeed the penetrated and vertical systems concepts would seem to be sufficiently important to warrant revision at the pre-theoretical level. It seems reasonable to presume, for instance, that the relative potency of systemic variables would be greater in penetrated systems than in those which are strictly of a national kind. Thus the pre-theory summarized in Table 5.1 could fruitfully be doubled in scope by subdividing each of the eight columns into ''penetrated'' and ''nonpenetrated'' categories and introducing eight new rankings which elevate the systemic variables,

say, one notch in each of the eight penetrated systems. Likewise, if the distinctive characteristics of the status and nonhuman resources areas have been correctly estimated, it is easy to envision still another expansion of the pre-theory—a twofold expansion in which societal variables are elevated one position in the rankings for status areas (because more members of the system are likely to be aroused to make more uncompromising demands) and lowered one rank in those for nonhuman resources areas (because fewer system members are likely to make less stringent demands). Table 5.2 presents these possible expansions of the pre-theory which the penetrated and vertical systems concepts facilitate.

While these concepts greatly complicate the task of theory building, they do not dictate or limit the kind of theory that can be constructed. As emphasized throughout, all we have done in this paper is to identify and amplify the materials out of which any theory of foreign policy must be fashioned. A wide range of theories can be built out of these materials, and nothing inherent in the latter determines the design, elegance, and utility of the former. These qualities must be supplied by the analyst, which is what makes the task of theory building awesome and challenging.

22.   U.S. Foreign Relations: Conflict, Cooperation, and Attribute Distances

R. J. RUMMEL

1. INTRODUCTION

In any one day, the foreign relations of the United States consist of a multitude of distinct actions. Some of them are consciously a part of the government's foreign policy, such as warning the Soviet Union on her overt military involvement in the Middle East prior to publicly announced discussions with Israel's foreign minister on the Israeli request for U.S. jet fighters. Other actions are separate from immediate foreign policy considerations and distinct from each other, such as a shipment of American automobiles to Denmark and twenty-five American students entering India for a year of foreign study. And still other actions are of such importance and consequence as to immediately affect most U.S. international relations, such as the sudden American attack on Viet Cong and North Vietnamese sanctuaries in Cambodia.

Obviously, the international relations of any one country, especially one as economically de-

veloped and powerful as the United States, will be diverse and multidimensional. How are we to make sense out of all these actions, for both the scholar and practitioner of international relations?

Traditionally, the scholar refines a conceptual framework of international relations which places these actions in relation to each other, orders them in a cause-effect hierarchy, and weights them in their prominence for practicing and understanding international politics.

He divides a nation's actions into public and private actions, relates them to immediate, short and long-run foreign policy goals, imbues those actions with consequences for the power and national interest of a nation, and categorizes them into causes, effects, conditions, or processes. The practitioner, less self-consciously theoretical and abstract, generally deals with international relations on a day-by-day basis, responding to actions of other nations when necessary to satisfy bureaucratic and political demands, innovating and initiating actions to meet contingencies, and restraining or channeling other actions as events require.

The conceptual world of the practitioner consists of individuals: decision makers, elites, and

Reprinted from R.J. Rummel, *Field Theory Evolving* (Beverly Hills Calif.: Sage Publications, 1977), pp. 260–268. Copyright © 1977 Sage Publications, Inc. Reprinted by permission of the publisher and author. Footnotes deleted.

influentials. A nation's economic development, political system, culture, and history are givens. International law and organizations, the number and variety of nations and their geographic separation, and the configuration of power and alliances are the context within which human beings barter, exchange, fight, negotiate, and cooperate. If the practitioner, as he does often, says that the United States has done such, or that the United States desires . . ., he knows this is a semantic convenience, an accepted and understood reification; and in effect he means that Dr. Henry Kissinger has influenced President Nixon to say . . . , or that Secretary Rogers initiated those diplomatic moves to placate Senator Fulbright. The practitioner's questions are generally not those of the scholar's. He is not, except in perhaps an intellectual sense, concerned with how the size of nations affects their trade, or even the relationship between economic development and foreign conflict behavior. He would prefer to know such things as who the likely successor to Mao is, what his past relationship and attitudes toward the United States and the Soviet Union have been, and what changes he is likely to make in China's foreign behavior.

In short, the practitioner conceptualizes and understands the diverse international relations at the *individual level*, as the daily interaction of human beings. Scholars, on the other hand, often are interested in the theoretical understanding of such actions at the *aggregate level*. They wish to theorize about these actions in the aggregate and relate them to the practitioners' givens. They wish to isolate the forces and indicators, to delineate the patterns and trends in aggregate actions, and to stipulate or discover the social and political laws of international relations.

While the individual-aggregate distinction does not sharply differentiate scholars and practitioners, since many scholars are concerned with developing theoretical and empirical knowledge at the individual level, it does distinguish levels of understanding and conceptualization of a nation's actions and focuses on a source of misunderstanding between practitioners and scholars themselves.

At the individual level, actions appear random, caused by idiosyncrasies of the personality involved, specific circumstances, or never-repeated events. Actions seem to be triggered by unique events, such as an assassination, or to be the plaything of chance. The behavior of nations, which consist of the actions of human beings, appears unpredictable, unlawful, and sometimes irrational.

At the aggregate level, however, many actions are structured; they are highly correlated, ordered, and patterned. They seem to be lawful and subject to scientific study and prediction. On the whole, aggregate international relations appear more regular than random, more to be explained by deterministic equations than probabilistic statistics.

This transformation in perspective which takes place as one shifts his vision from an individual to an aggregate level might be best illustrated by an example from physics. Gas molecules seem to move in an unordered, random fashion, as capricious as human behavior in international relations. At an aggregate level, however, the random molecular motions are patterned, ordered in their totality, enabling us to assert Boyle's law that gas pressure on a container times the volume equals a constant (at constant temperature).

The shift in appearance of international relations between the individual and aggregate perspectives causes difficulty in communication. A practitioner or scholar whose paradigm is individual-centered neither appreciates nor understands the scholar's emphasis on scientific theory and laws. Predict international relations? Absurd. Who could have predicted Sukarno's erratic and highly personal actions? Who could have forecast the rise of a Hitler, Stalin, Mao, or Castro? On the other hand, the scholar summing across a number of actions, standardizing them, and comparing across countries and years knows he has strong relationships. His correlations often exceed in magnitude those of the other social sciences and lead him to be impatient with the belief in the unpredictability of human behavior.

Certainly, both the individual and aggregate perspectives can complement and supplement each other. Aggregate level research contributes an understanding and a conceptual framework of the context within which individual actions take place. It can define the direction of aggregate behavior, the range of alternative directions (alternative worlds), and the crucial variables (such as energy consumption or national income) whose shift in values might provide calmer waters for the ship of state.

For the scholar, the practitioner's world should be the testing ground of aggregate research and theory. While study can proceed at the aggregate level, international relations, after all, consist of the actions and problems of people. It is at the practitioner's level that the crucial tests of the aggregate perspective must be applied, for of what use are concepts of integration and social distance, correlations between trade and economic development, dimensions of size and foreign conflict behavior, and nearly perfect multiple correlations if they give no guidance to human affairs, solve no problems, provide no solutions?

(This may be the first expression of my growing pragmatic outlook. As I worked over the years with a variety of quantitative techniques, I realized how slight changes in a research design [changes in mode of transformation data scaling, coefficient of correlation, and so on] surprisingly could alter one's findings for the same data. Not even a completely mathematical theory was sufficient to dictate all the aspects of a research design. This experience, in conjunction with a growing dissatisfaction with model building and the quantitative analysis of others not anchored in any meaningful social problem, turned me toward pragmatism. Given the arbitrariness of so many of our scientific decisions, given that science can become [and has for some social scientists] a closed system of criteria, I began to feel that there must be some outside basis for judging our findings, and to believe that this external criterion is the ability of our results to help man with his problems.)

This long introduction is to set the stage for the field theory of U.S. conflict and cooperation to be presented and tested here, for this will use an aggregate level perspective with which most will be unfamiliar. It will treat international rela-

tions as a deterministic system and pose within the representation to be developed a fundamental proposition of foreign relations. As applied above, while the discussion from this point on will develop an aggregate theory, it is recognized that an individual world of everyday actions and decisions exists and that ultimately the ability to solve some of the problems of this world will be the final test by fire.

(I was still as strong a determinist at this point as with the first paper in 1965. I still felt comfortable in saying to my students "In theory, man's behavior is fully determined by . . . ." This perspective was soon transformed under the influence of the reading I did in preparation for writing *The Dynamic Psychological Field* [1975].)

2. INTERNATIONAL RELATIONS AS A SOCIAL SPACE

Most attempts to develop aggregate theories of nations' actions have worked at a conceptual level not far removed from that of diplomats, politicians, and journalists. Power, national interest, nationalism, conflict, cooperation, integration, international law, international organization, politics, geographical distance, regionalism, threats, war, and the like are usually the major ingredients of aggregate theories. Like sociology, economics, and psychology, international relations has been gifted with men like Karl Deutsch, Ernst Haas, Morton Kaplan, Charles McClelland, Lewis Fry Richardson, Bruce Russett, J. David Singer, and Quincy Wright, who with great insight wove such concepts into theories. It is to their credit that their insights have expanded our understanding and research in international relations. It does not detract from their contribution if we now build on their efforts by shifting our conceptual framework to a new plane further removed from daily affairs, and one that introduces constructs and imbeds traditional concepts like power within an explicit logical framework allowing deduction and falsification by observation.

Decades ago, Arthur Bentley (1954) observed that the study of human affairs could benefit from thinking in terms of a social space—like physical space with dimensions, movements, locations, and spatial relationships. Social space, however, would define man's social world not in terms of physical location, but in terms of his characteristics and behavior. Others, such as Sorokin (1943), have since employed the concept of social space. Tolman (1951) has proposed a behavior space comprising individuals, their behavior and perceptions. Parsons's theory of action explicitly conceives of a social space, with his pattern variables being the dimensions of this space. Lewin (1964) has in his field theory proposed a life space of social behavior, a topological space that defines the context of behavior. And Dodd (1947) has built a complex notation describing "societal phenomena" in a social space.

Influenced by the theoretical works of the sociologist Parsons and psychologist Thurstone (1935), Quincy Wright was the first international relations theorist to represent international relations as a social space in Bentley's sense, which Wright (1955:543) calls an analytic field:

> The analytic field approach to the study of international relations . . . implies that each international organization, national government, association, individual or other 'system of action,' or 'decision maker' may be located in a multidimensional field. Such a field may be defined by co-ordinates, each of which measures a political, economic, psychological, sociological, ethical, or other continuum influencing choices, decisions, and actions important for international relations.

Wright went on to specify what these coordinates might be and to locate nations in the resulting space on the basis of subjective estimates. Much of the factor analytic work in international relations, as Wright suggested could be done, has been implicitly filling in Wright's analytic field with coordinates (dimensions) based on aggregate data.

The representation of international relations as a social space is powerful. It enables the systematization of observations, the development of mathematical theory tied to methods for testing, and the picturing of the relationships involved. A social space of international relations will be the first aggregate *construct* I will use in representing U.S. foreign actions.

In developing this social space notion, one metasociological assumption is relevant. Let us assume that in explaining the behavior of nations the *principle of relative values* operates. That is, the behavior and attributes of nations are relative. It is not the absolute economic development nor power of a nation which should be taken into consideration (most nations today are more developed and powerful than any one nation two hundred years ago), for example, but its relative power vis-a-vis some explicit other nation. And the action of one nation to another should be considered in relation to its other actions, as well as in relation to the object's behavior and that of all other nations. As we shall see, the notion of social space allows the principle of relative values to be simply incorporated.

First, consider that the foreign actions and attributes of the United States are part of the social space of nations. The United States then is located in this space in terms of its actions to other nations and its relative attributes. Second, conceptually divide the social space into behavior and attribute subspaces. The attribute subspace, which will henceforth be called attribute space, defines the location of the United States (and other nations) in terms of her relative values on all her attributes and the intercorrelation among these attributes for all nations. The origin of the space lies at the average values for the attributes. Thus, the GNP, area, population, defense budget, censorship, number of political parties, number of riots, number of Roman Catholics, etc. of the United States will locate her in this space relative to the values that other nations, the *potential objects of her actions*, have on these attributes.

As in physical space in which all the motions and spatial relationships among things are defined by three physical dimensions (ignoring time), the relationship between attributes and relative location of nations in attribute space is defined by a number of dimensions. Figure 5.4 shows the United States and five potential objects of her actions located in attribute space on two dimensions, called economic development and power bases. These two dimensions have repeatedly been delineated in attempts to define the attribute space of nations as the comparison of a number of studies has shown (Russett, 1967; Rummel,

1972). Attributes most highly correlated with the economic development dimension are energy consumption per capita, telephones per capita, and gross national product per capita. Those elements most correlated with the power bases dimension are national income, population, area, men under arms, and size of the defense budget. Not shown in Figure 5.4, but a third major dimension found to define attribute space, is political orientation, which is highly correlated with censorship, freedom to oppose the government, and proportion of communist party members. The three dimensions together—economic development, power bases, and political orientation—subsume over 40% of the variation of nations on their attributes.

Keeping attribute space in mind, for the moment, let us move to a second basic construct (where the first is social space), that of *dyad*. A dyad is a coupling of two nations together in terms of the actions of one to the other. It is an actor-object pair of nations. In terms of U.S. actions, US → China, US → USSR, US → Greece, are such dyads, where each object is coupled separately with the United States by U.S. actions toward it.

The concept of dyad now allows the behavior of a nation's subspace, henceforth to be called behavior space, to be defined. Behavior space locates all dyads relative to each other in terms of their actions. The principle of relative values is involved here also, where the origin of behavior space lies at the average values for each behavior (such as threats). Figure 5.5 shows the relative position of five dyads involving the United States as actor on two behavior space dimensions, exports and official conflict behavior.

FIGURE 5.4

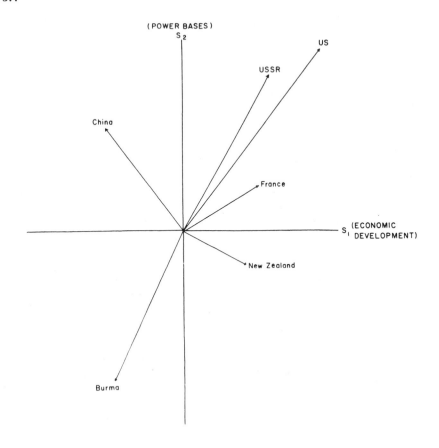

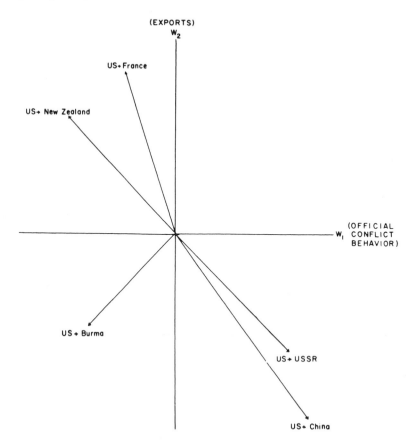

FIGURE 5.5

3. HYPOTHESES ABOUT INTERNATIONAL RELATIONS

So far, I have proposed an aggregate level representation of U.S. actions and attributes as existing in a social space, conceptually divisable into attribute and behavior spaces, and embodying the principle of relative values and the concept of dyads. This representation can now be used to tie together six hypotheses about a nation's international relations.

The first hypothesis is that the foreign behavior of a nation is linked to certain characteristics of a nation, specifically its economic development, size, and political system (whether the polity is open or closed). This hypothesis is from Rosenau's (1966) building block, which he calls the "pre-theory" approach to tying together international relations and comparative politics. For Rosenau, the three characteristics are basic for understanding the outputs of a nation. In particular, the profile a nation has on these characteristics will determine the ranking of idiosyncratic, role, governmental, societal, and systemic variables in explaining the outputs. Rosenau does not specify the manner of this linkage, for clearly he is trying to present concepts and considerations that a theory can incorporate and not a theory itself, nor does he consider how such a linkage might be tested. In other words, the hypothesis is open for considerable interpretation, and this we will do later.

The second hypothesis has to do with the concept of distance, as it has been applied in the social sciences to explain behavior. The basic idea is that the similarities between people in socioeconomic and cultural activities determine behavior; that prejudice is a function of dissimilarities in characteristics, and that interaction is the greater the more homologous the people.

The concept of distance has been employed by Quincy Wright to define the *relationships* between nations (1955:127), and particularly to develop a model of the probability of war. He proposes that the relations between two nations is a function of eight distances: Technological, Strategic, Psychological, Political, Social, Intellectual, Legal, and Expectancy (1965:332). He combined these distances in a differential equation, subjectively estimated the eight distances between the great powers in July 1939, and found that the "relative probability of war at that date was highest for Japan-USSR (.96), Germany-USSR (.86), and Germany-France (.82)" (1965:348). This work of Wright and the general connections between behavior and such distances suggest the hypothesis that the actions of nations are a function of a variety of distances between them.

The third hypothesis has to do with social stratification. Following the work on class and stratification in sociology, Johan Galtung (1964) and colleagues (Galtung, Araujo, and Schwartzman, 1966; Schwartzman, 1966; Gleditsch, 1969) have defined the international system as a status system in which nations are located on status dimensions. They then propose that the behavior of nations to each other is a function of their relative status positions. For example, if wealth, power, and prestige are status dimensions of international relations, as proposed by Lagos (1963), then the behavior of the United States to the USSR will be a consequence of the relative profiles of the United States and USSR across these three status dimensions. The third hypothesis is then that the actions of one state to another are a function of their relative statuses.

The fourth hypothesis has to do with the central thesis of international relations: the configuration of power among nations determines their policy and behavior. That power considerations structure international politics has been attested to by scholars and practitioners alike. That power is basic is a fact of practical experience and scholarly study. That power is measurable, constrainable in equations, and a concept leading to testable predictions of nation behavior, however, has not at all been established.

One of the more explicit theories of power has been offered by A.F.K. Organski (1968). He argues that nations are ranked in a power pyramid and that the international order is largely shaped by those at the top. International conflict then comes about when a nation lower down in the pyramid is changing in its power in a way to threaten to displace the more dominant nation and when there are few bonds to tie the two nations together. For Organski, international politics is shaped by the relative and changing power between nations and the bonds that bind them. This theory, then, suggests the fourth hypothesis: a nation's conflict and cooperation with another nation are the result of their relative power and cooperative ties.

The next hypothesis embodies the general orientation of those working on international and regional integration (Russett, 1963, 1967; Deutsch et al., 1957; Jacob and Teune, 1964). The fundamental notion is that the interaction and cooperation leading to political integration result from, among other things, a high level of social and cultural homogeneity, similarity in political attitudes and values, and geographical proximity. Metaphorically, like marry like. Based on this perspective, the sixth hypothesis is that the relative cooperation between nations is related to the degree of similarity between them and their geographical distance.

To assert that geographical distance conditions international relations is trite. To specify how it does so is no easy matter (Wohlstetter, 1968). Does geographical distance influence the relations between nations as astronomical distance between planets in conjunction with their mutual gravity influences the relative motion of planets? Does geographical distance only set up boundaries of behavior (Sprout and Sprout, 1962)? Or does distance provide a gradient of behavior (Boulding, 1962)? Rather than adopt any of these alternative functions at this point, I will make explicit the general hypothesis: the relations between nations are conditioned by the geographical distance between them.

To recapitulate, the six relevant hypotheses of international relations are:

1. Foreign policy behavior is a function of economic development, size, and political system.

2. The behavior of one nation to another is a function of distances.

3. The behavior of one nation to another is a function of relative status.

4. A nation's conflict and cooperation with another nation are results of their relative power and cooperative ties.

5. The relative cooperation between nations is related to their homogeneity and geographical distance.

6. The relations between nations are conditioned by the geographical distance between them. . . .

REFERENCES

BENTLEY, A. F. 1954. *Inquiry Into Inquiries: Essays in Social Theory*. Edited by S. Rutner. Boston: Beacon Press.

BOULDING, K. E. 1962. *Conflict and Defense*. New York: Harper and Row.

DEUTSCH, K. W. et al. 1957. *Political Community and the North Atlantic Area: International Organization in the Light of Historical Experience*. Princeton: Princeton University Press.

DODD, S. C. 1947. *Dimensions of Society*. New York: Macmillan.

GALTUNG, J. 1964a. Summit Meetings and International Relations. *Journal of Peace Research* 1:36–54.

——, M. MORA Y ARAUJO, AND S. SCHWARTZMAN. 1966. The Latin-American System of Nations: A Structural Analysis. *Journal of Social Research*.

GLEDITSCH, N. P. 1969. Rank and Interaction: A General Theory with Some Application to the International System. Paper presented at the Third Conference of the International Peace Research Association. Karlovy Vary, Czechoslovakia (September 21–23).

JACOB, P. E., AND H. TEUNE. 1964. The Integrative Process: Guidelines for Analysis of the Bases of Political Community.'' In *The Integration of Political Communities*, ed. P. E. Jacob and J. V. Toscano. Philadelphia: Lippincott.

LAGOS, G. 1963. *International Stratification and Underdeveloped Countries*. Chapel Hill: University of North Carolina Press.

LEWIN, K. 1964. *Field Theory in Social Science*. Edited by Dorwin Cartwright. New York: Harper Torchbooks.

ORGANSKI, A. F. K. 1968. *World Politics* . 2nd edition. New York: Alfred A. Knopf.

ROSENAU, J. 1966. Pre-Theories and Theories of Foreign Policy. In R. B. Farrell, ed., *Approaches to Comparative and International Politics*. Evanston, Ill.: Northwestern University Press.

RUMMEL, R. J. 1972. *Dimensions of Nations*. Beverly Hills, Calif.: Sage.

RUSSETT, B. M. 1963. *Community and Contention: Britain and America in the Twentieth Century*. Cambridge, Mass.: MIT Press.

—— 1967. *International Regions and the International System*. Chicago: Rand McNally.

SCHWARTZMAN, S. 1966. International Development and International Feudalism: The Latin American Case. *Proceedings of the IPRA Inaugural Conference*. Assen, Netherlands: Van Gorcum.

SOROKIN, P. A. 1943. *Sociocultural Causality, Space, Time*. Durham, N.C.: Duke University Press.

SPROUT, H. AND M. SPROUT. 1962. *Foundations of International Politics*. New York: D. Van Nostrand.

THURSTONE, L. 1935. *The Vectors of Mind*. Chicago: University of Chicago Press.

TOLMAN, E. C. 1951. A Psychological Model. In T. Parsons and E. A. Shils, eds., *Toward a General Theory of Action*. New York: Harper and Row.

WOHLSTETTER, A. 1968. Illusions of Distance. *Foreign Affairs* 46 (January).

WRIGHT, Q. 1955. *The Study of International Relations*. New York: Appleton-Century-Crofts.

—— 1965. *A Study of War* (2nd edition) Chicago: University of Chicago Press.

6
CRISIS

23.   International Crisis
as a Situational Variable

CHARLES F. HERMANN

1

Interpreters of international politics have discussed numerous variables in their efforts to understand the variety of actions taken in the name of nation-states and other international actors. Single acts of foreign policy as well as patterns of interaction have been explained in terms of goals and national interests, the available national capabilities, the type of government, the personalities of national leaders, the influential nongovernmental agents within a country, or the human and nonhuman environment outside the country. One cluster of variables of potential value in explaining the behavior of international actors characterizes the situation that provides the occasion for action. Situational analysis, as it has been applied in other areas, assumes that the ac-

tion of an agent (in this case an international actor) is a function of the immediate situation it confronts.

With appreciation for the multiplicity of variables operating in international politics and with the availability of multivariate techniques of analysis, students of world affairs have increasingly avoided reliance on simplistic, single-factor explanations of their subject. No reversal of this trend is intended in this discussion of situational analysis. Rather this essay suggests that for the explication of some foreign policy actions, specific situational variables should be examined together with other factors. Situational variables are among a number of independent variables that can be expected to contribute significantly in accounting for variation in international actions.

Assuming that a researcher plans to include reference to the immediate situation, what specific variables can he use to characterize the event? Some time ago Snyder and his associates observed: "We ought to recognize that a systematic frame of reference for the study of international politics will require several typologies, one of which will be concerned with situations." As a

Excerpted from James N. Rosenau, ed., *International Politics and Foreign Policy*, revised edition (New York: Free Press, 1969), pp. 409–421. Copyright © 1969 by The Free Press, a division of Macmillan Publishing Co., Inc. Reprinted with permission of Macmillan Publishing Co., Inc. and the author. Footnotes deleted.

step in the development of a typology of situations, individual categories of situations can be isolated and defined. Crisis constitutes one possible category if only because it has been analyzed so frequently by observers of international politics. . . .

A number of reasons can be offered for [the] state of affairs in the study of crisis. First, only the vaguest common meaning appears attached to the concept. Since many analysts fail to define crisis at all, the reader is left to infer from the context that the situation concerns some "critical" or "urgent" problem. In the attempt to call attention to every important issue, we suffer from the indiscriminate use of the term "crisis." Second, many individuals who write about crisis seem to believe in the uniqueness of every situation. At least they find unique the combination of properties necessary to provide a satisfactory explanation of a specific event. For example, in discussing some implications of economic theory for international relations, Aron observes: "It has not yet been proven that 'crisis situations' are all alike. It is possible that each crisis is unique or, if you prefer, has its own particular story. . . ." If we foster the conviction that each crisis is totally distinct from those encountered in the past and to be encountered in the future, then it is not surprising that we have little accumulated knowledge about crises. Third, the prevailing mode of analysis has been the detailed case history of a single crisis. Despite the satisfaction gained by reading a thorough and well-written case study, this method of analysis makes it unnecessary for the writer to consider how the crisis under examination compares with other situations. Not only is the development of empirically verifiable generalizations by the original author hampered, but the absence of parallel construction between case studies makes it difficult for hypotheses to be abstracted by the reader of several studies.

These difficulties must be overcome if crisis is to be used as a situational variable accounting for certain foreign policy behaviors of nations. Although this essay deals primarily with the problems of definition and analysis, the question concerning the uniqueness of events requires brief consideration.

Every situation is novel when all its properties are considered. Even two simple situations—one a carefully executed replication of the other—differ in numerous ways. Between these occurrences, time will have elapsed. The earth and solar system will have moved. Human actors will be older and will have had intervening experiences. Given the novelty of simple, controlled situations, it is clear that countless differences exist between two complex international events such as the Berlin blockade of 1948 and Khrushchev's ultimatum on Berlin in 1958. Man would be unable to cope with his daily existence, however, if he did not treat most new situations as comparable to some situations he has met or learned about in the past. For purposes of evaluation and action, all humans categorize events according to a limited number of properties and ignore the rest. . . . If we *correctly* recognize a few critical properties of an international situation which identify it as a member of a general set of situations, we may establish many things about it even without examining many other qualities that make it unique.

2

Definitions of crisis which identify a specific class of situations can be constructed with reference to either of two approaches which are among those prevalent in the contemporary study of international politics. These two are the systemic and decision-making approaches. . . .

We shall stipulate that a system is a set of actors (for example, nations, international organizations, and so on) interacting with one another in established patterns and through designated structures. In any given international political system, critical variables must be maintained within certain limits or the instability of the system will be greatly increased—perhaps to the point where a new system will be formed. A crisis is a situation which disrupts the system or some part of the system (that is, a subsystem such as an alliance or an individual actor). More specifically, a crisis is a situation that creates an abrupt or sudden change in one or more of the basic systemic variables. . . .

The characterization of crisis from the systemic approach suggests the relationship of the concept to such terms as change and conflict. Because crises engage one or more of the critical variables necessary to maintain the existing pattern of relationships between actors, they necessarily can effect significant changes in the international system. Whether or not a crisis actually produces significant change depends on a number of factors such as the nature of the modified variables, the existing destabilizing factors, and the available techniques for crisis management. Just as not all crises lead to important changes, not all significant changes are crises. A gradual shift in the rate of exchange between nations could ultimately have a profound effect on the system, despite small increments of change at any given point in time. The association of crisis with abrupt change also bears on its relationship to conflict. A conflict between parties that continues at a relatively constant level of intensity would not constitute a crisis, but a sudden shift in the level of hostilities—most notably from peace to war—would be a crisis at least for the subsystem comprised of the combatants. . . .

If a class of crisis situations can be operationally defined from the guidelines discussed above, what contribution might this variable make to the analysis of international political systems? The structures and processes that maintain an international system may be more or less subject to the sudden stresses imposed by crisis. The question then arises as to what structures and processes are most "sensitive" to crisis situations. Sensitivity can vary in several ways including the tendency for some parts of the system to be more frequently exposed to crises. For example, interactions between actors who seek alterations in their international status are more prone to crises than interactions between actors who have accepted their status positions. Sensitivity also develops because some elements of a system can vary less than others without exceeding critical thresholds. For example, a system may be able to withstand considerably greater variation in the degree of conflict between smaller states than it can between major states. Essentially these questions concern the effect of crisis on system stability and transformation. . . .

3

As the name suggests, central to the decision-making approach is the process by which decisions are made on questions of policy. Also basic to this organizing framework are the persons who, as individuals or in some collective form, constitute the authoritative decision-makers. The decision-makers behave according to their interpretation of the situation, not according to its "objective" character as viewed by some theoretical omnipotent observer. Therefore, in attempting to explain how different kinds of situations influence the type of choice that is made, the analyst must interpret the situation as it is perceived by the decision-makers.

The use of crisis as a situational variable which partially explains the policy-makers' decision is not unlike the stimulus-response model familiar to psychologists. Crisis acts as a stimulus; the decision represents a response. In the usual experimental application of this model, the researcher varies an event or act which is used to account for any observed variation in the respondent's behavior. Applying this model to the interaction between policy makers of two nation-states, several political scientists expanded the paradigm to include: (1) the stimulus or actual policy of the initiating state, (2) the perception of that stimulus by the decision-makers in the recipient state, (3) the response or actual reply of the recipient state, and (4) the perception of that response by the decision-makers in the initiating state. As in this modification of the stimulus-response model, the definition of crisis required by the decision-making approach must take into account the screening processes of human perceptions.

Those analysts who have studied crisis using the decision-making framework display no more agreement regarding the definition of crisis than do their counterparts who have applied the systemic approach. As before, we stipulate a definition which delimits a class of situations and contains some of the properties frequently associated with crisis. Specifically, a crisis is a situation that (1) threatens high-priority goals of the decision-making unit, (2) restricts the amount of time available for response before the decision is transformed, and (3) surprises the members of the decision-making unit by its occurrence. Threat, time, and surprise all have been cited as traits of crisis, although seldom have all three properties been combined. Underlying the proposed definition is the hypothesis that if all three traits are present then the decision process will be substantially different than if only one or two of the characteristics appear. Contained in the set of events specified by this definition are many that observers commonly refer to as crises for American policy-makers, for example, the 1950 decision to defend South Korea, the 1962 Cuban missile episode, and the 1965 decision to send marines to the Dominican Republic. But other situations would not be considered crises for policy-makers in the United States; the 1958 ultimatum on Berlin, the extended Greek-Turkish-Cypriot dispute, and the mission in 1964 to rescue Europeans in Stanleyville (Congo) are illustrative in this regard. The exclusion of these and other situations that do not contain at least one of the three traits does not deny the importance of these situations or the significant consequences of the resulting decisions. The classification of them as noncrises simply indicates that these situations may be different with respect to the decision process in some systematic ways from those included in the crisis set.

Before hypothesizing how the decision process in crisis differs from noncrisis, we must return to the perceptual problem. The proposed definition clearly refers to the decision-makers' perceptions of crisis situations, but how can this definition be implemented? The ideal answer is as obvious as it is difficult to achieve. Through interviews the researcher would get decision-makers to assess the amount of threat, time, and surprise they thought a given situation involved. Even if interviews should not be feasible, however, perceptual data on each crisis trait can be developed through the use of the public statements of policy-makers,

their memoirs, and reports of their perceptions by other political leaders and by journalists.

Once we assume that the decision-makers' perceptions of a situation can be measured, a phenomenological question arises: Do the elements of the definition represent actual properties of situations as well as images in the minds of policy-makers? That is, do these qualities represent measurable stimuli independent of perceptions? Experimental data have been assembled elsewhere that offer an affirmative reply to this inquiry. Without reviewing that evidence we may note that situations do vary in the extent to which they obstruct goals sought by policy-makers, and hence, situations differ in measurable threat. Moreover, most situations contain dynamic elements which lead to their evolution after a measurable period of time regardless of whether these aspects of the situations are recognized by the affected decision-makers. Finally, the frequency with which similar events have occurred in the past and the existence of contingency planning are indicators of the amount of potential surprise contained in a situation. In short, the three crisis traits can be measured directly as properties of the situation or indirectly as perceptions of the decision-makers.

Because situations differ in their degree of threat, in their duration through time, and in their amount of surprise, each of the three traits that define a crisis can be conceived as one extreme on a dimension with scale positions for every possible quantity of each property. When taken together at right angles, these three scales form a three dimensional space in which all situations can be located according to their degree of threat, time, and awareness (surprise). In Figure 6.1, this space has been closed to form a cube, the eight corners of which represent all possible combinations of the extreme values of the three dimensions. Thus, the corners of the cube represent ideal types of situations with respect to threat, time, and awareness. Few, if any, actual situations can be considered to correspond to these ideal types, but as the location in the cube of a specific situation approaches one of the corners, that situation can be treated as influencing decision-making in a manner similar to the ideal type.

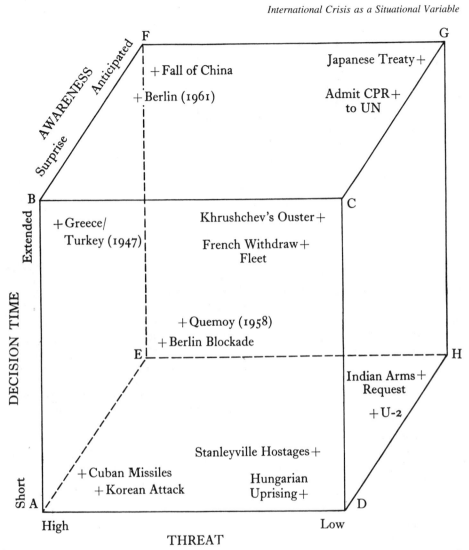

FIGURE 6.1   A situational cube representing the three dimensions of threat, decision time, and awareness, with illustrative situations from the perspective of American decision-makers. (*Note:* The representation of a three-dimensional space in a two-dimensional diagram makes it difficult to interpret the locations of the situations; their positions should not be considered exact in any case.)

A. Crisis Situation
   High Threat/Short Time/Surprise

B. Innovative Situation
   High Threat/Extended Time/Surprise

C. Inertia Situation
   Low Threat/Extended Time/Surprise

D. Circumstantial Situation
   Low Threat/Short Time/Surprise

E. Reflexive Situation
   High Threat/Short Time/Anticipated

F. Deliberative Situation
   High Threat/Extended Time/Anticipated

G. Routinized Situation
   Low Threat/Extended Time/Anticipated

H. Administrative Situation
   Low Threat/Short Time/Anticipated

To illustrate the location of a situation along a dimension, consider the element of decision time in both the Korean crisis of 1950 and the Cuban crisis of 1962. As the South Korean army crumbled before the North Korean advance, the initial optimism of American decision-makers changed to a realization that unless the United States intervened quickly the invaders would control the entire peninsula. The first meeting with the President to discuss the Korean situation occurred on Sunday evening, June 25. After a series of steps taken in the next several days to support the faltering South Korean army, President Truman decided early Friday morning, June 30, to commit American ground forces. Although Truman and his advisers considered the time to be extremely short, other situations such as the detection of a launched ballistic missile attack could offer even less time for decision. Thus, on the time dimension the Korean decision would be located near the short time end of the scale, but would not be at the most extreme point. The Cuban missile crisis also presented short decision time because, as the American policy-makers observed, once the missiles were operational they would be extremely difficult to remove without the possibility that some of them would be launched in retaliation. With missiles prepared for firing, the situation facing the leaders of the United States would be drastically altered. The first presidential session on that crisis occurred on the morning of Tuesday, October 26; the following Tuesday President Kennedy issued the "Proclamation of the Interdiction of Offensive Weapons" that ordered the blockade to begin the next morning. In actual time the decision in the missile crisis was more extended than that in the Korean crisis. If the decision-makers' perceptions of available time are used, some evidence indicates that the Korean crisis as compared to the Cuban crisis involved even less time than estimates based on clock or calendar. Despite these differences, the perceived time for both decisions puts them near the extreme of short time and both decision processes could be expected to bear resemblance to ideal type situations involving short decision time.

Hypothesized differences in decision-making introduced by crisis can be indicated by comparing crises with the other types of situations represented by the corners of the cube in Figure 6.1 The more decision-makers perceive a situation to approximate the specified characteristics of crisis, the more applicable the following comments should be.

Crisis Situations

In a crisis, with its extreme danger to national goals, the highest level of governmental officials makes the decision. The time limitations together with the ability of these high-ranking decision-makers to commit the government allow them to ignore usual bureaucratic procedures. Information about the situation is at a premium because of the short time for collecting new intelligence and the absence of the serious data-gathering that precedes expected situations of importance. To a greater degree than in other situations the inputs that provide the basis for choice must be other than information about the immediate situation. For example, decision-makers may have a tendency to rely on incomplete analogies with previous situations or on their prior judgments about the friendliness or hostility of the source of the crisis. Although some substantive disagreements may occur among the policy-makers, personal antagonisms remain subdued because of a felt need for ultimate consensus. Compared to the policies made in response to other situations, crisis decisions tend more toward under- or overreaction. An extreme response is encouraged by certain constraints imposed by the decision process (e.g., minimal information, increased importance of the decision-makers' personalities). The high stakes of a crisis decision and the uncertainty surrounding the outcome lead the decision-makers to remain quite anxious after the decision. Consequently, they expend considerable energy in the post-decision phase seeking support for their policy from allies and others.

Innovative Situations

A situation perceived to contain high threat and surprise but an extended amount of time can be described as encouraging an innovative decision. The threat to high-priority objectives increases the likelihood that the situation will receive the attention of the most able men available and, similarly, that considerable energy will be devoted to investigating the problem. Unlike a crisis decision, the greater time allows the government to undertake considerable search—a process motivated by the threat. Occasionally individuals in an agency charged with conducting foreign policy have programs or ideas that they have been unable to gain support for under normal conditions. A situation of the innovative type, for which there is no planned response and an openness to new ideas, will be sought by such individuals as an opportunity to obtain acceptance for their proposals. As in crises, ad hoc groups may be organized for the consideration of the situation, but they are not as free as crisis decision-makers to ignore normal administrative procedures.

Consider the following illustrations of innovative decisions. The deteriorating economic and political situation in Western Europe became increasingly visible to policy-makers in Washington during the last months of 1946. Against this background on February 21, 1947, the British surprised American officials by notifying them that beginning the first of April, Britain would be forced to discontinue financial assistance to embattled Greece. The same note also indicated that the British government would be unable to supply all the military assistance required by Turkey. That incident resulted in what Jones has called "the fifteen weeks" that culminated in the Marshall Plan. A second example of an innovative decision followed Nasser's nationalization of the Suez Canal in July 1956. That situation appears to have been perceived as a high-threat, surprise situation by decision-makers in Britain and France. They apparently felt that the decision time was sufficiently extended to explore several possible alternatives (e.g., the users' conference, a United Nations resolution) while coordinating their military operations that led to the dramatic attack on Egypt, October 31.

Inertia Situations

Situations perceived as involving low threat, extended time, and surprise often lead to inertia

decisions, that is, to decisions not to act or to discussions that never result in a decision. The surprise quality of the situation makes less likely the existence of preparations appropriate for coping with it. Being unexpected, no agency or bureau may see the situation as salient to its own plans. As a result the situation may be discussed by the various offices to which it is referred without the commitment of any agency. A decision is further inhibited by the absence of any sense of urgency. Given the number of policy situations at any given time that pose considerable danger to the objectives of policy-makers, this type of situation has difficulty being assigned a place on the crowded agenda of men with the authority to commit the state. Actual situations which, from the American perspective, approach the prototype for inertia decisions include the fall of Khrushchev on October 15, 1964 and De Gaulle's sudden withdrawal of the French Mediterranean Fleet from NATO in 1959. The latter situation was an annoyance to American objectives, but by itself was not recognized as a serious threat. Nor did it seem likely that De Gaulle would soon alter the situation if no American decision was made immediately.

Circumstantial Situations

Circumstantial decisions are increasingly likely in situations that policy-makers recognize as involving low threat, short time, and surprise. Like crises these are situational conditions that require a quick decision if a choice is to be made before the situation is transformed in some manner that makes action more difficult. But unlike crises, and more like inertia decisions, the stakes in the present type of situation are not high. A failure to make the "right" decision in time is not seen as leaving important national goals in jeopardy. Under these conditions whether or not the nation's policy-makers reach a decision depends on other circumstances that exist at the time the situation is recognized. In other words, the three situational variables are not likely to be critical determinants in the low threat, short time, and surprise configuration.

The captives held at Stanleyville in the Congo during November 1964 and the Hungarian revolt in November 1956 both created some threat to American objectives. On balance, however, these two situations must be located near the corner of the cube in Figure 6.1 designated "circumstantial." Both situations illustrate the importance of other factors in determining the response. When the uprising occurred in Hungary, policy-makers in the United States were preoccupied with the Anglo-French-Israeli assault on Egypt and the Suez Canal. They made no decision on the Hungarian issue until after the presence of Soviet troops had radically altered that situation. By contrast, the availability of Belgian troops and the interest of their government in cooperating with the United States to prevent the threatened murder of the European and American hostages resulted in 600 Belgian paratroopers being flown to Stanleyville on November 24, 1964, in aircraft furnished by the United States.

Reflexive Situations

The first four classes of situations involved surprise; the remaining four (located at the back of the cube in Figure 6.1) mark the opposite end of the awareness dimension. The lower left-hand corner of the cube represents situations that are recognized by policy-makers as containing high threat, short time, and anticipation. This situational configuration increases the probability of reflexive decisions. With decision time at a premium, no elaborate search routines or consultations are possible to disclose methods for coping with the situation. In this sense the decision process is similar to that for crises, the difference being that for reflexive decisions the policy-makers have expected the situation to occur. Because they will experience a serious threat to their goals if it does develop, the policy-makers probably produce a contingency plan in the period before the situation emerges. Once the situation appears, minor alterations may be made in the proposed plan, but time pressures deny decision-makers the chance to consider major alternatives. In fact, the knowledge that they have already considered the problem may lead policy-makers to an almost reflexive response. Under these circumstances the decision process will be more rapid than in a crisis.

The blockade of Berlin in 1948 provides an example. American decision-makers perceived the threat to their objectives to be severe. They also recognized decision time to be restricted both by the dwindling supply of essential commodities in Berlin and by the need for a rapid response to assure Europeans of the commitment of the United States. As early as January 1948, the Soviets introduced various restrictions on transportation moving through East Germany to Berlin. By early April, General Clay had proposed to Washington an airlift to Berlin—at least for American dependents—if access on the ground were denied. When the Soviets began to stop traffic on June 24, Clay called for an airlift to begin the following day as an interim measure. After a month, the President and his advisers agreed to continue this temporary measure on an increased scale for the duration of the blockade. The confrontation over the Taiwan Straits in 1958 may be another illustration of a situation containing the characteristics that lead to a reflexive decision. Policy-makers in the United States considered the shelling of Quemoy and Matsu islands—which began on August 23—as a serious threat requiring a quick decision if the islands were to be defended. American intelligence detected clues of the forthcoming assault during the first days of August, which added to the sense of anticipation already created by previous encounters. When the shelling of the islands began, the United States quickly responded by reinforcing the Seventh Fleet, which was operating in the area. Although engaging in overstatement, Stewart Alsop revealed the reflexive nature of the American reaction with his observation: "There is little real significance in the inner history of the 1958 crisis, simply because the basic decisions had already been made in 1954 and 1955."

Deliberative Situations

The combination of high threat, extended time, and anticipation often results in a decision process that can be described as deliberative. The reaction of decision-makers parallels that for the innovative decision in many respects. High threat increases the probability that the situation receives careful attention, but unlike a crisis, the deliberations are not limited to a small group of the highest-ranking officials. Consideration of the problem occurs at different levels and in different agencies. The time available for discussion both prior to the actual appearance of the situation (as a result of anticipation) and after it emerges (as a result of extended decision time) can lead to organizational difficulties. Many groups in and out of government may become committed to a particular method of handling the problem. As the following examples indicate, deliberative situations increase the likelihood of hard bargaining between groups with alternative proposals.

In August 1949, the Soviet Union achieved its first nuclear explosion. That threatening event had been anticipated by the American government, but had not been expected until 1952 or 1953.In the next several months it became evident to the American government that the civil war in China would result in a Communist regime on the Chinese mainland. With the background of the Soviet atomic explosion, the actual formation of the Chinese People's Republic created an anticipated situation for United States policy-makers of high threat and extended time. The response to the situation included the preparation of NSC-68, a document that makes a series of policy recommendations on the basis of a comprehensive statement of national strategy. These recommendations for rearmament involving large increases in military expenditures became the subject of an extensive debate within the Truman administration during the spring of 1950—a debate that was ultimately resolved by the attack on South Korea. The Soviet ultimatum on June 4, 1961, created a similar type of situation. The Soviet government warned that it would sign a separate peace treaty with East Germany within six months unless the Western powers withdrew their military forces from Berlin which was to become a demilitarized city. The U.S.S.R had made a similar demand in November 1958. Moreover, Khrushchev for months before the formal note was dispatched had boasted that he would sign such a treaty. Despite the anticipated quality of the situation and the relatively extended period of time for decision, the American decision-makers perceived it as quite threatening. The decision process in response to this situation involved consid-erable internal dissent among United States policy-makers as well as sharp divisions between the Western allies.

Routinized Situations

A diagonal running through the center of the cube in Figure 6.1 which has crisis decisions at one end has routinized decisions located at the other extreme. Routinized decisions frequently occur in low threat, extended time, and anticipated situations. Many, but not all, situations of this type are anticipated because they reappear with considerable regularity. Agencies charged with the conduct of foreign policy develop programmed routines for meeting recurrent low threat situations. Because established procedures are available, these situations tend to be dealt with by policy-makers at the lower and middle levels of the organization. The decision process follows one of two general patterns. In the first pattern decision-makers treat the problem in the same manner as they have treated previous situations of the same genus. Execution of the recommended course of action follows prompt agreement, unless temporary delays develop because policy-makers, whose approval is required, are engaged in more urgent business. If the situation lacks precedent or becomes the pawn in an interagency dispute, it follows the second pattern. Under these circumstances it may never come to a decision or may lie fallow until personnel change. Fear of bureaucratic obstruction provides one reason why policy-makers offer strong resistance to proposals for altering the response to an issue for which there are established procedures. For the United States the question of admitting Communist China to the United Nations is a routinized decision regularly considered before the General Assembly convenes. Efforts to change the American response to this situation—as in 1961—have met with opposition in the government. The signing of a peace treaty with Japan offers another example. American policy-makers, some of whom had anticipated the problem since the closing days of World War II, began formulating a response when the situation arose in 1947. But differences developed over the issue. Not until September 1951 was the United States able to call the San Francisco Conference at which forty-eight nations signed the treaty of peace with Japan.

Administrative Situations

The final corner of the situational cube represents low threat, short time, and anticipation—a combination that usually results in a decision process described in this essay as administrative. Administrative decisions engage middle-level officials of foreign policy organizations, men who have the authority to energize selected parts of the decision machinery for quick responses to situations that contain limited threat. Efforts to seek out new information about the situation are limited by the short decision time and by the relatively low priority of low threat situations in gaining access to the government's facilities for search. In a fashion similar to reflexive decisions, the treatment of an administrative decision depends on the extent to which policy-makers have taken advantage of their expectation that the situation is likely to occur. If they anticipate that the situation will involve minimal threat, policy-makers may be reluctant to invest much time in the preparation of a possible response. On the other hand, when a low threat situation materializes they have less of a felt need for some kind of action than do the participants in a reflexive decision. Hence, those engaged in an administrative decision are unlikely to act at all unless they are confident that the proposed response is appropriate to the situation. In brief, a low threat, short time, anticipated situation will mobilize existing work groups who will not engage in any significant amount of bargaining or search and who will reach a decision only if they are confident in their choice at the time it is made.

On May 1, 1960, when American decision-makers received notification that a U-2 reconnaissance aircraft was missing over the Soviet Union, the situation for them involved low threat, short time, and anticipation. The possibility that a U-2 might be lost over the U.S.S.R. had been considered previously. On the assumption that the Soviets would be unable to produce any substantial evidence regarding the plane's mission, United States policy-makers had prepared a series of guidelines for a cover story. The credibility of the cover story would be weakened if it were held until the Soviets made specific charges rather than being released immediately at the time the plane went down. Thus, a quick decision was made to issue the cover story. That the decision-makers had confidence in the released statement is suggested by their repetition of the story after the Soviets announced they had shot down a spy plane. Once the pilot and other evidence were produced the situation was radically changed. A second illustration of the administrative type of situation is the Indian request for arms during the October 1962 border conflict with China. The issue of military aid to India had been extensively explored during the previous months, especially since May when it appeared that India might turn to the Soviet Union for military support. When Prime Minister Nehru made an urgent appeal to the United States on October 29, the United States decision followed with such speed that the first shipments arrived within the week. This American decision was made while the highest levels of the government remained involved in the Cuban missile crisis.

We should reiterate that the statements about the decision processes that develop in response to various types of situations are hypotheses which may or may not be confirmed by further research. Thus, the statement about confidence in administrative decisions could be recast in the customary form for hypotheses as follows: The less threat and decision time and the more anticipation that decision-makers perceive in a given situation, the greater will be their initial confidence in any decision made about that situation. We hypothesize that situational variables increase the tendency for the occurrence of a certain kind of process or decision, but these variables alone may not determine the outcome. Other variables reinforce or alter the influence of the specified situational variables. It is possible, of course, that the effect of some situational configurations—perhaps crisis—is so strong that the impact of other variables seldom changes the situational effect on the decision. The question of how much variance in decisions is accounted for by particular situational variables is a matter for empirical research.

The situational cube offers one technique for increasing the cumulative knowledge about crises using the decision-making approach. The use of any classification scheme encourages the analyst to compare a particular situation with others he believes to be similar in specified qualities and to distinguish it from those assumed to be different. Many classifications for differentiating crises from other situations may prove to be of little use in explaining various types of decisions and will be discarded in favor of better alternatives. This process itself is valuable in increasing our knowledge about the important attributes of situational variables.

The examples used for the situational cube illustrate that previously written case studies can provide material for evaluating hypotheses about the effect of crises on decisions once these propositions have been advanced. As in the systemic approach, however, certain problems arise in reinterpreting a series of prepared studies, each describing an individual situation. The original authors may have excluded important information necessary for inspection of the hypotheses or they may have attached different meanings to important variables. If the same analyst examines a number of cases with the hypotheses in mind, some of these problems are overcome. Nevertheless, as we move from the statement of hypotheses about crisis as a situational variable to the rigorous testing of these hypotheses, the case study necessarily must be augmented by other methods of analysis. This requirement, together with more exact definitions of the situational variable, seems necessary for further crisis analysis using either the systemic or decision-making approaches.

24. Perception and Action
in the 1914 Crisis

OLE R. HOLSTI, ROBERT C. NORTH, AND RICHARD A. BRODY

. . . .
RELATING PERCEPTIONS TO BEHAVIOR: THE INTERACTION MODEL

We are interested not only in what national decision makers *perceive*—or say they perceive—about themselves and others. We are also interested in what they actually *do*. How are these perceptual and action elements to be brought together systematically and correlated for meaningful analysis? Basically, we are interested in internation "communication" in the sense that this concept can be used to characterize all transactions between nations. This indicates that both the verbal *and* the physical acts have information potential. The acts of one nation can be considered as inputs to other nations. The basic problem is this: given some input to a nation, what additional information do we need to account for the nation's foreign policy response?

Excerpted from J. David Singer, ed., *Quantitative International Politics*, (New York: Free Press, 1968), pp. 132–139, 141, 145–147,152–158. Copyright © 1968 by The Free Press, a Division of Macmillan Publishing Co., Inc. Reprinted with permission of Macmillan Publishing Co., Inc. Most footnotes deleted.

The conceptual framework we have selected for such analysis is a two-step mediated stimulus-response (S–r : s–R) model. These elements are as follows: A stimulus (S) is an event in the environment which may or may not be perceived by a given actor, and which two or more actors may perceive and evaluate differently. A stimulus may be a physical event or a verbal act. The stimuli relevant to international politics tend to originate with the acts of other nations (or are perceived as) directed toward a nation in question. This is not to say that domestic problems (for example, pressure for tariffs) have no relevance. Rather, it is to assert that the impetus for most decisions, especially in crisis, is extra-national. Input behavior (S) can be described in terms of the clarity and salience of the stimulus. Clarity is a function of both the nature of the act, and its intensity. Is the act physical or verbal? Is it at a high or low level of intensity? These characteristics may play a considerable part in determining the manner in which the nation-state responds (R). On the other hand, physical acts of moderate to high intensity may have a low level of salience; even a very clear stimulus may find the actors focused elsewhere. For example, during the early weeks of the 1914 crisis, British decision makers were primarily concerned with the Ulster situation rather than the events on the Continent.

A response (*R*) is an action of an actor, without respect to his intent or how either he or other actors may perceive it. Both *S*'s and *R*'s are non-evaluative and non-affective. For example, on July 29, 1914, Russia, in response to the declaration of war, ordered a partial mobilization of the southern district (*R*). Although the intention behind it was only to deter Austria-Hungary from invading Serbia, this action served as a stimulus (*S*) to Germany, which, within hours, responded by threatening a mobilization of its own (*R*).

In the model, the perception (*r*) of the stimulus (*S*) within the national decision system corresponds to the "definition of the situation" in the decision-making literature (Snyder, *et al.*, 1962; March and Simon, 1958). For example, during the crisis leading up to World War I, Germany perceived that Russia was threatening German borders. Finally, (*s*) represents the actor's expressions of his own intentions, plans, actions, or attitude toward another actor; for example, Germany asserted an intention of supporting Austria-Hungary. Both (*r*) and (*s*) carry evaluative and affective loadings. In the case of the Russian partial mobilization (*R*), although the intent behind it (*s*) was aimed solely at Austria-Hungary, it was perceived (*r*) as a serious threat by German decision-makers, who expressed their own intent (*s*) to take similar action. Three days later Germany ordered a general mobilization (*R*).

Operationally, it would be much simpler, of course, to confine oneself only to *S* and *R*, as do many traditional theories of international politics. In many situations and for many decision-makers the best predictor of state A's action response toward state B will be the nature of state B's actions. If the latter were unambiguously dangerous, one would expect them to be negatively valued by almost any individual or group in a decision-making role. Predicting President Roosevelt's response to the attack on Pearl Harbor would not be difficult. However, not all—or even most—inter-nation actions are so unambiguous. Consider, for example, Chamberlain's and Churchill's perceptions of Hitler's invitation to confer at Munich on the fate of Czechoslovakia.

There have been serious doubts about the feasibility of quantifying perceptual and affective data, and the inclination, until recently, has been to emphasize "hard" variables and aggregate data: to measure gross national products and populations, or to count troops or planes or ships or megatons, and assume that decision-makers respond to the "objective" value assigned to these capabilities by the investigator. As important as these "objective" data are, they may fail to take into sufficient account how human beings react to the factors discussed above. Many of the crucial problems of international politics concern such questions as decision-making, communication, and negotiation under varying conditions of stress. For this purpose, valuable indicators of tension are subjective ones, that is, those revealed by the decision-makers themselves. "Objective"

FIGURE 6.2 The Interaction Model.

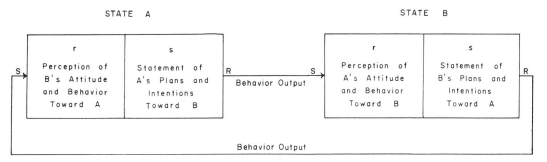

indicators of tensions, such as rising defense budget, while useful as supplementary information, may not indicate that a particular decision-maker felt himself to be under the pressure of high stress. Moreover, objective data are usually compiled on an annual, quarterly, or monthly basis. These indices may well be used to reveal the trend toward an environment conducive to crisis (Wright, 1957; K. J. Holsti, 1963; Deutsch, 1960; Russett, 1963)—such as Europe in 1914 or the cold war since 1945—but are less useful for the intensive study of a *short* time period. Thus it is particularly important for the investigator who seeks to analyze short-term changes in the international system—such as the crisis situation—to incorporate subjective data into his model.

COLLECTING THE PERCEPTUAL DATA

The selection of the 1914 crisis as the initial case in which to attempt rigorous quantitative analyses of conflict at the international level was based on several considerations. The available documentation relating to the outbreak of World War I surpasses that of any crisis of similar magnitude. Among the major nations involved, only the Serbian archives have remained relatively inaccessible to the investigator. Moreover, a generation of careful scholarship has produced published and readily accessible document collections of unquestioned authenticity, including those of Austria-Hungary (1930), France (1936), Great Britain (1926), Germany (Montegals and Schücking, 1924), and Russia (1934). The forged, altered, or incomplete collections—produced by the various governments while passions and charges of "war guilt" still ran high—have been superseded. Finally, the crisis is a classic example of war through escalation. The minor war between Austria-Hungary and Serbia—which crisis-hardened European diplomats expected to remain localized—engulfed nearly the entire continent within ten days. The existing international system—still referred to by many as the classic example of a functioning "balance of power" system—

was unable to cope with the situation as it had previously done in the recurring Balkan crises. While extensive war plans had been drawn up by the various general staffs, there is little evidence that any European decision maker wanted or expected a general war—at least in 1914.

The perceptual data were derived in whole from documents authored by selected British, French, Russian, German, and Austro-Hungarian decision makers. Those persons filling key roles such as head of state, head of government, or foreign minister were selected, unless there was a clear indication—from such standard sources as Fay (1928) or Albertini (1953)—that the person had no part whatsoever in the formulation of decisions. In addition, certain other persons who played a prominent part in the events were added. The complete list of decision-makers whose messages were subjected to content analysis is found in Table 6.1.

One issue that must be resolved in a satisfactory manner in research which is so heavily dependent upon diplomatic documents is that of *sampling*. Three potential sources of error are present. First, do the published documents represent a faithful sample of the communication between decision-makers? One difficulty is represented by that portion of communication which is not recorded—for example, face-to-face conversations, telephone messages, or conferences in which no official minutes are recorded. While the basic "sense" of such communication can often be cross-checked against diaries, memoirs, or other such sources, this type of communication represents a source of sampling error of generally unknown proportions.

A second potential source of sampling error is found in the adequacy of document collections themselves. Possible sources of loss are those attributable to misfiling or destruction of documents—either intentionally or inadvertently—and bias or carelessness by those commissioned to collect and publish them. Even in the case of intentionally destroyed documents, however, the historian or social scientist is not helpless. For example, if A destroys his copy of a message sent to B, it should still be found among B's documents.

TABLE 6.1 1914 Decision-Makers Selected for Documentary Content Analysis

Position[a]	Austria Hungary	Germany	England	France	Russia
Head of State	Franz Joseph	Wilhelm II	George V	Poincaré	Nicholas II
Head of Government	Stürgkh[b] Tisza	Bethmann-Hollweg	Asquith	Viviani	
Secretary for Foreign Affairs	Berchtold	Jagow	Grey	Viviani	Sazonov
Undersecretary for Foreign Affairs	Forgach Macchio Hoyos	Zimmermann Stumm	Nicolson	Bienvenu-Martin Berthelot Ferry	
Minister of War/Chief of General Staff	Conrad	Moltke		Messimy	Sukhomlinov
Others			Haldane[c]		

[a]Position refers to functionally equivalent roles, not to formal titles, which vary from nation to nation.

[b]Stürgkh was Austro-Hungarian Minister-President; Tisza was Hungarian Prime Minister.

[c]Lord Chancellor.

The documents published in various collections used in this study of the 1914 crisis appear to be complete. . . .

A third source of potential sampling error is in the selection of documents for content analysis by the investigator. The data in the present paper are derived from the *complete* universe, rather than a sample thereof: the *verbatim text* of published documents meeting the criteria of authorship and time (June 27–August 4).

The initial step in the exploitation of these documents was to devise perceptual units that could be defined, recognized by separate investigators, counted, and ranked along scales of more-to-less intensity. The units used in these analyses of international crisis—the *perceptions*—have been abstracted from the documents in terms of the following elements: *the perceiving party or actor; the perceived party or actors; the action or attitude; and the target party or actor.* For example, the assertion by a Russian decision maker that "The Austrian, as well as German, hope is for the ultimate annihilation of Serbia," was coded as follows:

Perceiver	Perceived	Action or Attitude	Target
Russia	Austrian	hope is for the ultimate annihilation of	Serbia
Russia	German	hope is for the ultimate annihilation of	Serbia

The 1914 documents yielded over 5,000 such cognitive and affective perceptions.

The analysis of these data has gone through three fairly distinctive states: (1) the use of only *frequency* of perceptions; (2) the recoding of the documents, and scaling of the perceptions for the *intensity* of various attributes; and (3) correlational analyses between perceptions and the various types of "*hard*" and *action* data.

Using frequency of themes as a technique of analysis, an initial paper tested two basic hypotheses about the relationships between perceptions of threat and perceptions of capability in international crisis (Zinnes, North, Koch, 1961). Theodore Abel, in his survey of decisions to go to war—including the case of 1914—had concluded that, "in no case is the decision precipitated by emotional tensions, sentimentality, crowd behavior, or other irrational motivations" (1941, p. 855). The evidence presented in that initial study strongly supported a contrary hypothesis: *If perceptions of anxiety, fear, threat, or injury are great enough, even the perception of one's own inferior capability will fail to deter a nation from going to war.*

Using perceptual data—but no action data—from the 1914 crisis, Dina A. Zinnes tested four hypotheses about the relationships between perceptions of hostility and expressions of hostility by key decision-makers (Zinnes, 1963). In the 1914 case it was found that a nation-state tends to express hostility to the degree that it sees itself to be the target of another state's hostility; and such a nation-state, on identifying the source of perceived injury, tends then to express hostility toward the perceived offending state.

Although these studies reinforced the belief that content analysis of documentary material provides a rich source of data, they also revealed the importance of measuring *intensity* as well as *frequency* of perceptions. Thus the entire set of documents was recoded for perceptions of: hostility, friendship, frustration, satisfaction, and desire to change the *status quo*. Each item was next typed on a separate card and masked to conceal the identity of the various actors. Thus the example cited above would appear as:

X's hope is for the ultimate annihilation of *Z*
Y's hope is for the ultimate annihilation of *Z*

The entire set of cards for each category (for example, hostility) was then scaled for intensity by a series of three judges on a forced-distribution scale of 1 to 9 by the Q-Sort technique (Block, 1961). The quantitative results were then aggregated into twelve time periods, each containing approximately one twelfth of the documentation.

After the complete recoding and scaling of the 1914 documents, the hypotheses relating perceptions of capability and injury were re-examined. It was found that decision-makers of each nation most strongly felt themselves to be the victims of injury precisely at that time when its leaders were making policy decisions of the most crucial nature (Holsti and North, 1965). As mentioned, perceptions of its inferior capability did not deter a nation such as Germany from going to war. The Kaiser's desperate reaction to the events which were engulfing him—perhaps best characterized by his assertion, "If we are to bleed to death, England shall at least lose India" (Montgelas and Schücking, 1924, p. 350)—is the reaction of a decision-maker under such severe stress that any action is preferable to the burden of the sustained tension.

This reaction in the face of an adversary's greater capabilities—a reaction strikingly familiar to instances in the Peloponnesian Wars, the wars

between Spain and England during the sixteenth century, and the Japanese decision to strike at Pearl Harbor (Holsti, 1963)—are not unrelated to the dilemmas of our own age of missiles and nuclear warheads. These findings underscore the need for re-examining that "common sense" and almost irresistible "conventional wisdom" which argues that deterrence is merely a matter of piling up more and/or better weapons than the opponent can amass.

COLLECTING THE BEHAVIORAL DATA

These initial studies were based solely on perceptual data, without a systematic attempt to correlate them against other data. Critics of content analysis have frequently pointed to the lack of studies in which inferences based on content data are tested against independent material (Berelson, 1952, p. 74–75). For example, is there any significant relationship between what policy-makers say and write, and the actual decisions they make? If there is not, then the value of content analysis as a research technique is placed in serious doubt. The next reasonable step, therefore, was to examine the relationship between perceptions and a series of "hard" indices. Financial data such as stock and bond prices, gold movements, commodity futures, interest rates, and other items lend themselves to this purpose. Reliable data on these indicators, measured and reported on a daily basis, are readily accessible.

The relationship between the level of tension, revealed through the content analysis of documents, and political decision-making may be investigated directly or indirectly. The direct approach involves a search for correlation between the results of the content analysis and such actions as troop movements, mobilization, breaking of diplomatic relations and the like. The indirect approach involves a correlation of the "soft" variables with a set of indices which are presumed to be sensitive to international tension levels.

The financial indicators discussed here are of the latter type. Although they respond to events other than international political crises, the history of 1914 rules out other causes of fluctuation. Given fluctuations of financial indicators, correlated with increases and decreases in international tension, these indicators can be used to check the validity of content analysis data. If the latter covary both with the political/military actions of nations participating in the crisis and with the fluctuations of financial indicators that respond to the tensions born of these actions, confidence in the content analysis techniques is substantially enhanced.

The results of the investigation of these indirect relationships follow.

The Flow of Gold

. . . When the movement of gold is compared to the daily fluctuations in the intensity of perceived hostility there is a significant correlation ($r_s = .85$). It is interesting to note, for example, that the drop in perceiver hostility on Monday, July 27, is matched by a sharp rise in the influx of gold. During the preceding weekend many observers and participants, including the Kaiser and Winston Churchill, had felt that the Serbian reply to the ultimatum marked the end of the crisis. Similarly the steady rise in hostility starting on July 28 corresponds to the withdrawal of gold in panic proportions. . . .

The Prices of Securities

The data analyzed here consist of twenty of the most important stocks and bonds for Serbia, Russia, France, Germany, Austria-Hungary, England, and Belgium, traded on the London, St. Petersburg, Paris, Berlin, Vienna and Brussels exchanges. To facilitate interpretation, the price of each security is given as a percentage of its value during the pre-crisis week (June 20–26). The index is the average value for the twenty securities. When the composite index is compared to the fluctuations in the intensity of perceived hostility, there is again an evident similarity. The decrease in perceived hostility on July 27 is matched by a slight rise in the value of securities. Some individual shares of those nations most intimately involved in the Austro-Serbian dispute rose quite markedly—Serbian Bonds (2.5%), Russian Bonds (2.5%), and Austrian Credit Shares (1.7%). Subsequently there was a virtual

collapse in prices, corresponding to the rise in perceived hostility. The figures on the extent of the collapse in the last few days of the crisis are actually stated conservatively. In the first place, many of the quoted prices were, according to observers, nominal and thus higher than the actual price for which one could sell his securities (*Economist*, August 1, 1914, p. 231). Secondly, for the purpose of the index, the price of a security that was no longer traded—usually due to the closing of various exchanges—are carried through July 30 at the last quoted price. . . .

In contrast, the paper losses in values of the stocks and bonds of the major participants in the crisis were staggering. In the ten-day period ending July 30, the value of 387 representative British stocks fell by £188,000,000. By July 25, the value of the securities of twenty-three German industrial firms had dropped from £79,000,000 to £65,900,000—and the worst was yet to come! In one sense the "cost" of the war reached catastrophic proportions even before the first shot was fired (*Economist*, August 1, 1914, p. 229; August 29, 1914, p. 383). Thus the comparison with the securities of belligerents and neutrals during the crisis strongly suggests that the virtual collapse of prices during July 1914 was directly related to rising international tensions. . . .

RELATING PERCEPTION AND MILITARY ACTION

The next step was to test the basic interaction ($S–r : s–R$) model with the data. Students of conflict have frequently asserted that parties acting in crisis situations reveal more or less consistent patterns of rising tensions and escalation leading to violence (Boulding, 1962; Richardson, 1960). Within the context of international politics, the line of reasoning can be summarized as follows: If state A—correctly or incorrectly—perceives itself threatened by state B, there is a high probability that A will respond with threats of hostile action. As state B begins to perceive this hostility directed toward itself, it is probable that B, too, will behave in a hostile (and defensive) fashion. This threatening behavior by B will confirm for A that its initial perceptions were correct, and A will be inclined to increase its hostile (and defensive) activity. Thereafter, the exchanges between the two parties will become increasingly negative, threatening, and injurious (North, 1962).

An initial and partial test of this sequence of interaction was carried out by correlating perceptual, or affective, data from 1914 with the spiral of military mobilizations just prior to the outbreak of World War I (North, *et al.*, 1964). The findings suggest that mobilizations accounted for a considerable part—but by no means all—of the variance in hostility. There was a steady rise in hostility *prior to* any acts of mobilization, and thus, to some degree, the decision makers were responding to verbal threats and diplomatic moves, rather than to troop movements, in earlier phases of the crisis. This study thus revealed the necessity of correlating perceptual data with other types of action data. It also underscored the importance of testing hypotheses in other crisis situations, since there was little in the 1914 data to suggest under what conditions the exchange of threats leads to "de-escalation," as appears to have happened in the October, 1962, Cuban crisis, rather than to a conflict spiral.

The action data (S and R in the model) were expanded to include all events of a military character involving nations in the 1914 crisis either as agents or targets of actions. These were gathered from standard military histories of the period (Edmunds, 1937; McEntee, 1937; Frothingham, 1924) and such usually reliable newspapers as the *New York Times, Times* (London), and *Le Temps* (Paris). Wherever possible the reports were verified in an authoritative history of the crisis (Albertini, 1953). If serious doubt existed about the accuracy of an item—in the closing days of the crisis newspapers were filled with many unsubstantiated charges and countercharges—the item was discarded. As with the documentary data, the action data were coded in a uniform format; that is, according to the *agent* of action, the *action*, and the *target* of action. Unless the target of action was *explicit*, it was coded as general. The coding yielded three hundred and fifty-four military actions, of which the following are examples:

Agent	Action	Target
French Chamber	approves a 3-year military law	(general)
German fleet	leaves Norway for home ports	(general)
Austrian army	bombarded	Belgrade
Churchill (Britain)	orders shadowing in the Mediterranean of	two German battle-cruisers
Germany	declares war on	France

. . . For purposes of combining action and perceptual data in the $S–r : s–R$ model, both the s and r stages in the model are operationalized solely in terms of the hostility variable. Previous studies involving multivariant analysis, which have revealed hostility to be the best predictor of action, are supported in the present study. With violence of action as the dependent variable, only the rank-order correlation coefficient for hostility ($rs = .66$) is statistically significant. A convenient starting point is to assume congruence across the $S–r : s–R$ model. In these terms it is postulated—however tentatively—that a given amount of violence (or any other quality which the investigator wishes to measure) in an environmental stimulus (S) will yield an appropriate level of expressed affective response (r) which, in turn, will stimulate an expressed "intent" (s) of like affective loading and a response (R) at about the same level of violence as the original stimulus (S). Where data from historical crisis situations provide incongruent patterns across the model, other sources of variance must be sought to account for the discrepancy between the expected and obtained relationship. . . .

Previous studies have suggested that in situations where two or more actor-nations are minimally engaged or involved in an interaction, the environmental stimulus (S) may yield an accurate prediction of an actor-nation's response (R). Stated somewhat differently, S may be the best predictor of R in circumstances where the actor-nations perceive that neither the penalties nor the rewards are likely to be of any great significance (Zaninovich, 1964).

The first hypothesis specifies the conditions under which the degree of congruence between S and R is high or low.

The correlation between input action (*S*) and policy response (*R*) will be better in a situation of low involvement than in one of high involvement.

This suggests that in the *low* involvement situation, the analysis of perceptions (*s* and *r*) may be less crucial, and that "objective" criteria may give the analyst adequate information. Rummel's (1964) findings that domestic data predict state behavior fairly well—except under conditions of high conflict—can be interpreted as lending support to this hypothesis.

Of the two coalitions engaged in the crisis, the Triple Entente was engaged for a much shorter period. During the month between June 27 and July 27, that coalition revealed a total of only 40 perceptions of hostility compared to 171 for the Dual Alliance; in the late period (July 28 to August 4) the figures were 229 and 270 respectively.[1] This certainly coincides with the historians' consensus.

. . . The degree of congruence between *S* and *R* for the less-engaged coalition, the Triple Entente, is considerably lower ($r_s = .463$) than that for the Dual Alliance ($r_s = .678$). Several explanations are possible. First, at least two members of the Triple Entente—England and France—acted (*R*) with a high level of violence only relatively late in the crisis period, withholding action until the threat (*S*) from the Dual Alliance was quite clearly defined.

On the other hand, the actions of the Dual Alliance—and particularly Austria-Hungary's actions in the early and middle part of the crisis period leading to a hoped-for local war—were not commensurate with the level of violence displayed by either Serbia or other members of the Triple Entente. There were two overlapping crises which became one at midnight August 4. The first was the result of a rather deliberately planned local war that had little to do with the actions of the other major powers and in which the members of the Triple Entente were only minimally engaged; the second resulted in an unplanned escalation into general war, engulfing all the nations.

A second hypothesis including the *S* and *R* (action) stages of the model is concerned not only with congruence or lack of congruence, but with the direction of differences.

In a situation of low involvement, policy response (*R*) will tend to be at a lower level of violence than the input action (*S*), whereas in a high-involvement situation, the policy response (*R*) will tend to be at a higher level of violence than the input action (*S*).

In terms of the events of 1914, the hypothesis suggests that the nations of the Triple Entente would under-respond to actions from the other side, whereas those of the Dual Alliance would be over-reacting to the threat from the Triple Entente. A Mann-Whitney *U* Test (Siegel, 1956, pp. 116–127) to compare the magnitude of the difference between input (*S*) and output (*R*) action reveals that the values for the Dual Alliance are indeed consistently negative (indicating over-reaction), whereas those of the Triple Entente are positive (under-reaction) on balance.

The inability to predict reactions (*R*) solely on the basis of action (*S*) suggests an examination of the relationship between action, perceptual, and situational variables.

Where such lack of congruence between input and output action exists, the intervening perceptions may perform either an accelerating or decelerating function. This suggests the hypothesis that

In the low-involvement situation, *r* will tend to be at a lower level than *S*, whereas in the high-involvement situation *r* will tend to be higher than *S*.

Intuitively the hypothesis makes sense. In a period of relative calm and low involvement, perceptual distortion will probably tend in the direction of under-perception; one may even be lulled into a false sense of security by failing to perceive a real threat. The British and French reaction to Nazi Germany—until the aggressive actions of Hitler became so unambiguous that even Chamberlain and Daladier perceived the danger—is a case in point. During a period of intense stress, on the other hand, when all fingers are near or on the trigger, even the most innocent action may

---

[1] $\chi^2 = 45.8$, and with $df = 1$, $P = < .001$. [This is statistically significant—ED.].

be perceived as a threat of great magnitude. This pattern is much like that exhibited by Kaiser Wilhelm during the intense crisis leading up to World War I. Although possessor of the world's second ranking navy, at one point he perceived the presence of a few Russian torpedo boats in the Baltic as adequate cause for alerting the entire German fleet (Montgelas and Schücking, 1924, p. 223).

The hypothesis is supported by the 1914 data. Table 12[2] reveals the difference beween the level of input action (S) and perceptions of those actions (r). The leaders of the Dual Alliance consistently overperceived the level of violence in the actions of the Triple Entente. On the other hand, the Triple Entente tended to underperceive the actions of the other coalition.

The same hypothesis can also be tested in a somewhat different way. The first six periods (June 27–July 27) have been described as those in which the members of the Dual Alliance were highly involved with the events in the Balkans, whereas those of the Triple Entente were not. On the other hand, during the culminating periods of the crisis (July 28–August 4), nations in both alliances were being drawn into war. Thus, if the hypothesis is correct, differences in the way in which actions (S) are perceived (r) by nations of the two coalitions should be greatest during the early stages of the crisis. When the data in Table 12 are reanalyzed in this manner, the hypothesis is again supported. The difference between the two coalitions in regard to the S–r link during the early period is statistically significant ($U = 4$, $p = .013$), whereas in the later period it is not ($U = 11$, $p =$ n.s.).

A further hypothesis within the model relates perceptions of one's own intent, with perceptions of the intent of others. Boulding (1959), Osgood (1962), and many others have pointed to the propensity of nations to perceive their own intentions in the best light possible, while attributing more hostile motives to those of others.

To the extent that there is a difference between perceptions of the other's policy (r) and statements of own intent (s), perceptions of hostility in r will tend to be higher than in s in *both* the low-involvement and the high-involvement situations.

The figures in Table 13 support the hypothesis both in that the level of perceived hostility for (r) is consistently higher than for (s), and in that there is no significant difference between the two coalitions.[3] The final intervening perceptual link in the model is that between the perception of one's own behavior (s) and the level of violence in the actual response (R). The hypothesis is that

In the situation of low involvement, statements of intent (s) will tend to be higher than action responses (R), whereas in the high-involvement situation, s will tend to be lower than R.

Again there is at least intuitive support for the hypothesis. In a situation of high involvement, whether the action is essentially cooperative or conflictual, the effort one makes often far surpasses stated intent. The efforts of war-torn Western European nations after 1945 toward rebuilding economies, establishing supranational organizations, and contributing to the defense of Europe during the period of most severe Soviet threat undoubtedly exceeded the plans and intentions of most leaders. In the case where one feels little stress, on the other hand, the propensity of promises to run ahead of performance appears enhanced. The subsequent European unwillingness to raise NATO divisions, even to the promised and planned level can, at least in part, be attributed to a situation of less likelihood of massive Soviet invasion of Western Europe.

Table 14,[4] however, reveals that there is, in fact, no difference between the two coalitions in regard to the s–R linkage. In both cases, R is consistently higher than s; that is, the states in both coalitions tended to react at a higher level of violence than suggested by the statements of intent by their various leaders.

[2]Table 12, which has been deleted, shows a statistically significant relationship: $U = 32$, $p = < .025$—ED.

[3]Table 13, which has been deleted, shows no statistically significant relationship: $U = 67$, $p =$ n.s.—ED.

[4]Table 14, which has been deleted, shows that $U = 50$, $p =$ n.s.—ED.

SUMMARY OF FINDINGS

The analysis of the 1914 crisis began with an assumption basic to most traditional theories of international politics—that is, the assumption of congruence between input (*S*) and output (*R*) action. The data revealed, however, a significant difference between the two coalitions corresponding to the different levels of involvement in the situation. . . .

Having failed to account for the escalation from a local incident to a general war with only the action variables, the perceptual variables (*r*) and (*s*) were analyzed. The various links across the model were examined and no significant difference between the two coalitions in regard to the *s*–*R* step was found: (*R*) was higher than (*s*) in both cases. As predicted, there was little difference between the Triple Entente and Dual Alliance in the *r*–*s* link, both perceiving themselves as less hostile than the other coalition. A significant difference did appear at the *S*–*r* step, however. The leaders of the Dual Alliance consistently over-perceived the actions of the Triple Entente. Thus the *S*–*r* link served a ''magnifying'' function. The decision-makers of the Triple Entente, on the other hand, tended to under-perceive the actions of the Dual Alliance. This difference in perceiving the environment (the *S*–*r* link) is consistent with the pronounced tendency of the Dual Alliance to respond at a higher level of violence than the Triple Entente. . . .

REFERENCES

ABEL, THEODORE. 1941. The Element of Decision in the Pattern of War. *American Sociological Review.* (Dec): 853–859.

ALBERTINI, LUIGI. 1953. *The Origins of the War of 1914.* 3 vols. New York: Oxford University Press.

BERELSON, BERNARD. 1952. *Content Analysis in Communication Research* New York: Free Press.

BLOCK, JACK. 1961. *The Q-Sort Method in Personality Assessment and Psychiatric Research.* Springfield, Ill.: Charles Thomas.

BOULDING, KENNETH E. 1962. *Conflict and Defense.* New York: Harper and Row.

_____. 1959. National Images and International Systems, *Journal of Conflict Resolution* 3: 120–131.

DEUTSCH, KARL W. 1960. Toward an Inventory of Basic Trends and Patterns in Comparative and International Politics. *American Political Science Review* 54: 34–57.

EDMUNDS, SIR JAMES E. 1937. *Official History of the War, Military Operations: France and Belgium 1914.* 3d ed. London: Macmillan.

FAY, SIDNEY B. 1928. *The Origins of the World War.* New York: Macmillan.

FROTHINGHAM, THOMAS C. 1924. *The Naval History of the World War: Offensive Operations, 1914–1915.* Cambridge, Mass.: Harvard University Press.

HOLSTI, KALEVI J. 1963. The Use of Objective Criteria for the Measurement of International Tension Levels. *Background* 7: 77–96.

HOLSTI, OLE R. 1963. The Value of International Tension Measurement. *Journal of Conflict Resolution* 7:608–617.

_____, AND ROBERT C. NORTH. 1965. Perceptions of Hostility and Economic Variables. *Comparing Nations*, ed. Richard L. Merritt. New Haven: Yale University Press.

McENTEE, GIRARD L. 1937. *Military History of the World War.* New York: Scribner's.

MARCH, JAMES G., AND HERBERT A. SIMON. 1958. *Organizations.* New York: John Wiley.

MONTGELAS, MAX., AND WALTER SCHÜCKING, eds. 1924. *Outbreak of the World War: German Documents Collected by Karl Kautsky.* New York: Oxford University Press.

NORTH, ROBERT C. 1962. Decision-making in Crises: An Introduction. *Journal of Conflict Resolution* 6: 197–200.

_____, RICHARD A. BRODY AND OLE R. HOLSTI. 1964. Some Empirical Data on the Conflict Spiral. *Peace Research Society Papers.* I: 1–14.

OSGOOD, CHARLES E. 1962. *An Alternative to War or Surrender.* Urbana, Ill.: University of Illinois Press.

RICHARDSON, LEWIS F. 1960. *Arms and Insecurity.* Chicago: Quadrangle.

RUMMEL, RUDOLPH J. 1964. Testing Some Possible Predictors of Conflict Behavior within and between Nations. *Peace Research Society Papers I*: 79–111.

RUSSETT, BRUCE M. 1963. *Community and Contention: Britain and America in the Twentieth Century.* Cambridge, Mass.: MIT Press.

SIEGEL, SIDNEY. 1956. *Nonparametric Statistics for the Behavioral Sciences.* New York: McGraw-Hill.

SNYDER, RICHARD C., H. W. BRUCK, AND BURTON SAPIN, eds. 1962. *Foreign Policy Decision-Making.* New York: Free Press.

WRIGHT, QUINCY. 1957. Design for a Research Proposal on International Conflict and the Factors Causing Their Aggravation or Amelioration. *Western Political Quarterly* 10: 263–275.

ZANINOVICH, GEORGE. 1964. An Empirical Theory of State Response: The Sino-Soviet Case. PhD. dissertation, Stanford University.

ZINNES, DINA A., ROBERT C. NORTH, AND HOWARD E. KOCH, JR. 1961. Capability, Threat and the Outbreak of War. In James N. Rosenau, ed., *International Politics and Foreign Policy: A Reader in Research and Theory*. New York: Free Press.

_____ . 1963. Expression and Perception of Hostility in Inter-State Relations. Ph.D. dissertation, Stanford University.

25. The Beginning, Duration, and Abatement of International Crises: Comparisons in Two Conflict Arenas

Charles A. McClelland

CRISIS BETWEEN PEACE AND WAR

In the relations between sovereign nations there is no more visible and important development than the transition from peace to war. When a series of events having the potential of this transition is recognized, national governments give close attention to all utterances and occurrences that appear to relate to the prospect of a change to war. Also, public interest becomes focused on the train of events leading along "the road to war." With gratifying frequency, the anticipated transition does not run its full course. It turns out to be a false prelude; the involved parties somehow find escape routes to avert a showdown and hence the shift from peace to war does not occur. Over the past century the concept of *international crisis* has come into use in international politics

Excerpted from Charles F. Hermann, ed., *International Crises: Insights from Behavioral Research*, (New York: Free Press, 1972), pp. 83–105. Copyright © 1972 by The Free Press, a Division of Macmillan Publishing Co., Inc. Reprinted with permission of Macmillan Publishing Co., Inc. and the author. Footnotes deleted.

to identify this transition. A crisis refers to both a real prelude to war and an averted approach toward war. Crises are most commonly thought of as interpositions between the prolongation of peace and the outbreak of war. . . .

THE SYSTEMIC APPROACH TO THE STUDY OF CRISES

Different research approaches need to be called into play to deal with different aspects of crisis problems and with the several distinctions noted above. For some questions about crises the most direct approach is in the study of the foreign policies of the participants. Given the relevant records of the decision makers of governments involved in a crisis, the study of the intentions, the perceptions, the incoming information, and the decisions of the participants would tell most of the story of how the crisis happened and what role, if any, it played in a transition between peace and war. Although important parts of the data having to do with policy processes, perceptions, information, intentions, and alternative courses of action are usually guarded from the public view, research on crisis decision making has been going forward with considerable success. Many of the studies reported in this volume have been done from the decision-making or "actor" point of view. Another approach is to develop analyses from the standpoint of "system" phenomena.

The main characteristic of the systemic approach to crisis is its preoccupation with the exchanges of words and deeds occurring in the arena of conflict. It is the "external behaviors" of the parties in the conflict that are given full attention. Those who concentrate on crisis decision-making problems deal mainly with *intra-unit* situations and processes whereas the students of international systems primarily investigate *inter-unit* phenomena. Of course, both intra-unit and inter-unit analyses should eventually be joined and synthesized, but at present there is an advantage in having different approaches to discover as much as possible according to these different perspectives. A division of labor is justified. Some problems are handled more effectively by one basic approach and some are more easily studied according to the other orientation. Different combinations of data are made and different organizing concepts are utilized. A practical reason for developing at least two kinds of attacks on the research problems of international crises is that large amounts of data need to be collected and analyzed and the separating of intra-unit and inter-unit materials helps to keep the work to manageable proportions.

The systemic approach followed in the reporting of research in this chapter ignores the impact of public opinion, the effects of informal and nongovernmental pressures, and the part played by the organizational, perceptual, motivational, and personality aspects of crisis behavior. No attention is given to the process of making decisions within governments under crisis conditions. The focus is on the interflow of actions and responses of the crisis participants.

Findings will be presented to show how an international crisis can be identified and distinguished from at least some pseudo-crisis. Then the problem of accounting for changes in behavior which are thought to be important in the abatement phases of crises is considered from a systemic point of view.

THE BERLIN AND TAIWAN CONFLICT ARENAS

The research has been given specific direction through the study and comparison of two arenas of international conflict. One is the Berlin conflict. International crises are generally considered to have occurred in the long struggle to control Berlin and the accesses to the city. Data pertaining to the actions and responses of the contending parties were gathered for the period from January 1, 1948, through December 31, 1963. The other conflict arena that has been studied is that of the Taiwan Straits between 1950 and 1964. Reported interactions of the contending parties were gathered in the same general way as for the Berlin confrontations. Public sources (mainly contemporary news reports) were used in making these chronological collections of data. The selection of items was guided by the question: "Who did what to whom and when?" Both verbal actions and physical actions (deeds) were collected. During the sixteen years included in the analysis of the Berlin conflict 1,791 interaction items were identified; for the fifteen years of the Taiwan Straits conflict 2,625 items were recorded. The Berlin material was restricted somewhat by a selection of items related directly to access—that is, the events concerning movement and transport within, to, and from the occupied city. This limitation stemmed from the requirements of an earlier inquiry of subsystem phenomena for which the Berlin data were originally collected.

Far too much information was acquired to permit incorporating all of it into narrative accounts. The idea needs emphasis that the purpose of collecting the information was not to construct some historical descriptions of events but, rather, to allow the building of something resembling box scores of actions and responses. The research was attentive to the external behaviors of the conflict participants and has exploited quantitative information on the performance records of these participants in the two arenas of conflict. . . .

Very important from the standpoint of the research problem of identifying real crises has been the frequent fluctuations in the actions of the contesting parties in the two arenas. The underlying motivations of the contestants appear to have remained quite constant, at least in terms of the determination to displace and to resist displacement, but the campaigns to attain these goals have varied greatly across time periods. On five different occasions the confrontations have become active and intense to the extent that news commentators at the time characterized the situations as "crises."

In 1948 the Soviet occupation authorities in Berlin gave orders which resulted in the attempt to seal the city against access from the Western zones of Germany and beyond. The famous Soviet blockade and the countering Western airlift of supplies then followed. The blockade was lifted in 1949 by agreement between the Western and Soviet governments and the airlift was no longer needed.

Late in 1954 Communist China launched an effort to gain possession of a number of small islands along the China coast. In the "Tachens crisis" of 1955, the mainland regime succeeded partly in its objective although strenuous objections and resistance came from both the Nationalist Chinese and the United States.

Another attempt to possess the Nationalist terrain was made in 1958 when a large artillery barrage from the mainland was directed mostly at the Quemoy group of islands. This attack was so heavy and continuous that the Nationalist troops stationed on the big island of Quemoy were cut off from supplies and access from Taiwan. The Quemoy crisis was centered on this action and the efforts made to break through or halt the Communist Chinese attack. Minor diplomatic accommodations were made in a series of exchanges between Communist China and the United States; the Quemoy crisis declined before the end of 1958.

At about the time of the abatement of the Quemoy crisis the confrontation in the Berlin arena was intensified. In November 1958 the Soviet Union served notice on the Allied powers in Berlin that the occupation status of the city was to be ended and six months were allowed for Allied cooperation in concluding the occupation. Otherwise, the Soviet Union proposed to act unilaterally and to turn over its Berlin affairs to the East Germans. The press proclaimed this "Deadline crisis" the worst since 1948. Nevertheless, the deadline passed without serious consequences and perhaps face was saved sufficiently by the convening of a foreign ministers' conference in May 1959 to mark the decline and end of that particular episode.

In August 1961 the Berlin arena again became very active when the East began the construction of the wall, running for miles through the city and cutting the movement of Berliners between the East and West sectors. Many incidents occurred involving the occupation forces. On one day late in October 1961, Soviet and American military units were in a tense and extreme confrontation for several hours. Few observers failed to call the Berlin Wall affair a "crisis."

These five occasions, then, provide material for research. The most recent pair of crises—Quemoy and the Berlin Wall—are of particular interest. Much experience in the thrust and parry of crisis interchange had accumulated before their occurrence and, presumably, these two crises illustrate the seasoned skills of the involved parties at crisis and conflict. If there are patterns of behavior that took shape earlier in these affairs, the two crises late in the series should reflect them. We should be able to demonstrate from the data whether or not some basic questions can be answered. Is it possible to identify crises by means other than the general feel of the situation or the judgments of contemporary observers and participants? Can the occurrence of a crisis be established by noting changes in the streams of action and response of the participants? In a chronic international conflict that is seldom far from a state of war, are there notable differences in behavior that mark a crisis?

THE QUANTITY AND VARIETY OF EVENTS

The most obvious way to approach these questions about observable changes in behavior is to look into the frequency of occurrence of the interactions within specified time periods. We can obtain results from the quantity of events data at once. The reader can identify "crisis years" in the two arenas by noting the main variations in Tables 6.2 and 6.3.

Even as rough a measure as the annual frequencies of occurrence of acts suggests that 1948 and 1961 stand apart in the Berlin arena. The same is true for 1955 and 1958 in the Taiwan arena. The single casualty of the annual frequency indicator of crisis is the 1958–1959 Deadline crisis at Berlin. Clearly, the Soviet ultimatum did not have much effect on the access interactions. It did not trigger a crisis if a crisis is to be defined by a sudden increase in the frequency of interactions. On the other hand, the strength of the crisis years as measured by the volume of activity is shown by the fact that the two crisis years of 1948 and 1961 at Berlin took up 35.6 per cent of the total volume of the action in the period 1948–1963 while the two years of 1955 and 1958 constituted 51 percent of the Taiwan total (1950 through 1964).

One possibility is that world news reporting becomes more attentive and, therefore, more voluminous during certain periods. The amount of news that sometimes is *not* reported is a very difficult problem to approach. In any case the simple volume indicator which increases appreciably in times ordinarily regarded as crisis periods is useful. It would be better if another indicator were used, particularly if it could show with more precision when international crises have started and how long they have lasted. In earlier research reports we have called the indicator capable of these accomplishments a *variety measure*. The development of the variety measure depends on the categorization of the actions and responses by type for the conflict participants.

Obviously, there could be several different ways to group 4,416 reported events in the two conflict arenas. The method followed in the research was to develop a list of different *kinds* of actions and responses found in the data. Some acts are so definite and clear that classifying them under a heading presents no difficulties. For example, the delivery of a protest note by one government to another is a common occurrence and is readily typed as a PROTEST. On the other hand, a category such as REQUEST turns out to be a composite which puts together several specific subtypes of acts such as "ask for information," "ask for material help," "request action," "appeal to," and "seek policy support." The single word REQUEST does not truly describe all that is subsumed. At present the classification system consists of sixty specific types of acts committed by participants in international politics. Our current practice is to group these more generally under twenty-two not-entirely-descriptive labels as follows: YIELD, COMMENT, CONSULT, APPROVE, PROMISE, GRANT, REWARD, AGREE, PROPOSE, REJECT, ACCUSE, PROTEST, DENY, DE-

TABLE 6.2   Annual Totals of Acts Committed in the Berlin Arena, 1948–1963

	1948	1949	1950	1951	1952	1953	1954	1955	1956	1957	1958	1959	1960	1961	1962	1963
East*	210	81	87	61	128	58	22	38	10	11	14	23	43	149	88	39
West†	144	44	57	39	69	36	16	27	7	7	7	22	33	135	63	23
Both	354	125	144	100	197	94	38	65	17	18	21	45	76	284	151	62

* "East" includes East Germany, East Berlin, and the Soviet Union.

† "West" includes West Germany, West Berlin, the United States, France, and Great Britain.

TABLE 6.3   Annual Totals of Acts Committed in the Taiwan Arena, 1950–1964

	1950	1951	1952	1953	1954	1955	1956	1957	1958	1959	1960	1961	1962	1963	1964
U.S.S.R. and Communist China	47	30	5	11	188	297	87	81	399	104	74	50	45	34	28
U.S. and Nationalist China	85	30	18	27	176	291	64	53	298	26	23	11	19	13	10
Both	132	60	23	38	364	588	151	134	697	130	97	61	64	47	38

MAND, WARN, THREATEN, DEMONSTRATE, RE-
DUCE RELATIONSHIP, EXPEL, SEIZE, and FORCE.
The Berlin analysis was done in part with a shorter
list of eighteen types of acts and with somewhat
different labels. The Taiwan analysis employed
a list of twelve types at one stage of the work but
new research on the Taiwan data has used the
current categorization. In addition, the standard
time unit used in counting the number of acts was
shortened from a year to a month for the development of the variety measure results. Later in the
reporting, the time unit will be changed to a day
when the details of crisis periods are examined.

Because the interaction data are organized
chronologically, it is possible to count the frequencies of occurrences of acts, month by month,
through the years 1948–1963 and 1950–1964 for
the respective conflict arenas and for the respective behaviors of the participants. To simplify
reporting, we have made the confrontations and
crises two-sided affairs by counting the acts of
all parties together on one side of the conflict and
the acts of the other parties together on the other
side of the conflict. Thus *East* and *West* are labels
which reflect the combining although they may
seem not entirely appropriate in the Taiwan case.
To illustrate, in the Berlin arena in June 1962,
West produced seven PROTESTS, two DEMANDS,
two SEIZES, two REQUESTS, and a scattering of
single acts in other categories for a total of seventeen. *East*, in the same arena and the same month,
committed eight SEIZES, nine YIELDS, four DE-
MANDS, two ACCUSES, and a scattering of single
acts in other categories for a total of twenty-nine.
In order to remove the effect of variations in the
volume of activity from time period to time
period, we converted the frequency counts to percentages of the whole. Thus, in the illustration
given above, *West*'s PROTESTS were 7/17 or 41.1
per cent of the whole, *East*'s DEMANDS were
4/29 or 13.8 per cent, and so on for the other
categories. Thereafter, the percentages were
transformed to corresponding logarithmic numbers to the base two.

There are two main reasons for converting the
percentages to the corresponding logarithmic
numbers. First, this operation permits a measurement to be achieved that allows comparisons on
a common basis of changes in interactions in two

or more international conflict arenas and at different time periods. Second, it has a normalization
effect on the data so that small frequencies are
somewhat enhanced and large frequencies are
somewhat diminished. To illustrate the first advantage, let us consider a hypothetical case in
which a party in a conflict could do only five
different kinds of acts: *A, B, C, D,* and *E.* Let us
say that this party committed fifty acts in a given
time period. One possible distribution appears in
Table 6.4. Although an observed instance with
exactly equal distribution might be unusual, it
could happen. Another distribution that one might
observe appears in Table 6.5. Tables 6.4 and 6.5
show equal and unequal distributions of the same
number of acts. The sums of the logarithmic numbers reflect the difference. The difference between
the sum of the logarithmic numbers for any unequal distribution (as in Table 6.5) and a similar
sum of the logarithmic numbers for an equal distribution (as in Table 6.4) provides the basis for
the variety measure. We compare an observed
sum such as that shown in Table 6.5 against the
"standard" of Table 6.4 by taking the ratio:
1.652/2.320 or .712.

TABLE 6.4 Example of Equal Distribution across
the Categories

	No. of Acts in Category	Per cent	Log_2
A	10	20	.464
B	10	20	.464
C	10	20	.464
D	10	20	.464
E	10	20	.464
Sum	50	100	2.320

TABLE 6.5 Example of Unequal Distribution
across the Categories

	No. of Acts in Category	Per cent	Log_2
A	12	24	.494
B	5	10	.066
C	5	10	.066
D	13	26	.505
E	15	30	.521
Sum	50	100	1.652

This ratio result (.712) is called "relative uncertainty" or *Hrel*. The uncertainty aspect is contained in the observation that in the equal probability instance, there is no way to judge if further occurrences would be more likely to fall in one category rather than another. In the distribution in Table 6.5, one can see that *A, D,* and *E* would be likely to receive more future occurrences than *B* and *C*. Hence it is said that "uncertainty is reduced" in this case. The smaller the *Hrel* figure, the "more certain" it is (i.e., the more the distribution departs from the equal condition). A common sense way to view a series of *Hrel* numbers is to think in terms of a "fanning out" toward equality of the distribution across the category system with the larger figures and a "channeling in" of the distribution toward relatively frequent occurrences in fewer categories with the smaller figures. As the ratio approaches 1,000, it suggests not only that almost everything that could happen has been occurring but also that the behaviors have shown increasing signs of disorderliness. The information measures do not tell us what the particular lack of ordering is, but they do give us a technical indication of a large amount of "variety" in the emissions. As the ratio decreases toward .000, the suggestion is that (1) there may be present a large amount of highly patterned and repetitive behavior and limited variety in the action, or (2) very little is occurring.

A long series of analyses has been carried out with the variety measure to establish how it functions on the data of the Berlin and Taiwan conflict arenas. The basic results are these:

1. With occasional exceptions, an *Hrel* of .700 or higher is associated with crisis months and only with crisis months. One or both parties will achieve this ratio or higher.

2. If we operationalize the beginning and duration of international crises with this *Hrel* criterion of .700 and higher, we are able to state when a particular crisis began and how long it lasted:

a. The Berlin Blockade crisis began in April 1948 and lasted through August 1948.
b. The Deadline crisis of 1958–1959 was not a crisis.
c. The Berlin Wall crisis began in August 1961 and lasted through September 1961.
d. Calculated with a twelve-type category system (the Berlin data were organized on an eighteen-type category system), the Tachens crisis of 1955 began in January and extended through March.
e. The Quemoy crisis began in September 1958 and concluded by the end of October 1958.

3. According to the calculations, only three months (April, May, and October 1948) in all the noncrisis time periods of the Berlin arena went over the .700 mark. Some questions may be raised about the months of April and May 1948 when the *Hrel* figures ranged between .738 and .784, yet the initial blockade announcement came late in June. Ordinarily, warning signs, if that is what they were in 1948, do not precede the dramatic onset of a crisis.

4. According to the calculations, only the month of June 1955 of all the noncrisis time periods of the Taiwan arena exceeded the .700 level while August 1958, the month of the beginning of the massive bombardment of Quemoy, did not reach the crisis level.

5. All noncrisis periods, except as just noted, have monthly *Hrel* figures below .700. . . .

It would be worthwhile if one could determine by quantitative analysis whether or not turning points in crises can be located. In the two cases in hand, the shifts of the thirteenth and fourteenth days might be the beginnings of the decline of the crisis. This observation leads us to speculate on the behavioral characteristics of an abatement phase in international crises. Further, we wonder if uptrends and downtrends in noncrisis periods in a given conflict arena are anything like uptrends (crisis mounting) and downtrends (crisis abating) in crisis episodes. Is there anything to be found in the data which would permit measurements of crisis abatement processes against the up-and-down fluctuations of noncrisis conflict?

PATTERNS OF CRISIS ABATEMENT

Pattern relationships in international politics are discussed sometimes as if they had been thoroughly investigated. How formidable the task is of actually carrying out intensive research on such relationships can be readily illustrated with the span of the subject matter of this chapter. We would have to consider 22 behavioral variables (or 60, if the subtypes are used) in various combinations, generated in two conflict arenas by nine main participants through four international crises and numerous subcrises across a span of time of about twenty years. This is enough complexity to challenge almost any amount of investigative enterprise and virtuosity. No doubt, a large number of relationships could be ferreted out of the data. The skeptic's question remains always to be faced in these matters: Is it worth all the effort and trouble to make such searches and to produce findings that, for the most part, can be regarded as only trivial?

Prevailing opinion seems to be that the important historical events of international relations follow each other in a unique succession with the result that productive comparisons across time are more in the nature of accidents than revelations of reality. The task of investigating regularities or recurrences such as turning points and changes in patterns of crisis behavior involves the possibility that one may be looking for something that is not there. In undertaking an inquiry of this sort, one needs to simplify things to avoid becoming overwhelmed with the work of analyzing quantities of complicated details and at the same time to direct research conservatively toward demanding tests which, if they produce poor results, will strongly suggest the wisdom of abandoning the project. In other words, a preliminary survey has much to recommend it. The following is a report on an effort of that type.

Simplification has been achieved and information has been combined in a way that should greatly reduce the likelihood of finding repetitive patterns. The actions and responses of all the conflict participants have been lumped together, although it is clear from the data already presented that the opposing sides did not behave similarly. The shifts of behavior of one side might either amplify or diminish the evidence of shifts of the other side. Whole year comparisons are going to be made against day-to-day data. It has been assumed, without any real knowledge of the matter, that the shifts from uptrend to downtrend behaviors in the Berlin Wall and Quemoy crises are located where the *Hrel* figures suggest they are. We shall want to test the assumption against the data, of course. Finally, the interaction data have

been reorganized into a set of a very few simple and manageable categories. By drastically reducing our information, we have reordered all data within the framework of just five behavioral alternatives. These are:

1. *Conflict deeds* including the active physical events of violent force, seizure, expulsion, negative sanctions which intend to punish opponents and reduce relationships, and the shows of potential force as in demonstrations and mobilizations. Thus we have grouped together the data previously categorized under DEMONSTRATE, REDUCE RELATIONSHIP, EXPEL, SEIZE, and FORCE and we shall call this grouping CONFLICT for the present purpose.

2. *Verbal combat* which reflects the actions and responses of parties in conflict but are not active physical events. For present purposes, this grouping is called CONFRONTATION and it encompasses the interaction categories of REJECT, ACCUSE, PROTEST, DENY, DEMAND, WARN, and THREATEN.

3. *Probing, exploratory, and supportive acts* which move away from confrontation and violent conflict and contain the means for approaching settlement, abatement, accommodation, postponement, or conclusion of conflict. Here we call this grouping ATTEMPTS TO SETTLE; it contains the categories of APPROVE, CONSULT, PROMISE, REQUEST, and PROPOSE.

4. *Acts which mark outcomes*, however temporary and partial, of confrontation and conflict. This grouping is named SETTLEMENT and includes the items categorized previously under the headings of YIELD, GRANT, REWARD, and AGREE.

5. *Expressions which convey information and state positions and intentions* related to the conflict arena, but without the attributes of the other four groupings. Merely talking about the conditions in a conflict arena and stating one's place in the action may appear to be of little importance but such utterances often have an influencing purpose behind them and, perhaps, also serve the functions of release and orientation. The interaction category COMMENT is the sole member of this grouping. . . .

From a systemic standpoint, a reasonable definition of international crisis is that it is a particular kind of alteration of the pattern of the interflowing actions between conflict parties. The change takes place in a short time and is large enough to be recognized. Thus the uptrend stage of a crisis (if there is such) should establish a change from the noncrisis condition to the crisis condition and the downtrend should be another change of state in the interaction flow, perhaps different from both the uptrend and the noncrisis situations. A test of these possibilities can be made by comparing the crisis stages with the average noncrisis behavior pattern of the conflict arena. The noncrisis frequencies and averages appear in the first two columns of Tables 6.6 and 6.7. The values of crisis years have been removed and, in the Taiwan case, the data of 1954 have also been excluded because the increase in interactions in 1954 clearly led to the Tachens crisis of early 1955. How the hypothesized uptrend and downtrend phases in the Berlin Wall and Quemoy crises varied from the noncrisis averages of the respective conflict arenas is revealed by comparing the subsequent columns in Tables 6.6 and 6.7 with the first two columns.

The data in these tables confirm turning points in the crises previously located by the variety measure. The evidence is more convincing in the Taiwan-Quemoy comparisons than in the Berlin data. Yet both indicate substantial shifts in the distributions across the five behavioral categories. Conflict deeds increased slightly in the uptrend phase of the crises and decreased more strongly in the downtrend or abatement phase. Very interesting is the fact that in the downtrend phase the reported acts of force, show of force, and direct violence are fewer than the noncrisis average. Interactions that fall within the ATTEMPT TO SETTLE and SETTLEMENT categories increased in the shift across the turning point from crisis uptrend to crisis downtrend. In both cases crisis abatement was accompanied by more than average amounts of harsh language directed at opponents, as is shown in the CONFRONTATION data. One is led to suspect that conflict parties in international crises are sometimes inclined to cover their retreats from violent deeds with a barrage of complaints, protests, accusations, denials, rejections, warnings, and threats. Overall, the usual pattern of behavior in noncrises is not like the

pattern of behavior in crises, the crisis engagement patterns differ from the abatment patterns, and the patterns throughout in the two conflict arenas are unlike.

The last step in this preliminary survey of crisis turning points and patterns consisted of an exploration of particular noncrisis periods when marked fluctuations appeared to have occurred. These were used for matching against changes of pattern within the crises. We concentrated only on the examination of the abatement phases of the Berlin Wall and Quemoy crises and compared them with downtrend periods of noncrisis in the two conflict arenas.

A search was made through the quantity and variety data for noncrisis time to locate the years that were not preludes or aftermaths of crises and that had a shift from a high level of interaction to a lower level. One instance was found in the Taiwan arena data: the high activity level of 1950 was followed by a marked decrease in 1951. In the Berlin arena, the best instance was found in the high activity of 1952 followed by the low activity of 1953. These downturns of Taiwan (1951) and Berlin (1953) were the only clear choices that could be made from the yearly data. The suggestion of a downtrend in activity seems to imply relaxation of conflict. The analogy with the abatement phase of a crisis following a turning point is obvious. The differences in behavior patterns of 1950–1951 and 1952–1953 provide change indicators to be applied against the crisis downtrend evidence. The essential information is the up-down differences of noncrisis and crisis; Tables 6.8 and 6.9 organize these data conveniently for the two conflict arenas.

The data for the downtrend effects are simple enough in these tables to allow direct observation of certain tendencies. The abatement process in both noncrisis and crisis situations in the two conflict arenas contains some similarities. The reported instances of forceful and violent actions decreased and the reported instances of settlement efforts increased. There are also a few systematic contrasts. Noncrisis abatement shows a somewhat unexpected decline of acts in the SETTLEMENT category while crisis abatement exhibits a modest increase in this area, as one might expect on a

TABLE 6.6   Changes between Noncrisis, Crisis Upswing, and Crisis Downswing for Berlin Arena

	No. of Acts in Noncrisis	% of Acts in Noncrisis*	% of Acts in Crisis Engagement†	% of Acts in Crisis Abatement‡	Difference between Noncrisis and Engagement	Difference between Noncrisis and Abatement	Difference between Engagement Downtrend and Abatement Phases of Crisis
Conflict	422	36.6	38.5	25.7	1.9	−10.9	12.8
Confront	393	34.1	52.3	52.3	18.2	18.2	0.0
Attempt Set.	60	5.2	0.0	4.6	−5.2	−0.6	−4.6
Settlement	206	17.9	7.7	9.2	−10.2	−8.7	−1.5
Comment	72	6.2	1.5	8.2	−4.7	2.0	−6.7

*Noncrisis percentages are based on the number of acts made by all parties during the years between 1948–1963 when data of crisis periods have been excluded.

†Crisis upswing percentages are based on the number of acts made by all parties during the first 12 days of the Berlin Wall crisis.

‡Crisis downswing percentages are based on the number of acts made by all parties during the succeeding 25 days of the Berlin Wall crisis.

TABLE 6.7   Changes between Noncrisis, Crisis Upswing, and Crisis Downswing for Taiwan Arena

	No. of Acts in Noncrisis	% of Acts in Noncrisis*	% of Acts in Crisis Engagement†	% of Acts in Crisis Abatement‡	Difference between Noncrisis and Engagement	Difference between Noncrisis and Abatement	Difference between Engagement Downtrend and Abatement Phases of Crisis
Conflict	472	48.4	52.0	21.7	3.6	−26.7	30.3
Confront	251	25.8	32.6	42.8	6.8	17.0	−10.2
Attempt Set.	157	16.1	3.1	20.5	−13.0	4.4	−17.4
Settlement	34	3.5	2.1	7.8	−1.4	4.3	−5.7
Comment	60	6.2	10.2	7.2	4.0	1.0	3.0

*Noncrisis percentages are based on the number of acts made by all parties during the years between 1950–1964 when data of crisis periods have been excluded.

†Crisis upswing percentages are based on the number of acts made by all parties during the first 13 days of the 1958 Quemoy crisis.

‡Crisis downswing percentages are based on the number of acts made by all parties during the succeeding 15 days of the 1958 Quemoy crisis.

common sense basis. The data indicate that tendencies in one conflict arena are different from those in another conflict arena. Thus abatement in the Taiwan arena included small declines in official explanations and policy comments but small increases in these behaviors in the Berlin arena. Increased verbal combat during the abatement phase appears to have been characteristic in the Taiwan arena but not as much so in the Berlin arena.

The difference figures for noncrisis abatement within each conflict arena show that the changes in pattern are much alike. Just how alike these changes are is not a critical consideration in a preliminary study such as this. Only in a more ambitious and complex analysis involving more cases and much more detailed data would it become important to adopt a specific method to establish the degree of pattern shift similarity. Nevertheless, the extent of downtrend pattern re-

TABLE 6.8   Up-Down Changes in Berlin Arena (1952–1953) and the Wall Crisis

	1952 Uptrend %	1953 Downtrend %	Differ-ence	Wall Crisis Uptrend; First 12 Days %	Wall Crisis Downtrend; Next 25 Days %	Differ-ence
Conflict	30.3	29.0	−1.3	38.5	25.7	−12.8
Confront	36.2	29.1	−7.1	52.3	52.3	0.0
Attempt Set.	5.4	18.3	12.9	0.0	4.6	4.6
Settlement	21.1	15.0	−6.1	7.7	9.2	1.5
Comment	7.0	8.6	1.6	1.5	8.2	6.7

TABLE 6.9   Up-Down Changes in Taiwan Arena (1950–1951) and the Quemoy Crisis

	1950 Uptrend %	1951 Downtrend %	Differ-ence	Quemoy Crisis Uptrend; 1st 13 Days %	Quemoy Crisis Downtrend; Next 15 Days %	Differ-ence
Conflict	55.3	43.3	−12.0	52.0	21.7	−30.3
Confront	21.2	31.6	10.4	32.6	42.8	10.2
Attempt Set.	6.8	15.0	8.2	3.1	20.5	17.4
Settlement	6.8	3.3	−3.5	2.1	7.8	5.7
Comment	9.8	6.7	−3.1	10.2	7.2	−3.0

semblance was calculated, using the simplified Taiwan and Berlin materials. The main purpose was to explore an approach to more complicated analyses which the preliminary survey now suggests should be undertaken. . . .

THE DIRECTION OF FURTHER WORK

The findings from two case studies do not establish any reliable generalizations beyond the cases. No matter how intensive is the research, the investigation of one or two conflict arenas is insufficient. The outcomes of the preliminary survey of crisis turning points and pattern changes are, therefore, interesting, encouraging, and inconclusive. It is clear that further inquiries concerning the structures of action and the relations within international crises should now be turned to more

cases. More crisis situations need to be analyzed to ascertain whether or not the patterning and recurring tendencies demonstrated for the Berlin Wall and Quemoy crisis will hold widely. The liability of the moment is in the paucity of data organized for the type of analysis presented in this chapter. The facts are available but gathering and ordering them involve a substantial outlay of time and research resources. The difficulty will have to be overcome because, without a comparative study of many crises, almost all conclusions about their behavioral characteristics will remain merely tentative.

The next step in pattern analysis requires the removal of the simplifications in the preliminary survey. The demonstration that there are some fairly steady patterns in crisis behavior warrants the expense and trouble of more detailed research. It is possible that more sensitive or more decisive indicators of crisis patterns and crisis changes are to be found within that detail. The survey dealt with the whole configuration of crisis interaction. Obviously, the performance of each of the major conflict participants should be traced. Joint performance relationships should be delineated more precisely by some means.

A significant result of the studies reported here is the discovery of the potential importance of noncrisis data in forecasting some aspects of crisis behavior. One might expect some regularity and continuity in chronic conflict situations between countries but explicit demonstrations of such similarities have been lacking over time. The field of investigation will be much widened if lesser encounters and confrontations of international politics are included within the study of crises. The number of cases for investigation will be greatly increased and it is not beyond the realm of possibility that there will be success in establishing operational codes and behavioral tendencies of nations that take part in the perennial contests of international politics. Eventually, subcrisis analysis may contribute to the understanding of all the interpositional phenomena lying between peace and war.

7

WAR

26. Of the Naturall Condition of Mankind, as Concerning Their Felicity, and Misery

THOMAS HOBBES

Nature hath made men so equall in the faculties of body, and mind; as that though there bee found one man sometimes manifestly stronger in body, or of quicker mind than another; yet when all is reckoned together, the difference between man, and man, is not so considerable, as that one man can thereupon claim to himselfe any benefit, to which another may not pretend, as well as he. For as to strength of body, the weakest has strength enough to kill the strongest, either by secret machination, or by confederacy with others, that are in the same danger with himselfe.

And as to the faculties of the mind, (setting aside the arts grounded upon words, and especially that skill of proceeding upon generall, and infallible rules, called Science; which very few have, and but in few things; as being not a native faculty, born with us; nor attained, (as Prudence,) while we look after somewhat els,) I find yet a greater equality amongst men, than that of strength. For Prudence, is but Experience; which equall time, equally bestows on all men, in those

things they equally apply themselves unto. That which may perhaps make such equality incredible, is but a vain conceipt of ones owne wisdome, which almost all men think they have in a greater degree, than the Vulgar; that is, than all men but themselves, and a few others, whom by Fame, or for concurring with themselves, they approve. For such is the nature of men, that howsoever they may acknowledge many others to be more witty, or more eloquent, or more learned; Yet they will hardly believe there be many so wise as themselves: For they see their own wit at hand, and other mens at a distance. But this proveth rather that men are in that point equall, than unequall. For there is not ordinarily a greater signe of the equall distribution of any thing, than that every man is contented with his share.

From this equality of ability, ariseth equality of hope in the attaining of our Ends. And therefore if any two men desire the same thing, which neverthelesse they cannot both enjoy, they become enemies; and in the way to their End, (which is principally their owne conservation, and sometimes their delectation only,) endeavour to de-

From *Leviathan*, Part I. Chapter 13.

stroy, or subdue one an other. And from hence it comes to passe, that where an Invader hath no more to feare, than an other mans single power; if one plant, sow, build, or possesse a convenient Seat, others may probably be expected to come prepared with forces united, to dispossesse, and deprive him, not only of the fruit of his labour, but also of his life, or liberty. And the Invader again is in the like danger of another.

And from this diffidence of one another, there is no way for any man to secure himselfe, so reasonable, as Anticipation; that is, by force, or wiles, to master the persons of all men he can, so long, till he see no other power great enough to endanger him: And this is no more than his own conservation requireth, and is generally allowed. Also because there be some, that taking pleasure in contemplating their own power in the acts of conquest, which they pursue farther than their security requires; if others, that otherwise would be glad to be at ease within modest bounds, should not by invasion increase their power, they would not be able, long time, by standing only on their defence, to subsist. And by consequence, such augmentation of dominion over men, being necessary to a mans conservation, it ought to be allowed him.

Againe, men have no pleasure, (but on the contrary a great deale of griefe) in keeping company, where there is no power able to over-awe them all. For every man looketh that his companion should value him, at the same rate he sets upon himselfe: And upon all signes of contempt, or undervaluing, naturally endeavours, as far as he dares (which amongst them that have no common power to keep them quiet, is far enough to make them destroy each other,) to extort a greater value from his contemners, by dommage; and from others, by the example.

So that in the nature of man, we find three principall causes of quarrell. First, Competition; Secondly, Diffidence; Thirdly, Glory.

The first, maketh men invade for Gain; the second, for Safety; and third, for Reputation. The first use Violence, to make themselves Masters of other mens persons, wives, children, and cattell; the second, to defend them; the third, for trifles, as a word, a smile, a different opinion, and any other signe of undervalue, either direct in their Persons, or by reflexion in their Kindred, their Friends, their Nation, their Profession, or their Name.

Hereby it is manifest, that during the time men live without a common Power to keep them all in awe, they are in that condition which is called Warre; and such a warre, as is of every man, against every man. For WARRE, consisteth not in Battell onely, or the act of fighting; but in a tract of time, wherein the Will to contend by Battell is sufficiently known: and therefore the notion of *Time*, is to be considered in the nature of Warre; as it is in the nature of Weather. For as the nature of Foule weather, lyeth not in a showre or two of rain; but in an inclination thereto of many dayes together; So the nature of War, consisteth not in actual fighting; but in the known disposition thereto, during all the time there is no assurance to the contrary. All other time is PEACE.

Whatsoever therefore is consequent to a time of Warre, where every man is Enemy to every man; the same is consequent to the time, wherein men live without other security, than what their own strength, and their own invention shall furnish them withall. In such condition, there is no place for Industry; because the fruit thereof is uncertain: and consequently no Culture of the Earth; no Navigation, nor use of the commodities that may be imported by Sea; no commodious Building: no Instruments of moving, and removing such things as require much force: no Knowledge of the face of the Earth; no account of Time; no Arts; no Letters; no Society; and which is worst of all, continuall feare, and danger of violent death; And the life of man, solitary, poore, nasty, brutish, and short.

It may seem strange to some man, that has not well weighed these things; that Nature should thus dissociate, and render men apt to invade, and destroy one another: and he may therefore, not trusting to this Inference, made from the Passions, desire perhaps to have the same confirmed by Experience. Let him therefore consider with himselfe, when taking a journey, he armes himselfe, and seeks to go well accompanied; when going to sleep, he locks his dores; when even in his house he locks his chests; and this when he knowes there bee Lawes, and publike Officers, armed, to revenge all injuries shall bee done him; what opinion he has of his fellow subjects, when he rides armed; of his fellow Citizens, when he locks his dores; and of his children, and servants, when he locks his chests. Does he not there as much accuse mankind by his actions, as I do by my words? But neither of us accuse mans nature in it. The Desires and other Passions of man, are in themselves no Sin. No more are the Actions, that proceed from those Passions, till they know a Law that forbids them: which till Lawes be made they cannot know: nor can any Law be made, till they have agreed upon the Person that shall make it .

It may peradventure be thought, there was never such a time, nor condition of warre as this; and I believe it was never generally so, over all the world: but there are many places, where they live so now. For the savage people in many places of *America*, except the government of small Families, that concord whereof dependeth on naturall lust, have no government at all; live at this day in that brutish manner, as I said before. Howsoever, it may be perceived what manner of life there would be, where there were no common Power to feare; by the manner of life, which men that have formerly lived under a peacefull government, use to degenerate into, in a civill Warre.

But though there had never been any time, wherein particular men were in a condition of warre one against another; yet in all times, Kings, and Persons of Soveraigne authority, because of their Independency, are in continuall jealousies, and in the state and posture of Gladiators; having their weapons pointing, and their eyes fixed on one another; that is, their Forts, Garrisons, and Guns, upon the Frontiers of their Kingdomes; and continuall Spyes upon their neighbours; which is a posture of War. But because they uphold thereby, the Industry of their Subjects; there does not follow from it, that misery, which accompanies the Liberty of particular men.

To this warre of every man against every man, this also is consequent; that nothing can be Unjust. The notions of Right and Wrong, Justice and Injustice have there no place. Where there is no common Power, there is no Law: where no Law, no Injustice. Force, and Fraud, are in warre, the two Cardinall vertues. Justice, and Injustice are none of the faculties neither of the Body, nor Mind. If they were, they might be in a man that were alone in the world, as well as his Senses, and Passions. They are Qualities, that relate to men in Society, not in Solitude. It is consequent also to the same condition, that there be no Propriety, no Dominion, no *Mine* and *Thine* distinct; but onely that to be every mans, that he can get; and for so long, as he can keep it. And thus much for the ill condition, which man by meer Nature is actually placed in; though with a possibility to come out of it, consisting partly in the Passions, partly in his Reason.

The Passions that encline men to Peace, are Feare of Death; Desire of such things as are necessary to commodious living; and Hope by their Industry to obtain them. And Reason suggesteth convenient Articles of Peace, upon which men may be drawn to agreement. These Articles, are they, which otherwise are called the Lawes of Nature: whereof I shall speak more particularly, in the two following Chapters.

27.   Thoughts for the Times on War and Death

SIGMUND FREUD

Swept as we are into the vortex of this wartime, our information one-sided, ourselves too near to focus the mighty transformations which have already taken place or are beginning to take place, and without a glimmering of the inchoate future, we are incapable of apprehending the significance of the thronging impressions, and know not what value to attach to the judgments we form. We are constrained to believe that never has any event been destructive of so much that is valuable in the commonwealth of humanity, nor so misleading to many of the clearest intelligences, nor so debasing to the highest that we know. . . .

The individual who is not himself a combatant—and so a wheel in the gigantic machinery of war—feels conscious of disorientation, and of an inhibition in his powers and activities. I believe

From *The Collected Papers of Sigmund Freud*, Vol. 4., pp. 288–304. Copyright © 1959 by Basic Books, Inc., by arrangement with the Hogarth Press Ltd. and The Institute of Psychoanalysis. Reprinted by permission of the publisher. Translated by E. Colburn Mayne. First published early in 1915 in *Imago*, Vol. 5; reprinted in *Sammlung*, 4th Series.

that he will welcome any indication, however slight, which may enable him to find out what is wrong with himself at least. I propose to distinguish two among the most potent factors in the mental distress felt by noncombatants, against which it is such a heavy task to struggle, and to treat them here: the disillusionment which this war has evoked: and the altered attitude towards death which this—like every other war—imposes on us.

When I speak of *disillusionment*, everyone at once knows what I mean. One need not be a sentimentalist; one may perceive the biological and psychological necessity of suffering in the economics of human life, and yet condemn war both in its means and in its aims, and devoutly look forward to the cessation of all wars. True, we have told ourselves that wars can never cease so long as nations live under such widely differing conditions, so long as the value of indivdual life is in each nation so variously computed, and so long as the animosities which divide them represent such powerful instinctual forces in the mind.

And we were prepared to find that wars between the primitive and the civilized peoples, between those races whom a colour-line divides, nay, wars with and among the undeveloped nationalities of Europe or those whose culture has perished—that for a considerable period such wars would occupy mankind. But we permitted ourselves to have other hopes. We had expected the great ruling powers among the white nations upon whom the leadership of the human species has fallen, who were known to have cultivated world-wide interests, to whose creative powers were due our technical advances in the direction of dominating nature, as well as the artistic and scientific acquisitions of the mind—peoples such as these we had expected to succeed in discovering another way of settling misunderstandings and conflicts of interest. Within each of these nations there prevailed high standards of accepted custom for the individual, to which his manner of life was bound to conform if he desired a share in communal privileges. These ordinances, frequently too stringent, exacted a great deal from him, much self-restraint, much renunciation of instinctual gratification. He was especially forbidden to make use of the immense advantages to be gained by the practise of lying and deception in competition with his fellow-men. The civilized state regarded these accepted standards as the basis of its existence; stern were its proceedings when an impious hand was laid upon them; frequent the pronouncement that to subject them even to examination by a critical intelligence was entirely impracticable. It could be assumed, therefore, that the state itself would respect them, nor would contemplate undertaking any infringement of what it acknowledged as the basis of its own existence. . . .

Then the war in which we had refused to believe broke out, and brought—disillusionment. Not only is it more sanguinary and more destructive than any war of other days, because of the enormously increased perfection of weapons of attack and defence; but it is at least as cruel, as embittered, as implacable as any that has preceded it. It sets at naught all those restrictions known as International Law, which in peace-time the states had bound themselves to observe; it ignores the prerogatives of the wounded and the medical service, the distinction between civil and military

sections of the popultion, the claims of private property. It tramples in blind fury on all that comes in its way, as though there were to be no future and no goodwill among men after it has passed. It rends all bonds of fellowship between the contending peoples, and threatens to leave such a legacy of embitterment as will make any renewal of such bonds impossible for a long time to come.

Moreover, it has brought to light the almost unbelievable phenomenon of a mutual conprehension between the civilized nations so slight that the one can turn with hate and loathing upon the other. Nay, more—that one of the great civilized nations is so universally unpopular that the attempt can actually be made to exclude it from the civilized community as *barbaric*, although it long has proved its fitness by the most magnificent co-operation in the work of civilization. We live in the hope that the impartial decision of history will furnish the proof that precisely this nation, this in whose tongue we now write, this for whose victory our dear ones are fighting, was the one which least transgressed the laws of civilization— but at such a time who shall dare present himself as the judge of his own cause?

Nations are in a measure represented by the states which they have formed; these states, by the governments which administer them. The individual in any given nation has in this war a terrible opportunity to convince himself of what would occasionally strike him in peacetime—that the state has forbidden to the individual the practice of wrong-doing, not because it desired to abolish it, but because it desires to monopolize it, like salt and tobacco. The warring state permits itself every such misdeed, every such act of violence, as would disgrace the individual man. It practises not only the accepted stratagems, but also deliberate lying and deception against the enemy; and this, too, in a measure which appears to surpass the usage of former wars. The state exacts the utmost degree of obedience and sacrifice from its citizens, but at the same time treats them as children by maintaining an excess of secrecy, and a censorship of news and expressions of opinion that renders the spirits of those thus intellectually oppressed defenceless against every unfavourable turn of events and every sinister rumour. It absolves itself from the guarantees and contracts it had formed with other states, and makes unabashed confession of its rapacity and lust for power, which the private individual is then called upon to sanction in the name of patriotism.

Nor may it be objected that the state cannot refrain from wrong-doing, since that would place it at a disadvantage. It is no less disadvantageous, as a general rule, for the individual man to conform to the customs of morality and refrain from brutal and arbitrary conduct; and the state but seldom proves able to indemnify him for the sacrifices it exacts. It cannot be a matter for astonishment, therefore, that this relaxation of all the moral ties between the greater units of mankind should have had a seducing influence on the morality of individuals; for our conscience is not the inflexible judge that ethical teachers are wont to declare it, but in its origin is *dread of the community* and nothing else. When the community has no rebuke to make, there is an end of all suppression of the baser passions, and men perpetrate deeds of cruelty, fraud, treachery, and barbarity so incompatible with their civilization that one would have held them to be impossible.

Well may that civilized cosmopolitan, therefore, of whom I spoke, stand helpless in a world grown strange to him—his all-embracing patrimony disintegrated, the common estates in it laid waste, the fellow-citizens embroiled and debased!

In criticism of his disillusionment, nevertheless, certain things must be said. Strictly speaking, it is not justified, for it consists in the destruction of—an illusion! We welcome illusions because they spare us emotional distress, and enable us instead to indulge in gratification. We must not then complain if now and again they come into conflict with some portion of reality, and are shattered against it.

Two things in this war have evoked our sense of disillusionment; the destitution shown in moral relations externally by the states which in their interior relations pose as the guardians of accepted moral usage, and the brutality in behaviour shown by individuals, whom, as partakers in the highest form of human civilization, one would not have credited with such a thing.

Let us begin with the second point and endeavour to formulate, as succinctly as may be, the point of view which it is proposed to criticize. How do we imagine the process by which an individual attains to a higher plane of morality? The first answer is sure to be: He is good and noble from his very birth, his very earliest beginnings. We need not consider this any further. A second answer will suggest that we are concerned with a developmental process, and will probably assume that this development consists in eradicating from him the evil human tendencies and, under the influence of education and a civilized environment, replacing them by good ones. From that standpoint it is certainly astonishing that evil should show itself to have such power in those who have been thus nurtured.

But this answer implies the thesis from which we propose to dissent. In reality, there is no such thing as *eradicating* evil tendencies. Psychological—more strictly speaking, psychoanalytic—investigation shows instead that the inmost essence of human nature consists of elemental instincts, which are common to all men and aim at the satisfaction of certain primal needs. These instincts in themselves are neither good nor evil. We but classify them and their manifestations in that fashion, according as they meet the needs and demands of the human community. It is admitted that all those instincts which society condemns as evil—let us take as representatives the selfish and the cruel—are of this primitive type.

These primitive instincts undergo a lengthy process of development before they are allowed to become active in the adult being. . . .

The transformation of *bad* instincts is brought about by two co-operating factors, an internal and an external. The internal factor consists in an influence on the bad—say, the egoistic—instincts exercised by erotism, that is, by the human need for love, taken in its widest sense. By the admixture of *erotic* components the egoistic instincts are transmuted into *social* ones. We learn to value being loved as an advantage for which we are willing to sacrifice other advantages. The external factor is the force exercised by upbringing, which advocates the claims of our cultural environment, and this is furthered later by the direct pressure of that civilization by which we are surrounded.

Civilization is the fruit of renunciation of instinctual satisfaction, and from each newcomer in turn it exacts the same renunciation. Throughout the life of the individual, there is a constant replacement of the external compulsion by the internal. The influences of civilization cause an ever-increasing transmutation of egoistic trends into altruistic and social ones, and this by an admixture of erotic elements. In the last resort it may be said that every internal compulsion which has been of service in the development of human beings was originally, that is, in the evolution of the human race, nothing but an external one. Those who are born today bring with them as an inherited consitution some degree of a tendency (disposition) towards transmutation of egoistic into social instincts, and this disposition is easily stimulated to achieve that effect. A further measure of this transformation must be accomplished during the life of the individual himself. And so the human being is subject not only to the pressure of his immediate environment, but also to the influence of the cultural development attained by his forefathers. . . .

Civilized society, which exacts good conduct and does not trouble itself about the impulses underlying it, has thus won over to obedience a great many people who are not thereby following the dictates of their own natures. Encouraged by this success, society has suffered itself to be led into straining the moral standard to the highest possible point, and thus it has forced its members into a yet greater estrangement from their instinctual dispositions. They are consequently subjected to an unceasing suppression of instinct, the resulting strain of which betrays itself in the most remarkable phenomena of reaction and compensation formations. In the domain of sexuality, where such suppression is most difficult to enforce, the result is seen in the reaction-phenomena of neurotic disorders. Elsewhere the pressure of civilization brings in its train no pathological results, but is shown in malformations of character, and in the perpetual readiness of the inhibited instincts to break through to gratification at any suitable opportunity. Anyone thus compelled to act continually in the sense of precepts which are not the expression of instinctual inclinations, is living,

psychologically speaking, beyond his means, and might objectively be designated a hypocrite, whether this difference be clearly known to him or not. It is undeniable that our contemporary civilization is extraordinarily favourable to the production of this form of hypocrisy. One might venture to say that it is based upon such hypocrisy, and that it would have to submit to far-reaching modifications if people were to undertake to live in accordance with the psychological truth. Thus there are very many more hypocrites than truly civilized persons—indeed, it is a debatable point whether a certain degree of civilized hypocrisy be not indispensable for the maintenance of civilization, because the cultural adaptability so far attained by those living today would perhaps not prove adequate to the task. On the other hand, the maintenance of civilization even on so questionable a basis offers the prospect of each new generation achieving a farther-reaching transmutation of instinct, and becoming the pioneer of a higher form of civilization.

From the foregoing observations, we may already derive this consolation—that our mortification and our grievous disillusionment regarding the uncivilized behaviour of our world-compatriots in this war are shown to be unjustified. They were based on an illusion to which we had abandoned ourselves. In reality our fellow-citizens have not sunk so low as we feared, because they had never risen so high as we believed. That the greater units of humanity, the peoples and states, have mutually abrogated their moral restraints naturally prompted these individuals to permit themselves relief for a while from the heavy pressure of civilization and to grant a passing satisfaction to the instincts it holds in check. This probably caused no breach in the relative morality within their respective national frontiers.

We may, however, obtain insight deeper than this into the change brought about by the war in our former compatriots, and at the same time receive a warning against doing them an injustice. For the evolution of the mind shows a peculiarity which is present in no other process of development. When a village grows into a town, a child into a man, the village and the child become submerged in the town and the man. Memory alone can trace the earlier features in the new image; in reality the old materials or forms have been superseded and replaced by new ones. It is otherwise with the development of the mind. Here one can describe the state of affairs, which is a quite peculiar one, only by saying that in this case every earlier stage of development persists alongside the later stage which has developed from it; the successive stages condition a co-existence, although it is in reference to the same materials that the whole series of transformations has been fashioned. The earlier mental state may not have manifested itself for years, but none the less it is so far present that it may at any time again become the mode of expression of the forces in the mind, and that exclusively, as though all later developments had been annulled, undone. This extraordinary plasticity of the evolution that takes place in the mind is not unlimited in its scope; it might be described as a special capacity for retroversion—for regression—since it may well happen that a later and higher stage of evolution, once abandoned, cannot be reached again. But the primitive stages can always be re-established; the primitive mind is, in the fullest meaning of the word, imperishable.

What are called *mental diseases* inevitably impress the layman with the idea of destruction of the life of mind and soul. In reality, the destruction relates only to later accretions and developments. The essence of mental disease lies in a return to earlier conditions of affective life and functioning. An excellent example of the plasticity of mental life is afforded by the state of sleep, which every night we desire. Since we have learnt to interpret even absurd and chaotic dreams, we know that whenever we sleep we cast off our hard-won morality like a garment, only to put it on again next morning. This divestiture is naturally unattended by any danger because we are paralysed, condemned to inactivity, by the state of sleep. Only through a dream can we learn of the regression of our emotional life to one of the earliest stages of development. . . .

Thus the transformations of instinct, on which our cultural adaptability is based, may also be permanently or temporarily undone by the experiences of life. Undoubtedly, the influences of war are among the forces that can bring about such regression: therefore we need not deny adaptability for culture to all who are at the present time displaying uncivilized behaviour, and we may anticipate that the refinement of their instincts will be restored in times of peace. . . .

Having in this way come to understand once more our fellow-citizens who are now so greatly alienated from us, we shall the more easily endure the disillusionment which the nations, those greater units of the human race, have caused us, for we shall perceive that the demands we make upon them ought to be far more modest. Perhaps they are reproducing the course of individual evolution, and still today represent very primitive phases in the organization and formation of higher unities. It is in agreement with this that the educative factor of an external compulsion towards morality, which we found to be so effective for the individual, is barely discernible in them. True, we had hoped that the extensive community of interests established by commerce and production would constitute the germ of such a compulsion, but it would seem that nations still obey their immediate passions far more readily than their interests. Their interests serve them, at most, as rationalizations for their passions; they parade their interests as their justification for satisfying their passions. Actually why the national units should disdain, detest, abhor one another, and that even when they are at peace, is indeed a mystery. I cannot tell why it is. It is just as though when it becomes a question of a number of people, not to say millions, all individual moral acquirements were obliterated, and only the most primitive, the oldest, the crudest mental attitudes were left. Possibly only future stages in development will be able in any way to alter this regrettable state of affairs. But a little more truthfulness and upright dealing on all sides, both in the personal relations of men to one another and between them and those who govern them, should also do something towards smoothing the way for this transformation. . . .

28. Warfare Is Only an Invention— Not a Biological Necessity

Margaret Mead

Is war a biological necessity, a sociological inevitability or just a bad invention? Those who argue for the first view endow man with such pugnacious instincts that some outlet in aggressive behavior is necessary if man is to reach full human stature. It was this point of view which lay back of William James's famous essay, "The Moral Equivalent of War," in which he tried to retain the warlike virtues and channel them in new directions. A similar point of view has lain back of the Soviet Union's attempt to make competition between groups rather than between individuals. A basic, competitive, aggressive, warring human nature is assumed, and those who wish to outlaw war or outlaw competitiveness merely try to find new and less socially destructive ways in which these biologically given aspects of man's nature can find expression. Then there are those who take the second view: warfare is the inevitable concomitant of the development of the state, the struggle for land and natural resources of class

societies springing, not from the nature of man, but from the nature of history. War is nevertheless inevitable unless we change our social system and outlaw classes, the struggle for power, and possessions; and in the event of our success warfare would disappear, as a symptom vanishes when the disease is cured.

One may hold a sort of compromise position between these two extremes; one may claim that all aggression springs from the frustration of man's biologically determined drives and that, since all forms of culture are frustrating, it is certain each new generation will be aggressive and the aggression will find its natural and inevitable expression in race war, class war, nationalistic war and so on. All three of these positions are very popular today among those who think seriously about the problems of war and its possible prevention, but I wish to urge another point of view, less defeatist perhaps than the first and third, and more accurate than the second: that is, that warfare, by which I mean recognized conflict between two groups *as groups*, in which each group puts an army (even if the army is only fifteen pygmies) into the field to fight and kill,

Reprinted from *Asia* 40/8 (August 1940) pp. 402–405 by permission of the author's estate. Also reprinted in *Anthropology, A Human Science* (Princeton: D. Van Nostrand Co., 1964), pp. 126–133.

if possible, some of the members of the army of the other group—that warfare of this sort is an invention like any other of the inventions in terms of which we order our lives, such as writing, marriage, cooking our food instead of eating it raw, trial by jury or burial of the dead, and so on. Some of this list any one will grant are inventions: trial by jury is confined to very limited portions of the globe; we know that there are tribes that do not bury their dead but instead expose or cremate them; and we know that only part of the human race has had the knowledge of writing as its cultural inheritance. But, whenever a way of doing things is found universally, such as the use of fire or the practice of some form of marriage, we tend to think at once that it is not an invention at all but an attribute of humanity itself. And yet even such universals as marriage and the use of fire are inventions like the rest, very basic ones, inventions which were perhaps necessary if human history was to take the turn that it has taken, but nevertheless inventions. At some point in his social development man was undoubtedly without the institution of marriage or the knowledge of the use of fire.

The case for warfare is much clearer because there are peoples even today who have no warfare. Of these the Eskimo are perhaps the most conspicuous examples, but the Lepchas of Sikkim described by Geoffrey Gorer in *Himalayan Village* are as good. Neither of these peoples understands war, not even defensive warfare. The idea of warfare is lacking, and this idea is as essential to really carrying on war as an alphabet or syllabary is to writing. But whereas the Lepchas are a gentle, unquarrelsome people, and the advocates of other points of view might argue that they are not full human beings or that they had never been frustrated and so had no aggression to expand in warfare, the Eskimo case gives no such possibility of interpretation. The Eskimo are not a mild and meek people; many of them are turbulent and troublesome. Fights, theft of wives, murder, cannibalism, occur among them—all outbursts of passionate men goaded by desire or intolerable circumstance. Here are men faced with hunger, men faced with loss of their wives, men faced with the threat of extermination by other men, and here are orphan children, growing up miser-

ably with no one to care for them, mocked and neglected by those about them. The personality necessary for war, the circumstances necessary to goad men to desperation are present, but there is no war. When a traveling Eskimo entered a settlement he might have to fight the strongest man in the settlement to establish his position among them, but this was a test of strength and bravery, not war. The idea of warfare, of one *group* organizing against another *group* to maim and wound and kill them was absent. And without that idea passions might rage but there was no war.

But, it may be argued, isn't this because the Eskimo have such a low and undeveloped form of social organization? They own no land, they move from place to place, camping, it is true, season after season on the same site, but this is not something to fight for as the modern nations of the world fight for land and raw materials. They have no permanent possessions that can be looted, no towns that can be burned. They have no social classes to produce stress and strains within the society which might force it to go to war outside. Doesn't the absence of war among the Eskimo, while disproving the biological necessity of war, just go to confirm the point that it is the state of development of the society which accounts for war, and nothing else?

We find the answer among the pygmy peoples of the Andaman Islands in the Bay of Bengal. The Andamans also represent an exceedingly low level of society; they are a hunting and food-gathering people; they live in tiny hordes without any class stratification; their houses are simpler than the snow houses of the Eskimo. But they knew about warfare. The army might contain only fifteen determined pygmies marching in a straight line, but it was the real thing none the less. Tiny army met tiny army in open battle, blows were exchanged, casualties suffered, and the state of warfare could only be concluded by a peace-making ceremony.

Similarly, among the Australian aborigines, who built no permanent dwellings but wandered from water hole to water hole over their almost desert country, warfare—and rules of "international law"—were highly developed. The student of social evolution will seek in vain for his obvious causes of war, struggle for lands, struggle for power of one group over another, expansion of population, need to divert the minds of a populace restive under tyranny, or even the ambition of a successful leader to enhance his own prestige. All are absent, but warfare as a practice remained, and men engaged in it and killed one another in the course of a war because killing is what is done in wars.

From instances like these it becomes apparent that an inquiry into the causes of war misses the fundamental point as completely as does an insistence upon the biological necessity of war. If a people have an idea of going to war and the idea that war is the way in which certain situations, defined within their society, are to be handled, they will sometimes go to war. If they are a mild and unaggressive people, like the Pueblo Indians, they may limit themselves to defensive warfare; but they will be forced to think in terms of war because there are peoples near them who have warfare as a pattern, and offensive, raiding, pillaging warfare at that. When the pattern of warfare is known, people like the Pueblo Indians will defend themselves, taking advantage of their natural defenses, the *mesa* village site, and people like the Lepchas, having no natural defenses and no idea of warfare, will merely submit to the invader. But the essential point remains the same. There is a way of behaving which is known to a given people and labeled as an appropriate form of behavior; a bold and warlike people like the Sioux or the Maori may label warfare as desirable as well as possible; a mild people like the Pueblo Indians may label warfare as undesirable; but to the minds of both peoples the possibility of warfare is present. Their thoughts, their hopes, their plans are oriented about this idea, that warfare may be selected as the way to meet some situation.

So simple peoples and civilized peoples, mild peoples and violent, assertive peoples, will all go to war if they have the invention, just as those peoples who have the custom of dueling will have duels and peoples who have the pattern of vendetta will indulge in vendetta. And, conversely, peoples who do not know of dueling will not fight duels, even though their wives are seduced and their daughters ravished; they may on occasion commit murder but they will not fight duels. Cultures which lack the idea of the vendetta will not meet

every quarrel in this way. A people can use only the forms it has. So the Balinese have their special way of dealing with a quarrel between two individuals: if the two feel that the causes of quarrel are heavy they may go and register their quarrel in the temple before the gods, and, making offerings, they may swear never to have anything to do with each other again. Today they register such mutual "not-speaking" with the Dutch government officials. But in other societies, although individuals might feel as full of animosity and as unwilling to have any further contact as do the Balinese, they cannot register their quarrel with the gods and go on quietly about their business because registering quarrels with the gods is not an invention of which they know.

Yet, if it be granted that warfare is after all an invention, it may nevertheless be an invention that lends itself to certain types of personality, to the exigent needs of autocrats, to the expansionist desires of crowded peoples, to the desire for plunder and rape and loot which is engendered by a dull and frustrating life. What, then, can we say of this congruence between warfare and its uses? If it is a form which fits so well, is not this congruence the essential point? But even here the primitive material causes us to wonder, because there are tribes who go to war merely for glory, having no quarrel with the enemy, suffering from no tyrant within their boundaries, anxious neither for land nor loot nor women, but merely anxious to win prestige which within that tribe has been declared obtainable only by war and without which no young man can hope to win his sweetheart's smile of approval. But if, as was the case with the Bush Negroes of Dutch Guiana, it is artistic ability which is necessary to win a girl's approval, the same young man would have to be carving rather than going out on a war party.

In many parts of the world, war is a game in which the individual can win counters—counters which bring him prestige in the eyes of his own sex or of the opposite sex; he plays for these counters as he might, in our society, strive for a tennis championship. Warfare is a frame for such prestige-seeking merely because it calls for the display of certain skills and certain virtues; all of these skills—riding straight, shooting straight, dodging the missiles of the enemy and sending one's own straight to the mark—can be equally well exercised in some other framework and, equally, the virtues—endurance, bravery, loyalty, steadfastness—can be displayed in other contexts. The tie-up between proving oneself a man and proving this by a success in organized killing is due to a definition which many societies have made of manliness. And often, even in those societies which counted success in warfare a proof of human worth, strange turns were given to the idea, as when the plains Indians gave their highest awards to the man who touched a live enemy rather than to the man who brought in a scalp— from a dead enemy—because the latter was less risky. Warfare is just an invention known to the majority of human societies by which they permit their young men either to accumulate prestige or avenge their honor or acquire loot or wives or slaves or sago lands or cattle or appease the blood lust of their gods or the restless souls of the recently dead. It is just an invention, older and more wide-spread than the jury system, but none the less an invention.

But, once we have said this, have we said anything at all? Despite a few instances, dear to the hearts of controversialists, of the loss of the useful arts, once an invention is made which proves congruent with human needs or social forms, it tends to persist. Grant that war is an invention, that it is not a biological necessity nor the outcome of certain special types of social forms, still, once the invention is made, what are we to do about it? The Indian who had been subsisting on the buffalo for generations because with his primitive weapons he could slaughter only a limited number of buffalo did not return to his primitive weapons when he saw that the white man's more efficient weapons were exterminating the buffalo. A desire for the white man's cloth may mortgage the South Sea Islander to the white man's plantation, but he does not return to making bark cloth, which would have left him free. Once an invention is known and accepted, men do not easily relinquish it. The skilled workers may smash the first steam looms which they feel are to be their undoing, but they accept them in the end, and no movement which has insisted

upon the mere abandonment of usable inventions has ever had much success. Warfare is here, as part of our thought; the deeds of warriors are immortalized in the words of our poets; the toys of our children are modeled upon the weapons of the soldier; the frame of reference within which our statesmen and our diplomats work always contains war. If we know that it is not inevitable, that it is due to historical accident that warfare is one of the ways in which we think of behaving, are we given any hope by that? What hope is there of persuading nations to abandon war, nations so thoroughly imbued with the idea that resort to war is, if not actually desirable and noble, at least inevitable whenever certain defined circumstances arise?

In answer to this question I think we might turn to the history of other social inventions, and inventions which must once have seemed as firmly entrenched as warfare. Take the methods of trial which preceded the jury system: ordeal and trial by combat. Unfair, capricious, alien as they are to our feeling today, they were once the only methods open to individuals accused of some offense. The invention of trial by jury gradually replaced these methods until only witches, and finally not even witches, had to resort to the ordeal. And for a long time the jury system seemed the one best and finest method of settling legal disputes, but today new inventions, trial before judges only or before commissions, are replacing the jury system. In each case the old method was replaced by a new social invention; the ordeal did not go out because people thought it unjust or wrong, it went out because a method more congruent with the institutions and feelings of the period was invented. And, if we despair over the way in which war seems such an ingrained habit of most of the human race, we can take comfort from the fact that a poor invention will usually give place to a better invention.

For this, two conditions at least are necessary. The people must recognize the defects of the old invention, and some one must make a new one. Propaganda against warfare, documentation of its terrible cost in human suffering and social waste, these prepare the ground by teaching people to feel that warfare is a defective social institution.

29. The Use of Mathematics
Arms Races

Lewis F. Richardson

THE USE OF MATHEMATICS

Literary people have sometimes wrongly supposed that mathematical expressions can be used to describe the actions of only such objects as follow laws of a rigid mechanical, deterministic type in all particulars. The answer to that assertion is the growth of statistical science and its applications to life-insurance, to the molecular chaos in a gas, and to many other features of social life, of biology, and of physics. The usual condition for mathematical treatment is that, if the individual phenomena are not determinate, then they must be numerous. An appreciation of the service rendered by mathematics to economics will be found in Marshall's *Principles of Economics* (1910). It therefore seems reasonable to inquire whether mathematical language can also express the behavior of people in another situation where they act together in large groups, namely in relation to war.

From *Arms and Insecurity* (Pacific Grove, Calif.: Boxwood Press, 1960), pp. xvii–xviii,12–17,19. Reprinted by permission of the Boxwood Press. Citations deleted.

William James even went so far as to use mathematics in his discussion of free will (1902). "The facts," he wrote, "may be most briefly symbolized thus, P standing for the propensity, I for the ideal impulse, and E for the effort:

$$I \text{ per se} < P.$$
$$I + E > P."$$

To have to translate one's verbal statements into mathematical formulae compels one carefully to scrutinize the ideas therein expressed. Next the possession of formulae makes it much easier to deduce the consequences. In this way absurd implications, which might have passed unnoticed in a verbal statement, are brought clearly into view and stimulate one to amend the formula. An additional advantage of a mathematical mode of expression is its brevity, which greatly diminishes the labor of memorizing the idea expressed. If the statements of an individual become the subject of a controversy, this definiteness and brevity lead to a speeding up of discussions over disputable points, so that obscurities can be cleared away, errors refuted, and truth found and expressed more quickly than could have been done had a more cumbrous method of discussion been pursued. Mathematical expressions have, however, their special tendencies to pervert thought: the definiteness may be spurious, existing in the equations but not in the phenomena to be described; and the brevity may be due to the omission of the more important things, simply because they cannot be mathematized. Against these faults we must constantly be on our guard. It will probably be impossible to avoid them entirely, and so they ought to be realized and admitted.

A fundamental rule of scientific method is Ockham's so-called "razor," to the effect that: "Entities are not to be postulated without necessity." For shaving off the superabundant growth of mathematical uncertainties and difficulties I have made frequent appeal to an analogous rule: "Formulae are not to be complicated without good evidence." This is a diffident and groping empiricism. A much bolder view of simplicity is to be found in the works of Harold Jeffreys (1939).

Mathematics has been used in this book both inductively to summarize facts, and deductively to trace the consequences of hypotheses. By mistaking the intention it is possible to complain that the inductions do not follow from the previous hypotheses, and that the deductions go beyond the known facts. Certainly that is so, but it is no cause for complaint, rather for rejoicing.

Those who say, "You can prove anything by statistics," should instead say, "Unfortunately we do not understand statistical method sufficiently well to enable us to distinguish arguments that are genuine from those that are false."

To anyone who believes that words are the proper medium of expression I commend the following exercise: Translate into words $Ax^2 + Bx + C = 0$, remembering that x, A, B, C are not words. Proceed in words, not using any algebraic symbols, to find and prove the solution of the equation. Read your words to schoolboys who are approaching, but have not yet done, quadratic equations. Set them examples in words alone.

There are people who despise theories and take a pride in their adherence to facts. Even such a person must admit that the ordinary process of recognition involves an element of theory. Has he never recognized in the street an acquaintance who showed no recognition in return? Or cut open an egg to find it uneatable? Such mistakes draw our attention to our false theories; and indicate that our correct recognitions involve correct theories. All ordinary political discussions are chock-full of theories, most of them unspoken. Pure mathematicians on the contrary strive to make their assumptions explicit. Dare we do that in matters which touch our feelings?

ARMS RACES

It is an old Proverb *Maxima bella ex levissimis causis:* the greatest Feuds have had the smallest Beginnings.
WILLIAM PENN (1693)

1. FREE WILL

CHAIRMAN: I now call on Dr. Richardson to explain his science of foreign politics.

CRITIC: Sir! I beg to move the previous question: that we do not waste our time on such an absurdity. How can anyone possibly make scientific statements about foreign politics? These are questions of right, of loyalty, of power, of the dignity of free choice. They touch a little on law but are far beyond the reach of any science.

AUTHOR: I admit that the discussion of free choice is better left to the dramatists. But nowadays science does usefully treat many phenomena that are only in part deterministic—witness the many social applications of statistics and the astounding progress of theories as to the probable position of an electron.

CRITIC: The electron? That surely is irrelevant. On glancing at your summary, I see mathematical equations with the symbol t in them. Does t stand for time?

AUTHOR: You have guessed rightly.

CRITIC: Can you predict the date at which the next war will break out?

AUTHOR: No, of course not. The equations are merely a description of what people would do if they did not stop to think. Why are so many nations reluctantly but steadily increasing their armaments as if they were mechanically compelled to do so? Because, I say, they follow their traditions, which are fixtures, and their instincts, which are mechanical and because they have not yet made a sufficiently strenuous intellectual and moral effort to control the situation. The process described by the ensuing equations is not to be thought of as inevitable. It is what *would occur if instinct and tradition were allowed to act uncontrolled*. In this respect the equations have some analogy to a dream. For a dream often warns an individual of the antisocial acts that his instincts would lead him to commit, if he were not wakeful.

CRITIC: Dreams, if you like. But why equations? History is not mechanical.

> The world's like a horse.
> We balance on a stirrup
> To manage the course
> Of Power in Europe.

AUTHOR: Wait until you see the statistics of arms races!

CRITIC: This author has the wrong background, for he appears to have been trained in physical science, which is the study of what merely exists whereas the proper training is strategy, the art of confounding our enemies. For we are sure always to have lots of enemies.

AUTHOR: Mr. Chairman, that last sentence is, in the phraseology of the lawcourts, my case. For those who neglect the objective good of the whole, in order to study strategy, are likely always to have lots of enemies.

CHAIRMAN: I think we might go on.

2. LINEAR THEORY OF TWO NATIONS

Introduction

This theory is about general tendencies common to all nations; about how they resent defiance, how they suspect defense to be concealed *aggression*, how they respond to imports by sending out exports; about how expenditure on armaments is restrained by the difficulty of paying for them; and, lastly, about grievances and their queer irrational ways, so that a halting apology may be received as though it were an added insult.

A rule of the theoretical game is that a nation is to be represented by a single variable, its outward attitude of threatening or co-operation. So the great statesmen, who collect, emphasize, and direct the national will, need not be mentioned by name. This is politics without personalities.

The various motives which lead a nation in time of peace to increase or decrease its preparations for war may be classified according to the manner of its dependence on its own existing preparations and on those of other nations. For simplicity, the nations are here regarded as forming two groups. There are motives such as revenge or dissatisfaction with the results of treaties; these motives are independent of existing armaments. Then there is the very strong motive of fear, which moves each group to increase its armaments because of the existence of those of the opposing group. Also there is rivalry, which, more than fear, attends to the difference between the armaments of the two groups rather than to the magnitude of those of the other group. Lastly, there is always a tendency for each group to reduce its armaments in order to economize expenditure and effort.

What the result of all these motives may be is not at all evident when they are stated in words. It is here that mathematics can give powerful aid.

But before the mathematician can get to work on the problem, the data must be stated precisely; and precision may seem inappropriate to sociology. Would it not be more polite to remain content with a modest vagueness? No! For, unless our statements are in terms so precise that it would be possible in them to make a definite mistake, it will be impossible in them to make a definite advance in science.

Permit me to discuss a generalized public speech, fictitious but typical of the year 1937. The Defense Minister of Jedesland, when introducing his estimates, said:

The intentions of our country are entirely pacific. We have given ample evidence of this by the treaties which we have recently concluded with our neighbors. Yet, when we consider the state of unrest in the world at large and the menaces by which we are surrounded, we should be failing in our duty as a government if we did not take adequate steps to increase the defenses of our beloved land.

We have now to translate that into mathematics. At first sight there might seem to be no way of doing it, and, on second thoughts, perhaps too many ways. But we can shave the problem clean with Ockham's razor. This principle in its usual form runs "entities are not to be multiplied without necessity." Mathematical physics has progressed by trying out first the simplest formulae that described the broad features of the early experiments and by leaving complicated formulae to wait for more accurate experiments. By "entities" let us understand terms and coefficients in formulae, and let us restate Ockham's rule as "formulae are not to be complicated without good evidence" or briefly "try out the easiest formulae first."

Now the simplest representation of what that generalized defense minister said is this:

$$dx/dt = ky \qquad \ldots (1)$$

where t is time, x represents his own defenses, y represents the menaces by which he is surrounded, and k is a positive constant, which will be named a "defense coefficient." Let us for simplicity assume that what he euphemistically called "sur-

roundings" is, in fact, a single nation. Its defense minister asserts similarly that

$$dy/dt = kx \qquad \ldots (2)$$

If x and y are ever both positive, they then, according to equations (1) and (2), are both increasing; and so they will become more positive, and go on increasing faster and faster without any end to the process.[1] The system described by equations (1) and (2) is evidently unstable. In fact, we know that the process of increasing defenses was altered by the outbreak of war. A failure of equations to describe both small and very large disturbances is familiar in many departments of applied mathematics and need not unduly dispirit us: for example, Hooke's law is important in connection with the strength of materials, although it does not describe fracture.

But can we really believe that the international system is inevitably unstable? Surely the cost of armaments exercises some restraint. Leading statesmen have expressed this opinion. Thus Mr. Winston Churchill (1923) records that on 3 November 1909, while he was President of the Board of Trade, he began a minute to the Cabinet with these words:

Believing that there are practically no checks upon German naval expansion except those imposed by the increasing difficulties of getting money, I have had the enclosed report prepared with a view to showing how far those limitations are becoming effective. It is clear that they are becoming terribly effective.

Again, the German Chancellor, Prince Bülow (1914), wrote:

It is just possible that the effect of convulsively straining her military resources to the uttermost may, by reacting on the economic and social conditions of France, hasten the return of pacific feelings. . . . Should the three-year

---

[1] A quantitative argument, which is not necessary for the understanding of this introduction, but which some readers may prefer, goes as follows. The general solution of equations (1) and (2) is

$$\begin{aligned} x &= Ae^{kt} + Be^{-kt}, &\ldots (3)\\ y &= Ae^{kt} - Be^{-kt} &\ldots (4) \end{aligned}$$

If at t_0 both x and y are positive, then so is $x + y$ and therefore also A. But $k > 0$. So, as $t \rightarrow \infty$, both $x \rightarrow \infty$ and $y \rightarrow \infty$.

military service entail an income tax, this would also probably have a sobering effect.

So let the equations be improved into

$$dx/dt = ky - \alpha x, \qquad \ldots (5)$$
$$dy/dt = lx - \beta y, \qquad \ldots (6)$$

where α and β are positive constants representing the fatigue and expense of keeping up defenses, and k and l are positive defense coefficients, which we now regard as possibly unequal.

Let us compare this statement with some opinions of statesmen. Sir Edward Grey, who was British Foreign Secretary when World War I broke out, afterward wrote (Grey, 1925):

The increase of armaments that is intended in each nation to produce consciousness of strength, and a sense of security, does not produce these effects. On the contrary, it produces a consciousness of the strength of other nations and a sense of fear. . . . The enormous growth of armaments in Europe, the sense of insecurity and fear caused by them—it was these that made war inevitable. . . . This is the real and final account of the origin of the Great War.

Sir Edward Grey's statement is symbolized by the terms in k and l. Compare also Thucydides' account of the cause of the Peloponnesian war: "The real though unavowed cause I believe to have been the growth of Athenian power, which terrified the Lacedaemonians and forced them into war . . ." (Jowett, 1881). When this opinion of Sir Edward Grey was quoted by Mr. Noel Baker, M.P., in the House of Commons on 20 July 1936, Mr. L. S. Amery, M.P., said in reply:

With all respect to the memory of an eminent statesman, I believe that statement to be entirely mistaken. The armaments were only the symptoms of the conflict of ambitions and ideals, of those nationalist forces, which created the war. The War was brought about because Serbia, Italy, Rumania passionately desired the incorporation in their States of territories which at that time belonged to the Austrian Empire and which the Austrian Government were not prepared to abandon without a struggle. France was prepared if the opportunity ever came to make an effort to recover Alsace-Lorraine. It was in those facts, in those insoluble conflicts of ambitions and not in the armaments themselves that the cause of the War lay.

Mr. Amery's objections should, I think, be met, not by leaving out Sir Edward Grey's terms, but by inserting additional terms, namely, g and h, to represent grievances and ambitions, provisionally regarded as constants, so that the equations become:

$$dx/dt = ky - \alpha x + g, \qquad \ldots (7)$$
$$dy/dt = lx - \beta y + h. \qquad \ldots (8)$$

These equations were published in 1935 (Richardson, 1935*a, b*), as a simplification of an earlier theory (Richardson, 1919).

In *Generalized Foreign Politics*, written in the years 1937–1939, the g and h were called the "grievances." Many people think that this was too sympathetic a name for what they call "aggressive intentions." From the mathematical point of view, g and h represent any motives which, while affecting warlike preparations, remain constant independently of the amount of such preparations at home or abroad. From the psychological point of view such motives could include deeply rooted prejudices, standing grievances, old unsatisfied ambitions, wicked and persistent dreams of world conquest, or, on the contrary, a permanent feeling of contentment. This list is too long to be recited on every occasion; so, for short, g and h are still usually called the "grievances"—a name which indicates that g is a positive number when its side is dissatisfied and a negative number when the prevailing mood of that side is contentment.

A well-known literary man objected that grievances and ambitions are imponderables; so what sense could there be in regarding them as measurable? The answer is that x and y can be counted, in men or money, and that x and y are partly the numerical effects of those "imponderables."

The preparations for war of the two groups may be regarded as the rectangular co-ordinates of a particle in an "international plane," so that every point in this plane represents one conceivable instantaneous international situation. The differential equations are then the equations of motion of the particle.

A hint will now be taken from Plato's advice concerning astronomy (*Republic*). We shall pursue foreign politics with the help of problems, just as we pursue geometry, but tentatively.

If g, h, x, y are all made zero simultaneously, the equations show that x and y remain zero. That ideal condition is *permanent peace by disarmament and satisfaction*. It has existed since 1817 on the frontier between the United States and Canada; also since 1905 on the frontier between Norway and Sweden (for the treaties see *League of Nations Armaments Year-Book* [1937].

The equations further imply that *mutual disarmament without satisfaction* is not permanent, for, if x and y instantaneously vanish, $dx/dt = g$ and $dy/dt = h$.

Unilateral disarmament corresponds to putting $y = 0$ at a certain instant. We have at that time

$$dx/dt = -ax + g, \quad dy/dt = lx + h.$$

The second of these equations implies that y will not remain zero if the grievance h is positive; later, when y has grown, the term ky will cause x to grow also. So, according to the equations, unilateral disarmament is not permanent. This accords with the historical fact that Germany, whose army was reduced by the Treaty of Versailles in 1919 to 100,000 men, a level far below that of several of her neighbors, insisted on rearming during the years 1933–36.

A *race in armaments*, such as was in progress in 1912, occurs when the defense terms predominate in the second members of the equations. If those were the only terms, we should have

$$dx/dt = ky, \quad dy/dt = lx,$$

and both x and y would tend to the same infinity, which, if positive, we may interpret as war. But, for large x and y, linearity may fail. . . .

Development of the Theory

The Opposite to War. The generalizing spirit of mathematics is very suggestive. It draws our attention to the possiblity of "negative preparedness for war" and invites us to assign a name to it and to inquire whether the above general statements still hold true when the signs of the variables are changed. As a preliminary, let us consider, not nations, but only two people, and let us compare quarreling with falling in love. If

hatred may be regarded as negative love, these two activities are opposite. Yet there are important resemblances between them. The chief stimulus to falling deeply in love is any sign of love from the other person, just as the chief stimulus to becoming more annoyed is any insult or injury from the other person. When quarreling is represented by $dx/dt = ky$, and $dy/dt = lx$, these same two equations with k and l still positive can also represent falling in love. For if x and y are ever both negative, they then, according to the equations, are both becoming more negative and will continue to do so, faster and faster, without any end to the process, as far as it is described by the equations.

Now, returning to the study of nations, we notice that the classical antithesis of "war and peace" is not appropriate here. For war is an intense activity, whereas peace, in the sense of a mere tranquil inattention to the doings of foreigners, resembles zero rather than a negative quantity. Negative preparedness for war must mean that the group directs toward foreigners an activity designed to please rather than to annoy them. Thus a suitable name for negative preparedness for wars seems to be "co-operation."

Just as armaments provoke counter-armaments, so assistance evokes reciprocal assistance; for example, imports and exports tend to equality. Also there is a tendency to reduce co-operation on account of the fatigue and expense which it involves. Thus it appears that the general statements remain broadly true when the preparedness changes from positive to negative. The most extensive form of international co-operation is foreign trade. There exist also more than 500 international associations, having little or no connection with one another but listed by the League of Nations (1936). The extreme form of international co-operation, corresponding to the infinity opposite to war, would appear to be a world-state, as imagined, for instance, by H. G. Wells in his book *The Shape of Things To Come* (1933).

Quarreling is here regarded as a positive activity, making friends as a negative activity. That happened because the equations were first written during World War I. It might be better to reverse the convention of signs. But the change has not been made in this book. . . .

30. Causes of War

QUINCY WRIGHT

Wars arise because of the changing relations of numerous variables—technological, psychic, social, and intellectual. There is no single cause of war. Peace is an equilibrium among many forces. Change in any particular force, trend, movement, or policy may at one time make for war, but under other conditions a similar change may make for peace. A state may at one time promote peace by armament, at another time by disarmament; at one time by insistence on its rights, at another time by a spirit of conciliation. To estimate the probability of war at any time involves, therefore, an appraisal of the effect of current changes upon the complex of intergroup relationships throughout the world. Certain relationships, however, have been of outstanding importance. Political lag deserves attention as an outstanding cause of war in modern civilization.

Reprinted from *A Study of War*, abridged edition, by Quincy Wright (Chicago: University of Chicago Press, 1965), pp. 351–360. By permission of The University of Chicago Press. Copyright © 1942 and 1965 The University of Chicago Press.

1. POLITICAL LAG

There appears to be a general tendency for change in procedures of political and legal adjustment to lag behind economic and cultural changes arising from technological progress. The violent consequences of this lag can be observed in primitive and historic societies, but its importance has increased in modern times. The expansion of contacts and the acceleration of change resulting from modern technology have disturbed existing power localizations and have accentuated the cultural oppositions inherent in social organization. International organization has not developed sufficiently to adjust by peaceful procedures the conflict situations which have arisen. This lag is related to the usual lag of value systems behind scientific and technological progress, accounting for the great transitions in civilizations. . . .

War tends to increase in severity and to decrease in frequency as the area of political and legal adjustment (the state) expands geographically unless that area becomes as broad as the area of continuous economic, social, and cultural contact (the civilization). In the modern period peoples in all sections of the world have come into the continuous contact with one another. Although states have tended to grow during this period, thus extending the areas of adjustment, none of them has acquired world-wide jurisdiction. Their growth in size has increased the likelihood that conflicts will be adjusted, but it has also increased the severity of the consequences of unadjusted conflicts. Fallible human government is certain to make occasional mistakes in policy, especially when, because of lack of universality, it must deal with conflicts regulated not by law but by negotiation that must function within an unstable balance of power among a few large units. Such errors have led to war.

War tends to increase both in frequency and in severity in times of rapid technological and cultural change because adjustment, which always involves habituation, is a function of time. The shorter the time within which such adjustments have to be made, the greater the probability that they will prove inadequate and that violence will result. War can, therefore, be attributed either to the intelligence of man manifested in his inventions which increase the number of contacts and the speed of change or to the unintelligence of man which retards his perception of the instruments of regulation and adjustment necessary to prevent these contacts and changes from generating serious conflicts. Peace might be kept by retarding progress so that there will be time for gradual adjustment by natural processes of accommodation and assimilation, or peace might be kept by accelerating progress through planned adjustments and new controls. Actually both methods have been tried, the latter especially within the state and the former especially in international relations.

Sovereignty in the political sense is the effort of a society to free itself from external controls in order to facilitate changes in its law and government which it considers necessary to meet changing economic and social conditions. The very efficiency of sovereignty within the state, however, decreases the efficiency of regulation in international relations. By eliminating tensions within the state, external tensions are augmented.

International relations become a "state of nature." War therefore among states claiming sovereignty tends to be related primarily to the balance of power among them.

Behind the power equilibrium are others, disturbances in any of which may cause war. These include such fundamental oppositions as the ambivalent tendency of human nature to love and to hate the same object and the ambivalent tendency of social organization to integrate and to differentiate at the same time. They also include less fundamental oppositions such as the tendency within international law to develop a world-order and to support national sovereignty and the tendency of international politics to generate foreign policies of both intervention and isolation. Elimination of such oppositions is not to be anticipated, and their continuance in some form is probably an essential condition of human progress. Peace, consequently, has to do not with the elimination of oppositions but with adequate methods of adjusting them.

The lag of adjusting procedures behind a change of conditions is a general cause of war. The persistence of this lag is due in part to the actual or presumed service of war to human groups. War has been thought (1) to serve sociological functions, (2) to satisfy psychological drives, (3) to be technologically useful, and (4) to be legally rational.

2. SOCIOLOGICAL FUNCTIONS OF WAR

Animal warfare is explained by the theory of natural selection. The behavior pattern of hostility has contributed to the survival of certain biological species, and consequently that behavior has survived. In the survival of other species other factors have played a more important role.

Among primitive peoples, before contact with civilization, warfare contributed to the solidarity of the group and to the survival of certain forms of culture. When population increased, migrations or new means of communication accelerated external contacts. The warlike tribes tended to survive and expand; furthermore, the personality traits of courage and obedience which developed among the members of these tribes equipped them for civilization.

Among peoples of the historic civilizations war contributed both to the survival and to the destruction of states and civilizations. Its influence depended upon the stage of the civilization and the type of military technique developed. Civilized states tended to fight for economic and political ends in the early stages of the civilization, with the effect of expanding and integrating the civilization. As the size and interdependence of political units increased, political and economic ends became less tangible, and cultural patterns and ideal objectives assumed greater importance. Aggressive war tended to become a less suitable instrument for conserving these elements of the civilization. Consequently, defensive strategies and peaceful sentiments developed, but in none of the historic civilizations were they universally accepted. War tended toward a destructive stalemate, disintegrating the civilization and rendering it vulnerable to the attack of external barbarians of younger civilizations which had acquired advanced military arts from the older civilization but not its cultural and intellectual inhibitions.

In the modern period the war pattern has been an important element in the creation, integration, expansion, and survival of states. World civilization has, however, distributed a singularly destructive war technique to all nations, with the consequence that the function of war as an instrument of integration and expansion has declined. Efforts to break the balance of power by violence have increasingly menaced the whole civilization, and yet this balance has been so incalculable that such efforts have continued to be made. Atomic weapons may have deprived war of any social function and made its consequences more calculable.

3. PSYCHOLOGICAL DRIVES TO WAR

Human warfare is a pattern giving social sanction to activities which involve the killing of other human beings and the extreme danger of being killed. At no period of human development has this pattern been essential to the survival of the individual. The pattern is a cultural acquisition, not an original trait of human nature, though many hereditary drives have contributed to the pattern. Of these, the dominance drive has been of especial importance. The survival of war has been due to its function in promoting the survival of the group with which the individual identifies himself and in remedying the individual problem arising from the necessary repression of many human impulses in group life. The pattern has involved individual attitudes and group opinion. As the self-consciousness of personality and the complexity of culture have increased with modern civilization, the drive to war has depended increasingly upon ambivalences in the personality and inconsistencies in the culture.

A modern community is at the same time a system of government, a self-contained body of law, an organization of cultural symbols, and the economy of a population. It is a government, a state, a nation, and a people.

Every individual is at the same time subject to the power and authority of a government and police, to the logic and conventions of a law and language, to the sentiments and customs of a nation and culture, and to the caprices and necessities of a people and its economy. If he fights in war, he does so because one of these aspects of the community is threatened or is believed by most of those who identify themselves with it to be threatened. It may be that the government, the state, the nation, and the people are sufficiently integrated so that there is no conflict in reconciling duty to all of these aspects of the community. But this is not likely because of the analytical character of modern civilization which separates military and civil government, the administration and the judiciary, church and state, government and business, politics and the schools, and religion and education. Furthermore, it may be that the threat is sufficiently obvious so that no one can doubt its reality, but this is seldom the case. The entities for whose defense the individual is asked to enlist are abstractions. Their relations to one another and the conditions of their survival are a matter of theory rather than of facts. People are influenced to support war by language and symbols rather than by events and conditions.

It may therefore be said that modern war tends to be about words more than about things, about potentialities, hopes, and aspirations more than about facts, grievances, and conditions. When the war seems to be about a particular territory, treaty, policy, or incident, it will usually be found that this issue is important only because, under the circumstances, each of the belligerents believed renunciation of its demand would eventually threaten the survival of its power, sovereignty, nationality, or livelihood. War broke out in 1939, not about Danzig or Poland, but about the belief of both the German people and their enemies that capacity to dictate a solution of these issues would constitute a serious threat to the survival of the power, ideals, culture, or welfare of the group which submitted to this dictation.

Even more remote from the needs of the individual and the state was the bearing of a campaign to expand the Roman frontier into Gaul, the Moslem frontiers into Africa, the Christian frontiers into Palestine, or the Communist frontier into central Europe. The meaning of Rome, of Islam, of Christendom, or of communism had to be understood by a considerable public. The importance of such increases in territory, population, and glory had to be inculcated by education of all those influencing policy, even though the prospect of immediate rewards to the active participants was obvious.

In the modern situation far more conceptual construction is necessary to make war appear essential to the survival of anything important. War, therefore, rests, in modern civilization, upon an elaborate ideological construction maintained through education in a system of language, law, symbols, and values. The explanation and interpretation of these systems are often as remote from the actual sequence of events as are the primitive explanations of war in terms of the requirements of magic, ritual, or revenge. War in the modern period does not grow out of a situation but out of a highly artificial interpretation of a situation. Since war is more about words than about things, other manipulations of words and symbols might be devised to meet the cultural and personality problems for which war offers an increasingly inadequate and expensive solution.

4. TECHNOLOGICAL UTILITY OF WAR

The verbal constructions which have had most to do with war in the modern period have been those which center about the words "power," "sovereignty," "nationality," and "living." These words may be interpreted as attributes, respectively, of the government, the state, the nation, and the people. By taking any one as an absolute value, the personality may be delivered from the restlessness of ambivalence and from the doubts and perplexities which arise from the effort to reconcile duty to conflicting institutions and values, particularly in times of rapid change. Although the relation of war to the preservation of any of these entities requires considerable interpretation, the validity of the interpretation varies with respect to the four entities.

The power of the government refers to its capacity to make its decisions effective through the hierarchy of civil and military officials. In a balance-of-power structure of world politics even a minor change in the relative power position of governments is likely to precipitate an accelerating process, destroying some of the governing elites and augmenting the power of others. If a government yields strategic territory, military resources, or other constituents of power to another without compensating advantage, it is quite likely to be preparing its own destruction. The theory which considers war a necessary instrument in the preservation of political power is relatively close to the facts. The most important technological cause of war in the modern world is its utility in the struggle for power.

The sovereignty of the state refers to the effectiveness of its law. This rests immediately on customary practices and on the prestige and reputation for power of the state rather than upon power itself. Sensitiveness about departures from established rules about honor and insult to reputation has a real relation to the preservation of sovereignty. A failure to resent contempt for rights or aspersions on prerogatives may initiate a rapid decline of reputation and increase the occasions when power will actually have to be resorted to if the legal system is to survive. Thus in the undeveloped state of international law, self-help and the war to defend national honor had a real relation to the survival of states prior to the nuclear age.

Nationality refers to the expectations of identical reactions to the basic social symbols by the members of the national group. It has developed principally from common language, traditions, customs, and values and has often persisted through political dismemberment of the group. Although national minorities have usually resisted the efforts of the administration and the economic system of the state to assimilate them, these influences may in time be successful. Thus, the use of force to preserve the power of the government and the sovereignty of the state which supports a given nationality may be important to the preservation of the latter. War, however, has been less useful to preserve nationality than to preserve power or sovereignty.

Living refers to the welfare and economy of a people. The argument has often been made that war is necessary to assure a people an area sufficient for prosperous living. Under the conditions of the modern world, this argument has usually been fallacious. The problem of increasing the welfare of a people has not depended upon the extension of political power or legal sovereignty into new areas but rather upon the elimination of the costs of war and depression, improvements in technology and land utilization, and a widening of markets and sources of raw materials far beyond any territories or spheres of interest which might be acquired by war. Population pressure, unavailability of raw materials, and loss of markets are more often the effect of military preparation than the cause. Although it is true, in a balance-of-power world, that economic bargaining power may increase with political power, yet it has seldom increased enough to compensate for the cost of maintaining a military establishment, of fighting occasional wars, and of impairing confidence in international economic stability. Through most of modern history people, even if conquered, have not ceased to exist and to consume goods. Efforts toward economic self-sufficiency and toward the forced migration, extermination, or enslavement of conquered peoples have, however, added to the reasonableness of conventional war for the preservation of the life of peoples.

Modern civilization offers a group more alternatives to war in most contingencies than did earlier civilizations and cultures. Resort to war, except within the restricted conception of necessary self-defense, is rarely the only way to preserve power or sovereignty and even more rarely the only way to preserve nationality or economy. War is most useful as a means to power and progressively less useful as a means to preserve sovereignty, nationality, or economy. That economic factors are relatively unimportant in the causation of war was well understood by Adolf Hitler:

Whenever economy was made the sole content of our people's life, thus suffocating the ideal virtues, the State collapsed again. . . . If one asks onself the question what the forces forming or otherwise preserving a State are in reality, it can be summed up with one single characterization: the individual's ability and willingness to sacrifice himself for the community. But that these virtues have really nothing whatsoever to do with economics is shown by the simple realization that man never sacrifices himself for them; that means: one does not die for business, but for ideals.

5. LEGAL RATIONALITY OF WAR

Which of the entities for which men fight is most important for men? Is there any criterion by which they may be rationally evaluated? Political power has been transferred from village to tribe, from feudal lord to king, from state to federation. Is it important today that it remain forever with the national governments that now possess it? The transfer of power to a larger group, the creation of a world police, under an international organization adequate to sanction a law against agression, appears a condition for eliminating a major cause of war.

Legal sovereignty also has moved from city-state to empire, from baronial castle to kingdom, from state to federation. To the individual the transfer of authority over his language and law to a larger group, although it has brought regret or resentment, has assured order, justice, and peace in larger areas and has increased man's control of his environment, provided that authority has been exercised with such understanding and deliberation as to avoid resentments arising to the point of revolt.

Nationality, in the broadest sense of a feeling of cultural solidarity, has similarly traveled from village to tribe, city-state, kingdom, nation, empire, or even civilization; but when it has become too broad, it has become too thin to give full satisfaction to the human desires for social identification and distinctiveness. There is no distinctiveness in being a member of the human race. Few would contemplate a world of uniform culture with equanimity. Geographical barriers and historic traditions promise for a long time to preserve cultural variety even in a world-federation, though modern means of communication and economy have exterminated many quaint customs and costumes. The need of cultural variety and the love of distinctive nationality suggest that a world police power is more likely to be effective if controlled by a universal federation than by a universal empire.

The area from which individuals have obtained their living has expanded from the village to the tribal area to the kingdom and empire, until, in the modern world, most people draw something from the most remote sections of the world. This widening of the area of exchange has augmented population and standards of living. Diminution of this area, such as occurred when the Roman Empire disintegrated into feudal manors, has had a reverse effect. The economist can make no case for economic walls, if economy is to be an instrument of human welfare rather than of political power, except in so far as widespread practices on the latter assumption force the welfare-minded to defend their existing economy by utilizing it temporarily as an instrument of power.

It may be questioned whether a rational consideration of the symbols, for the preservation of which wars have been fought, demonstrates that they have always been worth fighting for or that fighting has always contributed to their preservation. The actual values of these entities as disclosed by philosophy and the actual means for preserving them as disclosed by science have been less important in causing war than popular beliefs engendered by the unreflecting acceptance of the implications of language, custom, symbols, rituals, and traditions.

31. Accounting for International War: The State of the Discipline

J. DAVID SINGER

In the early 1930s, when Quincy Wright in America and Lewis Richardson in England began their respective investigations into the causes of war, they were not only unaware of one another's work; they were, of necessity, equally unaware of the radical change that their studies would produce in the field of war and peace research. With perhaps the exception of Jean de Bloch—whose *Future of War* (1899) sought all too successfully to predict what warfare would look like on the basis of a systematic examination of previous wars—and Pitirim Sorokin (1937)—whose focus was on the relationship between long cycles in cultural patterns and fluctuations in war and revolution over several thousand years—Wright (1942) and Richardson (1941 and 1960a, b) mark the first traceable efforts to bring scientific method to bear on international conflict. While physical phenomena had been studied in an essentially scientific fashion for several centuries, and biological phenomena for nearly a century, social phenomena had remained largely the domain of theological speculation, moral imperative, and

Reprinted from the *Journal of Peace Research* 18/1 (1981), pp. 1–3, 6–18, by permission of Universitetsforlaget, Oslo, and the author.

conventional folklore. But even as economics and sociology began to emerge as systematic sciences, followed in due course by the study of national political systems, international politics remained one of the most backward of disciplines.

This state of affairs was, and often still is, explained in terms of the intractability of the material; not only does much of the behavior occur in secret, but the material, structural, and cultural conditions associated with the international system are allegedly too spread out in time and in space to permit direct observation. But that explanation is incomplete. Political elites, it can be assumed, preferred things this way, partly because it made diplomatic bargaining easier and partly because political power brokers have typically shown an almost visceral reluctance to operate in the open. But if any event dramatically exposed the incompetence of these elites and the dangers of their secret diplomacy, it was World War I. While the most visible (and audible) result of this exposure was the Wilsonian call for "open covenants, openly arrived at," another message was received by Wright and Richardson.

As I interpret their prefatory remarks, each had begun to appreciate that another reason for secrecy was that the decision makers often did not "know what they were doing"; that is, even after lengthy domestic debate over foreign or military policy, the elites made recurrently erroneous predictions as to the consequences of their actions. Further, these two scholars arrived at a judgment that was not only generous, but probably correct: that the problem lay not so much with the stupidity or ambition of the foreign policy elites, but more with their ignorance. In addition, they observed that this ignorance was not peculiar to the practitioners alone; the scholarly community was hardly better off.

Having arrived at these general conclusions, it was natural that they would then have some caustic observations on the absence of evidence, and the heavy reliance on "brilliant, witty political discussion" (Richardson, 1960a, p. v.). This British meteorologist and pacifist also noted that "many of those who are considered to be experts on foreign affairs do not base their opinions on historical facts, but on some sort of instinctive reasoning." But, as the subsequent research of each makes clear, they saw the need for something more than historical facts, as gathered and interpreted by the standard diplomatic historian or political analyst. If the behavior of governments in the international setting was to become less destructive, the knowledge base from which they worked would have to be greatly improved. That is, if decision makers could more accurately predict—on the basis of historically observed regularities and theoretical inferences therefrom—the consequences of their decisions, there might be a decline in the frequency and magnitude of war. Even if that knowledge base served only to help challenge and question the assumptions behind our decisions, the error rate might be reduced. Of course, while the acquisition and codification of such knowledge would be necessary, neither Wright nor Richardson thought that it would be sufficient; decision makers and attentive publics would also have to be able and willing to understand, evaluate, and apply that knowledge.

1. TYPOLOGIES AND TAXONOMIES

Given, then, the need for a more solid knowledge base in the emerging inter-disciplinary field of war/peace studies, where do we stand now? What kinds of knowledge have we acquired and how adequately has it been codified into theoretically coherent form? What are the dominant orientations, and what are the more promising of these? In order to address these questions, we need some sort of organizing framework, within which we can differentiate the several theoretical orientations as well as summarize our knowledge to date. The variety of frameworks is, of course, quite large, and people gravitate to one or another of them for all sorts of reasons, scientific or otherwise: nationality, social class, age, gender, education, personality, academic identity, foundation and governmental fashions, and even (!) on the basis of prior research findings.

1.1 A Familiar Typology

One of the more familiar ways of classifying—and often, selecting from among—the possible approaches, is to divide them into the standard categories of technological, economic geographic, political, demographic, ideological, psychological, etc. As suggested, the advocates of any of these approaches often arrive at their position as a result of disciplinary affiliation, reflecting the oft-implicit premise that the academic discipline that one selects reflects one's "belief" that *its* major explanatory variables will account for virtually all sorts of social outcomes. Choosing such a typology and one of its approaches may, however, reflect nothing more than the conviction that one studies best those phenomena that one knows best, and that such partial models and their findings must eventually be integrated into those generated within the other social sciences.

But regardless of the motives and assumptions, we usually end up with a typology that helps to perpetuate and legitimize these parochial orientations and to encourage the appearance, disappearance, and reappearance of those "theories" that are all too typical of the no-growth, non-cumulative disciplines. Thus we find heavy, if not sole reliance on such factors as power discrepancies (Blainey, 1973), surplus capital (Lenin, 1939), business cycles (Secerov, 1919), demographic pressures (Organski, 1968), resource needs (Choucri & North, 1975), elite personalities

(Stoessinger, 1978), national moods (Klingberg, 1952; McClelland, 1961), misperceptions (White, 1968), and so forth. These at least have the virtue of resting upon variables that show some *variation* across time and place. But other alleged models of a single-variable sort fail to even recognize that a phenomenon as irregularly (and infrequently) distributed across time and space as war cannot be explained on the basis of relatively *in*variant phenomena. Thus, it is difficult to take seriously such putative explanations as the human drive for power (Morgenthau, 1948) or territory (Ardrey, 1966), the instinct of aggressiveness (Lorenz, 1967), or libidinous drive (Fornari, 1974).

In addition to the fact that most of the above orientations are rarely examined empirically, are seldom related to other explanations (Nelson & Olin, 1979; Silberner, 1946), ignore the multi-dimensional complexities of the war-inducing process, show insufficient variation in their "explanatory variables," and are overly responsive to current events, political pressures, and funding agency fads, they usually suffer from another fatal flaw. That is, they tend to overlook the critical distinction between international *conflict* and international *war*. While conflicts can arise out of an impressive range of social incompatibilities, the processes that lead to so frequent an event as conflicts are not necessarily those that lead to so infrequent an event as war. In a global system that is so poorly integrated in the structural or cultural sense, the relatively high frequency of serious international conflicts and military confrontations (about 225 involving the major powers alone since the Congress of Vienna) need not surprise us, whereas the relatively low frequency of war (fewer than 30 among those same powers in those 160-odd years) surely calls forth our curiosity.

Then there is the distinction between necessary conditions and sufficient ones (Deutsch & Senghaas, 1971). Many conditions are *necessary* for modern war: the fact that humans can behave aggressively and that many of them do seek power or territory under the proper stimuli; the availability of transport and weapons technology; centralized decision authority; some sort of credible justification; and so forth. While these may well

be certain necessary conditions, it is far from clear that any single factor is *sufficient* to carry a conflict across the threshold to war.

We need, therefore, a typology that: (a) recognizes the qualitative differences among competition, rivalry, and dispute on the one hand, and sustained military combat on the other, and that (b) also recognizes the complex interplay of necessary and/or sufficient conditions reflecting a wide range of material, structural, cultural, and behavioral phenomena. In addition, it should aid in integrating what we *have* discovered with what we *hope* to discover, and if possible, illuminate the research path that links the two. A discrete check list will not suffice; an integrated, but multitheoretical, framework would seem to be essential. Let us turn, then, to a scheme derived from the general systems literature that might possibly help us to organize what we know, and think we know, and to help stimulate the most appropriate next steps. . . .

1.3 Measuring the Incidence of International War

. . . Surprising as it may seem, scholars have been speculating on the causes of war for centuries before they tried to ascertain its empirical distribution, and even today many of our theoretical disagreements stem partly from the failure to identify our population of cases, and from differing conceptions and definitions of our outcome variable (Blechman & Kaplan, 1978; Bloomfield & Leiss, 1969; Bouthoul, 1951; Kende, 1971; Urlanis, 1960). But following on the work of Sorokin, Richardson, and Wright, the Correlates of War project at Michigan has assembled what seems to be the population of international (interstate, imperial, and colonial) and civil wars involving one or more sovereign states any place in the world since the Congress of Vienna, and has presented the coding rules, resulting data, and summary statistics (Singer & Small, 1972; Small et al., forthcoming).

In that handbook (*Wages of War*), we differentiate among four basic indicators of the incidence of war. The first is that of *frequency*, and is measured by the onset of sustained military hostilities between authorized armed forces of two or more sovereign national states culminating in at least 1,000 battle deaths. The second is *severity*, and is measured by the number of battle deaths resulting from a qualifying war; the third is *magnitude* measured in terms of nation-months of war; and the fourth is that of *intensity*, measured in battle deaths per nation-month or per capita. While frequency is measured only in the context of a given time and space domain, the other three indicators of the incidence of war can be applied to a given war as well as to all of the qualifying wars that occur in a specified time and space domain. In most, but not all of the studies summarized here, the Correlates of War data base and indicators have been used, and unless the choice of indicator makes an appreciable difference, the results will be reported in terms of the simplest indicator of war: its frequency.

Yet another consideration when seeking to account for the fluctuations in a given phenomenon is the extent to which they show a discernible regularity across time or space. While I would not accept the proposition that goodness of fit between a given distribution and one or another statistical model permits a legitimate inference as to the *processes that produced* that distribution, such regularities can certainly be suggestive (Horvath, 1968; Voevodsky, 1969; Weiss, 1963). Perhaps the most suggestive fit would be that of periodicity, on the assumption that a strong cyclical pattern might imply a degree of inexorability in international warfare. And, given the frequency with which cyclical patterns have been asserted, as well as the variety of inferences drawn from these putative patterns (Alcock, 1972; Davis et al., 1978; Denton & Phillips, 1968; Dewey, 1964), it may be worth reporting the results of a fairly systematic search for them. Simply put, we have found only the weakest trace of periodicity in the incidence of all international warfare over these 160 years, with a barely discernible cycle of 20-odd years (Singer & Small, 1972). More important, when we look at the war experiences of the more war-prone nations one at a time, virtually every conceivable technique fails to produce evidence for any kind of regularity (Singer & Cusack, 1980). Thus, it is perfectly true that there are peaks and troughs in the time plots of

war at both the national and the systemic levels, but the time intervals between those peaks and/or troughs are of sufficiently random length to support the sceptical conclusions of Sorokin (1937, p. 359) and Richardson (1960a, pp. 129–30 and 140). I would not, however, want to foreclose further research into the question, especially from the war expansion and contagion perspective. That is, despite the diverse results—stemming from diverse domains, indicators, and techniques—the evidence for *addiction* to war on the part of the system or any nation seems weak. But a close reading of Davis, Duncan, and Siverson (1978) and Siverson and King (1980) suggests that more complex models of *diffusion and contagion*—via alliance bonds—might well stand against the empirical test.

If war itself does not appear and re-appear in a regular cyclical fashion, it is unlikely that it results to any important extent from *any other* single-factor cycle, be it commercial, agricultural, climatic, or demographic. Rather, if there are indeed cyclical phenomena at work, there must be *several* of them involved in this process (Hart, 1946; Sorokin, 1937), with their concatenations falling at relatively irregular intervals. While there seems to be no concentrated research effort in this direction at the moment, it certainly appears to be worth pursuing further, perhaps when more is known regarding the time-space distributions of some of the more promising explanatory variables. Let us, then, attempt a brief and admittedly selective survey of these latter as they impinge on the incidence of international war.

2. FINDINGS TO DATE ON THE INCIDENCE OF WAR

To reiterate a point that has already been noted, there is no substitute for a good theoretical model when laying out an empirical investigation, but when we are not nearly far enough along to even specify the key variables of such a model, we have little choice but to work within a multi-theoretical framework and get on with our more inductive efforts. The problem now is one of identifying the results of the inductive work to date, some (but not all) of which has been shaped by the proposed framework, and to see how far it permits us to summarize and synthesize these diverse findings. We will work with three of the levels of aggregation noted earlier, and within each, look at the extent to which the several classes of variables seem to be accounting historically for the incidence of war. And, reflecting my strong suspicion that variables of a systemic and dyadic sort will turn out to be more powerful than those at the national and the decision-making levels of aggregation, let me deal with the finding at these levels in that order.

While it is often a rule of thumb to look first at the phenomena that are closest—in space or time—to the outcome we seek to explain, there seem to be reasonable grounds for *not* doing so in the case of war. While these grounds are far from conventional and the evidence for them is sparse, space limitations permit only stark assertions here; for a more detailed justification, see Singer (1961 and 1976). First, I assume that there is a great deal of homogeneity in the intellectual style of foreign policy/national security decision makers from nation to nation and from decade to decade over the past century or so. Similarly, there seems to be a remarkable homogeneity in the decision rules that nations follow, especially when they are in conflict, again irrespective of such allegedly critical distinctions as regime type, national culture and ideology, and level of economic development (Rosenau, 1966). These two assumptions suggest that we will not find a great deal of variation at the decisional and national levels, and therefore should not expect the attributes of nations or their decision makers to be very powerful in explaining so varying an outcome as war/no war.

A second consideration that follows quite logically is that most of the variation in the behavior of nations in conflict will be accounted for, not by their internal attributes, but by variation in their environment. That environment can, in turn, be viewed as having two basic components; the dyadic relationship with another nation, and the regional or global systemic context in which the conflicting nation finds itself. From this, it fol-

lows that we might expect to find the dyadic relationship and the properties of the system to carry us further in accounting for the incidence of international war than would the attributes of the nations or their decision making organizations (Zinnes, 1980a). Thus, we will begin with the systemic environment and examine some of the empirical evidence to date, and then move on to the effects of dyadic phenomena. But, to reiterate, the selection is intended to be more representative and suggestive than exhaustive.

2.1 Systemic Attributes

Despite the possible attractiveness of the above argument, few other investigators into the war/peace question have accepted it, and as a result, a fair fraction of research on the systemic conditions associated with war has emanated so far largely from the Michigan Correlates of War project. Further, of the three types of systemic conditions—material, structural, and cultural—most of the reproducible evidence to date reflects the structural dimension (Sullivan, 1976). Unfortunately, there is little systematic work on such material attributes of the system as weapons technology, industrial development, resource limits, climate, or demographic patterns. Similarly, outside of some preliminary efforts by Kegley et al. (1979), Choi (1978), and Gantzel (1972) little effort has been invested in the search for systematic connections between cultural conditions and the incidence of war. On the other hand, researchers of a scientific bent have been as assiduous in their examination of structural correlates of war as their methodologically traditional colleagues, and it is to that literature that we now turn.

Perhaps the most plausible of the system's structural attributes in the war/peace context is that of the configurations generated by alliance bonds, with those generated by distributions of power following closely behind. Looking first at the structural characteristic known as bipolarity, we usually have in mind the extent to which the nations in a given geographical region, or in the major power sub-set (a functional "region"), or world-wide, are clustered into two clearly opposed coalitions. While there are several definitions of bipolarity and rather diverse operational indicators, it generally implies the degree of conformity to an "ideal" condition in which all of the nations are—via military alliance—in one or another of two equally powerful coalitions with no alliance bonds between the polar blocs, and full bondedness *within* each. While such a set of conditions has never obtained, the reasoning is that even an approximation would so severely hamper the conflict resolving efficacy of the pluralistic cross-cutting, multiple balancing mechanism of the system as to make conflict escalation and war much more likely (Deutsch & Singer, 1964; Waltz, 1964; Rosecrance et al., 1974; Kaplan, 1957; Liska, 1956). But like all too many theoretical hunches in the world politics field, there is an equally plausible counter-argument: that so clearly bipoloar a system structure would eliminate all ambiguity as to who is on whose side, or as to the possibility of military victory, that war would just never be considered. Rather, according to this orientation, war occurs when there is ambiguity, either because behavior becomes less predictable and governments stumble into war, or because governments have a "drive toward certainty," and war helps to clarify the picture.

In any event, the research findings to date only partially resolve the theoretical disagreements. In one of the first systematic analyses, Singer and Small (1968) found that the relationship between their indicators of polarity and war differed in the 19th and 20th centuries. In the earlier epoch, higher polarity levels tended to be followed by lower levels of international war, but in the period since 1900, fluctuations in the incidence of war were *positively* associated with the fluctuations in polarity. In a follow-up, Wallace (1973) used a somewhat different indicator of polarity and found a curvilinear association, with war levels generally associated with very high bipolarity scores or very low ones, suggesting—for the entire 1816–1965 period—that there may be an optimal level of three or four relatively discernible alliance clusters, with war levels quite low when those intermediate conditions obtain. In a third and more recent analysis of the question, Bueno de Mesquita (1978) found that fluctuations in war were accounted for less by the *level* of bipolarity

in the system than by the direction and rate of change in the alliance configurations that might produce such bipolarity. That is, the amount of war in the system since the Congress of Vienna tended to rise when the "tightness" of alliance clusters was on the increase. Even more confusing are Levy's finding (1979) that bipolarity makes for maximum stability and unipolarity for maximum war, and Wayman's finding (1981) that cluster polarity exercises a different effect than power polarity. Perhaps Ostrom and Aldrich (1978, p. 765) summarize things best in reporting that "our results have a distinctly negative flavor."

As might be expected, there are several interesting extensions of the bipolarity-war hypothesis. The simplest is that since alliances involving one set of major powers will generally be in opposition to other majors, the greater the percentage of major powers in alliance, the greater the bipolarity of the system as a whole, and thus the greater (or lesser) will be the incidence of war in the ensuing years. Once again, the empirical findings are mixed; Singer and Small (1968) found that their alliance aggregation indicator, which was indeed highly correlated with their bipolarity index, predicted positively to the incidence of war in the 1900–1945 period, but negatively in the 1816–1899 period. Imposing more stringent analytical tests and slightly different indicators, Ostrom and Hoole (1978) turned up similar, but considerably weaker patterns.

A more complex version of this systemic hypothesis can be interpreted in two ways. One is that the concentration of military and industrial capabilities tends to follow the concentration of national coalitions and groupings (especially the majors), and that the concentration of these capabilities should have the same effect on the incidence of war as the concentration of the nations into a small number of tight polar groupings. While this isomorphism does occur from time to time, it is not constant enough to make this interpretation very compelling. Thus, one takes a more generalized view and treats both types of concentration as producing a high degree of *clarity* in the system's structure. And to the extent that the systemic environment is clear and unambiguous as to (a) who will fight on which side if a conflict escalates to war, and (b) which side will probably win that war, the decision makers are thought to be less likely to either entertain the war option or to merely stumble into war.

Regardless of the theoretical interpretation, the empirical investigations lead once more to inconsistent results. And, as before, a major anomaly is the inter-century one. In the 19th century, high concentration of capabilities in the hands of a very few powers makes for increases in the incidence of war, while more equal distributions are associated with *low* levels of war (Singer, Bremer and Stuckey, 1972). But in the period 1900–1965, high concentrations lead to low levels of warfare and low concentrations are associated with higher levels of war. In a follow-up study, Champion and Stoll (1980) went a step further and: (a) introduced an important control variable, classifying each major power as either "satisfied" or "dissatisfied" on the eve of each war as reflected in the historians' consensus; and (b) calculated the concentrations in terms of *coalitions*, rather than concentrations in terms of the nations separately and individually. These modifications appreciably enhanced the post-dictive power of the capability distribution model across the full time period, suggesting that if the blocs have indeed been accurately identified and the powers accurately classified on the "satisfaction" dimension, this systemic factor may be of considerable importance. But as the authors remind us, the validity of these additional indicators remains to be more fully demonstrated. In an interesting variation on this theme, Cannizzo (1978) examined the effect of such capability configurations on the major powers individually, and found that these were far from uniform; concentrations and changes therein strongly affected France, Italy, and Austria-Hungary, for example, while having little impact on the war experiences of England, Japan, and Russia. Wayman (1981) found that wars occurring under conditions of high concentration are less severe than those occurring when capabilities are more evenly distributed.

Another factor—related to the others in the sense that it taps the structural clarity dimension—is that of status inconsistency, aggregated to the systemic level. In two of the earlier investigations, Wallace (1973a) and East (1972) found moderately

clear associations between the incidence of international war and the extent to which the rank scores of the nations on the material capability and diplomatic importance dimensions were inconsistent with one another. That is, the more similar the systemic pecking orders on power and on prestige, the less war-prone the system was in the years following. On the other hand, the inquiries by Ray (1974) and Gochman (1980) produced more ambiguous results, perhaps due in part to the use of different indicators.

2.2 Dyadic Conditions

While there is a clear conceptual difference between the structural characteristics of a system and the relationships among the component units of the system, it is worth reiterating their empirical and conceptual connections. As noted earlier, most systemic properties rest upon, and can be inferred from, the links and bonds among the components, and while some scholars have sought their indicators of system structure in the triad (Harary, 1961), most of the data-based work has been restricted to the more manageable "two-body problem," to borrow from the vocabulary of physics. Following the distinction noted earlier, we will treat dyadic conditions of a relational sort first, and then turn to those of a comparative sort, resting not on the links, but on the similarities, between nations.

As to the former, we again find the familiar emphasis upon alliance bonds, followed by the bonds created via membership in discernible diplomatic clusters, trading blocs, and international organizations. First, we discover that, in general, nations with formal and long-standing alliance bonds experience a significantly higher frequency of war than do those without them (Singer & Small, 1966); on the other hand, Sabrosky (1980) found that nations that were allied to one another had a very low probability of going to war against one another. Neither case suggests anything as to the *intentions* of the alliance makers (Singer & Bueno de Mesquita, 1973). Looking at another type of bond, Skjelsbaek (1971) found that war oppponents tended to decrease their shared intergovernmental organization memberships in the five-year period preceding the onset of war, and

Singer and Wallace (1970) found that while most IGOs were founded *after* the terminaton of war, there was virtually no relationship between the number of them in the system and the amount of interstate war experienced in the subsequent five years. More surprisingly, Gochman (1980) found that militarized disputes between major trading partners were *more* likely to escalate to war than were disputes between states that did not heavily trade with each other.

Shifting from the role of dyadic bonds and associations in accounting for the incidence of war to that of similarities and differences, the ubiquitous dimension of power again captures most of our attention. The theoretical argument is rather direct: even though sub-military conflict seems to be no more likely between nations of very unequal strength than between those of approximate parity, this factor should become more critical as the war threshold is approached. The familiar dictum is that the weaker *dare* not fight and the stronger *need* not; the corollary is that one purpose of war is to ascertain which party is stronger when any doubt does exist.

While the evidence on this question is relatively consistent, the final word has hardly been said. For example, Garnham (1976a) found that equality in population reduced the likelihood of dyadic war, but that equality in geographical size or industrial base did not, in the 1816–1965 period. Controlling for geographical contiguity, however, both he (1976b) and Weede (1976), as well as Barringer (1972) and Wright (1965), found that nations that were approximately equal in material capabilities were significantly more likely to carry their disputes to war than were nations of discernible *dis*parity. Further, Stoll and Champion (1977) found that serious disputes were more likely to escalate to war if the weak side was the initiator of the dispute; disputes initiated by the stronger side were less likely to end in war. Mihalka (1976) found that once military force was threatened or used, the greater the disparity in capabilities of the disputants, the less likely the dispute was to escalate to hostilities. More recently, Singer and his colleagues (1979a) found that while only 13% of all major power militarized disputes since 1816 escalated to war, that figure rose to 20% when the parties were approximately equal in military terms, and to 75% if such parity was combined with rapid military buildup during the three years prior to the dispute.

A second emphasis in this literature is more diffuse, but worth noting briefly, given the theoretical pervasiveness of its assumptions. That is, the more similar two nations are in terms of certain political or cultural attributes, the more friendly their relationship might be expected to be, and the more friendly they are, the less frequently or severely might they be expected to wage war against one another. Here, too, Richardson (1960a) was the first to look into the question systematically, and he found little historical evidence to support the classical view. For the period 1820–1949 and using his population of 300-odd wars and military disputes, he found that neither a common language nor a common religion had a depressing effect on the incidence of dyadic war (pp. 230–31). To the contrary, as he himself demonstrated (pp. 285–86) and as others have confirmed (Gleditsch and Singer, 1975), geographical contiguity is the confounding variable. That is, since geographical neighbors are not only more likely to be culturally similar but also to have more sources of conflict and to be more accessible to one another's armies, it follows that such similarities should actually be related to dyadic war in the *positive* direction (Gantzel, 1972).

These findings lead, in turn, to another of the more interesting paradoxes in research to date. Reference is to the effect of common boundaries, with the reasonable hypothesis that the greater the number of immediate neighbors a nation has, the more frequently it will be drawn into warfare against one or another of them. While Richardson's data (1960a, p. 177) tend to support this hypothesis, the findings of Starr and Most (1978) do not. Rather, they find an *inverse* relationship between a nation's war proneness and the number of immediate neighbors. Nor should these results be surprising, when we consider that the number of direct neighbors is physically a function of a land-locked nation's geographic size vis-à-vis that of its neighbors. The longer its boundaries, the greater the numbr of others that can border on it, and the smaller these latter are, the more numerous they can be. From this, it follows that the greater will be the discrepancy between its size (and strength, all else being equal) and theirs, and given the finding that war is more likely between equals, it again follows that the frequency of war *should* be lower.

2.3 National Attributes and Relationships

In an earlier section I indicated that national attributes seemed less crucial in accounting for war than either systemic or dyadic conditions, and before summarizing the evidence to date, let me expand on that assertion. Briefly put, the exigencies of survival in an international system of such inadequate organization and with so pervasively dysfunctional a culture require relatively uniform response. That is, for a national entity to adapt to and survive in such an environment, it must achieve a fair degree of political mobilization, military preparedness, and political centralization. Despite great differences in tradition and culture, or great apparent differences in political regime and economic arrangements, these external considerations tend to reinforce the essential domestic similarity of national states, regardless of their size, strength, level of economic development, etc.

To what extent does the empirical evidence to date support this alleged lack of cross-national variation in the attributes that might be associated with the incidence of war? On the one hand, certain of these attributes do seem to be related to the frequency and/or severity of national war experiences (Richardson, 1960a; Rummell, 1972), with overall military-industrial capabilities the most potent predictor. In a systematic examination of the relationship between a six-dimensional index of such capabilities and war proneness since the Congress of Vienna, Bremer (1980) found a very strong positive correlation between the strength of nations (including industrial development and military preparedness) and their tendency to go to war. Using a more restricted indicator, reflecting the size of the military establishment, and using more general indicators of foreign conflict, several studies further confirm this positive association with national strength (Naroll, 1969; Choucri and North, 1975; Small, 1978; Weede, 1970).

On the other hand, if we turn to more complex models that might link national characteristics to war proneness, the findings are considerably more ambiguous. Applying the sociological concept of status inconsistency to nations whose material capabilities are high and whose attributed diplomatic status scores are low (or vice-versa), neither Ray (1974) nor Gochman (1980) found any consistent pattern. Another domestic characteristic that has often been thought of as contributing to national war proneness is that of domestic instability. Yet no investigation identified much of an association until Wilkenfeld (1973) controlled for regime type, and found, for part of the post-World War II period, several clear associations. However, looking at regime type alone and examining the full 1816–1965 period, Small and Singer (1974) found that autocratic and democratic regimes were equally likely to both initiate wars and to become embroiled in them, but Haas (1965) found, at least for the twentieth century, that democratic regimes were less war prone than authoritarian ones. He also concludes in the same study that wealthy urbanized nations, especially during periods of social strain, are particularly susceptible to war involvement.

Shifting from attributes of an essentially internal sort to external relationships, the dimension most often examined is that of alliance bonds. In studies covering members of the interstate system since 1816, both Singer and Small (1966) and Siverson and King (1978) find a strong positive association between alliance involvement and war proneness; this is not to suggest that the relationship rests on the high reliability of alliance commitments (Sabrosky, 1980). And, given the well-known association between high capabilities and high alliance involvement, as well as that between capabilities and war proneness, this should come as no surprise. On a related dimension and picking up the geographical variables summarized earlier in the dyadic context, Richardson (1960a) found a positive relationship between the number of neighbors a nation had and the frequency of its wars from 1820 to 1945, and Wesley (1969), Weede (1970), Midlarsky (1975), and Starr and Most (1978) found relatively similar patterns for comparable spatial-temporal domains. Finally, Gleditsch and Singer (1975) examined the effect of a nation's mean distance from all other sovereign members of the system, and they, too, found a positive relationship; the more centrally located they were, the more war they experienced.

The tentative inference from this limited set of studies is that such basic geo-strategic factors as location and strength seem to be of importance, but that despite persuasive arguments to the contrary (Rosenau, 1966), domestic factors of a less material sort would appear to be rather negligible in accounting for the war proneness of individual nations.

2.4 Behavioral and Interactional Patterns

To this juncture, our focus has been on the extent to which the frequency and magnitude of war might be accounted for historically by the contextual and ecological variables: fluctuations in systemic, dyadic, or national conditions. Following the check list implied in the taxonomy, this leaves untouched the question of behavior itself: to what extent can we account for war by the actions and interactions of the nations? Given the emphasis on diplomatic and military behavior in the speculative literature on war, one might expect to find a respectable body of empirical work on the question. The fact that we do *not*, however, need not be very surprising. First of all, behavioral phenomena are more elusive and seem to be more difficult to observe and measure. Second, a good many researchers suspect that behavioral patterns are so heavily determined by the ecological conditions summarized above that these former will account for very little variation in our outcome. Third, and closely related, is the suspicion that we can treat ecological variables as surrogates of behavior, given their assumed covariation, and thus avoid all of the grief associated with the observation and meaurement of behavior.

Be that as it may, there is a modest body of empirical work in which behavior patterns serve as predictors, and once again Richardson offers a convenient point of departure. Perhaps his most important contribution is found in the posthumous *Arms and Insecurity* (1960b), where he derives and then puts to the test a simple differential equation designed to capture the essence of an interactive arms race. Vis-à-vis the arms expenditure patterns preceding the two World Wars, the model offers a fairly good fit, and generally supports the notion that each protagonist's annual increase will be a function of the other's absolute expenditure in the previous year, controlling for a fatigue factor and an exacerbation factor.

These analyses have stimulated the development of a rich and diverse array of follow-up models, a fair number of which have been tested against various 19th and 20th century arms interaction processes. While it would require a major review article to summarize and interpret this body of research (Kurakawa, 1978; Luterbacher, 1974; Zinnes, 1980b) two general conclusions seem justified. One is that we have not yet been able to separate the effects of the domestic and foreign stimuli at the various stages of arms races, and the other is that we have yet to differentiate between the profiles or "signatures" of those that *have* ended in war and those that have not (Singer, 1970). But two important findings have resulted from Wallace's work in this area. In an earlier study (1973), he not only found that status inconsistency levels in the international system predicted system-wide increases in military expenditures, but also that these increases predicted in turn the incidence of war. In a later analysis (1979) Wallace found that if two nations started a military confrontation, their likelihood of crossing the war threshold was considerably lower if they were not in an arms race with one another, but much higher if they were.

An even more elusive problem arises when we shift from military expenditures and arms acquisition to less easily observed behavior such as the diplomatic moves and counter-moves associated with the escalation of conflict. But a satisfactory coding and scaling scheme has been developed (Leng and Singer, 1977). In some preliminary analyses, Leng (1980) found that the use of threats had a higher probability of ending in war when met with a defiant counter-threat, whereas there is no clear association between the mere frequency of threats and the onset of war. In an earlier set of investigations, North et al. (1964) combined behavior and perception in order to examine their reciprocal effects in a number of crises, particularly that preceding World War I. In general, they found a propensity toward over-estimation of the adversary's intentions (compared with his actual behavior) and an under-estimation of his relative capabilities, the combination of which leads to escalatory behavior.

Not surprisingly, and despite the attention of diplomatic historians and traditional political scientists, the systematic examination of the relationship between behavioral phenomena and war has lagged discernibly behind that of the other three sets of factors discussed earlier. While the explanation lies partially in the observation and measurement problem noted above, this lag also reflects the reasonable idea that the more we first discover regarding the effects of the ecological conditions, the greater the theoretical mileage we will obtain from subsequent analyses of the behavioral and interactional phenomena.

3. CONCLUSION

While this summary hardly suggests that we are well on the way to understanding the causes of war and conditions of peace (to use Wright's phrase), some modest optimism would not be completely out of place. That is, despite the limited amount of research and the relative lack of convergence in our findings, there are two grounds for believing that we are no longer moving in non-cumulative circles. First, we are finally seeing systematic research that rests on reproducible evidence, and after several centuries of pre-operational speculation, this is to be applauded. Second, despite the diversity of theoretical orientations, there seems to be a growing awareness that the resulting paradigms and investigations need not be incompatible.

On the one hand, my sense is that researchers in the war-peace sector are increasingly aware of the difference between explaining the *high* incidence of recurrent conflict and rivalry of a non-military sort, and explaining the low—but destructive—incidence of war. The range of models intended to address the former question is, admittedly, impressive in its diversity. But that, in my judgment, is a less critical problem; conflict is ubiquitous in all social systems and the problem is not to prevent it, but to reduce the frequency

with which it becomes socially destructive. Thus, when we shift from conflict in general to war in particular, we find a diminished and more manageable array of theoretical models (Burton, 1962; Hoffmann, 1965; Holsti, 1972; Kaplan, 1957; Wallensteen, 1973; Midlarsky, 1975; Russett, 1974). And, on the other hand, a close scrutiny of these models shows a remarkable overlap, if not convergence. To illustrate, let me mention some of the emphases found in the literature most frequently: realpolitik, arms race, power transition, economic development, and imperialism. There are indeed those who insist that such models are not only inconsistent with one another logically and empirically, but also not even subject to comparative analysis and testing. There are even those who insist on a different epistemology and assert that the western scientific method is inappropriate to the examination of rival models and hypotheses. But my suspicion is that their numbers and influence are on the wane, and that a compelling theoretical convergence could encourage a more open-minded examination of the empirical evidence.

In order to move toward such a theoretical convergence, two prior steps would seem necessary. First, we need to identify the extent to which these competing models rest upon similar explanatory variables. Given the Babel-like discourse of theorizers and practitioners, this might appear to be impossible. But as systematic empirical work goes forward, one inexorable consequence is the translation of ideologically loaded verbalization into operationally defined variables, and the evidence to date is that devotees of rather diverse approaches can agree on (at least) the face validity of these indicators. Moreover, it looks as if a rather wide range of putatively explanatory concepts can be validly translated into identical indicators. Thus, "defining our terms" and operationalizing our variables may well reveal a considerable degree of convergence amongst theoretical models that have often been thought of as hopelessly divergent and incomparable.

Second, we need to recognize that at rock bottom the most important difference amongst the contending causes of war models is that of the foreign policy decision process. That is, each model assumes—often implicitly—a different class of decision makers in power, and each postulates a different set of decision rules. Thus, one strategy might be to conceive of the policy making process in terms of interest aggregation, with the decision makers seen as trying to respond to and balance a complex array of international incentives and constraints vis-à-vis an equally complex array of domestic interests, including their own. Once those assumptions and postulations have been teased out of the verbal models, our highly general paradigm might then be converted into operational versions of the several more specific models. Note that we have assumed, to this juncture, a high degree of homogeneity in decision makers and the rules they employ, but to move closer to a full explanation, that assumption would have to be relaxed.

These assumptions, however, should be put to the empirical/historical test directly, and this is why the research described in the body of this paper can be so valuable. It is one thing to observe and then classify the backgrounds and interest group affiliations of foreign policy elites in a wide range of nations across an appreciable span of time; while this research task is far from complete, it is clearly manageable. But the decision rules that they employ, and the utilities that they assign to various outcomes in the economic, diplomatic, and military sectors will remain forever beyond the range of *direct* observation. Thus, we have little choice but to rely on careful inference, and the most solid basis for inferring their decision criteria will be found in the sort of evidence discussed above, especially when embedded in computerized representations of the historical process (Alker and Brunner, 1969; Bremer, 1977), *Under which systemic, dyadic, and national conditions do which foreign policy elites respond to which behavioral stimuli of which other nations in which specific fashion?* The more fully we can answer these empirical questions, the more reliably can we infer the decision rules that are at work. And the more we can check these inferences against those that are embedded in the rival models, the closer we can get to their confirmation and disconfirmation.

This brief overview leaves out a great deal of important detail, just as our survey of the evidence to date is far from complete; a more complete picture emerges in three recent volumes from the Michigan project: *Explaining War,* 1979; *Correlates of War I: Research Origins and Rationale,* 1979; and *Correlates of War II: Testing Some Realpolitik Models,* 1980. But these pages should serve to remind us that the causes-of-war question is not only a researchable one, soluble in principle. They also serve to remind us that the task is finally under way, and if the scientific talent and the necessary support can be mobilized, we may yet be in time to put an end to one of the most destructive and dysfunctional activities known to human history.

REFERENCES

ALCOCK, N. Z. 1972. *The War Disease.* Oakville, Canada: Canadian Peace Research Institute.

ALKER, H., AND R. BRUNNER. 1969. Simulating international conflict. *International Studies Quarterly* 13/1: 70–110.

ARDREY, R. 1966. *The Territorial Imperative.* New York: Atheneum.

BARRINGER, R. E. 1972. *War: Patterns of Conflict.* Cambridge, Mass.: MIT Press.

BLAINEY, G. 1973. *The Causes of War.* New York: Free Press.

BLECHMAN, B. M. AND S. S. KAPLAN. 1978. *Force Without War.* Washington, D.C.: Brookings Institute.

BLOCH, I. 1899. *The Future of War.* New York: Doubleday & McClure.

BLOOMFIELD, L. AND A. LEISS. 1969. *Controlling Small Wars.* New York: Knopf.

BOUTHOUL, G. 1951. *Les Guerres: Elements de Polemologie.* Paris: Payot.

BREMER, S. A. 1977. *Simulated Worlds.* Princeton, N.J.: Princeton University Press.

——. 1980. National capabilities and war proneness. In *Correlates of War II: Testing Some Realpolitik Models,* ed. J. D. Singer. New York: Free Press.

BREMER, S. A., J. D. SINGER, AND U. LUTERBACHER. The population density and war proneness of European nations 1816–1965. *Comparative Political Studies* 6/3: 329–348.

BUENO DE MESQUITA, B. 1978. Systemic polarization and the occurrence and duration of war. *Journal of Conflict Resolution* 22/2: 241–267.

BUENO DE MESQUITA, B. 1981. *The War Trap*. New Haven, Conn: Yale University Press.

BURTON, J. W. 1962. *Peace Theory*. New York: Knopf.

CANNIZZO, C. 1978. Capability distribution and major power war experience, 1816–1965. *Orbis, 21/4:* 947–957.

CHAMPION, M. AND R. STOLL. 1980. Capability concentration, alliance bonding, and conflict among the major powers. In *Alliances and International Conflict,* ed. A. N. Sabrosky. Philadelphia: Foreign Policy Research Institute.

CHOI, K. L. 1978. *An Empirical Investigation of the Relationship Between International Legal Norms Relevant to the Control of Violence and the Amount of International War.* Seoul, Korea: Department of Political Science and Diplomacy, mimeo.

CHOUCRI, N. AND R. C. NORTH. 1975. *Nations in Conflict*. San Francisco: W. H. Freeman.

DAVIS, W., G. DUNCAN, AND R. SIVERSON. 1978. The dynamics of warfare, 1816–1965. *American Journal of Political Science* 22/4: 772–792.

DENTON, F. H. AND W. PHILLIPS. 1968. Some patterns in the history of violence. *Journal of Conflict Resolution* 12/2: 182–195.

DEUTSCH, K. W. AND J. D. SINGER. 1964. Multipolar power systems and international stability. *World Politics* 16/3: 390–406.

———, AND D. SENGHAAS. 1971. A framework for a theory of war and peace. In *Search for World Order,* ed. A. Lepawsky et al. New York: Appleton-Century-Crofts, pp. 23–46.

DEWEY, E. R. 1964. *The 177-Year Cycle in War, 600 B.C.–A.D. 1957.* Pittsburgh: Foundation for the Study of Cycles.

EAST, M. A. 1972. Status discrepancy and violence in the international system: An empirical analysis. In *The Analysis of International Politics,* ed. V. Davis et al. New York: Free Press. pp. 299–319.

FORNARI, F. 1974. *Psychoanalysis of War*. Garden City, N.Y.: Doubleday.

GALTUNG, J. 1964. A structural theory of aggression. *Journal of Peace Research* 1/2: 95–119.

GANTZEL, K. J. 1972. *System und Akteur: Beiträge zur Vergleichenden Kriegsursachenforschung.* Düsseldorf: Bertelsmann.

GARNHAM, D. 1976a. Dyadic International War, 1816–1965: The role of power parity and geographical proximity. *Western Political Quarterly* 29/2: 231–242.

———. 1976b. Power parity and lethal international violence 1969–1973. *Journal of Conflict Resolution* 20/3: 379–394.

———. 1979. *The Causes of War: Systemic Findings.* Milwaukee, Wisconsin: University of Wisconsin Department of Political Science.

GLEDITSCH, N. P. AND J. D. SINGER. 1975. Distance and international war 1816–1965. *Proceedings of the International Peace Research Association, fifth general conference, Oslo*: 481–506.

GOCHMAN, C. S. 1980. Status, capabilities, and major power conflict. In *Correlates of War II: Testing Some Realpolitik Models,* ed. J. D. Singer. New York: Free Press.

HAAS, M. 1965. Societal approaches to the study of war. *Journal of Peace Research* 4: 307–323.

HARARY, F. 1961. A structural analysis of the situation in the Middle East in 1956. *Journal of Conflict Resolution* 5/2: 167–78.

HART, H. 1946. Depression, war, and logistic trends. *American Journal of Sociology* 52: 112–122.

HOFFMANN, S. 1965. *The State of War*. New York: Praeger.

HOLSTI, O. 1972. *Crisis, Escalation, War*. Montreal: McGill-Queens University Press.

HORVATH, W. J. 1968. A statistical model for the duration of wars and strikes. *Behavioral Science* 13/1: 18–28.

KAPLAN, M. A. 1957. *System and Process in International Politics*. New York: John Wiley.

KEGLEY, C. W. ET AL., EDS. 1975. *International Events and the Comparative Analysis of Foreign Policy.* Columbia, S.C.: University of South Carolina Press.

KEGLEY, C. W. 1979. Measuring transformations in the global legal system. In *Law Making In The Global Community*, ed. M. G. Onuf. Princeton: Princeton University Press.

KEGLEY, C. W., G. A. RAYMOND, AND K. L. CHOI. 1979. Fluctuations in Legal Norms and Arbital Behavior, 1825–1970: Indicators of major power conflict? Columbia, S.C.: Department of Political Science.

KENDE, I. 1971. Twenty-five years of local wars. *Journal of Peace Research* 8: 5–22.

KLINGBERG, F. L. 1952. The historical alternation of moods in American foreign policy. *World Politics* 4/2: 239–273.

KUROKAWA, S. 1978. A simple model of arms races: Richardson's model revisited. Prepared for delivery at the Hiroshima, Japan Conference of the Peace Science Society (International).

LENG, R. J. 1980. Influence strategies and interstate conflict. In *The Correlates of War II: Testing Some Realpolitik Models,* ed. J. D. Singer. New York: Free Press.

LENG, R. J. AND J. D. SINGER. 1977. Towards a multi-theoretical typology of international behavior. In *Mathematical Approaches to International Relations,* ed. Bunge, Galtung & Malitza. Bucharest: Romanian Academy of Social & Political Sciences: 71–93.

LENIN, V. I. 1939. *Imperialism.* New York: International Publishers.

LEVY, J. S. 1979. The polarity of the system and international stability. International Studies Association. Mimeo.

LISKA, G. 1956. *International Equilibrium.* Cambridge, Mass.: Harvard University Press.

LORENZ, K. 1967. *On Aggression.* New York: Bantam Books.

LUTERBACHER, U. 1974. *Dimensions Historiques de Modèles Dynamiques de Conflit.* Leiden: A. W. Sijthoff.

McCLELLAND, D. 1961. *The Achieving Society.* New York: Free Press.

MIDLARSKY, M. I. 1975. *On War.* New York: Free Press.

MIHALKA, M. 1976. *Interstate Conflict in the European State System, 1816–1970.* Ph.D. dissertation, University of Michigan.

MORGENTHAU, H. J. 1948. *Politics Among Nations* New York: Alfred A. Knopf.

NAROLL, R. 1974. *Military Deterrence in History.* Albany: State University of New York Press.

NELSON, K. L. AND S. C. OLIN. 1979. *Why War? Ideology, Theory and History.* Berkeley, Calif.: University of California Press.

NORTH, R. C., R. A. BRODY, AND O. R. HOLSTI. 1964. Some empirical data on the conflict spiral. *Peace Research Society Papers.* 1: 1–14.

ORGANSKI, A. F. K. 1968. *World Politics.* New York: Alfred A. Knopf.

OSTROM, C., AND J. H. ALDRICH. 1978. The relationship between size and stability in the major power international system. *American Journal of Political Science.* 22: 743–771.

OSTROM, C., AND F. HOOLE. 1978. Alliances and war revisited: A research note. *International Studies Quarterly.* 22: 215–235.

RAY, J. L. 1974. Status inconsistency and war involvement in Europe, 1816–1970. *Peace Science Society Papers.* 23: 69–80.

———. 1980. The measurement of system structure. In *The Correlates of War II: Testing Some Realpolitik Models,* ed. J. D. Singer. New York Free Press.

RICHARDSON, L. F. 1941. Frequency of occurrence of wars and other total quarrels. *Nature* 148: 37–59.

———. 1960a. *Statistics of Deadly Quarrels.* Pittsburgh: Boxwood.

———. 1960b. *Arms and Insecurity.* Pittsburgh: Boxwood.

ROSECRANCE, R., ET AL. 1974. *Power, Balance of Power and Status in Nineteenth Century International Relations.* Beverly Hills, Calif.: Sage.

ROSENAU, J. N. 1966. Pre-theories and theories of foreign policy. In *Approaches to Comparative and International Politics,* ed. R. B. Farrell. Evanston, Ill.: Northwestern University Press.

RUMMEL, R. J. 1972. *The Dimensons of Nations.* Beverly Hills, Calif.: Sage.

RUSSETT, B. M. 1974. *Power and Community in World Politics.* San Francisco: Freeman.

SABROSKY, A. D. 1980. Interstate alliances: their reliability and the expansion of war. In *Correlates of War II: Testing Some Realpolitik Models,* ed. J. D. Singer. New York: Free Press.

SECEROV, S. 1919. *Economic Phenomena Before and After War.* London: Rutledge.

SILBERNER, E. 1946. *The Problem of War in Nineteenth Century Economic Thought.* Princeton, N.J.: Princeton University Press.

SINGER, J. D. 1961. The level-of-analysis problem in international relations. *World Politics* 14/1: 77–92.

———. 1970. The outcome of arms races: A policy problem and a research approach. *Proceedings of the International Peace Research Association, Third General Conference,* 2: 137–46.

———. 1971. *A General Systems Taxonomy for Political Science.* Morristown: N.J.: General Learning Press.

———. 1976. The correlates of war project: Continuity, diversity and convergence. In *Quantitative International Politics: An Appraisal,* ed. F. Hoole and D. Zinnes, pp. 21–66. New York: Praeger.

———, ED. 1979. *Correlates of War I: Research Origins and Rationale.* New York: Free Press.

———, ED. 1979. *Explaining War.* Beverly Hills, Calif.: Sage.

_____. 1979a. *The Management of Serious International Disputes*. Ann Arbor, Mich.: University of Michigan Department of Political Science.

_____, ED. 1980. *Correlates of War II: Testing Some Realpolitik Models*. New York: Free Press.

_____, S. A. BREMER AND J. STUCKEY. 1972. Capability distribution, uncertainty and major power war, 1820–1965. In *Peace, War & Numbers,* ed. B. M. Russett. Beverly Hills, Calif.: Sage, 19–48.

_____, AND B. BUENO DE MESQUITA. 1973. Alliances, Capabilities, and War: A Review and Synthesis. *Political Science Annual* 4: 237–280.

_____, AND T. CUSACK. 1981. Periodicity, inexorability, and steersmanship in international war. In *From National Development to Global Community,* ed. R. Merritt and B. M. Russett.

_____, AND M. SMALL. 1968. Alliance aggregation and the onset of war, 1815–1945. In *Quantitative International Politics: Insights and Evidence,* ed. J. D. Singer. New York: Free Press.

_____, AND M. SMALL. 1972. *The Wages of War: A Statistical Handbook,* 1816–1965. New York: John Wiley.

_____, AND M. WALLACE. 1970. Intergovernmental organization and the preservation of peace, 1816–1964: Some bivariate relationships. *International Organization* 24/3: 520–47.

SIVERSON, R., AND J. KING. 1980. Attributes of national alliance membership and war participation, 1815–1965. *American Journal of Political Science* 24/1: 1–15.

SKJELSBAEK, K. Shared membership in intergovernmental organizations and dyadic war, 1865–1964. In *The United Nations: Problems & Prospects*. St. Louis: University of Missouri Center for International Studies.

SMALL, M. 1978. Does size make a difference? In *Studien i Dansk Udenrigspolitik,* ed. N. Amstrup and I. Faurby. Aarhus, Denmark: Forlaget Politika.

_____, AND J. D. SINGER. 1976. The war proneness of democratic regimes. *Jerusalem Journal of International Relations* 1/4: 49–69.

SOROKIN, PITRIM A. 1937. *Social and Cultural Dynamics: Fluctuations of Social Relationships, War and Revolution,* Vol. 3. New York: American Book.

STARR, H., AND B. MOST. 1978. A return journey. *Journal of Conflict Resolution* 22/3: 441–468.

STOESSINGER, J. G. 1978. *Why Nations Go to War*. New York: St. Martin's.

STOLL, R., AND M. CHAMPION. 1977. Predicting the escalation of serious disputes to international war: Some

preliminary findings: Philadelphia: North American Peace Science Conference.

SULLIVAN, M. 1976. *International Relations: Theories and Evidence*. Englewood Cliffs, N.J.: Prentice-Hall.

_____. 1978. The Causes of War: An Evaluation of the State of Theory. Tucson: University of Arizona, Department of Political Science.

URLANIS, B. T. 1960. *Wars and the Population of Europe*. Moscow: Government Publishing.

VOEVODSKY, J. 1969. Quantitative behavior of warring nations. *Journal of Psychology* 72: 269–292.

WALLACE, M. D. 1973a. *War and Rank Among Nations*. Lexington, Mass.: Heath.

_____. 1973b. Alliance polarization, cross-cutting, and international war, 1815–1964. *Journal of Conflict Resolution* 17: 4.

_____. 1979. The role of arms races in the escalation of disputes into war: Some new evidence. *Journal of Conflict Resolution* 23/1: 3–16.

WALLENSTEEN, P. 1973. *Structure and War*. Stockholm: Roben and Sjogren.

WAYMAN, F. 1981. Bipolarity, multipolarity and the threat of war. In *Power, Pacts, and War*. ed. A. N. Sabrosky. Boulder, Colo.: Greenwood Press.

WEEDE, E. 1970. Conflict behavior of nation states. *Journal of Peace Research*. 3:229–236.

_____. 1976. Overwhelming preponderance as a pacifying condition among contiguous Asian dyads, 1950–1969. *Journal of Conflict Resolution* 20/3: 395–412.

WEISS, H. K. 1963. Stochastic models for the duration and magnitude of a deadly quarrel. *Operations Research* 11/1: 101–121.

WESLEY, J. P. 1969. Frequency of wars and geographic opportunity. In *Theory & Research on the Causes of War*. ed. D. G. Pruitt and R. C. Snyder.

WHITE, R. K. 1968. *Nobody Wanted War*. Garden City, N.Y.: Doubleday.

WILKENFELD, J. 1973. Domestic and foreign conflict. In *Conflict Behavior and Linkage Politics,* ed. J. Wilkenfeld, pp. 107–123. New York: McKay.

WRIGHT, Q. 1942. *A Study of War,* 2 vols. Chicago: University of Chicago Press. Revised ed. 1965.

_____. 1965. The escalation of international conflicts. *Journal of Conflict Resolution* 9/4: 434–449.

ZINNES, D. 1980a. Empirical evidence on the outbreak of international violence. In *Handbook of Political Conflict,* ed. T. Gurr. New York: Free Press.

_____. 1980b. 'Three Puzzles in Search of a Researcher.' Bloomington, Indiana, mimeo.

8

IMPERIALISM

32. The Place of Imperialism in History

V. I. LENIN

We have seen that in its economic essence imperialism is monopoly capitalism. This in itself determines its place in history, for monopoly that grows out of the soil of free competition, and precisely out of free competition, is the transition from the capitalist system to a higher socioeconomic order. We must take special note of the four principal types of monopoly, or principal manifestations of monopoly capitalism, which are characteristic of the epoch we are examining.

Firstly, monopoly arose out of the concentration of production at a very high stage. This refers to the monopolist capitalist associations, cartels, syndicates and trusts. We have seen the important part these play in present-day economic life. At the beginning of the twentieth century, monopolies had acquired complete supremacy in the advanced countries, and although the first

From *Imperialism: The Highest Stage of Capitalism*, Chapter 10. Published in Volume 22 of the *Collected Works* (Moscow: Progress Publishers, 1964), pp. 298–304. Translated by Yuri Sdobnikov. Footnotes deleted.

steps towards the formation of the cartels were taken by countries enjoying the protection of high tariffs (Germany, America), Great Britain, with her system of free trade, revealed the same basic phenomenon, only a little later, namely, the birth of monopoly out of the concentration of production.

Secondly, monopolies have stimulated the seizure of the most important sources of raw materials, especially for the basic and most highly cartelised industries in capitalist society: the coal and iron industries. The monopoly of the most important sources of raw materials has enormously increased the power of big capital, and has sharpened the antagonism between cartelised and noncartelised industry.

Thirdly, monopoly has sprung from the banks. The banks have developed from modest middleman enterprises into the monopolists of finance capital. Some three to five of the biggest banks in each of the foremost capitalist countries have achieved the "personal link-up" between industrial and bank capital, and have concentrated in their hands the control of thousands upon thousands of millions which form the greater part of the capital and income of entire countries. A financial oligarchy, which throws a close network of dependence relationships over all the economic and political institutions of present-day bourgeois society without exception—such is the most striking manifestation of this monopoly.

Fourthly, monopoly has grown out of colonial policy. To the numerous "old" motives of colonial policy, finance capital has added the struggle for the sources of raw materials, for the export of capital, for spheres of influence, i.e., for spheres for profitable deals, concessions, monopoly profits and so on, economic territory in general. When the colonies of the European powers, for instance, comprised only one-tenth of the territory of Africa (as was the case in 1876), colonial policy was able to develop by methods other than those of monopoly—by the "free grabbing" of territories, so to speak. But when nine-tenths of Africa had been seized (by 1900), when the whole world had been divided up, there was inevitably ushered in the era of monopoly possession of colonies and, consequently, of particularly intense struggle for the division and the redivision of the world.

The extent to which monopolist capital has intensified all the contradictions of capitalism is generally known. It is sufficient to mention the high cost of living and the tyranny of the cartels. This intensification of contradictions constitutes the most powerful driving force of the transitional period of history, which began from the time of the final victory of world finance capital.

Monopolies, oligarchy, the striving for domination and not for freedom, the exploitation of an increasing number of small or weak nations by a handful of the richest or most powerful nations—all these have given birth to those distinctive characteristics of imperialism which compel us to define it as parasitic or decaying capitalism. More and more prominently there emerges, as one of the tendencies of imperialism, the creation of the "rentier state," the usurer state, in which the bourgeoisie to an ever-increasing degree lives on the proceeds of capital exports and by "clipping coupons." It would be a mistake to believe that this tendency to decay precludes the rapid growth of capitalism. It does not. In the epoch of imperialism, certain branches of industry, certain strata of the bourgeoisie and certain countries betray, to a greater or lesser degree, now one and now another of these tendencies. On the whole, capitalism is growing far more rapidly than before; but this growth is not only becoming more and more uneven in general, its unevenness also manifest itself, in particular, in the decay of the countries which are richest in capital (Britain).

In regard to the rapidity of Germany's economic development, Riesser, the author of the book on the big German banks, states:

The progress of the preceding period (1848–70), which had not been exactly slow, compares with the rapidity with which the whole of Germany's national economy, and with it German banking, progressed during this period (1870–1905) in about the same way as the speed of the mail coach in the good old days compares with the speed of the present-day automobile . . . which is whizzing past so fast that it endangers not only innocent pedestrians in its path, but also the occupants of the car.

In its turn, this finance capital which has grown with such extraordinary rapidity is not unwilling, precisely because it has grown so quickly, to pass on to a more "tranquil" possession of colonies which have to be seized—and not only by peaceful methods—from richer nations. In the United States, economic development in the last decades has been even more rapid than in Germany, *and for this very reason*, the parasitic features of modern American capitalism have stood out with particular prominence. On the other hand, a comparison of, say, the republican American bourgeoisie with the monarchist Japanese or German bourgeoisie shows that the most pronounced political distinction diminishes to an extreme degree in the epoch of imperialism—not because it is unimportant in general, but because in all these cases we are talking about a bourgeoisie which has definite features of parasitism.

The receipt of high monopoly profits by the capitalists in one of the numerous branches of industry, in one of the numerous countries, etc., makes it economically possible for them to bribe certain sections of the workers, and for a time a fairly considerable minority of them, and win them to the side of the bourgeoisie of a given industry or given nation against all the others. The intensification of antagonisms between imperialist nations for the division of the world increases this urge. And so there is created that bond between imperialism and opportunism, which revealed itself first and most clearly in Great Britain, owing to the fact that certain features of imperialist development were observable there much earlier than in other countries. Some writers, L. Martov, for example, are prone to wave aside the connection between imperialism and opportunism in the working-class movement—a particularly glaring fact at the present time—by resorting to "official optimism" (*à la* Kautsky and Huysmans) like the following: the cause of the opponents of capitalism would be hopeless if it were progressive capitalism that led to the increase of opportunism, or, if it were the best-paid workers who were inclined towards opportunism, etc. We must have no illusions about "optimism" of this kind. It is optimism in respect of opportunism; it is optimism which serves to conceal opportunism. As a matter of fact the extraordinary rapidity and the particularly revolting character of the development of opportunism is by no means a guarantee that its victory will be durable: the rapid growth of a painful abscess on a healthy body can only cause it to burst more quickly and thus relieve the body of it. The most dangerous of all in this respect are those who do wish to understand that the fight against imperialism is a sham and humbug unless it is inseparably bound up with the fight against opportunism.

From all that has been said . . . on the economic essence of imperialism, it follows that we must define it as capitalism in transition, or, more precisely, as moribund capitalism. It is very instructive in this respect to note that bourgeois economists, in describing modern capitalism, frequently employ catchwords and phrases like "interlocking," "absence of isolation," etc., "in conformity with their functions and course of development," banks are "not purely private business enterprises; they are more and mmore outgrowing the sphere of purely private business regulation." And this very Riesser, whose words I have just quoted, declares with all seriousness that the "prophecy" of the Marxists concerning "socialization" has "not come true"!

What then does this catchword "interlocking" express? It merely expresses the most striking feature of the process going on before our eyes. It shows that the observer counts the separate trees, but cannot see the wood. It slavishly copies the superficial, the fortuitous, the chaotic. It reveals the observer as one who is overwhelmed by the mass of raw material and is utterly incapable of appreciating its meaning and importance. Ownership of shares, the relations between owners of private property "interlock in a haphazard way." But underlying this interlocking, its very base, are the changing social relations of production. When a big enterprise assumes gigantic proportions, and, on the basis of an exact computation of mass data, organises according to plan the supply of primary raw materials to the extent of two-thirds, or three-fourths, of all that is necessary for tens of millions of people; when the raw materials are transported in a systematic and organised manner to the most suitable places of production, sometimes situated hundreds or thousands of miles from each other; when a single centre directs all the consecutive stages of processing the material right up to the manufacture of numerous varieties of finished articles; when these products are distributed according to a single plan among tens and hundreds of millions of consumers (the marketing of oil in America and Germany by the American oil trust)—then it becomes evident that we have socialisation of production, and not mere "interlocking"; that private economic and private property relations constitute a shell which no longer fits its contents, a shell which must inevitably decay if its removal is artificially delayed, a shell which may remain in a state of decay for a fairly long period (if, at the worst, the cure of the opportunist abscess is protracted), but which will inevitably be removed.

The enthusiastic admirer of German imperialism, Schulze-Gaevernitz, exclaims:

Once the supreme management of the German banks has been entrusted to the hands of a dozen persons, their activity is even today more significant for the public good than that of the majority of the Ministers of State. . . . (The "interlocking" of bankers, ministers, magnates of industry and rentiers is here conveniently forgotten.) If we imagine the development of those tendencies we have noted carried to their logical conclusion we will have: the money capital of the nation united in the banks; the banks themselves combined into cartels; the investment capital of the nation cast in the shape of securities. Then the forecast of that genius Saint-Simon will be fulfilled: "The present anarchy of production, which corresponds to the fact that economic relations are developing without uniform regulation, must make way for organisation in production. Production will no longer be directed by isolated manufacturers, independent of each other and ignorant of man's economic needs; that will be done by a certain public institution. A central committee of management, being able to survey the large field of social economy from a more elevated point of view, will regulate it for the benefit of the whole society, will put the means of production into suitable hands, and above all will take care that there be constant harmony between production and consumption. Institutions already exist which have assumed as part of their functions a certain organisation of economic labour, the banks." We are still a long way from the fulfilment of Saint-Simon's forecast, but we are on the way towards it: Marxism, different from what Marx imagined, but different only in form.

A crushing "refutation" of Marx, indeed, which retreats a step from Marx's precise, scientific analysis to Saint-Simon's guess-work, the guess-work of a genius, but guess-work all the same.

33. A Structural Theory of Imperialism

Johan Galtung

1. INTRODUCTION

This theory takes as its point of departure two of the most glaring facts about this world: the tremendous inequality, within and between nations, in almost all aspects of human living conditions, including the power to decide over those living conditions; *and* the resistance of this inequality to change. The world consists of Center and Periphery nations; and each nation, in turn, has its centers and periphery. Hence, our concern is with the mechanism underlying this discrepancy, particularly between the center in the Center, and the periphery in the Periphery. In other words, how to conceive of, how to explain, and how to counteract inequality as one of the major forms of *structural violence*. Any theory of liberation from structural violence presupposes theoretically and practically adequate ideas of the dominance

Reprinted from "A Structural Theory of Imperialism" by Johan Galtung, *Journal of Peace Research* [8]/2 (1971), pp. 81–91,106–109, by permission of Universitetsforlaget, Oslo. Footnotes deleted.

system against which the liberation is directed; and the special type of dominance system to be discussed here is *imperialism*.

Imperialism will be conceived of as a dominance relation between collectivities, particularly between nations. It is a sophisticated type of dominance relation which cuts across nations, basing itself on a bridgehead which the center in the Center nation establishes in the center of the Periphery nation, for the joint benefit of both. It should not be confused with other ways in which one collectivity can dominate another in the sense of exercising power over it. Thus, a military occupation of B by A may seriously curtail B's freedom of action, but is not for that reason an imperialist relationship unless it is set up in a special way. The same applies to the *threat* of conquest and possible occupation, as in a balance of power relationship. Moreover, *subversive* activities may also be brought to a stage where a nation is dominated by the pin-pricks exercised against it from below, but this is clearly different from imperialism.

Thus, imperialism is a species in a genus of dominance and power relationships. It is a subtype of something, and has itself subtypes to be explored later. Dominance relations between nations and other collectivities will not disappear with the disappearance of imperialism; nor will the end to one type of imperialism (e.g. political, or economic) guarantee the end to another type of imperialism (e.g. economic or cultural). Our view is not reductionist in the traditional sense pursued in marxist-leninist theory, which conceives of imperialism as an economic relationship under private capitalism, motivated by the need for expanding markets, and which bases the theory of dominance on a theory of imperialism. According to this view, imperialism and dominance will fall like dominoes when the capitalistic conditions for economic imperialism no longer obtain. According to the view we develop here, imperialism is a more general structural relationship between two collectivities, and has to be understood at a general level in order to be understood and counteracted in its more specific manifestations—just like smallpox is better understood in a context of a theory of epidemic diseases, and these diseases better understood in a context of general pathology.

Briefly stated, imperialism is a system that splits up collectivities and relates some of the parts to each other in relations of *harmony of interest*, and other parts in relations of *disharmony of interest*, or *conflict of interest*.

2. DEFINING "CONFLICT OF INTEREST"

"Conflict of interest" is a special case of conflict in general, defined as a situation where parties are pursuing incompatible goals. In our special case, these goals are stipulated by an outsider as the "true" interests of the parties, disregarding wholly or completely what the parties themselves say explicitly are the values they pursue. One reason for this is the rejection of the dogma of unlimited rationality: actors do *not* necessarily know, or they are unable to express, what their interest is. Another, more important, reason is that rationality is unevenly distributed, that some may dominate the minds of others, and that this may lead to "false consciousness." Thus, learning to suppress one's own true interests may be

a major part of socialization in general and education in particular.

Let us refer to this true interest as LC, *living condition*. It may perhaps be measured by using such indicators as income, standard of living in the usual materialistic sense—but notions of *quality of life* would certainly also enter, not to mention notions of *autonomy*. But the precise content of LC is less important for our purpose than the definition of conflict of interest:

There is *conflict*, or *disharmony of interest*, if the two parties are coupled together in such a way that the LC *gap* between them is *increasing*;

There is *no conflict*, or *harmony of interest*, if the two parties are coupled together in such a way that the LC *gap* between them is *decreasing down to zero*. . . .

. . . There is the problem of what to do with the case of a *constant gap*. The parties grow together, at the same rate, but the gap between them is constant. Is that harmony or disharmony of interest? We would refer to it as disharmony, for the parties are coupled such that they will not be brought together. Even in they *grow* parallel to each other it is impossible to put it down as a case of harmony, when the distribution of value is so unequal. On the contrary, this is the case of disharmony that has reached a state of equilibrium. . . .

And then, in conclusion: it is clear that the concept of interest used here is based on an ideology, or a *value premise of equality*. An interaction relation and interaction structure set up such that inequality is the result is seen as a coupling not in the interest of the weaker party. This is a value premise like so many other value premises in social science explorations, such as "direct violence is bad," "economic growth is good," "conflict should be resolved," etc. As in all other types of social science, the goal should not be an "objective" social science freed from all such value premises, but a more honest social science where the value premises are made explicit.

3. DEFINING "IMPERIALISM"

We shall now define imperialism by using the building blocks presented in the preceding two sections. In our two-nation world, imperialism can be defined as one way in which the Center nation has power over the Periphery nation, so as to bring about a condition of disharmony of interest between them. Concretely, *Imperialism* is a relation between a Center and a Periphery nation so that

(1) there is *harmony of interest* between the *center in the Center* nation and the *center in the Periphery* nation,

(2) there is more *disharmony of interest* within the Periphery nation than within the Center nations,

(3) there is *disharmony of interest* between the *periphery in the Center* nation and the *periphery in the Periphery* nation.

. . . This complex definition, borrowing largely from Lenin, needs spelling out. The basic idea is, as mentioned, that the center in the Center nation has a bridgehead in the Periphery nation, and a well-chosen one: the center in the Periphery nation. This is established such that the Periphery center is tied to the Center center with the best possible tie: the tie of harmony of interest. They are linked so that they go up together and down, even under, together. How this is done in concrete terms will be explored in the subsequent sections. . . .

In the Periphery nation, the center grows more than the periphery, due partly to how interaction between center and periphery is organized. Without necessarily thinking of economic interaction, the center is more enriched than the periphery—in ways to be explored below. However, for part of this enrichment, the center in the Periphery only serves as a transmission belt (e.g. as commercial firms, trading companies) for value (e.g. raw materials) forwarded to the Center nation. This value enters the Center in the center, with some of it drizzling down to the periphery in the Center. Importantly, there is less disharmony of interest in the Center than in the Periphery, so that *the total arrangement is largely in the interest of the periphery in the Center.* Within the Center the two parties may be opposed to each other. But in the total game, the periphery see themselves more as the partners of the center in the Center than as the partners of the periphery in the Periphery—and this is the essential trick of that game. Alliance-formation between the two peripheries is avoided, while the Center nation becomes more and the Periphery nation less cohesive—and hence less able to develop long-term strategies.

Actually, concerning the three criteria in the definition of imperialism as given above, it is clear that no. (3) is implied by nos. (1) and (2). The two centers are tied together and the Center periphery is tied to its center: that is the whole essence of the situation. If we now presuppose that the center in the Periphery is a smaller proportion of that nation than the center in the Center, we can also draw one more implication: *there is disharmony of interest between the Center nation as a whole and the Periphery nation as a whole.* But that type of finding, frequently referred to, is highly misleading because it blurs the harmony of interest between the two centers, and leads to the belief that imperialism is merely an international relationship, *not a combination of intra- and inter-national relations.* . . .

4. THE MECHANISMS OF IMPERIALISM

The two basic mechanisms of imperialism both concern the *relation* between the parties concerned, particularly between the nations. The first mechanism concerns the *interaction relation* itself, the second how these relations are put together in a larger interaction structure:

(1) the principle of *vertical interaction relation*

(2) the principle of *feudal interaction structure.* . . .

To study whether the interaction is symmetric or asymmetric, on equal or unequal terms, *two* factors arising from the interaction have to be examined:

(1) *the value-exchange between the actors—inter-*actor effects

(2) *the effects inside the actors—intra-*actor effects. . .

It is certainly meaningful and important to talk in terms of unequal exchange or asymmetric interaction, but not quite unproblematic what its precise meaning should be. For that reason, it may be helpful to think in terms of three stages or types of exploitation, partly reflecting historical *processes* in chronological order, and partly reflecting types of *thinking* about exploitation.

In the first stage of exploitation, A simply engages in looting and takes away the raw materials without offering anything in return. If he steals out of pure nature there is no human interaction involved, but we assume that he forces "natives" to work for him and do the extraction work. It is like the slave-owner who lives on the work produced by slaves—which is quantatively not too different from the land-owner who has land-workers working for him five out of seven days a week.

In the second stage, A starts offering something "in return." Oil, pitch, land, etc. is "bought" for a couple of beads—it is no longer simply taken away without asking any questions about ownership. The price paid is ridiculous. However, as power relations in the international systems change, perhaps mainly by bringing the power level of the weaker party up from zero to some low positive value, A had to contribute more: for instance, pay more for the oil. The question is now whether there is a cut-off point after which the exchange becomes equal, and what the criterion for that cut-off point would be. Absence of subjective dissatisfaction—B says that he is now content? Objective market values or the number of man-hours that have gone into the production on either side?

There are difficulties with all these conceptions. But instead of elaborating on this, we shall rather direct our attention to the shared failure of all these attempts to look at *intra*-actor effects. Does the interaction have enriching or impoverishing effects *inside* the actor, or does it just lead to a stand-still? This type of question leads us to the third stage of exploitation, where there may be some balance in the flow between the actors, but great differences in the effect the interaction has within them. . . .

If the first mechanism, the *vertical interaction relation*, is the major factor behind inequality, then the second mechanism, the *feudal interaction structure*, is the factor that maintains and rein-

forces this inequality by protecting it. There are four rules defining this particular interaction structure:

(1) interaction between Center and Periphery is *vertical*
(2) interaction between Periphery and Periphery is *missing*
(3) multilateral interaction involving all three is *missing*
(4) interaction with the outside world is *monopolized* by the Center, with two implications:
   (a) Periphery interaction with other Center nations is *missing*
   (b) Center as well as Periphery interaction with Periphery nations belonging to other Center nations is *missing*. . . .

Some important *economic* consequences of this structure should be spelled out.

First and most obvious: the *concentration on trade partners*. A Periphery nation should, as a result of these two mechanisms, have most of its trade with "its" Center nation. In other words, empirically we would expect high levels of *import concentrations* as well as *export concentration* in the Periphery, as opposed to the Center, which is more free to extend its trade relations in almost any direction—except in the pure case, with the Periphery of other Center nations.

Second, and not so obvious, is the *commodity concentration:* the tendency for Periphery nations to have only one or very few primary products to export. This would be a trivial matter if it could be explained entirely in terms of geography, if e.g. oil countries were systematically poor as to ore, ore countries poor as to bananas and coffee, etc. But this can hardly be assumed to be the general case: Nature does not distribute its riches that way. There is a historical rather than a geographical explanation to this. A territory may have been exploited for the raw materials most easily available and/or most needed in the Center, and this, in turn, leads to a certain social structure, to communication lines to the deposits, to trade structures, to the emergence of certain center groups, (often based on ownership of that particular raw material), and so on. To start exploiting a new kind of raw material in the same territory might upset carefully designed local balances; hence, it might be easier to have a fresh start for that new raw material in virgin territory with no bridgehead already prepared for imperialist exploits. In other to substantiate this hypothesis we would have to demonstrate that there are particularly underutilized and systematically underexplored deposits precisely in countries where one type of raw materials has already been exploited.

The combined effect of these two consequences is a *dependency* of the Periphery on the Center. Since the Periphery usually has a much smaller GNP, the trade between them is a much higher percentage of the GNP for the Periphery, and with both partner and commodity concentration, the Periphery becomes particularly vulnerable to fluctuations in demands and prices. At the same time the center in the Periphery depends on the Center for its supply of consumer goods. Import substitution industries will usually lead to consumer goods that look homespun and unchic, particularly if there is planned obsolescence in the production of these goods in the Center, plus a demand for equality between the two centers maintained by demonstration effects and frequent visits to the Center.

However, the most important consequence is political and has to do with the systematic utilization of feudal interaction structures as a way of protecting the Center against the Periphery. The feudal interaction structure is in social science language nothing but an expression of the old political maxim *divide et impera*, divide and rule, as a strategy used systematically by the Center relative to the Periphery nations. How could—for example—a small foggy island in the North Sea rule over one quarter of the world? By isolating the Periphery parts from each other, by having them geographically at sufficient distance from each other to impede any real alliance formation, by having separate deals with them so as to tie them to the Center in particularistic ways, by reducing multilateralism to a minimum with all kinds of graded membership, *and* by having the Mother country assume the role of window to the world.

However, this point can be much more clearly seen if we combine the two mechanisms

and extend what has been said so far for relations between Center and Periphery *nations* to relations between center and periphery *groups* within nations. Under an imperialist structure the two mechanisms are used not only between nations but also within nations, but less so in the Center nation than in the Periphery nation. In other words, there is vertical division of labor within as well as between nations. And these two levels of organization are intimately linked to each other (as A. G. Frank always has emphasized) in the sense that the center in the Periphery interaction structure is also that group with which the Center nation has its harmony of interest, the group used as a bridgehead.

Thus, the combined operation of the two mechanisms at the two levels builds into the structure a subtle grid of protection measures against the major potential source of 'trouble', the periphery in the Periphery. To summarize the major items in this grid:

1. the general impoverishment of pP brought about by vertical division of labor within the Periphery nation, and particularly by the high level of inequality (e.g. differential access to means of communication) and disharmony of interest in the Periphery nation;

2. the way in which interaction, mobilization, and organization of pP are impeded by the feudal structure *within* Periphery nations;

3. the general impoverishment of the Periphery nation brought about by vertical division of labor, particularly in terms of means of destruction and communication;

4. the way in which interaction, mobilization, and organization of the Periphery nations are impeded by the feudal interaction structure *between* nations

    a. making it difficult to interact with other Periphery nations "belonging" to the same Center nations,

    b. making it even more difficult to interact with Periphery nations "belonging" to other Center nations:

5. the way in which it is a fortiori difficult for the peripheries in Periphery nations to interact, mobilize, and organize

a. intra-nationally because of (1) and (2),
b. inter-nationally because of (3) and (4),
c. in addition; because the center in the Periphery has the monopoly on international interaction in all directions and cannot be counted on to interact in the interest of its own periphery;
6. the way in which pP cannot appeal to pC or cC either because of the disharmony of interest.

Obviously, the more perfectly the mechanisms of imperialism within and between nations are put to work, the less overt machinery of oppression is needed and the smaller can the center groups be, relative to the total population involved. *Only imperfect, amateurish imperialism needs weapons; professional imperialism is based on structural rather than direct violence.* . . .

10. CONCLUSION: SOME STRATEGIC IMPLICATIONS

From a general scheme, we cannot arrive at more than general policy implications that can serve as guide-lines, as strategies. More concreteness is needed to arrive at the first tactical steps. But theory developed in peace research should lead to such guide-lines; if it merely reflects what is empirical, not what is potential, then it is not good theory.

Our point of departure is once more that the world is divided into have's and have-not's, in have and have-not nations. To decrease the gap, one aspect of the fight against structural violence, redistribution by taking from the have's and giving to the have-not's is not enough: the structure has to be changed. The imperialist structure has inter-national as well as intra-national aspects and will consequently have to be changed at both levels.

However, let us start with the international changes needed, for a point of departure. Following closely the analysis of the mechanisms of imperialism in order to establish anti-mechanisms, we get Table 8.1.

TABLE 8.1 Strategies for Structural Change of the International Dominance System

I. HORIZONTALIZATION

1. Horizontalization Center-Periphery

a. *exchange on more equal terms*, either by reducing the division of labor, or by more horizontal division of labor that would equalize spin-off effects. Concretely this would mean that Center nations would have to start importing processed products from Periphery nations, and engage in intra- rather than inter-sector trade, and even intra- rather than inter-commodity trade.

b. *reduction of vertical interaction*, down to total de-coupling in case exchange on more equal terms is unacceptable or does not work.

c. *self-reliance*, partly in order to develop import substitutes, and partly in order for Periphery nations to define themselves what products they need rather than adapting the preference scales developed in the Center.

II. DEFEUDALIZATION

a. *exchange on equal terms*, intra- rather than inter-sector, but obviously at a lower level where degree of processing is concerned than under 1.a. above. It may imply exchanges of raw materials, or exchanges of semi-processed goods. Obviously, which Periphery country should interact horizontally with which other Periphery countries would depend on the nature of the economic exchange and the concrete geo-political situation.

b. *development of viable organization of Periphery countries for international class conflict*. Such organizations seem to depend for their viability not only on commitment to an ideology (rejection of past and present as well as visions for the future), but also seem to function better if they are built around an exchange relation of the type indicated in 2.a. The exact purpose of the organization would be to force Center nations to change their policies in the direction of 1.a., and also to command a better redistribution of capital and technology from the Center. This would also be the organization that could organize a strike on the delivery of raw materials in case Center nations do not conform with these types of structural changes, as an analogy to the denial of human manpower typical of the intra-national strikes.

3. Multilateralization Center-Periphery

a. *multinational, symmetric organization should be established wherever possible,* the system of international organizations should be taken out of phase 3 and moved towards phase 4. These organizations would serve as concrete instruments for horizontal relationships between Center and Periphery, and between Periphery and Periphery.

b. *destruction of multi-national asymmetric organizations* if they do not change in the direction of 3.a. above by withdrawal of Periphery participation.

c. *self-reliance with the Periphery itself building multinational symmetric organizations,* retaining some contact with the Center for conflict articulation. This pattern might also apply to the UN and the UN Agencies unless they pursue policies of the types indicated above.

d. *establishment of global or trans-national organizations* that could serve to globalize the world's means of communication and means of production in order to establish a universally accessible communication network and a production system that would give top priority to the needs of the periphery of the Periphery.

4. Extra-bloc activity

a. *Periphery-Center contacts extended to other Centers,* but in accordance with the program indicated in 1.a. and 1.b. above.

b. *Periphery-Periphery contacts extended to other Periphery countries,* but in accordance with points 2 and 3 above. For the latter the Algiers Group of 77 would be an important, although weak model, and the conferences of non-aligned states another. At the first conference in Beograd in 1961 there were 25 participants, at the second in 1964 in Cairo 47 participants, and at the 1970 Lusaka conference there were 54 participants (the number of observers was, 3, 10, and 12 respectively).

Again, at this general level it is impossible to indicate the first steps that would lead from vertical, feudal interaction towards horizontalization and defeudalization. These are guidelines only.

And their implementation should certainly not be seen as a sufficient condition for a process of genuine development to start in the Periphery, with the possible result that the gap between Center and Periphery may be decreasing again, but as a necessary condition. Very many of the findings in "liberal" development theory may become valid precisely when today's periphery nations become autonomous through structural change. Hence, the basic formulas of horizontalization and defeudalization are necessary conditions, not panaceas.

But another question that certainly has to be asked is what this presupposes in terms of intra-national strategies. In one sense the answer is simple: Table 8.1 also applies to the relation between center and periphery within a nation, not only between nations. As such it gives four general guide-lines for a revolutionary process that would abolish the exploitation of the periphery by the Center.

But this is too abstract, so let us return to the question in more concrete terms. The major difficulty with the international strategies in Table 8.1 is obviously that these would not be in the interest of the center in the Periphery. Nothing in these strategies would guarantee them the living conditions they already enjoy, very often on par with (or even above) the living conditions of the center in the Center. They would have all reasons to resist such changes. In fact, from a purely human point of view this group is perhaps the most exposed group in the whole international system, on the one hand the pawn and instrument of the center in the Center and on the other hand the exploiters of the periphery in the Periphery. In such a cross-pressure it seems reasonable to expect that the group will sooner or later have to choose sides. Either it will have to relocate and join the center in the Center, or it will have to stand in solidarity with the periphery in the Periphery.

We can now, building on the *criteria* of imperialism, formulate a new set of strategies that would have more immediate domestic implications and support the international strategies of Table 8.1, as shown in Table 8.2.

TABLE 8.2 Strategies for Structural Change of the Intra-national Dominance System.

I. REDUCED HARMONY BETWEEN THE CENTERS

1. *Reduction to neutral or no relationship*

This type of situation arises often when there is a crisis in the center of the Center, for instance due to internal war in the Center or external war between two or more Center nations. In this situation the Periphery attains some kind of autonomy because the Center can no longer exercise minute control—as seems to be the case for many countries in Latin America during the Second World War.

2. *Change to negative relationship between the centers*

In the general theory it has been postulated that there is "harmony" between the two centers, but social relations being complex such a harmony is hardly ever complete. There may be some privileges that cC reserve for themselves (such as taxation *without* representation) or some privileges that cP reserve for themselves (such as the right to maintain a slavery or racist society). In general tensions may arise precisely because the model of complete harmony and similarity is not realized. The result may be a *nationalist* fight for liberation from the Center country, and this fight may even attain a populist character if cP can manage to interpret the conflict as a threat to the Periphery nation as a whole, not only to its center. If the Center engages in destructive behavior against the Periphery, such as economic warfare (with economic sanctions as a special case) or even military warfare, a homogenization of the Periphery may occur, sufficient to conceal the disharmony of interest built into the Periphery.

II. REDUCED DISHARMONY IN THE PERIPHERY

3. *Violent revolution in the Periphery*

According to this formula the internal disharmony of interest is eliminated by eliminating cP as a class, by using means of force. This can be done partly by killing them, partly by means of imprisonment, and partly by giving them the chance to relocate, for instance by using their ties with cC so as to settle where they really belong—in the Center. A new regime is then introduced which perhaps may have its center, but certainly not a center that is tied with relations of harmony to the old cC.

4. *Non-violent revolution in the Periphery*

In this approach cP are not eliminated as persons, but as a part of the Periphery structure because the rest of the Periphery nation refuses to interact with them. They become non-functional socially rather than eliminated in a physical sense. To give them new tasks in a new society becomes an important part of the non-violent revolution.

5. *Cooperation between the peripheries in the Periphery*

Since international relations are so dominated by the centers in the Periphery, more of international relations has to be carried out by the peoples themselves in patterns of non-governmental foreign policy. The Havana-based *Tricontinental* (OSPAAAL) is an important example.

But in general we would believe more in Periphery-generated strategies than in the Center-generated ones, since the latter may easily lead to a new form of dependence on the Center.

III. CHANGES IN THE CENTER

6. *Increased disharmony in the Center*

In this case pC may no longer side with cC as it should according to nationalist ideology in the Center, but find that the Periphery nation in general and pP in particular is the natural ally. It is difficult to see how this can have consequences that could be beneficial to the Periphery unless the two countries are contiguous, or unless this might be a factor behind the types of development outlined in I,1 and I,2 above.

7. *Changes in the goals of the Center*

In this case there is no assumption of changes in the level of internal disharmony in the Center. The

Center might itself choose to stop imperialist policies, not because it is forced to do so from below (the Center by the Periphery, or cC by pC as above), but out of its own decision. Thus, cC might see that this is a *wrong* policy to pursue, e.g. because of the exploitation it leads to, because of the dangers for world peace, because of relations to other nations, etc. Or, there may be internal reasons: the Center might reduce its economic growth and change towards a politics of justice. Anti-centers, or the periphery in the Center might decide to boycott further economic growth because of its consequences in terms of negative spin-off effects (pollution, exploitation of man). There are many possibilities, and they may combine into quite likely contributions towards a disruption of the system. But in general we would believe more in Periphery-generated strategies than in Center-generated ones, since the latter may easily lead to a new form of dependence on the Center.

At this point we choose to stop. These strategies . . . are only presented here in brief outline in order to indicate what to us seems to be a crucial criterion against which any theory should be tested: is it indicative of a practice, does it indicate who the actors behind that practice could be? A theory should not only be evaluated according to its potential as a reservoir of hypothesis implications to be tested against present reality (data), but as much—or perhaps more—as a reservoir of policy implications to be tested against potential reality (goals, values). What we have tried to do here is an effort in both directions.

34. From *NATIONS IN CONFLICT*

Nazli Choucri and Robert C. North

The purpose of this chapter is to present the conceptual framework within which we have analyzed the policies and actions contributing to war. In general there seem to be at least three major processes that generate conflict and warfare among nations: domestic growth and the external expansion of interests; competition for resources, markets, superiority in arms, and strategic advantage; and the dynamics of crisis.

One of our problems has been to avoid essentially linear causal assumptions—we are interested in dynamic relationships, in which feedback mechanisms are continuously in play. We believe that among great powers the fundamental processes, even allowing for variations in detail, mode, and style of behavior, are universal enough not to be affected themselves by modes, styles, or most events.

From *Nations in Conflict* by Nazli Choucri and Robert C. North (San Francisco: W.H. Freeman, 1975), pp. 14–25. Copyright © 1975 by W.H. Freeman and Company. All rights reserved. Reprinted by permission of the publisher. Footnotes deleted.

By themselves, some of the propositions put forward in this chapter may seem self-evident; it is only when they are considered together that the implications for international conflict and war become fully apparent. We do not believe that war is in any sense inevitable, but our findings do suggest that the tap roots of large-scale violence reach far down into the basic structure of societies and are shaped by human population, technology, and access to resources.

Because individuals are the ultimate source of all increases in population, all advances in knowledge and skills, all social, political, and economic change, and therefore of the behavior of nations, the individual is our basic unit of analysis. All the variables in this study are aggregations of what individual humans have done. (Nevertheless, individuals and the society of which they are a part are intensely interactive. What the individual does or does not do affects the conditions and dispositions of the state, and the conditions and dispositions of the state affect the attitudes and behavior of individuals.)

Man is critically dependent on his physical environment. As biological organisms, humans have certain basic needs, namely, air, food, water, and territory. *In a growing population there will be an increasing demand for basic resources.* In addition to plants and animals required for food, human beings acquire other, harder-to-get resources; the technology of this acquisition brings about both environmental and social changes. A society that can produce electronic computers is likely to be organized quite differently than a society in which steam engines represent the highest level of technology, and even more differently than societies with only crude hand tools. Advances in technology tend not only to increase the range and amount of resources available to a society, but to influence individual and social behavior as well.

Advances in technology often lead to a greater concentration of population. Moreover, historically, the denser the population and the higher the level of technology, the greater is the division and institutionalization of labor. Bureaucratization seems to develop with increases in both the levels and density of population and the advancement of technology.

The more advanced the level of technology in a society, the greater will be the kinds and quantity of resources needed by society to sustain that technology and advance it further. At the same time, demands are likely to increase as technology alters a society's perception of its "needs." Each new level of technology influences manufacturing, transportation, and communication, creating social change and thus new economic and political institutions. Advances in technology, when combined with increases in population, often contribute to the dilemma of rising demands and insufficient domestic resources.

A society (especially one with a growing population) with insufficient resources within its own territory will be seriously constrained in its activities unless it finds some way of acquiring the resources it demands. Whether and how a society reaches for resources beyond its sovereignty is conditioned by location, level of population, level of technology, and the resources, technology, needs, power, and friendliness of neighboring states.

Overall, the entire history of man has been characterized by growth—that is, by larger populations, more advanced technologies, the ability to employ larger amounts of energy for human purposes, and the tendency to demand larger amounts and a wider range of resources and finished products—all requiring more complex modes of governance.

One function of governments is to articulate priorities and to establish these by influencing the allocation of technology, resources, and labor and thus shape national capabilities. Examples of capabilities are agriculture, the skills and implements of trade, the techniques and capital for sophisticated finance, light industry, heavy industry, specific enterprises such as the manufacture of chemicals or textiles, and naval and military establishments. Governments directly influence these allocations through the spending of public monies and through tax policy, and indirectly through, for example, wage and price controls, rationing of commodities, and restrictions on imports and exports.

Ordinarily, natural resources, capital, labor, and technology are limited, so that choices have to be made with respect to the development of national capabilities. These choices reveal the actual or operational, in contrast to the professed, values of a society. Often, the choices become institutionalized and difficult to alter in any significant way. Moreover, they are reinforced insofar as existing capabilities determine what other capabilities can be developed to meet growing demands.

When demands are unmet and existing capabilities are insufficient to satisfy them, new capabilities may have to be developed. But a society can develop particular capabilities (including resources) *only if it has the necessary existing capabilities to do so.* Moreover, if national capabilities cannot be attained at a reasonable cost within national boundaries, they may be sought beyond. Any activity—selling wheat, buying oil, investing capital, increasing the labor force, or moving troops—takes on new meaning once it is extended into foreign territory. We use the term lateral pressure to refer to the process of foreign expansion of any activity.

There are three aspects of this process that must be distinguished: (1) the *disposition* to extend activities beyond national boundaries; (2) the particular *activities* that result from the disposition to act; and (3) the *impact* that these activities have on the people of another country and their environment. When we discuss lateral pressure in this study we shall be explicitly concerned with the *measurable activities* of this process—although the other two aspects should be kept in mind.

Lateral pressure can be manifested in many different types of activities, depending on the nature of the demands that are not being satisfied domestically and on the capabilities that are available. Lateral pressure is not likely to be expressed unless both demands and capabilities are above some threshold. A society may demand particular commodities that are unavailable domestically, but be wholly lacking in the capabilities—the capital, the credit, the commercial institutions, the shipping facilities, and so forth—required to obtain those commodities. In such a case the demand for those commodities will not generate lateral pressure. On the other hand, a society may demand certain commodities (cotton and rubber, for example) that are unavailable domestically *and* have the capabilities for acquiring them. In this case the combination of demand and capabilities will create the *predisposition* to reach beyond national boundaries to satisfy demands. Now there are two major possibilities. The predisposition may be acted on—the desired resources are acquired—or the country may be prevented from doing so by another state. Thus, if a country demanding resources also lacks the naval or military capabilities necessary to overcome resistance by another country, the *predisposition* for lateral pressure will not be acted on.

Virtually any mode in which lateral pressure is expressed—commercial activities, dispatch of troops into foreign territory, establishment of naval or military bases, acquisition of colonial territory, even missionary activities—may contribute to international conflict and violence. Obviously, however, some activities are more likely than others to lead to violence. Moreover, international differences in the extent and intensity of lateral pressure contribute substantially to international conflict.

Conceivably, a country generating many demands and possessing capabilities appropriate for pursuing activities abroad may "turn inward." It may not require any great amount of resources from beyond its borders; it may use techniques to uncover hitherto inaccessible resources or find new uses for its resources; it may locate sufficient capital investment fields at home; it may not require foreign markets for its goods; or it may exchange international competition for power, prestige, and status. It would be difficult, however, to identify modern, industrialized countries that do not manifest strong, extensive lateral pressure in some form.

Lateral pressure may be expressed in many types of activities other than those associated with the search for raw materials, markets, or living space. During the great period of world exploration in the sixteenth century, some Europeans were as interested in finding Christians as spices; others wanted military or naval bases, or simply adventure. Nevertheless, Christianization was ordinarily undertaken by societies that were equally interested in spices (or some other product) and, more importantly, were able to build ships and mount large expeditions. Today, as well as during the nineteenth century, business has often "gone abroad" for cheaper labor and resources, new markets and fresh opportunities for investment. As in the sixteenth century, today's foreign commerce may also be connected with a desire for national security, status, prestige, or military advantage. Lateral pressure can therefore be the outcome of both public (or national) and private aims.

For some supporters of colonial policies in nineteenth-century Europe the "policy of colonial expansion was undoubtedly good business." For others, a strong colonial policy was a patriotic ideal, the "pride of standing in the front rank of the nations which were shaping the world of the future, the delight in ruling and the excitement of competing with foreign rivals. . . ." In either case, a policy of growth and expansion was difficult to reverse, once undertaken. National growth can generate a strong demand for greater growth and thus create ever higher demands for resources. Surpluses for such resources as labor and capital generate demands for further research and development, exploration, investment and other enterprise and growth.

The disposition toward foreign activities is not always sound economically. A nation's foreign policy may encourage foreign activities solely for national prestige. Foreign activities may be profitable only so long as the government, often at a huge cost to the taxpayer, protects trade routes and maintains a secure environment for overseas enterprises.

An industrialized country with strong military capabilities may extend its activities into (and even establish domination over) a country with a much larger population that generates comparatively higher demands, but which has a less advanced technology and lower level of industrialization. For example, although the population of India was larger than that of Britain, England enjoyed a considerable advantage over India by virtue of a difference in technological efficiency.

After the Renaissance a relatively few European countries (and, more recently, the United States and Japan) were able to extend their interests throughout the world. This expansion of interests was so widespread and long-lasting that it became institutionalized through colonies, protectorates, lease-holds, unequal alliances, client-state arrangements, and exploitative trade. Many white men thus inferred that they were innately superior, and were preordained to preside over and exploit societies with lower capability.

Although lateral pressure encompasses some of the propositions about imperialism put forward by J. A. Hobson, V. I. Lenin, and others, the two concepts are not synonymous. The demands of a capitalist economy may contribute to lateral pressure in important ways, but capitalism is not a necessary condition for lateral pressure; both pre-capitalist and socialist societies may generate lateral pressure. Similarly, although class conflict may contribute to lateral pressure, it is not a necessary condition.

As a nation or empire extends its activities, and hence its interests, the feeling may develop among the leaders of such a state or the citizenry or both, that these "national interests" ought to be protected. National interests tend to be intensely subjective among those who define and proclaim them, so that it is often extremely dif-

ficult to predict which interests are likely to be defended by arms. The critical factor in determining the importance to a nation of an interest is not the kind of interest, but the existence of the feeling that the interest must be defended (and then the intensity of this feeling, measured by the social costs that a nation is willing to incur in the defense of this interest).

The protection of national interests in far off places may lead to war between colonial powers and their subject populations, or to attempts at attracting, equipping, and financing local power elites benefiting from foreign control. During the late nineteenth and early twentieth centuries, Britain, France, and Germany engaged in such activities throughout much of Africa and Asia. For example, the Afghan Wars were to a large extent a manifestation of British and Russian expansionism in Central Asia. The history of French control in Indochina and British domination in Burma and Siam offer other examples.

Large differences in capabilities between countries mean grossly unequal political and economic relations between them. In most cases of intensive interaction between societies, the nation with vastly greater capabilities tends to dominate the other, even when domination is not a deliberate policy. Such relations invite the domination and exploitation of the weaker country by the stronger. Differences in capabilities between major powers are likely to have a different meaning. *When two or more major powers extend their respective interests outward, there is a strong probability that these interests will be opposing, and the activities of these nations may collide.* These activities may be diplomatic, commercial, military, or so forth, and thus involve quite different levels of intensity. Depending upon the intensity, such conflicts of interests and activities may contribute to the outbreak of war between strong countries, or between their client states, or both. The Fashoda Incident, the Moroccan Crisis, and the Bosnian Crisis of 1908—1909 are examples of military confrontations resulting from conflicts of interest between major powers before WWI.

Collisions can lead to the withdrawal of one (or both) of the parties, an agreement between them, or continuing conflict. In general the stronger the lateral pressure manifested by rival countries, the greater is the likelihood of the intensification of competition of conflict over territory, resources, markets, political or diplomatic influence, military or naval power, status, or prestige. Such behavior tends to be characteristic of the international relations of powerful states and empires.

The more intense the competition becomes, the greater is the likelihood that it will lead to arms competition, crisis, or possibly armed conflict. Major wars often emerge from a two-fold process: internally generated pressures, and mutual comparison, competition, rivalry, and conflict on a number of salient dimensions. Each of these processes is closely related to the other, and each can be accounted for to a remarkable degree by the interaction among three variables: population, technology, and access to resources.

Thus, international competition and conflict are closely linked to domestic growth, with the result that a country's domestic and foreign activities are likely to be intensely interdependent. Just as domestic growth may contribute to a country's foreign activities, so its foreign activities, in conflict with those of other countries, may generate further domestic demands and growth.

Although any activity by one country in or near the boundary of another country, or within the sphere of interest of another, may generate conflict and even violence, some activities are likely to have a stronger influence on international affairs than others. During the years between 1870 and 1914 we would expect that colonial expansion would be especially important for its effect on relations among the major powers. In another era, other manifestations of lateral pressure might be more important—troops overseas, military bases on foreign territory, outside investment in former colonial areas, military aid, technical assistance. In the late nineteenth and early twentieth centuries competition for colonial territory and spheres of control was the principal international concern. A major factor in Bismarck's turn to imperialism and colonialism may have been the fear that "if he failed to authorize the hoisting of the German flag, the flag of another European power would quickly go up." The British, leaders of the world's largest empire, felt threatened on many occasions when it appeared that some other power might secure a territorial advantage in some part of the world.

States and empires do not stand still relative to one another in population, technology, territory, resources, military capability, or strategic advantage. Compared with each other, some are growing while others are declining, and thus the condition of the international system is perpetual change. A nation may find itself at a relative disadvantage in the world competition for resources, markets, prestige, or strategic superiority. In this eventuality, such a nation's leaders will look for means of improving the nation's relative position. This may involve increases in military or naval capabilities, or improvements in heavy industry. One method of increasing capabilities is to secure favorable alliances. Such bonds normally imply the pooling of some capabilities for the maintenance of shared interests. In defense alliances, the partners are able to complement one another's military capabilities.

Alliances are not always formed only to enhance national capabilities. Alliances, treaties and other international compacts are often concluded to end or moderate conflicts of interests. But although these arrangements may ameliorate conflict, they may also create conflict. Whenever some compact is achieved between two nations not previously allied, it is likely to damage relations between at least one of the parties and any rivals, unless comparable compacts are made with these. Under such circumstances, the alignment of one group of nations may encourage other nations to create a competing bloc. Although relationships improved between Britain and France after 1904 and between Britain and Russia after 1907 as a result of alliances, none of these three powers achieved alliance with Germany. In such a case the amelioration of conflict among only some powers may be suspected of contributing in the long run to conflict among all the powers.

Broad alliance patterns (including distribution of capabilities within and across alliance boundaries) may define the structure of the international system. From the viewpoint of a nation's leaders, a strong or strategically placed ally may be viewed as organic to their own national power. A leading power may seek an alliance to prevent a growing power from overtaking it in some area, or a grow-

take a stronger power. There is usually a price for alliances, however, since international compacts impose some constraints upon a nation's activities.

Competition may give rise to "antagonizing," the term given by Arthur Gladstone to "the process by which each side forms an increasingly unfavorable picture of the other as evil, hostile, and dangerous." No matter which side initiates the process, antagonizing tends to become mutual. "When one side criticizes, distrusts, ridicules, or denounces the other, the other side is likely to reply in kind." The more intense the competition and antagonizing, the greater is the probability of interactions being transformed from insult to injury. Thereafter, "when one side takes actions which are or threaten to be harmful to the other side, the other side is even more likely to reply in kind."

With respect to the interactions between two rival countries, the difference between them on any salient dimension—territorial acquisition, trade, armaments, prestige, etc.—can be a powerful factor in motivating further competition or conflict. *An increase in the political, economic or military strength and effectiveness of one nation will tend to generate new demands in the rival nation and a disposition among its leaders to increase appropriate capabilities.* For example, if Nation A with a higher naval budget than Nation B adds further increments, Nation B is likely to increase its naval budget. Also, if Nation B with a lower budget tries to catch up with A, then the latter is likely to add increments in an effort to maintain its advantage. Nevertheless, we show in Part III that arms increases are sometimes better-explained by domestic growth factors than by international competition.

A nation may respond to an increase in the strength and effectiveness of another nation, e.g., trade, by increasing its own strength and effectiveness in a wholly different area, e.g., colonial territory, military strength, or naval power. This possibility tends to complicate the Richardson-type model of arms races in that increases in the military budgets (or shipping tonnage, etc.) of nations may be attributable to increases by a rival nation in some area *other than* military capability.

The interdependency between a country's domestic growth and military expenditures, on the one hand, and the interdependency between military budgets of rival countries are of considerable importance in the great-power system prior to WWI. Most of the major powers were growing or expanding on a number of dimensions—in colonial territory, military expenditures, trade, and so forth. The stronger these tendencies were after 1900—the more the European countries absorbed available territory for colonialization, the higher their military and naval budgets grew, and the stiffer the competition for the world's resources became—the more some leaders saw the possibilities for further growth threatened and their own policy options narrowing, rather than expanding along with the increased power of their nations. The larger the colonial commitments and spheres of interest of Britain and France, for example, the greater was the dissatisfaction of German leaders, who saw the area of unclaimed territories rapidly diminishing. The greater the armaments expenditures of one major power, the stronger the feeling of commitment was likely to be on the part of its rivals to increase their own military expenditures. Finally, as the powers began to adhere to one or another alliance, the more limited appeared to be the possibilities for negotiation and peaceful diplomacy between alliances.

National decisions are frequently thought of as being made in direct response to some perceived threat by another nation, or as steps directed toward certain widely shared and explicit goals, such as "survival of country." But the processes involved in policy formation and action are often exceedingly complex. National decision, even in an authoritarian state, are usually the outcome of communications—often indirect, subtle, and difficult to trace—among the head of state, his advisers and agents, and the citizenry. Such data as levels and rates of change in population, technology, trade, investment, and colonial expansion are in every case the accumulation and aggregation of the effects of decisions made by individual human beings acting singly, in partnership, or in small groups.

The size of a nation's population at any given time is an outcome of millions of private decisions ("conscious" or "unconscious") to have or not have children. So, too, a country's general level of technology is the outcome of large numbers of research and production enterprises undertaken by individuals working singly, in private firms, and in agencies of government. The decision of ten million Germans to have a second cup of coffee could affect their country's relations with Brazil. In a modern state problems of national security are analyzed by hundreds and perhaps thousands of different institutions. Furthermore, different approaches to national defense are taken simultaneously by dozens or hundreds of research and planning centers in and out of government, and in imperfect communication with one another. Thus, a nation's military budget can be as much the outcome of the personal ambition and interests of bureaucrats in war and navy departments as it is of interactions with rival powers. Often, the accumulation of countless individual decisions creates tendencies that were not planned or foreseen. Despite these complexities, since this study focuses on the interaction of certain macro-level events—growth, expansion, and competition of nations—we shall be concerned only with the *outcomes* of decision-making processes and not with decision-making itself.

National attributes (the levels and rates of change of certain variables) can provide valuable data for studying the processes that lead to war. Chapter 2 presents profiles of the national attributes of the six major European powers during the 45 years prior to WWI. These profiles are an important consideration in the history of the interaction of these powers (presented in Part II) and are the data base for our quantitative analysis (reported in Part III).

Despite our best efforts, the propositions put forward here are crude, and greater precision is required before we can approach a true theory. Our thoughts, observations, assumptions, and propositions constitute at best a "proto-theory." The specific components (variables) of the processes we are studying are presented in Table 8.3. In Part III we introduce an operational model (a system of simultaneous equations) designed to capture some of the complexities of the interdependency and interaction of these components. Even then, we assume that our tentative theory will be only a first cut into the problem, and that the propositions will have to be subjected to much more testing than that reported in this book.

TABLE 8.3 The Conceptual Model

Components of the Model	Description-Rationale	Measure[a]
Expansion	Demands resulting from the interactive effects of population and technological growth give rise to activities beyond national borders.	Colonial area.
Conflict of interest	Expanding nations are likely to collide in their activities outside national boundaries; such collisions have some potential for violence.	Metricized measure of violence in *intersections* (conflicts specifically over colonial issues) between major powers.
Military capability	States, by definition, have military establishments; these grow as a result of domestic growth and competition with military establishments of other nations.	Military budgets.
Alliance	Nations assess their power, resources, and capabilities in comparison with other nations and attempt to enhance themselves through international alliances.	Total alliances.
Violence-behavior	Nations engage in international violence as a consequence of expansion, military capability, and alliances.	Metricized measure of violence in actions directed toward all other nations.[b]

[a]Data are established for *each* nation and aggregated *annually* for the years 1870–1914. . . .

[b]Target nations include not only the six major powers in the study, but all states.

35.   From *THE MODERN WORLD-SYSTEM*

Immanuel Wallerstein

Theorizing is not an activity separate from the analysis of empirical data. Analyses can only be made in terms of theoretical schema and propositions. On the other hand, analyses of events or processes must include as a starting point a whole series of specific values of certain of the variables, on the basis of which one can explain how the final outcomes were arrived at. In order to convey the historical explanation with clarity, it is often the case that one has to assume or glide over the exposition of the formal interrelations between variables.

Consequently, it often makes sense to review the material a second time more briefly and abstractly at the conclusion. No doubt this should be useful to the reader. But it is even more important for the author, in forcing a degree of rigor in the analysis whose absence might readily pass unnoticed amidst the complexity of detail. The empirical material treated thus far has surely been

Reprinted from *The Modern World-System*, text edition (New York: Academic Press, 1976), pp. 229–239, by permission of the publisher and the author. Copyright © 1976 by Academic Press, Inc.

complex—indeed, far more complex than it was possible to portray. Hence, I propose to review what I have been arguing in this book.

In order to describe the origins and initial workings of a world system, I have had to argue a certain conception of a world-system. A world-system is a social system, one that has boundaries, structures, member groups, rules of legitimation, and coherence. Its life is made up of the conflicting forces which hold it together by tension, and tear it apart as each group seeks eternally to remold it to its advantage. It has the characteristics of an organism, in that it has a life-span over which its characteristics change in some respects and remain stable in others. One can define its structures as being at different times strong or weak in terms of the internal logic of its functioning.

What characterizes a social system in my view is the fact that life within it is largely self-contained, and that the dynamics of its development are largely internal. The reader may feel that the use of the term "largely" is a case of academic weaseling. I admit I cannot quantify it. Probably no one ever will be able to do so, as the definition is based on a counterfactual hypothesis: If the system, for any reason, were to be cut off from all external forces (which virtually never happens), the definition implies that the system would continue to function substantially in the same manner. Again, of course, substantially is difficult to convert into hard operational criteria. Nonetheless the point is an important one and key to many parts of the empirical analyses of this book. Perhaps we should think of self-containment as a theoretical absolute, a sort of social vacuum, rarely visible and even more implausible to create artificially, but still and all a socially-real asymptote, the distance from which is somehow measurable.

Using such a criterion, it is contended here that most entities usually described as social systems—"tribes," communities, nation-states—are not in fact total systems. Indeed, on the contrary, we are arguing that the only real social systems are, on the one hand, those relatively small, highly autonomous subsistence economies not part of some regular tribute-demanding system and, on the other hand, world-systems. These latter are to be sure distinguished from the former because they are relatively large; that is, they are in common parlance "worlds." More precisely, however, they are defined by the fact that their self-containment as an economic-material entity is based on extensive division of labor and that they contain within them a multiplicity of cultures.

It is further argued that thus far there have only existed two varieties of such world-systems: world-empires, in which there is a single political system over most of the area, however attenuated the degree of its effective control; and those systems in which such a single political system does not exist over all, or virtually all, of the space. For convenience and for want of a better term, we are using the term "world-economy" to describe the latter.

Finally, we have argued that prior to the modern era, world-economies were highly unstable structures which tended either to be converted into empires or to disintegrate. It is the peculiarity of the modern world-system that a world-economy has survived for 500 years and yet has not come to be transformed into a world-empire—a peculiarity that is the secret of its strength.

This peculiarity is the political side of the form of economic organization called capitalism. Capitalism has been able to flourish precisely because the world-economy has had within its bounds not one but a multiplicity of political systems.

I am not here arguing the classic case of capitalist ideology that capitalism is a system based on the noninterference of the state in economic affairs. Quite the contrary! Capitalism is based on the constant absorption of economic loss by political entities, while economic gain is distributed to "private" hands. What I am arguing rather is that capitalism as an economic mode is based on the fact that the economic factors operate within an arena larger than that which any political entity can totally control. This gives capitalists a freedom of maneuver that is structurally based. It has made possible the constant economic expansion of the world-system, albeit a very skewed distribution of its rewards. The only alternative world-system that could maintain a high level of productivity and change the system of distribution would involve the reintegration of the levels of political and economic decision-making. This would constitute a third possible form of world-system, a socialist world government. This is not a form that presently exists, and it was not even remotely conceivable in the sixteenth century.

The historical reasons why the European world-economy came into existence in the sixteenth century and resisted attempts to transform it into an empire have been expounded at length. We shall not review them here. It should however be noted that the size of a world-economy is a function of the state of technology, and in particular of the possibilities of transport and communication within its bounds. Since this is a constantly changing phenomenon, not always for the better, the boundaries of a world-economy are ever fluid.

We have defined a world-system as one in which there is extensive division of labor. This division is not merely functional—that is, occupational—but geographical. That is today, the range of economic tasks is not evenly distributed throughout the world-system. In part this is the consequence of ecological considerations, to be sure. But for the most part, it is a function of the social organization of work, one which magnifies and legitimizes the ability of some groups within the system to exploit the labor of others, that is, to receive a larger share of the surplus.

While, in an empire, the political structure tends to link culture with occupation, in a world-economy the political structure tends to link culture with spatial location. The reason is that in a world-economy the first point of political pressure available to groups is the local (national) state structure. Cultural homogenization tends to serve the interests of key groups and the pressures build up to create cultural-national identities.

This is particularly the case in the advantaged areas of the world-economy—what we have called the core-states. In such states, the creation of a strong state machinery coupled with a national culture, a phenomenon often referred to as integration, serves both as a mechanism to protect disparities that have arisen within the world-system, and as an ideological mask and justification for the maintenance of these disparities.

World-economies then are divided into core-states and peripheral areas. I do not say peripheral *states* because one characteristic of a peripheral area is that the indigenous state is weak, ranging from its nonexistence (that is, a colonial situation) to one with a low degree of autonomy (that is, a neo-colonial situation).

There are also semiperipheral areas which are in between the core and the periphery on a series of dimensions, such as the complexity of economic activities, strength of the state machinery, cultural integrity, etc. Some of these areas had been core-areas of earlier versions of a given world-economy. Some had been peripheral areas that were later promoted, so to speak, as a result of the changing geopolitics of an expanding world-economy.

The semiperiphery, however, is not an artifice of statistical cutting points, nor is it a residual category. The semiperiphery is a necessary structural element in a world-economy. These areas play a role parallel to that played, *mutatis mutandis*, by middle trading groups in an empire. They are collection points of vital skills that are often politically unpopular. These middle areas (like middle groups in an empire) partially deflect the political pressures which groups primarily located in peripheral areas might otherwise direct against

core-states and the groups which operate within and through their state machineries. On the other hand, the interests primarily located in the semiperiphery are located outside the political arena of the core-states, and find it difficult to pursue the ends in political coalitions that might be open to them were they in the same political arena.

The division of a world-economy involves a hierarchy of occupational tasks, in which tasks requiring higher levels of skill and greater capitalization are reserved for higher-ranking areas. Since a capitalist world-economy essentially rewards accumulated capital, including human capital, at a higher rate than "raw" labor power, the geographical maldistribution of these occupational skills involves a strong trend toward self-maintenance. The forces of the marketplace reinforce them rather than undermine them. And the absence of a central political mechanism for the world-economy makes it very difficult to intrude counteracting forces to the maldistribution of rewards.

Hence, the ongoing process of a world-economy tends to expand the economic and social gaps among its varying areas in the very process of its development. One factor that tends to mask this fact is that the process of development of a world-economy brings about technological advances which make it possible to expand the boundaries of a world-economy. In this case, particular regions of the world may change their structural role in the world-economy, to their advantage, even though the disparity of reward between different sectors of the world-economy as a whole may be simultaneously widening. It is in order to observe this crucial phenomenon clearly that we have insisted on the distinction between a peripheral area of a given world-economy and the external arena of the world-economy. The external arena of one century often becomes the periphery of the next—or its semiperiphery. But then too core-states can become semiperipheral and semiperipheral ones peripheral.

While the advantages of the core-states have not ceased to expand throughout the history of the modern world-system, the ability of a particular state to remain in the core sector is not beyond challenge. The hounds are ever to the hares for the position of top dog. Indeed, it may well be that in this kind of system it is not structurally possible to avoid, over a long period of historical time, a circulation of the elites in the sense that the particular country that is dominant at a given time tends to be replaced in this role sooner or later by another country.

We have insisted that the modern world-economy is, and only can be, a capitalist world-economy. It is for this reason that we have rejected the appellation of "feudalism" for the various forms of capitalist agriculture based on coerced labor which grow up in a world-economy. Furthermore, although this has not been discussed in this volume, it is for this same reason that we will, in future volumes, regard with great circumspection and prudence the claim that there exist in the twentierh century socialist national economies within the framework of the world-economy (as opposed to socialist movements controlling certain state-machineries within the world-economy).

If world-systems are the only real social systems (other than truly isolated subsistence economies), then it must follow that the emergence, consolidation, and political roles of classes and status groups must be appreciated as elements of this *world*-system. And in turn it follows that one of the key elements in analyzing a class or a status-group is not only the state of its self-consciousness but the geographical scope of its self-definition.

Classes always exist potentially *(an sich)*. The issue is under what conditions they become class-conscious *(für sich)*, that is, operate as a group in the politico-economic arenas and even to some extent as a cultural entity. Such self-consciousness is a function of conflict situations. But for upper strata open conflict, and hence overt consciousness, is always *faute de mieux*. To the extent that class boundaries are not made explicit, to that extent it is more likely that privileges be maintained.

Since in conflict situations, multiple factions tend to reduce to two by virtue of the forging of alliances, it is by definition not possible to have three or more (conscious) classes. There obviously can be a multitude of occupational interest groups which may organize themselves to operate within the social structure. But such groups are really one variety of status-groups, and indeed often overlap heavily with other kinds of status-groups such as those defined by ethnic, linguistic, or religious criteria.

To say that there cannot be three or more classes is not however to say that there are always two. There may be none, though this is rare and transitional. There may be one, and this is most common. There may be two, and this is most explosive.

We say there may be only one class, although we have also said that classes only actually exist in conflict situations, and conflicts presume two sides. There is no contradiction here. For a conflict may be defined as being between one class, which conceives of itself as the universal class, and all the other strata. This has in fact been the usual situation in the modern world-system. The capitalist class (the *bourgeoisie*) has claimed to be the universal class and sought to organize political life to pursue its objectives against two opponents. On the one hand, there were those who spoke for the maintenance of traditional rank distinctions despite the fact that these ranks might have lost their original correlation with economic function. Such elements preferred to define the social structure as a non-class structure. It was to counter this ideology that the bourgeoisie came to operate as a class conscious of itself.

But the bourgeoisie had another opponent, the workers. Whenever the workers became conscious of themselves as a class, which was not too frequently in the sixteenth century, they defined the situation as a polarized two-class situation. In such circumstances, the bourgeoisie found itself in a deep tactical dilemma. To the extent that they maintained their own *class*-consciousness, they abetted by this fact workers' class-consciousness, and thereby risked undermining their own political position. To the extent that, in order to deal with this problem, they muted their class-consciousness, they risked weakening their position vis-à-vis the tenants of traditional high rank.

The process of the crystallization of class-consciousness of a bourgeoisie, thinking of itself as a universal class, drawing its members from all social ranks, has been illustrated in our discussions of the emergence of the gentry as a social category in Tudor England or the rise of the burghers in the northern Netherlands. One of the ways they supported their claim to be a universal class was by the development of national sentiment, which gave a cultural veneer to their claim.

The deep dilemma of a bourgeoisie trapped by insurrection on the left, so to speak, and fearing an alliance between its two sets of opponents taking the form of regionalist claims, has been illustrated in our discussions of France in the "second" sixteenth century. The bourgeoisie there opted for temporary retreat. They perhaps had no viable alternative. But this retreat was to have its long term consequences in the later social radicalism of the French revolution (however momentary), and in the long-run lag in economic development of France behind England.

Our examples here are of bourgeoisies that became conscious, but concious within the bounds of a nation-state. This was clearly not the only choice. They could have become conscious of themselves as a world class. And many groups pushed for such a definition. On the one hand, there were the various communities of international merchant-bankers. On the other hand, there were the many sets of capitalist farmers in the peripheral areas.

In the heyday of Charles V, there were many in the Low Countries, in southern Germany, in northern Italy and elsewhere who tied their hopes to the imperial aspirations of the Hapsburgs (some prudentially keeping a foot in the door of the Valois as well). If these groups remained a social stratum and did not yet form a conscious class, they were moving in that direction, and it seemed only a matter of time. But with the failure of empire, the bourgeoisies of Europe realized that their economic and social future was tied to the core-states. And those who, by virtue of their ethnic-religious affiliations, could turn to the national state as their arena of political operation did so.

As for the capitalist farmers of the periphery, they would gladly have thought of themselves as part of an international gentry class. They willingly sacrificed local cultural roots for participation in "world" cultures. But to constitute an international class, they needed the cooperation of the capitalist strata of the core-states, and this was not to be forthcoming. So increasingly these peripheral capitalist farmers became the antiquated and snobbish Spanish-American *hacenderos* or east European nobility of later centuries, retreating from potential international class-consciousness into local status solidarities—which served well the interests of Western European bourgeoisies.

Geographic concentration of particular economic activities serves as a continuing pressure to status-group formation. When the local dominant strata are threatened by any incipient class-consciousness of lower strata, emphasis on local culture serves well to deflect local internal conflict, creating instead local solidarity against the outside. If, in addition, these local dominant strata feel themselves oppressed by higher strata of the world-system, they are doubly motivated to pursue the creation of a local identity.

Obviously, one does not construct an identity out of thin air. One builds on what one finds—in terms of language, religion, and distinctive life-styles. Nonetheless, it is quite clear that both linguistic and religious homogeneity and passion *(a fortiori* devotion to separate life-styles) are social creations which cannot be accounted for as simple continuities of tradition eternal. They are social creations molded with difficulty in times of travail.

The sixteenth century was such a time of travail in much of Europe. It was of course the era of the Reformation and the Counter-Reformation. It was the era of great religious civil wars. It was the era of international religious "parties." But in the end, as the dust settled, all the religious upheaval resulted in a pattern of relative religious homogeneity of the various political entities within the framework of international laissez-faire—*cuius regio eius religio.*

We have tried to indicate in our discussion of various specific developments why various forms of Protestantism ended up as the religion of the core-states (except France, and again why) and Catholicism as the religion of the periphery and semiperiphery. We have been skeptical that the tenets of the various theologies had too much to do with it, although they may have facilitated the task. Rather the tenets of the theologies, as they evolved in practice as opposed to their original conception, reflected and served to sustain the roles of the various areas in the world-system.

It is often said that Charles V missed a great opportunity of creating a united German Protestant state by attempting to remain an arbiter of the religious split instead of a protagonist. But such a critique neglects the fact that Charles V sought to create a world-empire, not a core-state within a world-economy. Empires thrive on multiple religions reflecting multiple roles, few of which are concentrated within specific political boundaries. National homogeneity within international heterogeneity is the formula of a world-economy.

At least this is the formula at the simple beginnings. Core-states because of their complex internal division of labor begin to reflect the pattern of the system as a whole. In the sixteenth century, England was already moving in the direction of becoming Britain, which would have regional homogeneity within a relative heterogeneity for the nation as a whole.

Religion does not have to be the defining cultural trait of the major status-groups; one can use language. Language indeed began to play such a role in the sixteenth century, and its importance was to increase as the centuries passed. Religious reinforcement of role specialization in a world-economy has, however, advantages over linguistic reinforcement. It interferes less with the ongoing communications process within the world-economy. And it lends itself less (only less) to isolationist closures, because of the underlying universalist themes of world religions.

The European world-economy of the sixteenth century tended overall to be a one-class system. It was the dynamic forces profiting from economic expansion and the capitalist system, especially those in the core-areas, who tended to be class-conscious, that is to operate within the political arena as a group defined primarily by their common role in the economy. This common role was in fact defined somewhat broadly from a twentieth-century perspective. It included persons who were farmers, merchants, and industrialists. Individual entrepreneurs often moved back and forth between these activities in any case, or combined them. The crucial distinction was between these men, whatever their occupation, principally oriented to obtaining profit in the world market, and the others not so oriented.

The "others" fought back in terms of their status privileges—those of the traditional aristocracy, those which small farmers had derived from the feudal system, those resulting from guild monopolies that were outmoded. Under the cover of cultural similarities, one can often weld strange alliances. Those strange alliances can take a very activist form and force the political centers to take account of them. We pointed to such instances in our discussion of France. Or they can take a politically passive form that serves well the needs of the dominant forces in the world-system. The triumph of Polish Catholicism as a cultural force was a case in point.

The details of the canvas are filled in with the panoply of multiple forms of status-groups, their particular strengths and accents. But the grand sweep is in terms of the process of class formation. And in this regard, the sixteenth century was indecisive. The capitalist strata formed a class that survived and gained *droit de cité*, but did not yet triumph in the political arena.

The evolution of the state machineries reflected precisely this uncertainty. Strong states serve the interests of some groups and hurt those of others. From, however, the standpoint of the world-system as a whole, if there is to be a multitude of political entities (that is, if the system is not a world-empire), then it cannot be the case that all these entities be equally strong. For if they were, they would be in the position of blocking the effective operation of transnational economic entities whose locus were in another state. It would then follow that the world division of labor would be impeded, the world-economy decline, and eventually the world-system fall apart.

It also cannot be that *no* state machinery is strong. For in such a case, the capitalist strata would have no mechanisms to protect their interests, guaranteeing their property rights, assuring various monopolies, spreading losses among the larger population, etc.

It follows then that the world-economy develops a pattern where state structures are relatively strong in the core areas and relatively weak in the periphery. Which areas play which roles is in many ways accidental. What is necessary is that in some areas the state machinery be far stronger than in others.

What do we mean by a strong state-machinery? We mean strength vis-à-vis other states within the world-economy including other core-states, and strong vis-à-vis local political units within the boundaries of the state. In effect, we mean a sovereignty that is *de facto* as well as *de jure*. We also mean a state that is strong vis-à-vis any particular social group within the state. Obviously, such groups vary in the amount of pressure they can bring to bear upon the state. And obviously certain combinations of these groups control the state. It is not that the state is a neutral arbiter. But the state is more than a simple vector of given forces, if only because many of these forces are situated in more than one state or are defined in terms that have little correlation with state boundaries.

A strong state then is a partially autonomous entity in the sense that it has a margin of action available to it wherein it reflects the compromises of multiple interests, even if the bounds of these margins are set by the existence of some groups of primordial strength. To be a partially autonomous entity, there must be a group of people whose direct interests are served by such an entity: state managers and a state bureaucracy.

Such groups emerge within the framework of a capitalist world-economy because a strong state is the best choice between difficult alternatives for the two groups that are strongest in political, economic, and military terms: the emergent capitalist strata, and the old aristocratic hierarchies.

For the former, the strong state in the form of the "absolute monarchies" was a prime customer, a guardian against local and international brigandage, a mode of social legitimation, a preemptive protection against the creation of strong state barriers elsewhere. For the latter, the strong state represented a brake on these same capitalist strata, and upholder of status conventions, a maintainer of order, a promoter of luxury.

No doubt both nobles and bourgeois found the state machineries to be a burdensome drain of funds, and a meddlesome unproductive bureaucracy. But what options did they have? Nonetheless they were always restive and the immediate politics of the world-system was made up of the pushes and pulls resulting from the efforts of both groups to insulate themselves from what seemed to them the negative effects of the state machinery.

A state machinery involves a tipping mechanism. There is a point where strength creates more strength. The tax revenue enables the state to have a larger and more efficient civil bureaucracy and army which in turn leads to greater tax revenue—a process that continues in spiral form. The tipping mechanism works in other directions too—weakness leading to greater weakness. In between these two tipping points lies the politics of state-creation. It is in this arena that the skills of particular managerial groups make a difference. And it is because of the two tipping mechanisms that at certain points a small gap in the world-system can very rapidly become a large one.

In those states in which the state machinery is weak, the state managers do not play the role of coordinating a complex industrial–commerical–agricultural mechanism. Rather they simply become one set of landlords amidst others, with little claim to legitimate authority over the whole.

These tend to be called traditional rulers. The political struggle is often phrased in terms of tradition versus change. This is of course a grossly misleading and ideological terminology. It may in fact be taken as a general sociological principle that, at any given point of time, what is thought to be traditional is of more recent origin than people generally imagine it to be, and represents primarily the conservative instincts of some group threatened with declining social status. Indeed, there seems to be nothing which emerges and evolves as quickly as a "tradition" when the need presents itself.

In a one-class system, the "traditional" is that in the name of which the "others" fight the class-conscious group. If they can encrust their values by legitimating them widely, even better by enacting them into legislative barriers, they thereby change the system in a way favorable to them.

The traditionalists may win in some states, but if a world-economy is to survive, they must lose more or less in the others. Furthermore, the gain in one region is the counterpart of the loss in another.

This is not quite a zero-sum game, but it is also inconceivable that all elements in a capitalist world-economy shift their values in a given direction simultaneously. The social system is built on having a multiplicity of value systems within it, reflecting the specific functions groups and areas play in the world divisions of labor.

We have not exhausted here the theoretical problems relevant to the functioning of a world-economy. We have tried only to speak to those illustrated by the early period of the world-economy in creation, to wit, sixteenth-century Europe. Many other problems emerged at later stages and will be treated, both empirically and theoretically, in later volumes.

In the sixteenth century, Europe was like a bucking bronco. The attempt of some groups to establish a world-economy based on a particular division of labor, to create national states in the core areas as politico-economic guarantors of this system, and to get the workers to pay not only the profits but the costs of maintaining the system was not easy. It was to Europe's credit that it was done, since without the thrust of the sixteenth century the modern world would not have been born and, for all its cruelties, it is better that it was born than that it had not been.

It is also to Europe's credit that it was not easy, and particularly that it was not easy because the people who paid the short-run costs screamed lustily at the unfairness of it all. The peasants and workers in Poland and England and Brazil and Mexico were all rambunctious in their various ways. As R. H. Tawney says of the agrarian disturbances of sixteenth-century England: "Such movements are a proof of blood and sinew and of a high and gallant spirit. . . . Happy the nation whose people has not forgotten how to rebel."

The mark of the modern world is the imagination of its profiteers and the counter-assertiveness of the oppressed. Exploitation and the refusal to accept exploitation as either inevitable or just constitute the continuing antinomy of the modern era, joined together in a dialectic which has far from reached its climax in the twentieth century.

IV
The Search
for Peace

Throughout the ages, one of the goals of international relations inquiry has been to find a way to bring about peace. Chapters 9 through 12 present four approaches to peace that have attracted attention in our own day: the balance of power, nuclear deterrence, world government, and world community. Each of these approaches entails a peace proposal or set of proposals that can be evaluated in terms of its viability and feasibility. A proposal can be said to be viable if, once implemented, it will actually bring about peace. In other words, a proposal is viable if, in principle, it will work. A proposal can be said to be *feasible* if it *can* be implemented—in other words, if it is sufficiently practical and not too costly. Unfortunately, the solutions that often appear to be the most viable, like world government, do not seem very feasible; and the solutions which can be implemented, like deterrence, may not be viable.

Despite many noble attempts, war has obviously not been eliminated. Therefore, many peace proposals seek not to abolish war but to mitigate its effects. They try to do this by constraining the capability of each side (balance of power and nuclear deterrence), by circumscribing the conditions under which war will be used as an instrument of policy and the methods by which it will be fought (nuclear deterrence and limited war), or by providing alternative means of conflict resolution and an atmosphere that encourages peaceful change (world government and world community).

Perhaps the oldest mechanism for preserving the peace has been the maintenance of a balance of power. As long ago as the time of Thucydides, the breakdown of a balance of power was seen as a cause of war:

What made war inevitable was the growth of Athenian power and the fear which this caused in Sparta.[1]

Throughout European history, and particularly in the last four centuries, the balance of power has been cited as a justification for policy and has been lauded by some as the only realistic proposal for maintaining peace. Nevertheless, it has been fraught with problems. At the practical level, it has not provided a very permanent solution; wars have occurred throughout the last four centuries. Those who have argued in favor of the viability of the balance of power have maintained that these wars occurred when the balance was disrupted. This contention is not very persuasive, since it concedes that a balance may be difficult to implement at the point at which it is needed most—when war threatens. Thus, this argument saves the viability of the proposal, but sacrifices its feasibility. Conversely, others have argued that the balance can be implemented, but that it will not prevent war; states will fight each other whether they are equal or unequal in capability.

At the conceptual level, the proposal has difficulties because it means different things. Some see it as an automatic and natural phenomenon, like Adam Smith's invisible hand; if one nation increases in power, one or more other nations will move to match and counter that power. Others view it as a conscious policy that decision makers must meticulously follow if it is to work. Still others see it as a popular symbol with which to marshal support and rationalize a position that has been taken for other reasons. In this guise, the balance of power is a form of propaganda.[2]

Regardless of whether, in Ernst Haas's words, it is a prescription, an empirical concept, or propaganda, it is unclear why the balance of power should work. Thucydides and other ancients commented that if one state gained too much power there would be nothing to stop it from subjecting all others. This certainly points out a potential danger, but it does not follow that peace will be produced from a balance. All a balance will prevent is an "easy" victory. War may, and often does, occur among relative equals. This has led many scholars to argue that security can be attained not through a balance of power, but only through a preponderance of power. The other side will only be prevented from attacking if it knows it will lose the war. While this argument makes sense, what is to prevent the preponderant power from attacking?

These kinds of conceptual and theoretical problems, coupled with the balance of power's limited historical success, have undermined scholarly confidence in the balance of power as a peace proposal. Indeed, it can be argued that neither a balance of power nor a preponderance of power is associated with peace, but rather each is associated with different types of war! From this perspective, the balance of

---

[1]Thucydides, *History of the Peloponnesian War,* translated by Rex Warner (Harmondsworth: Penguin Books, 1954), p. 25.

[2]These points are made by Ernst Haas, in "The Balance of Power: Prescription, Concept, or Propaganda?" *World Politics* 5 (1953), pp. 442–477. Similar criticisms were made in the eighteenth century by Johann Heinrich Gottlob von Justi; see Per Maurseth, "Balance of Power Thinking from the Renaissance to the French Revolution," *Journal of Peace Research,* No. 2, (1964) pp. 131–132.

power has been associated with total wars like the Peloponnesian War, the Punic Wars, the Thirty Years War, the Napoleonic Wars, and World Wars I and II. These were wars of rivalry among relative equals. Conversely, a preponderance of power has been associated with imperial wars of conquest. A balance of power may prevent the latter wars in the short run, but in so doing often produces conditions that lead to total wars between rivals.

The selections in Chapter 9 examine some of these issues in detail. The 1572 essay by David Hume reviews ancient commentators to elucidate the balance-of-power principle and illustrates how the concept was viewed in eighteenth-century England. Significantly, Hume saw the English attempt to balance power as easily subject to abuse, and criticized the English government for its excessive hostility and unnecessary wars. In an article that provides an overview of his important 1957 book, *System and Process in International Politics*, Morton Kaplan employs systems language to analyze the balance of power. He describes how the basic elements of the European balance of power can be viewed as a system of behavior that is supported by a given structure, and how a change in the structure can produce different systems. Kaplan's main contribution is to provide political scientists with a set of propositions that elaborate in systematic fashion the role of power in shaping world politics. Since some of his six systems are more peaceful than others, his work is also useful for those who seek to avoid or limit war through a change in the system. Finally, in a cogent analysis, A.F.K. Organski explains why the balance of power usually does not bring peace. He then goes on to present the famous power-transition thesis, which states that war is most likely when the dominant or most powerful nation is being surpassed by a rising nation. If this thesis is true, then it is clear that the balance of power is often only a stopgap measure before a major war.

With the advent of nuclear weapons, balance-of-power thinking received a new lease on life. The nuclear balance of terror, although horribly frightening, seemed to achieve the positive aspects of both the balance of power and the preponderance of power without the negative aspects. As long as each side was able to absorb an initial attack and to retaliate, power was relatively equal, as in the balance of power. Thus, wars of conquest could be prevented. Conversely, the tremendous destructive capability of nuclear weapons insured that both sides would lose a nuclear war. As long as this mutual assured destruction was in place, each side had, in effect, a preponderance of power. Thus, wars of rivalry could be prevented.

Chapter 10 reprints the most influential and relevant thought on these questions. The chapter begins with a selection from Clausewitz, the eighteenth-century military theorist, because his work has been seen as particularly relevant to the nuclear dilemma. Now that war can be so catastrophic and final, it is important to remember exactly what war is, how it is related to politics, and what functions it serves. Clausewitz addressed these questions for his century; his insistence that ''war is a mere continuation of policy by other means,'' has been particularly relevant to nuclear theorists because it makes it clear that the purpose of force is to win a set of political decisions.

In the late 1950s and early 1960s, a group of American scholars examined issues concerning nuclear weapons and developed what became in effect an American doctrine of deterrence. The work of Bernard Brodie, Herman Kahn, Thomas Schelling, and Henry Kissinger is of special importance. Brodie was among the first to perceive that nuclear weapons would change old notions of the balance of power and make strategy even more important. Herman Kahn, in his work at the RAND Corporation, was one of the main architects of nuclear deterrence. In the selection reprinted here, he defines three types of deterrence and the underlying logic of each. One of the problems that Kahn points out in this analysis and in his larger work, *On Thermonuclear War*, is that if deterrence against direct attack works, then it is hard to believe that the United States would risk nuclear annihilation to protect a Berlin, let alone a Taiwan.

This was known as the problem of credibility and was the focus of much of the work of Thomas Schelling, who was also associated with RAND. Schelling pointed out that it is easier to deter someone from taking an action than it is to compel them to do something. His elucidation of this distinction between deterrence and "compellence," along with his work on credibility, make Schelling as important a figure as Herman Kahn.

Although it appeared that the United States was successful in deterring Soviet threats to Berlin and Chinese attacks on Taiwan with threats of massive retaliation, the problem of credibility and the risks associated with this strategy were troublesome. In two major books, *Nuclear Weapons and Foreign Policy* and *The Necessity for Choice*, Henry Kissinger defines the problems associated with massive retaliation and seeks to resolve them by providing the United States with an option between nuclear war and surrender—conventional military force. In the selection reprinted here, he delineates the way in which a limited war must be fought in order to avoid escalation to a nuclear confrontation.

The deductive arguments of Brodie, Kahn, and Schelling, coupled with the public pronouncements of John Foster Dulles and later of Robert McNamara, gradually transformed nuclear deterrence from a theory and policy into a dogma and doctrine. Yet there was little empirical evidence to support it. The first major test was conducted by Bruce Russett and is reprinted here.[3] He examines the conditions under which deterrence was successful in both the nuclear and prenuclear periods. Although primarily suggestive, the article was important because of its insistence that empirical claims should be tested systematically rather than simply accepted through repetition; its finding that some aspects of deterrence theory were incorrect is also notable.

More influential were the comparative case studies conducted eleven years later by Alexander George and Richard Smoke. In a changed political atmosphere, their analyses raised very serious questions about the empirical accuracy of much of deterrence doctrine. Their review of American actions shows that deterrence theory provided decision makers with insufficient guidance, and that decision makers often deviated from the guidance that was provided. If deterrence theory is unable to

---

[3]For an update, see Paul Huth and Bruce Russett, "What Makes Deterrence Work? Cases from 1900 to 1980," *World Politics* 36 (July 1984), pp. 496–526.

accurately describe and explain the actions of American decision makers, then it is doubtful that it could predict how the Russians or Chinese would react in a nuclear confrontation. Yet it is precisely this informatin that it purports to provide. The selection reprinted here is from their conclusion.

The implications of George and Smoke's analysis are very disturbing, because nuclear deterrence has been the basis upon which the West has sought to avoid nuclear war. Critics of nuclear strategy, like Anatol Rapoport, have often pointed out the risks of conducting diplomacy at the brink; but if decision makers do not even make the kinds of cost-benefit calculations upon which deterrence is based, then the risks are even greater. It may very well be that the absence of a nuclear war between the U.S. and U.S.S.R. has not been due simply to nuclear deterrence, but to other irenic factors like: the fact that the U.S. and U.S.S.R. are not continguous and are not fighting over territory, that they are willing to accept a de facto division of Europe, that they do not seriously attempt to overthrow each other's governments, and that they are prepared to lose limited wars in the periphery to avoid escalation to total war. If this is the case, then nuclear proliferation is even more dangerous than we had thought, because it is not likely that these irenic factors will be present among other nations.

Historically, the most common proposal for ending war has been to create a world government and to establish international law. Dante, Hobbes, Rousseau, and Kant all discussed this proposal in a trenchant manner. The heart of the argument lies in the assumption that, in a state of anarchy (the absence of government and law), war occurs naturally because there is nothing to prevent it; it occurs whenever a side is willing to fight rather than lose. Thus, in an anarchic state, war provides the same function as government does—a way of making decisions authoritatively. According to this argument, world government and international law can become a substitute for war if nations will accept them as nonviolent and binding bases for reaching political agreement. To provide empirical support for this argument, proponents of world government often point to the relative absence of domestic violence within nations that have legitimate governments. They argue that, just as domestic government put an end to the state of nature within a given territory, so can world government end global anarchy.

The problem with this proposal seems to lie not so much in its viability—it probably would work if a world government could be created and its decisions accepted—but in its feasibility—how can a world government be created? Contemporary critics of world government and international law have regarded this proposal as utopian, because the conditions necessary for creating an effective world government or enforcing international law do not exist. Such realist critics as Reinhold Niebuhr and Hans Morgenthau have argued that the League of Nations and the United Nations could not become a proto–world government, because government presupposes community. Since there was and is no world community, there can be no world government. Realist as well as other critics point out that the mere existence of government will not prevent violence—as revolutions and civil wars make abundantly clear. It is necessary to discover the conditions that produce *effective* government. In recent years, these criticisms have led some scholars to investigate the causes of community formation and its consequences for the prospects of creating government. Some hoped that such knowledge could be used to aid in the development of a world community, which could then serve as a foundation for the creation of a world government. At the time of its formation, UNESCO was actually charged with such a mission. By 1950, this lofty goal and similar ones in the United Nations were swept away by the Cold War.

While the feasibility of world government is an obvious problem, many have also questioned its desirability. Some do not want peace at the price of justice, or equality, or freedom, or some other value they hold dear. Likewise, they may be hesitant to join a government or support a law that benefits others more than themselves, or that institutionalizes the status quo and makes change difficult, or that reduces their autonomy and places the right to make decisions into the hands of an international body. For all these reasons, there is very little support for a world government among nations in today's world.

Chapter 11 presents three selections on international law and world government. The first is by Hugo Grotius, who is commonly recognized as the father of international law. Grotius was a seventeenth-century Dutch jurist best known for promulgating the principle of freedom of the seas and for establishing the foundation of modern international law. The selection reprinted here is from his prolegomena to *The Law of War and Peace*, first published in 1625. In it, he makes the argument that international law, as a reflection of natural law, is in the best interest of all nations. The second selection, by Grenville Clark and Louis Sohn, was first published in 1958; it presents the case for converting the United Nations into a quasi–world government. In the last selection, Inis Claude delineates some of the difficulties in drawing an analogy between domestic government and world government. In particular, he points out that advocates of world government, like Clark and Sohn, often ignore the fact that government is based not so much on the "rule of law" as on the "rule of politics." Two of Claude's books, *Swords into Plowshares* (1956) and *Power and International Relations* (1962), the latter of which is represented in the selection reprinted here, were considered major studies of international organization in the post–World War II period.

Chapter 12 presents selections from the two leading scholars of inter-nation integration—the process by which two or more nations establish sufficient cultural, social, economic, and political ties to create a sense of community. The process was seen by David Mitrany as an important step toward creating peace. He offered the functionalist argument that cooperation in one area, especially in a nonpolitical area, would "spill over" into cooperation in another area. The creation of the European Coal and Steel Community (ECSC) and later of the European Common Market as a way of ending war in Western Europe spurred empirical research on the integration process and its relationship to peace. In the forefront of this effort were Karl Deutsch and Ernst Haas. Deutsch was noted for his use of a cybernetic approach to the study of integration—that is, a focus on how information is communicated and transferred to give rise to a community. In the selection presented here, he defines *integration* and the other major concepts that form the basis of his approach. Haas has been associated with those who have taken a neofunctionalist approach. The neo-functionalists have examined the empirical accuracy of some propositions initially suggested by Mitrany. In the selection here, Haas traces the integration process in Western Europe, and examines its relationship to cooperation and its applicability to the world as a whole.

The proposals for peace that are discussed in this part of the book have been chosen because they are relevant to the question that has overshadowed much of world politics since the mid–twentieth century—whether nuclear annihilation can be avoided. Much of the scholarship suggests that the balance of power is neither a viable nor feasible mechanism for avoiding conventional war. At the nuclear level, the balance-of-power proposal has been replaced by the notion of nuclear deterrence, which has been widely credited with preventing war between the United States and the U.S.S.R. The extent to which deterrence actually works is now being questioned. The fact that the two nations have avoided nuclear war may have nothing to do with the principles of deterrence. If that is the case, then nuclear proliferation is quite ominous, because deterrence cannot be relied upon. This has led some to seek nuclear disarmament and world government. As we have seen, however, the political conditions for this do not seem ripe. All this suggests that international relations theory cannot offer any permanent solutions. Can it offer any guidance?

Here it is possible to be more optimistic. International relations theory provides two fundamental insights that can serve as a guide to behavior. The first, from the balance of power and nuclear deterrence literature, is that nations and other political actors must, at a minimum, be prepared to militarily defend their interests if they are to have any hope of attaining them. In international politics, virtue—or reason—is not a substitute for power. The second, from the idealist notions of world government and international law, is that rules and norms can provide an escape from the state of nature and its intermittent war. The struggle for power can be mitigated and the use of violence limited by institutionalizing law and procedures for making political decisions.

By melding these two insights, the following two-step strategy can be derived. First, in order to avoid a nuclear war and to attain an acceptable peace, each side must be prepared to fight rather than to surrender; both sides must be convinced that they can only lose a nuclear war; neither side may believe that nuclear coercion can produce a victory that is worth the risks of nuclear war; and both sides must be willing to tolerate the position of the other on certain fundamental issues in order to compromise on other issues.

Once this phase has been completed, it will be possible to enter a second phase, which is the establishment of global regimes based on the acceptance of certain rules and norms about how nations can compete and, if necessary, fight with each other. The purpose of these regimes would be to resolve outstanding political issues. A single global regime that covered all issues would be a world government, and that is not feasible. A variety of global regimes seems more likely, each with different rules and participants, and each confined to an identifiable set of issues.

The most important regime would be the one on nuclear war and associated issues. The attempt at detente by Nixon, Kissinger, and Brezhnev was clearly an inchoate form of such a regime. If a detente regime were successful, it might be extended and expanded to a concert of power that would seek to prevent or limit conventional wars among minor powers. A concert like this might operate in much the same manner as the Concert of Europe did in 1815, and might eventually include the most important European states, Japan, China, and perhaps regional powers in the Third World. Other regimes would be devoted to the oceans, economic questions, energy, development, food, telecommunications, and so forth. Indeed, in some of these areas, such as the oceans, a new body of international law is being developed; in others, including economics, energy, and food, new norms and structures are being created. The ways in which these more functionalist issues are resolved, and the manner in which the United States and the Soviet Union resolve the Cold War will provide important precedents for the future avoidance of nuclear war. The key point, as Claude and philosophers like Edmund Burke would insist, is that the creation of such regimes must be worked out in practice and on the basis of experience, not by the imposition of rationalistic schemes; only then will they have any chance of being feasible. This brief discussion should indicate that international relations theory can provide insight and guidance for these intractable problems. Whether those insights will be used wisely or perniciously will depend upon the actions of world leaders, their followers, and mass political movements.

FOR FURTHER READING

Balance of Power:

1. JOHANN HEINRICH GOTTLOB von JUSTI. *Die Chimäre des Gleichgewichts von Europa* (1758).

2. ERNST B. HAAS. The Balance of Power: Prescription, Concept, or Propaganda? *World Politics* 5 (1953): 442–477.

3. EDWARD V. GULICK. *Europe's Classical Balance of Power*. Ithaca, N.Y.: Cornell University Press, 1955.

4. RICHARD ROSECRANCE. *Action and Reaction in World Politics*. Boston: Little Brown, 1963.

Nuclear Deterrence:

5. BERNARD BRODIE. The Atomic Bomb and American Security. Memorandum No. 18, Yale Institute of International Studies, 1945.

6. CHARLES E. OSGOOD. Suggestions for Winning the Real War with Communism. *Journal of Conflict Resolution* 3 (1959): 295–325.

7. THOMAS C. SCHELLING. *The Strategy of Conflict*. New York: Oxford University Press, 1960. *Arms and Influence*. New Haven: Yale University Press, 1966.

8. ANATOL RAPOPORT. *Fights, Games and Debates*. Ann Arbor: University of Michigan Press, 1960. *Strategy and Conscience*. New York: Schocken Books, 1964.

International Law, World Government, and World Community:

9. DANTE ALIGHIERI (1256–1321). *On World Government* (De Monarchia) (ca. 1310–1313). Indianapolis: Bobbs-Merrill, 1976.

10. JEAN JACQUES ROUSSEAU (1712–1778). *A Lasting Peace through the Federation of Europe* (1761).

11. EMMERICH DE VATTEL (1714–1767). *The Law of Nations* (1758).

12. IMMANUEL KANT. (1724–1804). *Perpetual Peace* (1795). Indianapolis: Bobbs-Merrill, 1957.

13. REINHOLD NIEBUHR. The Myth of World Government. *The Nation* 162 (1946): 312–314.

14. HANS KELSEN. *Principles of International Law*. New York: Rinehart, 1952.

15. INIS L. CLAUDE, JR. *Swords Into Plowshares*. New York: Random House, 1956.

16. HENRY KISSINGER. *A World Restored*. Boston: Houghton Mifflin, 1957.

17. HAYWARD R. ALKER, JR. AND BRUCE M. RUSSETT. *World Politics in the General Assembly*. New Haven: Yale University Press, 1965.

18. HEDLEY BULL. Society and Anarchy in International Relations. In *Diplomatic Investigations*, edited by Herbert Butterfield and Martin Wight. Cambridge, Mass.: Harvard University Press, 1966.

19. ROBERT O. KEOHANE AND JOSEPH S. NYE, JR. Transnational Relations and World Politics: A Conclusion. In *Transnational Relations and World Politics*, edited by R. Keohane and J. Nye, Jr.. Cambridge, Mass.: Harvard University Press, 1972.

20. ROBERT W. COX, HAROLD K. JACOBSON ET AL. *The Anatomy of Influence: Decision Making in International Organization*. New Haven: Yale University Press, 1973.

CHAPTER

9

THE BALANCE OF POWER

36. Of the Balance of Power

DAVID HUME

It is a question whether the *idea* of the balance of power be owing entirely to modern policy, or whether the *phrase* only has been invented in these later ages? It is certain, that XENOPHON, in his Institution of CYRUS, represents the combination of the ASIATIC powers to have arisen from a jealousy of the encreasing force of the MEDES and PERSIANS; and though that elegant composition should be supposed altogether a romance, this sentiment, ascribed by the author to the eastern princes, is at least a proof of the prevailing notion of ancient times.

In all the politics of GREECE, the anxiety, with regard to the balance of power, is apparent, and is expressly pointed out to us, even by the ancient historians. THUCYDIDES represents the league, which was formed against ATHENS, and which produced the PELOPONNESIAN war, as entirely owing to this principle. And after the decline of ATHENS, when the THEBANS and LACEDEMONIANS disputed for sovereignty, we find, that the

ATHENIANS (as well as many other republics) always threw themselves into the lighter scale, and endeavoured to preserve the balance. They supported THEBES against SPARTA, till the great victory gained by EPAMINONDAS at LEUCTRA; after which they immediately went over to the conquered, from generosity, as they pretended, but in reality from their jealousy of the conquerors.

Whoever will read DEMOSTHENES'S oration for the MEGALOPOLITANS, may see the utmost refinements on this principle, that ever entered into the head of a VENETIAN or ENGLISH speculatist. And upon the first rise of the MACEDONIAN power, this orator immediately discovered the danger, sounded the alarm throughout all GREECE, and at last assembled that confederacy under the banners of ATHENS, which fought the great and decisive battle of CHAERONEA.

It is true, the GRECIAN wars are regarded by historians as wars of emulation rather than of politics; and each state seems to have had more in view the honour of leading the rest, than any

From *Essays: Moral, Political, and Literary*, Part II, Essay 7. First published in 1752. Footnotes deleted.

well-grounded hopes of authority and dominion. If we consider, indeed, the small number of inhabitants in any one republic, compared to the whole, the great difficulty of forming sieges in those times, and the extraordinary bravery and discipline of every freeman among that noble people; we shall conclude, that the balance of power was, of itself, sufficiently secured in GREECE, and needed not to have been guarded with that caution which may be requisite in other ages. But whether we ascribe the shifting of sides in all the GRECIAN republics to *jealous emulation* or *cautious politics*, the effects were alike, and every prevailing power was sure to meet with a confederacy against it, and that often composed of its former friends and allies.

The same principle, call it envy or prudence, which produced the *Ostracism* of ATHENS, and *Petalism* of SYRACUSE, and expelled every citizen whose fame or power overtopped the rest; the same principle, I say, naturally discovered itself in foreign politics, and soon raised enemies to the leading state, however moderate in the exercise of its authority.

The PERSIAN monarch was really in his force, a petty prince, compared to the GRECIAN republics; and therefore it behoved him, from views of safety more than from emulation, to interest himself in their quarrels, and to support the weaker side in every contest. This was the advice given by ALCIBIADES to TISSAPHERNES, and it prolonged near a century the date of the PERSIAN empire; till the neglect of it for a moment, after the first appearance of the aspiring genius of PHILIP, brought that lofty and frail edifice to the ground, with a rapidity of which there are few instances in the history of mankind.

The successors of ALEXANDER showed great jealousy of the balance of power; a jealousy founded on true politics and prudence, and which preserved distinct for several ages the partition made after the death of that famous conqueror. The fortune and ambition of ANTIGONUS threatened them anew with a universal monarchy; but their combination and their victory at IPSUS saved them. And in subsequent times, we find that, as the Eastern princes considered the GREEKS and MACEDONIANS as the only real military force, with whom they had any inter-

course, they kept always a watchful eye over that part of the world. The PTOLEMIES, in particular, supported first ARATUS and the ACHAEANS, and then CLEOMENES king of SPARTA, from no other view than as a counter-balance to the MACEDONIAN monarchs. For this is the account which POLYBIUS gives of the EGYPTIAN politics.

The reason, why it is supposed, that the ancients were entirely ignorant of the *balance of power*, seems to be drawn from the ROMAN history more than the GRECIAN; and as the transactions of the former are generally more familiar to us, we have thence formed all our conclusions. It must be owned, that the ROMANS never met with any such general combination or confederacy against them, as might naturally have been expected from the rapid conquests and declared ambition; but were allowed peaceably to subdue their neighbours, one after another, till they extended their dominion over the whole known world. Not to mention the fabulous history of their ITALIC wars; there was, upon HANNIBAL's invasion of the ROMAN state, a remarkable crisis, which ought to have called up the attention of all civilized nations. It appeared afterwards (nor was it difficult to be observed at the time) that this was a contest for universal empire; yet no prince or state seems to have been the least alarmed about the event or issue of the quarrel. PHILIP of MACEDON remained neuter, till he saw the victories of HANNIBAL; and then most inprudently formed an alliance with the conqueror, upon terms still more imprudent. He stipulated, that he was to assist the CARTHAGINIAN state in their conquest of ITALY; after which they engaged to send over forces into GREECE, to assist him in subduing the GRECIAN commonwealths.

The RHODIAN and ACHAEAN republics are much celebrated by ancient historians for their wisdom and sound policy; yet both of them assisted the ROMANS in their wars against PHILIP and ANTIOCHUS. And what may be esteemed still a stronger proof, that this maxim was not generally known in those ages; no ancient author has remarked the imprudence of these measures, nor has even blamed that absurd treaty above-mentioned, made by PHILIP with the CARTHAGINIANS. Princes and statesmen, in all ages, may, before-hand, be blinded in their reasonings with regard to events: But it is somewhat extraordinary, that historians, afterwards, should not form a sounder judgment of them.

MASSINISSA, ATTALUS, PRUSIAS, in gratifying their private passions, were, all of them, the instruments of the ROMAN greatness; and never seem to have suspected, that they were forging their own chains, while they advanced the conquests of their ally. A simple treaty and agreement between MASSINISSA and the CARTHAGINIANS, so much required by mutual interest, barred the ROMANS from all entrance into AFRICA, and preserved liberty to mankind.

The only prince we meet with in the ROMAN history, who seems to have understood the balance of power, is HIERO king of SYRACUSE. Though the ally of ROME, he sent assistance to the CARTHAGINIANS, during the war of the auxiliaries: "Esteeming it requisite," says POLYBIUS, "both in order to retain his dominions in SICILY, and to preserve the ROMAN friendship, that CARTHAGE should be safe; lest by its fall the remaining power should be able, without contrast or opposition, to execute every purpose and undertaking. And here he acted with great wisdom and prudence. For that is never, on any account, to be overlooked; nor ought such a force ever to be thrown into one hand, as to incapacitate the neighbouring states from defending their rights against it." Here is the aim of modern politics pointed out in express terms.

In short, the maxim of preserving the balance of power is founded so much on common sense and obvious reasoning, that it is impossible it could altogether have escaped antiquity, where we find, in other particulars, so many marks of deep penetration and discernment. If it was not so generally known and acknowledged as at present, it had, at least, an influence on all the wiser and more experienced princes and politicians. And indeed, even at present, however generally known and acknowledged among speculative reasoners, it has not, in practice, an authority much more extensive among those who govern the world.

After the fall of the ROMAN empire, the form of government, established by the northern conquerors, incapacitated them, in a great measure, for farther conquests, and long maintained each

state in its proper boundaries. But when vassalage and the feudal militia were abolished, mankind were anew alarmed by the danger of universal monarchy, from the union of so many kingdoms and principalities in the person of the emperor CHARLES. But the power of the house of AUSTRIA, founded on extensive but divided dominions, and their riches, derived chiefly from mines of gold and silver, were more likely to decay, of themselves, from internal defects, than to overthrow all the bulwarks raised against them. In less than a century, the force of that violent and haughty race was shattered, their opulence dissipated, their splendor eclipsed. A new power succeeded, more formidable to the liberties of EUROPE, possessing all the advantages of the former, and labouring under none of its defects; except a share of that spirit of bigotry and persecution, with which the house of AUSTRIA was so long, and still is so much infatuated.

In the general wars, maintained against this ambitious power, GREAT BRITAIN has stood foremost; and she still maintains her station. Beside her advantages of riches and situation, her people are animated with such a national spirit, and are so fully sensible of the blessings of their government, that we may hope their vigour never will languish in so necessary and so just a cause. On the contrary, if we may judge by the past, their passionate ardour seems rather to require some moderation; and they have oftener erred from a laudable excess than from a blameable deficiency.

In the *first* place, we seem to have been more possessed with the ancient GREEK spirit of jealous emulation, than actuated by the prudent views of modern politics. Our wars with FRANCE have been begun with justice, and even, perhaps, from necessity; but have always been too far pushed from obstinacy and passion. The same peace, which was afterwards made at RYSWICK in 1697, was offered so early as the year ninety-two; that concluded at UTRECHT in 1712 might have been finished on as good conditions at GERTRUYTEN-BERG in the year eight; and we might have given at FRANKFORT, in 1743, the same terms, which we were glad to accept of at AIX-LA-CHAPELLE in the year forty-eight. Here then we see, that above half of our wars with FRANCE, and all our public debts, are owing more to our own imprudent vehemence, than to the ambition of our neighbours.

In the *second* place, we are so declared in our opposition to FRENCH power, and so alert in defence of our allies, that they always reckon upon our force as upon their own; and expecting to carry on war at our expence, refuse all reasonable terms of accommodation. *Habent subjectos, tanquam suos : viles, ut alienos*. All the world knows, that the factious vote of the House of Commons, in the beginning of the last parliament, with the professed humour of the nation, made the queen of HUNGARY inflexible in her terms, and prevented that agreement with PRUSSIA, which would immediately have restored the general tranquility of EUROPE.

In the *third* place, we are such true combatants, that, when once engaged, we lose all concern for ourselves and our posterity, and consider only how we may best annoy the enemy. To mortgage our revenues at so deep a rate, in wars, where we were only accessories, was surely the most fatal delusion, that a nation, which had any pretension to politics and prudence, has ever yet been guilty of. That remedy of funding, if it be a remedy, and not rather a poison, ought, in all reason, to be reserved to the last extremity; and no evil, but the greatest and most urgent, should ever induce us to embrace so dangerous an expedient.

These excesses, to which we have been carried, are prejudicial; and may, perhaps, in time, become still more prejudicial another way, by begetting, as is usual, the opposite extreme, and rendering us totally careless and supine with regard to the fate of EUROPE. The ATHENIANS, from the most bustling, intriguing, warlike people of GREECE, finding their error in thrusting themselves into every quarrel, abandoned all attention to foreign affairs; and in no contest ever took part on either side, except by their flatteries and complaisance to the victor.

Enormous monarchies are, probably, destructive to human nature; in their progress, in their continuance, and even in their downfall, which never can be very distant from their establishment. The military genius, which aggrandized the monarchy, soon leaves the court, the capital, and the center of such a government; while the wars are carried on at a great distance, and interest so small a part of the state. The ancient nobility, whose affections attach them to their sovereign, live all at court; and never will accept of military employments, which would carry them to remote and barbarous frontiers, where they are distant both from their pleasures and their fortune. The arms of the state, must, therefore, be entrusted to mercenary strangers, without zeal, without attachment, without honour; ready on every occasion to turn them against the prince, and join each desperate malcontent, who offers pay and plunder. This is the necessary progress of human affairs: Thus human nature checks itself in its airy elevation: Thus ambition blindly labours for the destruction of the conqueror, of his family, and of every thing near and dear to him. The BOURBONS, trusting to the support of their brave, faithful, and affectionate nobility, would push their advantage, without reserve or limitation. These, while fired with glory and emulation, can bear the fatigues and dangers of war; but never would submit to languish in the garrisons of HUNGARY or LITHUANIA, forgot at court, and sacrificed to the intrigues of every minion or mistress, who approaches the prince. The troops are filled with CRAVATES and TARTARS, HUSSARS and COSSACS; intermingled, perhaps, with a few soldiers of fortune from the better provinces: And the melancholy fate of the ROMAN emperors, from the same cause, is renewed over and over again, till the final dissolution of the monarchy.

37. Some Problems of International Systems Research

Morton A. Kaplan

This essay will attempt to provide a brief and non-technical account of some of the theoretical models employed in *System and Process in International Politics*, to indicate some of the problems of a theoretical nature to which these models give rise, and to provide a preliminary account of some research efforts that are intended to test these models. Although these models are not intended to deal with problems of political unification and do not permit a systematic exploration of that subject, the research so far conducted permits an occasional inference with respect to that subject and these will be adumbrated at the end of this paper.

1

A number of theoretical considerations underlie this essay. One is that some pattern of repeatable or characteristic behavior does occur within

Excerpted from "Some Problems of International Systems Research," by Morton A. Kaplan, first published in *International Political Communities: An Anthology* (Garden City, N.Y.: Anchor, 1966), pp. 469–486. Reprinted by permission of the author. Footnotes deleted.

the international system. Another is that this behavior falls into a pattern because the elements of the pattern are internally consistent and because they satisfy needs that are both international and national in scope. A third is that international patterns of behavior are related, in ways that can be specified, to the characteristics of the entities participating in international politics and to the functions they perform. A fourth is that international behavior can also be related to other factors such as military and economic capability, communication and information, technological change, demographic change, and additional factors long recognized by political scientists.

Just as it is possible to build alternative models of political systems, e.g., democratic or totalitarian, and of family systems, e.g., nuclear families, extended families or monogamous or polygamous families, so it is possible to build different models of international systems. The models can be given an empirical interpretation and the specific propositions of the models can be tested.

The aspiration to state testable propositions in the field of international politics is useful provided some degree of caution is observed concerning the kinds of propositions one proposes to test. For instance, can a theory of international politics yield a prediction of a specific event like the Hungarian revolution of October 1956? The answer probably must be negative. Yet why make such a demand of theory?

Two basic limitations upon prediction in the physical sciences are relevant to this problem. In the first place, the mathematics of complicated interaction problems has not been worked out. For instance, the physical scientist can make accurate predictions based on general formulas with respect to the two-body problem, more complicated and less general predictions with respect to the three-body problem, and only very *ad hoc* predictions concerning larger numbers of bodies. The scientist cannot predict the path of a single molecule of gas in a tank of gas.

In the second place, the physical scientist's predictions are predictions concerning an isolated system. He does not predict that so much gas will be in the tank, that the temperature or pressure of the tank will not be changed by someone, or even that the tank will remain in the experimental room. He predicts what the characteristic behavior of the mass of gas molecules will be if stated conditions of temperature, pressure, etc., hold.

The engineer deals with systems in which many free variables enter. If he acts wisely—for instance, in designing aircraft—he works within the constraints imposed by the laws of physics. But many aspects of exact design stem from experiments in wind tunnels or practical applications of past experiences rather than directly from the laws of physical science.

A theory of international politics normally cannot be expected to predict individual actions, because the interaction problem is too complex and because there are too many free variables. It can be expected, however, to predict characteristic or modal behavior within a particular kind of international system. Moreover, the theory should be able to predict the conditions under which the system will remain stable, the conditions under which it will be transformed, and the kinds of transformations that may be expected to take place.

2

Six alternative models of international systems are presented in this section. These models do not exhaust the possibilities. They are, however, intended to explore the continuum of possibilities. In their present stage of development the models are heuristic. Yet, if they have some degree of adequacy, they may permit a more meaningful organization of existing knowledge and more productive organization of future research. Only two of the models—the "balance of power" system and the loose bipolar system—have historical counterparts.

"Balance of Power" System

The first system to be examined is the "balance of power" international system. Quotation marks are placed around the term to indicate its metaphoric character.

The "balance of power" international system is an international social system that does not have as a component a political sub-system. The actors within the system are exclusively national actors, such as France, Germany, Italy, etc. Five national actors—as a minimum—must fall within the classification "essential national actor" to enable the system to work.

The "balance of power" international system is characterized by the operation of the following essential rules, which constitute the characteristic behavior of the system: (1) increase capabilities, but negotiate rather than fight; (2) fight rather than fail to increase capabilities; (3) stop fighting rather than eliminate an essential actor; (4) oppose any coalition or single actor that tends to assume a position of predominance within the system; (5) constrain actors who subscribe to supranational organizational principles; and (6) permit defeated or constrained essential national actors to re-enter the system as acceptable role partners, or act to bring some previously inessential actor within the essential actor classification. Treat all essential actors as acceptable role partners.

The first two rules of the "balance of power" international system reflect the fact that no political sub-system exists within the international social system. Therefore, essential national actors must rely upon themselves or upon their allies for protection. However, if they are weak, their allies may desert them. Therefore, an essential national actor must ultimately be capable of protecting its own national values. The third essential rule illustrates the fact that other nations are valuable as potential allies. In addition, nationality may set limits on potential expansion.

The fourth and fifth rules give recognition to the fact that a predominant coalition or national actor would constitute a threat to the interests of other national actors. Moreover, if a coalition were to become predominant, then the largest member of that coalition might also become predominant over the lesser members of its own coalition. For this reason members of a successful coalition may be alienated; they may also be able to bargain for more from the losers than from their own allies.

The sixth rule states that membership in the system is dependent upon only behavior that corresponds with the essential rules or norms of the "balance of power" system. If the number of essential actors is reduced, the "balance of power" international system will become unstable. Therefore, maintaining the number of essential national actors above a critical lower bound is a necessary condition for the stability of the system. This is best done by returning to full membership in the system defeated actors or reformed deviant actors.

Although any particular action or alignment may be the product of "accidents," i.e., of the set of specific conditions producing the action or alignment, including such elements as chance meetings or personality factors, a high correlation between the pattern of national behavior and the essential rules of the international system would represent a confirmation of the predictions of the theory.

Just as any particular molecule of gas in a gas tank may travel in any direction, depending upon accidental bumpings with other molecules, particular actions of national actors may depend upon chance or random conjunctions. Yet, just as the general pattern of behavior of the gas may repre-

sent its adjustment to pressure and temperature conditions within the tank, the set of actions of national actors may correspond to the essential rules of the system when the other variables take the appropriate specified values.

By shifting the focus of analysis from the particular event to the type of event, seemingly accidental events may become part of a meaningful pattern. In this way, the historical loses its quality of uniqueness and is translated into the universal language of science.

The number of essential rules cannot be reduced. The failure of any rule to operate will result in the failute of at least one other rule. Moreover, at this level of abstraction, there does not seem to be any other rule that is interrelated with the specified set in this fashion.

Any essential rule of the system is in equilibrium with the remaining rules of the set. This does not imply that particular rules can appear only in one kind of international system. The first two rules, for instance, also apply to bloc leaders in the bipolar system. However, they are necessary to each of the systems and, in their absence, other rules of the two systems will be transformed.

The rules of the system are interdependent. For instance, the failure to restore or to replace defeated essential national actors eventually will interfere with the formation of coalitions capable of constraining deviant national actors or potentially predominant coalitions.

The equilibrium of the set of rules is not a continuous equilibrium but one that results from discrete actions over periods of time. Therefore, the possibility of some change operating to transform the system becomes great if sufficient time is allowed.

Apart from the equilibrium within the set of essential rules, there are two other kinds of equilibrium characteristic of the international system: the equilibrium between the set of essential rules and the other variables of the international system and the equilibrium between the international system and its environment or setting.

If the actors do not manifest the behavior indicated by the rules, the kind and number of actors will change. If the kind or number of actors changes, the behavior called for in the rules cannot be maintained. Some changes in capabilities and information, for instance, may be compatible with the rules of the system, while others may not. If the value of one variable changes—for instance, the capabilities of a given coalition—the system may not maintain itself unless the information of some of the actors changes correspondingly. Otherwise a necessary "counter-balancing" shift in alignment may not take place. Some shifts in the pattern of alliance may be compatible with the rules of the system and others may not.

The rules, in short, are equilibrium rules for the system. This does not, however, imply that the rules will be followed by the actors because they are equilibrium rules, unless an actor has an interest in maintaining the equilibrium of the system. The constraints on the actor must motivate it to behave consonantly with the rules; or, if one or more actors are not so motivated, the others must be motivated to act in a way which forces the deviant actors back to rule-consonant behavior. Thus the rules may be viewed normatively, that is, as describing the behavior which will maintain the equilibrium of the system or as predictive, that is, as predicting that actors will so behave if the other variables of the system and the environment are at their equilibrium settings. If the other variables of the system and the environment are not at their equilibrium settings, deviant behavior is expected.

It is relatively easy to find historical examples illustrating the operation of the "balance of power" system. The European states would have accepted Napoleon had he been willing to play according to the rules of the game. The restoration of the Bourbons permitted the application of rule three. Had this not been possible, the international system would immediately have become unstable. Readmission of France to the international system after restoration fulfilled rule six.

The European concert, so ably described by Mowat, illustrates rule one. The *entente cordiale* illustrates rule four and the history of the eighteenth and nineteenth centuries rule two. Perhaps the best example of rule three, however, can be found in the diplomacy of Bismarck at Sadowa, although his motivation was more complex than the rule alone would indicate. It is not the purpose of this essay to multiply historical illustrations. The reader can make his own survey to determine whether international behavior tended to correspond to these rules during the eighteenth and nineteenth centuries.

The changes in conditions that may make the "balance of power" international system unstable are: the existence of an essential national actor who does not play according to the rules of the game, such as one who acts contrary to the essential rules of the system; in the example discussed, a player who seeks hegemony; failures of information which prevent a national actor from taking the required measures to protect its own international position; capability changes that become cumulative and thus increase an initial disparity between the capabilities of essential national actors; conflicts between the prescriptions of different rules under some conditions; difficulties arising from the logistics of the "balancing" process, the small number of essential actors, or an inflexibility of the "balancing" mechanism.

An important condition for stability concerns the number of essential national actors. If there are only three, and if they are relatively equal in capability, the probability that two would combine to eliminate the third is relatively great. Although the two victorious nations would have an interest in limiting the defeat of the third and in restoring it to the system as an acceptable role partner, they might not do so. Since this might not happen, the penalty for being left out of an alliance would be high and even the hazards of being in an alliance relatively great. Even if a nation were in one alliance, it might be left out of the next. Therefore this would be a system in which each victorious nation might attempt to gain as much as it could from the war as a protection against what might happen in the next round. Moreover, each victorious nation would attempt to double-cross the other in order to obtain a differential advantage. There would be a premium upon deceit and dishonesty. On the other hand, the addition of some other nations to the system would remove many of the pressures and add to the stability of the system.

Coalitions with many members may thus regard loosely attached members with equanimity. The role of the non-member of the coalition will also be tolerated. When there are a large number of loosely attached actors or non-members of an alliance any change of alliance or addition to an alliance can be "counter-balanced" by the use of an appropriate reward or by the cognition by some national actor of danger to its national interest.

When, however, there are very few loosely attached or non-member actors, a change in or an addition to an alignment introduces considerable tension into the international system. Under these circumstances, it becomes difficult to make the necessary compensatory adjustments.

For the same reasons, coalition members will have more tolerance for the role of "balancer," i.e., the actor who implements rule four, if the international system has a large number of members and the alignments are fluid. Under these conditions, the "balancer" does not constitute a lethal threat to the coalition against which it "balances." If, however, there are only a few essential actors, the very act of "balancing" may create a permanent "unbalance." In these circumstances the tolerance of the system for the "balancing" role will be slight and the "balance of power" system will become unstable.

Instability may result, although the various national actors have no intention of overthrowing the "balance of power" system. The wars against Poland correspond to the rule directing the various national actors to increase their capabilities. Since Poland was not an essential national actor, it did not violate the norms of the system to eliminate Poland as an actor. The Polish spoils were divided among the victorious essential national actors. Nevertheless, even this co-operation among the esesential national actors had an "unbalancing" effect. Since the acquisitions of the victorious actors could not be equal—unless some exact method were found for weighting geographic, strategic, demographic, industrial, material factors, etc., and determining accurately how the values of these factors would be projected into the future—a differential factor making the system unstable could not easily be avoided.

Even the endeavor to defeat Napoleon and to restrict France to her historic limits had some effects of this kind. This effort, although conforming to rules four, five, and six, also aggrandized Prussia and hence upset the internal equilibrium among the German actors. This episode may have triggered the process which later led to Prussian hegemony within Germany and to German hegemony within Europe. Thus, a dynamic process was set off for which shifts within alignments or coalitions were not able to compensate.

The logistical or environmental possibilities for "balancing" may be decisive in determining whether the "balancing" role within the "balance of power" international system will be filled effectively. For example, even had it so desired, the Soviet Union could not have "balanced" Nazi pressure against Czechoslovakia without territorial access to the zone of potential conflict. In addition, the intervening actors—Poland and Rumania—and possibly also Great Britain and France regarded Soviet intervention as a threat to their national interests. Therefore, they refused to co-operate.

It is possible that a major factor accounting for British success in the "balancing" role in the nineteenth century lay in the fact that Great Britain was predominantly a naval power and had no territorial ambitions on the European continent. These facts increased the tolerance of other national actors for Britain's "balancing" role. As a preponderant maritime power, Great Britain could interfere with the shipping of other powers and could transport its small army; it also was able to use its naval capabilities to dispel invading forces. Even so, Palmerston discovered occasions on which it was difficult to play the "balancing" role either because it was difficult to make effective use of Britain's limited manpower or because other powers displayed little tolerance for the role.

The "balance of power" system has the following consequences. Alliances tend to be specific, of short duration, and to shift according to advantage and not according to ideology (even within war). Wars tend to be limited in objectives. There is a wide range of international law that applies universally within the system. Among the most significant rules of applicable law are those dealing with the rules of war and the doctrine of non-intervention.

The "balance of power" system in its ideal form is a system in which any combination of actors within alliances is possible so long as no alliance gains a marked preponderance in capabilities. The system tends to be maintained by the fact that even should any nation desire to become predominant itself, it must, to protect its own interests, act to prevent any other nation from accomplishing such an objective. Like Adam Smith's "unseen hand" of competition, the international system is policed informally by self-interest, without the necessity of a political sub-system.

The rise of powerful deviant actors, inadequate counter-measures by non-deviant actors, new international ideologies, and the growth of supranational organizations like the Communist bloc with its internationally organized political parties, sounded the death knell for the "balance of power" international system.

Loose Bipolar System

In its place, after an initial period of instability, the loose bipolar system appeared. This system differs in many important respects from the "balance of power" system. Supranational actors participate within the international system. These supranational actors may be bloc actors like NATO or the Communist bloc or universal actors like the United Nations. Nearly all national actors belong to the universal actor organization and many—including most of the major national actors—belong to one or the other of the major blocs. Some national actors, however, may be non-members of bloc organizations.

In distinction to the "balance of power" international system, in which the rules applied uniformly to all national actors, the essential rules of the loose bipolar system distinguish, for instance, between the role functions of actors who are members of blocs and those who are not.

In the "balance of power" system, the role of the "balancer" was an integrating role because it prevented any alliance from becoming predominant. In the ideal form of the system, any national actor is qualified to fill that role. In the loose bipolar system, however, the integrating role is a mediatory role. The actor filling it does not join on one side or the other but mediates between the contending sides. Therefore, only non-bloc members or universal actor organizations can fill the integrative role in the loose bipolar system.

The functioning of the loose bipolar system depends upon the organizational characteristics of the supranational blocs. If the two blocs are not hierarchically organized, the loose bipolar system tends to resemble the "balance of power" system, except that the shifting of alignments takes place around two fixed points. Such shifting is limited by the functional integration of facilities, since a shift may require the destruction of facilities and the reduction of the capabilities of the shifting national actor. Shifting in alignment tends also to be limited by geographic and other logistic considerations. Nevertheless, the bloc actors constitute relatively loose organizations and the international system itself develops a considerable flexibility.

If one bloc has some hierarchical organizational features and the other is not hierarchically organized, a number of consequences can be expected. The hierarchical or mixed hierarchical bloc will retain its membership, since functional integration will be so great that it would be difficult for satellite members to withdraw or to form viable national entities if they did. The relative permanence of membership in the bloc constitutes a threat to non-members. Therefore, such a bloc is unlikely to attract new members except as a consequence of military absorption or political conquest by a native political party which already had associate membership in the bloc through the medium of an international party organization. The relatively irreversible characteristics of membership in such a bloc constitute a threat to all other national actors, whether associated in a bloc or not.

The non-hierarchical bloc has a looser hold over its members but is more likely to enter into co-operative pacts of one kind or another with non-bloc members. The pressure emanating from the hierarchically organized bloc, however, is likely to force the non-hierarchical organized bloc to integrate its bloc activities more closely and to extend them to other functional areas, or alternatively is likely to weaken and undermine the bloc.

If both blocs subscribe to hierarchical integrating rules, their memberships become rigid and only uncommitted states can, by choosing an alignment, change the existing line-up. Any action of this sort, however, would tend to reduce the flexibility of the international system by eliminating nations not included in blocs. Non-bloc member actors therefore would be more likely to support one or the other of the blocs on specific issues than to support either in general. If both blocs are hierarchically organized, their goals are similar—hierarchical world organization—and incompatible, since only one can succeed in leading such a world system.

With only two major groupings in the bipolar system, any rapid change in military capabilities tends to make this system unstable. For this reason, possession of second-strike nuclear systems by both major blocs is a factor for stability within the system.

The rules of the loose bipolar system follow:

1. All blocs subscribing to hierarchical or mixed hierarchical integrating principles are to eliminate the rival bloc.

2. All blocs subscribing to hierarchical or mixed hierarchical integrating principles are to negotiate rather than to fight, to fight minor wars rather than major wars, and to fight major wars—under given risk and cost factors—rather than to fail to eliminate the rival bloc.

3. All bloc actors are to increase their capabilities relative to those of the opposing bloc.

4. All bloc actors subscribing to non-hierarchical organizational principles are to negotiate rather than to fight to increase capabilities, to fight minor wars rather than to fail to increase capabilities, but to refrain from initiating major wars for this purpose.

5. All bloc actors are to engage in major war rather than to permit the rival bloc to attain a position of preponderant strength.

6. All bloc members are to subordinate objectives of the universal actor to the objectives of their bloc in the event of gross conflict between these objectives but to subordinate the objectives of the rival bloc to those of the universal actor.

7. All non-bloc member national actors are to co-ordinate their national objectives with those of the universal actor and to attempt to subordinate the objectives of bloc actors to those of the universal actor.

8. Bloc actors are to attempt to extend the membership of their bloc but to tolerate the non-member position of a given national actor if the alternative

is to force that national actor to join the rival bloc or to support its objectives.

9. Non-bloc member national actors are to act to reduce the danger of war between the bloc actors.

10. Non-bloc members are to refuse to support the policies of one bloc actor as against the other except in their roles as members of a universal actor.

11. Universal actors are to reduce the incompatibility between the blocs.

12. Universal actors are to mobilize non-bloc member national actors against cases of gross deviation, e.g., resort to force by a bloc actor. This rule, unless counterbalanced by the other rules, would enable the universal actor to become the prototype of a universal international system.

Unlike the "balance of power" international system, there is a high degree of role differentiation in the loose bipolar system. If any of the roles is pursued to the exclusion of others, the system will be transformed. If one bloc actor eliminates another, the system may be transformed into a hierarchical system. If the universal actor performs its functions too well, the system may be transformed into a universal international system. Other variations are possible.

The consequences of the loose bipolar system are as follows. Alliances tend to be long-term, to be based on permanent and not on shifting interests, and to have ideological components. Wars, except for the fear of nuclears, would tend to be unlimited. However, the fears concerning nuclear escalation are so great that there is, in fact, a greater dampening of war than in the "balance of power" system. Thus, wars tend to be quite limited; and even limited wars are rare. In the field of law, there are fewer restrictions on intervention than in the "balance of power" system and the limitations which do exist stem largely from the fear of escalation. The universal organization is used primarily for mediation and to some extent for war dampening.

Tight Bipolar System

The tight bipolar international system represents a modification of the loose bipolar system in which non-bloc member actors and universal actors either disappear entirely or cease to be significant. Unless both blocs are hierarchically organized, however, the system will tend toward instability.

There is no integrative or mediatory role in the tight bipolar system. Therefore there will tend to be a high degree of dysfunctional tension in the system. For this reason, the tight bipolar system will not be a highly stable or well-integrated system.

Universal System

The universal international system might develop as a consequence of the functioning of a universal actor organization in a loose bipolar system. The universal system, as distinguished from those international systems previously discussed, would have a political system as a subsystem of the international social system. However, it is possible that this political system would be of the confederated type, i.e., that it would operate on territorial governments rather than directly on human individuals.

The universal international system would be an integrated and solidary system. Although informal political groupings might take place within the system, conflicts of interest would be settled according to the political rules of the system. Moreover a body of political officials and administrators would exist whose primary loyalty would be to the international system itself rather than to any territorial sub-system of the international system.

Whether or not the universal international system is a stable system depends upon the extent to which it has direct access to resources and facilities and upon the ratio between its capabilities and the capabilities of the national actors who are members of the system.

Hierarchical System

The hierarchical international system may be democratic or authoritarian in form. If it evolves from a universal international system—perhaps because the satisfactions arising from the successful operation of such a universal international system lead to a desire for an even more integrated

and solidary international system—it is likely to be a democratic system. If, on the other hand, the hierarchical system is imposed upon willing national actors by a victorious or powerful bloc, then the international system is likely to be authoritarian.

The hierarchical system contains a political system. Within it, functional lines of organization are stronger than geographical lines. This highly integrated characteristic of the hierarchical international system makes for greater stability. Functional cross-cutting makes it most difficult to organize successfully against the international system or to withdraw from it. Even if the constitution of the system were to permit such withdrawal, the integration of facilities over time would raise the costs of withdrawal too high.

Unit Veto System

Consider a world in which some twenty-odd nations have nuclear systems capable of a not incredible first strike. That is, each nation would have a nuclear system that would not completely reduce enemy forces in a first strike but that might nonetheless reduce the enemy forces so much, if everything went according to plan, that a war begun by a first strike might be contemplated. However, even a successful first strike would then leave a nation launching such an attack, because of its depleted arsenal, quite vulnerable to attack by a third nation—an attack that might not be unlikely either if its own attack had been without provocation or if the other nation were malevolent. In any event, the vulnerability of the attacker to subsequent attack by a third state would tend to inhibit such a first strike except in the most extremely provocative circumstances.

There would be little need for specific alliances in this world. To the extent that alliances did occur, one would expect them to be of a non-ideological nature. Nations might ally themselves in pacts establishing an obligation to retaliate against any "aggressor" who launched a nuclear attack, which exceeded certain specified proportions, against an alliance member.

In this system one does not expect large counter-value or counter-force wars. If nuclear weapons are used at all, they will tend to be used in limited retaliations for purposes of warning or in other strictly limited ways. The wars that do occur will tend to be non-nuclear and limited in geographic area and means of war-fighting. Sub-limited wars will occur more often than actual wars.

The system, however, might seem to have some potentiality for triggering wars or for catalytic wars. That is, if one nation engages in a counter-force attack, this in some views would likely trigger an attack on it by a third state. Or an anonymous attack or accident might catalyze a series of wars. These possibilities cannot be denied, particularly if tensions within the system become high. Nonetheless first strikes and accidental wars are unlikely because credible first-strike forces will not exist and because adequate command and control systems will be available. Thus the nuclear systems will be relatively stable against accidents. An anonymous attack will be a theoretical possibility but not a practicable one unless many nations develop polaris forces—that is, forces such than an attack cannot be attributed to a particular nation. Even so, it would seem difficult to identify the rational motive for attack in such a world. An anonymous attack would not seem to have any reasonable political motive, since, by definition, the aggressor could not identify himself and thus secure the benefits arising from threats. Numerous nervous rivals would remain, and the attack might very well trigger a holocaust.

Because of the adequacy of nuclear systems and the relative unimportance of alliances, when contrasted with the "balance of power" international system, interventions would not be as ominous as in that system and therefore would not be as strongly interdicted. But since the gains resulting from such interventions would be smaller than in the loose bipolar system, they are unlikely to become characteristic of this system.

The danger of escalation, moreover, would tend to limit them. If universal organizations exist in this system, they would act as mediators, as would non-involved states whether nuclear or non-nuclear. In general, though, the universal organization would have fewer and less important functions than in the loose bipolar system. Nations equipped with nuclear forces in the unit veto system will tend to be self-sufficient and to reject outside pressures, even in coming from universal organizations. In particular, the functions of the universal organization dealing with political change will tend to be minimized. This will be reinforced by the disappearance of the colonial question as an important issue in world politics.

The foreign policies of the great nuclear powers will tend to be isolationist. Alliances, as specified, will recede in importance. Hegemonial ambitions will be curbed—primarily by an obvious inability to achieve them. Protective functions will tend to be shifted to "other" shoulders, when aggression does occur, since no "natural" assignment of this function will be possible. (That is, almost any one of the nuclear powers could play the role; there is no particular pressure on any particular nation to assume it.)

One would expect nations such as the Soviet Union and China to be less revolutionary, as the prospects for revolutionary solidarity receded even further, and as the frictions between nuclear powers, regardless of ideology, increased. As a consequence nations such as the United States would have less incentive to resist changes in the status quo.

The domestic corollary of the above would involve publics suspicious of foreign nations, relatively uninterested in the morals of quarrels or in social change external to the nation, and lacking the assurance necessary for an articulated goal-oriented foreign policy. . . .

38.   The Power Transition

A.F.K. ORGANSKI

. . . It is claimed that a balance of power brings peace. We have seen that there were periods when an equal distribution of power between contenders actually existed or was thought to have existed by the parties involved, but examination revealed that these periods were the exception rather than the rule. Still closer examination reveals that they were periods of war, not periods of peace.

In the 18th century, the last century of the period called the golden age of the balance of power, there were constant wars. In the 19th century, after the Napoleonic Wars, there was almost continuous peace. The balance of power is usually given a good share of the credit for this peaceful century, but as we have seen, there was no balance at all, but rather a vast preponderance of power in the hands of England and France. A local balance of power between France and Germany erupted into the Franco-Prussion War, and German miscalculations that her power balanced that

Excerpted from *World Politics* by A.F.K. Organski (New York: Knopf, 1958), pp. 292–93, 325–33, 338. Copyright © 1958 by A.F.K. Organski. Reprinted by permission of Alfred A. Knopf, Inc. and the author.

of her probable enemies resulted in World War I, bringing an end to the century of peace.

In the years between the two World Wars, we again and peace and a preponderance of power on the side of the Allies. Once Germany rose again to the point where the power of the Axis nations in fact approximated that of the European allies, war broke out again, the attack predicated on the erroneous assumption that the power of the United States was not involved. Now we are again in the period of peace, where the United States holds the preponderance of power.

The relationship between peace and the balance of power appears to be exactly the opposite of what has been claimed. The periods of balance, real or imagined, are periods of warfare, while the periods of known preponderance are periods of peace. If this is true, the time to worry about the dangers of a third world war is not now, when the predominance of the West is so obvious, but in the future, when industrialization may bring the Communist world abreast of us in power.

The claim that a balance of power is conducive to peace does not stand up. Indeed, it is not even logical. It stands to reason that nations will not fight unless they believe they have a good chance of winning, but this is true for both sides only when the two are fairly evenly matched, or at least when they believe they are. Thus a balance of power increases the chances of war. A preponderance of power on one side, on the other hand, increases the chances for peace, for the greatly stronger side need not fight at all to get what it wants, while the weaker side would be plainly foolish to attempt to battle for what it wants. . . . [One of] the conditions that make for international peace. . . is *not* an equal distribution of power.

There is one last point that must be raised about the balance of power. According to the theory, the danger of aggression is to be expected from the stronger nation. A powerful nation intent on maximizing its power is expected to press its advantage and make war upon its neighbors if it ever succeeds in achieving a clear preponderance of power. Here again, the facts do not back up the theory. Nations with preponderant power have indeed dominated their neighbors, but they have not been the ones to start the major wars that have marked recent history. This role has fallen almost without exception to the weaker side. The theory of the balance of power provides no possible explanation for Germany's action in the two World Wars or for Japan's attack upon the United States. It does not explain the two great wars of recent history. . . .

We are now in position to understand more clearly why the usual distribution of power in the world has not been a balance but rather a preponderance of power in the hands of one nation and its allies. And we can understand why world peace has coincided with periods of unchallenged supremacy of power while the periods of approximate balance have been the periods of war. As we have noted, wars occur when a great power in a secondary position challenges the top nation and its allies for control. Thus the usual major conflict is between the top nation (and its allies) and the challenger that is about to catch up with it in power.

In some respects the international order has striking similarities with that of a national society; it is legitimized by an ideology and rooted in the power differential of the groups that compose it.

Peace is possible only when those possessing preponderant power are in firm control and are satisfied with the *status quo* or with the way in which it promises to develop in a peaceful context. Peace is threatened whenever a powerful nation is dissatisfied with the *status quo* and is powerful enough to attempt to change things in the face of opposition from those who control the existing international order.

Degree of power and degree of satisfaction, then, become important national characteristics to be considered when trying to locate the nations that are most likely to disturb world peace. We can classify all the nations of the world in terms of these two characteristics, achieving four categories which turn out to be of major importance in international politics.

CLASSIFICATION OF NATIONS: 1. THE POWERFUL AND SATISFIED

The international order is best visualized if one thinks of a pyramid with one nation at the top and many nations at the bottom. Those at the top of the pyramid are most powerful and those at the bottom least powerful. As we move downward in terms of power, the number of nations in each layer is greater than the number in the layer above it. . . .

Together, the dominant nation and the great powers allied with it make up our first group of nations: the powerful and the satisfied. At present, this group includes the United States, Britain, France (though France is falling fast into the position of a middle power), and, since their defeat in World War II, Western Germany, Italy, and Japan. Satisfaction is, of course, a relative term. Perhaps no nation is ever completely satisfied, but in a general way it can be said that these nations are satisfied with the present international order and its working rules, for they feel that the present order offers them the best chance of obtaining the goals they have in mind. The dominant nation is necessarily more satisfied with the existing international order than with any other since it is to a large extent *her* international order. Other nations (such as England and France today) may be satisfied because they realized their full power potential before the present order was established, and thus their power assured them a full measure of what they regarded as their rightful share of benefits. Still other great powers (such as the defeated Axis powers) may be considered satisfied because they can no longer hope to achieve the domination they once sought and are thus content to accept a place in the international order that seems likely to allow them substantial rewards.

2. THE POWERFUL AND DISSATISFIED

Some of the great powers, however, are not satisifed with the way things are run on the international scene, and they make up our second category, that of the powerful and dissatisfied. From this group come the challengers who seek to upset the existing international order and establish a new order in its place. When nations are dissatisfied and at the same time powerful enough to possess the means of doing something about their dissatisfaction, trouble can be expected.

As we have seen in our brief historical sketch, the nations that are powerful and dissatisfied are usually nations that have grown to full power after the existing international order was fully established and the benefits already allocated. These parvenus had no share in the creation of the international order, and the dominant nation and its supporters are not usually willing to grant the newcomers more than a small part of the advantages they receive. Certainly they are unwilling to share the source of all their privileges: the rule of international society. To do so would be to abandon to a newcomer the preferred position they hold. As far as the dominant nation is concerned and, even more pointedly, as far as great nations that support the dominant nation are concerned, the challengers are to be kept in their place.

The challengers, for their part, are seeking to establish a new place for themselves in international society, a place to which they feel their growing power entitles them. Often these nations have grown rapidly in power and expect to continue to grow. They have reason to believe that they can rival or surpass in power the dominant

nation, and they are unwilling to accept a subordinate position in international affairs when dominance would give them much greater benefits and privileges.

A rapid rise in power thus produces dissatisfaction in itself. At the same time, a rapid rise in power is likely to be accompanied by dissatisfaction of a different sort. In the present period such rapid rises have been brought about largely through industrialization. Rapid industrialization, however, produces many internal strains and grievances, and the temptation is great for the national government of a nation undergoing such changes to channel some of the dissatisfaction into aggressive attitudes and actions toward the outside in order to divert criticism from the government or other powerful groups within the nation. Industrialization is the source of much of the international "trouble" of the present period, for it expands the aspirations of men and helps to make them dissatisfied with their lot and at the same time it increases their power to do something about their dissatisfactions, i.e., to wrest a greater share of the good things of life from those who currently control them.

The role of challenger, of course, is not a permanent role, nor is it one that all great powers go through. Some of the great powers never fill it. These are the nations that accept a supporting role in the dominant international order, nations we have classified as "powerful and satisfied." Dissatisfied, powerful nations, however, are likely to become challengers, at least for a time. Those who succeed become dominant (and so satisfied) nations eventually. Those who fail conclusively may fall back and accept a secondary supporting role in the international order they have tried to overturn, as Germany appears to have done after two defeats, thus joining the ranks of the satisfied and the powerful by a different path. However, as long as they remain outside the dominant international order and have hopes of overturning it or taking over its leadership through combat, such nations are serious threats to world peace. It is the powerful and dissatisfied nations that start world wars. . . .

Peace, then, is most likely to be maintained when the powerful and satisfied nations together with their allies enjoy a huge preponderance in power over the challenger and its allies, i.e., when the power of those who support the *status quo* is so great that no military challenge to them could hope to achieve success. War is most likely when the power of the dissatisfied challenger and its allies begins to approximate the power of those who support the *status quo*.

It must be stressed that such a peace is not necessarily a peace with justice. Protestations to the contrary notwithstanding, dominant nations are interested primarily in their own welfare, not in that of the rest of the world, and the two are not always compatible. Nor is the challenger necessarily on the side of right. Challengers often claim to speak for all of oppressed humanity, for all the underdogs who suffer under the existing international order, but they, too, are primarily interested in their own welfare, and once a new international order is successfully established, the underdogs are likely to find that they are still underdogs who have merely exchanged one set of world leaders for another.

Nor is peace exactly synonymous with the maintenance of the *status quo*. . . .[C]hange is constant. The international distribution of power is constantly shifting and with it many of the other arrangements that depend upon power. The possibilities of peaceful change should not be under estimated, but neither should the frequency with which major changes are brought about through war. As the challenger grows more powerful, it begins to demand new arrangements and changes in the international order which will give it a larger share of the benefits it desires. In theory, those who dominate the existing international order could make way for the newcomer and welcome it into the top ranks, giving up some of their privileges in the process. In practice, however, such action is rare. The challenger demands a place at the top and is rebuffed. Desiring change and unable to bring it about peacefully, the challenger all too often turns to war.

It might be expected that a wise challenger, growing in power through internal development, would hold back from threatening the existing international order until it had reached a point where it was as powerful as the dominant nation and its allies, for surely it would seem foolish to attack while weaker than the enemy. If this expectation were correct, the risk of war would be greatest when the two opposing camps were almost exactly equal in power, and if war broke out before this point, it would take the form of a preventive war launched by the dominant nation to knock off a competitor before it became strong enough to upset the existing international order.

In fact, however, this is not what has happened in recent history. Germany, Italy, and Japan attacked the dominant nation and its allies long *before* they equalled them in power, and the attack was launched by the challengers, not by the dominant camp. If history repeats itself, the next world war will be started by the Soviet Union and it will be launched *before* the Soviet bloc is as powerful as the United States and its allies, thus diminishing the chances of a Communist victory. However, history may not repeat itself, for the Soviet Union is not Germany, and there are other factors involved besides the relative power of the two camps. . . .

Thus wars are most likely when there is an approaching balance of power between the dominant nation and a major challenger. However, there are other factors which also operate to make war more or less likely. Specifically, war is most apt to occur: if the challenger is of such a size that at its peak it will roughly equal the dominant nation in power; if the rise of the challenger is rapid; if the dominant nation is inflexible in its policies; if there is no tradition of friendship between the dominant nation and the challenger; and if the challenger sets out to replace the existing international order with a competitive order of its own.

10

NUCLEAR DETERRENCE AND POLITICO-MILITARY STRATEGY

39. On the Nature of War

KARL VON CLAUSEWITZ

WHAT IS WAR?

1. Introduction.

We propose to consider first the single elements of our subject, then each branch or part, and, last of all, the whole, in all its relations—therefore to advance from the simple to the complex. But it is necessary for us to commence with a glance at the nature of the whole, because it is particularly necessary that in the consideration of any of the parts their relation to the whole should be kept constantly in view.

2. Definition.

We shall not enter into any of the abstruse definitions of War used by publicists. We shall keep to the element of the thing itself, to a duel. War is nothing but a duel on an extensive scale.

_____

From *On War*, Book I, Chap. 1, the J.J. Graham translation of 1874, republished in London in 1909.

If we would conceive as a unit the countless number of duels which make up a War, we shall do so best by supposing to ourselves two wrestlers. Each strives by physical force to compel the other to submit to his will: each endeavours to throw his adversary, and thus render him incapable of further resistance.

War therefore is an act of violence intended to compel our opponent to fulfil our will.

Violence arms itself with the inventions of Art and Science in order to contend against violence. Self-imposed restrictions, almost imperceptible and hardly worth mentioning, termed usages of International Law, accompany it without essentially impairing its power. Violence, that is to say, physical force (for there is no moral force without the conception of States and Law), is therefore the *means*; the compulsory submission of the enemy to our will is the ultimate *object*. In order to attain this object fully, the enemy must be disarmed, and disarmament becomes therefore the immediate object of hostilities in theory. It takes the place of the final object, and puts it aside as something we can eliminate from our calculations.

3. Utmost Use of Force.

Now, philanthropists may easily imagine there is a skilful method of disarming and overcoming an enemy without causing great bloodshed, and that this is the proper tendency of the Art of War. However plausible this may appear, still it is an error which must be extirpated; for in such dangerous things as War, the errors which proceed from a spirit of benevolence are the worst. As the use of physical power to the utmost extent by no means excludes the co-operation of the intelligence, it follows that he who uses force unsparingly, without reference to the bloodshed involved, must obtain a superiority if his adversary uses less vigour in its application. The former then dictates the law to the latter, and both proceed to extremities to which the only limitations are those imposed by the amount of counteracting force on each side.

This is the way in which the matter must be viewed and it is to no purpose, it is even against one's own interest, to turn away from the considertion of the real nature of the affair because the horror of its elements excites repugnance. . . .

Therefore, if we find civilised nations do not put their prisoners to death, do not devastate towns and countries, this is because their intelligence exercises greater influence on their mode of carrying on War, and has taught them more effectual means of applying force than these rude acts of mere instinct. The invention of gunpowder, the constant progress of improvements in the construction of firearms, are sufficient proofs that the tendency to destroy the adversary which lies at the bottom of the conception of War is in no way changed or modified through the progress of civilisation.

We therefore repeat our proposition, that War is an act of violence pushed to its utmost bounds[1]; as one side dictates the law to the other, there arises a sort of reciprocal action, which logically

---

[1] By this Clausewitz means that there is no limit to the use of force.—ED.

must lead to an extreme. This is the first reciprocal action, and the first extreme with which we meet.

4. The Aim Is to Disarm the Enemy.

We have already said that the aim of all actions in War is to disarm the enemy, and we shall now show that this, theoretically at least, is indispensable.

If our opponent is to be made to comply with our will, we must place him in a situation which is more oppressive to him than the sacrifice which we demand; but the disadvantages of this position must naturally not be of a transitory nature, at least in appearance, otherwise the enemy, instead of yielding, will hold out, in the prospect of a change for the better. Every change in this position which is produced by a continuation of the War should therefore be a change for the worse. The worst condition in which a belligerent can be placed is that of being completely disarmed. . . .

. . . As long as the enemy is not defeated, he may defeat me; then I shall be no longer my own master; he will dictate the law to me as I did to him. This is the second reciprocal action, and leads to a second extreme.

5. Utmost Exertion of Powers.

If we desire to defeat the enemy, we must proportion our efforts to his powers of resistance. This is expressed by the product of two factors which cannot be separated, namely, *the sum of available means* and *the strength of the Will*. The sum of the available means may be estimated in a measure, as it depends (although not entirely) upon numbers; but the strength of volition is more difficult to determine, and can only be estimated to a certain extent by the strength of the motives. Granted we have obtained in this way an approximation to the strength of the power to be contended with, we can then take a review of our own means, and either increase them so as to obtain a preponderance, or, in case we have not the resources to effect this, then do our best by increasing our means as far as possible. But the adversary does the same; therefore, there is a new mutual enhancement, which, in pure conception, must create a fresh effort towards an extreme. This is the third case of reciprocal action, and a third extreme with which we meet.

6. Modification in the Reality.

Thus reasoning in the abstract, the mind cannot stop short of an extreme, because it has to deal with an extreme, with a conflict of forces left to themselves, and obeying no other but their own inner laws. If we should seek to deduce from the pure conception of War an absolute point for the aim which we shall propose and for the means which we shall apply, this constant reciprocal action would involve us in extremes, which would be nothing but a play of ideas produced by an almost invisible train of logical subtleties. . . . But everything takes a different shape when we pass from abstractions to reality. . . .

7. War Is Never an Isolated Act.

With regard to the first point, neither of the two opponents is an abstract person to the other, not even as regards that factor in the sum of resistance which does not depend on objective things, viz., the Will. This Will is not an entirely unknown quantity; it indicates what it will be to-morrow by what it is to-day. War does not spring up quite suddenly, it does not spread to the full in a moment, each of the two opponents can, therefore, form an opinon of the other, in a great measure, from what he is and what he does, instead of judging of him according to what he, strictly speaking, should be or should do. . . .thus these deficiencies, having an influence on both sides, become a modifying principle.

8. War Does Not Consist of a Single Instantaneous Blow.

The second point gives rise to the following considerations:

If War ended in a single solution, or a number of simultaneous ones, then naturally all the preparations for the same would have a tendency to the extreme, for an omission could not in any way be repaired; the utmost, then, that the world of reality could furnish as a guide for us would be the preparations of the enemy, as far as they are known to us; all the rest would fall into the domain of the abstract. But if the result is made up from several successive acts, then naturally that which precedes with all its phases may be taken as a measure for that which will follow, and in this manner the world of reality again takes the place of the abstract, and thus modifies the effort towards the extreme. . . .

. . . the possibility of gaining a later result causes men to take refuge in that expectation, owing to the repugnance in the human mind to making excessive efforts; and therefore forces are not concentrated and measures are not taken for the first decision with that energy which would otherwise be used. Whatever one belligerent omits from weakness, becomes to the other a real objective ground for limiting his own efforts, and thus again, through this reciprocal action, extreme tendencies are brought down to efforts on a limited scale.

9. The Result in War Is Never Absolute.

Lastly, even the final decision of a whole War is not always to be regarded as absolute. The conquered State often sees in it only a passing evil, which may be repaired in after times by means of political combinations. How much this must modify the degree of tension, and the vigour of the efforts made, is evident in itself.

10. The Probabilities of Real Life Take the Place of the Conceptions of the Extreme and the Absolute.

In this manner, the whole act of War is removed from the rigorous law of forces exerted to the utmost. If the extreme is no longer to be apprehended, and no longer to be sought for, it is left to the judgment to determine the limits for the efforts to be made in place of it, and this can only be done on the data furnished by the facts of the real world by the *laws of probability*. Once the belligerents are no longer mere conceptions, but individual States and Governments, once the War is no longer an ideal, but a definite substantial procedure, then the reality will furnish the data to compute the unknown quantities which are required to be found.

From the character, the measures, the situation of the adversary, and the relations with which he is surrounded, each side will draw conclusions by the law of probability as to the designs of the other, and act accordingly.

11. The Political Object Now Reappears.

Here the question which we had laid aside forces itself again into consideration (*see* No. 2), viz., *the political object of the War*. The law of the extreme, the view to disarm the adversary, to overthrow him, has hitherto to a certain extent usurped the place of this end or object. Just as this law loses its force, the political object must again come forward. If the whole consideration is a calculation of probability based on definite persons and relations, then the political object, being the original motive, must be an essential factor in the product. The smaller the sacrifice we demand from our opponent, the smaller, it may be expected, will be the means of resistance which he will employ; but the smaller his preparation, the smaller will ours require to be. Further, the smaller our political object, the less value shall we set upon it, and the more easily shall we be induced to give it up altogether.

Thus, therefore, the political object, as the original motive of the War, will be the standard for determining both the aim of the military force and also the amount of effort to be made. This it cannot be in itself, but is so in relation to both the belligerent States, because we are concerned with realities, not with mere abstractions. One and the same political object may produce totally different effects upon different people, or even upon the same people at different times; . . .

23. War Is Always a Serious Means for a Serious Object. Its More Particular Definition.

. . .The War of a community—of whole Nations, and particularly of civilised Nations—always starts from a political condition, and is called forth by a political motive. It is, therefore, a political act. Now if it was a perfect, unrestrained, and absolute expression of force, as we had to deduce it from its mere conception, then the moment it is called forth by policy it would step into the place of policy, and as something quite independent of it would set it aside, and only follow its own laws, just as a mine at the moment of explosion cannot be guided into any other direction than that which has been given to it by preparatory arrangements. This is how the thing has really been viewed hitherto, whenever a want of harmony between policy and the conduct of a War has led to theoretical distinctions of the kind. But it is not so, and the idea is radically false. War in the real world, as we have already seen, is not an extreme thing which expends itself at one single discharge; it is the operation of powers which do not develop themselves completely in the same manner and in the same measure, but which at one time expand sufficiently to overcome the resistance opposed by inertia or friction, while at another they are too weak to produce an effect; it is therefore, in a certain measure, a pulsation of violent force more or less vehement, consequently making its discharges and exhausting its powers more or less quickly—in other words, conducting more or less quickly to the aim, but always lasting long enough to admit of influence being exerted on it in its course, so as to give it this or that direction, in short, to be subject to the will of a guiding intelligence. Now, if we reflect that War has its root in a political object, then naturally this original motive which called it into existence should also continue the first and highest consideration in its conduct. Still, the political object is no despotic lawgiver on that account; it must accommodate itself to the nature of the means, and though changes in these means may involve modification in the political objective, the latter always retains a prior right to consideration. Policy, therefore, is interwoven with the whole action of War, and must exercise a continuous influence upon it, as far as the nature of the forces liberated by it will permit.

24. War Is a Mere Continuation of Policy by Other Means.

We see, therefore, that War is not merely a political act, but also a real political instrument, a continuation of political commerce, a carrying out of the same by other means. All beyond this which is strictly peculiar to War relates merely to the peculiar nature of the means which it uses. That the tendencies and views of policy shall not be incompatible with these means, the Art of War in general and the Commander in each particular case may demand, and this claim is truly not a trifling one. But however powerfully this may react on political views in particular cases, still it must always be regarded as only a modification of them; for the political view is the object, War is the means, and the means must always include the object in our conception.

25. Diversity in the Nature of Wars.

The greater and the more powerful the motives of a War, the more it affects the whole existence of a people. The more violent the excitement which precedes the War, by so much the nearer will the War approach to its abstract form, so much the more will it be directed to the destruction of the enemy, so much the nearer will the military and political ends coincide, so much the more purely military and less political the War appears

to be; but the weaker the motives and the tensions, so much the less will the natural direction of the military element—that is, force—be coincident with the direction which the political element indicates; so much the more must, therefore, the War become diverted from its natural direction, the political object diverge from the aim of an ideal War, and the War appear to become political. . . .

27. Influence of this View on the Right Understanding of Military History, and on the Foundations of Theory.

We see, therefore, in the first place, that under all circumstances War is to be regarded not as an independent thing, but as a political instrument; and it is only by taking this point of view that we can avoid finding ourselves in opposition to all military history. This is the only means of unlocking the great book and making it intelligible. Secondly, this view shows us how Wars must differ in character according to the nature of the motives and circumstances from which they proceed. . . .

40.   The Three Types of Deterrence

HERMAN KAHN

TYPE 1 DETERRENCE (DETERRENCE AGAINST A DIRECT ATTACK)

It is important to distinguish three types of deterrence. The first of these is: Type 1 Deterrence, or deterrence against a direct attack.

Most experts today argue that we must make this type of deterrence work, that we simply cannot face the possibility of a failure. Never have the stakes on success or failure of prevention been so high. Although the extreme view, that deterrence is everything and that alleviation is hope-is questionable, clearly Type 1 Deterrence must have first priority.

Typically, discussions of the capability of the United States to deter a direct attack compare the pre-attack inventory of our forces with the pre-attack inventory of the Russian forces—that is, the number of planes, missiles, army divisions, and

submarines of the two countries are directly compared. This is a World War I and World War II approach.

The really essential numbers, however, are estimates of the damage that the retaliatory forces can inflict after being hit. Evaluation must take into account that the Russians could strike *at a time and with tactics of their choosing*. We strike back with a *damaged* and perhaps *un-co-ordinated* force which must conduct its operations in the *post-attack environment*. The Soviets may use *blackmail* threats to intimidate our response. The Russian defense is completely *alerted*. If the strike has been preceded by a tense period, their active defense forces have been *augmented* and their cities have been at least partially *evacuated*. Any of the emphasized words can be very important, but almost all of them are ignored in most discussions of Type 1 Deterrence.

The first step in this calculation—analysis of the effects of the Russian strike on U.S. retaliatory ability—depends critically on the enemy's tactics and capabilities. The question of warning is generally uppermost. Analyses of the effect of the

Excerpted from "The Nature and Feasibility of War and Deterrence," by Herman Kahn, in Walter Hahn and John Neff, eds., *American Strategy in the Nuclear Age* (Garden City, N.Y.: Anchor, 1960), pp. 225–229, 233–237. Reprinted by permission of the author.

enemy's first strike often neglect the most important part of the problem by assuming that warning will be effective and that our forces get off the ground and are sent on their way to their targets. Actually, without effective warning, attrition on the ground can be much more important than attrition in the air. The enemy may not only use tactics that limit our warning but he may do other things to counter our defensive measures, such as interfering with command and control arrangements. Thus it is important in evaluating enemy capabilities to look not only at the tactics that past history and standard assumptions lead us to expect but also at any other tactics that a clever enemy might use. We should not always assume what Albert Wohlstetter has called "U.S.-preferred attacks" in estimating the performance of our system. We should also look at "U.S.S.R.-preferred attacks"—a sensible Soviet planner may prefer them!

The enemy, by choosing the timing of an attack, has several factors in his favor. He can select a *time* calculated to force our manned-bomber force to retaliate in the daytime, when his day fighters and his air-defense systems will be much more effective. In addition, he can choose the *season* so that his post-war agricultural problems and fallout-protection problems will be less difficult.

The second part of the calculation—consequences of the lack of co-ordination of the surviving U.S. forces—depends greatly on our tactics and the flexibility of our plans. If, for example, our offensive force is assigned a large target system, so that it is spread thinly, and if because of a large or successful Russian attack the Russians have succeeded in destroying much of our force, many important Russian targets would go unattacked. If, on the other hand, to avoid this we double or triple the assignment to important targets, we might overdestroy many targets, especially if the Soviets had not struck us successfully. For this and other reasons, it would be wise to evaluate the damage and then retarget the surviving forces. Whether this can be done depends critically on the timing of the attack, the nature of the targeting process, and our post-attack capability for evaluation, command, and control. . . .

Another point that may be of great importance is that modern nuclear weapons are so powerful that even if they don't destroy their target, they may change the environment so as to cause the retaliating weapons to be inoperable. The various effects of nuclear weapons include blast, thermal and electromagnetic radiation, ground shock, debris, dust, and ionizing radiation—any of which may affect people, equipment, propagation of electromagnetic signals, and so on. One might say that the problem of operating in a post-attack environment after training in the peacetime environment is similar to training at the Equator and then moving a major but incomplete part (that is, a damaged system) to the Arctic and expecting this incomplete system to work efficiently the first time it is tried. This is particularly implausible if, as is often true, the intact system is barely operable at the Equator (that is, in peacetime).

In addition to attacking the system, the enemy may attempt to attack our resolve. Imagine, for example, that we had a pure Polaris system invulnerable to an all-out simultaneous enemy attack (invulnerable by assumption and not by analysis) and the enemy started to destroy our submarines one at a time at sea. Suppose an American President were told that if we started an all-out war in retaliation, the Soviets could and would destroy every American because of limitations in our offense and our active and passive defenses. Now if the President has a chance to think about the problem, he simply cannot initiate this kind of war even with such provocation.

One of the most important and yet the most neglected elements of the retaliatory calculation is the effect of the Russian civil-defense measures. The Russians are seldom credited with even modest preparedness in civil defense. A much more reasonable alternative that would apply in many situations—that the Russians might at some point evacuate their city population to places affording existing or improvisable fallout protection—is almost never realistically examined. If the Russians should take steps to evacuate their cities, the vulnerability of their population would be dramatically reduced.

The Soviets also know that they can take an enormous amount of economic damage and be set back only a few years in their development. Not only did they do something like this after World War II, but, what is even more impressive, they fought a war *after* the Germans had destroyed most of their existing military power and occupied an area that contained about 40 per cent of the prewar Soviet population—the most industrialized 40 per cent.

The difficulties of Type 1 Deterrence arise mainly from the fact that the deterring nation must strike second. These difficulties are compounded by the rapidity with which the technology of war changes and the special difficulty the defender has in reacting quickly and adequately to changes in the offense. The so-called missile gap illustrates the problem. The Russians announced in August 1957 that they had tested an ICBM. Evidence of their technical ability to do this was furnished by Sputnik I, sent aloft in October of that year. Early in 1959 Khrushchev boasted that the Soviet Union had intercontinental rockets in serial production. We have little reason to believe that they won't have appreciable numbers of operational ICBMs about three years after their successful test— which would be in August 1960. . . .

TYPE 2 DETERRENCE (DETERRENCE OF EXTREME PROVOCATION)

A quite different calculation is relevant to U.S. Type 2 Deterrence, although it is still a Soviet calculation (but this time a Soviet calculation of an American calculation). Type 2 Deterrence is defined as using strategic threats to deter an enemy from engaging in very provocative acts other than a direct attack on the United States itself. The Soviet planner asks himself: If I make this very provocative move, will the Americans strike us? Whether the Soviets then proceed with the contemplated provocation will be influenced by their estimate of the American calculation as to what happens if the tables are reversed. That is, what happens if the Americans strike and damage the Russian strategic air force and the Russians strike back un-co-ordinated in the teeth of an alerted U.S. air defense and possibly against an evacuated U.S. population? If this possibility is to be credible to the Soviets, it must be because they recognize that their own Type 1 Deterrence can fail. If Khrushchev is a convinced adherent of the balance-of-terror theory and does not believe that his Type 1 Deterrence can fail, then he may just go ahead with the provocative action.

It is important to realize that the operation of Type 2 Deterrence will involve the possibility that the United States will obtain the first strategic strike or some temporizing move, such as evacuation. Many people talk about the importance of having adequate civil and air defense to back our foreign policy. However, calculations made in evaluating the performance of a proposed civil- and air-defense program invariably assume a Russian surprise attack and—to make the problem even harder—a surprise attack directed mostly against civilians. This is unnecessarily pessimistic. The calculation in which one looks at a U.S. first strike in retaliation for a Russian provocation is probably more relevant in trying to evaluate the role that the offense and defense play in affecting some important aspects of foreign policy.

Under this assumption, if we have even a moderate nonmilitary defense program, its performance is likely to look impressive to the Russians and probably to most Europeans. For example, the crucial problem of obtaining adequate warning will have been greatly lessened, at least in the eyes of the Soviets. They are also likely to think that we have more freedom than we will have. The Soviets may believe that we are not worried by the possibility that they will get strategic or premature tactical warning. This could be true in spite of the fact that in actual practice such an attack would probably involve a considerable risk that the Soviets would get some warning. Any planning would have to be tempered by the sobering realization that a disclosure or mistake could bring a pre-emptive Russian attack.

The possibility of augmenting our active and passive defense is very important. That is, rather than striking the Russians if they do something very provocative, we might prefer to evacuate our city population to fallout protection, "beef up" our air defense and air offense, and then tell the Russians that we had put ourselves into a much stronger position to initiate hostilities. After we had put ourselves in a position in which the Russian retaliatory strike would inflict much less than a total catastrophe, the Russians would have just three broad classes of alternatives:

1. To initiate some kind of strike.
2. To prolong the crisis, even though it would then be very credible that we would strike if they continued to provoke us.
3. To back down or compromise the crisis satisfactorily.

Hopefully the Soviets would end up preferring the third alternative, because our Type 1 Deterrence would make the first choice sufficiently unattractive and our Type 2 Deterrence would do the same for the second.

TYPE 3 DETERRENCE (DETERRENCE OF MODERATE PROVOCATION)

Type 3 Deterrence might be called "*tit-for-tat* deterrence." It refers to those acts that are deterred because the potential aggressor is afraid that the defender or others will then take limited actions, military or nonmilitary, that will make the aggression unprofitable.

The most obvious threat that we could muster under Type 3 Deterrence would be the capability to fight a limited war of some sort. Because this subject is complicated and space is limited, I will not discuss this particular Type 3 Deterrence capability—although it is important and necessary. Instead, I shall consider some of the nonmilitary gambits open to us.

Insofar as day-to-day activities are concerned, the things that seemingly regulate the other man's behavior are nonmilitary. For example, among other things, a potential provocation may be deterred by any of the following effects or reactions:

1. Internal reactions or costs.
2. Loss of friends or antagonizing of neutrals.
3. Creation or strengthening of hostile coalitions.
4. Lowering of the reaction threshold of potential opponents.
5. Diplomatic or economic retaliation.
6. Moral or ethical inhibitions.
7. An increase in the military capability of the potential opponent.

Space permits discussion of only the last subject, which is both very important and badly neglected. It has become fashionable among the more sober military experts to regard mobilization capabilities as examples of wishful thinking. And indeed, in the few *hours* or *days* of a modern war, large-scale production of military goods will not be possible.

What deters the Russians from a series of Koreas and Indochinas? It is probably less the fear of a direct U.S. attack with its current forces than the probability that the United States and her allies would greatly increase both their military strength and their resolve in response to such crises. The deterrent effect of this possibility can be increased by making explicit preparations so that we can increase our strength very rapidly whenever the other side provokes us. For example, in June 1950 the United States was engaged in a great debate on whether the defense budget should be 14, 15, or 16 billion dollars. Along came Korea. Congress quickly authorized 60 billion dollars, an increase by a factor of four!

No matter what successes the Communist cause had in Korea, that authorization represents an enormous military defeat for the Soviets. However, it was almost three years before that authorization was fully translated into increased expenditures and corresponding military power. It is very valuable to be able to increase our defense expenditures, but this ability becomes many times more valuable if authorizations can be translated into military strength in a year or so. If the Russians know that deterioration in international relations will push us into a crash program, they may be much less willing to let international relations deteriorate. The problem is: Would we have time to put in a useful program? After all, the basic military posture (including installations) must be of the proper sort if it is to be possible to expand it within a year or so to the point where it is prepared to fight a war in addition to being able to deter one. Our current posture (1960) is probably far from optimal for doing this.

If preparations like these were at least moderately expensive and very explicit, the Russians might find it credible that the United States would initiate and carry through such a program if they were provocative even, say, on the scale of Korea or less. The Russians would then be presented with the following three alternatives:

1. They could strike the United States before the build-up got very far. This might look very unattractive, especially since the build-up would almost certainly be accompanied by an increased alert and other measures to reduce the vulnerability of SAC.
2. They could try to match the U.S. program. This would be very expensive.
3. They could accept a position of inferiority. Such an acceptance would be serious, since the United States would now have a "fight the war" capability as well as a "deter the war" capability.

In each case the costs and risks of their provocation would have been increased, and it is likely that the Soviets would take these extra costs and risks into account before attempting any provocation. If they were not deterred, we could launch the crash program. Then we would be in a position to correct the results of their past provocation or at least to deter them in the future from exploiting these results.

It might be particularly valuable to have credible and explicit plans to institute crash programs for civil defense and limited-war capabilities. It seems to be particularly feasible to maintain inexpensive and effective mobilization bases in these two fields, and the institution of a crash program would make it very credible to the Russians, our allies, and neutrals that we would go to war at an appropriate level if we were provoked again.

This is one of the major threats we can bring to bear on the Russians. If we are not aware that we have this threat, if we believe that doubling the budget would really mean immediate bankruptcy or other financial catastrophe, then the Russians can present us with alternatives that may in the end result in their winning the diplomatic, political, and foreign-policy victory. It is important that we understand our own strengths as well as our possible weaknesses.

41.   The Problems of Limited War

1

Perhaps the basic problem of strategy in the nuclear age is how to establish a relationship between a policy of deterrence and a strategy for fighting a war in case deterrence fails. From the point of view of its impact on the aggressor's actions, maximum deterrence can be equated with the threat of maximum destructiveness. From the point of view of a power's readiness to resist aggression, the optimum strategy is one which is able to achieve its goals at minimum cost. The temptation of strategic doctrine is to seek to combine the advantages of every course of action: to achieve maximum deterrence but also to do so at minimum risk.

Ever since the end of our atomic monopoly, however, this effort has been thwarted by the impossibility of combining maximum destructive-

ness with limited risk. The greater the horror of our destructive capabilities, the less certain has it become that they will in fact be used. In such circumstances deterrence is brought about not only by a physical but also by a psychological relationship: deterrence is greatest when military strength is coupled with the willingness to employ it. It is achieved when one side's readiness to run risks in relation to the other is high; it is least effective when the willingness to run risks is low, however powerful the military capability. It is, therefore, no longer possible to speak of military superiority in the abstract. What does "being ahead" in the nuclear race mean if each side can already destroy the other's national substance? What is the strategic significance of adding to the destructiveness of the nuclear arsenal when the enormity of present weapons systems already tends to paralyze the will?

Given the power of modern weapons, a nation that relies on all-out war as its chief deterrent imposes a fearful psychological handicap on itself. The most agonizing decision a statesman can face is whether or not to unleash all-out war; all pressures will make for hesitation, short of a direct

Excerpted from *Nuclear Weapons and Foreign Policy* by Henry A. Kissinger, pp. 114–125, 139–144. Copyright © 1957,1958 by Council on Foreign Relations, Inc. Published by Doubleday Anchor Books for the Council on Foreign Relations. Reprinted by permission of the Council on Foreign Relations.

attack threatening the national existence. And he will be confirmed in his hesitations by the conviction that, so long as his retaliatory force remains intact, no shift in the territorial balance is of decisive significance. Thus both the horror and the power of modern weapons tend to paralyze action: the former because it will make few issues seem worth contending for; the latter because it causes many disputes to seem irrelevant to the over-all strategic equation. The psychological equation, therefore, will almost inevitably operate against the side which can extricate itself from a situation *only* by the threat of all-out war. Who can be certain that, faced with the catastrophe of all-out war, even Europe, long the keystone of our security, will seem worth the price?

As the power of modern weapons grows, the threat of all-out war loses its credibility and therefore its political effectiveness. Our capacity for massive retaliation did not avert the Korean War, the loss of northern Indochina, the Soviet-Egyptian arms deal, or the Suez crisis. Moreover, whatever the credibility of our threat of all-out war, it is clear that all-out thermonuclear war does not represent a strategic option for our allies. Thus a psychological gap is created by the conviction of our allies that they have nothing to gain from massive retaliation and by the belief of the Soviet leaders that they have nothing to fear from our threat of it. . . .

The power of modern weapons thus forces our statesmanship to cope with the fact that absolute security is no longer possible. Whatever the validity of identifying deterrence with maximum retaliatory power, we will have to sacrifice a measure of destructiveness to gain the possibility of fighting wars that will not amount to national catastrophe. Policy, it has been said, is the science of the relative. The same is true of strategy, and to understand this fact, so foreign to our national experience, is the task history has set our generation.

2

What strategic doctrine is most likely to enable us to avoid the dilemma of having to make a choice between all-out war and a gradual loss of positions, between Armageddon and defeat without war? Is limited war a conceivable instrument of policy in the nuclear period? Here we must analyze precisely what is meant by limited war. . . .

A limited war . . . is fought for specific political objectives which, by their very existence, tend to establish a relationship between the force employed and the goal to be attained. It reflects an attempt to *affect* the opponent's will, not to crush it, to make the conditions to be imposed seem more attractive than continued resistance, to strive for specific goals and not for complete annihilation.

Limited war presents the military with particular difficulties. An all-out war is relatively simple to plan because its limits are set by military considerations and even by military capacity. . . .

The more the military plan on the basis of crushing the enemy even in a limited area, the more the political leadership will recoil before the risks of taking *any* military action. The more limited war is conceived as a "small" all-out war, the more it will produce inhibitions similar to those generated by the concept of massive retaliation. The prerequisite for a policy of limited war is to reintroduce the political element into our concept of warfare and to discard the notion that policy ends when war begins or that war can have goals distinct from those of national policy.

To what extent can the nuclear age leave room for a policy of intermediate objectives? Do any of the factors apply today which in the past made possible a diplomacy of limited objectives and a military policy of limited wars?

In the great periods of European cabinet diplomacy, between the Treaty of Westphalia and the French Revolution and between the Congress of Vienna and the outbreak of the First World War, wars were limited because there existed a political framework which led to a general acceptance of a policy of limited risks. . . .

Today, as we have seen, we lack both stable power relationships and a legitimate political order on whose tenets all major powers are agreed. But these shortcomings may be outweighed by a third factor, the fear of a thermonuclear war. Never have the consequences of all-out war been so obvious, never have the gains seemed so out of relation to the sacrifices. . . .

3

The conduct of limited war has two prerequisites: a doctrine and a capability. So long as we consider limited war as an aberration from the ''pure'' case of all-out war we will not be ready to grasp its opportunities and we will conduct the wars we do fight hesitantly and ambiguously, oscillating between the twin temptations to expand them (that is, to bring them closer to our notion of what war should be like) or to end them at the first enemy overture.

A doctrine for limited war will have to discard any illusions about what can be achieved by means of it. Limited war is not a cheaper substitute for massive retaliation. On the contrary, it must be based on an awareness that with the end of our atomic monopoly it is no longer possible to impose unconditional surrender at an acceptable cost.

The purpose of limited war is to inflict losses or to pose risks for the enemy out of proportion to the objectives under dispute. The more moderate the objective, the less violent the war is likely to be. This does not mean that military operations cannot go beyond the territory or the objective in dispute; indeed, one way of increasing the enemy's willingness to settle is to deprive him of something he can regain only by making peace. But the result of a limited war cannot depend on military considerations alone; it reflects an ability to harmonize political and military objectives. An attempt to reduce the enemy to impotence would surely lead to all-out war.

Nevertheless, a strategic doctrine which renounces the imposition of unconditional surrender should not be confused with the acceptance of a stalemate. The notion that there is no middle ground between unconditional surrender and the *status quo ante* is much too mechanical. To be sure, a restoration of the *status quo ante* is often the simplest solution, but it is not the only possible one. The argument that neither side will accept a defeat, however limited, without utilizing every weapon in its arsenal is contradicted both by psychology and by experience. There would seem to be no sense in seeking to escape a limited defeat through bringing on the cataclysm of an all-out war, particularly if all-out war threatens a

calamity far transcending the penalties of losing a limited war. It simply does not follow that because one side stands to lose from a limited war it could gain from an all-out war. On the contrary, both sides face the same dilemma: that the power of modern weapons has made all-out war useless as an instrument of policy, except for acts of desperation. . . .

There exist three reasons, then, for developing a strategy of limited war. First, limited war represents the only means for preventing the Soviet bloc, at an acceptable cost, from overrunning the peripheral areas of Eurasia. Second, a wide range of military capabilities may spell the difference between defeat and victory even in an all-out war. Finally, intermediate applications of our power offer the best chance to bring about strategic changes favorable to our side. . . .

6

Limited war is not simply a question of appropriate military forces and doctrines. It also places heavy demands on the discipline and subtlety of the political leadership and on the confidence of the society in it. For limited war is psychologically a much more complex problem than all-out war. In an all-out war the alternatives will be either surrender or unqualified resistance against a threat to the national existence. To be sure, psychological factors will largely determine the relative willingness to engage in an all-out war, and the side more willing to run risks may gain an important advantage in the conduct of diplomacy. However, once the decision to fight is taken, a nation's physical ability to conduct war will be the most important factor in the outcome.

In a limited war, on the other hand, the psychological equation will be of crucial importance, not only with respect to the decision to enter the war but throughout the course of military operations. A limited war among major powers can be kept limited only by the conscious choice of the protagonists. Either side has the physical power to expand it, and to the extent that each side is willing to increase its commitment in preference either to a stalemate or to a defeat, the war will gradually become an all-out one. The restraint which keeps a war limited is a psychological one: the consequences of a limited victory or a limited defeat or a stalemate—the three possible outcomes of a limited war—must seem preferable to the consequences of an all-out war.

In a limited war the choices are more varied than in an all-out conflict and their nature is more ambiguous. Victory offers no final solution, and defeat does not carry with it the penalty of national catastrophe. The side which is more willing to risk an all-out war or can convince its opponent of its greater readiness to run that risk is in the stronger position. Even when the willingness of both sides to run risks is equal at the beginning of the war, the psychological equation will constantly be shifting, depending on the course of military operations. Because the limitation of war is brought about by the fear of unleashing a thermonuclear holocaust, the psychological equation is, paradoxically, constantly shifting *against* the side which seems to be winning. The greater the transformation it seeks, the more plausible will become the threat by its opponent of launching an all-out war. The closer that the loser in a limited war is brought to the consequences which he would suffer by defeat in an all-out war, the less he will feel restrained from resorting to extreme measures.

At the same time, the winning side may become increasingly reluctant to test the opponent's willingness to resort to all-out war. The better its position, the more secure it will feel and the less it will be willing to take the risks of an all-out war. The more precarious the position of the losing side becomes, the more likely it will be to raise its commitment toward the level of an all-out war. Success in limited war requires, therefore, that the opponent be persuaded that national survival is not at stake and that a settlement is possible on reasonable terms. Otherwise the result is almost certain to be either stalemate or all-out war.

If an opponent attaches great importance to an area in dispute—or is thought to attach great importance to it—he will have a distinct psychological advantage in a limited war. This was the case with China's role in Korea. Some areas may be thought so important to one of the contenders that they will be protected by the belief of the opponent that any attack on them will lead to a general war.

Protection for these areas will be achieved less by local defense than by the over-all strategic balance. This has been the case up to now with Western Europe with respect to the United States or with the satellite regions with respect to the U.S.S.R. As total war poses increasingly ominous prospects, however, the over-all strategic balance will be a less and less adequate protection to threatened areas, for ever fewer regions will seem worth this price. As the implications of all-out war with modern weapons become better understood, security for many areas will increasingly depend on the capability for local action. Limited war would thereby become a test of the determination of the contenders, a gauge of the importance they attach to disputed issues. If one side attaches greater importance to an area or an issue and is willing to pay a higher price, and if it possesses a capability for waging a limited war, it may well achieve a favorable shift in the strategic equation.

The key to a successful policy of limited war is to keep the challenge to the opponent, whether diplomatic or military, below the threshold which would unleash an all-out war. The greater the risk in relation to the challenge, the less total the response is likely to be. The more the challenge approximates the risks posed by all-out war, the more difficult it will be to limit the conflict. A policy of limited war therefore presupposes three conditions: the ability to generate pressures other than the threat of all-out war; the ability to create a climate in which survival is not thought to be at stake in each issue; and the ability to keep control of public opinion in case disagreement arises over whether national survival is at stake. The first condition depends to a considerable extent on the flexibility of our military policy; the second on the subtlety of our diplomacy; the third will reflect the courage of our leadership. . . .

A long history of invulnerability has accustomed us to look at war more in terms of the damage we can inflict than of the losses we might suffer. The American people must be made aware that with the end of our atomic monopoly all-out war has ceased to be an instrument of policy, except as a last resort, and that for most of the issues likely to be in dispute our only choice is between a strategy of limited war or inaction. It would be tragic if our government were deprived of freedom of maneuver by the ignorance of the public regarding the consequences of a course from which it would recoil if aware of all its implications. This is all the more true since the same ignorance which underlies the demand for all-or-nothing solutions might well produce panic if our people were unexpectedly brought face-to-face with the consequences of an all-out war. Conversely, a public fully aware of the dangers confronting it and forearmed psychologically by an adequate civil defense program will be better prepared to support a more flexible national policy.

Whatever aspect of our strategic problem we consider—mitigating the horrors of war, creating a spectrum of capabilities to resist likely Soviet challenges—we are brought to recognize the importance of developing a strategy which makes room for the possibility of limited war. Creating a readiness for limited war should not be considered a matter of choice but of necessity. It results from the impossibility of combining both maximum force and the maximum willingness to act.

A strategy which makes room for the possibility of fighting limited wars will not eliminate the precariousness of our situation. In the nuclear age the best strategy can provide only a relative security, for the threat of all-out war will always loom in the background as a last resort for either side. Moreover, as nuclear technology becomes more widely diffused, other and perhaps less responsible powers will enter the nuclear race. The fear of mutual destruction, today the chief deterrent to all-out war for the major powers, may prove less effective with nations who have less to lose and whose negotiating position might even be improved by a threat to commit suicide.

Even among the major powers the strategy outlined in this chapter will not be easy to implement. It presupposes a military capability which is truly graduated. It assumes a diplomacy which can keep each conflict from being considered the prelude to a final showdown. And it requires strong nerves. We can make a strategy of limited war stick only if we leave no doubt about our readiness and our ability to face a final showdown.

42.   The Calculus of Deterrence

Bruce M. Russett

A COMPARATIVE STUDY OF DETERRENCE

A persistent problem for American political and military planners has been the question of how to defend "third areas." How can a major power make credible an intent to defend a smaller ally from attack by another major power? Simply making an explicit promise to defend an ally, whether that promise is embodied in a formal treaty or merely in a unilateral declaration, is not sufficient. There have been too many instances when "solemn oaths" were forgotten in the moment of crisis. On the other hand, more than once a major power has taken up arms to defend a nation with whom it had ties appreciably less binding than a formal commitment.

Some analysts like Herman Kahn maintain that the determining factor is the nature of the overall strategic balance. To make credible a promise to defend third areas the defender must have overall strategic superiority; that is, he must be able to strike the homeland of the attacker without sustaining unacceptable damage to himself in return (Kahn, 1960). This analysis implies, of course, a strategy which threatens to retaliate, even for a local attack, directly on the home territory of the major power antagonist. Advocates of a strategy of limited warfare retort that, in the absence of clear strategic superiority, the capacity to wage local war effectively may deter attack.

Other writers, notably Thomas C. Schelling, have suggested that the credibility of one's threat can be considerably enhanced by unilateral actions which would increase the defender's loss if he failed to keep his promise (Schelling, 1960). One of the best examples is Chiang Kai-shek's decision in 1958 to station nearly half his troops on Quemoy and Matsu. While the islands were of questionable intrinsic importance, the presence of so much of his army there made it virtually impossible for Chiang, or his American ally, to abandon the islands under fire.

Reprinted from "The Calculus of Deterrence," by Bruce M. Russett, *Journal of Conflict Resolution* 7/2 (June 1963), pp. 97–109. (Copyright © 1963 by the University of Michigan) with permission of Sage Publications, Inc. and the author. Footnotes deleted.

All of these explanations tend to stress principally the military elements in what is a highly complex political situation. There are, however, numerous nonmilitary ways in which one can strengthen one's commitment to a particular area. A government can make it a matter of prestige with its electorate. A nation might even deliberately increase its economic dependence upon supplies from a certain area, the better to enhance the credibility of a promise to defend it. W. W. Kaufmann's classic piece identified the elements of credibility as a power's capabilities, the costs it could inflict in using those capabilities, and its intentions as perceived by the enemy. In evaluating the defender's intentions a prospective attacker will look at his past actions, his current pronouncements, and the state of his public opinion (Kaufmann, 1956, pp. 12-38).

Kaufmann's formulation is better than simpler ones that stress military factors almost exclusively, but it needs to be expanded and made more detailed. One must particularly examine the potential costs to the defending power if he does not honor his commitments. In addition, propositions about factors which determine the credibility of a given threat need to be tested systematically on a comparative basis. On a number of occasions, for example, an aggressor has ignored the threats of a major power "defender" to go to war to protect a small nation "pawn" even though the defender held both strategic superiority and the ability to fight a local war successfully. Hitler's annexation of Austria in 1938 is just this kind of case, and one where the aggressor was correct, moreover.

In this paper we shall examine all the cases during the last three decades where a major power "attacker" overtly threatened a pawn with military force, and where the defender either had given, prior to the crisis, some indication of an intent to protect the pawn or made a commitment in time to prevent the threatened attack. A threat may be believed or disbelieved; it may be a bluff, or it may be sincere. Often the defender himself may not be sure of his reaction until the crisis actually occurs. We shall explore the question of what makes a threat credible by asking which threats in the past have been believed and which disregarded. Successful deterrence is defined as

an instance when an attack on the pawn is prevented or repulsed without conflict between the attacking forces and regular combat units of the major power "defender." ("Regular combat units" are defined so as not to include the strictly limited participation of a few military advisers.) With this formulation we must ignore what are perhaps the most successful instances of all—where the attacker is dissuaded from making any overt threat whatever against the pawn. But these cases must be left aside both because they are too numerous to be treated in detail and because it would be too difficult to distinguish the elements in most cases. Who, for example, really was the "attacker"? Was he dissuaded because of any action by the defender, or simply by indifference? Such questions would lead to too much speculation at the expense of the careful analysis of each case in detail

Deterrence fails when the attacker decides that the defender's threat is not likely to be fulfilled. In this sense it is equally a failure whether the defender really does intend to fight but is unable to communicate that intention to the attacker, or whether he is merely bluffing. Later we shall ask, from the viewpoint of the attacker, which threats ought to be taken seriously. At this stage we shall simply examine past cases of attempted deterrence to discover what elements are usually associated with a threat that is believed (or at least not disbelieved with enough confidence for the attacker to act on his disbelief) and therefore what steps a defender might take to make his threats more credible to his opponent. Table 10.1 lists the cases for consideration.

These cases are not, of course, comparable in every respect. Particularly in the instances of successful deterrence the causes are complex and not easily ascertainable. Nevertheless, a systematic comparison, undertaken cautiously, can provide certain insights that would escape an emphasis on the historical uniqueness of each case.

Deterrence in Recent Decades

First, we may dismiss as erroneous some frequent contentions about the credibility of deterrence. It is often said that a major power will fight only to protect an "important" position,

TABLE 10.1   Seventeen Cases—1935–1961

Pawn	Year	Attacker(s)	Defender(s)
		SUCCESS	
Iran	1946	Soviet Union	United States Great Britain—Secondary
Turkey	1947	Soviet Union	United States
Berlin	1948	Soviet Union	United States Great Britain } France } Secondary
Egypt	1956	Great Britain France	Soviet Union[a]
Quemoy-Matsu	1954–55 1958	Communist China	United States
Cuba	1961	United States (support of rebels)	Soviet Union
		FAILURE—PAWN LOST	
Ethiopia	1935	Italy	Great Britain France
Austria	1938	Germany	Great Britain France Italy
Czechoslovakia	1938	Germany	Great Britain France
Albania	1939	Italy	Great Britain
Czechoslovakia	1939	Germany	Great Britain France
Rumania	1940	Soviet Union	Great Britain
Guatemala	1954	United States (support of rebels)	Soviet Union
Hungary	1956	Soviet Union	United States
		FAILURE—WAR NOT AVOIDED	
Poland[b]	1939	Germany	Great Britain France
South Korea	1950	North Korea (supported by China & Soviet Union)	United States
North Korea	1950	United States	Communist China

[a]Despite its efforts to restrain the attackers, the United States was not a "defender" in the Suez affair. It neither supplied arms to the Egyptians before the crisis nor gave any indication that it would employ military force against Britain and France. In fact, the United States government explicitly ruled out the use of military coercion. See *New York Times*, November 7, 1956.

[b]Possibly the Polish case is not really a failure at all, for Hitler may have expected Britain and France to fight but was nevertheless prepared to take the consequences. A. J. P. Taylor presents an extreme version of the argument that Hitler expected Poland and/or Britain and France to give in (Taylor, 1961).

and not to defend some area of relatively insignificant size or population. As we shall see below, this is in a nearly tautological sense true—if, by "important," we include the enmeshment of the defender's prestige with the fate of the pawn, the symbolic importance the pawn may take on in the eyes of other allies, and particular strategic or political values attached to the pawn. But if one means important in terms of any objectively measurable factor like relative population or Gross National Product, it is not true.

As Table 10.2 shows, in all of our cases of successful deterrence—Iran, Turkey, Berlin, Egypt, Quemoy-Matsu, and Cuba—the pawn's

TABLE 10.2   Size (Population and Gross National Product) of Pawn in Relation to Defender(s)

Pawn	Defender(s)	Pawn's Population as Percent of Defender's Population	Pawn's G.N.P as Percent of Defender's G.N.P.
		SUCCESS	
Iran	United States	12	a
	Great Britain	37	4
Turkey	United States	13	1.7
Berlin	United States	1.5	a
	Great Britain	4	3
	France	5	3
Egypt	Soviet Union	12	2
Quemoy-Matsu	United States	a	a
Cuba	Soviet Union	3	1.5
		FAILURE—PAWN LOST	
Ethiopia	Great Britain	28	1.8
	France	31	2
Austria	Great Britain	14	7
	France	16	8
	Italy	16	17
Czechoslovakia (1938)	Great Britain	30	14
	France	34	16
Albania	Great Britain	2	a
Czechoslovakia (1939)	Great Britain	23	11
	France	26	12
Rumania	United Kingdom	33	11
Guatemala	Soviet Union	1.6	a
Hungary	United States	6	1.0
		FAILURE—WAR NOT AVOIDED	
Poland	Great Britain	73	25
	France	82	29
South Korea	United States	14	a
North Korea	Communist China	2	3

[a]Less than 1 percent

Sources: Population—United Nations, 1949, pp. 98–105; United Nations, 1962, pp. 126–37). G.N.P.—Norton Ginsburg (Ginsburg, 1962, p. 16). G.N.P. data are approximate and sometimes estimated.

population was well under 15 per cent, and his G.N.P. less that 5 per cent of that of the principal defender. (Britain was not Iran's chief protector.) Yet in five of the eleven cases where the attacker was not dissuaded the territory in question represented over 20 per cent of the defender's population (Ethiopia, Czechoslovakia in the Sudeten crisis and again in 1939, Poland, and Rumania). Poland in 1939 constituted the largest prize of all, yet Hitler may not have been convinced that Britain and France would go to war to save it.

Nor can one discover any special strategic or industrial importance of the pawn only in cases of success. Austria and both Czechoslovakian cases met these criteria but were nevertheless overrun, and the United States did not expect Communist China to fight for North Korea, despite its obvious strategic significance.

Clearly too, it is not enough simply for the defender to make a formal promise to protect the pawn. Only in one case of success was there what could be described as a clear and unambiguous commitment prior to the actual crisis (Berlin). In the others the commitment was either ambiguous (Iran, Cuba, Quemoy-Matsu) or not made until the crisis was well under way (Turkey, Egypt). The United States' principal precrisis commitment to Iran was the Big Three communique from Teheran in 1943 (written chiefly by the American delegation) guaranteeing Iranian "independence, sovereignty, and territorial integrity." Britain was allied with Iran, but the Russians recognized that any effective resistance to their plans would have to come from the United States rather than from an exhausted Britain. In July 1960 Khrushchev warned that the Soviet Union would retaliate with missiles if the United States attacked Cuba, but this was later qualified as being "merely symbolic" and the precise content of Soviet retaliation was left undefined. Neither Congress nor the President has ever stated the exact circumstances under which our formal guarantees of Taiwan would apply to the offshore islands.

Yet in at least six cases an attacker has chosen to ignore an explicit and publicly acknowledged commitment binding the defender to protect the pawn. Britain, France, and Italy were committed by treaty to Austria, France by treaty to Czechoslovakia in 1938, France by treaty and Britain by executive agreement to Czechoslovakia in 1939, Britain by executive agreement to Rumania, Britain, and France by treaty with Poland, and China by public declaration to North Korea. In three others there was at least an ambiguous commitment on the "defender's" part that might have been more rigorously interpreted. By a treaty of 1906 Britain, France, and Italy pledged themselves to "cooperate in maintaining the integrity of Ethiopia," Britain and Italy agreed in 1938 to "preserve the status quo in the Mediterranean" (including Albania), and in the 1950s American officials made references to "liberating" the satellites that were tragically overrated in Hungary. Of the failures, in fact, only Guatemala and possibly South Korea lacked any verbal indication of their "protectors'" willingness to fight. (In these instances, the defenders showed their concern principally by sending arms to the pawns before the attack.) The analyst who limited his examination to the present cases would be forced to conclude that a small nation was as safe without

an explicit guarantee as with one. At least such guarantees existed in fewer instances of success (one in six) than in cases of failure (six of eleven).

We must also examine the proposition that deterrence is not credible unless the defender possesses over-all strategic superiority; unless he can inflict far more damage on an aggressor than he would suffer in return. It is true that the successful deterrence of attack is frequently associated with strategic superiority, but the Soviet Union had, at best, strategic equality with the United States at the time of the Bay of Pigs affair. While Russia was clearly superior to Britain and France when it threatened to attack them with rockets in 1956, it just as clearly did not have a credible first strike force for use against their American ally.

Furthermore, in at least five cases where the attacker was not dissuaded, it nevertheless appears that the defender definitely had the ability to win any major conflict that might have developed (in the cases of Ethiopia, Austria, Czechoslovakia in 1938, Albania, and South Korea) and in two others (Czechoslovakia in 1939 and Hungary) the defender had at least a marginal advantage. (*Post hoc* analysis of the relevant documents indicates this superiority was more often perceived by the attacker, who went ahead and took the chance it would not be used, than by the defender. Hitler consistently recognized his opponents' strength and discounted their will to use it.)

Even less is it necessary for the defender to be able to win a limited local war. Of all the cases of success, only in Egypt could the defender plausibly claim even the ability to fight to a draw on the local level. In the other instances the defender could not hope to achieve equality without a long, sustained effort, and local superiority appeared out of reach. Yet in at least two failures the defenders, perhaps individually and certainly in coalition, had local superiority (Ethiopia and Austria) and in four others (Czechoslovakia in 1938, Albania, and the Korean cases) the defenders seemed to have been more or less on a par with their prospective antagonists.

Yet if these two kinds of capabilities—local and strategic—are analyzed together, it would seem that a defender may not be clearly inferior in both and yet hope to restrain an attacker. Although the Soviet Union could not dream of meeting the United States in a limited war in the Caribbean, at least in 1961 its strategic nuclear capabilities seemed roughly on a par with America's. And although Russia was inferior to Britain-France-United States on the strategic level, Soviet chances of at least matching their efforts in a local war over Egypt seemed a little brighter. Success requires at least apparent equality on one level or the other—this is hardly surprising—but when we remember that even superiority on both levels has often been associated with failure we have something more significant. *Superiority*, on either level, is not a condition of success. *Equality* on at least one level is a *necessary*, but by no means *sufficient*, condition. The traditionally conceived purely military factors do not alone make threats credible.

Nor, as has sometimes been suggested, does the kind of political system in question seem very important, though it does make some difference. Often, it is said, a dictatorial power can threaten much more convincingly than a democracy because the dictatorship can control its own mass media and present an apparently united front. Democracies, on the other hand, cannot easily suppress dissenting voices declaring that the pawn is "not worth the bones of a single grenadier." This argument must not be overstated—four of our successful cases of deterrence involved a democracy defending against a dictatorship. Yet in all of these cases the democracy possessed strategic superiority, whereas the other two successes, by a dictatorship, were at best under conditions of strategic equality for the defender. And in all but two (North Korea and Guatemala) of the eleven failures the defender was a democracy. Thus a totalitarian power's control over its citizens' expression of opinion may give it some advantage, if not a decisive one—particularly under conditions when the defender's strategic position is relatively weak.

INTERDEPENDENCE AND CREDIBILITY

With some of these hypotheses discarded we may now examine another line of argument, the credibility of deterrence depends upon the economic,

political, and military interdependence of pawn and defender. Where visible ties of commerce, past or present political integration, or military cooperation exist, an attacker will be much more likely to bow before the defender's threats—or if he does not bow, he will very probably find himself at war with the defender.

Military Cooperation

In every instance of success the defender supported the pawn with military assistance in the form of arms and advisers. In one of these cases, of course (Berlin) the defenders actually had troops stationed on the pawn's territory. The military link with Iran was somewhat tenuous, for Teheran received no shipments of American military equipment until after the 1946 crisis was past. Yet an American military mission was stationed in the country at the time, and 30,000 American troops had been on Iranian soil until the end of 1945 (Kirk, 1952, p. 150). America had given a tangible, though modest, indication of her interest in Iran. But in only five of the eleven failures were there significant shipments of arms to the pawn. France extended large military credits to Poland, and the British gave a small credit ($20 million) to Rumania. The Americans and the Chinese sent both arms and advisers to their Korean protégés. The Soviets sent small arms to Guatemala but no advisers, and they did not give any explicit indication of an intent to intervene in any American move against the Guatemalan government. A French military mission was stationed in Prague before and during the two Czechoslovakian crises, but no substantial amount of French equipment was sent (in part because of the high quality of the Czechoslovakian armament industry). In none of the other failures was there any tangible military interdependence. Some degree of military cooperation may not always be sufficient for successful deterrence, but it is virtually essential.

Political Interdependence

This is a helpful if not essential condition. Four of the instances of successful deterrence include some kind of current or recent political tie in addition to any current alliance. Western troops were stationed in Berlin and the three Western powers participated in the government of the city by international agreement. America and Nationalist China had been allies in a recent war. Turkey became allied with the Big Three toward the end of World War II. Iran had been occupied by British troops until early 1946 and American troops until the end of 1945. In the case of failures only four of eleven pawns had any significant former tie with a defender. Britain and Rumania were allies in World War I, as were the U.S.S.R. and Guatemala in World War II. Obviously, neither of these ties was at all close. The other two, however, were marked by rather close ties. United States forces occupied South Korea after World War II, and the R.O.K. government was an American protégé. The Communist Chinese had close party and ideological ties with the North Korean regime, and not too many decades previously Korea had been under Chinese sovereignty.

Economic Interdependence

We shall work with a crude but simple and objective measure of economic interdependence. In 1954 all countries of the world, other than the United States, imported a total of $65 billion of goods, of which 16 per cent came from the United States. South Korea, however, took 35 per cent of its total imports from the United States, a figure well above the world average. This will be our measure: does the pawn take a larger than average proportion of its imports from the defender or, vice versa, does the defender take a larger than average proportion of its imports from the pawn? To repeat, this is a crude measure. It does not tell, for example, whether the defender is dependent upon the pawn for a supply of a crucial raw material. But there are few areas of vital economic significance in this sense—almost every commodity can be obtained from more than one country, though not always at the same price—and attention to over-all commercial ties gives a broad measure of a country's general economic state in another. In none of the cases where this test does not show general economic interdependence is there evidence that the defender relied heavily on the pawn for a particular product.

In five of the six cases of successful deterrence either the pawn took an abnormally high proportion of its imports from the defender or vice versa. In the remaining case, the Iranian economy was closely tied to Britain if not to the United States, but in only three of the eleven failures was there interdependence between pawn and defender. A higher than average proportion of Austria's trade was with Italy, though not with France and Britain, the other two parties bound by treaty to preserve her integrity. Both Korean regimes also traded heavily with their defenders. Economic interdependence may be virtually essential to successful deterrence.

DIVINING INTENTIONS

Briefly we may also examine the question from the viewpoint of the attacker. If the defender's threat is not challenged, one may never know whether it truly expresses an intention to fight or whether it is merely a bluff. Perhaps the defender himself would not know until the circumstances actually arose. But we can examine the eleven cases where deterrence was not sufficiently credible to prevent attack. Previously we asked what differentiated the instances when the attacker pressed on from those in which he restrained his ambitions. Now, what distinguishes the cases where the defender actually went to war from those where he did not?

"Size," as defined earlier, again is not crucial. Poland, for which Britain and France went to war, was a very large prize but neither North nor South Korea represented a significant proportion of its defender's population or G.N.P. Of the eight instances where the defender's bluff was successfully called, four of the pawns (Ethiopia, Czechoslovakia on both occasions, and Rumania) represented over 20 percent of the defender's population and four (Austria, Czechoslovakia both times, and Rumania) over 5 percent of its G.N.P. Proportionately "large" pawns were more often the subject of "bluffs" than of serious intentions. Nor is there necessarily a formal, explicit commitment in cases which result in war. There were such commitments over Poland and North Korea, but South Korea is an obvious exception. And there was such a commitment in the case of half the "bluffs" (Austria, Czechoslovakia twice, and Rumania), and a vague, ambiguous one in three other cases (Ethiopia, Albania, Hungary).

The state of the military balance does not seem to have much effect either. In at least four "bluffs" (Ethiopia, Austria, Czechoslovakia in 1938, and Albania) the defenders were clearly superior *over-all* and in two other cases (Czechoslovakia in 1939 and Hungary) they were at least marginally so. Yet despite their bad military position Britain and France fought for Poland in 1939. And although the Chinese made some bold "paper tiger" talk they really could have had few illusions about their position should the United States counter their move into North Korea with its full conventional and nuclear might. In no instance where a defender fought did he have the ability to win a quick and relatively costless *local* victory. But in the two cases where the defender probably did have this ability (Ethiopia and Austria) he did not employ it. Neither does the defender's political system appear to matter much. The Chinese fought to defend North Korea, but dictatorships did nothing to protect Austria and Guatemala.

Yet bonds of interdependence—economic, political, land military—do turn out to be highly relevant. In every case where the defender went to war he had previously sent military advisers and arms to the pawn. Only four of the eight "bluffs" were marked by either of these activities, and none by a significant level of both. The two Koreas both had important prior political ties to their eventual defenders, but only two of the instances of "bluffs" (Rumania and Guatemala) were marked by even very weak ties of previous alliance. The two Korean states also were closely tied economically to their defenders, but of all the seven instances of bluffs, only Italy-Austria show a bond of similar strength. Again it is the nature of the defender-pawn relationship, rather than the attributes of either party separately, that seem most telling in the event.

We must be perfectly clear about the nature of these ties. Certainly no one but the most inveterate Marxist would assert that the United States entered the Korean War to protect its investments and economic interests. The United States went

to war to protect a state with which it had become closely identified. It was rather heavily involved economically in Korea, and its prestige as a government was deeply involved. It had occupied the territory and restored order after the Japanese collapse; it had installed and supported an at least quasi-democratic government; and it had trained, organized, and equipped the army. Not to defend this country in the face of overt attack would have been highly detrimental to American prestige and to the confidence governments elsewhere had in American support. Even though it had made no promises to defend Korea (and even had said it would not defend it in a general East-West war) the American government could not disengage itself from the fate of the Korean peninsula. Despite the lack of American promises, the American "presence" virtually guaranteed American protection.

MAKING DETERRENCE CREDIBLE

It is now apparent why deterrence does not depend in any simple way merely upon the public declaration of a "solemn oath," not merely on the physical means to fight a war, either limited or general. A defender's decision whether to pursue a "firm" policy that risks war will depend upon his calculation of the value and probability of various outcomes. If he is to be firm the prospective gains from a successful policy of firmness must be greater, when weighted by the probability of success and discounted by the cost and probability of war, than the losses from retreat. The attacker in turn will determine whether to press his attack in large part on his estimate of the defender's calculation. If he thinks the chances that the defender will fight are substantial he will attack only if the prospective gains from doing so are great.

The physical means of combat available to both sides are far from irrelevant, for upon them depend the positions of each side should war occur. A defender's commitment is unlikely to be believed if his military situation is markedly inferior to his enemy's. Yet even clear superiority provides no guarantee that his antagonist will be dissuaded if the defender appears to have relatively little to lose from "appeasement." At the time of the Austrian crisis Neville Chamberlain could tell himself not only that appeasement was likely to succeed, but that prospective losses even from its possible failure were not overwhelming. In particular, he failed to consider the effects appeasement would have on Britain's other promises to defend small nations. By autumn 1939, however, it was clear that further appeasement would only encourage Hitler to continue to disregard British threats to fight, as British inaction over Austria in fact had done.

Under these circumstances the effectiveness of the defender's threat is heavily dependent on the tangible and intangible bonds between him and the pawn. If other factors are equal, an attacker will regard a military response by the defender as more probable the greater the number of military, political, and economic ties between pawn and defender. No aggressor is likely to measure these bonds, as commercial ties, in just the way we have sketched them here, but he is most unlikely to be insensitive to their existence.

Strengthening these bonds is, in effect a strategy of raising the credibility of deterrence by increasing the loss one would suffer by not fulfilling a pledge. It illustrates in part why the American promise to defend Western Europe, with nuclear weapons if necessary, is so credible even in the absence of overwhelming American strategic superiority. Western Europe is certainly extremely important because of its large, skilled population and industrial capacity. Yet it is particularly important to the United States because of the high degree of political and military integration that has taken place in the North Atlantic Area. The United States, in losing Western Europe to the Communists, would lose population and industry, and the credibility of its pledges elsewhere. To put the case another way, America has vowed to defend both Japan and France from external attack, and there is much that is convincing about both promises. But the latter promise is somewhat more credible than the former, even were one to assume that in terms of industrial capacity, resources, strategic significance, etc., both countries were of equal importance. The real, if not wholly tangible, ties of the United States with France make it so.

Interdependence, of course, provides no guarantee that the defender's threat will be believed. There have been a few cases where an attacker chose to ignore a threat even when relatively close interdependence existed. But if one really does want to protect an area it is very hard to make that intention credible *without* bonds between defender and pawn. If the United States wishes to shield a country it will be wise to "show," and even to increase, its stake in that country's independence. Because the strength of international ties is to some degree controllable, certain policy choices, not immediately relevant to this problem, in fact take on special urgency. Implementation of the Trade Expansion Act, allowing the American government to eliminate tariffs on much of United States trade with Western Europe, will have more than an economic significance. By increasing America's apparent and actual economic dependence on Europe it will make more credible America's promise to defend it from attack.

The particular indices of economic, military, and political integration employed here are less important in themselves than as indicators of a broader kind of political and cultural integration, of what K. W. Deutsch refers to as mutual sympathy and loyalties, "we-feeling," trust, and mutual consideration (Deutsch, 1954, pp. 33-64). These bonds of mutual identification both encourage and are encouraged by bonds of communication and attention. Mutual attention in the mass media, exchanges of persons (migrants, tourists, students, etc.), and commercial activities all make a contribution. Mutual contact in some of these areas, such as exchange of persons, tends to promote contacts of other sorts, and often produces mutual sympathies and concern for each other's welfare. This process does not work unerringly, but it does work frequently nevertheless. And these mutual sympathies often are essential for the growth of a high level of commercial exchange, especially between economically developed nations rather than nations in an essentially colonial relationship with each other.

In addition to the loss of prestige and of tangible assets, there is yet another way in which a defender may lose if he fails to honor his pledge.

New Yorkers would sacrifice their own self-esteem if they fail to defend Californians from external attack; some of the same feeling applies, in lesser degree, to New Yorkers' attitudes toward Britishers. Though broad and intangible, this kind of relationship is nonetheless very real, and knowledge of it sometimes restrains an attacker.

Communication and attention both produce and are produced by, in a mutually reinforcing process, political and cultural integration. The appendix to this paper demonstrates the degree to which economic, military, and political interdependence are correlated. All this raises the "chicken and egg" kind of question as to which comes first. In such a "feedback" situation there is no simple answer; sometimes trade follows the flag, sometimes the flag follows trade (Russett, 1963, ch.4). Yet these are also to some extent independent, and the correlation is hardly perfect. From the data available one cannot identify any single factor as essential to deterrence. But as more are present the stronger mutual interdependence becomes, and the greater is the attacker's risk in pressing onward.

REFERENCES

DEUTSCH, KARL W. 1954. *Political Community at the International Level.* Garden City, N.Y.: Doubleday.

GINSBURG, NORTON. 1962. *Atlas of Economic Development.* Chicago: University of Chicago Press.

KAHN, HERMAN. 1960. *On Thermonuclear War.* Princeton, N.J.: Princeton University Press.

KAUFMANN, W. W. ed. 1956. *Military Policy and National Security.* Princeton, N.J.: Princeton University Press.

KIRK, GEORGE. 1952. *The Middle East in the War: Royal Institute of International Affairs Survey of International Affairs, 1939–46.* New York: Oxford University Press.

RUSSETT, BRUCE M. 1963. *Community and Contention: Britain and America in the Twentieth Century.* Cambridge, Mass.: MIT Press.

SCHELLING, THOMAS C. 1960. *The Strategy of Conflict.* New York: Oxford University Press.

TAYLOR, A. J. P. 1962. *The Origins of the Second World War.* New York: Atheneum.

UNITED NATIONS. *Demographic Yearbook, 1948.* New York: United Nations, 1949.

_____ . *Demographic Yearbook, 1961.* New York: United Nations, 1962.

APPENDIX:

Presence or Absence of Various Factors Alleged to Make Deterrent Threats Credible

	ATTACKER HOLDS BACK						ATTACKER PRESSES ON									Defender Fights		
							Defender Does Not Fight											
	Iran	Turkey	Berlin	Egypt	Quemoy-Matsu	Cuba	Ethiopia	Austria	Czechoslovakia (1938)	Albania	Czechoslovakia (1939)	Rumania	Guatemala	Hungary	Poland	South Korea	North Korea
Pawn 20% + of Defender's Population	*						x	x		x		x			x		
Pawn 5% + of Defender's G.N.P.								x	x		x	x			x		
Formal Commitment Prior to Crisis	?	x		?	?		?	x	x	?	x	x		?	x		x
Defender Has Strategic Superiority	x	x	x		x		x	x	x	x	?		?		x		
Defender Has Local Superiority							x	x	?	?						?	?
Defender Is Dictatorship				x		x	*						x				x
Pawn-Defender Military Cooperation	x	x	x	x	x	x		x			x	x	x		x	x	x
Pawn-Defender Political Interdependence	x	x	x		x							x	x			x	x
Pawn-Defender Economic Interdependence	*	x	x	x	x	x	*									x	x

Key: x Factor present
   ? Ambiguous or doubtful
   * Factor present for one defender

43. The Gap Between Deterrence Theory and Deterrence Policy

Alexander L. George and Richard Smoke

Much of part one of this study revolved around the theme that the contemporary abstract, deductivistic theory of deterrence is inadequate for policy application, notwithstanding its having been offered in a normative-prescriptive mode. The eleven cases we have now examined indicate the kinds of complexities which arise when the United States makes actual deterrence attempts, complexities which in many respects are not addressed by the abstract theory of deterrence.

To be sure, deterrence theorists have always acknowledged that like any other theory theirs, too, simplifies reality. It does not suffice, however, to stop with such a caveat. In addition, there is an obligation, recognized by most deterrence theorists, to go further and identify those aspects of deterrence phenomena in real-life settings which may be critical for determining deterrence outcomes but which are not encompassed by the simplifying assumptions of the theory in its pre-

Reprinted from *Deterrence in American Foreign Policy* by Alexander L. George and Richard Smoke (New York: Columbia University Press, 1974), pp. 503–508. Reprinted by permission of the publisher and the senior author. Footnotes deleted.

sent form. This difficult task, all the more necessary since deterrence theory has offered guidelines for policy-making, has not been satisfactorily accomplished. At the same time, it must be recognized that prudent and successful application of deterrence strategy to real-life situations is highly problematic without a clear grasp of precisely those complexities which deterrence theory simplifies or ignores.

It is not surprising, therefore, that the simplifying assumptions of prescriptive deterrence theory should have seriously restricted its relevance and usefulness for foreign policy-making. The inability of deterrence theorists to make an adequate analysis of the gap between the assumptions of their theory and the complexities of deterrence behavior in real life has necessarily left that important task in the hands of policy-makers. Left to their own devices, American policy-makers have filled this gap as best they could in their own way, and the results have often been unfortunate. Moreover, deterrence *strategy*, as applied by policy-makers, bears only a loose resemblance to the primitive, abstract, only partly developed deterrence *theory*. Hence neither the successes nor the failures of deterrence strategy in American foreign policy can be attributed to the influence of formal deterrence theory, which has stopped well short of the level of detail required of a policy-relevant theory and therefore has had only modest influence.

As a prescriptive theory, deterrence theory remains incomplete and unsatisfactory. It has become increasingly clear that initial statements of the theory merely adumbrated a starting point and that the necessary development and refinement of the theory did not follow. (It is instructive to reflect on this experience and what it implies more broadly for the goal of developing policy-relevant theory for different aspects of international politics. . . .

Let us briefly recall seven simplifying assumptions of abstract deterrence theory . . . ;

Assumption 1: Each side in the deterrence situation is a unitary, purposive actor. (This assumption overlooks the fact that the policy behavior of governments is affected by the dynamics of organizational behavior and internal governmental politics.)

Assumption 2: The payoffs and choices of action by the actors in the deterrence situation can be deduced by assuming a single general "rationality."

Assumption 3: General deterrence theory can be useful to policy-makers, even though it does not define the scope or relevance of deterrence strategy as an instrument of foreign policy.

Assumption 4: The major threat to the defending power's interests lies in its opponents' capacity for launching military attacks.

Assumption 5: Deterrence commitments are always a simple "either-or" matter, i.e., either the defending power commits itself or it does not; if it does, then the commitment is strong, unequivocal, unqualified, and of indefinite duration.

Assumption 6: The deterring power can rely upon threats to persuade the opponent not to alter the status quo.

Assumption 7: The critical and only problematical task of deterrence strategy is to achieve credibility of commitment.

The assumptions of prescriptive deterrence theory have often had to be discarded or modified by the policy-maker in diagnosing specific situations. A few examples will suffice to indicate the poor or even misleading quality of formal deterrence theory for the situational diagnoses needed in policy-making. Against the second assumption just listed, we noted in Part Two the chronic difficulty American policy-makers experienced in trying to estimate how the opponent calculated the risks of his options. In all three Berlin cases, the Korean War, and the Cuban missile crisis, American policy-makers were surprised by the action the opponent took. In each case American officials had thought the opponent would not act as he did because such action would entail high risks. In fact, there is reason to believe that in each of these cases the opponent regarded his initiative as a low-risk strategy through which he was confident of controlling and avoiding unwanted risks of greater magnitude. It is evident that to make the diagnoses needed in assessing situations, the policy-maker cannot work on the assumption that all actors operate with the same kind of "rationality." Rather, the policy-maker needs more discriminating theoretical models of how particular opponents behave in conflict situations.

With respect to the third assumption, our case studies suggest, to the contrary, that the scope and relevance of deterrence strategy for foreign policy needs to be strictly and carefully defined. Our case histories of the Eisenhower Doctrine for the Middle East and the Communist Chinese intervention in Korea both illustrate the risks of U.S. overreliance on deterrence strategy. The deterrence commitment embodied in the Eisenhower Doctrine paradoxically increased internal political instability in some of the Middle Eastern countries which it was designed to help. Our study of Chinese intervention in Korea emphasizes that deterrence strategy cannot be a reliable substitute for a sensible foreign policy or be used, as Truman and Acheson did in that case, to avoid the consequences of a dangerously provocative foreign policy error. Only a timely abandonment of the policy of trying to unify Korea by force could have reliably reduced the danger of war with Communist

China by removing or substantially reducing its motivation to intervene.

More broadly, the American policy of containment during the Cold War suffered badly from a *failure to define limits to the scope and relevance of deterrence strategy*. While containment logically required some use of deterrence strategy, the need for selective, discriminating use of deterrence to uphold containment gave way to a rigid attempt to exclude loss of any territory, even the offshore islands lying a few miles off mainland China. The deformation of containment led to a proliferation of American deterrence commitments throughout the world and, as George Kennan was to complain, also to a "militarization" of containment. As we noted in our account of the Taiwan Strait crisis of 1954–1955, the American effort to extend containment from Europe to Asia invited serious new risks because of the different structure of the situation, which was dangerously fluid and not neatly structured, as Europe was, for a classical *defensive* application of deterrence strategy. Because the Chinese civil war remained unresolved, the American effort to employ deterrence strategy on behalf of the Nationalist regime on Taiwan resulted in a confusion of containment with "liberation," thereby increasing tensions and inviting crisis.

Finally, as our account of the origins of the Cuban missile crisis stressed, the risks and untoward consequences of too heavy a reliance by both sides on deterrence strategy and strategic power during the Cold War to achieve a broad range of foreign policy objectives contributed to bringing about the most dangerous confrontation of the two nuclear superpowers.

In contrast to the fifth assumption, regarding the "either-or" character of commitments, our case studies indicate that policy-makers need a much more complex understanding of the nature of commitments both in order to convey their own commitments more effectively and to diagnose better the commitments other actors are making. . . .

As for the sixth assumption, which concerns the central role of threats in deterrence strategy, we argue to the contrary that the policy-maker would be better served in the conduct of foreign policy by a broader influence theory. A variety of policy means should be considered for reducing, rechanneling, accommodating, deterring, or frustrating challenges to different kinds of interests, not just deterrent threats. The need for threatening sanctions cannot be properly judged by the policy-maker on the basis of a prescriptive theory that confines itself to indicating that such threats are likely to be necessary to deter encroachments on one's interests. A policy-maker who diagnoses conflict situations solely from the standpoint of how to make more effective use of threats will find that threats are often irrelevant or dysfunctional. This irrelevance of deterrence threats was evident in the Middle East crises of 1957–1958. Some of their harmful consequences are suggested by the Berlin crisis of 1961; after it was over President Kennedy wondered whether some of the moves he had taken to signal resolution had not aggravated the crisis by forcing Khrushchev to undertake similar moves.

In certain situations, moreover, threats may be provocative. The threats the United States and its allies made in 1941 to deter Japan from further encroachments against Asian countries were all too potent and credible to Japanese leaders. They decided they had no choice but to resort to a still more ambitious strategy and attack the United States. But the fact that deterrent threats against a highly motivated opponent are sometimes ineffectual or may boomerang does not permit us to conclude that deterrent threats will surely be more effective against a cautious opponent who confines himself to low-risk and controlled-risk options. In the Quemoy and the Cuban missile crises, threats did not deter the controlled low-risk strategies the opponents were engaged in.

A policy-maker who invariably relies upon threats to deter encroachments on his interests is likely in some situations to pay a high price for temporary deterrence successes which do not really remove the sources of the conflict. We called attention to this in our accounts of the Taiwan Strait and Quemoy crises of 1954–1955 and 1958. A deterrence success of this kind buys time for efforts to restructure the situation after the crisis subsides, in order to defuse its conflict potential. Failure to utilize a temporary deterrence success to alter the situation invites a repetition of the crisis in the future, perhaps under new circumstances in which resort to deterrence strategy may be even more costly and ineffectual.

Viewed from a broader perspective on international relations, therefore, controlled crises of the kind we have seen in Berlin and the Taiwan Strait often have a *catalytic* function for bringing about changes that are necessary if war is to be avoided in the longer run. While deterrence may be necessary to avoid the dangers of "appeasement" under pressure, a deterrence success in such crises creates dangers of another kind if it encourages the defending power to ignore the need for utilizing other policy approaches in the ensuing noncrisis period to find more viable, mutually acceptable solutions to the conflict of interests.

11

INTERNATIONAL LAW
AND WORLD GOVERNMENT

44. Prolegomena to
The Law of War and Peace

HUGO GROTIUS

1. The municipal law of Rome and of other states has been treated by many, who have undertaken to elucidate it by means of commentaries or to reduce it to a convenient digest. That body of law, however, which is concerned with the mutual relations among states or rulers of states, whether derived from nature, or established by divine ordinances, or having its origin in custom and tacit agreement, few have touched upon. Up to the present time no one has treated it in a comprehensive and systematic manner; yet the welfare of mankind demands that this task be accomplished. . . .

3. Such a work is all the more necessary because in our day, as in former times, there is no lack of men who view this branch of law with contempt as having no reality outside of an empty name. On the lips of men quite generally is the saying of Euphemus, which Thucydides quotes, that in the case of a king or imperial city nothing

is unjust which is expedient. Of like implication is the statement that for those whom fortune favours might makes right, and that the administration of a state cannot be carried on without injustice.

Furthermore, the controversies which arise between peoples or kings generally have Mars as their arbiter. That war is irreconcilable with all law is a view held not alone by the ignorant populace; expressions are often let slip by well-informed and thoughtful men which lend countenance to such a view. Nothing is more common than the assertion of antagonism between law and arms. . . .

5. Since our discussion concerning law will have been undertaken in vain if there is no law, in order to open the way for a favourable reception of our work and at the same time to fortify it against attacks, this very serious error must be briefly refuted. In order that we may not be obliged to deal with a crowd of opponents, let us assign to them a pleader. And whom should we choose in preference to Carneades? . . .

Carneades, then, having undertaken to hold a brief against justice, in particular against that

---

Excerpted from *The Law of War and Peace*, by Hugo Grotius. Translated by Francis W. Kelsey in 1925 for the Carnegie Endowment for International Peace. Reprinted by permission of the publisher. Footnotes deleted.

phase of justice with which we are concerned, was able to muster no argument stronger than this, that, for reasons of expediency, men imposed upon themselves laws, which vary according to customs, and among the same peoples often undergo changes as times change; moreover that there is no law of nature, because all creatures, men as well as animals, are impelled by nature toward ends advantageous to themselves; that, consequently, there is no justice, or, if such there be, it is supreme folly, since one does violence to his own interests if he consults the advantage of others.

6. . . . Man is, to be sure, an animal, but an animal of a superior kind, much farther removed from all other animals than the different kinds of animals are from one another; evidence on this point may be found in the many traits peculiar to the human species. But among the traits characteristic of man is an impelling desire for society, that is, for the social life—not of any and every sort, but peaceful, and organized according to the measure of his intelligence, with those who are of his own kind; this social trend the Stoics called "sociableness." Stated as a universal truth, therefore, the assertion that every animal is impelled by nature to seek only its own good cannot be conceded. . . .

8. This maintenance of the social order, which we have roughly sketched, and which is consonant with human intelligence, is the source of law properly so called. To this sphere of law belong the abstaining from that which is another's, the restoration to another of anything of his which we may have, together with any gain which we may have received from it; the obligation to fulfil promises, the making good of a loss incurred through our fault, and the inflicting of penalties upon men according to their deserts.

9. From this signification of the word law there has flowed another and more extended meaning. Since over other animals man has the advantage of possessing not only a strong bent towards social life, of which we have spoken, but also a power of discrimination which enables him to decide what things are agreeable or harmful (as to both things present and things to come), and what can lead to either alternative: in such

things it is meet for the nature of man, within the limitations of human intelligence, to follow the direction of a well-tempered judgement, being neither led astray by fear or the allurement of immediate pleasure, nor carried away by rash impulse. Whatever is clearly at variance with such judgement is understood to be contrary also to the law of nature, that is, to the nature of man.

10. To this exercise of judgement belongs moreover the rational allotment to each man, or to each social group, of those things which are properly theirs, in such a way as to give the preference now to him who is more wise over the less wise, now to a kinsman rather than to a stranger, now to a poor man rather than to a man of means, as the conduct of each or the nature of the thing suggests. Long ago the view came to be held by many, that this discriminating allotment is a part of law, properly and strictly so called; nevertheless law, properly defined, has a far different nature, because its essence lies in leaving to another that which belongs to him, or in fulfilling our obligations to him.

11. What we have been saying would have a degree of validity even if we should concede that which cannot be conceded without the utmost wickedness, that there is no God, or that the affairs of men are of no concern to Him. . . .

15. Again, since it is a rule of the law of nature to abide by pacts (for it was necessary that among men there be some method of obligating themselves one to another, and no other natural method can be imagined), out of this source the bodies of municipal law have arisen. For those who had associated themselves with some group, or had subjected themselves to a man or to men, had either expressly promised, or from the nature of the transaction must be understood impliedly to have promised, that they would conform to that which should have been determined, in the one case by the majority, in the other by those upon whom authority had been conferred.

16. What is said, therefore, in accordance with the view not only of Carneades but also of others, that

> Expediency is, as it were, the mother
> Of what is just and fair,

is not true, if we wish to speak accurately. For the very nature of man, which even if we had no lack of anything would lead us into the mutual relations of society, is the mother of the law of nature. But the mother of municipal law is that obligation which arises from mutual consent; and since this obligation derives its force from the law of nature, nature may be considered, so to say, the great-grandmother of municipal law.

The law of nature nevertheless has the reinforcement of expediency; for the Author of nature willed that as individuals we should be weak, and should lack many things needed in order to live properly, to the end that we might be the more constrained to cultivate the social life. But expediency afforded an opportunity also for municipal law, since that kind of association of which we have spoken, and subjection to authority, have their roots in expediency. From this it follows that those who prescribe laws for others in so doing are accustomed to have, or ought to have, some advantage in view.

17. But just as the laws of each state have in view the advantage of that state, so by mutual consent it has become possible that certain laws should originate as between all states, or a great many states; and it is apparent that the laws thus originating had in view the advantage, not of particular states, but of the great society of states. And this is what is called the law of nations, whenever we distinguish that term from the law of nature. . . .

For since, by his own admission, the national who in his own country obeys its laws is not foolish, even though, out of regard for that law, he may be obliged to forgo certain things advantageous for himself, so that nation is not foolish which does not press its own advantage to the point of disregarding the laws common to nations. The reason in either case is the same. For just as the national, who violates the law of his country in order to obtain an immediate advantage, breaks down that by which the advantages of himself and his posterity are for all future time assured, so the state which transgresses the laws of nature and of nations cuts away also the bulwarks which safeguard its own future peace. Even if no advantage were to be contemplated from the keeping of the law, it would be a mark of wisdom, not of folly, to allow ourselves to be drawn towards that to which we feel that our nature leads.

19. Wherefore, in general, it is by no means true that

> You must confess that laws were framed
> From fear of the unjust,

a thought which in Plato some one explains thus, that laws were invented from fear of receiving injury, and that men are constrained by a kind of force to cultivate justice. . . .

45. From *World Peace Through World Law*

GRENVILLE CLARK AND LOUIS B. SOHN

INTRODUCTION

By Grenville Clark

This book sets forth a comprehensive and detailed plan for the maintenance of world peace in the form of a proposed revision of the United Nations Charter. The purpose is to contribute material for the world-wide discussions which must precede the adoption of universal and complete disarmament and the establishment of truly effective institutions for the prevention of war.

At the outset, it may be helpful to explain: *first,* the underlying conceptions of this plan for peace; and *second,* the main features of the plan whereby these conceptions would be carried out.

The fundamental premise of the book is identical with the pronouncement of the President of the United States on October 31, 1956: "There

Reprinted by permission of the publishers from *World Peace Through World Law*, third edition, by Grenville Clark and Louis B. Sohn (Cambridge, Mass.: Harvard University Press, 1966), pp. xv–xvii. Copyright © 1958, 1960, 1966 by the President and Fellows of Harvard College.

can be no peace without law." In this context the word "law" necessarily implies the law of a world authority, i.e., law which would be uniformly applicable to all nations and all individuals in the world and which would definitely forbid violence or the threat of it as a means for dealing with any international dispute. This world law must also be law in the sense of law which is capable of enforcement as distinguished from a mere set of exhortations or injunctions which it is desirable to observe but for the enforcement of which there is no effective machinery.

The proposition "no peace without law" also embodies the conception that peace cannot be ensured by a continued arms race, nor by an indefinite "balance of terror," nor by diplomatic maneuver, but only by universal and complete national disarmament together with the establishment of institutions corresponding in the world field to those which maintain law and order within local communities and nations.

A prime motive for this book is that the world is far more likely to make progress toward genuine peace, as distinguished from a precarious armed truce, when a *detailed* plan adequate to the purpose is available, so that the structure and functions of the requisite world institutions may be fully discussed on a world-wide basis. Consequently, this book comprises a set of definite and interrelated proposals to carry out complete and universal disarmament and to strengthen the United Nations through the establishment of such legislative, executive and judicial institutions as are necessary to maintain world order.

UNDERLYING PRINCIPLES

The following are the basic principles by which Professor Sohn and I have been governed.

First: It is futile to expect genuine peace until there is put into effect an effective system of *enforceable* world law in the limited field of war prevention. This implies: (a) the complete disarmament, under effective controls, of each and every nation, and (b) the simultaneous adoption on a world-wide basis of the measures and institutions which the experience of centuries has shown to be essential for the maintenance of law and order, namely, clearly stated law against violence, courts to interpret and apply that law and police to enforce it. All else, we conceive, depends upon the acceptance of this approach.

Second: The world law against international violence must be explicitly stated in constitutional and statutory form. It must, under appropriate penalties, forbid the use of force by any nation against any other for any cause whatever, save only in self-defense; and must be applicable to all individuals as well as to all nations.

Third: World judicial tribunals to interpret and apply the world law against international violence must be established and maintained, and also organs of mediation and conciliation,—so as to substitute peaceful means of adjudication and adjustment in place of violence, or the threat of it, as the means for dealing with all international disputes.

Fourth: A permanent world police force must be created and maintained which, while safeguarded with utmost care against misuse, would be fully adequate to forestall or suppress any violation of the world law against international violence.

Fifth: The complete disarmament of all the nations (rather than the mere "reduction" or "limitation" of armaments) is essential for any solid and lasting peace, this disarmament to be accomplished in a simultaneous and proportionate manner by carefully verified stages and subject to a well-organized system of inspection. It is now generally accepted that disarmament must be universal and enforceable. That it must also be complete is no less necessary, since: (a) in the nuclear age no mere reduction in the new means of mass destruction could be effective to remove fear and tension; and (b) if any substantial national armaments were to remain, even if only ten per cent of the armaments of 1960, it would be impracticable to maintain a sufficiently strong world police force to deal with any possible aggression or revolt against the authority of the world organization. We should face the fact that until there is *complete* disarmament of every nation without exception there can be no assurance of genuine peace.

Sixth: Effective world machinery must be created to mitigate the vast disparities in the economic condition of various regions of the world, the continuance of which tends to instability and conflict.

The following supplementary principles have also guided us:

Active participation in the world peace authority must be universal, or virtually so; and although a few nations may be permitted to decline active membership, any such nonmember nations must be equally bound by the obligation to abolish their armed forces and to abide by all the laws and regulations of the world organization with relation to the prevention of war. It follows that ratification of the constitutional document creating the world peace organization (whether in the form of a revised United Nations Charter or otherwise) must be by a preponderant majority of all the nations and people of the world.

The world law, in the limited field of war prevention to which it would be restricted, should apply to all individual persons in the world as well as to all the nations,—to the end that in case of violations by individuals without the support of their governments, the world law could be invoked directly against them without the necessity of indicting a whole nation or group of nations.

The basic rights and duties of all nations in respect of the maintenance of peace should be clearly defined not in laws enacted by a world legislature but in the constitutional document itself. That document should also carefully set forth not only the structure but also the most important powers of the various world institutions established or authorized by it: and the constitutional document should also define the limits of those powers and provide specific safeguards to guarantee the observance of those limits and the protection of individual rights against abuse of power. By this method of "constitutional legislation" the nations and peoples would know in advance within close limits what obligations they would assume by acceptance of the new world system, and only a restricted field of discretion would be left to the legislative branch of the world authority.

The powers of the world organization should be restricted to matters directly related to the maintenance of peace. All other powers should be reserved to the nations and their peoples. This definition and reservation of powers is advisable not only to avoid opposition based upon fear of possible interference in the domestic affairs of

the nations, but also because it is wise for this generation to limit itself to the single task of preventing international violence or the threat of it. If we can accomplish that, we should feel satisfied and could well leave to later generations any enlargement of the powers of the world organization that they might find desirable.

While any plan to prevent war through total disarmament and the substitution of world law for international violence must be fully adequate to the end in view, it must also be *acceptable* to this generation. To propose a plan lacking in the basic essentials for the prevention of war would be futile. On the other hand, a plan which, however ideal in conception, is so far ahead of the times as to raise insuperable opposition would be equally futile. Therefore, we have tried hard to strike a sound balance by setting forth a plan which, while really adequate to prevent war, would, at the same time, be so carefully safeguarded that it *ought* to be acceptable to all nations.

It is not out of the question to carry out universal and complete disarmament and to establish the necessary new world institutions through an entirely new world authority, but it seems more normal and sensible to make the necessary revisions of the present United Nations Charter.

46. World Government

INIS L. CLAUDE JR.

THE ANALOGY OF NATIONAL STATE AND WORLD STATE

The theory of world government is essentially analogical; it proposes to reproduce the national state on an international scale, and it looks to the operation of government as an instrument of order within national society for clues as to the means by which global order might be achieved. This clearly means that the preliminary problem for the designer of global institutions and processes is to develop an understanding of national institutions and processes. How does government function within the national state? How then might government function within the world state?

It should be acknowledged that government might not function in the same manner, or with the same degree of success, in the larger as in the smaller setting, and that devices and techniques quite different from those normally

Excerpted from *Power and International Relations* by Inis L. Claude, Jr. (New York: Random House, 1962), pp. 255–271. Copyright © 1962 by Random House, Inc. Reprinted by permission of the publisher. Footnotes deleted.

associated with government might be found appropriate for international order-keeping. Champions of world government frequently seem too much concerned about the persuasiveness of advocacy to make these acknowledgments. Such dogmatic assurance that effective global institutions can be simply defined as national government writ large is as regrettable in intellectual terms as it may be satisfying in emotional terms, and one might reasonably ask for less dedication and more qualification. However, it must be stressed that this sort of ideological exuberance is not inherent in the position itself. One can legitimately ask what can be learned from national governmental experience that *might* usefully be adopted or adapted for the purpose of building a system of world order, without indulging in the illusion that the national and international problems are perfectly comparable or that solutions are perfectly transferable from the one level to the other. Indeed, I should argue that one *must* do so, for we are not so well supplied with promising ideas for solving the problem of war that we can afford to neglect the possibility that decisively valuable insights might be gained in this way. Whatever its defects, the world government school of thought has to its credit the achievement of directing attention to this important question.

It is a striking fact that most commentators, whether they are numbered among the dedicated promoters of the world government movement or among those who look more dispassionately upon the theory of world government, tend to visualize national government as an instrumentality for dealing with individuals when they consider the question of the transferability of governmental techniques to the global level. Asking "What, if anything, can we learn from domestic government that might be relevant to the problem of world order?", they begin by noting that states have judges and policemen who undertake to cope with individual criminals. There is little difference on this score between those who conceive world government as dealing exclusively with individual law-breakers and those who contemplate a world organization concerned with enforcing orderly conduct upon states instead of, or in addition to, individuals; the ideal presumably is to enable a world government to relate itself to the objects of its regulatory action, whether individuals, states, or both, as an effective national government relates itself to individuals. . . .

It is strange that those who have been most devoted to the idea that the solution of the problem of relations among states is to be found in the creation of a global version of the national state have displayed so little interest in the peace-among-groups aspect of domestic government. It would seem to be almost self-evident that national societies are most comparable to the international society when they are viewed as pluralistic rather than atomistic communities, and that the problem of civil war is the closest domestic analogue of the problem of international war. If one is concerned about preventing an aggressive state from disrupting world peace, it would be more natural, I suggest, to turn one's thoughts to the prevention of large-scale rebellion against the public order in a federal system than to the prevention of armed robbery in a well-governed city. How, then, is one to explain the concentration of attention upon the analogy of domestic government as a regulator of individual behavior?

To some degree, this peculiar focus appears to be the product of an utterly unsophisticated conception of government. In schoolboyish fashion, one sees government as a legislature, a code of law, a policeman, a judge, and a jail; those who misbehave are arrested and punished. The social discipline of government is located essentially at the end of the night stick wielded by the cop on the corner. If this works in Kalamazoo, why should it not work on a world-wide scale, with a global cop intimidating potential criminals everywhere, or controlling states assimilated to the position of individual offenders in Kalamazoo?

This explanation ought not to be pushed too far. Many prominent advocates of world government are thoroughly cognizant of the complexity of the modern governmental process; they are men whose image of government takes in the intricacies of public affairs in Washington as well as the simplicities of the street-corner situation in Kalamazoo. How is it that men such as these consider the problem of world government as if it were a large-scale reproduction of the problem of domestic law-enforcement against individuals?

A clue may perhaps be found in the intimate association between the idea of world government and the fashionable theme of a world rule of law. *Law* is a key word in the vocabulary of world government. One reacts against anarchy—disorder, insecurity, violence, injustice visited by the strong upon the weak. In contrast, one postulates law—the symbol of the happy opposites to those distasteful and dangerous evils. Law suggests properly constituted authority and effectively implemented control; it symbolizes the supreme will of the community, the will to maintain justice and public order. This abstract concept is all too readily transformed, by worshipful contemplation, from one of the devices by which societies seek to order internal relationships, into a symbolic key to the good society. As this transformation takes place, law becomes a magic word for those who advocate world government and those who share with them the ideological bond of dedication to the rule of law—not necessarily in the sense that they expect it to produce magical effects upon the world, but at least in the sense that it works its magic upon them. Most significantly, it leads them to forget about *politics*, to play down the role of the political process in the management of human affairs, and to imagine that somehow *law*, in all its purity, can displace the soiled devices of politics.

Inexorably, the emphasis upon law which is characteristic of advocates of world government carries with it a tendency to focus upon the relationship of individuals to government; thinking in legal terms, one visualizes the individual apprehended by the police and brought before the judge. The rejection, or the brushing aside, of politics involves the neglect of the pluralistic aspect of the state, for the political process is preeminently concerned with the ordering of relationships among the groups which constitute a society. In short, it would appear to be the legal orientation of world government theory which produces its characteristic bias against treating government as an instrument for dealing with groups.

The effect of the *rule of law* stress in discouraging attention to politics, with its pluralistic implications, is illustrated by the contention of Clark and Sohn that the representatives constituting the General Assembly of their projected world organization would, after a transitional period of voting largely along national lines, ''more and more tend to vote in accordance with their individual judgment as to the best interests of all the people of the world, as in the case of national parliaments where the interests of the whole nation are usually regarded as of no less importance than the interests of a particular section or group.'' One cannot deny that legislators sometimes exercise individual judgment or that they sometimes show great devotion to the general interest, but one would expect commentary on this subject to reflect awareness of the phenomenon of political parties. . . .

The political process by which governments attempt to manage the relationships of segments of society with each other and with the society as a whole, with all the pulling and hauling, haggling and cajoling that it involves, is not so neat and orderly, so dignified and awe-inspiring, as the law-enforcement process by which they assert authority over individuals. But it is a vitally important aspect of the role of government, and the

one which bears the closest relation to the problem of establishing order in international affairs. It is ironical that those who have done most to stimulate consideration of the possible applicability of the lessons of domestic governmental experience to the problem of world order have been so enamored of the concept of law that they have neglected and discouraged consideration of the most relevant aspect of that experience. . . .

Looking specifically at the United States, I suggest that the tributes which are regularly paid to the ''rule of law'' should more realistically be paid to the ''rule of politics.'' In a society of contending groups, law is *not* the only effective way of preventing violence, or even the most important method; instead, politics is the device which has proved most useful. The American Civil War was the result of a failure of political adjustment among sectional forces, not of a breakdown of law enforcement against individuals. . . .

Americans today regard civil war as unthinkable; the threat and reality of such internal disorder has become a historical memory. This fundamental change of outlook does not derive from conviction that the United States Government is vastly more capable of enforcing law against individuals or segments of society in the 1960s than it was in the 1860s. Rather, it seems to me to be based upon confidence in the adequacy of our political process for working out compromises and promoting accommodations of interest among the diverse and overlapping groups which constitute American society. . . .

One of the lessons of governmental experience is that coercion can seldom be usefully invoked against significant collectivities which exhibit a determination to defend their interests, as they conceive them, against the public authority. The order-keeping function of government is not fulfilled by the winning of a civil war, but by its prevention. If groups cannot be coerced without the disruption of the order which government exists to maintain, it does not follow that the alternative tactic of coercing individuals should be adopted. What follows is rather that the difficult task of ordering group relationships by political means should be attempted. . . .

I would conclude that theorists of world government are not mistaken in their insistence that one should look to domestic governmental experience for clues as to the most promising means for achieving world order, but that they tend to misread the lessons of that experience. In some instances, they treat the domestic problem of crime prevention as comparable to the international problem of war, and draw from national experience the conclusion that the central function of a world government would be to maintain order by enforcing legal restrictions upon individual behavior. In other instances, they note the domestic problem of coping with dissident groups, acknowledge its comparability to the problem of dealing with aggressive states, and suggest that the governmental pattern requires that a central authority be equipped with adequate military force to coerce any possible rebellion within the larger society.

In contrast, I would argue that the prevention of civil war is the function of national government most relevant to the problem of ordering international relations, that governments cannot and do not perform this function by relying primarily upon either police action against individuals or military action against significant segments of their societies, and that governments succeed in this vitally important task only when they are able to operate an effective system of political accommodation. . . .

This conception treats government not as a monopoly of power which effectuates a rule of law, but as the focal point of a political process. If the history of national government tells us anything about the problem of achieving international order, it seems to me to be this: There is no substitute for policital adjustment as a means of managing relationships among the units which constitute complex human societies, and there is no magic formula for producing either the kind of society which lends itself to ordering in this manner or the kind of institutional system which can effectively preside over the process of adjustment.

I do not contend that this analysis demonstrates the invalidity of the concept, or that it disproves the desirability of a system of world government. It does, I think, call into question the assumption that the task of devising an adequate theoretical scheme for world order has been completed—that

we know the answer to the problem, and now face only the issue of whether, and how, the answer can be translated from theory into reality. To say that the institution of government in international affairs would transform that realm from a world of politics into a world of law seems to me to deny the lessons of experience with governed national societies, and to lead to false expectations regarding the means by which relations among states may be regulated. To say that the management of power in international relations cannot be achieved except by concentrating an effective monopoly of power in a central agency, which thus becomes capable of maintaining order by the threat of bringing overwhelming coercion to bear against any and all dissident elements, seems to me to misstate the position which governments occupy in national societies and to overstate both the requirements and the possibilities of the centralization of coercive capacity in the global society. To say that governments succeed, if they do and when they do, in maintaining order by sensitive and skillful operation of the mechanisms of political adjustment seems to me to be correct—but it does not point the way to a revolutionary new system of international relations, or promise a dramatic escape from the perils of international conflict. The idealized concept of government which advocates of world government expound exists primarily in their own minds; few actual governments are very government-like in their terms. The more mundane version of government which I have described is not wholly missing even in the international sphere; in my terms, the United Nations is not entirely ''un-government–like.'' Government, defined in terms of the function of promoting order through political management of inter-group relations, is a matter of degree. Looking at it in this way, we can say that British society enjoys a high degree of government, that Indonesian society suffers from having achieved only a precarious minimum of government, and that the international society is in dire peril because of the manifest inadequacy of the level of government which it has thus far reached.

In the final analysis, it appears that the theory of world government does not *answer* the question of how the world can be saved from catastrophic international conflict. Rather, it helps us to *restate* the question: How can the world achieve the degree of assurance that inter-group conflicts will be resolved or contained by political rather than violent means that has been achieved in the most effectively governed states? This is a valuable and provocative restatement of the question—but it ought not to be mistaken for a definitive answer.

12
WORLD COMMUNITY

47. From *Political Community and the North Atlantic Area*

KARL W. DEUTSCH ET AL.

THE PROBLEM

We undertook this inquiry as a contribution to the study of possible ways in which men some day might abolish war.

From the outset, we realized the complexity of the problem. It is difficult to relate "peace" clearly to other prime values such as "justice" and "freedom." There is little common agreement on acceptable alternatives to war, and there is much ambiguity in the use of the terms "war" and "peace." Yet we can start with the assumption that war is now so dangerous that mankind must eliminate it, must put it beyond serious possibility. The attempt to do this may fail. But in a civilization that wishes to survive, the central problem in the study of international organization is this: How can men learn to act together to eliminate war as a social institution?

This is in one sense a smaller, and in another sense a larger, question than the one which occupies so many of the best minds today: how can we either prevent or avoid losing "the next war"? It is smaller because there will, of course, be no chance to solve the long-run problem if we do not survive the short-run crisis. It is larger because it concerns not only the confrontation of the nations of East and West in the twentieth century, but the whole underlying question of relations between political units at any time. We are not, therefore, trying to add to the many words that have been written directly concerning the East-West struggle of the 1940–1950s. Rather, we are seeking new light with which to look at the conditions and processes of long-range or permanent peace, applying our findings to one contemporary problem which, though not so difficult as the East-West problem, is by no means simple: peace *within* the North Atlantic area.

Whenever a difficult political problem arises, men turn to history for clues to its solution. They do this knowing they will not find the whole answer there. Every political problem is unique, of

From *Political Community and the North Atlantic Area* by Karl W. Deutsch et al., pp. 3–9. Copyright © 1957 by Princeton University Press. Reprinted by permission of Princeton University Press.

course, for history does not "repeat itself." But often the reflective mind will discover situations in the past that are essentially similar to the one being considered. Usually, with these rough parallels or suggestive analogies, the problem is not so much to find the facts as it is to decide what is essentially the same and what is essentially different between the historical facts and those of the present.

When most people discuss war and history in the same breath, they are likely to adopt one of two extreme positions. Some say that because history shows a continuous record of war, it indicates nothing but more of the same for the future. Others say that history shows a persistent growth in the size of the communities into which men organize themselves, and that this trend will continue until the world is living peacefully in a single community. Neither of these conclusions seems warranted on its face, though both contain some truth.

There is plenty of room between such extreme interpretations of history. Yet we know of no thorough investigation into the ways in which certain areas of the world have, in the past, "permanently" eliminated war. Historians, especially diplomatic historians, have covered a great deal of ground in explaining how wars were avoided for long and short periods of time, but they have not gone into detail in explaining how and why certain groups have permanently stopped warring. Those who believe that international war is here to stay may be correct. But we may point out that war *has* been eliminated permanently, for all practical purposes, over large areas. If we could be sure of results, we would find it worth our while to spend many millions of man-hours and many millions of dollars in studying how this condition came about and how it might be extended over larger and larger areas of the globe. Thus far no such effort has been made, and no techniques for it have been perfected. In the course of our study, therefore, we had to develop our own techniques. This book is the first result of a limited but somewhat novel inquiry.

We are dealing here with political communities. These we regard as social groups with a process of political communication, some machinery for enforcement, and some popular

habits of compliance. A political community is not necessarily able to prevent war within the area it covers: the United States was unable to do so at the time of the Civil War. Some political communities do, however, eliminate war and the expectation of war within their boundaries. It is these that call for intensive study.

We have concentrated, therefore, upon the formation of "security-communities" in certain historical cases. The use of this term starts a chain of definitions, and we must break in here to introduce the other main links needed for a fuller understanding of our findings.

A SECURITY-COMMUNITY is a group of people which has become "integrated."

By INTEGRATION we mean the attainment, within a territory, of a "sense of community" and of institutions and practices strong enough and widespread enough to assure, for a "long" time, dependable expectations of "peaceful change" among its population.

By SENSE OF COMMUNITY we mean a belief on the part of individuals in a group that they have come to agreement on at least this one point: that common social problems must and can be resolved by processes of "peaceful change."

By PEACEFUL CHANGE we mean the resolution of social problems, normally by institutionalized procedures, without resort to large-scale physical force.

A security-community, therefore, is one in which there is real assurance that the members of that community will not fight each other physically, but will settle their disputes in some other way. If the entire world were integrated as a security-community, wars would be automatically eliminated. But there is apt to be confusion about the term "integration."

In our usage, the term "integration" does not necessarily mean only the merging of peoples or governmental units into a single unit. Rather, we divide security-communities into two types: "amalgamated" and "pluralistic."

By AMALGAMATION we mean the formal merger of two or more previously independent units into a single larger unit, with some type of common government after amalgamation. This common government may be unitary or federal. The United States today is an example of the amalgamated type. It became a single governmental unit by the formal merger of several formerly independent units. It has one supreme decision-making center.

The PLURALISTIC security-community, on the other hand, retains the legal independence of separate governments. The combined territory of the United States and Canada is an example of the pluralistic type. Its two separate governmental units form a security-community without being merged. It has two supreme decision-making centers. Where amalgamation occurs without integration, of course a security-community does not exist.

Since our study deals with the problem of ensuring peace, we shall say that any political community, be it amalgamated or pluralistic, was eventually SUCCESSFUL if it became a security-community— that is, if it achieved integration—and that it was UNSUCCESSFUL if it ended eventually in secession or civil war.

Perhaps we should point out here that both types of integration require, at the international level, some kind of organization, even though it may be very loose. We put no credence in the old aphorism that among friends a constitution is not necessary and among enemies it is of no avail. The area of practicability lies in between.

Integration is a matter of fact, not of time. If people on both sides do not fear war and do not prepare for it, it matters little how long it took them to reach this stage. But once integration has been reached, the length of time over which it persists may contribute to its consolidation.

It should be noted that integration and amalgamation overlap, but not completely. This means that there can be amalgamation without integration, and that there can be integration without amalgamation. When we use the term "integration or amalgamation" in this book, we are taking a short form to express an alternative between integration (by the route of either pluralism or amalgamation) and amalgamation short of integration. We have done this because unification movements in the past have often aimed at both of these goals, with some of the supporters of the movements preferring one or the other goal at different times. To encourage this profitable ambiguity, leaders of such movements have often used broader symbols such as "union," which

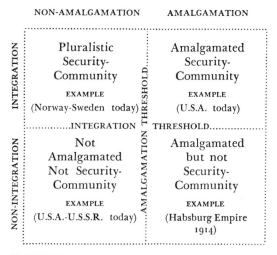

FIGURE 12.1

would cover both possibilities and could be made to mean different things to different men.

One of our basic premises is that whatever we can learn about the process of forming security-communities should be helpful in an indirect way not only to planners, but also to existing international organizations. If the way to integration, domestic or international, is through the achievement of a sense of community that undergirds institutions, then it seems likely that an increased sense of community would help to strengthen whatever institutions—supranational or international—are already operating. When these institutions are agencies for enforcement of the public will, we encounter that ancient and tantalizing puzzle: who polices the police? Can we make certain that agreements, freely entered into, will be reliably enforced or peacefully changed? Until we can do this, war may be called upon to do the job, liquidating the disputing parties instead of the dispute.

Everyone knows that political machinery already exists for reaching international decisions, and that these decisions cannot always be enforced after they are decided upon. Likewise, judicial machinery also exists which could be used for settling any international dispute without force; but states cannot be brought before a court against their will, nor made to abide by its judgment. It is equally true that enforcement or compliance can be achieved for a time without willing acceptance, as in the case of a strong state against a weak one. But without steady acceptance by large numbers of people, compliance is bound to be ineffective or temporary.

A situation of compliance, then, presupposes general agreement about something. Perhaps the "something" has to be the substance of the matter being complied with, or perhaps merely the legitimacy of the enforcing agent, or even the rightfulness of the procedure being used. Once men have attained this condition of agreement with regard to a social institution for enforcement of the public will, and have stabilized this condition, that institution would seem to be reliably supported: the police are effectively policed. This kind of institution—perhaps the most crucial of all—represents the force organized on behalf of the community. In our terms, a sense of community would have been achieved to a high degree—perhaps high enough to be considered as integration.

It is the object of our inquiry to learn as much as possible about how such a condition has been reached under various circumstances at various times. Through this study, we hope to learn how that condition could be approached more closely in the present world.

48.   International Integration:
The European and the Universal Process

ERNST B. HAAS

I. EUROPEAN AND UNIVERSAL
INTEGRATION

The established nation-state is in full retreat in Europe while it is advancing voraciously in Africa and Asia. Integration among discrete political units is a historical fact in Europe, but disintegration seems to be the dominant *motif* elsewhere. Cannot the example of successful integration in Europe be imitated? Could not the techniques of international and supranational cooperation developed in Luxembourg, Paris, and Brussels be put to use in Accra, Bangkok, and Cairo, as well as on the East River in New York? Or, in a different perspective, will not the progress of unity in Europe inevitably have its integrating repercussions in other regions and at the level of the United Nations even without efforts at conscious imitation?

Excerpted from "International Integration: The European and Universal Process," by Ernst B. Haas, *International Organization* 15/3 (1961), pp. 366–378, 389–392. Revised by the author. Copyright © 1962, World Peace Foundation. Reprinted by permission of the MIT Press, Cambridge, Massachusetts, and the author.

Such a development would be most satisfying. Presumably it would contribute to world peace by creating ever-expanding islands of practical cooperation, eventually spilling over into the controversy-laden fields which threaten us directly with thermonuclear destruction. The functionalist theory of international peace might be put to work by a generalization of the European mode of post-1945 international cooperation. Further, those who hope to contribute to the peaceful solution of conflict could take much solace from such a development, for the post-1945 European mode of resolving conflicts among states has demonstrated that "there often comes a moment when there is a simultaneous revolution of interests on both sides and unity precipitates itself," to quote Mary Follett.

Before abandoning ourselves to such pleasant speculation, however, we would do well to state systematically what we have learned about the causes of European integration and then to investigate where else these causes might be operative. This effort calls for some definitions.

We are interested in tracing progress toward a terminal condition called *political community*.

Successful nation-states constitute such communities and subsequent amalgamations of several such states may also form communities. A variety of constitutional and structural factors are compatible with this notion; political community exists when there is likelihood of internal peaceful change in a setting of contending groups with mutually antagonistic claims. The process of attaining this condition among nation-states we call *integration,* the process whereby political actors in several distinct national settings are persuaded to shift their loyalties, expectations, and political activities toward a new and larger center, whose institutions possess or demand jurisdiction over the pre-existing national states. It should be noted that the objective economic, social, and communications "factors" often identified with "integration," in my scheme, are conditions typical of an ongoing political community. At best they may serve as indicators to help us assess the progress of integration. . . .

Conflict resolution is a particularly interesting indicator for judging progress along the path of integration. A close study of negotiating processes in international relations suggests the prevalence of three types of compromise, each indicative of a certain measure of integration.

1. The least demanding we may call accommodation on the basis of the minimum common denominator. Equal bargaining partners gradually reduce their antagonistic demands by exchanging concessions of roughly equal value. Gains and losses are easily identified, but the impact of the transaction never goes beyond what the *least* cooperative bargaining partner wishes to concede. This mode of compromise is typical of classic diplomatic negotiations.

2. Accommodation by "splitting the difference" carries us a little farther along the path of integration. As before, demands are reduced and concessions of roughly equal value exchanged among autonomous bargaining units. But in this mode of compromise the mediatory services of a secretary-general or *ad hoc* international expert study group may be admitted by the parties. Conflict is resolved, not on the basis of the will of the least cooperative, but somewhere between the final bargaining positions. This type of negotiation is prevalent in international economic organi-

zations and in other dealings permitting financial identification of gains or losses, such as the formulation of a scale of assessments for Members of the United Nations.

3. Finally, accommodation on the basis of deliberately or inadvertently upgrading the common interests of the parties takes us closest to the peaceful change procedures typical of a political community with its full legislative and judicial jurisdictions, lacking in international relations. . . .

In terms of results, this mode of accommodation maximizes what I have elsewhere called the "spill-over" effect of international decisions: policies made pursuant to an initial task and grant of power can be made real only if the task itself is expanded, as reflected in the compromises among the states interested in the task. In terms of method, the upgrading of the parties' common interests relies heavily on the services of an institutionalized mediator, whether a single person or a board of experts, with an autonomous range of powers. It thus combines intergovernmental negotiation with the participation of independent experts and spokesmen for interest groups, parliaments, and political parties. It is this combination of interests and institutions which we shall identify as "supranational." The initial creation of such an agency, of course, demands a creative compromise among the states parties to the effort, based on the realization that certain common interests cannot be attained in any other way. This in turn presupposes that identical and converging policy aims, rather than antagonistic ones, predominated at the moment when the supranational organization was set up.

Each of these modes of accommodation, in addition to specifying a type of outcome relating to intensities of integration, also is typified by appropriate institutional mechanisms. There exists, moreover, a fourth prominent procedural device—parliamentary diplomacy—which is capable of producing any of the three outcomes. Parliamentary diplomacy, as Dean Rusk defined it, implies the existence of a continuing organization with a broad frame of reference, public debate, rules of procedure governing the debate, and the statement of conclusions in a formal resolution arrived at by some kind of majority vote. When bodies like the UN or the Council of Europe define a conflict situation by filtering discussion through this machinery they may also be setting the limits within which eventual settlement comes about, though parliamentary diplomacy rarely defines the actual terms of the settlement. Instead it mobilizes political mediatory forces—the uncommitted states, parties, groups, or persons—whose voice in the settlement process is given volume by the reluctance of the parties to the dispute to annoy the mediating forces. Since the institutional context in which parliamentary diplomacy can be practiced maximizes the representation of a variety of interests emanating from the same nation, it opens up areas of maneuver which are fore closed in negotiations exclusively conducted by carefully instructed single agents of foreign ministries. To that extent it facilitates a greater amount of integration even though it does not necessarily produce outcomes which upgrade common interests.

Where can these modes of accommodation be identified in the history and institutions of European integration?

II. THE LESSON OF EUROPEAN INTEGRATION

Clearly all these modes of accommodation are part of the European pattern of international adjustment. While they do not provide the only indicators of degrees of integration, they appear to be particularly strategic ones in that they focus on decision-making, thereby acting as a summary of, and an abstraction upon, other factors which could also be used as indicators. Broadly speaking, international institutions maximizing decision-making by means of the second and third modes yield the greatest amount of progress toward the goal of political community.

Parliamentary diplomacy is the chief contribution to European unity which can be credited to the various parliamentary assemblies. They have not meaningfully controlled their various executives nor have they legislated in any real sense, though they have attempted and partially exercised powers in both these fields. But they have acted as a spur to the formation of new voluntary elite groups across national boundaries—the European political groups—and the interplay among these has produced a type of diplomatic problem-solving which takes its inspiration from parliamentary resolutions and is able to upgrade common interests. As examples we may cite the work of the Council of Europe in relation to the Saar, in refugee relief and resettlement, and in the relaxation of frontier formalities. We may add the work of the Nordic Council in the negotiation of the now superseded Nordic Common Market Agreement. But let it be admitted at the same time that the total contribution of parliamentary diplomacy is not very great. It found no institutional outlet at all in the Organization for European Economic Cooperation (OEEC); yet that organization's contribution to integration was substantial even though it operated primarily on the level of accommodation by "splitting the difference."

The most successful institutions in Europe are the "Communities" of the Ten, constitutional hybrids which once caused nightmares to the public lawyer. They facilitate the resolution of conflict by virtue of all three modes, but the upgrading of common interests is their true contribution to the art of political integration. All fundamental decisions are made by the Councils of Ministers. But they are decisions based on continuous compromise, constantly informed by generally respected expert bodies with constitutional powers of their own and in constant contact with supranational voluntary associations and interest groups. The character of decision-making stimulates interest groups to make themselves heard; it spurs political parties in Strasbourg and Brussels to work out common positions; it creates an enormous pressure on high national civil servants to get to know and establish rapport with their opposite numbers; and it sharpens the sensitivities of the legal profession to European norms and political processes in preparation for the inevitable flood of litigation before the Court of Justice. In short, many of the decisions are integrative in their immediate economic consequences *as well as* in the new expectations and political processes which they imply. It is this indirect result which is maximized by the mixture of institutions which usually achieves accommodation at a higher level of agreement as compared to the initial bargaining positions of the parties. Earlier decisions, including the ones constituting the Communities, spill over into new functional contexts, involve more and more people, call for more and more inter-bureaucratic contact and consultation, thereby creating their own logic in favor of later decisions, meeting, in a pro-community direction, the new problems which grow out of the earlier compromises.

Intergovernmental institutions of the classic variety, even when assisted by respected international civil servants and advisory boards, have not been able to match this performance. The North Atlantic Treaty Organization (NATO) and OEEC, for reasons to be explored, have continued to make their contribution to integration by means of compromises based on techniques found also in the United Nations. They have transcended these only in relation to certain tasks hinging around the direct implications of the welfare state.

This brings us face to face with the key question of which organizational *functions*, or tasks, have contributed most to the process of integration in Europe. The superficial answer clearly points to the field of economics; but by no means all organizations with an economic competence have performed equally well and few of them solve their problems on the basis of upgrading common interests. Parliamentary diplomacy has apparently been of importance in advancing economic integration only in the Nordic Council; OEEC functioned on the basis of "splitting the difference" or compromising on the level of the minimum common denominator in all areas except those relating to currency convertibility and the removal of quotas (in which common interests were indeed upgraded). The European Free Trade Association (EFTA) has not taken strides comparable to those of the European Economic Community (EEC) and the European Coal and Steel Community (ECSC).

Not merely economic tasks, therefore, but the degree of functional specificity of the economic task is causally related to the intensity of integration. The more specific the task, the more likely important progress toward political community. It is not enough to be concerned with the reduction of trade barriers or the forecasting of industrial productivity. Specificity of task is essential, with respect to such assignments as creating a common market for narrowly defined products, unifying railway rates, removing restrictive practices in certain branches of industry, removing import quotas by fixed percentage points during fixed periods, and the like. Functional specificity, however, may be so trivial as to remain outside the stream of human expectations and actions vital for integration. This would seem to be the case with the standardization of railway rolling stock, for example, or the installation of uniform road signs. The task, in short, must be both specific and economically important in the sense of containing the potential for spilling over from one vital area of welfare policy into others.

Non-economic tasks have shown themselves much more barren. . . .

This survey of the functional lessons of European integration leads to the inevitable conclusion that functional contexts are autonomous. Integrative forces which flow from one kind of activity do not necessarily infect other activities, even if carried out by the same organization. OEEC could not repeat in the field of tariff bargaining the results it obtained on questions of convertibility. NATO cannot transfer its success in planning strategy for new weapons systems to the standardization of the enlistment period; and ECSC has shown itself more adept in negotiating cumulative compromises on the creation of a common market than on short-run solutions for the coal crisis. Decisions made by identical officials, in organizations with a stable membership, in a non-revolutionary socio-ideological setting with similar institutional characteristics nevertheless vary sharply, in terms of their integrative impact, depending on the functional context. If this is true even in the European setting, how much more true is it likely to be in the United Nations. But the converse proposition is equally important: the autonomy of functional contexts means that disintegration in one range of relations among certain states does not necessarily imply parallel disintegration in other relations among the same states. . . .

The attempt to compare the European experience with efforts elsewhere compels attention to the environment in which the process of integration is taking place, what some scholars call the "background" factors. This investigation will show that while "Europe"—in the largest sense of the nineteen countries west of the Iron Curtain—possesses no completely common factors at all, significant islands of almost identical environmental factors exist among certain of them.

Social structure provides one set of factors. With the exception of Greece, Turkey, Portugal, parts of Spain, and southern Italy, the western European social scene is dominated by pluralism. Articulate voluntary groups, led by bureaucratized but accessible elites, compete with each other more or less rationally for political power and social status. The population is mobilized and participates in this process through affiliation with mass organizations. In the countries mentioned, however, effective and functionally diffuse social relations prevail.

Economic and industrial development furnishes a second set of factors. With the exception of the same countries plus Ireland, we are dealing with a very high level of economic development—including that of the countries in which the dominant products are agricultural—from the point of view of productivity, investment, and consumption. Significantly correlated with industrialization we find the usual high degree of urbanization and ever-growing demands for government services and durable consumer goods. We also find increasing demands on limited natural resources and greater dependence on foreign (or regional) trade. . . .

Ideological patterns provide the final set of factors. Since policies of integration are, in the first instance, advanced or blocked by the activities of political parties and their ministers, parties may be used as an index of ideological homogeneity. A given cluster of countries is ideologically "homogeneous" if the divisions among the parties are, very roughly, the same among all the countries in the cluster, when the principles professed and the concrete socio-economic interests represented by the parties are roughly analogous on both sides of a frontier. Given this definition, the Scandinavian countries emerge as ideologically homogeneous among themselves (with the partial exception of Iceland) but quite dissimilar from the rest of Europe. The Benelux countries, West Germany, Switzerland,

and Austria seem homogeneous and seem to have considerable affinity for Italy and France, even though Italy and France have large Communist parties. Portugal, Greece, Spain, and Turkey lack the typical European socio-economic structure and therefore the appropriate party systems; they do not fit into any neat ideological package. The British and Irish parties show some affinity for their continental colleagues, especially the socialists, but the patterns of interest aggregation and political style differ sufficiently to prevent the positing of a homogeneous pattern. We therefore have two large ideological clusters: (1) Scandinavia, and (2) the Six (plus Switzerland and Austria), as well as a number of single national systems whose characteristics seem *sui generis*.

Let us relate these environmental patterns to the integration process. Integration proceeds most rapidly and drastically when it responds to socio-economic demands emanating from an industrial-urban environment, when it is an adaptation to cries for increasing welfare benefits and security born by the growth of a new type of society. In the words of two European scholars:

For decades industrialism has been revising the workways and consuming habits of people everywhere. It has enabled cities to grow and the urban way of life to spread. Urbanism is the great outreaching dynamic, breaking down isolation and encroaching upon tradition. Modern industrial urbanism is innately inimical to any isolation. It demands access and stimulates mobility. As earlier it resisted being confined to city walls, now it resists being confined to limited political areas. This resistance to confinement is greater than the resistance against the encroachments. In the measure that industrial urbanism has gained in this contest against the rooted barriers—in that measure integration is needed. The effort toward European integration reflects this need of industrial urbanism for wider organization.

I reject the teleological aspects of this statement. In terms of a social process based on rational human perceptions and motives, no mere concept "calls for" or "needs" anything: a discrete set of group motives, converging with motives of cognate groups from across the border, results in a certain pattern of policy; the aims and the policy reflect demands born from the environment, and the later policies may well change the environment in a wholly unintended fashion. Only in this sense, then, does industrial urbanism favor integration. Because the modern ''industrial-political'' actor fears that his way of life cannot be safeguarded without structural adaptation, he turns to integration; but by the same token, political actors who are neither industrial, nor urban, nor modern in their outlook usually do not favor this kind of adaptation, for they seek refuge instead in national exclusiveness.

Thus, countries dominated by a non-pluralistic social structure are poor candidates for participation in the integration process. Even if their governments do partake at the official level, the consequences of their participation are unlikely to be felt elsewhere in the social structure. Hence the impact of European integration, in all its aspects, has been minimal in Portugal, Turkey, and Greece. Finally, sufficient ideological homogeneity for value-sharing among important national elite groups is essential for rapid integration. The implications for Europe are obvious as reflected in the differential rates of progress toward political community which have been made within Scandinavia, with the Ten, and within Benelux compared to the all-European level represented by OEEC, NATO, and the Council of Europe.

In addition to these environmental considerations, which relate to the internal characteristics of the region undergoing integration, there are often external environmental factors of importance. Fear of a common enemy is an absolutely necessary precondition for integration in military organization: without the Soviet Union there would have been no NATO. But the common enemy may be a more subtle manifestation, such as fear of external groupings of culturally and economically suspect forces: such considerations were not irrelevant to the ''third force'' argument which entered the integration process among the Ten and is apparent in the convergence of interests which resulted in the Organization for Economic Cooperation and Development (OECD). While external environments produce motives favoring integration, they are never sufficient in themselves to explain the rate and intensity of the process.

Institutions, functions, and environments provide useful categories for arranging the human data among which our various modes of accommodation made themselves felt; but they do not exhaust the list of crucial given factors of which we are all aware and without which the process of integration simply cannot be discussed. Variations in national policy, for instance, are fundamental to the life of international organizations, especially in agencies which do not possess the institutional power to influence significantly the policy aims of their member states. However, this truism should not be rendered in the all too common form which asserts that differences in *power* among members determine organizational behavior and the speed and direction of organizational response. Variations in national policy provide a power determinant, not in absolute terms, but only with respect to the functional strength of particular states in relation to the specific task of the organization. The military and economic power of the United States in NATO, for instance, is a meaningful ingredient in the life of that organization only when it is brought to bear on infrastructure or procurement negotiations. The fact remains, nonetheless, that changes in the policy needs experienced by member states, reflecting as they do the pressures of the home and of the international environments, create definite phases in the life of international organizations.

Therefore, lessons about integrative processes associated with one phase do not generally carry over into the next because the specific policy context—often short-range—determines what is desired by governments and tolerated by them in terms of integrative accommodations. This, in turn, forces us to the conclusion that types of accommodation, and the associated procedural norms of an organization, developed in one phase of its life do not necessarily carry over into the next. There is no dependable, cumulative process of precedent formation leading to ever more community-oriented organizational behavior, unless the task assigned to the institutions is inherently expansive, thus capable of overcoming the built-in autonomy of functional contexts and of surviving changes in the policy aims of member states. . . .

The lesson of European integration can be summarized as follows:

1. *Institutionally,* supranational bodies most readily lend themselves to accommodation on the basis of upgrading common interests. This is equally true of intergovernmental bodies which permit certain of their expert commissions the role usually associated with the Communities of the Ten, such as the OEEC Steering Board for Trade, the Council of Europe's Commissioner for Refugees, and WEU's Armaments Control Agency. These institutions are least susceptible to the alternation of phases and most likely to develop cumulative decision-making precedents.

2. *Functionally,* specific economic tasks resolving policy differences emerging from previous imperfect compromises on welfare questions, but involving large mass interests, are most intimately related to rapid integration. Conflicts may be resolved by all the usual methods, but upgrading common interests predominates. The tendency toward autonomy of tasks can be overcome only by building into the institutions specific assignments which maximize the spill-over process.

3. *Environmentally,* integration fares best in situations controlled by social groupings representing the rational interests of urban-industrial society, groups seeking to maximize their economic benefits and dividing along regionally homogeneous ideological-political lines. Changing national policy inhibits integration unless compensated by strong central institutions maximizing the spill-over process.

Obviously, integration may take place and has taken place among nations which have few of these characteristics and through international organizations which depart little from the classic intergovernmental pattern. But the pace and intensity of such integration is pallid in such a context as compared to the situation in which all optimal conditions are met. Hence it should come as no surprise that the Communities of the Ten represent the most, and the Council of Europe the least, successful organizations in a European spectrum in which all organizations make some contribution to some aspect of the integration process. . . .

V. INTEGRATION AS A DISCONTINUOUS PROCESS

Five major conclusions can be drawn from this discussion. Processes which yield optimal progress toward the end of political community at the European level simply cannot be reproduced in other contexts because the necessary preconditions exist to a much lesser degree. Therefore, European integration will proceed at a much more rapid pace than universal integration. Further, other regions with strongly varying environmental factors are unlikely to imitate successfully the European example.

However, it is by no means clear that slightly different functional pursuits, responding to a different set of converging interests, may not also yield integration. The Soviet and Latin American examples suggest that this may be the case. But it is also true that if regional integration continues to go forward in these areas, it will obey impulses peculiar to them and thus fail to demonstrate any universal "law of integration" deduced from the European example.

Integration at the universal level obeys still different impulses. It flows from much more intense conflict than the regional process, in deference to the heterogeneity of the environment in which it unrolls. Consequently, the areas of common interest are more difficult to isolate and the proper specific functions harder to define. In view of the prevalence of phases it then becomes very hazardous to forecast any even and consistent pattern of integration.

The UN effort suffers from the built-in defect that the very economic development and technical aid activities which at the moment constitute its integrative task may create the kind of national environment in which *less* integration will take place a generation from now. To the extent that the UN effort strengthens national economies and administrative structures it actually may *reduce* the final integrative component. Functionally specific economic tasks found to provide progress toward a political community in Europe may thus have the opposite final effect at the world level. Whether, in some future UN phase, space and nuclear tasks would produce more integration remains an open question.

The element of discontinuity among the various processes is increased by the continued autonomy of the universal and regional decision-making contexts. . . .there is no overwhelming evidence that the members of a cohesive regional system remain united in the UN, nor is there evidence that normally weak and heterogeneous regional systems may not perform cohesively in New York. In short, the contexts remain separate and distinct in the minds of policy-makers, a feature hardly conducive to the elaboration of a unified and global integration process.

A final element of discontinuity must be frankly exposed. Regional integration, because it proceeds more rapidly and responds to a greater number of optimal factors, may eventually slow down universal integration altogether. The regional process may create a relatively small number of integrated political communities, facing each other in the UN system. In fact, the expanded UN task looking toward pooled economic development and regional agencies in Africa, Southeast Asia and elsewhere, may actually contribute to this trend. In that case, the growth of fewer and larger political communities will contribute to regional, but not to universal, peace. The universal system will remain what it now is: the arena for minimizing conflict and maximizing common interests in deference to the minimum common denominator.

APPENDIX: Collateral Reading in Major International Relations Texts

Chapters in *Classics of International Relations*	TEXTS:* Coplin (1980)	Dougherty-Pfaltzgraff (1981)	Hartmann (1983)	Holsti (1983)
1. Just War & Idealism		5		14
2. Realism	1, 12	3	1-3, 5, 13-15	2
3. Radical Critique				3
4. Science		1, 13		1
5. Foreign Policy	6, 7	11	4	1, 4-5, 7-8
6. Crisis	9			10, 12
7. War		7, 8	8	15
8. Imperialism	8	6	7	9
9. Balance of Power	2, 3	4	16-21,31	6
10. Deterrence		9, 12		11
11. International Law and World Government	5, 10, 11		6, 9-12	13
12. World Community	4	10		16

* William D. Coplin, (1980) *Introduction to International Politics*, 3rd ed.

James E. Dougherty and Robert L. Pfaltzgraff, Jr., (1981) *Contending Theories of International Relations*, 2nd ed.

Frederick H. Hartmann, (1983) *The Relations of Nations*, 6th ed.

K.J. Holsti, (1983), *International Politics: A Framework for Analysis*, 4th ed.

Walter S. Jones and Steven J. Rosen, (1982) *The Logic of International Relations*, 4th ed.

Charles W. Kegley, Jr. and Eugene R. Wittkopf, (1981) *World Politics: Trend and Transformation*.

Hans J. Morgenthau, (1975), *Politics Among Nations*, 5th ed., revised .

Frederic S. Pearson and J. Martin Rochester, (1984) *International Relations: The Global Condition in the Late 20th Century*.

Bruce Russett and Harvey Starr, (1981) *World Politics: The Menu for Choice*.

John Spanier, (1981) *Games Nations Play*, 4th ed.

Michael P. Sullivan, (1976) *International Relations: Theories and Evidence*.

	Jones-Rosen (1982)	Kegley-Wittkopf (1981)	Morgenthau (1975)	Pearson-Rochester (1984)	Russett-Starr (1981)	Spanier (1981)	Sullivan (1976)
(1.)			15-17				
(2.)	7	2	1, 3, 31-32	2	3-7		
(3.)							
(4.)			2		1-2	1-2	1, 8 appendix
(5.)	6	3, 10	4-10, 21	1, 4-6	8, 11, 12	13,16	2-4
(6.)				7	7	9	
(7.)	11	11	22	8	5, 13	10	
(8.)	12-13	4, 6-9	5	11, 13	4, 9, 16-17	11-12, 14-15	
(9.)	8-9	12	11-14	3	6	8	5
(10.)	10			12	14		7
(11.)	14-15	5, 13	18-20, 23-29	9-10	3	17, 19	
(12.)	16-17	14	30	14-15	15, 18-19	18,20	6

INDEX

Boldface type indicates a reading by the indexed author.